MOVING OUT OF POVERTY, VOLUME 4

# Rising from the Ashes
of Conflict

## About the Series

The Moving Out of Poverty series presents the results of new comparative research across more than 500 communities in 15 countries on how and why poor people move out of poverty. The findings lay the foundations for new policies that will promote inclusive growth and just societies, and move millions out of poverty.

The series was launched in 2007 under the editorial direction of Deepa Narayan, former senior adviser in the World Bank. She earlier directed the pathbreaking Voices of the Poor project.

Titles in the Moving Out of Poverty series:

# Moving
## *Out of*
# Poverty

**VOLUME 4**

## Rising from the Ashes
## of Conflict

Deepa Narayan *and* Patti Petesch, *editors*

A COPUBLICATION OF PALGRAVE MACMILLAN
AND THE WORLD BANK

# 504835492

©2010 The International Bank for Reconstruction and Development / The World Bank
1818 H Street, NW
Washington, DC 20433
Telephone: 202-473-1000
Internet: www.worldbank.org
E-mail: feedback@worldbank.org

A copublication of The World Bank and Palgrave Macmillan.

PALGRAVE MACMILLAN
Palgrave Macmillan in the UK is an imprint of Macmillan Publishers Limited, registered in England, company number 785998, of Houndmills, Basingstoke, Hampshire, RG21 6XS.

Palgrave Macmillan in the US is a division of St Martin's Press LLC, 175 Fifth Avenue, New York, NY 10010.

Palgrave Macmillan is the global academic imprint of the above companies and has companies and representatives throughout the world.

Palgrave® and Macmillan® are registered trademarks in the United States, the United Kingdom, Europe, and other countries.

ISBN: 978-0-8213-7631-7 *(softcover)*      eISBN: 978-0-8213-8112-0
ISBN: 978-0-8213-7839-7 *(hardcover)*      DOI: 10.1596/978-0-8213-7631-7
ISSN: None

Library of Congress Cataloging-in-Publication Data has been applied for.

**Cover design:** Drew Fasick
**Cover photograph:** Adrian Brooks/Imagewise

Printed in the United States

## Dedication

To the thousands of women, men, and youth who took the time
to share with us their experiences, their hopes, and their dreams

*and*

To Amartya Sen for inspiring the Moving Out of Poverty
research project and generations of scholars and
practitioners to value poor peoples' aspirations for
freedom and dignity

# Contents

## Boxes

## Figures

## Maps

# Tables

# Foreword

Lifting people out of poverty is one of the great challenges facing the international community today. It has become still more daunting in the context of the global financial crisis, which has severe implications for the poorest people in the world. Almost 1.4 billion people in developing countries live in poverty, according to recent estimates by the World Bank, and a significant part of this population lives in chronic poverty.

Reducing poverty in countries emerging from major political conflict presents an especially difficult challenge within the overall continuum of relief, rehabilitation, reconstruction, and development. But there are signs of hope. In communities and countries ravaged by conflict, some people do manage not only to survive and recover but even to improve their well-being and move out of poverty. This book helps explain how and why.

This is the fourth in a series of volumes emerging from the global Moving Out of Poverty study, which explores mobility from the perspectives of poor people who have moved out of poverty in more than 500 communities across 15 countries. The research on conflict-affected countries was managed by the Global Development Network in partnership with the World Bank. This volume includes an incisive analysis of the impact of major political conflict on poverty and mobility, backed up by in-depth case studies of six countries affected by significant violence during the 10-year study period. Deepa Narayan, Denis Nikitin, and Patti Petesch have done a brilliant job of synthesizing key findings and lessons based on the excellent work of the country-based researchers.

A particular strength of this volume is that it focuses on communities rather than countries. It thus fills a gap in the literature, which tends to be preoccupied with issues at the macro level and not at the micro level. The findings presented here will be of great interest to professionals, practitioners, and policy makers engaged in policy reforms in this crucial area as well as to students of poverty and development.

George Mavrotas
Chief Economist
Global Development Network
New Delhi

# Study Team and Acknowledgments

This book draws on the contributions of many people who supported the Moving Out of Poverty research project at different stages. The project was led and managed by Deepa Narayan, who served from 2002 through 2008 as senior adviser in the Poverty Reduction and Economic Management (PREM) Network of the World Bank, first in the Poverty Reduction Group and then in the vice president's office within PREM. She subsequently worked with the Global Development Network as project director. Patti Petesch served as the global study coordinator through 2006 and then remained engaged as a contributor to the Moving Out of Poverty series and co-editor of two volumes.

We gratefully acknowledge Lyn Squire and his successor, Gobind Nankani, of the Global Development Network for their support of the work on conflict-affected countries. We also thank Ramona Angelescu Naqvi and George Mavrotas for their involvement, Emcet Tas for research and project coordination, and Rajesh Grover and Naushad Khan for administrative support.

A number of local and international research institutes conducted the country studies. The lead researchers were Philibert de Mercey, Alejandra Val Cubero, and Najibullah Ziar (Afghanistan); Ingrid FitzGerald and So Sovannarith (Cambodia); Ana María Ibáñez, María Teresa Matijasevic, Sergio Iván Prada, and Carlos Ariel García (Colombia); Deepa Narayan and Binayak Sen (Assam, India); Sri Kusumastuti Rahayu and Vita Febriany (Indonesia); Erlinda Montillo-Burton, Chona R. Echavez, and Imelda G. Pagtulon-an (Philippines); and Prashan Thalayasingam (Sri Lanka). The contributions of the country researchers are so vital that we have listed their names separately in appendix A, along with the list of country reports that these teams produced.

The study was guided by experts in a series of methodological workshops. We are particularly grateful to Ashutosh Varshney, who served as an adviser to the conflict study. Patrick Barron and his colleagues at SMERU Research Institute worked with us to pilot the new conflict timeline data collection tool in Indonesia. Research workshops on the conflict study were held in February 2005 and April 2007. We would like to thank those who participated, including Ian Bannon, Luca Barbone, Susan Burgerman, Mark Chernick, Sarah Cliffe, Klaus Deininger, Nora Dudwick, Kai Kaiser, Monty Marshall, Erlinda Montillo-Burton, Caroline Moser, Borany Penh, David Pottebaum, Sri Kusumastuti Rahayu, Joseph Siegle, Claire Smith, Lyn Squire, Frances Stewart, Ashutosh Varshney, Per Wam, Bridget Welsh, Michael Woolcock, and William Zartman. We also thank Alexander Marc for convening a World Bank–wide meeting in June 2008 that allowed us to share our initial findings and receive feedback.

Several World Bank staff and others helped us initiate the country studies and/or provided technical guidance. They include Ian Bannon and Ana Paula Fialho Lopes on conflict-affected contexts; Nisha Agarwal, Jehan Arulpragasam, Patrick Barron, Tim Conway, Scott Guggenheim, and Mia Hyun on East Asia; Jairo A. Arboleda, Jaime Saavedra, and Maximo Torero on Latin America; and Christine Allison, Sanjib Baruah, Rachid Benmessaoud, Maitreyi Das, Dipak Dasgupta, Rinku Murgai, Ashish Narain, Ambar Narayan, V. J. Ravishankar, Shonali Sardesai, Abhijit Sen, Binayak Sen, and Tara Vishwanath on South Asia. We are also grateful to all the World Bank country directors who extended their support to the study.

Data analysis was a huge task. Lant Pritchett guided the quantitative data analysis for the global study, and the basic methodology was adapted for the conflict-affected countries; quantitative analysis for the conflict study was conducted by Denis Nikitin. The huge qualitative global data set was analyzed by two groups. The ACNielsen team in India coded the data after being trained by Soumya Kapoor in use of the Nudist software. The coding tree was developed with the help of several people, including Kaushik Barua, Chris Gibson, Soumya Kapoor, Molly Kinder, and Divya Nambiar. Manzoor Ali prepared printed packages for analysis. Training in other qualitative analyses was provided by Deepa Narayan and coordinated by Mohini Datt. Primary researchers included Huma Kidwai and Mahima Mitra. Other team members who provided valuable assistance at different phases of the conflict study included Ursula Casabonne, Reema Govil, Kyla Hayford, Divya Nambiar, Kazuhiro Numasawa, Yukti Pahwa, Brice Richards, Niti Saxena, Gitima Sharma, Sarah Sullivan, Emcet Tas, and Sunita Varada.

Six scholars reviewed part 1 of the book: Scott Guggenheim, Stathis Kalyvas, George Mavrotas, Gary Milante, Frances Stewart, and Michael Woolcock. Reviewers of the country chapters are acknowledged in the chapter endnotes. We owe a deep debt of gratitude to all, though any errors remain our responsibility.

The study was financed by a Post-Conflict Fund grant from the World Bank to the Global Development Network. Additional funds were provided by several donors. We especially wish to thank the government of Sweden, whose funds were untied. In addition, we gratefully acknowledge the governments of Denmark, Finland, the Netherlands, and Norway.

We thank the team at the World Bank Office of the Publisher, including Pat Katayama, Nancy Lammers, and Janet Sasser, who managed publication of this volume. We deeply appreciate Cathy Sunshine's meticulous editorial work and eye for detail that helped us through successive drafts and resulted in this book.

# Contributors

**Patrick Barron** is a social development specialist at the World Bank in Jakarta. He manages the Bank's programs in conflict-affected and postconflict areas of Indonesia, including a large program of support to the Aceh peace process. Since 2002 he has managed a mixed-methods research program aimed at understanding conflict and its impacts and evaluating the role of development programs in conflict prevention and peace building (see www.conflictanddevelopment.org). He has published extensively on conflict and development issues and advises other country teams on peace-building issues.

**Chona Echavez** is a senior research associate at the Research Institute for Mindanao Culture at Xavier University, Cagayan de Oro City, Philippines, where she is also a faculty member in the departments of Development Communication and Socio-Anthropology. At present, she is an Asia fellow and a visiting researcher at the Centre for Peace and Conflict Studies in Phnom Penh. Her interests include impact evaluations, gender- and culture-sensitive research, and evaluation tools for conflict-affected communities.

**Vita Febriany** is a researcher at the SMERU Research Institute in Jakarta, where she has worked for more than nine years. Her main research interests are related to poverty, health, education, and governance. She is currently involved in a study of the impact of the global financial crisis on Indonesia.

**Vanessa Joan Gray** is assistant professor of political science at the University of Massachusetts at Lowell. She specializes in resource and conflict issues in Colombia and has conducted dozens of interviews in three regions of that nation. Her current research is on transnational activist support for communities pursuing an alternative model of development in Cauca, Colombia.

**Katy Hull** is a consultant to the Poverty Reduction Group in the Poverty Reduction and Economic Management (PREM) Network of the World Bank. Her interests include human rights, democratization, and political institutions. She is a co-author of "Democracy and Poverty Reduction: Explorations on the Sen Conjecture" (with L. Barbone, L. Cord, and J. Sandefur, in *Political Institutions and Development: Failed Expectations and Renewed Hopes*, Edwin Elgar, 2007).

**Philibert de Mercey** has been working as a consultant on development issues in Afghanistan for the past five years. He has worked on numerous projects in the areas of rural development, rural livelihoods, and socioeconomic analysis, as well as program monitoring and evaluations. He recently taught in a master's program in international relations at the Institut d'Études Politiques de Paris (Paris Institute of Political Studies).

**Deepa Narayan** is project director of the 15-country World Bank study called Moving Out of Poverty: Understanding Freedom, Democracy, and Growth from the Bottom Up (see http://www.worldbank.org/movingoutofpoverty). From 2002 through 2008, she served as senior adviser in the Poverty Reduction and Economic Management (PREM) Network of the World Bank, first in the Poverty Reduction Group and subsequently in the vice president's office within PREM. Her interests include participatory development, community-driven development, and postconflict recovery. In addition to the Moving Out of Poverty series, her recent publications include *Ending Poverty in South Asia: Ideas that Work* (with E. Glinskaya, World Bank, 2007); *Measuring Empowerment: Cross-Disciplinary Perspectives* (World Bank, 2005); *Empowerment and Poverty Reduction: A Sourcebook* (World Bank, 2002); and the three-volume *Voices of the Poor* series (Oxford University Press, 2000–02).

**Denis Nikitin** has worked as a consultant to the World Bank for eight years. His research focuses on poverty analysis and public sector governance. He has contributed to poverty assessments in India, Kazakhstan, Malawi, and Romania, as well as to gender assessment in Bangladesh. He is currently working on a study documenting the exclusion faced by India's scheduled tribes.

**Patti Petesch** is a consultant with experience in policy design, program management, and research on global poverty, conflict, and gender issues. She is interested in the empowerment of poor men and women and in the structures and norms that support this. Currently she is working on gender, conflict, and peace-building issues. She served as study coordinator for the Voices of the Poor and Moving Out of Poverty research programs and co-edited several volumes in each series. Other recent publications include "Communities Where Poor People Prosper" (with D. Narayan and S. Paul, in *Moving Out of Poverty: The Promise of Empowerment and Democracy in India*, World Bank, 2009) and *Voices of the Poor from Colombia: Strengthening Livelihoods, Families, and Communities* (with J. Arboleda and J. Blackburn, World Bank, 2004).

**Sri Kusumastuti Rahayu** is a policy consultant to the World Bank's Conflict and Development program in Indonesia. Her role includes coordinating the policy advisory, capacity building, and dissemination aspects of the program and supporting research and evaluation activities as well as overall program management. Before joining the Bank in 2008, she was a senior researcher at the SMERU Research Institute in Jakarta, where she was involved in numerous studies related to social protections, poverty issues, and antipoverty programs.

**Emcet Oktay Tas** is a doctoral candidate and graduate teaching assistant at American University in Washington, DC. His fields of specialization are development, international economics, and political economy, with research interests in poverty dynamics, gender, and institutional development in developing countries. He has worked as a consultant to the Moving Out of Poverty study in the World Bank's Poverty Reduction Unit and in the Global Development Network. Currently, he is conducting research for the Swedish International Development Cooperation Agency (Sida) on gender aspects of the financial crisis.

**Prashan Thalayasingam** leads the Poverty and Conflict research program at the Centre for Poverty Analysis, an independent research institution in Colombo, Sri Lanka. His research areas include development in a conflict context, community conflict management systems, the historical development of conflict in Sri Lanka, and the politics of international aid. He was recently a visiting fellow at the Centre for Research on Inequality, Human Security and Ethnicity (CRISE) at Oxford University.

**Sunita Varada** is a private sector development specialist with a background in microfinance and competitiveness, as well as in rural and postconflict development. She has worked for the World Bank's Poverty Reduction unit, performing research and analysis for the Moving Out of Poverty study. At present, she consults for the Latin America Finance and Private Sector division of the World Bank. In addition to her current work in Central America, she has contributed to projects and research in various countries, including Angola, Brazil, India, and Turkey.

# Abbreviations

| | |
|---|---|
| $ | All dollar amounts are U.S. dollars unless otherwise indicated. |
| AFP | Armed Forces of the Philippines |
| AGP | Asom Gana Parishad (India) |
| ARMM | Autonomous Region in Muslim Mindanao (Philippines) |
| BBR | Bantuan Bangunan Rumah (Assistance with Housing Materials, Indonesia) |
| BPD | Badan Perwakilan Desa (village representative council, Indonesia) |
| BPS | Badan Pusat Statistik (Indonesian statistical bureau) |
| CAFGU | Civilian Armed Forces Geographical Unit (Philippines) |
| CDC | community development council (Afghanistan) |
| CPL | community poverty line |
| CRPF | Central Reserve Police Force (India) |
| ELN | Ejército de Liberación Nacional (National Liberation Army, Colombia) |
| FARC | Fuerzas Armadas Revolucionarias de Colombia (Revolutionary Armed Forces of Colombia) |
| FI | falling index |
| FPI | falling of the poor index |
| FRI | falling of the rich index |
| FRIP | falling of the rich into poverty index |
| GDP | gross domestic product |
| IDP | internally displaced person |
| IDT | Inpres Desa Tertinggal (Presidential Instruction for Neglected Villages, Indonesia) |
| IMT | International Monitoring Team (Philippines) |
| IPKF | Indian Peace Keeping Force (Sri Lanka) |
| JVP | Janatha Vimukthi Peramuna (People's Liberation Front, Sri Lanka) |
| KDP | Kecamatan Development Program (Indonesia) |
| LTTE | Liberation Tigers of Tamil Eelam (Sri Lanka) |
| MILF | Moro Islamic Liberation Front (Philippines) |
| MNLF | Moro National Liberation Front (Philippines) |
| MOP | moving out of poverty index |
| MPI | mobility of the poor index |

| | |
|---|---|
| MRI | mobility of the rich index |
| MRRD | Ministry of Rural Rehabilitation and Development (Afghanistan) |
| NGO | nongovernmental organization |
| NPI | net prosperity index |
| NPR | net poverty reduction |
| NSCN | National Socialist Council of Nagaland (India) |
| NSP | National Solidarity Program (Afghanistan) |
| OLS | ordinary least squares |
| PCA | principal components analysis |
| PRK | People's Republic of Kampuchea |
| PSP | percentage starting poor |
| RDS | Rural Development Society (Sri Lanka) |
| Rp | rupiah (Indonesia) |
| SULFA | Surrendered ULFA (India) |
| ULFA | United Liberation Front of Asom (India) |
| UNHCR | United Nations High Commissioner for Refugees |
| UNTAC | United Nations Transitional Authority in Cambodia |

# PART 1

# Building States from the Bottom Up in Conflict-Affected Countries

*Deepa Narayan*
*Denis Nikitin*
*Patti Petesch*

# Moving Out of Poverty in Conflict Communities

*The problem has not even been solved. Even though the memorandum of understanding is signed, the war is like a sleeping lion. It can get up at any time.*

— MEN'S DISCUSSION GROUP,
Manivali, Jaffna district, Sri Lanka, 2006

*Freedom is being ruined by those ruling the country. They do not let people think with their heads but with their stomachs because they are hungry. The other thing is weapons; there is no power of words, only power of weapons.*

— PEDRO, PARTICIPANT IN A DISCUSSION GROUP,
Villa Rosa, Cartagena municipality, Colombia

Violent conflict is devastation. But imagine, amid such devastation, more poor people moving out of poverty than in villages at peace. Imagine women emerging from their homes and the weight of centuries of tradition and becoming decision makers in village councils. Imagine old rivalries across social divides of religion and ethnicity getting buried in the rubble. Imagine local governments listening to ordinary people. Is this a utopian fantasy, or do new possibilities take shape when countries emerge from violent conflict?

The conventional wisdom backed by cumulative research is that conflict wreaks havoc on economies, polities, and societies. This is correct. But we may have missed a great deal by focusing only on national and global aggregates. When one looks closely at local communities in conflict-affected areas, a very different picture often emerges. This picture does not deny the devastation, the horror, and the pain of prolonged civil strife. But it also reveals many instances of hope amid devastation, and this in turn suggests ways to help people, communities, polities, and societies recover from civil conflict and build resilience at the local level.

The global Moving Out of Poverty study explores mobility from the perspectives and experiences of poor people who have moved out of poverty in more than 500 communities across 15 countries.[1] It is based on quantitative and qualitative data collected from 60,000 people through life stories, group discussions, and household questionnaires. In this fourth and final volume of the series, we focus on the subset of seven countries affected by conflict: Afghanistan, Cambodia, Colombia, India (the state of Assam), Indonesia (North Maluku), the Philippines (Mindanao island), and Sri Lanka.

We were interested in learning how civil conflict and political violence affect poor people's chances of moving out of poverty and the underlying

3

processes that produce mobility outcomes. We are fully aware that no two conflicts are alike, yet we feel that it is important to go beyond statements like "it all depends on the context." Context is important. At some peril, and guided by theory, we explore what factors in the context seem to be important—although they may not be equally important in all contexts, and may not be important at all in some contexts. We were surprised at what we found. It seems that when communities hit rock bottom and the old ways fall apart, for a short time there are possibilities of doing things in new ways that were not possible during peaceful times.

Even communities that have recently experienced high levels of civil conflict, political violence, and destruction may sometimes experience high levels of movement out of poverty. Overall, we found *no* significant difference between the rates at which people move out of poverty in peaceful and conflict-affected communities in our study. Overall, 32 percent of conflict communities and 31 percent of peaceful communities had high mobility rates. Fewer conflict communities (34 percent) than peaceful communities (41 percent) experienced very low mobility rates. In four of the countries, Indonesia, the Philippines, Colombia, and Sri Lanka, communities in conflict had higher mobility rates than peaceful communities.

These results are counterintuitive, and this book explores the underlying processes that may help explain them. We reach three overarching conclusions. First, people's immediate priority after conflict is to get on with their lives and livelihoods, reinvigorating their economic activities to ensure a future for their families and communities. Second, building a lasting peace depends on efforts to construct a legitimate, inclusive, accountable, participatory, and decentralized state from the bottom up that is functional in the far-flung peripheral areas of both low-income and middle-income countries. Third, rebuilding after civil conflict and political violence requires giving primacy to nation building, especially the construction of broad national identities that override religious or ethnic identities. This involves creating decentralized leadership committed to letting go of the past in thousands and thousands of recovering communities.

Broadly put, it is possible for poor people living in conflict-affected communities to move out of poverty if they live in countries with a strong democratic state that has the will and sufficient economic and military resources to reclaim and rebuild conflict-affected peripheral areas. Alternatively, if state capacity and resources are low, *sustained* international assistance may enable a legitimate state to create law and order, work across social divides to help poor people build permanent economic assets, and foster citizenship by creating legitimate local governance structures and a vibrant associational life. In such cases as well, poor people gain.

Our findings challenge much of the conventional wisdom about the development assistance strategies of governments, international agencies, and nongovernmental organizations (NGOs) in conflict and postconflict contexts. We highlight a few key findings.

First, people's top priority after basic security, law, and order is their own economic revival. Doling out a few seeds, a chicken, or a goat helps poor people cope, but it is not a strategy for quick and permanent wealth creation. It does not create the permanent assets that give people a stake in peace and enable them to leave poverty behind forever. Instead, people need support and advice to help them produce for markets. Much innovation is needed in supporting poor people's businesses and corporations, along with investment and innovation by the private sector and international corporations to create jobs and new partnerships with workers.

Second, people returning after conflict to burned-down homes and villages have lost everything, yet assistance strategies almost never provide direct, substantial transfers of cash or private assets in such situations. When they do, people forget their grievances more quickly, are more ready to forgive and heal old wounds, and develop a stake in maintaining peace. Families can focus their attention on expanding their economic assets rather than on merely surviving day to day and coping with the pain of their loss. Assistance programs that do provide income support typically offer small amounts and play a complicated game of calculating who deserves help and who does not. Narrowly defined targeting wastes resources, sows divisiveness in already divided societies, and invariably leaves out the poorest, who can seldom meet the conditions imposed. Often multiple agencies—governments, donors, and NGOs—working in the same communities solemnly dole out small amounts with different conditions, ignoring each other; local people watch, baffled, but still willing to take whatever they get. This approach has not helped.

Third, bottom-up approaches can change the culture of accountability in thousands of communities, even in war-torn contexts. The international community in the last two decades has increasingly focused on state accountability, yet indicators of improved governance at the national level have remained stable over a decade, except where there is a major regime change (as in Indonesia). There is little change within countries, although there is great variation across countries.[2] Yet international attention has focused almost exclusively on capital cities rather than on creating a culture of accountability in thousands of scattered communities. In addition, the international focus on the *forms* of democracy, particularly national elections, has been misguided. Elections in conflict communities hurt poor people's mobility. Changing dysfunctional polities into functioning democracies requires more than elections; it requires investment in strong local civic associations and support for them over time through access to information and functioning systems of justice. It requires changing norms and values. It requires local leaders in these communities who support and nurture community prosperity rather than capturing resources for themselves. Large-scale programs in the Philippines, Indonesia, and Afghanistan demonstrate that this is possible even in the most difficult conflict contexts.

Fourth, in conflict and postconflict contexts, neutrality is not enough; indeed it may be harmful. This is particularly true when conflicts are based on divisions between ethnic, religious, or other social groups. What is needed in these contexts is a pro-active effort to reach across fractured social lines early in the process, while there is still hope for burying old wounds. Help has to shift from platitudes to action. In one Philippine village visited for the study, Christians and Muslims built houses for each other and helped rehabilitate each other's places of worship. Such joint action can be deeply healing. When reconciliation processes support such actions, with mass media outreach appropriate to the context, a culture of peace rather than war may take hold. However, unless steps are taken to address the core political, economic, and social inequities between social groups, even the best reconciliation process will wear thin over time. These processes are not helped when development assistance in conflict contexts is slow in arriving, whereas the needs are dire and immediate.

Finally, local people know well that changing societies run by warlords into functioning, stable societies takes time. Development assistance and programming also must take a long-term view, over at least a decade if not more.

## Organization of the Book

This book examines 102 communities across seven middle-income and low-income countries affected by conflict. Part 1 is based on cross-country analysis, and part 2 presents country case studies.

The analysis is guided by the overall conceptual framework for the Moving Out of Poverty study, which considers mobility to be an outcome of the interaction between individual initiative, collective action, and local-level institutions (social, political, and economic). Social inequality mediates these relationships, and where the social fissures are deep, different types of inequalities overlap and result in horizontal inequalities.[3]

In conflict contexts, the role of the state is central. When countries are engulfed in civil war, the state loses its hold on the country, and its legitimacy and capacity to govern equitably and reestablish security are brought into question. Some conflicts remain on the periphery, but these often are a result of marginalization and are framed around issues of identity. All conflicts weaken the legitimacy of the state and drain national treasuries.

Since the role of the state is so central in recovery, part 1 of the book is organized around the issue of state building. Unlike most studies, which focus on the national level, we concentrate on what is happening at the community level. We build from below. Our findings are based on discussions with approximately 14,000 people in the 102 communities visited, using a variety of data collection methods. Hence the title of part 1, "Building States from the Bottom Up."

This introductory chapter describes the history of political conflict and violence in the seven countries. It then describes briefly the process we used to assign conflict ratings, the data limitations, and the patterns of mobility across conflict and nonconflict communities. Methodological details can be found in the volume appendixes, especially appendix B. Chapter 2 focuses on the importance of establishing a minimum level of security, law, and order to enable people to reclaim their lives. Chapter 3 makes the distinction between form and functions of democracy in low- and middle-income countries. Its findings, some of them counterintuitive, suggest how to move from dysfunctional politics to a democratic culture of accountability to citizens.

Chapter 4 turns to the much-neglected issue of nation building from below. The process is critical when social group differences underlie conflict or are an incipient source of tension. Even in contexts where conflict is based on social divides, there is some evidence that social divisiveness is declining. We examine the underlying mechanisms that can contribute to lessening social tensions even when conflict has been ignited by these very divisions. The role of local leaders emerges as paramount in seeding a culture of peace and reconciliation.

Chapter 5 focuses on the overall poor economic environment in conflict-affected contexts and the ways in which people cope. What emerges is a sharp mismatch between local people's priorities and the offerings of most aid programs. Chapter 6 focuses on problems with existing aid strategies and makes recommendations based on the study findings. It ends by describing how nationwide community-driven and peace-building programs provide a way to reknit socially divided communities into a nation and spread a culture of accountability from the bottom up. Chapter 7 summarizes key conclusions about development assistance for more effective economic recovery with poverty reduction, peace, and nation building.

## History and Nature of the Conflicts

The primary focus of the research reported in this volume is to explore the *consequences* of major political conflict with respect to poverty and mobility.[4] Unlike many studies, ours does not attempt to explain the *causes* of conflict. There is a vast and growing literature on that topic, and lively debate has followed Paul Collier's (1999) provocative claim that greed and the feasibility of violence, rather than grievance alone, are the main causes of civil war.[5] This debate across disciplines about the causes of conflict has implications for strategies used by governments and international agencies during postconflict recovery. One of the most important statistics to emerge from recent research is that in countries that have recently emerged from civil war, there is a 44 percent risk that violence will erupt again, and this risk continues for at least a decade after the end of the initial conflict (Collier et al. 2003, 83).[6] Thus, postconflict recovery strategies must include prevention of conflict as an overarching aim that affects their focus, timing, scale, and content over time.

The nature of civil conflict in the countries in our sample varied tremendously. The majority of the conflicts have persisted for more than two decades.

- In *Afghanistan,* conflict between the *mujahedeen* and the Soviet-backed government started in 1979, escalated after 1985, and ended in 1992. Violence raged between the various mujahedeen factions from 1992 to 1996, and between the mujahedeen and the Taliban from 1996 to 2001. Since 2006, when the study was conducted, there has been a dramatic deterioration in security, and currently over half the country is once again embroiled in conflict.
- *Cambodia* was wracked by civil war for almost a decade before the Khmer Rouge declared victory in 1975. In 1979 Vietnamese forces invaded and established the People's Republic of Kampuchea. Fighting involving the Khmer Rouge affected much of the country throughout the 1980s, and although a peace agreement was signed in 1991, armed conflict continued to threaten many regions into the 1990s.

- The armed conflict in *Colombia* dates back to at least 1964, with guerrillas of the FARC (Fuerzas Armadas Revolucionarias de Colombia) and the ELN (Ejército de Liberación Nacional) rising up from the Liberal and Communist parties, respectively. Right-wing paramilitary and drug-trafficking organizations also challenge state authority.
- In Assam, a state in the north of *India*, the United Liberation Front of Asom (ULFA) began fighting in the late 1980s for an independent state. It claims to represent all of the diverse ethnic and religious groups that populate the state, including Hindu and Muslim Assamese and Bengalis as well as tribal groups. A separate armed opposition group seeks to carve out a state for the Bodo people of Assam. There has been a resurgence of conflict in recent years.
- In *Indonesia*, religious and ethnic conflict erupted in the adjoining provinces of Maluku and North Maluku in January 1999 and lasted until 2002. The fighting was largely between local groups of Muslims and Christians, although clashes between Muslim sects also occurred.
- In the south of Mindanao, an island in the *Philippines*, armed groups including the Moro Islamic Liberation Front (MILF), the Moro National Liberation Front (MNLF), and Abu Sayyaf have waged a battle to create a separate Muslim homeland. The MNLF launched the secessionist conflict in the late 1960s and participated in peace talks that resulted in creation of the Autonomous Region in Muslim Mindanao in 1989.
- In *Sri Lanka*, the Liberation Tigers of Tamil Eelam (LTTE) began waging a secessionist struggle in 1983 from bases in the north and east of the country. At the time the study was conducted in late 2005, a cease-fire was quickly breaking down. In 2009 the government launched a major offensive against the LTTE in which the rebel leaders were killed, there were high civilian casualties, and thousands were displaced to refugee camps. The government then declared victory over the LTTE. There was also an earlier period of violent conflict between a Marxist revolutionary group and the government between 1989 and 1991.

Three of the conflicts, those in the Philippines, Sri Lanka, and Indonesia, engage the aspirations of minority ethnic or religious groups.[7] Four of the conflicts directly challenge the very notion of nationhood, as minority groups demand autonomous self-government on their own terms with an identity distinct from that of the current nation-state. The protracted conflicts, especially those in Assam, Colombia, the Philippines, and until very recently Sri Lanka, drain national resources and challenge the state's capacity to govern fairly in remote areas. Afghanistan experienced full civil war that affected all parts of the country, and Cambodia suffered genocide. The five other civil conflicts affected mostly areas in the periphery. Our sample of communities largely reflects the rural bias of most of these conflicts.

The wars in Cambodia and Afghanistan, in particular, took a staggering human toll. In the period from 1975 to 1979, an estimated 1 million to 2 million Cambodians were killed under the Khmer Rouge. During the period of Afghanistan's mujahedeen combat with Soviet-backed forces, from 1979 to 1992, over a million Afghans died and 2 million migrated. There are also estimates that 6 million Afghans fled the country for their lives during the 1996–2001 clashes between the mujahedeen and the Taliban. Colombia earns the distinction of having the most landmines of any country and the second-largest internally displaced population after Sudan. The death toll in Sri Lanka over the last 25 years of civil conflict is estimated to be 150,000. The death toll in the final weeks of fighting before the end of the civil conflict in 2009 remain elusive, but figures of 10,000 to 20,000 Tamil deaths are mentioned. Across Indonesia, where our study focuses on North Maluku, communal violence erupted approximately 465 times between 1990 and 2001, and violent events driven by separatist ambitions totaled more than 500 (NPRC 2005). Further details on the history and nature of the conflicts can be found in the country chapters.

The boundaries between "conflict" and "postconflict" in reality are blurred, both at the country level and, especially, at the community level. Even when cease-fires or national peace agreements have been signed, situations frequently change over time, as seen in Sri Lanka, the Philippines, Afghanistan, and Assam. One-third of the sample communities that were in conflict in 1995 were still in conflict at the time of the study in 2005, but a quarter had moved from conflict to peace or postconflict status. A smaller number of communities that were formerly peaceful had started experiencing some conflict.

## Community Conflict Ratings

*During the Taliban, people were tortured a lot. The effect of their government was that people were killed; their houses were destroyed; people were injured and became crippled or disabled; people suffered from psychological problems; and the Taliban were beating people in prisons.*
    —Discussion group, Shazimir, Kabul province, Afghanistan

In order to conduct comparative analyses across communities in these seven countries, and after much consultation and discussion with conflict experts, we standardized the criteria used to assign conflict ratings across communities. To qualify as high-conflict, a community had to have at least five deaths plus destruction of property or evacuation of the entire village due to political violence during the roughly 10-year observation period of 1995 to 2005. Each community was rated as high-conflict, low-conflict, or no-conflict by two researchers independently. Then, because six of the seven countries (all except Assam, India) contained only three low-conflict communities between them, we combined low- and high-conflict communities into a single "conflict" rating (table 1.1).[8]

We distinguish between political conflict and everyday crime and violence. Political conflict involves contestation over political power and decision making; as a result, it may take on stable institutional forms and sometimes creates economies of its own. Everyday crime and violence often involve a fight over resources, including access to farmland, forests, and fisheries.[9] Such violence may be organized, but it does not constitute a fight over political power, and we did not consider it to be political conflict. Communities affected *only* by everyday crime and violence were therefore given ratings of "no conflict."

While political violence affected only the sample communities labeled as conflict communities, everyday violence was more widespread, affecting

**TABLE 1.1**

**Distribution of study communities by country and presence of conflict**

*number of communities*

| Country | Conflict | Nonconflict | Total |
|---|---|---|---|
| Afghanistan | 4 | 2 | 6 |
| Assam | 35 | 15 | 50 |
| Cambodia | 5 | 4 | 9 |
| Colombia | 5 | 3 | 8 |
| Indonesia | 5 | 5 | 10 |
| Philippines | 8 | 2 | 10 |
| Sri Lanka | 5 | 4 | 9 |
| Total | 68 | 34 | 102 |

*Source:* Authors' analysis.
*Note:* Assam, a state of India, is listed under "countries" in our data tables.

56 percent of the "peaceful" communities that did not have political conflict. Everyday violence also occurred in many of the conflict communities, and in these places it often intertwined with political violence in ways that were hard to untangle.[10] Again, our data collection tools focused on the consequences of major political violence for households and communities rather than on a detailed understanding of its varied forms and causes.

An average conflict community experienced four separate periods of violence over the last 10 years, while an average nonconflict community experienced only two violent periods (table 1.2). When violence broke out, it lasted on average 6 to 12 hours in conflict communities but less than 6 hours in nonconflict ones. Consequently, the disruption of economic relations was considerably more severe in conflict-affected communities, where violence led to the closing of nearly all markets and shops for extended periods of time. In nonconflict communities, violence led to some closures but not as many. Additionally, conflict communities lingered for longer periods during which they feared an outbreak of renewed violence—two to three years out of the past decade in conflict communities, but only two to four weeks in nonconflict communities.

**TABLE 1.2**

**Nature of conflict over 10 years in conflict and nonconflict communities**

| Variable | Conflict | Nonconflict |
|---|---|---|
| Median duration of violence once it breaks out, over past 10 years | 6 to 12 hours | 1 to 6 hours |
| Conflict resulted in property damage (% of communities) | 71 | 46 |
| Conflict resulted in injuries (% of communities) | 85 | 69 |
| Average number of separate periods of violence per community, over past 10 years | 4 | 2 |
| Effect on daily functioning of markets, over past 10 years | Nearly all markets/ shops closed for extended periods of time | Some markets closed |
| Length of time during which community faced a risk of experiencing violent conflict, over past 10 years (median) | 2 to 3 years | 2 to 4 weeks |

*Source:* Community questionnaire.

## Study Design and Methods

### Focus on communities

Earlier volumes in this series focused primarily on factors associated with household mobility.[11] Since conflict is an event that affects everyone in a community (although different parts of a community may be differentially affected), the analysis in this volume focuses primarily on factors affecting communities rather than individuals or households.[12] Part 1 of the book examines communities across countries in conflict and nonconflict contexts. We report quantitative trends across countries, pointing out country differences sparingly. We primarily explore the relationships between factors in communities across conflict contexts, and we bring in country context through the qualitative data. Hence, when numbers are reported, these usually refer to communities and not households.

Clearly, the national context is important, and part 2 of the book is organized by country. Our sample is deliberately small, as we decided to explore a few communities in depth rather than attempt a wide investigation across a large number of communities. Countries were chosen to represent different types and intensities of conflict and different levels of income. Our attempt to conduct a study in Rwanda was poorly timed and unfortunately had to be discontinued, so our sample does not include an African country context. We examined 102 communities in total; sample sizes range from 6 to 10 communities per country, except for Assam, where the sample size is 50.[13] Within each country, communities were chosen to represent high- and low-growth areas and high-, low-, or no-conflict areas.[14] In each country, community-level sampling was informed by growth data, proxied by levels of infrastructure and other economic data, and by whatever data were available on conflict. While we took care to select communities that were representative of their areas, the sample is not nationally representative. This needs to be remembered, although for ease of reading we do not qualify our statements throughout the text.

There are four sampling issues. First, despite efforts by our country-based researchers to classify and select communities as peaceful or conflict-affected, using secondary data and other sources, in all of the countries such classification proved to be a difficult task. Community visits indicated that the data used for the sampling were not always reliable. Hence, some communities had to be dropped and were replaced by other communities that fit the sampling framework. Everywhere we found that "peace is not always peace, and conflict is not always conflict."

Second, our sample is numerically dominated by communities in Assam, and we take this into account in different ways. Extensive analysis on Assam as a case study has already been reported in volume 3 in the series, and hence we are familiar with the pattern of results for this context. In addition, for this chapter we conducted extensive analysis by country and also by Assam and non-Assam categorization of conflict and nonconflict communities. Where we observed important differences in patterns of relationships relying primarily on simple cross tabulations, we report them. In summarizing quantitative data through regression analysis, we include both country and regional dummies to take into account country effects.

Third, our quantitative analysis does not include Cambodia or Sri Lanka. The Cambodia study was based on a panel dataset, so it did not gather poverty data using subjective recall measures with our ladder of life tool (see below). Hence, while we have very useful descriptive information and quantitative data for Cambodia, we do not have quantitative data that are comparable to much of the data reported for the cross-country analyses. In Sri Lanka as well, we have only partial data because of the resurgence of major civil conflict in the north in early 2006, which truncated both the sample and the quantitative data collection. However, since we have extensive other data from both countries, we include them in our analyses of patterns and also in the country case studies in part 2 of the book.

Finally, conflicts affect the very structure of communities through death, displacement, and migration. We did not have the resources to trace people who did not return to their communities. However, we did conduct some analyses to understand how migration affects movement out of poverty at the community level. We found no difference between communities with more migration into the community and those with more migration out (appendix table F.1).[15]

Despite these limitations, we hope that the study provides some insights and will stimulate other comparative research efforts that focus on understanding community dynamics and how they affect the mobility of poor households in conflict contexts.

## Focus on subjective experiences

We give primacy to qualitative data and use the quantitative data as a summation device. The overall Moving Out of Poverty methodology involved use of 10 data collection techniques (see appendix B for a discussion of the study approach and the most important data collection methods, and appendix C for descriptions of all the methods). The different tools enabled us to triangulate information from different sources. Like all studies and all datasets, ours are not problem free. Qualitative data, like quantitative data, are subject to well-known errors of recall, desire to please, and desire to mislead. We discuss these issues in greater detail in volume 2 and will not revisit them here except to note that the stress and uncertainty of collecting data in conflict contexts undoubtedly compound these measurement challenges.

We privilege people's subjective experiences, both collective and individual. Our research results are based on 850 group discussions, 2,800 individual interviews, and 1,000 life stories. Discussion groups explored their community's history, including its history of conflict, how conflict affected the community, and what factors contributed to community prosperity or decline. Group discussions were also held on freedom, power, democracy, and livelihoods. In most places, separate discussion groups were held with men, women, and youth. At the same time, we listened to people's individual descriptions of their own lives—how and why they had remained stuck in poverty, had managed to move out of poverty, had fallen into poverty, or had remained well off. These included both household interviews and life stories.

To protect the privacy of participants, this book uses pseudonyms for the study communities (villages and barrios). Cities, municipalities, districts, departments, and provinces are identified by their real names.

## Definitions of poverty and community mobility indicators

The poverty statistics used in the study are based on people's subjective definitions of poverty and on a locally defined poverty line for each community, with no attempt at standardization across communities. We use a tool called the ladder of life to establish each community's own definition of poverty and wealth and determine who in the community qualifies as poor. In each community, ladder of life discussion groups were formed, usually with men and women separately. Participants create a figurative ladder of well-being for their own community, with the bottom step representing the poorest and worst-off households and the top step the wealthiest and best-off. They describe the household characteristics that define each step of the ladder and the typical ways in which households can move up or down the ladder.

Next, 100–150 household names in the community are randomly selected for sorting. The groups place each household on a step on the ladder according to its status today and at the beginning of a predefined period, typically 10 years ago.[16] After sorting the households, the group identifies a community poverty line (CPL). Households at steps below the line are considered poor, and those at steps above the line are considered not poor. Just as different discussion groups create ladders with different numbers of steps (usually four to six), they can set the poverty line wherever they think is appropriate for their own community.

The sorting of households in communities allows us to categorize each one in terms of its poverty mobility or lack of mobility during the study period. Households may have moved up or down or remained stuck at the same step of the ladder. Those that have moved, or fallen, may or may not have crossed the community poverty line. Throughout this book, we refer to four mobility categories:

- *Movers:* households that were poor initially but moved out of poverty by the end of the study period
- *Chronic poor:* households that were poor initially and remained poor
- *Never poor:* households that were not poor initially and remained not poor
- *Fallers:* households that were not poor initially but fell into poverty by the end of the period.

The distribution of households into these four categories allows us to calculate mobility rates for entire communities, using the mobility indexes in table 1.3. Further details of the methodology are available in appendix B.

## Mobility Rates in Conflict and Nonconflict Communities

Conventional wisdom and intuition tell us to expect no mobility or negative mobility in conflict contexts. But we did not find this to be true, on average, in the conflict-affected communities in our sample. Once violence ceases, poverty reduction is even more likely than in the localities that witnessed no conflict at all.

The moving out of poverty (MOP) index captures the share of a community's households that were poor in 1995 but moved up the ladder and across the community poverty line by the end of the study period, in 2005 or 2006. If 15 percent of a community's initially poor households escaped poverty during this period, the community's MOP would be 0.15. Depending on these percentages, communities were categorized as low, middle, or high MOP across the sample.

**TABLE 1.3**
**Summary indicators of mobility**

| | |
|---|---|
| MOP | Moving out of poverty index |
| | Measures extent of upward mobility by the poor across the CPL in a community. |
| | MOP = initially poor who move above CPL ÷ initially poor. |
| MPI | Mobility of the poor index |
| | Measures extent of upward mobility by those who were initially poor. |
| | MPI = initially poor who move up ÷ initially poor. |
| MRI | Mobility of the rich index |
| | Measures extent of upward mobility by those who were initially above the CPL (nonpoor or "rich" by the study's definition). |
| | MRI = initially rich who move up ÷ initially rich. |
| FI | Falling index |
| | Measures extent of all downward mobility in a community. |
| | FI = all households that move down ÷ total number of households. |
| FPI | Falling of the poor index |
| | Measures extent of downward mobility of the initially poor. |
| | FPI = initially poor who move down ÷ initially poor. |
| FRI | Falling of the rich index |
| | Measures extent of downward mobility of the rich. |
| | FRI = initially rich who move down ÷ initially rich. |
| FRIP | Falling of the rich into poverty index |
| | Measures extent of downward mobility of the rich across the CPL. |
| | FRI = initially rich who move below CPL ÷ initially rich. |
| NPI | Net prosperity index |
| | Measures extent of net upward mobility (upward less downward) in a community. |
| | NPI = (all households that move up − all households that move down) ÷ total number of households. |

Table 1.4 shows the extent of movement out of poverty in conflict and nonconflict communities. While it is logical to assume that few conflict-affected communities would show high rates of poverty escapes, this is not what we found. Rather, close to a third of the conflict communities were classified as having high MOP, slightly higher than the percentage of nonconflict communities with high MOP in the same countries. Our data thus do not suggest that during periods of conflict and recovery, poverty in a community always remains static or worsens. Also unexpectedly, we find fewer conflict communities (34 percent) than nonconflict communities (41 percent)

**TABLE 1.4**
**Distribution of study communities by conflict and MOP rating**
*percentage of communities*

| MOP rating | Conflict | Nonconflict | Total |
|---|---|---|---|
| Low MOP | 34 | 41 | 37 |
| Middle MOP | 34 | 28 | 32 |
| High MOP | 32 | 31 | 31 |
| Total | 100 | 100 | 100 |
| N | 61 | 29 | 90 |

*Source:* Ladder of life group discussions and authors' analysis.
*Note:* Pearson chi$^2$ = 0.545, Pr = 0.762. Percentages include Sri Lanka.

experiencing low MOP. The pattern of distribution is the same with and without the Assam communities (appendix table F.2).

In addition to the distribution of high- and low-MOP communities, we consider the mean MOP in conflict and nonconflict communities. The MOP index is higher on average in conflict communities, where 19 percent of households moved out of poverty, than in nonconflict communities, where only 16 percent did (table 1.5). This pattern holds and becomes even sharper when we consider conflict and nonconflict communities in the non-Assam portion of the sample only. The Assam communities tend to have, on average, lower MOP than the non-Assam communities, and this varies little across conflict and nonconflict contexts.

Next, we examine other useful indexes of mobility patterns across communities (table 1.6). We find that the mean initial level of poverty (percentage starting poor, or PSP) is lower in conflict communities than in nonconflict ones. It is striking to note that even the well-off groups seem to fare better in conflict communities. If you are above the poverty line, then your chances of

**TABLE 1.5**
**Mean MOP in conflict and nonconflict communities**

| Conflict rating | Total sample | Total without Assam | Assam only |
|---|---|---|---|
| Conflict | 0.19 | 0.32 | 0.10 |
| Nonconflict | 0.16 | 0.21 | 0.11 |
| Total | 0.18 | 0.28 | 0.11 |

*Source:* Ladder of life group discussions and authors' analysis.
*Note:* Total sample includes Sri Lanka.

**TABLE 1.6**
**Mean mobility indicators in conflict and nonconflict communities**

| Indicator | Conflict | Nonconflict | Total |
|---|---|---|---|
| MOP | 0.19 | 0.16 | 0.18 |
| FRIP | 0.20 | 0.27 | 0.22 |
| FRI | 0.24 | 0.35 | 0.28 |
| MRI | 0.17 | 0.12 | 0.16 |
| NPI | 0.16 | 0.22 | 0.18 |
| PSP | 0.71 | 0.78 | 0.73 |
| N | 61 | 29 | 90 |

Source: Ladder of life group discussions and authors' analysis.
Note: Includes Sri Lanka.

rising further are slightly higher in conflict contexts than in peaceful contexts. And importantly, the chances of well-off groups falling down slightly or all the way down into poverty are much lower in conflict contexts.

Finally, we examine the mobility rates in each of the six countries for which we had sufficient quantitative data (table 1.7). An interesting pattern emerges. In the three middle-income countries of Indonesia, Colombia, and the Philippines, conflict communities register higher poverty mobility rates than peaceful communities, with the difference being sharpest in Indonesia. In the two low-income countries, India and Afghanistan, there were no differences in mobility rates between conflict and nonconflict communities. In Sri Lanka, however, conflict communities have higher MOP than nonconflict communities.[17] Overall rates of escaping poverty were lowest in Assam (India) and highest in Afghanistan. It is remarkable that nearly half of the sample emerged from poverty in Afghanistan, where people experienced prolonged war, widespread destruction of property, and mass displacement at very high rates.

## Community MOP and Poverty

A priori, initial levels of poverty can be associated with upward mobility either positively or negatively. In a community with large numbers of poor people, if there is some improvement in the economic or political context that enables people to benefit from their own initiative, there are potentially many poor people who could do so and move up. This suggests that moving out of poverty rates will be higher in communities with a large proportion

**TABLE 1.7**

**Mean mobility indicators in conflict and nonconflict communities, by country**

| Country | Conflict rating | MOP | FRIP | FRI | MRI | NPI | PSP | N |
|---|---|---|---|---|---|---|---|---|
| Afghanistan | Conflict | 0.47 | 0.28 | 0.31 | 0.26 | 0.29 | 0.61 | 4 |
|  | Nonconflict | 0.48 | 0.29 | 0.34 | 0.24 | 0.29 | 0.58 | 2 |
|  | Total | 0.47 | 0.28 | 0.32 | 0.25 | 0.29 | 0.60 | 6 |
| Assam | Conflict | 0.10 | 0.16 | 0.21 | 0.10 | 0.07 | 0.71 | 35 |
|  | Nonconflict | 0.11 | 0.26 | 0.33 | 0.06 | 0 | 0.72 | 15 |
|  | Total | 0.11 | 0.19 | 0.24 | 0.09 | 0.05 | 0.72 | 50 |
| Colombia[a] | Conflict | 0.24 | 0.17 | 0.20 | 0.65 | 0.54 | 0.84 | 5 |
|  | Nonconflict | 0 | — | — | — | 0.70 | 1.00 | 3 |
|  | Total | 0.15 | 0.17 | 0.20 | 0.65 | 0.60 | 0.90 | 8 |
| Indonesia | Conflict | 0.38 | 0.14 | 0.19 | 0.25 | 0.29 | 0.58 | 5 |
|  | Nonconflict | 0.17 | 0.26 | 0.32 | 0.16 | 0.50 | 0.83 | 5 |
|  | Total | 0.27 | 0.20 | 0.25 | 0.21 | 0.40 | 0.70 | 10 |
| Philippines[b] | Conflict | 0.24 | 0.31 | 0.39 | 0.10 | 0.09 | 0.68 | 8 |
|  | Nonconflict | 0.20 | 0.53 | 0.62 | 0.07 | 0.11 | 0.82 | 2 |
|  | Total | 0.23 | 0.35 | 0.43 | 0.09 | 0.10 | 0.71 | 10 |
| Sri Lanka | Conflict | 0.40 | 0.28 | 0.36 | 0.19 | 0.28 | 0.81 | 4 |
|  | Nonconflict | 0.34 | 0.07 | 0.26 | 0.38 | 0.45 | 0.93 | 2 |
|  | Total | 0.34 | 0.20 | 0.32 | 0.31 | 0.34 | 0.85 | 6 |

*Source:* Ladder of life group discussions and authors' analysis.
a. The Colombian communities did not record any well-off people and hence the indexes on movement of the rich could not be calculated.
b. Conflict study only (a separate Philippines study was conducted in Bukidnon).

of poor people than in those where their proportion is smaller. Thus, MOP rates are likely to be higher in India than in Belgium simply because there are many more poor people in India.

This view, however, presumes that the poor have comparable resources to escape poverty in countries with high and low levels of poverty. In reality, it is likely that communities with widespread poverty will lack important resources necessary for upward mobility, and consequently higher levels of poverty would discourage poverty reduction. In our sample we find support for this latter view.

In figure 1.1 we plot the community MOP rates with the initial poverty rates for conflict and nonconflict communities. Two patterns are striking. The negative relationship between PSP and MOP outlined above seems to hold in

**FIGURE 1.1**

**MOP by initial poverty level, conflict and nonconflict communities**

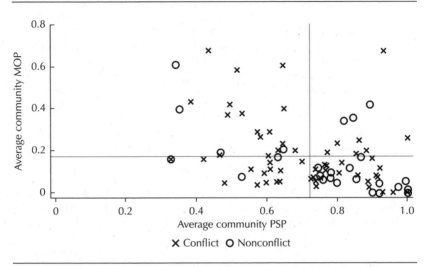

*Source:* Ladder of life group discussions and authors' analysis.
*Note:* PSP = percentage starting poor.

our sample of nonconflict communities, observed by the clustering of high PSP and low MOP in the right bottom quadrant. However, there is more variation in the relationship between PSP and community MOP for conflict-affected communities. It is this variance that we seek to understand.

In the remaining chapters of part 1, we explore why we sometimes see higher poverty mobility in conflict areas or no stark contrasts in mobility between conflict and nonconflict areas in the same country.

## Notes

1. The Moving Out of Poverty research program is a follow-up to the three-volume Voices of the Poor series, which explored the experience of poverty from the perspectives of 60,000 poor men and women. As in Voices of the Poor, the current study sought to learn directly from people in local communities, but this time our focus was on how and why people are able to move out of poverty, remained trapped in poverty, or fall back into poverty. Volume 1 of the series provides a multidisciplinary examination of current theories and empirical works about poor people's mobility (Narayan and Petesch 2007). Volume 2 presents the global synthesis of findings from our new data collection across 15 countries (Narayan, Pritchett, and Kapoor 2009). Volume 3 examines poverty dynamics

in 300 communities from four states in India: Andhra Pradesh, Assam, Uttar Pradesh, and West Bengal (Narayan 2009). Assam is a conflict-affected state, but the Assam study is reported in chapter 7 of volume 3 rather than here in volume 4. The Moving Out of Poverty Web site is at http://www.worldbank.org/movingoutofpoverty or http://go.worldbank.org/8K2Q8RYZ10.

2. See the annual reports of Freedom House and its political rights and civil liberties indexes for the study period (http://www.freedomhouse.org).

3. "Horizontal inequalities" is a term coined by Frances Stewart. For a detailed conceptual framework, see volumes 2 and 3 in the Moving Out of Poverty series (Narayan, Pritchett, and Kapoor 2009; Narayan 2009), as well as appendix B of this volume.

4. The decision to focus the study on countries or parts of countries affected by major political conflict rather than on more localized problems of crime and violence emerged from a February 2005 research workshop. The intention was to get as much variation as possible in geographic location and the nature of conflict. The actual country selection depended in part on the level of interest in the study shown by each country's government and by the World Bank country teams. Another factor was whether we could identify local research institutes with the interest, time, and capacities to carry out the multidisciplinary work.

5. The literature on causes of political conflict has become much more multidisciplinary in response to Collier and Hoeffler's (1998, 2004) empirical work supporting greed (or private profit motives) rather than grievance (or political, social, and economic exclusion and injustice) as the main driver of civil strife. For an overview of the evolving discourse sparked by the greed versus grievance discourse, see Arnson (2005). For explanations of conflict that focus on political or state capacity factors, see, for example, North, Wallis, and Weingast (2009) on the lack of institutions that enable open political and economic competition; Tilly (2003) on the importance of authoritarian (and authoritarian-like democratic) regimes and weak state capacities; and Horowitz (2000) on the polarizing effect of identity politics. For explanations that center on social factors, see Stewart (1998) on the role of disadvantaged social identities associated with a widening of political, economic, and social inequalities.

   Econometric analysis by Fearon and Laitin (2003) finds that the factors most associated with the onset of 127 civil wars between 1945 and 1999 were poverty, large populations, and weak central governments that lack the administrative and military/police capacities to contain rebellion, in part because of "inept and corrupt counterinsurgency practices" (76). Their models did not find ethnic or religious diversity, inequality, lack of democracy, poor civil liberties, or state discrimination against minorities to be good predictors of conflict.

6. There is much debate about the number, and other researchers suggest lower estimates. See Suhrke and Samset (2007).

7. Scholars have sought explanations of ethnic and religious differences as causes of civil war, but the evidence remains mixed. See Wood (2003) and Kalyvas (2008) for two useful reviews of this literature. Also relevant is Frances Stewart's recent edited volume, *Horizontal Inequalities and Conflict* (2008).

8. There are slight inconsistencies between the conflict ratings reported in this chapter and in the country chapters. To ensure consistency across the countries for the cross-country analysis informing part 1 of the book, every conflict rating was coded independently by two researchers. Minor discrepancies emerged with the country chapters, particularly around incidents of evacuation. An incident of mass displacement was not used to classify a community as high-conflict unless it was accompanied by reports of at least five deaths or a reasonable assumption that deaths had occurred based on reports of injuries and property destruction.

9. Sometimes other issues triggered everyday violence in the communities, ranging from accusations of witchcraft in Indonesia to family honor in Afghanistan and the Philippines. In East Java there were two vigilante-type murders after charges of witchcraft created widespread fear in the village. We labeled this community peaceful, however, because it was an isolated incident of violence in an otherwise (politically) peaceful community and region.

10. This finding is consistent with important work by Kalyvas (2006) demonstrating that the violent contest for territorial control by armed actors can often unleash or exacerbate diverse forms of "private" violence among local individuals and groups. These local actors may opportunistically use the surrounding mayhem in order to settle personal scores and advance personal agendas, including by fingering neighbors as "enemies." Only with considerable investments can outsiders begin to understand, and work to quell, locally rooted disorder.

11. In other volumes we report community-level effects, but by and large the focus is on households. The exception is chapter 3, "Communities Where Poor People Prosper," in volume 3 (Narayan, Petesch, and Paul 2009). Most studies of conflict focus on the macro level, but there is a burgeoning literature on household-level effects of conflict, much of which employs econometric techniques. Many of these studies can be found on the Web sites for the Households in Conflict Network and MICROCON. For example, see Justino (2006, 2008) and Brück and Schindler (2008) for a theoretical and empirical discussion of the different channels through which conflict affects households.

12. Narayan and Petesch (2007) provide an overview of the literature on mobility and find that community-level analysis is just starting to inform quantitative economic and sociological mobility research, though it has long been present in important qualitative work on mobility by sociologists and anthropologists. In 2009 the Pew Charitable Trusts Economic Mobility Project released a study of individuals that found very high rates of downward mobility among African Americans born to middle-class parents in the 1950s and 1960s; growing up in a high-poverty neighborhood emerged as the single most important explanatory factor for their reduced economic status (MacGillis 2009).

13. The India study was conducted in four states, with a special policy focus in each case. The studies were conducted on a larger sample because of the country's sheer population size. The availability of private sector data collection organizations with well-trained field teams enabled us to conduct the study in 50 to 110 communities in each state.

14. For a detailed discussion of the sampling framework, see appendix B.

15. It is plausible, especially in conflict communities, that those who stayed in their village were better fitted to endure hardship because of their accumulated assets, determination, or other advantages. We find that MOP levels are slightly higher in communities with higher levels of outward migration than in communities where there was no outward migration. However, *t*-test results indicate that the difference in mean MOP in communities with predominantly outward migration versus those with predominantly inward migration or no migration at all is insignificant. In comparing communities with outward migration in conflict and nonconflict contexts, we find that the mean MOP in the nonconflict communities (10 percent) is much lower than in the conflict communities (21 percent). This is likely to reflect very different reasons for outmigration in the two contexts. In nonconflict communities, community poverty and lack of opportunities probably push people out to seek chances elsewhere. In communities emerging from conflict, this is probably less true, at least initially, as people return with the expectation of reclaiming their properties and taking advantage of increased economic opportunities in peacetime.

16. The observation periods for the conflict country studies vary slightly but all are at least a decade; they are specified in each of the country chapters. To help people with recall, teams were instructed to pick an initial study year that coincides with a major event in the country, such as the coming to power of a new president. In Cambodia, however, the study built on an existing panel, so a baseline year of 2001 was used for sorting households, while 1993 was the baseline for group discussions of trends. The Colombia study examined mobility processes in six mostly new neighborhoods settled by large displaced populations, in addition to two conflict villages; baseline years for the new barrios vary from 4 to 10 years ago, depending on when they were formed.

17. For detailed country-level data, see the country chapters in part 2 of this volume.

# References

Arnson, C. J. 2005. "The Political Economy of War: Situating the Debate." In *Rethinking the Economics of War: The Intersection of Need, Creed and Greed*, ed. C. Arnson and I. W. Zartman, 1–22. Washington, DC: Woodrow Wilson Center Press; Baltimore: Johns Hopkins University Press.

Brück, T., and K. Schindler. 2008. "The Impact of Conflict and Fragility on Households: A Conceptual Framework with Reference to Widows." WIDER Research Paper 2008/83, United Nations University and World Institute for Development Economics Research, Helsinki.

Collier, P. 1999. "On the Economic Consequences of Civil War." *Oxford Economic Papers* 51 (1): 168–83.

Collier, P., V. L. Elliott, H. Hegre, A. Hoeffler, M. Reynal-Querol, and N. Sambanis. 2003. *Breaking the Conflict Trap: Civil War and Development Policy*. Washington, DC: World Bank; New York: Oxford University Press.

Collier, P., and A. Hoeffler. 1998. "On Economic Causes of Civil War." *Oxford Economic Papers* 50 (4): 563–73.

———. 2004. "Greed and Grievance in Civil War." *Oxford Economic Papers* 56 (4): 563–95.

Fearon, J. D., and D. D. Laitin. 2003. "Ethnicity, Insurgency and Civil War." *American Political Science Review* 97 (1): 75–90.

Horowitz, D. L. 2000. *Ethnic Groups in Conflict*. Berkeley: University of California Press.

Justino, P. 2006. "On the Links Between Violent Conflict and Chronic Poverty: How Much Do We Really Know?" HiCN Working Paper 18, Households in Conflict Network, University of Sussex, Brighton, UK.

———. 2008. "Poverty and Violent Conflict: A Micro Level Perspective on the Causes and Duration of Warfare." MICROCON Research Working Paper 6, Institute of Development Studies, University of Sussex, Brighton, UK.

Kalyvas, S. N. 2006. *The Logic of Violence in Civil War*. New York: Cambridge University Press.

———. 2008. "Ethnic Defection in Civil War." *Comparative Political Studies* 41 (8): 1043–68.

MacGillis, A. 2009. "Neighborhoods Key to Future Income, Study Finds." *Washington Post*, July 27, A6.

Narayan, D., ed. 2009. *Moving Out of Poverty: The Promise of Empowerment and Democracy in India*. New York: Palgrave Macmillan; Washington, DC: World Bank.

Narayan, D., and P. Petesch, eds. 2007. *Moving Out of Poverty: Cross-Disciplinary Perspectives on Mobility*. New York: Palgrave Macmillan; Washington, DC: World Bank.

Narayan, D., P. Petesch, and S. Paul. 2009. "Communities Where Poor People Prosper." In *Moving Out of Poverty: The Promise of Empowerment and Democracy in India*, ed. Deepa Narayan, 112–65. Washington, DC: World Bank.

Narayan, D., L. Pritchett, and S. Kapoor. 2009. *Moving Out of Poverty: Success from the Bottom Up*. New York: Palgrave Macmillan; Washington, DC: World Bank.

North, D. C., J. J. Wallis, and B. R. Weingast. 2009. *Violence and Social Orders: A Conceptual Framework for Interpreting Recorded Human History*. New York: Cambridge University Press.

NPRC (National Poverty Reduction Committee). 2005. "Strategi Nasional Penanggulangan Kemiskinan" (National Poverty Reduction Strategy). Komite Penanggulangan Kemiskinan (National Poverty Reduction Committee), Jakarta.

Stewart, F. 1998. "The Root Causes of Conflict: Some Conclusions." QEH Working Paper Series 16, Queen Elizabeth House, Oxford Department of International Development, University of Oxford, UK.

———, ed. 2008. *Horizontal Inequalities and Conflict: Understanding Group Violence in Multiethnic Societies*. New York: Palgrave Macmillan.

Suhrke, A., and I. Samset. 2007. "What's in a Figure? Estimating Recurrence of Civil War." *Journal of International Peacekeeping* 14 (2): 195–203.

Tilly, C. 2003. *The Politics of Collective Violence*. New York: Cambridge University Press.

Wood, E. J. 2003. "Review Essay: Civil Wars: What We Don't Know." *Global Governance* 9: 247–60.

# First Steps: Security, Law and Order, and Legitimacy

*No one wants to start a business because they don't know when they will have to give it up because of war.*

— **FEMALE YOUTH,**
Pothupana, Ampara district, Sri Lanka

*To us, law is a cheating formula that is used by the government or other authorities . . . If you try to follow the law, you are perceived to be stupid and have no brain and you become poor or remain poor.*

—**YOUNG MEN'S DISCUSSION GROUP,**
Chakboeng, Peam Ro district, Cambodia

A democratic state gets its legitimacy and mandate from its relations with citizens whom it represents and who in turn hold the state accountable. While laws provide the legal framework, societies function because most citizens accept an economic, political, and social compact with the state. This allows the state and society to interact without constant reference to law enforcement agencies and courts of law. Underlying values, norms, attitudes, and cultural practices guide behavior in order to maintain societal stability and keep conflict from turning into violence.

When civil conflict does erupt and persist, the authority and legitimacy of the state are called into question. Violence is no longer a state monopoly, as a variety of nonstate actors, from warlords to insurgents to individuals seeking to settle old personal scores, step into the melee. Chaos ensues, and civilian casualties mount.[1] As violence continues, the state progressively loses its capacity to protect citizens and their property and to guarantee basic rights to participate in the society, polity, and economy. The compact between citizens and the state collapses.[2]

Civil conflicts are often based on political, social, and economic marginalization of social groups. Grievances based on real or perceived inequality among groups provide a ready pool of recruits and can fuel the claims of insurgents. Identity politics emerge or harden. Many such groups demand their own sovereign territory carved out of the nation-state.

In postconflict contexts, therefore, two large, intertwined challenges face the state: state building and nation building. State building involves strengthening state capacity so that the state is present throughout the national territory, even in remote areas. A competent state ensures security, law, and order. It also provides infrastructure, basic services such as health and education, and an overall environment of stability and fairness in which citizens can pursue their livelihoods. Such a state, accountable to its citizens, must be reestablished for peace to prevail (Ghani and Lockhart 2008).

Nation building involves instilling a sense of national identity that is greater than and subsumes social group identity. It involves reknitting society through norms of fairness that ensure inclusion of all citizens and protection of their basic human rights, irrespective of their ethnicity, religion, tribe, caste, or gender.

## The Need for Security

*People have the fear of another war.*
    —Men's discussion group, Kaithamavi, Jaffna district, Sri Lanka

*The most important freedom is law and order. Law and order is very bad here and we cannot get any help from the law and order people. When theft or robbery or assault occurs in our village and we inform the police, they will not come without money or the cost of fuel. And if the police do come they harass the villagers.*
    —Men's discussion group, Baunrangi, Assam, India

The ordinary business of daily life in a community cannot happen without some measure of law and order. Farmers do not plant crops when they live in fear; businesses do not flourish when private property cannot be protected. Women and children stay indoors to stay safe. In every conflict-affected community visited for the study, people spoke about the breakdown of security and the unpredictability of their lives. Without security neither societies nor economies can flourish.

Providing law and order and enforcing the rules that govern society is the most basic function of governments. But when government fails in the task, the hunger for security and justice may cause communities to accept alternatives offered by insurgents and other nonstate groups. Even groups that are ruthless and brutal may win respect because of their ability to provide quick justice where there is no other recourse.

In this chapter, we first describe how people live in fear. We then discuss the behavior of security providers—the police and the army—and the mistrust that results when erstwhile armed rebels are elected to government posts. We discuss the capture of resources and corruption by state representatives; when those governing become the rule breakers, the pretense of accountability disappears and state legitimacy declines. Widespread lawlessness generates a deep desire to return to law and order and justice, which in some circumstances makes even brutal justice attractive. We then highlight gender-based violence and youth abduction. Finally, we explore how communities and countries have attempted to restore security in postconflict contexts. We move from the international to the local level, arguing that the success of international peacekeepers depends in part upon indigenous security strategies and the willingness of local leaders to cooperate.

## Living in fear

*The conflict caused fear and anxiety in the people. People got sick because of too much nervousness and fear.*
—Women's discussion group, Lomamoli,
Balabagan municipality, Philippines

*The biggest impact was economic. The market where we ran our business was closed. People were all afraid.*
—Men's discussion group, North Maluku province, Indonesia

The unpredictability of violence and the fear that violence may start up again paralyze people, preventing them from taking action and investing in the future. Businesses are shuttered, and children are held back from going to school. Daily life freezes in fear, and the fear outlasts peace agreements. When people live in fear, irrationality wins over rationality. In Barumangga, a village in North Maluku, Indonesia, a men's discussion group said that during the conflict, people became irrational and emotional because all their businesses were closed and they were afraid.[3] Almost everywhere, people spoke about the interweaving of economic and psychological trauma.

In Sri Lanka, in Welumbe, people spoke about the terror of having to leave everything behind to save their lives. "So we didn't bother about our livelihoods or our property, we just fled away to safe places or to the jungle. There were times when we spent days on top of trees. That was the time when we realized the uselessness of wealth and money. They cannot bring back a life lost. Death was what we feared." In Pothupana, Sri Lanka, a young men's discussion group added that during the war "we lived in fear, we used to run to the jungle to hide from terrorists, and we could not study properly."

In Tucampo, Mindanao, Philippines, a men's group described in great detail how fear never left them all through the conflict period. Before, during, and even after the displacement, they repeated again and again, fear never left them. Forced to leave their farms, people had no way of making a living. When they came back they found farms, animals, and trees destroyed by bombs and neglect. They could not concentrate on their work and the hours that they could spend working depended on the peace and order on a given day. "We visit our farms, but fear never left us. It affected our livelihoods because we could not concentrate on working at our farms since we were very cautious with our surroundings. Something might happen and we might have to run for our lives."

A women's discussion group in Glikati, Philippines, spoke of the casualties in their community: "They did not die because they got caught in the crossfire. They died because of health complications, for example, heart attacks triggered by nervousness and mental stress. But all these deaths were triggered by the conflict."

## Protectors of society: The police and the army

*Freedom means leading a free life in our birthplace. If we do not lose our virginity, honor, and self-respect at the hands of our soldiers, but get respectable behavior, that is freedom for us.*
   —Women's discussion group, Lakhanbar, Assam, India

*The police demand money at many checkpoints along the road, but it is not written in law that the police can get such and such amount from people along the road.*
   —Men's discussion group, Somrampi, Kampot district, Cambodia

When the army and the police commit atrocities, including indiscriminate torture and rape of ordinary people, or demand bribes, it signals a breakdown of the compact between the state and citizens. Such abuses break any bonds of trust and allegiance that people may have had with the state.[4] In communities in Sri Lanka, the Philippines, and Assam, people often found themselves caught in the crossfire and unable to distinguish clearly between the armed forces and the insurgents. Indeed, people often reported feeling as unsafe with the army as with other armed groups. The police often scored low in trust and sometimes were considered helpless watchers on the sidelines, at best.

In Morga, Assam, which is located near forests, a discussion group expressed fear of the ULFA (United Liberation Front of Asom) separatists, the

NSCN (National Socialist Council of Nagaland, another separatist group), and the CRPF (Central Reserve Police Force, India's elite paramilitary force).

> The problem is the free movement of the ULFA and NSCN extremists, because not only they but also the army and the CRPF torture us in the name of raid. We are sandwiched between the lawful and unlawful persons. The females constantly cry for fear of getting gang-raped by the enemy and CRPF and the extremists. The villagers are all unknown to the ULFA. But the CRPF think you may be ULFA. Now the villagers are constantly living in fear. Their minds are full of fear.

In another village, ULFA combatants dug a fishery pond on public lands. When these forces were pushed out by the army, villagers started using the fishery, only to be brutally attacked by the army when it stepped in to take over the fishery. Villagers then reported a long period of terror under the army presence that harmed the entire local economy: "People do not do business and other work for fear of the CRPF. If they go to this business in the morning time, they do not go out in the evening time, because the CRPF have arrested them and think them to be ULFA. The laborers' condition is same." Indeed, there was often little peace for the remote villages in the study that had the misfortune of being able to offer steady income to armed groups.

In Sampatnagar, Assam, local people referred to the army as the tall demons who "with bitter laughter used to strike people cruelly." In Gatakpur, people spoke of "the torture done by the militaries on the general people [when they act as] the false protector in search of ULFA terrorists." These abuses deeply alienated local people.

## When rebels become politicians

*People are still afraid and they don't express their problems or feelings openly. Some of our authorities now were also the authorities during the Taliban.*

—Discussion group, Morlaw Ghano,
Nangarhar province, Afghanistan

In some countries, former rebels have been invited to participate in the political process in order to address exclusion and marginalization. However, winning elections does not automatically change tendencies toward predatory behavior and violence, especially in an environment where governance and accountability are weak. In general, people wait to see how such groups will govern. In several communities in Afghanistan, people viewed the Taliban as masters of coercion who had robbed people of dignity and freedom. The Taliban regime was considered the worst in the country's history. There were massacres, people were taken out of their homes and beaten, and property was destroyed. Some people described psychological warfare in which the Taliban used fear to compel people to behave and dress in particular ways. Shirn Gul, a 47-year-old participant in a men's discussion group in Zakwak Ulya, said, "The Taliban is the opposite of freedom; their black turban is the opposite of freedom. Because the Taliban obliged people to go to the mosque and wear a black turban." Local elections, which the Taliban won in some places, did not suddenly cloak them with legitimacy. Many people remained distrustful.

In Assam, people in some areas expressed similar fears when the ULFA, competing in elections as SULFA ("Surrendered ULFA"), gained "political legitimacy."

## Capture of resources by state representatives

> *I could not claim my rights because they, the fishing authorities, had guns.*
> —A poor fisherman, Chakboeng, Peam Ro district, Cambodia

When elected leaders or other representatives of the state themselves capture resources, apply the law unfairly, or blatantly violate the law, accountability becomes a sham. Laws and rules are not worth observing if they are not considered legitimate.[5] In general, we found more dissatisfaction with higher authorities than with local authorities. The impunity and unfair advantage available to state agents extend also to those connected to them. In Cambodia, such untouchable individuals are said to have a "strong back." Discussion groups used this term to describe those who use their connections to others higher up in government to undertake illegal or immoral activities and to escape any consequences of these activities. The presence of "strong backs" keeps illegal activities going, destroys local livelihoods, and generates more crime, as people who obey the law are then considered stupid. Cambodian discussion groups describing this process expressed great frustration:

> Social morality has declined because people rely on their "strong back" and never listen to others. Moreover, people who have strong back are not afraid of doing wrong because they believe that when they do something wrong, their strong back will help them. It's a shield against any kind of action imposed on those who misbehave and engage in misconduct. For instance, if a nephew of the commune chief hits my head and I go to protest against him, I will be treated as a crazy man. (Kdadaum, Cambodia)

[People undertaking] large-scale illegal activities are untouchable because they have strong backing from high officials. Most of them are impossible to approach . . . too powerful . . . and it is impossible to break this relation under the current system. Many illegal fishing tools have recently been destroyed by the provincial Department of Forests and Fisheries in collaboration with commune authorities, but the owners were not arrested because they are untouchable. (Salvia Prey, Cambodia)

People have no power to make any complaint. If they do, no one listens to them. Money! Money! Money! There is no responsibility or accountability from authorities and government officials. (Somrampi, Cambodia)

These findings are reflected in the decline in ratings of trust and capture. In both 1995 and 2005, only one-third of movers and chronic poor in conflict-affected communities had great or very great trust in their local government officials. Moreover, this trust, particularly among movers, had declined over time. But even among movers, who presumably have been able to benefit from at least some resources flowing through local government, 61 percent perceive the local government to be captured by a few interests. These numbers are higher in conflict communities (figure 2.1).

**FIGURE 2.1**
**Trust in local government among movers and chronic poor in conflict and nonconflict communities, 1995 and 2005**

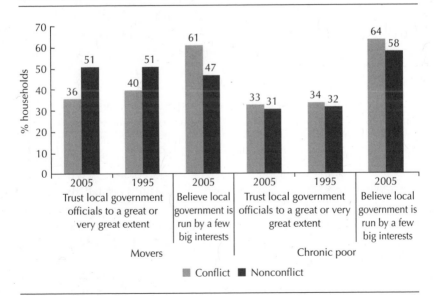

*Source:* Household questionnaire.

## Deterioration of law and order

*According to the laws, people have equal rights and freedom. But in practice the authorities just use the laws as a mat for sitting on. No one investigates a case. The one who has money is the winner of the case.*
— Discussion group of women and men,
Somrampi, Kampot district, Cambodia

Perceptions of unfairness and lack of accountability breed greater insecurity and violence as people grab resources and take the law into their own hands.

In some of the communities struggling with rampant lawlessness, we were astonished by the scale of illegal doings and the range of actors engaged. We learned about wealthy farmers, politicians, speculators, firms, and armed groups grabbing land; timber conglomerates and large fishing fleet owners colluding with local officials to clear forests and mine fish stocks in flagrant violation of regulations; local leaders, politicians, bureaucrats, and contractors pocketing relief and development funds with impunity; various armed forces and civilian thugs engaging in extortion and ambushes along trade routes; and violent youth gangs, including some with connections to armed groups, causing mayhem wherever they roamed. In communities with a thriving illegal drug economy, nearly everyone seemed to have a hand in it—insurgent and army commanders and soldiers, politicians, police, businessmen, landowners, farm workers, male youth. In some of the most resource-rich (and often remote) areas, people described many forms of seemingly institutionalized lawlessness.[6] In almost every case, an increase in random crime and violence was threaded into this difficult mix.

Some of the worst lawlessness was reported in Colombia. In the urban barrios, for example, people who had fled the countryside to escape armed conflict found themselves in the midst of a different type of war zone. Illegal armed groups vied for control of local councils, markets, and extortion rackets, with youth gangs sometimes serving as foot soldiers. In the barrio of Santa María, near Cartagena, peasants trying to cultivate small abandoned plots on surrounding lands were targets of murder, rape, and arson instigated by well-connected local landowners. Shop owners and activists also received death threats and were targeted in assassination waves. In El Mirador, a neighborhood of Pasto in the south of Colombia, residents described roving gangs with a dozen or more members, some as young as eleven and many addicted to drugs. "One can't go out because they'll rob you," reported a resident.

Children do not walk the street unaccompanied, and taxi drivers and shop owners refuse to conduct business in the barrio at night.

In several places we heard reports of armed groups taking over local economic activities or setting up their own. In such environments there seems to be little recourse for civilians unless they are politically connected or wealthy and can somehow get in on the action. When the owner of a plywood company in Assam, India, could no longer afford the exorbitant monthly payments to the ULFA and began to receive death threats, he knew better than to seek help from the police. He shut down the plant and laid off workers, and his managers negotiated a deal with the ULFA to turn over the large property. When the ULFA next moved to evict residents living along the perimeter of the plant, people looked to the police for help. But the police refused to intervene. Nor did they back the residents' initiatives to protest.

Accounts from Cambodia suggest that the reported rise in insecurity, crime, violence, and illegal economic activities in postconflict environments is understated and often persists for decades in environments of weak accountability. Tracked over the period from 1993 to 2001 (or a decade after the 1991 Paris Peace Agreements were signed), six of the nine Cambodian study communities reported declining peace and security and three reported increasing peace and security (FitzGerald et al. 2007). However, even in two of these "increasing peace" communities, crime, theft, and robbery actually increased and most poor villagers continued to live in fear. New forms of violence reflected the rise of corruption in the police and the courts and frequent collusion between these state agents and the elite. People also reported a breakdown of social morality, manifested in the increased theft of property (such as buffaloes, motorcycles, and fishing nets), assaults on women, and the emergence of male youth gangs that provoked fights between villages.

In the village of Sastaing, where rising peace was reported, a young woman summarized the situation of insecurity: "Nowadays, if we ask the question that between humans and ghosts which one do you fear, I will answer that I'm afraid of humans rather than ghosts. The ghost cannot cause any problems to me, while the humans can." In Kdadaum, a men's discussion group said, "Before the Khmer Rouge were defeated in 1998, we were not afraid of losing shoes, bicycles, and motorcycles, but now things have changed. We can no longer put those things in an unsecured place." Others reported increased land conflicts in which rich people grab poor people's lands "step by step" and corrupt policemen look the other way. In every community except one in Cambodia, people spoke about increased corruption and criminality throughout the "peaceful" study period.

**FIGURE 2.2**
**Lack of safety in conflict and nonconflict communities, 1995 and 2005**

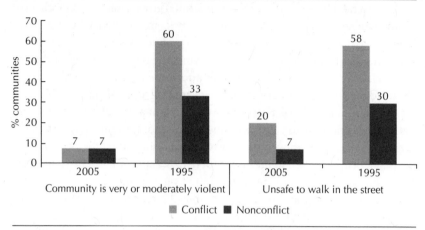

*Source:* Community questionnaire.

While discussants in Cambodia and Colombia told of persistent severe insecurity, insecurity was an issue in other places as well, where it tended to spike in certain periods. The conflict communities reported much higher levels of violence in 1995, but by 2005 this had dropped quite dramatically (figure 2.2). However, when asked directly about safety on the streets, 20 percent of the conflict communities still reported being moderately or very unsafe; this was reported by only 7 percent of the peaceful communities. Once violence ceases, as when peace agreements have been reached or victory has been declared, return to safety is not automatic. Unless law and order is effectively restored and enforced, insecurity will frequently continue in new forms.

## The thirst for quick justice

*The liberation of the community from the Philippines government and the subsequent implementation of the MILF form of governance under Shari'a law is the actualization of freedom.*
                    —Cairudin, age 33, member of a men's discussion group,
                              Abanang, Baloi municipality, Philippines

In many developing countries, access to formal justice systems, including courts, remains difficult. In India, for example, a staggering 28 million cases are pending in the courts (Mehta 2009). Obviously the situation is much worse in postconflict contexts. So deep is the yearning for justice, law, and order that in some places people preferred to be ruled by insurgent forces. With the insurgents in charge, they reasoned, at least some justice would be assured—and it would be quick.

Even brutal vigilante justice may be accepted if it resolves conflict rapidly. This includes shooting people who do not obey the rules clearly known to all. In poor Colombian barrios populated by internally displaced people, residents sometimes expressed appreciation for the unknown armed actors who would suddenly arrive at night to "take care of" violent drug addicts and others who were seen as endangering the community.

Some people in Muslim communities mentioned Islamic law as providing a welcome form of alternative justice. This emerged, for example, in the detailed case study mapping the institutional actors involved in the conflict in Abanang, Philippines. The Moro Islamic Liberation Front (MILF) had gained much sympathy during the war and cease-fire period in some communities. The MILF conducted a three-day consultation across the island of Mindanao that included all sectors of society, government organizations, nongovernmental organizations (NGOs), traditional leaders, and religious leaders. In a discussion group, men expressed their admiration for the MILF and their yearning for speedy justice. "I believe that the MILF can do more good for the communities affected by war," said one man. "They have good governance and the MILF justice system has solved more crimes than the existing one." Another explained that the MILF "will stop all the illegal activities. They will kill murderers, cut off parts of thieves, and recommend beheadings of anyone who commits adultery. If we follow the MILF bylaws we will prosper 100 percent."

Men and women in some Muslim communities also spoke about the gender inequalities embodied in Islamic law. In Kalisido, in peaceful East Java, Indonesia, Muslim women enjoy freedom to travel and work beyond their communities. But a 57-year-old man cautioned, "Women must dress in accordance with Islamic requirements. Men are free to socialize and come home at 11:00 p.m. and it doesn't matter, but if women come home at 10:00 p.m. they will be reprimanded." In Riah Khillaw, Afghanistan, women are scarcely visible outside their homes. There, young women in a discussion group expressed the belief that their religion was being misused and held out hope for greater equality: "Our people are always talking about Islam, but they don't know anything about what real Islam says about education and women. They do not know that Islam said education is necessary and important for both men and women. Women should take part in business, jobs, and politics. Islam gives us these rights but our people and parents take them away." In Muslim Thambulla, in the eastern part of Sri Lanka, a young woman lamented that "females have to ask permission [to leave their homes] and males always accompany us."

## Gender-based violence

*When someone knocks at the door during the night, we do not open the door quickly. We send the young boys and maidens to escape from the village, knowing that they will be tortured by the army. The military people come in a group to taste girls at midnight, like the cats come when they smell dried fish. They come when they know that maidens are present.*
—Men's discussion group, Gatakpur, Assam, India

While study discussants elaborated at length on many threats to community safety, there was a zone of silence around the issue of atrocities against women. Rape is so traumatic and so mixed up with shame and family honor that both men and women are reluctant to talk about it directly.[7] Unfortunately, there is growing evidence that women and girls, old and young, remain acutely vulnerable to sexual violence in postconflict settings.

In a few cases in the Philippines, Assam, Cambodia, Indonesia, and Sri Lanka, people reported that combatants had raped young girls and women in their localities. In Welumbe, Sri Lanka, where a Sinhalese insurgency raged in the 1980s, a discussion group recalled, "There were incidents of mothers and daughters getting raped in stark daylight while peeling cinnamon, the main livelihood. After this, people were too scared to go out into the land and work." In the village of Preysath, Cambodia, fear of rape by Khmer Rouge factions and other bandits hiding in the surrounding forests kept women close to their homes, a situation that persisted into the late 1990s.

In sharing his life story, a 58-year-old poor man from Pajikuchi, Assam, confided, "On the sixteenth of June at about 9:20 p.m. someone knocked on my door. I opened the door; three soldiers wearing civilian dress came in and hit me with the butt of a gun. After hitting me badly, they raped my wife. They left the home, and my wife went to the garden and took a rope in her hand to commit suicide. I caught her hand and tried to calm her down. After that, I reported it to the villagers. Nevertheless, the soldiers warned us that if I [told the authorities], they would kill me. This was the worst moment of my life."

Across communities, groups mentioned the imperative to first protect women and children. To do so, they used a range of strategies. In Afghanistan, villages came together and moved women and children en masse to border areas of Pakistan during the Taliban regime. In Lomamoli, Philippines, women and children hid in the nearby mountains during the day, while the men went out to work. When they set out at sunset to deliver food to their husbands, they wore dark clothes, especially black, so that men would not notice them.

### Youth abduction

*At the time of the Taliban, kidnapping increased. A lot of children were kidnapped and people were afraid for their children. That is why they did not want to send them to school.*

—Women's discussion group, Nasher Khan,
Nangarhar province, Afghanistan

Parents in conflict areas do all they can to protect their young from abduction by insurgents, often without success. The fear of abduction restricts movements of young people everywhere. In Sri Lanka, youth expressed frustration at their inability to move freely in and around their villages. Young men were subject to forced recruitment by different armed groups. Male youth in Manivali defined freedom as "the ability to go anywhere at any time." In Nilakulam, youth reported that "we do not let women move around on the roads after 8 p.m. to avoid incidents." In Nasher Khan in Nangarhar province, Afghanistan, Besmillah Khan, a farmer, reported that the Taliban not only collected unfair taxes, burned houses, and killed people but also "took away our young people to fight."

In Colombia, the lives of young people seem especially perilous. The danger of being recruited for war is so pressing that parents feel compelled to break up their households. Mothers flee with their sons and daughters to cities; fathers, if they haven't been caught up in the war, stay behind in the countryside to watch the property and do farm work, including on coca fields. A 48-year-old mother who had resettled in the barrio of El Gorrión recounted, "I have two big kids. The oldest one is 18 and my girl is 16. One day some strange people came and said they were going to take my kids to recruit them." In El Mirador, a barrio of Pasto, almost every displaced household interviewed for the study was headed by a woman. But whether Pasto was safer than the surrounding mountains was anybody's guess. Children who left school unescorted risked beatings and extortion at the hands of young men and boys who were out of school and out of work.

A poignant report came from a father in Nelutanga, Hambantota, in the southern part of Sri Lanka. The area was involved in a conflict with a Marxist revolutionary group between 1989 and 1991. The father narrated the following while drawing up the community conflict timeline:

> The youth are affected the most. Girls couldn't walk on the roads. The students from schools were taken away for protests. The school was closed for six months and an army camp was set up in the school for three months . . . My son was not that old at the time of the insurrection, but he was tall for his age. So I used to always bathe him whenever they came looking for him. There were days that I used to bathe my son more than five times a day. I told them that I was bathing my son, pretending he was very young.

## Restoring Security

*People were afraid, and totally controlled. The economy was ruined and many fled.*
       —Men's discussion group, Shazimir, Kabul province, Afghanistan

Reestablishing security and peace takes time and persistence. Postconflict environments are characterized by a potent mixture of poverty, wide availability of arms, an unleashing of pent-up private conflicts, and a breakdown of the social norms that ordinarily serve to curtail outward expressions of violence. In our study communities, several mechanisms emerged for restoring security. They ranged from international peacekeeping forces to zones of peace to initiatives taken by local informal leaders, either on their own or in cooperation with the army or police.

Sometimes, as in Indonesia, Assam, and Sri Lanka, memorandums of agreement were signed, some of which led to peace and security and some of which did not. Since our study did not focus on this issue a priori, we do not have enough detailed information to judge what makes a peace agreement effective. Four factors that seemed to be important were the presence of international peacekeepers (Afghanistan, the Philippines); the extent to which community leaders of different ethnic factions saw the agreements as fair (some communities in Indonesia and the Philippines); the extent to which the military and police were mobilized to keep the peace (Indonesia, Cambodia); and the extent to which demobilization of insurgents occurred together with their reintegration into social, political, and religious structures and processes (some communities in the Philippines, Assam, and Cambodia).

Unfortunately, cease-fires and peace agreements do not by themselves lead to security. Insurgents and army personnel often persist in violence and predation. In Kumputhiri, in eastern Sri Lanka, for example, villagers described having to pay the Liberation Tigers of Tamil Eelam (LTTE) two bags of rice for every acre they farmed. This stopped with the 2002 cease-fire, but villagers commented, "[Now] we have to pay 50 rupees to go to the woods to bring a cartload of firewood. But even though we pay 50 rupees, sometimes they catch us and ask us to pay 15,000, 20,000, or even 25,000 rupees to release the cart. If we go to argue with them they will kill us. In 2003 the LTTE killed three people who were safeguarding their cultivation lands. Now we have to pay 100 rupees to LTTE to bring a tractor load of quarry." In Manivali, in the north of Sri Lanka, the community staged protests and letter-writing campaigns after the cease-fire to get rid of the military base on their lands. But the Sinhalese army guards continued to threaten local Tamil women and men, and scores of residents remained unable to recover their homes and farmlands taken over by the army base.

## International peacekeeping

*Now we have the foreign forces who maintain security, and it is good.*
—Men's discussion group, Ramili Qali,
Parwan province, Afghanistan

*If LTTE captures someone we go to the police through the mosque committee. Then the police will inform the Norway people and they try to resolve the issue. In 2003 LTTE killed three people who were looking after their vegetable farm near the village. After that the government put a security point near the mosque. After that there were no security problems.*
—Men's discussion group, Kumputhiri,
Trincomalee district, Sri Lanka

Restoring security in both Afghanistan and the Philippines involved international peacekeeping forces after a peace agreement. In general, international peacekeepers enforce cease-fires and peace agreements, and their presence provides a check on excesses by armed forces and other armed groups. Sometimes they become involved in reconstruction as well. They are seen as outsiders who are present only temporarily and who have no stake in the society, and hence they are usually perceived to be fair. Recent research by Paul Collier (2009) and others concludes that expenditures on peacekeeping strongly and significantly reduce the risk that a postconflict situation will revert to war. Collier also concludes that peacekeeping troops may need to stay on for a decade, until there is economic recovery, in order to greatly reduce the chances of recurrent conflict.

In Afghanistan, in almost every community, U.S. and international forces were widely praised in 2006 for establishing security and ousting the Taliban. In addition, they were often trusted to be fair and to restore justice, as they were perceived to be outside the system. Commanders in some areas also dispensed assistance to local people, something highly appreciated during periods of extreme hardship. For example, in Zakwak Ulya, Herat, villagers said, "Foreign forces based in Herat airport always distributed food and medicines to people." In Shazimir, a member of a men's discussion group said, "The security situation is very good right now. I don't feel in danger these days. The government has collected the weapons from the illegal armed groups. There are numerous security checkpoints in the city. The coalition forces and ISAF [International Security Assistance Force] ensure good security in the city. There are lots of economic opportunities."[8]

In the Philippines, in the high-conflict community of Abanang, local people identified the presence of the International Monitoring Team (IMT), which arrived in the area in May 2004, as the number one reason for improved security. The team's mandate was to monitor cease-fire violations committed by the government and the MILF. A discussion group of men reported on the efficacy of the IMT in reducing the number of clashes between government troops and the MILF: "According to Newsbreak, two years before the IMT arrived, more than 100 violations of the cease-fire agreements were being committed [by both sides]. After they were established, the violations decreased significantly. There were only 15 incidents that have violated cease-fire agreements." After two years of operation, the IMT's influence had increased "because the residents trust them more than any other organization present in their place. The people felt more secure with their presence." One discussion group participant from Abanang hoped that the IMT would not be confined to monitoring the cease-fire but would also have authority to monitor the implementation of rehabilitation programs and community development programs in every conflict-affected community in Mindanao.

The presence of the IMT also reportedly ended the excesses of the Philippine Marines and military posted to protect the area. The discussion group said that the Marines and the military did dreadful things during the all-out war in 2000, burning houses, destroying property, and looting valuables left behind by people who evacuated. All agreed that the power of these groups declined after the arrival of the IMT: "Before, the Marines and military were very powerful, above all elements, and they had the control of every situation. But after the war, they lost their credibility because of the terrible things they had done."

Another factor may have played a role at least initially in establishing the legitimacy of the external peacekeepers. The international peacekeepers were from Islamic countries—Malaysia, Brunei, and Libya. Since the conflict in Mindanao was a war against Muslims in a predominantly Christian society, Muslims in the communities felt under siege, and the Muslim composition of the IMT may have been reassuring. The IMT also mediated the peace between the MILF and the government.

### Creating peace zones

*Before, at 4:00 in the afternoon, we would already take supper without lights. We would then wait for nightfall. At night, we started guarding for any attacks that might be done against us. At dawn, we could not walk home without any worry, because we would still have to be alert for any attack that we might encounter. We could not go to the mountains all by ourselves because someone would hunt us. There was really a big difference when the zone of peace was established . . . We only had a relaxed life when Uncle Bob declared Dubiading as a zone of peace. We were now able to go around the barangay, but only within its boundaries.*

*—Joselito, age 38, a militia member, Dubiading,*
*Picong municipality, Philippines*

Peace zones emerged in the Philippines in the mid-1970s and became better known in the mid-1980s as a way of containing feuds between warring families.[9] Over time, the method has became popular and accepted by NGOs, donors, and governments as a way to initiate a culture of peace in war-affected communities and provide resources for reconstruction. As peace zones are meant to be community initiated, local community leaders, as well as external actors, play a crucial role in supporting them.

The longest-established peace zone in our sample was in Dubiading, a community that is 95 percent Muslim and 5 percent Christian. Since the 1950s, the village had been threatened by a long-running, violent feud between two clans, one from each religious group. A 1-square-kilometer zone of peace was designated in 1976. The prime mover in this effort was Bob Anton, a local informal leader who had tremendous credibility in the village. A rich landowner, Bob was a respected community "uncle" and a rough-and-ready law enforcer rolled into one. Bob considers himself Christian, but his mother was Muslim, making him acceptable to both sides.

In 2003 the feud flared again, putting the entire village in danger. Bob's solution was to delineate a small area in which the warring parties would be permitted to fight. At first community members were incredulous that simply demarcating an area with flags would contain the violence, but over time this is exactly what happened. Discussion groups described a final clash in which the warring parties were a mere stone's throw from each other. Joselito, one of the discussion participants, described how events unfolded:

> The feuding families of the Kaya and Alando, who had been firing at each other nonstop for a week, were told not to fight inside the barangay because the civilians would be included. But they could not contain the rage that they felt for each other, so Bob Anton created a plan on how they could have their battle and keep the nonclan members safe. Uncle Bob gave them a boundary where they were allowed to fight. He divided Padian [the Muslim market] and placed a flag signifying the demarcation line of where they could fight. He told the conflicting parties that they could have their war as long as they do not cross the boundary line. While they were having a war on the other side, trade continued on the opposite side of the boundary line.

Other group members added,

> The families were also given an ultimatum on the number of days that they could have their battle. After that, they would have to stop and separate. The members of these families were also instructed to fire in specific directions to avoid hitting any civilians. On the other hand, the people living near the place chosen for the Kaya and Alando armed encounter were asked to move farther. If we look at this event closely, we seem to be looking at a movie taping with the director busy giving out instructions.

There were two casualties in this face-off, one from each family. Some houses were damaged, but none was set on fire; the families had been warned against arson because of the danger it would pose to other houses in the community. When the prescribed week was over, the clans stopped firing at each other. The death of the key personality in each group also motivated both families to end their battle. Negotiations followed the shootout, and although the feud was not completely resolved, there has been no further violence between these two families.

Dubiading's continuing effort to reach across the religious divide also paid off during the all-out war, when the village avoided major destruction. In 2002, an attack by the MILF on the village was imminent. Muslims living in the upland areas rushed down to warn the local militia—the Civilian Armed Forces Geographical Unit, or CAFGU—and the army, both of which were primarily Christian. The timely warning led to evacuation of the community, and the MILF guerrillas were defeated in a gunfight that lasted an hour. Community bonds had trumped religious affiliations. A Christian militia member said that to his surprise, his Muslim neighbors "thought of us like brothers."

The village women recalled that the night before the MILF attack, they sought shelter in one of the big houses owned by Bob Anton's extended family.

> We were already cautious of what's going to happen so we were on our guard. Gunshots began at 5:30 in the morning of March 15, 2002, and continued for more or less 10 minutes. By six o'clock the CAFGUs and army in the barangay cleared the area. This short-lived armed encounter between the MILFs and the military formally ended by the afternoon on the same day. No other shootouts followed after that episode.

Most of those who evacuated stayed in one of Bob's houses for a month or two, though some stayed for just one or two weeks. Afraid of tensions, Christians tended to stay longest. Not only did community cohesion keep the fighting out of Dubiading, but the village became a haven of peace and attracted those fleeing war in the surrounding area.

As Dubiading's experience illustrates, the success of peace zones depends upon strong local initiative and leaders and community acceptance of the rules of a peace zone. It also depends on the presence of the army and of a local militia armed by the army. In Lomamoli, local and international civil society organizations worked with local leaders to create a peace zone. Local community organizers received six months of training in how to instill a culture of peace in the community. In Kilaluna, where the population is 60 percent Christian, 30 percent indigenous, and 10 percent Muslim, the barangay leader played a key role in maintaining peace, together with the local CAFGU, the army, and the municipal authorities. Kilaluna also had a cease-fire monitoring group, including representatives from each of the three ethnic groups, to monitor violations after the all-out war subsided. However, in two other communities in Mindanao, the peace zone was declared by external leaders with little follow-up at the community level. In these circumstances, the formal designation of a zone of peace seems to have had less impact (see chapter 9).

## Multiple actors working together to restore peace

As noted earlier, the experience of Abanang in the Philippines highlights the role of international peacekeeping forces in restoring security. Digging deeper into this community's history, however, reveals a complex picture, with inter-action among many different actors who were involved either in conflict or in peacemaking. On average, 8 to 15 different actors were identified as involved in restoring security in many of the communities visited.

In Abanang, during the all-out war, nine different actors were drawn into restoring security (figure 2.3). After the IMT, the second most important actors in restoring peace were said to be the local government officials of Baloi municipality. The majority of discussants, though not all, believed that

**FIGURE 2.3**

**Leading actors involved in conflict and peacemaking in Abanang, Philippines**

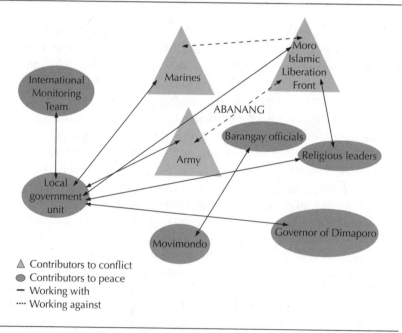

△ Contributors to conflict
● Contributors to peace
— Working with
···· Working against

*Source:* Discussion group, Abanang, Philippines.

these municipal officials were neutral before, during, and after the war and refrained from favoring either the government or the MILF. All agreed that the local officials played an important role as intermediaries between the different actors inside and outside the community. While the IMT remained the most trusted, the MILF was the next most trusted for resolving local conflict. Other actors included religious elders who tried to keep calm in the community and coordinate between the local government unit and the MILF leaders, but were not seen as effective peace brokers; the barangay officials who reportedly fled but who coordinated the involvement of the Italian NGO Movimondo; the governor of Dimaporo, who used the calamity fund to release money to build 96 houses burned down during the war; and the Marines and the military, both present near the area.

Finally, a year after the conflict, a CAFGU unit was organized, consisting mostly of former MILF members from the community who had "apparently" surrendered their guns. In this community, largely sympathetic to the MILF, the CAFGU was rated as providing security, protection, peace, and order. In some other communities the reports were more mixed.

### Community defense groups

*Aside from the peace covenant, the local government paved the way for us to organize a group [Umpia ko Iranun] that would help in maintaining the peace and security in this community.*

—A 39-year-old man, Bakimati,
Kapatagan municipality, Philippines

Providing security for civilians during conflict is a big job. Armies and police frequently train and arm local people and enroll them in local civil defense units. Such units are usually paid poorly, if they are paid at all, but they can provide work for unemployed ex-combatants and other local people. Sometimes communities mobilize their own defense or neighborhood watch groups. While self-defense forces are often greatly valued, there were a few reports that these groups have become laws unto themselves, dispensing vigilante justice without checks and balances.

"We don't have enough people guarding the village. We feel like the Tamil Tigers can come and kill us at any time," stated a discussion group participant from the Sinhalese town of Pothupana in the east of Sri Lanka. A former defense minister had provided the town with arms, and the village mobilized a group of men to operate out of the mosque. The town also had Home Guards, government troops stationed in border villages to guard against Tamil incursions. These combined forces, however, proved unable to resist a Tamil attack on the mosque that left five of the town's guards dead.

Well-coordinated civil defense activities emerged in North Maluku, Indonesia. Residents of Bodolenge, for instance, named five pillars of local security: family responsibilities, a civil defense group, community patrolling, special security responsibilities for their neighborhood heads, and installation of a bell or security post in each neighborhood. People in Galalolo, also in North Maluku, reported 10 years of experience with local security and night watch posts, but they took pains to explain that these were not intended for the ethnic strife that raged between 1999 and 2002. Instead, the security measures "were established in anticipation of bad behavior by young people, and in that respect they had proved quite effective." At the time of the conflict, however, Galalolo's guards became extremely active. In Kacokerre, a peaceful East Java village, local people said their only security precautions involved hiring "local thugs" for special events such as weddings. During periods of nonpolitical violence, however, Kacokerre officials set up a group of watchmen every night, with 10 to 15 men on guard at special posts.

Accounts from the Philippines are also laced with reports of communities taking up arms to defend themselves. In addition to signing a peace covenant, leaders in Bakimati received government support to organize a CAFGU defense group. In Lomamoli, at the height of the conflict, men stationed themselves in the village's multipurpose hall, and their wives would secretly bring food and water at night. As one woman explained, "We just whispered and made a signal for them to know that their food was ready. We did not want to get closer because we might be caught in crossfire."

## Conclusion

The end of war does not automatically bring peace and security. The biggest challenge for democratic states after major political conflict is to reestablish security, peace, and order and renew the state's compact of accountability with its citizens. Warring groups, and even the army and police, may have developed an appetite for mayhem and the opportunities for predation that it brings. If lawlessness continues, with armed actors looting and killing, the state loses its legitimacy and chaos prevails. In such a climate of fear and uncertainty, human rights are violated with impunity and neither individuals nor the private sector will make any economic investments in the future.

A disciplined army and police force are crucial to keeping the peace, particularly in the fragile initial phases, when the probability of a return to conflict is high. Such self-restraint on the part of the armed forces is more likely when there is some monitoring by a strong state or by external peacekeepers.

Ordinary people, meanwhile, just want to get on with their lives—farming, working, going to school, raising their families. This deep hunger for security and justice is central to peacemaking after civil war. Even weak governments can tap into community resolve to maintain peace, whether through peace zones or other means. In some cases international peacekeeping forces may be needed for several years to ensure that conflict does not flare up again. As villagers in Sri Lanka reminded us, even after the formal cessation of hostilities, wars are like sleeping lions that can wake up at any time.

## Notes

1. Scholars are increasingly turning to micro data to better understand the sharp rise and strong geographic variation in noncombatant deaths, a hallmark of contemporary wars. Humphreys and Weinstein (2006) surveyed 1,043 ex-combatants in Sierra Leone and found that high levels of abuse and violence during that war were exhibited by "warring factions that are unable to police the behavior of their members because they are more ethnically fragmented, rely on material incentives to recruit participants, and lack mechanisms to punish indiscipline" (429). Explanations that emphasize the importance of community ties and contestation do not find strong support in the data. Kalyvas's (2006) micro-level work on patterns of violence in the Greek civil war found that violence surged in places where neither of the rival armed groups could claim territorial control.

2. Ashraf Ghani and Clare Lockhart (2008), in their recent book on state failure, describe this situation well. "Many states have collapsed and are unable to provide even the most basic services to their citizens. The failure to maintain basic order not only makes fear a constant of daily life but also provides a breeding ground for a small minority to perpetuate criminality and terror" (4).

3. To protect the privacy of participants, this book uses pseudonyms for the study communities (villages and barrios). Cities, municipalities, districts, departments, and provinces are identified by their real names.

4. Kalyvas (2006) argues that armed groups practice indiscriminate violence when they lack the resources and capacities to engage in more selective use of violence. In addition, his work brings to light difficulties with poorly disciplined troops, which can sometimes encourage civilian and military defections to the enemy, thus undermining the armed group's support and control. Senseless killing, torture, maiming, looting, and rape all instill fear; in that sense they substitute for political legitimacy as a means of maintaining control, but at a cost. Lipset recognized the challenges of mediating social conflicts and ruling with legitimacy in deeply divided societies: "A stable democracy requires relatively moder-

ate tension among the contending political forces. And political moderating is facilitated by the capacity of a system to resolve key dividing issues before new ones arise . . . The more reinforced and correlated the sources of cleavage, the less likelihood for political tolerance" (1959, 97).

5. Lipset stresses that legitimacy "involves the capacity of a political system to engender and maintain the belief that existing political institutions are the most appropriate or proper ones for the society." This depends "in large measure upon the ways in which the key issues which have historically divided the society have been resolved" (1959, 86). De Tocqueville (1835) does not frame his observations of early American democracy around notions of legitimacy, but his views on the advantages of broad-based political participation, and the greater public spirit and respect for law that this can instill in a society, fit quite closely with the concept: "In America, the lowest classes have conceived a very high notion of political rights, because they exercise those rights; and they refrain from attacking the rights of others in order that their own may not be violated. While in Europe the same classes sometimes resist even the supreme power, the American submits without a murmur to the authority of the pettiest magistrate."

6. See Ross (2004) and Le Billion (2001) on the important role of natural resources in the onset and persistence of conflict.

7. Gender violence is a very sensitive subject in all cultures, and to get a full understanding of its scope and dimensions would require much more extensive work than we conducted. For an introduction to the methodological challenges in conducting research on gender-based violence, see Ward (2005). For a helpful overview of the forms and patterns of sexual violence in different war contexts and factors contributing to them, see Wood (2006).

8. The International Security Assistance Force is the NATO multinational army in Afghanistan. Its main roles are to help secure the country, train the Afghan National Army, and participate in the reconstruction effort.

9. See chapter 9 on the Philippines.

## References

Collier, P. 2009. *Wars, Guns, and Votes: Democracy in Dangerous Places*. New York: Harper Collins.

de Tocqueville, A. 1835. *Democracy in America*. Quoted in C. Cohen, *Communism, Fascism, and Democracy* (New York: Random House, 1972), 597.

FitzGerald, I., S. Sovannarith, C. Sophal, K. Sithen, and T. Sokphally. 2007. "Moving Out of Poverty? Trends in Community Well-being and Household Mobility in Nine Cambodian Villages." Cambodia Development Resource Institute (CDRI), Phnom Penh.

Ghani, A., and C. Lockhart. 2008. *Fixing Failed States: A Framework for Rebuilding a Fractured World*. New York: Oxford University Press.

Humphreys, M., and J. Weinstein. 2006. "Handling and Manhandling in Civil War." *American Political Science Review* 100 (3): 429–47.

Kalyvas, S. N. 2006. *The Logic of Violence in Civil War.* New York: Cambridge University Press.

Le Billion, P. 2001. "The Political Ecology of War: Natural Resources and Armed Conflicts." *Political Geography* 20: 561–84.

Lipset, S. M. 1959. "Some Social Requisites of Democracy: Economic Development and Political Legitimacy." *American Political Science Review* 53 (1): 69–105.

Mehta, P. B. 2009. "Citizenship and Accountability: The Case of India." In *Citizenship, Governance, and Social Policy in the Developing World,* ed. A. Dani and A. Varshney. Washington, DC: World Bank.

Ross, W. 2004. "What Do We Know about Natural Resources and Civil War?" *Journal of Peace Research* 41: 337–56.

Ward, J. 2005. "Conducting Population-Based Research on Gender-Based Violence in Conflict-Affected Settings: An Overview of a Multi-country Research Project." Prepared for an expert group meeting on violence against women organized by UN Division for the Advancement of Women, Economic Commission for Europe, and World Health Organization, Geneva, April 11–14.

Wood, E. J. 2006. "Variation in Sexual Violence during War." *Politics and Society* 34 (3): 307–41.

# Democracy: Big "D" and Little "d"

*We want a good exercise of power . . .
power that is practiced in a good and
right manner. Those who have the power
must respect other people's interests and
opinions. Power should not be used for
one's own interests.*

— COMMUNITY TIMELINE DISCUSSION GROUP,
Preysath, Kampong Svay district, Cambodia

*Civilians steal first and then they run.
Politicians run first [for office] and then
they steal.*

— WOMEN'S DISCUSSION GROUP,
Kilaluna, Carmen municipality, Philippines

All seven countries in our conflict sample are democracies. National democracies vary in their characteristics and in the length of time that they have been established; some are younger, some older. But all have certain core features in common: they have multiparty systems, to a greater or lesser extent, and they hold national elections to choose their political leaders.

A prime motivation in undertaking this study was to examine how democracy works in practice, to go below the "big D" of democracy at the national level to the "little d" of democracy at the local level. Just as with economic growth, we wanted to dig below national, regional, and state averages to focus on the community level where people live and work. And we wanted to look beyond the acclaimed marker of democracy, elections. Most important, we wanted to explore the relationship between democracy and movement out of poverty in conflict-affected communities.

There are two reasons for this community-focused approach. First, while national elections may be a good thing, the fact that they are held says nothing about how democracy functions on the ground. Elections, the most important symbol of democracy, unleash powerful forces that are messy and all about power. In fact, recent research has shown that elections are directly associated with increased violence, with the time immediately following an election being particularly dangerous.[1] Democracy has a peace-promoting effect in higher-income countries but may be destabilizing in low-income countries (Collier and Rohner 2008).

Second, national elections and representatives are too far removed from people in rural and remote communities. The presence of formal structures of democracy at the national level does not necessarily ensure equal opportunity for citizens to participate meaningfully in the democratic process. People's

53

interactions with representatives of the state (whether elected or not) take place primarily at the local level. At this level there is great variation in democratic functioning, irrespective of the form and functioning of democracy at the national level. A key finding from the cross-country analysis reported in volume 2 of this series is that 93 percent of the variation in responsiveness of local democracies is *within* each country, that is, across communities in a country, rather than across countries.[2]

While national policies set the political context, most countries around the world have embraced the need for a decentralized state in order to bring government closer to citizens. There is great variation in the extent to which authority, resources, and decisions are devolved to the local level. Local authorities also vary significantly in the extent to which they collect taxes from citizens.[3] In conflict contexts there are often deep social fissures along ethnic or religious lines, and the geographic distribution of excluded groups may be uneven. In such settings local government can deepen social divides, or it can help heal them by promoting political participation in government by all major groups and by extending equal treatment to all citizens irrespective of ethnicity or religion.[4]

This chapter examines the role of local democracies in conflict and nonconflict contexts. In democracies, elected representatives are expected to govern communities and countries on behalf of *all* citizens whose interests they represent and to whom they are accountable. These arrangements, when applied equally to all social groups and governed by an agreed set of rules, generally lead to legitimacy. To the extent that these agreements are broken with no repercussions, citizens lose trust in their elected representatives and the pact between citizens and elected representatives breaks down. What remains is the shell of democracy. Since the issue of accountability has already been discussed, we will not discuss it here in detail, except to examine the evidence and factors that reflect a lack of accountability and feed a vicious cycle of democratic breakdown.

We first examine whether poor people and others living in conflict contexts have democratic citizenship aspirations. They do. We organize the rest of our analysis around two concepts, distinguishing between the formal structures or *forms* of local democracy and the way democracy actually *functions.*

The first set of findings concerns the presence and effects of democratic structures, the *forms* of democracy. While widely prevalent, democratic structures seem to have perverse effects in conflict contexts. Local elections seem to *hurt* poor people's chances of moving out of poverty in both conflict and nonconflict contexts, even when these elections are perceived to be fair. In communities directly affected by conflict, having ethnically representative village councils also does not seem to help poor people's mobility, except when strong civic associations exist as a counterbalancing force. Clearly, the effects of the forms or structures of democracy differ sharply in conflict and nonconflict contexts in the same country.

Our second set of findings focuses on how democratic structures *function* in conflict contexts and whether they help or hinder poor people's movement out of poverty. Responsiveness of local government, the extent to which it takes into account people's concerns, is also perverse in conflict contexts; it is negatively related to poor people's mobility, but only in conflict contexts. We also find huge increases in corruption and bribery in all communities, a sign of weakening accountability that eventually erodes legitimacy. And finally, despite the dirty politics, people's participation in collective action and community meetings remains high.

Our third set of findings has to do with strong differences in how democracy functions in low-income and middle-income communities in our sample. Democratic functioning was superior on almost every count in the middle-income countries, even when the communities visited were as poor as communities in the low-income countries.

Finally, we report results from multivariate regressions that confirm the bivariate results and provide some guidance on how to make representative councils more accountable in conflict contexts. Results indicate that the presence of active people's associations makes councils more accountable and legitimate.

## People's Aspirations for Democracy and Citizenship

*Democracy means giving importance to people. It's when people still listen to each other. The importance of people means people are the ones who make the decisions on all important issues. It is a bottom-up approach . . . from the small items to the big items.*

—Discussion group of women and men, Sastaing,
Thma Koul district, Cambodia

*Democracy is only something that is at the beginning of our country's name and nothing more. The country's official name is the Democratic Socialist*

*Republic of Sri Lanka. This is the only place that there is democracy. It is just a word added to the name. It doesn't mean anything else.*
                                   —Discussion group of male and female youth,
                                         Nelutanga, Hambantota district, Sri Lanka

Very rarely did poor people have any difficulty articulating their understandings of freedom, democracy, and citizenship, concepts they see as closely related. Four elements emerged quite consistently in their definitions: assertion of people's rights and choice; equality across genders and social groups; equality before the law, and the rule of law applied equally to all; and elections. Elections are so taken for granted, however, that they are mentioned only in passing except in Afghanistan and to some extent in Indonesia, the newer democracies.

There were noticeable country differences in people's expectations and hopes for democracy. The greatest depression, cynicism, and hopelessness were expressed in Sri Lanka, followed closely by Assam and Colombia. In war-weary Sri Lanka, people in both high-conflict and low-conflict communities considered democracy an illusion. In Nelutanga,[5] a village in Hambantota district that suffered conflict during a Sinhalese insurgency in the late 1980s, a men's group said of democracy,

> Now it is only a term for us. Even the people who talk about it don't know the meaning of it. Now people don't have an interest to know about it. The people who speak the most about it are the people who abuse democracy the most. They don't even know what it means. It is an empty word now, without any meaning. People don't get excited about it anymore.

In Cambodia, by contrast, people still hoped that democracy would eventually bring justice and prosperity. In the middle-income countries of the Philippines and Indonesia, democracy received mixed reviews, but people voiced a basic optimism about local democracy. The greatest optimism was expressed in the youngest democracy, Afghanistan, where the English word "democracy" was most often used.[6] These responses, however, came in 2006, before the sharp deterioration of security in Afghanistan and the 2009 elections, which were marred by allegedly high levels of voter fraud.

Box 3.1 provides examples of people's definitions of democracy in two countries, Afghanistan and Indonesia. Their definitions highlight the right to choose, freedom, equality, fairness, and justice, as well as the aspiration to participate in decision making and hold elected leaders accountable.

**BOX 3.1**
**Definitions of *democracy* in Afghanistan and Indonesia**

## Afghanistan

*To have equal rights, freedom of expression, to implement rules on everyone in society.*

—Discussion group of men and women,
Shazimir, Kabul province

*In a democracy both men and women work together. Women walk without a veil and can go to school. In short, in a democracy men and women have the same rights.*

—Women's discussion group, Ramili Qali,
Parwan province

*Democracy is the government of the people, by the people, through the people.*

—Nezammuddin, a 37-year-old butcher,
Zakwak Ulya, Herat province

*Democracy is the equal implementation of the law over all the people.*

—Sultan Ahmad, a 55-year-old farmer,
Zakwak Ulya, Herat province

*Democracy is the freedom of the women.*

—Mullah Noor Mohamed, a 70-year-old farmer,
Zakwak Ulya, Herat province

*Democracy means that freedom should be equal for men and women. Democracy means everything should be done through rules and regulations. Democracy means women should be free according to Islamic rules.*

—Female youth discussion group, Ramili Qali,
Parwan province

*Democracy means to have a government established by election through votes.*

—Men's discussion group, Morlaw Ghano,
Nangarhar province

*continued*

**BOX 3.1**
*continued*

---

### Indonesia

*Democracy is people's aspirations. It is negotiation and tolerance; it is discussion; it is consensus; it is gotong royong [collective work].*

—Women's discussion group, Lupotogo,
North Maluku province

*Democracy is together expressing aspirations. Democracy is carrying out demonstrations.*

—Women's discussion group, Yasapira,
North Maluku province

*Democracy means together, meaning all decisions are in the common interest of the people. There must be agreement on goals, there must be meetings; the rationale must be clear, no interference. Agreement on decisions is the ultimate goal of democracy.*

—Women's discussion group, Kalisido,
East Java province

*Democracy is the people's voice. The dissemination of vision and mission, to choose and be chosen. And then if it is without consensus, it means that consensus doesn't work.*

—Men's discussion group, Barumangga,
North Maluku province

*Democracy is to carry the people's mandate. By carrying the people's mandate leaders feel responsible for expressing people's desires. Elect leaders who have a conscience, in order to yield leaders to carry people's mandate. Avoid inequality. Without justice the lies continue.*

—Male youth discussion group, Barumangga,
North Maluku province

*Democracy is important as a foundation to act, think, and express opinions. Democracy is freedom of expression.*

—Female youth discussion group, Kalisido,
East Java province

---

## Formal Features of Democracy

*We all went to vote for peace and we have peace now, but we are not happy because we have no money.*
> —Discussion group of men and women, Chakboeng,
> Peam Ro district, Cambodia

*There is always a fight at election time. Everybody wants to win.*
> —Japar, a 40-year-old man, Tucampo,
> Parang district, Philippines

To institute processes that meet democratic aspirations requires the creation of democratic structures. At the community level we consider three factors: the presence of local councils, whether elections have been held to select council heads, and whether these elections are perceived to be fair. We explore the extent to which the village councils are considered representative of different religious and ethnic groups, since this may be particularly important in divided societies recovering from conflict. We also explore the representation of women and poor people on the councils.

### Village councils and elections

*If ever there are changes, it is for the worse. One example is the election: the only change we see is the amount of money given by the candidate [to buy votes], and nothing else.*
> —Women's discussion group, Abanang,
> Baloi municipality, Philippines

Figure 3.1 examines the basic structures of local democracy, comparing the presence of local councils and elections in conflict and nonconflict contexts. Figure 3.2 shows whether this varies across communities with high and low rates of movement out of poverty (MOP). We set aside the middle MOP tercile in order to draw sharper comparisons.

Overall, 39 percent of conflict-affected communities in 2005 had village councils, a rate slightly lower than in nonconflict communities (44 percent). But the mere presence of village councils does not tell us whether local elections are held and whether these elections are perceived to be fair. On the latter two measures, conflict communities actually do better, with 77 percent of communities having elected village leaders and 73 percent having fairly elected village leaders. These numbers are systematically lower in the nonconflict communities, 70 percent and 65 percent, respectively. Hence, the formal

**FIGURE 3.1**

**Democratic structures present in conflict and nonconflict communities, 2005**

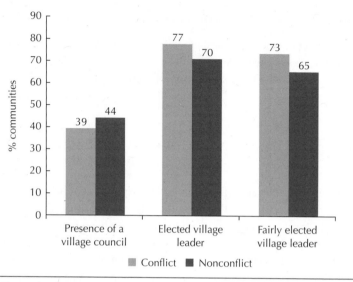

*Source:* Community questionnaire.

**FIGURE 3.2**

**Democratic structures by conflict and MOP rating, 2005**

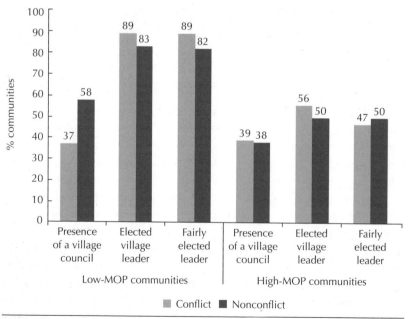

*Source:* Community questionnaire.

processes of democracy are quite well developed in conflict environments (see also appendix table F.3)

Since our primary interest is in understanding factors that affect poor people's mobility, we explored the relationship between these democratic structures and MOP (figure 3.2). In conflict communities there is no relationship between MOP and the presence of village councils in 2005. However, in nonconflict communities, there is a strong negative relationship between the presence of village councils and movement out of poverty. Notably, the presence of councils is higher in *low*-mobility peaceful communities (58 percent), indicating that community mobility may be worse in the presence of village councils. This relationship was the reverse in 1995: in conflict communities it was slightly negative and in nonconflict communities it was negative (see appendix table F.4). Thus, over time the relationship between MOP and the presence of local councils has become more positive in conflict contexts but more negative in nonconflict contexts.

In the case of whether leaders are elected, there are sharp differences by MOP level in conflict communities as well—albeit in the "wrong" direction (89 percent in low-MOP, 56 percent in high-MOP). The same is true for whether leaders are fairly elected in conflict communities (89 percent in low-MOP, 47 percent in high-MOP). This pattern also holds in nonconflict communities (for more detailed results, see appendix table F.4). *In both conflict and nonconflict communities, there is a statistically significant and negative association between moving out of poverty and elections and fair elections.*[7] Hence, we conclude that the formal structures of democracy, particularly elections, even elections perceived to be fair, are associated with lower mobility of poor people in both conflict and nonconflict contexts. This perverse relationship is stronger in conflict environments.[8]

## Why do elections hurt poor people?

> *Those who are cunning and sly, only they jump into politics armed, and sling mud upon themselves to thicken their hides. Then they start their rule of tyranny.*
>
> —A male youth, Morga, Assam, India

Most elections across the sample were not rigged. In fact, they were widely seen as fair. Nonetheless, elections, in general, seem to hurt poor people. To understand these perverse results we turn to the qualitative data across communities and to people's explanations of how local elections and local politicians function. Three key factors seem to be at work.

First, electoral outcomes are determined in part by the kind of people who enter politics and by what it takes to become a politician—money, party connections, and often guns. People in Assam described elections as a "choice between rascals." In such an environment elections cannot serve as an accountability mechanism. Candidates buy or muscle their way onto party lists, and neither voter base, nor performance, nor platforms matter.

Second, the norms around corruption and bribery seem to have changed. Local elections in several countries were marred by bribes for vote buying, and while this sometimes evoked disgust, such practices were considered normal and inevitable. In most cases, people said that they accepted gifts from all politicians and then voted for the one who was the least bad, or according to their own preferences.

And finally, neither the elected nor those who elect them have any expectations that politicians, once in office, will show an interest in public service or in delivery of basic services. It is widely accepted that the power of an elected office means money and that most elected officials will focus on enriching themselves and their cronies as quickly as possible, before their term is up. In communities in Colombia, older men said they have a choice between thieves and they choose those who they think will steal the least. Everywhere, politicians were identified as the most powerful people, able to do whatever they wanted without worrying about the law.

There is thus a sharp divergence between people's definitions of democracy and the reality they perceive around them. Many people appear to feel powerless and hopeless about their ability to change political systems. In fact, people express less optimism about the likelihood of positive changes in their political systems than about economic and social changes (figure 3.3).

## Good politicians, guns, and goons

*There is a direct relation between the development of the village and democracy. For example, Santosh Mohan Deve is the local member of Parliament from here. From his grants a lot of development has taken place, such as the high school, help for poor people, culverts, and roads.*
        —Women's discussion group, Kechula, Assam, India

In every country people were able to identify the ideal qualities that politicians should have, and they even named some local politicians who were dedicated to the development needs of their communities. In Riah Khillaw, Afghanistan, people said that "if a person comes and asks about the needs of the community and takes actions for the improvement of the community

**FIGURE 3.3**
**Optimism about improving conditions in the future**

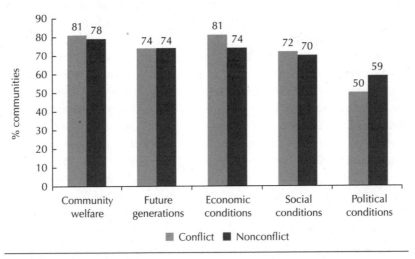

*Source:* Community questionnaire.

and links the community to the government, then he can become a politician." In Chakboeng, Cambodia, people wanted a good leader, "a good father or mother" who would lead them on the path to prosperity. Young Cambodian men wanted leaders who were well respected and capable and had the ability to bring about change.

In the Philippines, the barangay captain in Glikati was praised for helping, in "so many ways," all the people in the community who had to be evacuated to safety. In Bakimati, the barangay captain explained that it was now they, the people, who held the power because without them there would be no need for a barangay captain. "That is why he is doing everything for the barangay," a women's group commented. In Kilaluna, people had confidence in their local elected officials and said that if they had problems, the barangay officials immediately addressed them. In a few communities in Assam, people said that a politician should have a close relationship with society, think of the common people, and have a good character.

Sometimes communities get lucky and have leaders with these qualities. More often, local politicians are seen as benign but ineffective at best, and as ruthless and brutal at worst. In Garupara, Assam, where local politics is under the thumb of the "big man" of the village and panchayat decisions are made in his drawing room, people spoke bitterly about dysfunctional politics. "Sometimes people hate the AGP [Asom Gana Parishad, a political party] and give the votes to Congress [Party]. Next they hate the Congress and they vote for the AGP. But it's not true that people give votes to them as if they were Mahatma Gandhi. People elect these rascals helplessly, as there is no honest candidate."

In Assam, close to one-third of the communities said that those who used "goons, muscle power, and guns" were the ones who became politicians. Power was defined very simply as force. In Krishnanagar and Borakbari, Assam, people said that those who are associated with political parties enjoy more freedom "because they are the hooligans in our society and everyone is afraid of them. They capture everything by threatening people." In Kalodola, Assam, youth spoke about ULFA, an insurgent group, and SULFA ("Surrendered ULFA"), former insurgents who were encouraged to enter politics. "Sometimes thieves also become political leaders and later on they become quite powerful. ULFA and SULFA are also powerful, because with their guns they can threaten anyone for money and can also kill anyone they want." Not surprisingly, given the presence of guns in postconflict environments, acquiring power through guns was mentioned in other places as well.

In socially divided communities, local leaders may be particularly vicious in inflaming passions between ethnic or religious groups or along other divides as a means of mobilizing their own supporters and keeping themselves in power. People in several discussion groups highlighted this negative role of leaders in perpetuating violent conflict. The village of Bodolenge, in Indonesia's North Maluku province, is affected by Christian-Muslim conflict. A discussion group in the village noted that the pastor of the local church had advised Christians to take revenge. In Newsib, Philippines, also affected by religious conflict, Norping, a 67-year-old man in a discussion group, criticized both Christian and Muslim leaders: "I believe that our leaders manipulated the situation so that Christians and Muslims fight against each other. As I have observed, every time the conflict started to subside and the relationship between Christians and Muslims gets better, some groups from the Muslims or from the [mainly Christian] government would come, causing more conflict to our community."

In Borakbari, Assam, local leaders fomented further tension among religious groups after four Muslim youths forcibly took away four Hindu girls and married them. Some local Hindus said that if a Muslim youth marries a Hindu, he gets a hefty sum of Rs 50,000 from the local Muslim head as remuneration. The abductions resulted in riots, and political leaders, instead of working to resolve the matter, incited further hostilities. Social divisiveness deepened and the development of the village was severely affected.

Social divides do not always involve religion or ethnicity. In Villa Blanca, Colombia, the fight is between political leaders who cater to poor people displaced by armed conflict and those aligned with the homeless, who have a longer history in their localities.

The most consistent expectation among poor people was that their political leaders would fail to perform: that is, they would do little or nothing to help the communities that elected them. If they did bring in external resources for development, they would most likely skim off some 25 to 75 percent of the funds. Bribery was extremely widespread. In Afghanistan, 83 percent of households surveyed perceived that most or almost all local politicians take bribes. The share elsewhere ranged from 74 percent in Assam to a low of 40 percent in the Philippines.

In recent decades, numerous developing countries have implemented decentralization policies with the aim of improving government performance in delivering services. In their review of the literature, Bardhan and Mookherjee (2005) conclude that the effects of decentralization on corruption and services are highly context-specific. Recent studies in Colombia and Indonesia find that elections following decentralization are associated with a fight for power that has led to greater violence and corruption. In Colombia, researchers conclude that the decentralization reforms "misbehaved" in conflict contexts.[9] In our study in Colombia, less than a fifth of the households surveyed expressed confidence that their local politicians generally act in the public interest rather than in their own interest.[10] In the urban barrios there, people reported the murders or forced removal of beloved barrio leaders and the takeover of community boards (and their access to external resources) by "representatives" associated with armed groups.

As in the case of Colombia, some scholars of Indonesia argue that decentralization, and the rise in local government corruption that followed, sometimes triggered violence among rival ethnic-religious groups (Nordholt and Van Klinken 2007). The North Maluku communal violence was sparked by tensions over which groups would benefit most from a redistricting initiative and from the opportunities that the new government seat would provide. The discovery of gold in the area made the redistricting even more contentious.[11]

People everywhere saw politicians as having the money and power to do what they wanted and as being above the law because of their high (and low) connections. In the absence of any restraints and accountability, politicians are seen as seasonal, making promises during the campaign only to break them after the election. In conflict contexts, there are also signs that the recent decentralization processes may only make local democracy even more worthy of capturing.

## Representation: Ethnicity, Gender, and Poverty

*The MILF [Moro Islamic Liberation Front] are fighting for the right to self-determination.*
        —A 48-year-old man, Abanang, Baloi municipality, Philippines

*We do not have democracy at all. We have to speak in Sinhala, even in Jaffna. The army people arrest us if we speak Tamil sometimes. We have no freedom to speak our own language.*
        —A Tamil male youth, Kaithamavi, Jaffna district, Sri Lanka

We considered whether different social groups—meaning ethnic, religious, tribal, caste, racial, and language groups—are represented on village councils in the study communities. We also considered representation of women and poor people. Representation of these three broad categories increased markedly over the study period, especially representation of social groups (see figure 3.4 and also appendix table F.5).

**FIGURE 3.4**

**Representation on local councils in conflict and nonconflict communities, 2005**

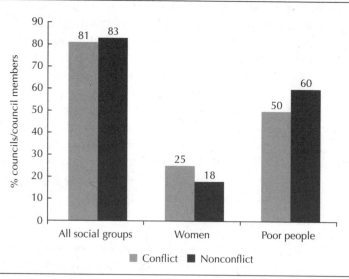

*Source:* Community questionnaire.
*Note:* "All social groups" refers to ethnic, religious, tribal, caste, racial, and language groups. Figures for social groups refer to the percentage of councils with representation. Figures for women and poor people refer to the percentage of council members.

### Representation of social groups

By 2005, more than 80 percent of existing village councils in both conflict and nonconflict contexts included representation from all social groups (ethnic, religious, caste, and so on) in the community. Overall, the percentage of village councils that were representative declined slightly in conflict contexts but increased in nonconflict contexts. Not surprisingly, the trends across countries varied. For instance, the share of representative councils increased in both Indonesia and Colombia, but in Indonesia the increase was due to increased representativeness in nonconflict settings, while in Colombia the improvement occurred in conflict settings. In Afghanistan, most of the village councils that existed were reported to be representative (appendix tables F.6 and F.7).

Among conflict communities, there was little variation in representation between the high- and low-mobility contexts (figure 3.5). The very slight

**FIGURE 3.5**

**Representation on local councils by conflict and MOP rating, 2005**

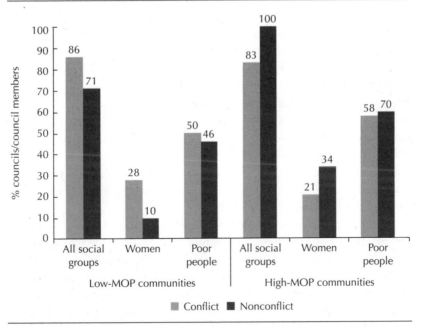

Source: Community questionnaire.

Note: "All social groups" refers to ethnic, religious, tribal, caste, racial, and language groups. Figures for social groups refer to the percentage of councils with representation. Figures for women and poor people refer to the percentage of council members.

difference with respect to social groups went in the "wrong" direction, that is, more councils had representation in low-MOP than in high-MOP contexts (86 percent versus 83 percent).[12] But in nonconflict contexts, the association between representation of social groups and high MOP was strongly positive. In the high-mobility nonconflict communities, 100 percent of the councils were representative, while in low-mobility nonconflict communities only 71 percent were (figure 3.5; see also appendix table F.8).

This suggests that diversity of representation in itself is not inimical to poverty reduction, growth, and prosperity. Rather, political structures get distorted in conflict contexts. In at least half of our sample, ethnic divides were the cause of conflict (in Sri Lanka, the Philippines, and Indonesia). Simmering tensions between ethnic groups were present in at least some of the other contexts, though often suppressed in the face of larger civil wars (in Afghanistan and Assam). For example, in Barumangga, Indonesia, a village beset by Christian-Muslim conflict, an intrasect clash among Muslims, and conflicts based on ethnic inequality, discussion groups said that people no longer trusted or respected each other or their local elected leaders. It is not surprising that the formal representation of warring groups on councils does not improve governance or bring prosperity to communities.

In the overall sample, both religious and ethnic polarization increased in conflict communities between 1995 and 2005. Polarization is measured as the size of the second-largest group (the largest minority) relative to the largest group (the majority).[13] Over time, a community whose second-largest group grows faster becomes more polarized using this index. This does not always happen: in Sri Lanka, for example, ethnic polarization decreased over time as communities across the conflict areas became consolidated by ethnicity, becoming predominantly Sinhalese, Tamil, or Muslim. Our regression analysis, discussed below, shows that religious polarization is significantly and negatively associated with movement out of poverty, but only in conflict communities (appendix tables F.9 and F.10).

Minority group representation on formal councils may slow down decision making and cooperation. This in turn may influence the mobility prospects of poor people, probably because of the inability of council members to work together to serve the public good, invest in local infrastructure, and attract resources to the community. In both Indonesia and the Philippines, ethnic and religious tensions were overcome in some communities by creating new decision-making structures, *outside* the village councils, that were trusted by all. In communities in North Maluku, Indonesia, this was Tim 30, a committee of 15 respected and trusted Muslims and 15 respected and trusted Christians. Their task was to interact with both the local council and the community to express aspirations, monitor assistance, and resolve tensions and conflict.

It is important to note that ethnic tension is not an inevitable outcome of ethnic diversity (Fearon and Laitin 2003). In nonconflict communities, ethnic representation on village councils does not have this slowing effect. In fact, in the non-Assam sample, both 10 years ago and now, all the high-MOP communities were representative, but the conflict communities in the non-Assam sample behaved like those in Assam, although to a lesser extent. Conflict worsens preexisting tensions between social groups, particularly when conflict is mobilized along ethnic lines. However, as noted, communities often blame politicians for fanning "sparks into fires" and keeping the ethnic flame burning and scorching.[14] A men's discussion group from the low-MOP village of Kahikuchi in Assam aptly described these dynamics:

> If there is collective effort in our community, then there must be progress. But there is another class of people who always separate people from each other. It is shown especially in politics; various political parties, whether it's AGP, BJP [Bhartiya Janta Party], or Congress . . . are trying to create divisions among the people of society. This kind of discrimination sometimes also hampers development work. If the group of supporters of one party gets a contract then the other party's supporter group opposes and pushes, and as a result both parties lose the work.

In political contexts where winners take all, there are no incentives for rivals on either side to play by the rules.

## Representation of women and poor people

*Women have seen a lot of changes. The most important of them is to have a female shura [council]. We have a female shura and women can participate in all the activities and solve any kind of problems.*
> —Discussion group of men and women, Zakwak Ulya,
> Herat province, Afghanistan

*Now women are working in the panchayat. It seems we, the women, are able to make complaints.*
> —Women's discussion group, Malujan, Assam, India

In conflict communities a revolution has taken place in terms of the number of women who are members of village councils. Many scholars have taken note of this shift.[15] In the conflict-affected communities across our sample, the proportion of village council members who are women more than tripled, from 8 percent of members in 1995 to 25 percent in 2005. The corresponding increase in nonconflict communities, 61 percent, was also substantial though less dramatic. In conflict contexts, the biggest shift occurred in Afghanistan, where the percentage of women on local councils went from 0 to 33 percent, followed by Indonesia (0 to 15 percent) and the Philippines (16 to 34 percent). Thus, in communities affected by conflict, one of the strongest social strictures regarding women's roles—their confinement to the private sphere—cracks open.[16]

Representation of poor people on village councils also shifted upward in 1995–2005, but here the progress has been greater in nonconflict communities. In conflict communities, the percentage of council members who are poor increased from 40 percent in 1995 to 50 percent in 2005; in nonconflict communities, the increase was from 38 to 60 percent.

Finally, as shown in figure 3.5, poor people's representation on councils is associated with higher mobility—more sharply in nonconflict contexts. In high-MOP nonconflict communities, 70 percent of village council members are poor, but in low-MOP communities, this is true for only 46 percent. In conflict communities, the corresponding figures are 58 percent in high-MOP communities and 50 percent in low-MOP communities. Hence, in conflict contexts the link between representation of poor people on village councils and mobility has grown positive over time (appendix table F.8).

## Functioning of Local Democratic Structures

> *We have rights to talk, to express our opinion on what is right and what is wrong. But if we have no money, our voice becomes bullshit.*
>
>     —Discussion group, Kdadaum, Santuk district, Cambodia

> *There is a link. Better democracy, like openness, transparency from the village head and his staff members, automatically will improve the prosperity of the people.*
>
>     —Discussion group, Barumangga,
>     North Maluku province, Indonesia

The structures of local democracy are in place even in conflict-affected communities. In fact, where elections were held, the large majority, 73 percent, reported that their local elections were fair. But these elections are associated with significantly lower mobility in conflict contexts. Clearly, it takes much more than an election to transform a local council into one that is functionally democratic: responsive, accountable, and participatory in its workings, with impacts that may translate into greater prosperity for poor people as well. Hence, we first examine if there are differences in democratic processes in conflict and nonconflict contexts, and then we examine the links to movement out of poverty.

We focus on the nexus between local leaders and communities. Approximately 20 percent of local leaders in both conflict and nonconflict contexts are currently considered very responsive, meaning they take into account concerns voiced by local people. In terms of trends over time, the pace of change toward greater responsiveness was faster in the conflict communities (figure 3.6).

**FIGURE 3.6**
**Responsiveness of local leaders in conflict and nonconflict communities, 2005**

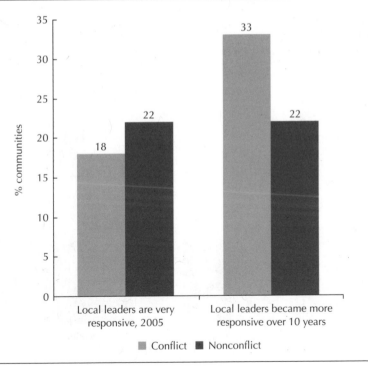

*Source:* Community questionnaire.

Yet, responsiveness in conflict contexts is *not* associated with high mobility. Rather, the direction of the relationship is inverse, that is, low mobility and high responsiveness go together (figure 3.7). This is not true for non-conflict communities in the same countries, where higher responsiveness is associated with higher mobility out of poverty.

In conflict communities, responsiveness may not translate into movement out of poverty for poor people, but there does appear to be some relation between responsiveness and local law and order. Communities in conflict contexts that were rated as having more responsive leaders also scored better on safety, that is, they were considered less dangerous than the communities with less responsive leaders (appendix table F.11). In conflict communities it is not clear that more responsive leaders necessarily bring about better local service provision, although in the nonconflict communities there does seem to be some relationship (appendix table F.12).

While responsiveness is clearly important in participatory or representative democracies, the notion that responsiveness by itself will bring prosperity

**FIGURE 3.7**
**Responsiveness of local leaders by conflict and MOP rating, 2005**

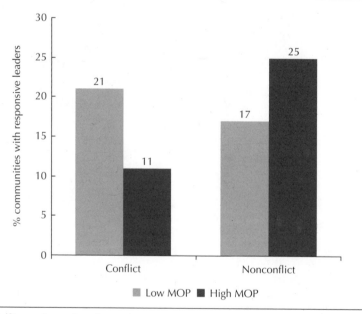

*Source:* Community questionnaire.

to a conflict-affected community may be far-fetched. Even the most good-hearted, voter-oriented leader may not be able to overcome all the disadvantages of a war-wracked community: poor infrastructure, lack of economic opportunities, poor government finances, and conflict.[17]

If responsiveness has risen modestly, corruption and bribery have risen immodestly. Approximately half of the conflict communities were corrupt in 1995; by 2005, 91 percent reported that most or almost all government officials were corrupt, a 79 percent increase in a decade. Nonconflict communities also saw a surge in corruption, from 44 percent to 74 percent, a 67 percent increase (table 3.1). The increase in bribe taking among local officials was even more spectacular, an 89 percent increase in conflict communities and a whopping 189 percent increase in nonconflict communities.

*Both corruption and bribery facilitate movement out of poverty in all communities in 2005, even when there were differences in earlier years* (figures 3.8 and 3.9). Bribe giving is particularly effective in conflict contexts. Given the state of local politics and politicians and the dire needs in communities emerging from conflict, this should be no surprise, but it is a surprise to see the pattern so clearly. Those poor people who have some resources are able to bribe their way out of poverty.

These findings give new meaning to the word "responsiveness" when applied to local government. The earlier discussion of people's descriptions of politicians fits this pattern of results.

**TABLE 3.1**

**Corruption and bribery in conflict and nonconflict communities, 1995 and 2005**

*percentage of communities*

| Indicator | Conflict | Nonconflict |
|---|---|---|
| *% reporting most or almost all local government officials are corrupt* | | |
| 2005 | 91 | 74 |
| 1995 | 51 | 44 |
| Change over 10 years | 79 | 67 |
| *% reporting that most or almost all local government officials take bribes* | | |
| 2005 | 48 | 58 |
| 1995 | 26 | 20 |
| Change over 10 years | 89 | 189 |

*Source:* Community questionnaire.

**FIGURE 3.8**

**Corruption and bribery by conflict and MOP rating, 1995 and 2005**

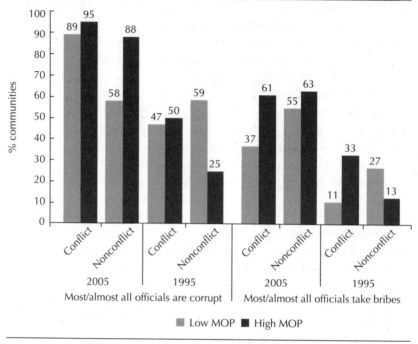

*Source:* Community questionnaire.

**FIGURE 3.9**

**Change in corruption and bribery, 1995–2005, by conflict and MOP rating**

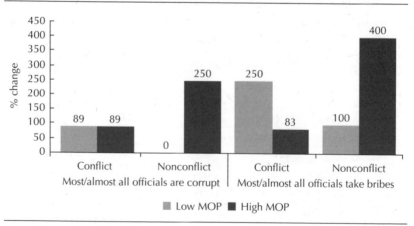

*Source:* Community questionnaire.

When reflecting on democracy and government performance in Cambodia, a discussion group of young women exclaimed,

> Governance—we have never heard the term "governance," but we have heard the term "corruption" . . . meaning that government officials get bribes from people. There are a lot of examples of corruption in our society. For example, if we have a conflict with someone who has a connection with powerful officials or has money to bribe them, then they will win the case. We the poor dare not file any complaint to the court because there will be no fairness anyway.

A young men's discussion group from Chakboeng said,

> We have heard from our parents that corruption occurs in every society or regime, but today it is getting worse and worse . . . because the pockets of the officials are open. So much foreign aid flows into our country but there are still only a few jobs available . . . We are still jobless.

Corruption is usually crass and bold, but it is sometimes a bit more subtle, as in this story told by Mus, an upright citizen, in conflict-affected Barumangga, Indonesia:

> In 2000 a member of the community brought 71 bottles of alcohol into Barumangga, so I reported the matter to the correct authorities. They checked up and found the proof. It was my wish that the bottles be destroyed immediately, on the spot, but the authorities decided to keep them as evidence . . . up to now I have no idea where the bottles went.

Despite all this evidence, it is still too soon to dismiss local democracy in these contexts as a lost cause. There are four reasons. One, as already pointed out, in nonconflict communities local government appears to be positive and helpful to poor people's mobility, especially when it is representative and responsive. This means that, depending on what happens in postconflict contexts, it is possible for functional democracy to take root at the local level.

Second, people do report improvements in local democracy. At the end of long discussions with groups about democracy, freedom, village councils, elections, and politicians, we asked people a few concluding questions. One of these focused on their assessment of democracy. We asked whether people had seen any changes in democracy and whether these changes had a positive, negative, or neutral impact. Despite everything that is wrong with democratic functioning, 53 percent of discussion groups in conflict areas that reported seeing a change in local democratic functioning said that these changes had positive impacts; this number went up to 67 percent in nonconflict communities (figure 3.10). These ratings are influenced by the ability of local leaders to bring some prosperity to individuals and to the community and by the extent to which central government provides resources that improve basic infrastructure, security, and the economic environment.

Third, poor people and ordinary citizens might still be the saving grace. It takes two sides to make democracy work: elected leaders who pay attention and are responsive, and citizens who are willing to participate in political and community decision making and affairs. People are clearly way ahead of their leaders, even in the most war-torn and war-weary communities. Their willingness to come together and participate in meetings to benefit the community far surpasses leader responsiveness. An extraordinary 76 percent of communities in conflict contexts report that people actually came together in community meetings to act for the greater benefit; in nonconflict communities

**FIGURE 3.10**

**Perceptions of democracy and civic engagement in conflict and nonconflict communities**

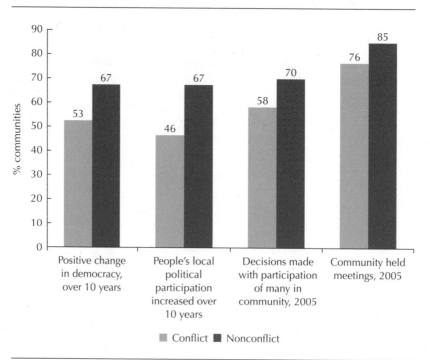

*Source:* Community questionnaire.

the incidence of such meetings is even higher, around 85 percent (figure 3.10). Representation of disadvantaged groups in community decision making is also broadening. This decision making will become more real when the political culture, norms, and incentives change so that politicians actually take their obligations as "public servants" seriously.

Finally, as noted earlier in figure 3.5, in nonconflict communities poor people's representation on councils is strongly associated with higher mobility. Overall, 70 percent of the high-MOP communities had poor people's participation on local councils, but this was true for only 46 percent of the low-MOP communities. For conflict communities, the pattern was the reverse 10 years ago, but in 2005 slightly more high-MOP communities had poor people represented on their councils. Hence, the trend even in conflict communities has become positive.

## How Local Democracy Functions in Countries with Different Income Levels

Recent literature seems to indicate that democracy is conflict-provoking at low-income levels.[18] The primary reason is that legitimacy, security, law and order, and accountability do not take hold. In this environment, there is little to stop those who lose elections from resorting to political violence, often along ethnic divides. Right after an election is the most dangerous time, and violence may paradoxically increase after this rite of democracy. This lawlessness in the political field discourages good people from entering politics. The equilibrium seems to shift with economic growth and development; in terms of per capita income, the magic number seems to be around $2,700 (Collier and Rohner 2008).

Is this true in our sample, and can we say anything about how to bring about greater accountability and security at the local level in low- and middle-income communities recovering from conflict?

Our findings provide support for this political science observation, highlighted recently by Collier (2009).[19] We first examine whether there are differences in violence levels between low-income and middle-income countries in our sample. The differences are striking: across both conflict and nonconflict communities, in both 1995 and 2005, levels of violence were higher in low-income than in middle-income countries. In 1995, on average, 59 percent of communities in low-income countries reported moderate to high levels of violence, compared to 36 percent of communities in middle-income countries. By 2005, none of the communities in middle-income countries

**TABLE 3.2**

**Levels of violence in low-income and middle-income countries, 1995 and 2005**

*percentage of communities*

| Level of violence/conflict rating | Low income | Middle income |
|---|---|---|
| *Village is very or moderately violent now* | | |
| Conflict | 10 | 0 |
| Nonconflict | 12 | 0 |
| Total | 11 | 0 |
| *Village was very or moderately violent 10 years ago* | | |
| Conflict | 69 | 39 |
| Nonconflict | 35 | 30 |
| Total | 59 | 36 |

*Source:* Community questionnaire.

reported moderate or high levels of violence, whereas 11 percent of communities in low-income countries still experience violence at this level (table 3.2).

Next we turn to the differences in forms or formal structures of democracy. With respect to the presence of village councils, the conflict communities in low-income countries do dramatically worse than the conflict communities in middle-income countries. However, the differences are not so sharp with respect to elections (figure 3.11; detailed data by year in appendix table F.13).[20] Low-income countries actually score better on fairness of elections and representation of social groups in both conflict and nonconflict contexts.

The differences between communities in low- and middle-income countries are even more striking in every aspect of the functioning of democracy (figure 3.12; appendix table F.13). The communities in low-income countries score lower on responsiveness and much higher on corruption and bribery, indicating perhaps an improvement in accountability of government in middle-income countries. It is also worth noting that while overall corruption rates double or triple in low-income countries, in middle-income countries corruption increases in conflict contexts but drops in nonconflict contexts. The difference between income levels with respect to bribery is even more dramatic. Again, while the numbers double or triple over time in the low-income countries, bribery reportedly disappears in nonconflict middle-income countries and increases only slightly in conflict communities in these countries.

**FIGURE 3.11**

**Formal democratic attributes by conflict rating and country income level, 2005**

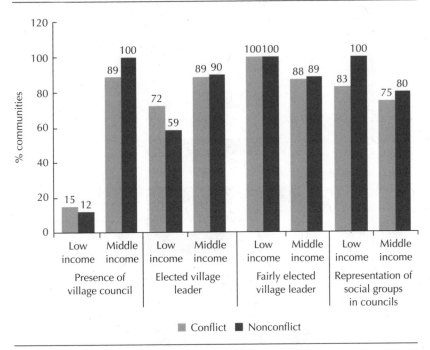

*Source:* Community questionnaire.

These findings are consistent with the wider literature as well as with our findings in India, which showed that as communities become more prosperous, local democracy becomes less exclusionary (Friedman 2005; Narayan, Pritchett, and Kapoor 2009).

Overall, 47 percent of conflict communities in low-income countries report positive changes in democracy, compared to 65 percent in middle-income countries. Given the great difficulties facing conflict-affected communities in low-income countries, these numbers should not be dismissed as insignificant.

Despite the persistent bad behavior of their political leaders, poor people in low-income countries continue to participate in community meetings at rates very similar to those in middle-income countries. They do so to exercise their rights and because they are hoping against hope that their voices may someday be heard and make a difference. People in low-income contexts remain the beacon of hope.

**FIGURE 3.12**
**Functional democratic attributes by conflict rating and country income level, 2005**

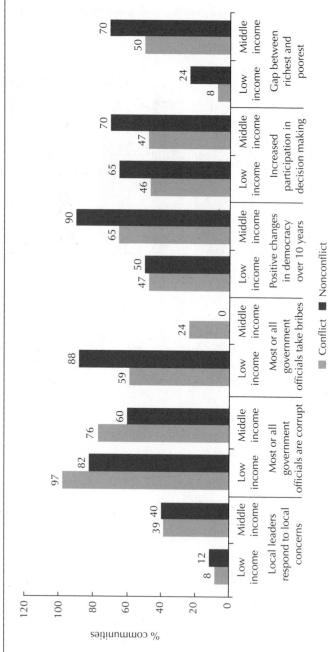

*Source:* Community questionnaire.

Low-income countries do better than middle-income countries in the size of the gap between the richest and poorest. It increased in only 8 percent of the low-income conflict communities, compared to 50 percent of the middle-income conflict communities. This is consistent with the vast literature pointing to an increase in income inequalities as incomes rise.

While overall income levels may strongly influence the performance of local democracy, this relationship is not inevitable. Afghanistan, a low-income country, behaved more like the middle-income countries in this regard, at least in the early days of democracy, the period considered most dangerous. And it is true that as international assistance to Afghanistan has slowed, both security and corruption have worsened dramatically. Colombia, one of our three middle-income countries, acts more like a low-income country, closer to Cambodia and Assam than to the Philippines and Indonesia. However, in Colombia our study focused primarily on very disadvantaged urban communities with large numbers of internally displaced people, while the sample communities in Indonesia and the Philippines were more economically heterogeneous. In the next section we look at the importance of overall poverty levels for mobility prospects, together with a range of other factors.

## Factors Affecting Community Mobility Rates

*We did go to vote . . . but we did not know or even care whether the electoral process was free and fair. We just thought and cared about how to make a living. We got nothing from the election, but just the black paint on our finger . . . We went to vote because we love our nation.*

—Youth discussion group, Chakboeng,
Peam Ro district, Cambodia

*There is no openness between the village head and the community, and hence there was a clash over the assistance from LML [Lembaga Mitra Lingkungan, Environmental Partners Institute]. If there was openness, then there would be a connection between democracy and prosperity. If there is no transparency in the leadership, there is no connection between democracy and prosperity.*

—Men's discussion group, Galalolo,
North Maluku province, Indonesia

We now present the results of multivariate regression analysis. Econometric modeling is useful because it enables us to assess simultaneously the role of several factors in helping communities reduce poverty, and then determine the most significant ones.

Because of the large number of economic, social, and political variables of interest, we use ordinary least squares (OLS) regressions as a summation device to examine the relationship between a set of factors and movement out of poverty.[21] These are correlates and we do not imply causation. As far as possible we use initial conditions for independent variables. Our dependent variable is the community-level moving out of poverty (MOP) rate; it is a continuous variable ranging from 0 to 100, based on the ladder of life exercise.

We often asked several questions about the same phenomenon. Rather than mine the data for the best fit, we did a principal components analysis (PCA) to combine the conceptually related variables into a single measure. Although there are limitations to PCA as a data reduction tool, it has the advantage of not referring to the dependent variable in the construction of the measure of the independent variable and hence is not data mining (for technical details, see appendix B).

The communities in our sample had large numbers of poor people in 1995; the percentage starting poor (PSP) ranged from 60 to 90 percent. However, when we plot community MOP with the PSP, we find great variation across the conflict countries. For example, the Philippines, Indonesia, and Assam all have similar percentages starting poor, approximately 70 percent. However, MOP for communities in Assam averages just 10 percent, while average MOP in the Philippines is double that (21 percent) and in Indonesia almost triple (27 percent). This variation was also true in our larger global sample (see volume 2), and it is this variation that needs to be explained. We turn then to our overall theoretical framework in which a community's poverty mobility is conceptualized as a product of local institutional factors—political, social, and economic—as well as factors related to collective and individual agency and assets.

We broadly follow the Moving Out of Poverty conceptual framework and the global specification developed to explain household-level mobility, with some modifications. Given that the sample of conflict communities is small (54), and the sample of nonconflict or peaceful communities in the conflict countries even smaller (26), we present four different models for comparative purposes in table 3.3. Model 1 represents only the conflict-affected communities. Model 2 combines conflict and nonconflict communities from the conflict countries, since our nonconflict sample is too small to run separate regressions. Model 3 presents the results from the larger global sample of only "peaceful countries" as a comparison. Model 4 presents the

entire sample of conflict and nonconflict countries, combined for comparative purposes and to reveal how our key variables of interest act across these
different samples. The model includes an Afghanistan dummy to control for
Afghanistan's very high MOP, which reflects that country's specificity; in addition, we use regional dummies to control for regional differences in MOP
unrelated to the other explanatory variables. We considered using specific
country dummies to control for fixed country effects; however, we found that
regional dummies capture well the broad geographic differences in MOP
while reducing the number of independent variables and therefore boosting
the degrees of freedom.

There are five important findings regarding the possible association of
different factors with community MOP rates. These factors include conflict,
access to economic opportunities, political structures and political culture,
people's participation in community meetings, and finally, political and religious associations and religious polarization.

## Conflict

Living in a conflict community is *not* associated with reduced mobility for
the poor, but living in a conflict-affected country does reduce poor people's
chances of escaping poverty. This finding is consistent with the results presented in chapter 1. The fact that conflict communities do not show lower
rates of MOP means that there are mechanisms present that foster poor people's mobility in these communities. The effects of conflict are examined by
introducing dummies for conflict communities in model 2 and dummies
for conflict communities and conflict countries in model 4. After we control
for the effects of other variables, the conflict community dummy is still not
significant, but the conflict country dummy is significant in our sample. This
is also similar to the results from simple cross tabs. In other words, the mere
fact of being located in a conflict-affected country affects the overall development of communities, even communities in localities not involved in direct
conflict, and lowers the overall rates of moving out of poverty.[22] It is worth
remembering that our samples are not representative of entire countries but
focus on a small set of communities to explore the relationship between
conflict and mobility.

## Poverty and access to economic opportunities

The proportion of the population starting poor in a community has a significant effect on MOP: the higher the initial poverty rate, the lower the MOP

**TABLE 3.3**

**Regression results for conflict and peaceful communities and countries**

| Independent variables | Conflict countries | | Peaceful countries[a] | All countries[b] |
|---|---|---|---|---|
| | Conflict communities | Conflict and nonconflict communities | | |
| | (1) | (2) | (3) | (4) |
| Strength of local economy 10 years ago (very weak=1, very strong=5) | −0.010 (0.016) | −0.002 (0.015) | −0.015 (0.012) | −0.012 (0.010) |
| Access to education (yes=1, no=0) | −0.004*** (0.001) | 0.000 (0.008) | 0.007 (0.007) | 0.007 (0.006) |
| Percent of village population starting poor (0 to 100) | −0.256* (0.094) | −0.286** (0.072) | −0.328** (0.111) | −0.330*** (0.096) |
| Index of social exclusion | −0.029 (0.014) | 0.006 (0.010) | 0.025* (0.013) | 0.018* (0.010) |
| Index of access to information, 10 years ago | −0.033 (0.023) | −0.019 (0.015) | 0.013** (0.004) | 0.008 (0.005) |
| Number of financial/ credit groups, 10 years ago | 0.053 (0.034) | 0.033 (0.022) | 0.002 (0.001) | 0.002 (0.001) |
| Number of religious groups, 10 years ago | 0.007 (0.019) | −0.003 (0.016) | −0.045*** (0.010) | −0.033** (0.013) |
| Number of political groups, 10 years ago | 0.033* (0.013) | 0.011 (0.012) | 0.006 (0.012) | 0.006 (0.010) |
| Number of ethnic groups, 10 years ago | 0.001 (0.013) | 0.013 (0.011) | −0.028 (0.019) | 0.022* (0.012) |
| Presence of village council, 10 years ago (yes=1, no=0) | −0.321* (0.133) | −0.113 (0.123) | −0.057 (0.032) | −0.058* (0.030) |
| Village council was representative, 10 years ago (yes=1, no=0) | 0.169** (0.051) | 0.127** (0.028) | 0.023 (0.020) | 0.039* (0.021) |
| Access to credit from friends (yes=1, no=0) | −0.015* (0.006) | 0.001 (0.019) | 0.043** (0.017) | 0.033 (0.020) |

**TABLE 3.3**
*continued*

| Independent variables | Conflict countries | | Peaceful countriesᵃ | All countriesᵇ |
|---|---|---|---|---|
| | Conflict communities | Conflict and nonconflict communities | | |
| Religious polarization (polarization=1, no polarization=0) | −0.188* | −0.094** | −0.066 | −0.075* |
| | (0.077) | (0.024) | (0.040) | (0.037) |
| Corruption, 10 years ago | 0.030* | 0.020 | 0.000 | 0.004 |
| | (0.013) | (0.018) | (0.012) | (0.010) |
| Village had organized community meetings, 10 years ago (yes=1, no=0) | 0.059 | 0.006 | 0.032* | 0.020 |
| | (0.034) | (0.038) | (0.016) | (0.014) |
| Afghanistan dummy | 0.501** | 0.314** | (dropped) | 0.322*** |
| | (0.123) | (0.085) | | (0.032) |
| Region East Asiaᶜ | 0.273** | 0.114 | 0.069* | 0.104*** |
| | (0.085) | (0.090) | (0.032) | (0.023) |
| Region Africa | (dropped) | (dropped) | 0.086*** | 0.072** |
| | | | (0.020) | (0.025) |
| Region Latin America | 0.335** | 0.181* | 0.342*** | 0.245*** |
| | (0.100) | (0.075) | (0.039) | (0.072) |
| Conflict country dummy (yes=1, no=0) | | | | −0.161*** |
| | | | | (0.040) |
| Conflict community dummy (yes=1, no=0) | | 0.051 | | 0.039 |
| | | (0.047) | | (0.045) |
| Constant | 0.274** | 0.269*** | 0.515*** | 0.508*** |
| | (0.062) | (0.047) | (0.091) | (0.078) |
| Number of observations | 54 | 80 | 321 | 401 |
| $R^2$ | 0.801 | 0.648 | 0.255 | 0.292 |

*Source:* Authors' analysis of community questionnaire.
a. This table includes regression results for a group of peaceful communities, that is, those located in countries not affected by conflict. These communities are genuinely insulated from political conflict (by our definition) because they experience political violence neither directly nor indirectly.
b. The "all countries" sample includes all communities in conflict countries plus the peaceful countries.
c. When used in regressions for the sample of conflict countries, regional dummies in Latin America include only Colombia; in East Asia, they include the Philippines and Indonesia. Since Afghanistan, which is in South Asia, is always included separately, the reference country is India in the overall and peaceful countries samples and Assam in the conflict countries sample.
*p < .10   **p < .05   ***p < .01

rate. This effect is quite strong in peaceful countries and moderate in conflict countries. In peaceful countries a 10 percent increase in the proportion of the population that is initially poor is associated with a reduction of 3.3 percent in MOP, while in conflict communities the reduction is less, 2.6 percent. This supports the trend of divergence in community mobility rates, since communities with a high proportion of poor in 1995 are slow to get ahead; high initial levels of poverty put a considerable brake on subsequent mobility. But this divergence is less sharp in conflict communities, consistent with the greater scope of upward mobility out of poverty in conflict contexts.

We also consider two other economic factors, the strength of the local economy and using friends as a source of credit. The strength of the local economy 10 years ago has a weak negative effect on MOP; in other words, communities that had strong local economies 10 years ago experienced slightly lower MOP. We probably do not see strong negative effects because it is not just the overall economic environment that matters, but poor people's access to opportunities within that environment. In fact, people in conflict contexts reported overall that while economic opportunities had increased over time, their access to economic opportunities had decreased.

Lack of access to credit often emerged as an obstacle to upward mobility in discussions of constraints in the economic environment. Therefore, we introduced an indicator to capture this: depending on friends as the most important source of credit. Supporting our argument that access to economic opportunities matters most, we find that in conflict-affected communities there is a significant negative relationship between dependence on friends for credit and movement out of poverty. At the same time, the relationship is strongly positive in peaceful countries. We speculate that in conflict settings, reliance on friends as the main source of credit implies lower access to formal sources of lending—hence the negative effect on mobility. In peaceful communities, the effect of credit from friends is positive, presumably because credit from friends complements formal sources of credit.

## Political structures and political culture

The dysfunctionality of the political context and the capture of political institutions in conflict environments come through very strongly in our regression results. Even after controlling for all other factors, the independent effect of village councils in conflict communities is significantly negative. *In conflict communities, having a village council is associated with a 32 percentage point decrease in MOP, the strongest negative effect of all factors considered in these contexts.* The effect is negative but much weaker and insignificant in other contexts. It only becomes significantly negative in the total sample that included the conflict countries (column 4 in table 3.3).[23]

Councils in conflict contexts do not always misbehave. When councils are representative of different ethnic groups, they have significant positive association with movement out of poverty. The presence of representative councils increases MOP by 17 percent, the strongest positive effect of all the variables included. The effect of the representative councils appears much stronger in the presence of multivariate controls than in the bivariate tables.

On further exploration we find that having no council is better than having an unrepresentative council for poor people's mobility. Village councils must be representative; otherwise, they become an economic and political liability. We also found that communities with representative councils are associated with greater access to political decision making and tend to have more dynamic social and economic associations (see appendix tables F.14, F.15, and F.16 for a summary of MOP in communities with representative and nonrepresentative councils).

In the extensive literature on governance, accountability, and transparency, the one factor on which theorists, practitioners, and policy makers generally agree is the importance of free availability of information to citizens.[24] Free flows of information to citizens about government actions encourage informed public scrutiny of government performance. Perversely, in conflict contexts, access to information has a negative sign, although it is not significant; in the peaceful countries, the sign is positive and significant. We speculate that in conflict contexts people lose trust in their councils, which are captured and unaccountable. In this overall context of fear and mistrust, access to information may just add to the confusion, or at the very least brings no tangible economic benefit.

There is a positive and statistically significant relationship between corruption and moving out of poverty, *but only in conflict contexts*. This confirms what discussion groups told us over and over again: those who can afford to connect with corrupt politicians gain access to government programs, private jobs, and other assistance. In the peaceful countries there is no relationship between community mobility rates and corruption.

## People's participation

People's participation in community meetings theoretically should make a difference to mobility, as local people know their problems. If they have a sense of ownership in decisions, they are much more likely to work to overcome problems, whether with broken hand pumps or the unsatisfactory performance of a teacher, nurse, or extension worker. When local people have control over funds and decisions, local projects are much more likely to reflect their priorities and make a difference. However, when decisions are made at night in "big men's" homes, participation in meetings becomes a sham, even though in the long run society gains from inculcating the habit of civic participation.

Given the capture of local village councils, it is not surprising that there is no relationship between people's participation in meetings and moving out of poverty in conflict contexts. However, in peaceful societies, people's ability to come together and take action for the benefit of the larger community contributes significantly and positively to mobility of the poor.

## Political and religious groups/associations and polarization

When state legitimacy is called into doubt, when the state fails to provide even the most basic services, and when private sector provision is also absent, people turn to one another to solve their problems and reclaim their rights. In the sample communities there were many different types of voluntary associations, from revolving credit groups to political, religious, and ethnic groups and associations. Given the ethnic nature of many conflicts, we were particularly interested in the composition of these associations and their effects on mobility. While we discuss these more completely in the next chapter, we highlight some key results here.

Our measure of religious polarization, which reflects the demographic relationship of the two largest religious groups in a community, is significantly and negatively associated with mobility of the poor in conflict contexts. Poor people who live in religiously polarized conflict communities have a much lower chance of moving out of poverty. In terms of orders of magnitude, a 10 percent increase in religious polarization reduces the mobility rates by 1.8 percent, a significant amount. This effect remains negative and significant in nonconflict communities within conflict countries, and it is negative but loses its significance in peaceful countries. The pattern indicates that religious demographics do not determine conflict destiny, but it is clear that religious markers of identity can be used by politicians to incite and ignite differences. History teaches us that once this happens, it is difficult to reverse.[25]

Controlling for the degree of religious polarization, we consider the effect of the number of religious and political associations. Independently of the negative effect of religious polarization, an increase in the number of political groups/associations in conflict settings was significantly and positively associated with moving out of poverty. In the absence of representative councils, it appears, people in some communities are organizing to claim their citizenship rights and access resources.

It is important to note that in the peaceful countries, and in the global sample of all countries, the number of religious groups (associations) in a community was significantly and negatively related to mobility. As we discuss in greater detail in chapter 4, religious groups contributed to tension in communities rather than playing a constructive role (as by providing credit or basic services); hence, the strong negative sign with religious groups (appendix table F.17). In conflict communities, this negative effect disappears. This is primarily because, as discussed in chapter 5 on the economic environment, some of these religious groups have in recent years become providers of small amounts of credit in the absence of other providers.

## The Mischief and Promise of Democracy

Democracy rests on a spirit of service and accountability. Elected representatives must serve the public good. And to make sure they do, citizens must serve as watchdogs.

Across the communities in our study, this spirit was broken. Citizens could only choose among "rascals" who bought or fought their way into power. The lack of law and order and the breakdown of justice systems meant few restraints could be imposed on the misbehavior of politicians. Citizens could not act as watchdogs in such an environment, no matter how close the government was brought to the people.

In the conflict countries, the hollowness of local democracy matters intensely. Local democratic structures "misbehave" and end up hurting the poor. Communities had less mobility when they had councils, elections, and even fair elections. And responsive politicians made no difference to poor people's mobility. What did show a positive association with mobility, in conflict-affected communities, was corruption. When political systems break down, it is everyone for himself or herself, and poor people, where possible, attempt to buy their way out of poverty.

There are three pieces of hopeful news, nevertheless. First, in the non-conflict communities within the conflict countries, democratic functioning seems more normal and has positive effects on poor people's mobility. Positive change in local-level democracy is possible. The culture of predatory leadership needs to shift and incentives need to be provided for more citizen-oriented leadership at the local level. Strong civic associations at the community level play a particularly important role in promoting this shift. People's associations can overcome even deep social divides, but such groups are unlikely to gain momentum and change political culture on their own unless they receive support through government or NGO programs.[26] Also needed are easily enforceable laws guaranteeing the public's right to information.[27]

Second, across the conflict-affected countries, people voted, attended meetings, and helped each other, hoping that their democracies might start working as they are supposed to. While they continue to vote, to believe, and to hope, they are less optimistic about the likelihood of positive changes in politics than about social or economic changes.

Third, as per capita incomes rise, democracy seems to function better. So once again, economic development matters. There seem to be virtuous circles apparent even in the poor communities visited in the middle-income countries.

The functioning of local democracy is not immutable. It can and does change, and in a relatively short time. Over 90 percent of the conflict-affected communities in our sample reported change, more than half of which was positive change. Local democracy can be made to work in ways that benefit poor people in conflict contexts. However, the challenge remains.

## Notes

1. Fragile democracies can be conflict-provoking (Snyder 2000; Stewart and O'Sullivan 1999). Paul Collier (2009) is the most recent to call attention to the relationship between elections and violence, emphasizing that violence most often escalates in the period *after* elections rather than during the campaign and voting. Mansfield and Snyder (2005) similarly draw attention to a country's vulnerability to violence during periods of democratic transition. Recent work by Amy Pate (2008) shows that governments that are characterized by a mix of authoritarian and democratic features are more than twice as likely as other governments to experience genocide or political events and nearly two and half times as likely to experience adverse regime change. Charles Tilly argues: "People in low-capacity undemocratic regimes usually suffer the most extensive losses from collective violence because their regimes allow so much room for petty tyranny (on the part of officeholders, warlords, and other predators) and also provide opportunities for profit taking outside intervention" (2003, 232). Also see Windsor (2007) for a review of some of the literature on the links between poverty, conflict, and democracy issues.

2. See "All Politics Is Local: How Better Governance Helps the Poor," chapter 6 in volume 2 of the Moving Out of Poverty series (Narayan, Pritchett, and Kapoor 2009).

3. Local resource mobilization is an important issue in its own right. It is particularly crucial as a means of supporting broad-based recovery in which excluded groups benefit as they contribute to public finances (Murshed 2002; Addison and Murshed 2003).

4. Econometric work by Fearon and Laitin (2003) finds that ethnically diverse countries display no greater propensity for civil war than other states at similar levels of economic development. For insightful analysis of how and why horizontal inequalities, and especially ethnic cleavages, do nonetheless spark strife in many contexts, and what can be done to ease them, see Stewart's edited volume (2008). Donald Horowitz (2000) provides a rich examination of why identity politics emerge and then often turn violent. He notes that political parties may begin with multiethnic support, but in societies with deep social divisions the parties often become ethnically based "irrespective of the initial wishes of party leaders and often in explicit contradiction to their ideas about the desirability of multiethnic organization" (30). Horowitz attributes these processes to voting patterns that reflect voter wishes and to the popular appeal of extremist ethnic positions rather than simply to leaders who use extreme positions to galvanize a base of support, as emphasized in much of the literature. In this sense, Horowitz informs political science theories about winning voter coalitions with primordial arguments about the roots of conflict.

5. To protect the privacy of participants, this book uses pseudonyms for the study communities (villages and barrios). Cities, municipalities, districts, departments, and provinces are identified by their real names.

6. There is no direct translation for "democracy" in Pashto or Dari. On rare occasions people used the Pashto word *woloswaki*, meaning "government by the people." Many people reported that they heard the word "democracy" on television or radio.

7. We examined the two-way relationship between elections and fair elections and MOP using the Pearson chi-square test. For elected leaders in conflict communities, the relationship is negative and significant in 2005 (chi-square 7.1, significant at 0.02) and also in 1995 (chi-square 6.8, significant at 0.03). In nonconflict communities, however, the difference is not statistically significant in either time period because of the way the middle-MOP communities behave (in 2005, chi-square 2.56, and in 1995, chi-square 3.18, not significant in either case). As far as fairly elected leaders, there is a significant negative relationship with MOP in conflict communities in both periods (in 2005, chi-square 8.96, significant at 0.01, and in 1995, chi-square 9.0, significant at 0.01). However, the differences are not significant in nonconflict contexts.

8. The relationship holds across the sample of communities and is not driven by Assam results.

9. Oslender's (2007) work traces increased violence in some locations in Colombia to paramilitary efforts to roll back the electoral gains of the left and to undermine resource rights granted to indigenous and Afro-Colombian populations that interfered with powerful agribusiness interests. Similarly, Siegle and O'Mahoney (2006) find that rural violence and instability intensified with decentralization as armed groups muscled their way into public office or local procurements.

10. Nor surprisingly, the better-off group that benefits more from capture was the only group whose median response indicated that public authorities *did* act in the public interest.

11. See chapter 10 for more details. At the aggregate level, Østby (2008) finds that horizontal inequalities seem to be particularly conflict-provoking in demo-

cratic regimes with electoral and political systems that are apparently politically inclusive.

12. This result is consistent with the political science and economics literatures that suggest that at the aggregate level, and more recently at the community level, ethnic diversity on decision-making boards reduces the effectiveness of decision making and investments. See particularly the study by Edward Miguel, in which he finds that Kenyan communities at mean levels of ethnic diversity have 40 percent fewer desks per primary school pupil than homogeneous communities, on average (Miguel 2001, 2004; Miguel and Gugerty 2005).

13. Imagine two communities, each of which has a majority group that accounts for 70 percent of its population. In community A, a single minority group makes up the remaining 30 percent, while in community B, there are several minority groups and the largest of them accounts for only 10 percent. Our measure would indicate that community A is more polarized (30/70=0.43) than community B (10/70=0.14).

14. See Ashutosh Varshney's (2002) exploration of intercommunal riots in Indian cities with roughly similar proportions of Hindus and Muslims in their population.

15. Conflicts often force women to take on roles that are traditionally in the male domain (see, for example, Bouta, Frerks, and Bannon 2005; Sørensen 1998). But there is also an important literature indicating that these new roles can be fleeting once conflict ends (see Strickland and Duvvury 2003 for an extensive bibliography on gender and conflict). More generally, scholars agree that gender quotas are changing norms for women's political participation. These policies have catapulted women into political roles in Afghanistan, which require women-only councils, and in India (but not yet Assam), which require women's membership on panchayats and reserve one-third of panchayat headships for women. However, in India there is mixed evidence as to whether the presence of women representatives makes elected bodies more responsive to women's needs. For example, Misra and Kudva (2008) report uneven impacts of gender quotas, and they attribute this to the weak capacities of the women panchayat members. They found that almost two-thirds were illiterate or minimally literate, with the exception of those in Orissa and the four southern states. On the other hand, Chattopadhyay and Duflo (2004) draw on econometric analysis to conclude that the women-headed gram panchayats in West Bengal and Rajasthan were more likely than those headed by men to invest in infrastructure of strong relevance to women's needs, such as water, electricity, and roads. They also find that women are more politically active in panchayats headed by women.

16. Hughes (2007) contends that postconflict periods can sometimes provide opportunities for women to play stronger political roles that go beyond openings created by the introduction of gender quotas.

17. We do find some evidence that in the overall sample of communities, improvements in infrastructure are associated with higher responsiveness, but the pattern for conflict communities is very mixed.

18. See note 1; also see Auvinen and Nafziger (1999).

19. The quantitative data on low-income countries are dominated by Assam.

20. The exception is fairly elected leaders, 100 percent in low-income Assam. This is in reality a very small sample, since Assam scored very low on the presence of local councils. Specifically, in 1995 only one Assam community had a village council; by 2005 there were three such communities.

21. OLS regressions also have the advantage that the coefficients can be interpreted easily. This is consistent with the analyses reported in earlier volumes in this series. See volume 2 (Narayan, Pritchett and Kapoor 2009), as well as appendix B of this volume, for technical details.

22. Collier, Chauvet, and Hegre (2008) estimate that civil wars cost between $60 billion and $250 billion. Collier and colleagues (2003, 17) find that during civil war, countries tend to grow 2.2 percentage points more slowly than countries at peace; after a typical war that lasts seven years, incomes would be approximately 15 percent lower than if the war had not occurred. There are many reasons for this, including property destruction and loss of productive assets (infrastructure, factories, and farmland are common war targets); diversion of public expenditures to the military; and depressed labor productivity due to health problems, disability, lost education, displacement, and migration. Indirect costs can include capital flight and reduced investments for prolonged periods due to what Collier calls a substantial "war overhang." In conflict contexts, where trust is shattered, cooperation and collective action may also decline (Holtzman and Nezam 2004). The Geneva Declaration Secretariat (2008) estimates that the cost of lost productivity and violent conflict and crime outside of war zones totals $95 billion per year.

23. A negative effect of the village council in the total sample but not in the peaceful countries only (column 3 of table 3.2) means that the strong negative effect of village councils in conflict countries drives the results of the whole sample.

24. See Reinikka and Svensson (2005) for an account of how increased public access to information on local school budgets led to dramatic reductions in corruption in Uganda.

25. For country-level results, see appendix table F.9.

26. Support can take different forms; see chapters 5 and 6 for examples of large-scale community-driven programs that focus on improving local governance. See also Narayan and Glinskaya (2007) for other examples of large-scale programs and Narayan, Pritchett, and Kapoor (2009) for an extensive review of the literature and evidence from other countries in the global sample.

27. There is an extensive literature on the causes of people's movements; see Tarrow (1994) and Meyer and Tarrow (1998).

# References

Addison, T., and S. M. Murshed. 2003. "Debt Relief and Civil War." *Journal of Peace Research* 40 (2): 159–76.

Auvinen, J., and E. W. Nafziger. 1999. "The Sources of Humanitarian Emergencies." *Journal of Conflict Prevention* 43 (3): 267–90.

Bardhan, P., and D. Mookherjee. 2005. "Decentralization, Corruption and Government Accountability." In *International Handbook on the Economics of Corruption*, ed. S. Rose-Ackerman, 161–88. Northampton, MA: Edward Elgar.

Bouta, T., G. Frerks, and I. Bannon. 2005. *Gender, Conflict and Development.* Washington, DC: World Bank.

Chattopadhyay, R., and E. Duflo. 2004. "Women as Policy Makers: Evidence from a Randomized Policy Experiment in India. *Econometrica* 72 (5): 1409–43.

Collier, P. 2009. *Wars, Guns, and Votes: Democracy in Dangerous Places.* New York: Harper Collins.

Collier, P., L. Chauvet, and H. Hegre. 2008. "The Security Challenge in Conflict-Prone Countries." Copenhagen Consensus 2008 Conflicts Challenge Paper, Copenhagen Consensus, Frederiksberg, Denmark.

Collier, P., V. L. Elliott, H. Hegre, A. Hoeffler, M. Reynal-Querol, and N. Sambanis. 2003. *Breaking the Conflict Trap: Civil War and Development Policy.* Washington, DC: World Bank; New York: Oxford University Press.

Collier, P., and D. Rohner. 2008. "Democracy, Development, and Conflict." *Journal of the European Economic Association* 6 (2/3): 531–40.

Fearon, J. D., and D. Laitin. 2003. "Ethnicity, Insurgency and Civil War." *American Political Science Review* 97 (1): 75–90.

Friedman, B. 2005. *The Moral Consequences of Economic Growth.* New York: Knopf.

Geneva Declaration Secretariat. 2008. *The Global Burden of Armed Violence.* Geneva: Geneva Declaration on Armed Violence and Development.

Holtzman, S., and T. Nezam. 2004. *Living in Limbo: Conflict-Induced Displacement in Europe and Central Asia.* Washington, DC: World Bank.

Horowitz, D. L. 2000. *Ethnic Groups in Conflict.* Berkeley: University of California Press.

Hughes, M. M. 2007. "Understanding the Positive Effects of Armed Conflict on Women's Parliamentary Representation." Paper presented at annual meeting of the American Sociological Association, New York, August 11.

Mansfield, E., and J. Snyder. 2005. *Electing to Fight: Why Emerging Democracies Go to War.* Cambridge, MA: MIT Press.

Meyer, D. S., and S. Tarrow. 1998. "A Movement Society: Contentious Politics for a New Century." In *The Social Movement Society: Contentious Politics for a New Century,* ed. D. S. Meyer and S. Tarrow, 1–28. Lanham, MD: Rowman and Littlefield.

Miguel, E. 2001. "Ethnic Diversity and School Funding in Kenya." Paper C01-119, Center for International Development Economics Research, University of California, Berkeley.

———. 2004. "Tribe or Nation? Nation Building and Public Goods in Kenya Versus Tanzania." *World Politics* 56 (3): 327–62.

Miguel, E., and M. K. Gugerty. 2005. "Ethnic Diversity, Social Sanctions, and Public Goods in Kenya." *Journal of Public Economics* 89 (11/12): 2325–68.

Misra, K., and N. Kudva. 2008. "En(Gendering) Effective Decentralization: The Experience of Women in Panchyati Raj in India." In *Planning and Decentralization: Contested Spaces for Public Action in the Global South,* ed. V. Beard, F. Miraftab, and C. Silver, 175–87. New York: Routledge.

Murshed, S. M. 2002. "Conflict, Civil War and Underdevelopment: An Introduction." *Journal of Peace Research* 39 (4): 387–93.

Narayan, D., and E. Glinskaya, eds. 2007. *Ending Poverty in South Asia: Ideas that Work.* Washington, DC: World Bank.

Narayan, D., L. Pritchett, and S. Kapoor. 2009. *Moving Out of Poverty: Success from the Bottom Up.* New York: Palgrave Macmillan; Washington, DC: World Bank.

Nordholt, H. S., and G. van Klinken. 2007. *Renegotiating Boundaries: Local Politics in Post-Soeharto Indonesia.* Leiden, Netherlands: KITLV Press.

Oslender, U. 2007. "Violence in Development: The Logic of Forced Displacement on Colombia's Pacific Coast." *Development in Practice* 17 (6): 752–64.

Østby, G. 2008. "Inequalities, the Political Environment, and Civil Conflict: Evidence from 55 Developing Countries." In Stewart 2008, 136–57.

Pate, A. 2008. "Trends in Democratization: A Focus on Instability in Anocracies." In *Peace and Conflict 2008,* ed. J. J. Hewitt, J. Wilkenfeld, and T. R. Gurr. Center for International Development and Conflict Management, University of Maryland. Boulder: Paradigm Publishers.

Reinikka, R., and J. Svensson. 2005. "Fighting Corruption to Improve Schooling: Evidence from a Newspaper Campaign in Uganda." *Journal of European Economic Association* 3 (2/3): 259–67.

Siegle, J., and P. O'Mahoney. 2006. "Assessing the Merits of Decentralization as a Conflict Mitigation Strategy." Paper prepared for USAID's Office of Democracy and Governance as a supporting study for revision of the *Decentralization and Democratic Local Governance Programming Handbook.* Development Alternatives, Washington, DC.

Snyder, J. L. 2000. *From Voting to Violence: Democratization and Nationalist Conflict.* New York: Norton.

Sørensen, B. 1998. "Women and Post-Conflict Reconstruction: Issues and Sources." Occasional Paper 3, War-Torn Societies Project, United Nations Research Institute for Social Development, Geneva.

Stewart, F., and M. O'Sullivan. 1999. "Democracy, Conflict and Development: Three Cases." In *The Political Economy of Comparative Development into the 21st Century,* ed. G. Ranis, S. C. Hu, and Y. P. Chu. Essays in Memory of John C. H. Fei, vol. 1. Northampton, MA: Edward Elgar.

Stewart, F., ed. 2008. *Horizontal Inequalities and Conflict: Understanding Group Violence in Multiethnic Societies.* New York: Palgrave Macmillan.

Strickland, R., and N. Duvvury. 2003. "Gender Equity and Peacebuilding: From Rhetoric to Reality: Finding the Way." Discussion paper prepared for the Gender Equity and Peacebuilding Workshop, International Center for Research on Women, Washington, DC.

Tarrow, S. 1994. *Power in Movement: Social Movements, Collective Action and Politics.* New York: Cambridge University Press.

Tilly, C. 2003. *The Politics of Collective Violence.* New York: Cambridge University Press.

Varshney, A. 2002. *Ethnic Conflict and Civic Life: Hindus and Muslims in India.* New Haven, CT: Yale University Press.

Windsor, J. L. 2007. "Breaking the Poverty-Insecurity Nexus: Is Democracy the Answer?" In *Too Poor for Peace? Global Poverty, Conflict and Security in the 21st Century,* ed. L. Brainard and Derek Chollet, 153–62. Washington, DC: Brookings Institution Press.

# Nation Building from Below: Identity, Unity, and Civic Engagement

*In Sri Lanka we divide people into groups according to their religion, nationality, race. We don't call ourselves Sri Lankans. But in America they are all Americans.*

—DISCUSSION GROUP OF MALE AND FEMALE YOUTH,
Welumbe, Matara district, Sri Lanka

*If there is a program in a village where there is a majority of Muslims, they benefit more than other ethnic groups. In a village where there is a majority of Tamil families, the Tamils get more benefit than other groups. There is no equal distribution.*

—FEMALE YOUTH DISCUSSION GROUP,
Thambulla, Ampara district, Sri Lanka

*We need to solve this ethnic problem. We need the country as it was before the war.*

—WOMEN'S DISCUSSION GROUP,
Pesavankalai, Mannar district, Sri Lanka

Conflict brings destruction and displacement. Conflict also brings disconnection and ruptures of different kinds, visible and invisible. We turn now to the invisible ruptures and their aftermath.

The human predilection for association is as old as humankind, and the earliest human beings lived and traveled in groups. This desire to associate results in formation of different types of groups for different purposes—families, clans, tribes, and castes, as well as groups based on geographic location, occupation, language, religion, ethnicity, or gender. As people generally prefer to associate with others like themselves, they develop and define their identities and group affinities with markers such as language, dress, rituals, and festivals.

It is important to recognize that these identities are *constructed* over time; hence they can and do change over time.[1] Moreover, in the modern world, people have multiple identities, and different identities may be relevant in different contexts. Being a Christian or a Muslim is important when it is time to attend a church or mosque for prayers. It is not necessarily important when it comes to farming, selling vegetables in the market, working in construction, or sending children to school—*unless* a group chooses to separate itself based on religious identity or more powerful groups mobilize to promote discrimination on religious grounds. It is this behavior of mobilizing around religious/ethnic identity that leads to religious/ethnic politics, leading in turn to many conflicts and civil wars in the world.[2]

While much attention has focused on the visible impacts of war, there has been little attention to its invisible social consequences, namely, the effects of conflict on the social organization and values of communities and societies. Understanding how social groups are affected by conflict and how they function in postconflict settings is important for three reasons. First, since many conflicts are sparked by ethnic tensions, it is important to understand how local communities manage such differences in the period after conflict. Communities that have experienced ethnic warfare vary widely in their ability to mediate local divides and achieve lasting harmony. Communities also vary in the extent to which they experience episodes of recurrent violence. Second, once connections between social groups have ruptured, healing is a long and difficult process—if it ever occurs. Finding ways to reknit diverse social groups into communities is essential, as it lays the foundation for nation building. Third, as discussed in the preceding chapter, politics and local democracy do not function the same way in conflict-affected communities as they do in nonconflict communities in the same country. Local democracies tend to be captured in conflict contexts, leading to violent fights over resources provided by governments or outside agencies; this may be the case even when local politicians are elected and local councils are formally representative.

In some countries, national political leaders have recognized the importance of investing in nation building right after independence. Over time, this investment has paid off in lower levels of conflict based on ethnicity. Recent research documents how national identity has triumphed over ethnic identity in Tanzania, whereas Kenya has been engulfed in ethnic clashes repeatedly. Researchers also point to Ghana as an example of successful nation building, while in neighboring Côte d'Ivoire ethnic fissures have led to destructive conflict (Langer 2008).[3]

In this chapter we focus on the sweeping social changes that can happen in communities as displaced people come back after hostilities have waned or a cease-fire is declared. Cases of toxic ethnic politics persisting long after conflict are well known: one need only think of Bosnia, Ireland, Kenya, Nigeria, Sri Lanka, Afghanistan, Indonesia, the Philippines, and parts of India. While touching briefly on some of these cases, we focus primarily on trying to understand some of the surprisingly positive shifts in social relations that emerged in our sample of communities, and on their implications for nation building.

We start with a case study of a community in the Philippines that experienced intense religious conflict but became relatively harmonious in the postconflict period. This sets the stage for an inquiry into why social divisiveness and social inequality were found to decline, at least temporarily, in many of the conflict-affected communities in our seven-country sample. Four interconnected factors appear to play a role: the leveling effects of war, the role of local leaders in promoting unity, a community's capacity to manage conflict and violence, and the explosion in civic participation. We then turn to three large programs that attempt to promote nation building from the bottom up in the communities. They provide some hope that nation building can be encouraged in other places by building bridges across social groups and reducing "horizontal inequalities" through fair and inclusive politics. We end with implications for policy.

## The Case of Paitatu, Philippines: A High-Conflict Community

*It is hard to imagine that a group of Christian pastors would help build a mosque, houses, and a water system for a Muslim community. I never heard of any religious group doing so much to break down barriers and bridge the gap between two historically opposed groups for the sake of peace.*

—Camlon, barangay captain, Paitatu,
Kauswagan municipality, Philippines

*Once the community is energized, people can do what seemed impossible before.*

—Women's discussion group, Paitatu,
Kauswagan municipality, Philippines

The population of Paitatu, on the island of Mindanao in the Philippines, consists overwhelmingly of Maranao Muslims, with a Christian minority of just 1 percent.[4] But the village is surrounded by Christian settlers, and tensions between Muslims and Christians in the area produced high levels of conflict for decades. The first outbreaks were related to land. Christians moved into the area in the 1970s and occupied a 24-hectare piece of land rich in coconut trees that Muslims had long harvested. The Christian settlers were allegedly supported and armed by the army, also made up primarily of Christians.

In 2000, during the "all-out war," the Moro Islamic Liberation Front (MILF) set up camp on one side of Paitatu, after which the army set up camp on the other side and attacked the MILF forces. The community, caught in the middle, evacuated just before the battle erupted. Thirteen people were killed and 100 were injured. The army, suspecting that the community was a MILF hideout, torched the village. All of the houses were leveled, along with the mosque and school; animals and vehicles were destroyed or stolen. People said that when they returned "there was nothing left to salvage."

A peace accord was signed with the MILF in 2000, but the land conflict between Christians and Muslims continued to fester. In 2005 a group of

Muslims ambushed some Christians while they were harvesting coconuts on the disputed 24 hectares, just the latest in a continuing sequence of retaliatory killings. Almost everyone has a family member who has been killed over land disputes. The conflicts reduced the incentive to invest in businesses, as people were never sure when violence might ignite again and require a new evacuation.

Despite the conflict, there has been some movement out of poverty, 19 percent. This is lower than in most of the other Philippine study communities, but remarkable nonetheless. During extensive group discussions, women, men, and youth in Paitatu cited three reasons for their increased prosperity. The first was development assistance, including housing and a water system provided by Christian groups. The second was the leadership of the barangay captain, who gradually gained the village's trust as people became convinced that he was "sincere and fair." The third was the increased solidarity and unity of the community, which came together in new ways despite continuing tensions over the 24 hectares.

Of these, the most central to the changes was the role of the relatively new barangay captain, Camlon Moner. A Muslim, he played a key role in building trust between Christians and Muslims and thus seeded the process of healing. He also leveraged his contacts with the government and with outside agencies to attract substantial assistance to the community. Hearing about the interfaith efforts and attracted by the prospect of intercommunal unity, nongovernmental organizations (NGOs) moved in to help. The reconstruction projects—the rebuilding of the mosque, the houses, and the water system—became a symbol of interfaith solidarity as people of both religions, including the army, did hands-on construction work.

The process did not begin auspiciously. As Camlon recounted,

> When Christians came here together with the government agencies to provide help [in May 2000], the people were suspicious. It took some time before we trusted their intention. We suspected that the Christians were building houses so that they could drive the Muslims out of this village for good or that they were using us to earn money from the government. The worst is that we suspected them of wanting to convert us to Christianity, and building houses for us is one good strategy to do so. However, when they built the mosque with us as the first structure for the village, we started to change our minds.

The mosque was the first reconstruction project undertaken by Christian pastors and their church members, who came from outside the village. The unusual sight of Christian pastors working with Muslim imams to build a

Muslim house of prayer shocked people into suspending judgment, though suspicions remained.

Once the mosque was finished, the focus shifted to building houses for the community. In the first batch of grants, only 12 houses could be built, and the allocation of houses rested with Camlon, the barangay captain. He decided to build one house for one family in each of the 12 major clans. All the houses were the same size. Camlon explained that he resisted pressure from his own relatives, who thought that they "should be the first beneficiaries of the housing program because of their social standing as former leaders of the village. That was the way it used to be in the village. But I refused them with this scheme because I wanted to make a difference in this village, so I made everything equal."

The housing project became a venue of collective action by Muslims and Christians and a symbol of Muslim-Christian unity. "Pastors and imams helped each other during the construction, unaffected by religious differences," said Camlon. Government agencies, the private sector, and community members all participated actively in the project. Instead of families erecting temporary shanties themselves after returning from evacuation, the government was now providing permanent housing; this increased people's trust in the government and the army. Villagers gained confidence that the army would not attack them again, since an attack would mean destroying houses that the army itself had built. The permanent houses, which were *larger and better* than the old shanties, also helped people let go of their anger at the army and the government and Christians in general for destroying their homes and village. A men's discussion group said, "During the war and for few months after that, we were so angry at the military for burning our houses. After the project we were happy because our houses were replaced with bigger ones. We did not contribute even a centavo for the construction of houses. We did not even know how to operate a chainsaw so the pastors did it for us. Our contribution was hauling lumber and assisting them in the construction."

The houses were built in a cluster rather than scattered. Earlier, people had built their temporary shanties at a distance from each other because of the nauseating stench from the open pit latrines. But the new houses had water-sealed flush toilets. This represented a tremendous advance in sanitation and convenience, and the recipients were delighted to have toilets like those of the "rich people." The improved sanitation also meant that the houses could be built close together. This is turn promoted community cohesion and safety as people interacted continuously, kept an eye on each other's children, could respond to screams, and shared information about community happenings. Trust, security, and attendance at community meetings all grew. And people's ratings of social divisiveness and inequality dropped.

The reconstruction projects also included a new water system. Christian pastors realized the severity of the water problem in the village, which required people to walk a long distance to a stream. Water also held religious significance for Muslims, who are required to perform ablutions with water before prayers five times a day. The pastors turned their attention to raising 1.8 million pesos from their Christian friends and from the United Nations Development Programme.

Camlon said that working together on the reconstruction projects lessened the grudges between Christians and Muslims. "Before, whenever we heard a Christian name, we would immediately feel angry because of the long experience of conflict we have with the Christians. Imagine three decades of violence. In these areas around this village alone, more than 150 Muslims have been killed by Christians. Almost every family here has relatives who were killed by Christians." The key to easing this anger was a consistent focus on projects that were visible and tangible, met high-priority needs in the community, benefited everyone in the community equally, and were completed quickly. Work on these projects converted suspicion and anger to trust and acceptance in just three years—a short span of time compared to the three decades of violence.

The power of peace, reconciliation, and community unity across warring groups goes beyond "warm fuzzies." It can have high payoffs, including avoiding war and conflict altogether. In 2003, when war broke out in neighboring communities surrounding Paitatu, the village remained peaceful, and there was no evacuation. As Camlon recalled,

> Our barangay was spared. This was unusual because in the past, whenever there were problems close to us, we were the first to evacuate. But that was not the case in 2003; it was the other way around. People sought refuge in our barangay and this became the evacuation center for more than half of that year.
>
> That was the turning point. People started believing that despite the wars going on around us, our barangay will not be affected. That experience removed the few doubts we still carried with us, and people felt a sense of security. People realized that the killings that happened before were a product of a violent situation. It has nothing to do with religion, which was shown by Christians coming here and asking what they could do to help. That really helped.

Despite the turnaround in the security situation and the increased assistance, Paitatu still has many poor people. The unresolved land conflict continues to simmer. But the improved climate in the village has allowed people to invest in the community and in building their incomes. Camlon concluded by saying, "We cannot deny that there are still a lot of people here who experience poverty. In fact you can see that for yourself. And it is a lie to say that we no longer need assistance. But life today is better than before. People are now secure and can concentrate on their livelihoods without fear of war and evacuation. The provision of basic services has resulted in economic stability."

## Declining Salience of Ethnic and Religious Identity

*We don't have democracy at all. We have to speak Sinhala, even in Jaffna. Army people arrest us if we don't speak Sinhala sometimes. We have no freedom to speak our own language.*
—Discussion group of Tamil youth, Kaithamavi,
Jaffna district, Sri Lanka

*I can no longer work at the port, because many of the laborers are from the Christian community. Sometimes I feel everyone's eyes are on me when I come to work.*
—Muhamad Basrum, a Muslim man, Lupotogo,
North Maluku province, Indonesia

Issues of subnational identity based on ethnicity or religion become salient when people belonging to these groups experience exclusion that is economic, political, social, or cultural. When many of these exclusions overlap, identity becomes a potent force for political mobilization and manipulation. Frances Stewart coined the term "horizontal inequalities" to refer to this phenomenon, which can persist for centuries in a given community or country (1998, 2002, 2008). She especially draws attention to the political dangers that emerge when inequalities are widely perceived to be rising.

Poor people, including participants in our discussions, know very well about inequality, but they often did not associate it with social groups. When inequality was discussed, people's definitions focused on the interconnections between inequalities. The definitions of economic inequality offered by discussion groups of male and female youth in Afghanistan are typical. "Inequality means not to be equal, not to be identical, not to be judged in an equal way," said a male youth group in Shazimir. "In this community there are inequalities of rights, inequalities of power, of economy and politics."

Youth in Nasher Khan commented, "Economic inequality makes for social inequality between those who have land and those who have no land. The differences are not good, because there will be hatred between the poor and the rich. Rich can behave arrogantly and not want to associate with the poor. This situation can create tension."

Ethnic issues rarely emerged in community discussions on the meaning of freedom, except occasionally in Afghanistan and Sri Lanka. In Afghanistan, people spoke about freedom from the behavioral restrictions imposed by the Taliban with respect to dress, beards, music and cinema, and freedom of movement for women. In Sri Lanka, definitions of freedom for the most part had to do with attaining peace; people said, "no peace, no development." In Cambodia and Colombia, there were almost no references to ethnic or social differences, but freedom from violence figured in several definitions. A more universal distinction made in discussions of freedom was the difference between the rich and the poor. The same pattern was found in discussions of power: again, ethnic issues were almost never mentioned, but money and the use of force figured prominently.

### Religious and ethnic polarization

*Spiritual freedom is getting along with others, apologizing. That is being free.*

—Laura, a 24-year-old woman, San Feliz,
Sincelejo municipality, Colombia

*Our people can't mingle with people of other communities. Our community is mainly busy fighting, and as a Muslim I don't receive the Kisan credit card loan. The government takes our community as illiterate and wicked. No, I have not joined any political party.*

—Jamaluddin Laskar, a well-off man,
Kechula, Assam, India

Despite the blurring of identity issues, polarization persists in many places, particularly in the context of the long, drawn-out conflicts in Cambodia, Colombia, and Assam. One common measure of ethnic and religious polarization is the relative sizes of the two largest groups in the community. The larger the minority (the second-largest group) in relation to the majority (the largest group), the higher the polarization. By this measure, across the countries in our sample, the conflict communities are more polarized than the peaceful communities (table 4.1; for detailed results, see appendix table F.9).

**TABLE 4.1**

**Religious and ethnic polarization in conflict and nonconflict communities**

*average polarization score*

| Conflict rating | Religious polarization | Ethnic polarization |
|---|---|---|
| Conflict | 14 | 26 |
| Nonconflict | 11 | 20 |

*Source:* Community questionnaire.

*Note:* Ethnic polarization captures membership in a caste, tribe, clan, or language group, while religious polarization is based on religious affiliation. Polarization measures the size of the second-largest group (the minority) relative to the largest group (the majority) in a community; the higher the percentage, the higher the polarization. In Indonesia, the second-largest group was not recorded in the community dataset, so ethnic and religious information from the community synthesis reports was used to compute polarization.

The difference between conflict and nonconflict communities was smallest in Assam, followed by Colombia. Assam has a complex structure of multiple and overlapping social identities. In Colombia, the main identity that emerged was based on internal displacement status, although differences are also perceived around regional origins and ethnicity. Displaced people across the Colombian study barrios report suffering acute discrimination due to their association with the rural war zones. In the Philippines and Indonesia there were differences along ethnic and religious lines, and in Afghanistan along ethnic lines. Sri Lanka has seen a consolidation of its communities along ethnic lines, so mixed communities of Tamils and Sinhala are now rare, particularly in the conflict-affected areas.

We were interested in how the extent of polarization may affect a community's moving out of poverty (MOP) rating. We find strong negative associations with religious polarization. These results are supported by the simple cross tabs reported in table 4.2, which show that religious polarization is

**TABLE 4.2**

**Religious polarization by MOP rating in conflict and nonconflict communities, 2005**

*average polarization score*

| Conflict rating | Low MOP | High MOP | Total |
|---|---|---|---|
| Conflict | 23 | 14 | 16 |
| Nonconflict | 9 | 2 | 11 |

*Source:* Community questionnaire.

*Note:* Polarization measures the size of the second-largest group (the minority) relative to the largest group (the majority) in a community. Also see the note to table 4.1.

more pronounced in low-MOP communities than in high-MOP communities, a pattern that holds for both conflict and nonconflict communities. As reported in the regression analysis, religious polarization is strongly and negatively associated with poverty mobility, particularly in conflict contexts. In other words, where religious polarization is high, fewer poor people move out of poverty. Clearly, religious polarization is not good news for the poor, and this is particularly true in conflict contexts. There was no clear pattern regarding ethnic polarization.

### Declining social divisiveness and inequality

*Ten years ago the Muslims did not join meetings; they did not even stay very long when they visited the center of the barangay. Now they join the barangay meetings and discussions like this. There are also more Muslims sending their children to school. More of them get educated.*
—A mixed Christian and Muslim discussion group,
Newsib, Tulunan municipality, Philippines

*We now have a gaon unnayan samiti. It has helped the villagers develop a sense of unity. Four to five years ago villagers were not willing to sit together, but now the situation has changed. People of different castes are sitting together to solve various problems and difficulties that hamper or dilute social culture, discipline, and the unity of our village.*
—Men's discussion group, Chakugoda,
Nalbari district, Assam, India

Despite the dampening effects of religious polarization, there are signs of hope. Not all social divisions lead to conflict. We asked a series of questions about whether social divisions existed and whether these differences had led to violence. Contrary to expectations, people reported that social differences of ethnicity, religion, and caste have *not increased* over time in conflict contexts, including communities where such differences led to violence in the past. In fact, in 2005 social differences were much lower in the conflict-affected communities than in the nonconflict communities. Social divisiveness instead had increased in nonconflict communities. Even though social group differences were reported to lead to violence sometimes, there were no sharp differences between conflict and nonconflict communities in this regard (table 4.3).

The second set of findings provides further cause for some optimism. Despite religious and ethnic polarization (a demographic variable), something

**TABLE 4.3**
**Measures of social cohesion and divisiveness in conflict and nonconflict communities**
*percentage of communities*

| Measure | Conflict | Nonconflict | Total |
|---|---|---|---|
| High or very high social divisiveness in 2005 | 7 | 15 | 10 |
| High or very high social divisiveness in 1995 | 7 | 11 | 8 |
| Social differences led to violence over 10 years | 18 | 15 | 17 |

*Source:* Community questionnaire.

very important is happening with respect to the social dynamics within the study communities. *Inequality among socially divided groups has decreased in these communities, and the decline is particularly dramatic in conflict contexts.* Religious inequality decreased in 25 percent of the conflict communities but in none of the nonconflict communities. Ethnic inequality decreased in 28 percent of the conflict communities but only in 4 percent of the nonconflict communities (table 4.4). The destruction of the social fabric of communities may actually be creating the possibility that less fractured communities will rise from the ashes of conflict.

There are other encouraging indicators of greater social inclusion. For example, 81 percent of conflict communities reported that social networks are more open to people in the community. The corresponding figure for nonconflict communities was 92 percent (see appendix table F.18).

**TABLE 4.4**
**Decrease in inequality among religious and ethnic groups over 10 years, in conflict and nonconflict communities**
*percentage of communities*

| Trend | Conflict | Nonconflict | Total |
|---|---|---|---|
| Inequality decreased among religious groups | 25 | 0 | 17 |
| Inequality decreased among ethnic groups | 28 | 4 | 21 |

*Source:* Community questionnaire.

## Mechanisms Leading to Social Change

*Freedom means to respect the rights of others.*
—Rustam, a 24-year-old man, Shazimir,
Kabul province, Afghanistan

After conflict in a community has ended, whether through a cease-fire or other means, it is sometimes possible for community members to heal old wounds and come together in new ways. In doing so, they override narrowly defined social affiliations with a broader and more community-wide sense of identity. It is this broadening of identity that lays the foundation for social cohesion and nation building. This process may take place in local communities even when turmoil continues at the national level.

How can this happen? Our analyses of hundreds of reports of group discussions about community prosperity, conflict timelines, freedom, power, prosperity, and livelihoods, as well as the national reports, revealed four mechanisms that seem to be at work. They are the leveling effects of war, the role of local leaders, local capacity to manage and mediate conflict, and civic engagement and unity.

### Leveling effects of war

*There is no room for progress. We always have to start from scratch every time we return from evacuation. But there is nothing we can do because our farm is here . . . I was forced to sell my motorcycle and my water buffalo. These two are essential for my livelihood but I have no choice. My family needs the money in order to survive.*
—Usman Baliwan, male, Glikati,
Pikit municipality, Philippines

*The poor have desires but they can't achieve them. The rich have desires, and they can fulfill them.*
—Women's discussion group, Tattantok,
East Java province, Indonesia

Even in societies marked by deep discrimination, there is a leveling effect across economic groups when communities are bombed or burned to the ground. Those who have more lose more, and those who have less lose less. And for a short time the income gap between the rich and the poor narrows dramatically (table 4.5).[5]

**TABLE 4.5**
**Trends in economic inequality and economic access over 10 years, in conflict and nonconflict communities**
*percentage of communities*

| Trend | Conflict | Nonconflict |
|---|---|---|
| Decrease in gap between richest and poorest | 63 | 37 |
| Less access to economic opportunities now | 45 | 15 |

*Source:* Community questionnaire.

## Role of local leaders

> *They [Maranaos and Christians] also recognized the freedom of each other's choice in terms of religion. For our church, the first contributors were Muslims. Muslims did the painting jobs. Muslims did the carpentry work, while the Christians were also doing the Muslim mosque. Here religion is no longer an issue to consider or reckon with.*
> —Bob, a 67-year-old informal leader, Dubiading,
> Picong municipality, Philippines

Whenever central planners or economists are told by field-based NGOs that local leadership really matters, eye rolling and lip curling start. The immediate retort is "What are the policy implications for producing such leaders, and how do you suggest *we* produce good local leaders in thousands of communities?"

In our analysis of the role of local leaders, we scanned the universe of community reports across countries and kept going back to them, digging deeper and deeper. Good local leaders emerged in many places. But it finally became clear that there was something different about the Philippines. It was the only country that produced local leaders who very deliberately went about overcoming social divides so that angry, hurt, and distrustful Christians and Muslims (and sometimes different Muslim groups) could work and live together in peace. Conflict-affected communities in the Philippines produced Camlon Moner, the barangay captain in Paitatu, and Bob Anton, the informal leader who spearheaded creation of a peace zone in Dubiading—and many others.

Both Camlon Moner and Bob Anton live in predominantly Muslim communities. Bob Anton described how the village of Dubiading, within just a few years, transformed from a place where the MILF carried out frequent killings and attacks to one where Muslims protect Christian families and fight for their rights. Members of the two religious groups now sometimes visit each other's homes to eat and listen to music together. He noted the shift in culture and values: "This is the only place where Christians are paid blood money when Muslims hurt them. I am referring to the whole province of Lanao del Sur." He continued, "You know, in Islam, [Muslims] are not supposed to be friendly with infidels. But here in Dubiading that is not what is happening. From cradle to grave [the two groups] are companions. In fact they have one cemetery. So that makes them unique. Here you do not easily hurt Christians, because the Muslims will retaliate." It is this reputation that enabled Dubiading to avoid repeated MILF attacks and to become instead a sanctuary for both Christian and Muslim evacuees from other villages.

There are almost no similarities between Camlon Moner and Bob Anton in terms of personal characteristics. Camlon is Muslim and Bob is Christian (though his mother is Muslim). Camlon is a young man, while Bob is 67. As a new leader, Camlon had to prove himself before he was trusted, and the community watched his actions carefully. Bob's reputation goes back almost 40 years and rests on the force of his personality, his impartiality, and his occasional use of extralegal punitive measures. Camlon is a barangay captain and Bob is an informal leader. Bob is wealthy and has enough homes to take in large numbers of evacuees; Camlon is middle-class.

Community leaders, both elected and informal, played important roles in other Mindanao communities as well. In Bakimati, the vice mayor would personally patrol the village on a motorcycle to ensure peace. In Kilaluna, the barangay captain's ability to coordinate closely with the military saved the village from destruction. In Lomamoli, also a peace zone, the former mayor ensured that community organizers received leadership training, and they quickly applied what they learned in collectively building a water project for the community. Lomamoli, like Dubiading, also hosted evacuees.

The million-dollar question is, why did this happen in the Mindanao region of the Philippines and not elsewhere?

The key in the Philippines is the spread of a *culture of peace* through the creation of peace zones. Rather than focusing only on a defensive strategy of policing and security forces, agencies and actors working in Mindanao embraced the concept of creating zones of peace. This started as an indigenous strategy in one community and spread to others as more and more agencies became involved in supporting the zones.[6]

Not all peace zones worked equally well, or at all, but the very notion led to new possibilities, new values, and a new framework for thinking. Decentralized local leaders played key roles in facilitating the culture of peace, especially by bringing warring factions together for consultations and community meetings. Facilitators, chosen both from the local government and from communities, received training in how to resolve conflict. Some were sent to communities that had already succeeded in overcoming tensions in order to learn from them. As the culture of peace spread, all those associated with the process started to be regarded as local heroes, well respected and well liked, creating further incentives for this type of leadership to emerge.

Even corrupt, discredited leaders from the old days started to change. In Dubiading, Bob took on a group of former Muslim leaders who had lost respect and trust because of their clannish attitudes, unfair justice, and corruption. He impressed upon them the importance of honor through earthy metaphors and helped build their skills in resolving local conflicts. Bob said, "People are now coming to us to solve family disputes because we now have very effective peace advocates in the peace committee. We have very effective people who have learned the values already. Little by little we were able to recover their lost reputation and ill image that they are corrupt and biased. All those things are slowly fading because of my close supervision of them. So eventually, they were able to regain their honor and the trust of the people."

Now let's return to the important question raised by central planners and economists. The answer is that *you* don't create leaders. You nurture an investment and societal climate with the right signals and incentives that will enable such leaders to emerge, leaders who embody a particular value set. As the cultural climate begins to shift, you make adjustments based on learning and *continue* for 20 to 40 years to provide an environment that will nurture the emergence of more such leaders. This is exactly what has happened in Mindanao. Whether this new culture continues to take root will depend on investment by successive governments. In addition, horizontal inequalities will also need to be addressed through public policy actions so that both real and perceived inequalities are reduced.

Fairness, nondiscrimination, and respect are always important, but these qualities become critical in contexts where conflict has persisted along ethnic or religious lines. Unless someone reaches across ethnic groups with a promise and practice of fairness and equal opportunity, old wounds fester and will erupt time and again. Across many communities in the Philippines and occasionally in other regions as well, we encountered local leaders, both informal and elected, who did just this.

In particular, they used the design and distribution of development assistance to bring hostile factions together. Outside agencies provided the assistance needed to actively support this process. Neutrality is not sufficient in conflict contexts. By reaching across social groups and including all in the benefits of aid, rather than targeting it to some, outsiders can help communities shift from a climate of war, revenge, and despair to one of peace, reconciliation, and hope.

These local leaders were engaged in nation building.

## Capacity to resolve disputes

*The Shura-e Masajed [Council of Mosques] has an important role in resolving disputes because all the people are obedient to their religion. The council members are very religious, hence trusted by everyone in the community. Besides the United Nations and the Red Cross, help was channeled to the people through this council.*

—Suraheb, a male laborer, Shazimir, Kabul province, Afghanistan

*The entire responsibility falls on the gaonbura [village head]. If any youth of the village has been taken captive by the army or the CRPF [paramilitary police], the gaonbura has to go to the police station to get the boy released or talk to the superintendent of police or the district police.*

—Bhupen, a participant in a men's discussion group, Lakhanbar, Assam, India

Official cease-fires and peace agreements are signs of hope. Whether they result in peace depends on the extent to which governments or international monitors enforce them by punishing violators. What is clear is that conflict areas remain unpredictable for a while after peace agreements and in general are less safe than nonconflict areas. As we reported in earlier sections, communities sometimes create defense parties to protect themselves, either independently or with financing from the army or police.

Conflict is a part of the development process. The ability to resolve disputes at the local level is essential to managing tensions in postconflict communities. In this section we explore community capacity to mediate and resolve conflicts and to access justice for those conflicts that cannot be resolved privately at the local level.

A large majority of conflict communities, 83 percent, reported having to deal with disputes that required intervention (table 4.6). Naturally, then,

TABLE 4.6
**Extent of disputes and involvement of youth in disputes over 10 years, in conflict and nonconflict communities**

*percentage of communities*

| Indicator | Conflict | Nonconflict | Total |
|---|---|---|---|
| Had disputes requiring mediation | 83 | 58 | 74 |
| Youth were involved in local crime and violence | 65 | 31 | 54 |

*Source:* Community questionnaire.

the capacity to satisfactorily resolve such conflicts is extremely important in returning to peace and achieving poverty reduction. In fact, among the conflict communities, more high-MOP than low-MOP communities experienced conflicts that needed resolution. A surprisingly high proportion of nonconflict communities, 58 percent, also experienced conflicts that required resolution.

Youth were involved in disputes in a majority of conflict communities, 65 percent, but in only 31 percent of the nonconflict communities. Clearly, communities in conflict contexts are much more likely to report disputes involving youth.[7] A number of factors may play a role, including the presence of ex-combatants, a breakdown in social and legal restraints, changing norms, and high levels of youth unemployment. In Colombia all the study communities reported youth involvement in violence requiring resolution, while in Afghanistan only 34 percent did. In other countries the numbers ranged from 60 to 75 percent.

Communities, as already illustrated, deploy a large and diverse array of actors to intervene in conflicts. Community leaders emerge the most prominently, mentioned by 71 percent of households.[8] Additionally, "respected leaders," and less frequently religious leaders, were mentioned across both conflict and nonconflict communities. Other actors mentioned were ethnic leaders, heads of associations, armed opposition groups, self-defense groups, and teachers. The police were mentioned quite frequently by movers (53 percent), but much more often in conflict contexts (appendix tables F.19 and F.20).

Skillful local leaders can resolve many disputes, but some conflicts and issues require multiple levels of intervention. In some places, steps have been taken to create new mechanisms for mediation, including new elected community councils in Afghanistan, Tim 30 in Indonesia, and new groups of Muslim elders in some communities in the Philippines.

Larger conflicts need functioning courts, tribunals, and systems of justice administered by or fully backed by the government. But there is a long way to go before the study communities will be able to have complete confidence in their justice systems. Courts received high "no confidence" ratings, around 40 percent, second only to local government officials (around 50 percent). People had more confidence in the police, who received only about a 30 percent "no confidence" rating (appendix table F.21).

When local dispute resolution fails and higher authorities do not step in, the maintenance of peace is jeopardized. We conclude this section by returning to the unresolved conflict over the 24 hectares of land in Paitatu, Philippines, which has been festering for 40 years. Camlon Moner, the barangay captain, called this conflict "sleeping dynamite." He appealed personally and in writing to higher government authorities to resolve the conflict, but no action was taken. He blames officials and politicians for neglecting the matter and even suspects them of using it as an excuse to incite violence.[9] He said, "There are even times when I think that this [dispute] is just used as dynamite here to ignite violence . . . The 24-hectares land dispute is not really the root of the problem. It has become the instrument that feeds the longtime clash between Muslims and Christians at the expense of many lives. The longer we ignore it, the bigger the problem gets. Today there is no confrontation in that area, but war could break out anytime. That is still dynamite lying in wait."

### Associational activity and civic engagement

*If you are alone, you will have problems. You will have problems in having yourself hired if people do not consider you part of the community.*
—A man who fell into poverty, Glikati,
Pikit municipality, Philippines

*There was a conflict, so we feel traumatized, but now we are free. We can do anything, but good things . . . Muslims can greet Christians. The spirit of gotong royong [mutual assistance] has returned.*
—Discussion group of men and women, Yasapira,
North Maluku province, Indonesia

In contexts of poverty and exclusion by the state, and where basic services such as water and law enforcement do not function, poor people have three choices: move away, try to manage on their own, or associate with others to cope at least a bit better with the problems of daily life. Poor people often organize informally or through mutual aid groups, cooperatives, and other associations, pooling their resources to survive. Increasingly, NGOs and governments are promoting such groups and providing them some assistance. We investigated the nature and extent of associational life in the study communities and the impact of such associations on poor people's efforts to move out of poverty.

There was a virtual explosion of civic groups and associations in our sample communities during the 10-year period. The mean number of associations more than doubled in the conflict-affected communities, from 3.8 to 8.5, and also increased in the nonconflict communities, from 5.6 to 9.0. Indonesia, well known for its *gotong royong* system in which communities come together for collective action, has the highest mean, 23 groups per community, on average. Afghanistan has the lowest, with 1 group. In societies where traditions of helping primarily involve informal clan or caste relations, these practices often do not get picked up in surveys or discussions of associational life. Such traditional practices include *koleman* in Indonesia, in which cash or in-kind contributions are collected for a specific purpose such as a wedding ceremony, with strict accounting and reciprocity.

We found associations engaged in a wide range of activities, which we classified into six categories. In conflict communities in 2005, the most common were groups concerned with livelihoods, which we called main economic activity groups. These were followed by political and financial groups (figure 4.1). The salience of economic groups is not surprising given the great

**FIGURE 4.1**

**Mean number of local associations by type in conflict and nonconflict communities, 1995 and 2005**

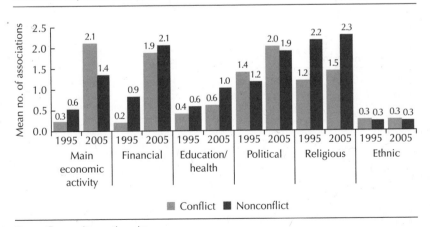

*Source:* Community questionnaire.

concern over livelihood activities in these contexts, a message that emerged strongly and that we highlight in chapter 5.

In nonconflict communities, on the other hand, religious groups were the most prevalent in 2005, followed by financial groups and political groups. Religious groups play important roles in community life almost everywhere. Religious groups were mentioned in Afghanistan, in Indonesia (particularly in Java), in the Philippines, and in Assam, where indigenous religions together with Buddhism, Hinduism, and Islam can be found.

In terms of the groups that grew the most, main economic activity groups and financial groups increased by over 710 percent in conflict-affected contexts, again communicating the hunger and desperation for help in securing livelihoods (table 4.7).

Finally, we turn to the relationship between associational life and poor people's ability to move out of poverty (figure 4.2 and appendix table F.22). Overall, the expansion in groups is greater in *low*-MOP communities: that is, the number of groups increased more sharply in communities where fewer people moved out of poverty. The association is particularly marked in conflict contexts. Since it is unlikely that groups cause poverty, the more likely explanation, supported by extensive previous research, is that poor people turn to groups to help them survive and cope but that the resource-strapped associations of poor people do not necessarily help them move out of poverty.[10]

**TABLE 4.7**

**Change in mean number of associations by type, 1995–2005, in conflict and nonconflict communities**

*percentage change*

| Type of association | Conflict communities | Nonconflict communities |
| --- | --- | --- |
| Main economic activity | 713 | 147 |
| Financial | 731 | 143 |
| Education/health | 54 | 75 |
| Political | 43 | 63 |
| Religious | 20 | 5 |
| Ethnic | 0 | 0 |
| Total | 121 | 59 |

*Source:* Community questionnaire.

**FIGURE 4.2**
**Change in mean number of all local associations by conflict and
MOP rating, 1995–2005**

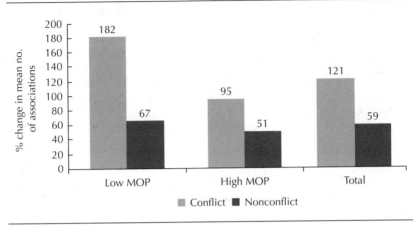

*Source:* Community questionnaire.

Table 4.8 shows the changes in types of associations by mobility and conflict rating. Once again, the big shifts are in economic and financial groups: the economic groups in conflict contexts grew by over 2,000 percent and the financial groups grew by 1,700 percent in low-MOP communities in

**TABLE 4.8**
**Change in mean number of each type of local association by conflict and
MOP rating, 1995–2005**
*percentage change*

| Type of association | Conflict communities | | Nonconflict communities | |
|---|---|---|---|---|
| | *Low-MOP* | *High-MOP* | *Low-MOP* | *High-MOP* |
| Main economic activity | 2,033 | 286 | 50 | 200 |
| Financial | 680 | 560 | 1,700 | 69 |
| Education/health | 45 | 80 | 100 | 38 |
| Political | 47 | 20 | 92 | 38 |
| Religious | 36 | 26 | 0 | 13 |
| Ethnic | 67 | –100 | 0 | — |

*Source:* Community questionnaire.

nonconflict areas (the means can be found in appendix table F.22). Clearly, this dramatic increase in groups has not yet helped move people out of poverty in the low-MOP communities. As discussed in chapter 5, micro-credit groups are plagued with many problems, including small loan sizes, complicated procedures, production activities not linked to markets, and product saturation.[11]

Finally, we turn to the issue of bonding versus bridging social capital and to local groups' linkages with actors and networks outside of the com-munity.[12] Since the divisions in our sample are based primarily on religion and ethnicity, we explored whether the composition of membership in the most important groups was more or less heterogeneous along these dimen-sions and whether greater heterogeneity was associated with more mobil-ity of the poor. In other words, do communities where the most important groups include members from all religions or all ethnicities have higher rates of MOP than communities where the key groups are religiously or ethnically exclusive?

In conflict contexts, we found that heterogeneous groups that include members from different religious groups are associated with higher MOP (20 percent), while groups that have members from only one religious group are associated with lower MOP (13 percent). The pattern is similar in non-conflict contexts and for ethnic heterogeneity as well (figure 4.3). Diversity in this case supports movement out of poverty, presumably because people cooperate rather than engage in conflict. The presence of different religious and ethnic groups creates "bridges."

Not all groups in conflict areas are able to overcome the trauma of con-flict ignited by religious/ethnic polarization and tensions. In the high-conflict village of Galalolo, Indonesia, where the population is 60 percent Christian and 40 percent Muslim, neither community participation in village meetings nor group functioning had returned to preconflict levels by 2005. In fact, the population had shrunk, as many families chose not to return to the village after the conflict. Prior to the conflict, the community had created a group to receive Rs 10 million from a government program for poor communities, but after the conflict the group could not come back together. The chairman of the group had put the funds in the bank just before the outbreak of fight-ing. When it became obvious that the group could not be reconstituted, he withdrew the cash and gave it first to a member of the armed forces so as to not be accused of absconding with the funds. The chairman said, "Because of the conflict, the group activities could not be done. So I divided the money

**FIGURE 4.3**
**MOP by religious and ethnic heterogeneity of most important associations in conflict and nonconflict communities**

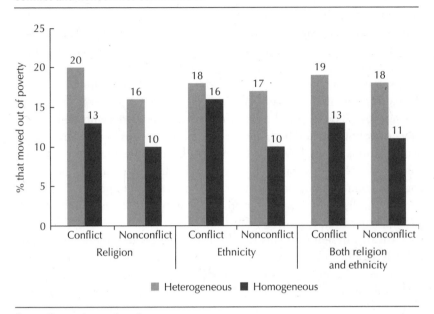

*Source:* Community questionnaire.

and gave to each member the amount of Rs 1 million. My share of the money was used to meet my needs when I was a refugee." The women's group said that they had not yet recovered the quality of their relationships prior to the conflict but that people were "tolerant" of each other.

## Large-Scale Nationwide Support to Community Groups

It is possible to provide assistance to small, isolated community groups that enables them to shift from helping their members cope to helping them move out of poverty. This happens when groups become more diverse and draw in people with different resources (bridging groups), and when they achieve some scale by connecting to each other and/or to external resources (linking groups). In addition to the community-driven peace zones in the Philippines, which also received substantial funds for community rehabilitation, we came across three other large-scale programs, in Afghanistan, Indonesia, and Sri Lanka. Only the first two, however, could be considered "community driven."

These two programs succeeded in the most difficult circumstances. The National Solidarity Program (NSP) was launched soon after the defeat of the Taliban in Afghanistan, and the Kecamatan Development Program (KDP) began at the height of the financial crisis in Indonesia. Neither program is perfect, but both became national flagships, reaching thousands of communities, improving local governance, building local infrastructure, and reducing corruption. Both are based on field research and on a design that allows changes based on learning. Both invest in field facilitators who are independent of politicians, and both involve community groups in decision making. These groups decide how to use block grants to address their most serious problems; the groups manage the funds and watch "their money" like hawks. Both programs require participation by women and poor people. Their most important distinguishing characteristic is community decision making and transparency in budgeting and contracting.

Clearly, design elements matter in the success of large-scale community development programs. Broadly participatory by design, KDP and NSP are creating decentralized leadership and community groups that help keep local government accountable. With more explicit focus and training on how to work across social divides in war-torn areas, such programs can strengthen community governance and build national identity from the bottom up. In Samurdhi, an income transfer program in Sri Lanka, however, narrow targeting has restricted participation and led to capture, with a divisive rather than unifying effect.

### The National Solidarity Program, Afghanistan

The National Solidarity Program in Afghanistan is a government program with a budget of nearly $1 billion. The project was started in 2003 on the initiative of Ashraf Ghani, then finance minister, to build the government's legitimacy in the eyes of citizens while the government was still getting established in Kabul. In the first year, the NSP started operation in 5,000 communities, and another 4,500 communities began participating in 2005.

The program facilitates the election of local people to community development councils (CDCs) and trains the council members in participatory development planning, accounting, procurement, management, and monitoring. CDCs open bank accounts to which block grants (ranging from $27,000 to $60,000) are transferred; these monies are then used for small-scale infrastructure programs chosen by local people. Communities contribute a minimum of 10 percent of total project costs. The training of the CDC members, provided by professional project facilitators, emphasizes transparency, and financial books can be audited at any time. The program's rates of return are around 20 percent and average subproject costs are 30 percent lower than other construction programs, due in part to local procurement. Independent audits show corruption is lower than in other aid projects. When projects are locally owned, even the Taliban hesitate before destroying them, afraid of losing village support.

The NSP currently reaches two out of three people in rural Afghanistan, operating in all 34 provinces. CDCs have been created in almost 22,000 communities, and 29,000 subprojects have been completed. Current problems include declining security in Afghanistan and a falloff in donor funds (21 international donors contribute to this program). There is also a need to change government bylaws so that in the long run government fiscal resources can be devolved to the CDCs to make them self-sustaining. The lack of funds for follow-up projects means that the culture of local democracy, transparent governance, and community ownership has not had a chance to become institutionalized.

## The Kecamatan Development Program, Indonesia

Afghanistan's NSP was designed by Scott Guggenheim, a World Bank anthropologist who also initiated the Kecamatan Development Program in Indonesia. KDP has become the world's largest community-driven development program, with a $1.6 billion budget. The design was inspired in part by a study on local-level institutions in Indonesia that showed that government-managed programs had high levels of corruption, high costs, did not respond to local needs, were not maintained, did not include the poor, and crowded out local initiative. Launched at perhaps the worst possible time, amid political upheaval and financial crisis in 1998, KDP quickly came to account for 75 percent of the World Bank's Indonesia portfolio. Going counter to the conventional wisdom, the program provided unprogrammed block grants to the lowest subdistrict level, which redistributed them to communities in response to community proposals.

In 2006, in response to the successes of KDP, the government of Indonesia launched the National Program for Community Empowerment (Program Nasional Pemberdayaan Masyarakat). It provides a single framework for all community-driven programs in Indonesia, with KDP and its variants providing the foundation. In conflict-affected Aceh, for instance, the program addresses peace-building processes and provides reintegration grants for ex-combatants.

In 2009 these community-driven programs will reach 140 million people in 59,000 villages, including those in war-torn areas. KDP is marked by an open menu of projects that can be chosen by community groups and by openness to experimentation, audits, evaluation, and reporting. Journalists can go to any village without notice and write about KDP. Audits show repeatedly that leakage is less than 1 percent, and construction costs run 56 percent less than equivalent works carried out by the Ministry of Public Works.[13]

## The Samurdhi program, Sri Lanka

There were other countries in the study with very large national welfare programs for their poor. We discuss only Sri Lanka's Samurdhi program, because its orientation—although not its scale—differs importantly from the approaches of the NSP and KDP. Samurdhi was introduced by the government of Sri Lanka in 1994 to reduce poverty and create employment for youth, women, and the disadvantaged. It is currently the largest welfare program in the country, costing 1 percent of gross domestic product. The program has three major components. The first and largest, accounting for 80 percent of the funds, is food stamps. The second is a savings and credit program operated through Samurdhi banks, with loans meant for business development. Third is a community infrastructure program that includes workfare and social development programs. Samurdhi agencies at each level of government administer the program, and they also engage a cadre of youth who are selected "under the specific recommendations of local politicians" (Glinskaya 2003, 8).

While implementation is meant to be participatory in nature, this is dampened by extensive means-testing requirements that call for assessments of individual incomes to determine eligibility for food stamps and related benefits. A recent evaluation shows that the design features, including having the local youth facilitators report to local politicians, subject the project to capture by local politicians, who use Samurdhi to reward party loyalists. There is substantial mistargeting of food stamps, as 44 percent are directed to households in better-off groups despite substantial administrative investments in targeting.[14] The credit program is also largely captured by the better-off, and there is little evidence that the program has reduced poverty or generated employment. Despite the fact that the program is implemented by the

Ministry of Nation Building, the bias in beneficiary selection is systematic and not random. Discrimination varies by ethnic membership: relative to Sinhalese households, Sri Lankan Tamils, Indian Tamils, and Muslims are less likely to receive Samurdhi (Glinskaya 2003, 19).[15]

## Conclusion

The focus on the role of national governments in development assistance has made citizens and citizen action invisible. The focus at the national level has made the local level invisible. The focus on politics has made society invisible. What has been missed in development assistance is half the picture: half the picture in terms of the consequences of conflict and half the picture in identifying appropriate solutions for postconflict recovery of societies that make up a nation.

What is invisible to the eye gets disregarded as not important. In contexts where conflicts are based on ethnic or religious grievances, it is critical to address issues of inequality, lessen tensions, and rekindle a culture of peace, reconciliation, and tolerance. This has to be done quickly, as soon as peace accords have been concluded; otherwise, anger and hatred at the loss of life and property will fester and give politicians new grievances to manipulate for their own petty ends.

Conflict may also open up possibilities, as the destruction of the social fabric brings about declines in inequality and in the salience of identity defined in religious and ethnic terms. This opening may not last long, however, as a new elite and new politicians hungry for power will soon emerge. Immediately after hostilities come to an end, there is a window of hope. If swift action is taken, the recovery period can be a turning point at which people begin to overcome past social divisions and build nations.

Country governments and multilateral and bilateral agencies that design large international programs for $200 million or more are impatient with bottom-up approaches because the presumption is that approaches such as community building, civic engagement, and peace building across conflicting groups cannot be done on a large scale, or at least cannot be done well on a large scale.

Community-driven programs that are implemented throughout the country can channel substantial resources quickly to communities to rebuild basic infrastructure and livelihoods. *How* this is done is critically important.

The best programs seek to bring about two cultural changes by instilling local democratic governance structures and by fostering a community-wide culture of peace and inclusion.

Cultures do not change overnight, so programs need to continue over at least a decade in order to rebuild trust, lives, and communities. Over time, nations emerge, and ethnicity becomes a subsidiary category.

## Notes

1. Lipset (1959) argued that democracy benefits from societies in which one-dimensional identities do not become salient, and it thrives in societies characterized by "multiple and politically inconsistent affiliations and loyalties." Amartya Sen, in *Identity and Violence* (2006), stresses the importance of political leaders who are able to acknowledge and make salient people's diverse identities, interests, and histories in order to instill trust and tolerance and resolve conflicts. Sen argues that even moderate governments run a risk when they turn to narrowly based religious or ethnic institutions to help solve essentially political and social problems of exclusion.
2. Frances Stewart (2008, 7) notes a dramatic increase in the proportion of conflicts that are termed "ethnic," from 15 percent in 1953 to 60 percent in 2005.
3. For analysis of issues of identity, ethnicity, and civil war, especially in Africa, also see Collier (2003), Collier and Hoeffler (2004), and Miguel (2004).
4. To protect the privacy of participants, this book uses pseudonyms for the study communities (villages and barrios). Cities, municipalities, districts, departments, and provinces are identified by their real names.
5. One of the most widely used measures of income inequality at the national level is the Gini index, which indicates the amount of income earned by different cohorts of the national income distribution. Results across countries have shown that Gini coefficients change very slowly, if at all, even though deeper distributional change and welfare impact may take place at the micro level (Ravallion 2001). Nonetheless, two recent exceptions to fairly constant aggregate income distributions are China and India, where the Gini coefficient rose as a result of sustained urban-based growth in the previous decades (Deaton and Drèze 2002; Meng, Gregory, and Wang 2005).
6. The idea of peace zones has spread to many parts of the world, and there is a growing literature on their establishment and impact. For a review, see *Zones of Peace* (Hancock and Mitchell 2007). A chapter in that volume by Avruch and Jose (2007) provides a history of over 80 peace zones in the Philippines. Bouvier (2009) offers a rich discussion of the varied peace efforts in Colombia, involving business leaders, community organizers, local officials, and women's groups.
7. See Tilly (2003) for a general discussion. Varshney, Panggabean, and Tadjoeddin (2004) find that youth clashes and drunken brawls were the most important triggers for deadly riots and ethnic community violence in Indonesia between 1990 and 2003.

8. Because of errors in this variable at the community level, we report responses from households by mobility group (see appendix tables F.19 and F.20).

9. See Varshney (2002) on Hindu-Muslim conflict in India for similar accounts of politicians inciting violence through a variety of actions (including inaction).

10. Earlier volumes in the Moving Out of Poverty series contain further discussion and findings on the weak links between poor people's collective action and movement out of poverty. For data from the global study, see "The Unfulfilled Potential of Collective Action," chapter 7 in volume 2 (Narayan, Pritchett, and Kapoor 2009). For data from India, see "Communities Where Poor People Prosper," chapter 3 in volume 3 (Narayan 2009). Molinas's (1998) study of 104 peasant cooperatives in Paraguay found that the poorer communities had better-performing organizations.

11. See volume 2 of the Moving Out of Poverty series (Narayan, Pritchett, and Kapoor 2009) for a more detailed discussion.

12. Bonding takes place between groups whose members share similar socioeconomic backgrounds. Such ties typically characterize poor people's associations, and the literature repeatedly finds that bonding groups provide vital supports that help the poor cope with everyday life. Bridging takes place between heterogeneous groups, including those with linkages outside the community. It is these bridging groups, according to the literature, that most frequently bring their members new resources, connections, and ideas, making them more effective springboards for poor people's mobility than the more homogeneous bonding groups (see Narayan 2002; Narayan and Cassidy 2001; Woolcock 1998).

13. For more information on KDP, see Guggenheim (2006), Guggenheim et al. (2004), and Indonesia KDP Task Team (2006).

14. The maximum grant is 1,000 rupees (approximately $10), which is given to a family of more than five members whose total monthly income is less than 500 rupees.

15. It is important to note, however, that many villages in the north and east began to receive Samurdhi programs only after the 2002 cease-fire.

## References

Avruch, K., and R. S. Jose. 2007. "Peace Zones in the Philippines." In Hancock and Mitchell 2007, 51–70.

Bouvier, V. M., ed. 2009. *Colombia: Building Peace in a Time of War.* Washington, DC: United States Institute of Peace.

Collier, P. 2003. *Breaking the Conflict Trap: Civil War and Development Policy.* New York: Oxford University Press; Washington, DC: World Bank.

Collier, P., and A. Hoeffler. 2004. "Greed and Grievance in Civil War." *Oxford Economic Papers* 56 (4): 563–95.

Deaton, A., and J. Drèze. 2002. "Poverty and Inequality in India: A Re-Examination." *Economic and Political Weekly,* September 7, 3729–48.

Glinskaya, E. 2003. "An Empirical Evaluation of the Samurdhi Program in Sri Lanka." Paper presented at the Second World Bank Conference on Inequality, Washington, DC, June 9–10. Originally prepared as a background paper for the Sri Lanka Poverty Assessment.

Guggenheim, S. 2006. "Crises and Contradictions: Understanding the Origins of a Community Development Project in Indonesia." In *The Search for Empowerment: Social Capital as Idea and Practice at the World Bank*, ed. A. Bebbington, M. Woolcock, S. Guggenheim, and E. Olson, 111–44. Bloomfield, CT: Kumarian Press.

Guggenheim, S., T. Wiranto, Y. Prasta, and S. Wong. 2004. "Indonesia's Kecamatan Development Program: A Large-Scale Use of Community Development to Reduce Poverty." Working Paper 30779, World Bank, Washington, DC.

Hancock, L., and C. Mitchell, eds. 2007. *Zones of Peace*. Bloomfield, CT: Kumarian Press.

Indonesia KDP Task Team. 2006. "Brief on KDP's Anti-Corruption Work." Social Development in East Asia and Pacific, World Bank, Washington, DC. http://go.worldbank.org/FRKE9CL4N0.

Langer, A. 2008. "When Do Horizontal Inequalities Lead to Conflict? Lessons from a Comparative Study of Ghana and Côte d'Ivoire." In Stewart 2008, 163–89.

Lipset, S. M. 1959. "Some Social Requisites of Democracy: Economic Development and Political Legitimacy." *American Political Science Review* 53 (1): 69–105.

Meng, X., R. Gregory, and Y. Wang. 2005. "Poverty, Inequality, and Growth in Urban China, 1986–2000." *Journal of Comparative Economics* 33 (4): 710–29.

Miguel, E. 2004. "Tribe or Nation? Nation Building and Public Goods in Kenya versus Tanzania." *World Politics* 56 (3): 327–62.

Molinas, J. R. 1998. "The Impact of Inequality, Gender, External Assistance and Social Capital on Local-Level Cooperation." *World Development* 26 (3): 413–31.

Narayan, D. 2002. "Bonds and Bridges: Social Capital and Poverty." In *Social Capital and Economic Development: Well-being in Developing Countries*, ed. J. Isham, T. Kelly, and S. Ramaswamy, 58–81. Northampton, MA: Edward Elgar.

———, ed. 2009. *Moving Out of Poverty: The Promise of Empowerment and Democracy in India*. New York: Palgrave Macmillan; Washington, DC: World Bank.

Narayan, D., and M. F. Cassidy. 2001. "A Dimensional Approach to Measuring Social Capital: Development and Validation of a Social Capital Inventory." *Current Sociology* 49 (2): 59–102.

Narayan, D., L. Pritchett, and S. Kapoor. 2009. *Moving Out of Poverty: Success from the Bottom Up*. New York: Palgrave Macmillan; Washington, DC: World Bank.

Ravallion, M. 2001. "Growth, Inequality and Poverty: Looking Beyond Averages." *World Development* 29 (11): 1803–15.

Sen, A. 2006. *Identity and Violence: The Illusion of Destiny*. New York: W. W. Norton.

Stewart, F. 1998. "The Root Causes of Conflict: Some Conclusions." QEH Working Paper Series 16, Queen Elizabeth House, Oxford Department of International Development, University of Oxford, UK.

———. 2002. "Horizontal Inequalities: A Neglected Dimension of Development." QEH Working Paper Series 81, Queen Elizabeth House, Oxford Department of International Development, University of Oxford, UK.

———, ed. 2008. *Horizontal Inequalities and Conflict: Understanding Group Violence in Multiethnic Societies*. New York: Palgrave Macmillan.

Tilly, C. 2003. *The Politics of Collective Violence*. New York: Cambridge University Press.

Varshney, A. 2002. *Ethnic Conflict and Civic Life: Hindus and Muslims in India*. New Haven, CT: Yale University Press.

Varshney, A., R. Panggabean, and M. Z. Tadjoeddin. 2004. "Patterns of Collective Violence in Indonesia (1990–2003)." UNSFIR Working Paper 04/03, United Nations Support Facility for Indonesian Recovery, Jakarta.

Woolcock, M. 1998. "Social Capital and Economic Development: Toward a Theoretical Synthesis and Policy Framework." *Theory and Society* 27 (2): 151–208.

# The Economic Environment

*Poverty is increasing in our society day by day. People are jobless, and the government is not creating jobs for people. When the economy is in a bad situation, everything goes in a bad situation.*

— SULTAN AHMAD, A 45-YEAR-OLD MALE LANDOWNER,
Zakwak Ulya, Herat province, Afghanistan

*The situation is deteriorating day by day. The Taliban are getting stronger and stronger, and they will start fighting massively in the future.*

— GHULAM RASOOL, A MALE WORKER,
Zakwak Ulya, Herat province, Afghanistan

The two comments from discussion groups in the Herat region of Afghanistan seem prescient. Since the 2006 field visits to Afghanistan, the Taliban have come back in force. Security has deteriorated across the country. The economy is in a steep decline, while international aid and attention have faltered and government corruption has spiked. One result is that desperate farmers in many areas of the country have turned to growing opium poppy for the booming drug trade.

Conditions in Afghanistan are among the worst we encountered, but poor economic environments are not unique to that country. Overall, the 102 communities visited are poor, even those in the middle-income countries of Colombia, Indonesia, and the Philippines. Most communities are marked by the near-absence of large private sector businesses and by the low availability of jobs. The conflict communities, however, are particularly disadvantaged. Added to their stark economic environments, they face the presence of large numbers of weapons and factions fighting for power and a deteriorated local governance context. It is not surprising, then, that the conflict communities rated their risk of future conflict to be much higher than did the nonconflict communities in the same countries. When people have nothing to lose and the future is so insecure, they have little stake in rebuilding society.

We highlight three sets of findings in this section. The first is the importance of livelihoods. Given the bad economic environment and the large numbers of poor in each community, people's most fervent hope is for solid sources of income. It is well established that the struggle to capture limited economic resources can lead to renewed violence and lawlessness in postconflict communities that lack strong governance. And poor people do resort to the illegal economy when possible in the absence of other viable economic opportunities. On the other hand, the destruction of old livelihoods and the mass displacement of communities can also open new paths. In particular, it can encourage or compel households to diversify away from agriculture or combine nonfarm work with agriculture. This can have beneficial effects for those who had previously relied solely on subsistence or small-scale farming.

Second, we find that youth, particularly young men, are frustrated in their quest for stable employment and self-respect in postconflict contexts. Not all turn to illegal activities, but the presence of numerous idle young men is widely associated with higher levels of local violence, with drinking and drugs, and in some contexts with gang activities. Many young women with restricted mobility outside their homes are equally frustrated, although they do not usually resort to violence or antisocial behaviors. Despite these obstacles to achieving their dreams, many youth remain stubbornly optimistic.

Finally, when asked what sort of assistance would be most helpful in recovery from conflict, 90 to 95 percent of discussion groups in the sample communities called for help with economic livelihoods and improving incomes. There is little evidence that aid strategies match these priorities. When governments and donor agencies do provide support with livelihoods, it is usually done on a small scale and so indifferently that it does not allow people to quickly build permanent assets that would enable them to escape poverty and keep from sliding back into it.

## Poor People in Poor Economic Contexts

*We are screwed over here. We have no economic opportunities. Over there we had services and schools for our kids, and here we don't. Some times there are conflicts because of that.*
—Gloria, a 35-year-old internally displaced woman, Villa Blanca,
Floridablanca municipality, Colombia

The vast majority of people in the communities visited are poor. And the vast majority of communities visited have poor economic environments.[1]

There was almost no difference between conflict and nonconflict communities with respect to the strength of their local economies in 2005 (table 5.1). When local economies were rated on a 5-point scale, only 12 percent

**TABLE 5.1**
**Indicators of general economic performance in conflict and nonconflict communities, 1995 and 2005**

| Indicator | Year | Conflict | Nonconflict |
|---|---|---|---|
| Local economy strong | 2005 | 12 | 11 |
| (% communities) | 1995 | 16 | 7 |
| Public works projects present | 2005 | 44 | 52 |
| (% communities) | 1995 | 12 | 15 |
| % of village population employed | 2005 | 4 | 4 |
| by government | 1995 | 3 | 4 |
| Private employers present | 2005 | 58 | 59 |
| (% communities) | 1995 | 48 | 56 |
| Hard or very hard to find jobs with | 2005 | 70 | 62 |
| private employers (% communities) | 1995 | 56 | 45 |
| Economic opportunities increased over 10 years (% communities) | | 37 | 44 |

*Source:* Community questionnaire.

of communities in conflict contexts and 11 percent in nonconflict contexts rated their economies as strong. Communities across conflict and nonconflict contexts did not differ in the presence of private employers; in both contexts approximately 40 percent of communities reported no private sector employers. However, many more communities in conflict contexts, 70 percent, reported that it was hard or very hard to find jobs with these private sector employers, mostly small businesses. This difficulty had increased over time. Fewer conflict communities (37 percent) than nonconflict communities (44 percent) reported an increase in economic opportunities over the past 10 years.

Although the numbers employed by government are low (around 4 percent in 2005), the government was providing at least some opportunities for daily employment through public works projects. Forty-four percent of conflict communities and 52 percent of nonconflict communities had at least one public works project that provided temporary jobs in construction to local people. Indeed, the most dramatic difference over time is the more than 250 percent increase in these government-provided public works projects (figure 5.1).

**FIGURE 5.1**
**Change in economic indicators in conflict and nonconflict communities,**
**1995–2005**

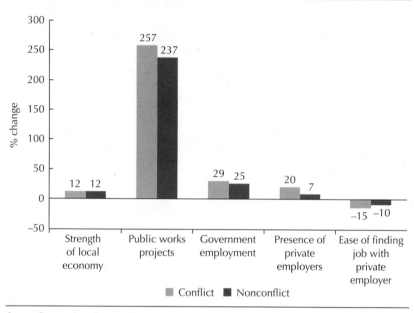

*Source:* Community questionnaire.

At the community level, we examine the relationship between strength of the local economy and the moving out of poverty (MOP) index. In stronger economies, which presumably offer more economic opportunities, there should be more movement out of poverty. At the community level, strength of the local economy is slightly higher in high-MOP communities in both conflict and nonconflict contexts and in both years, 1995 and 2005. However, this is not true for change in strength of the local economy over time (see appendix table F.23).

## Poor People's Lives and Livelihoods

*People want to work, not fight.*
          —Nadir Ali, a male shopkeeper in a men's discussion group,
                    Shazimir, Kabul province, Afghanistan

Poor people in rural areas across the study countries are primarily engaged in subsistence agriculture and menial labor. They work in fields, quarries, and brick kilns; transport goods and construction materials by head loading; and do many small odd jobs. The specific types of work differ depending on the agro-ecological zone, the season, and the weather, especially the rains.

Hunger is pervasive. Across the sample, 31 percent of the conflict communities and 33 percent of the nonconflict communities reported experiencing food shortages before the harvest. When probed for food shortages at any time of the year, one-third of communities again reported experiencing severe food shortages or periods of scarcity, with no significant differences between conflict and nonconflict communities.

In Lomamoli, Philippines, discussion groups described the community's poorest families as landless, working at menial and unstable jobs as farm laborers or tenant farmers.[2] Some are small-time fisherfolk who do not have their own fishing equipment and who catch enough only for their own consumption. Their wives sometimes find jobs like doing other people's laundry. In these families, the parents have little or no education and cannot afford to educate their children. They live in shanties or makeshift shelters and own no animals or furniture. They eat only twice a day, and if they miss a day's work they have nothing to eat. Hunger in these households is a fact of life. "They only drink coffee in the morning. Breakfast is taken at 10 or 11 o'clock in the morning, making it their lunch too. By the afternoon, these people would just go to their relatives to ask for food for dinner." They may also hunt game in the mountains, but if they do not catch anything they go hungry.

In remote La Soledad, Colombia, few options other than growing potatoes emerged after the army pushed the guerrillas out of the village. Augusto, a 51-year-old member of a men's discussion group, said, "Many people have left looking for money, to get coke, marijuana . . . The necessities, hunger . . . Maybe you have never had a kid crying from hunger. There is much poverty over here. If the government had not forgotten us, if there were some employment, the peasant would not have to go to the guerrillas, the paramilitaries, or to other departments to learn bad habits." In rural Los Rincones, Colombia, where a cattle feed factory had been the most important source of jobs in the town, discussion group participants named the shutting down of the factory after death threats and extortion as one of the most harmful events in the life of the community.

## Difficulties restarting incomes after conflict

*Before the war, we were known for our banana plantations, but after the conflict the bananas died. We don't know if it was the effect of the chemicals from the bombs or what. That's why now we depend only on our rice and corn plants.*

—Puti, a 36-year-old man, Tucampo,
Parang municipality, Philippines

*It is somewhat difficult for the poor to improve their lives because there are not enough employment opportunities available to them. Of course the poor want to be better than what they are, but they can do nothing to be able to survive besides wait for others to hire them.*

—Female youth discussion group, Kdadaum,
Santuk district, Cambodia

The communities visited experienced every kind of damage imaginable. In every study country except Colombia, there were at least one or two sample communities where many or most structures had been burned to the ground or severely damaged.[3] Livestock were killed or looted, crops set on fire, and landmines scattered across fields, pathways, and roads. In the Philippines, banana and coconut plantations were laid waste. A village in Afghanistan lost its lucrative grapevines. In Assam, a few tea plantations shut down in response to extortion, killing, kidnappings, and other harassment. Where factories existed, they often closed.

Mass displacements were reported in all the countries, although less so in Assam, India. When an evacuation lasts just weeks or months, people usually can come back to the land and start over; this was the case during some of the riots in North Maluku, Indonesia, and in certain communities of Colombia, the Philippines, and Sri Lanka. But when displacement drags on for a year or more, or when people cannot return to their village because of their ethnicity or religion, they suffer permanent and uncompensated loss of land and property. Their property may be occupied by other displaced families, sometimes belonging to different ethnic groups, or homes and farms may have been acquired under questionable deals. In some cases poor people have sold their land quickly and cheaply to the wealthy in order to buy their way to safety, as in Sri Lanka and Colombia. Large swaths of land may serve as bases for troops and remain under army or insurgent control for long periods, as in Sri Lanka and Assam.

Traditional livelihoods are also difficult to revive after conflict because of the absence of markets, lawlessness and new security restrictions, and declining natural resources. No agricultural activities can begin until landmines are cleared and the fear of attacks dissipates. In Manivali and Kaithamavi, Sri Lanka, coastal activities involving fishing, palm harvesting, and coir work (making of ropes) faced security restrictions, and it became too risky to transport goods by canoe. Restarting livestock husbandry and the growing of paddy rice and tobacco were also deemed too risky during the cease-fire. In the east of Sri Lanka, the Tamil Tigers charged villagers a fee to enter the forests and harvest wood and other forest products; even after paying the tolls, people reported that their loads were sometimes confiscated. Vital agricultural inputs are difficult to obtain and unaffordable, while traders pay low prices for crops and livestock if they pay at all. In the north and east of Sri Lanka, farmers were hurt by the influx of cheap farm goods from outside the conflict region, including tsunami rice relief from international donors. In Cambodia, fishing villages reported declines in fish stocks due to the use of illegal fishing nets and dynamite by large fishing fleets.

Life in urban areas was equally difficult. In Shazimir, a populous community on the rim of Kabul, Afghanistan, most men depended on unskilled daily wage labor wherever they could find it. Some turned to vending cheap goods on handcarts and in tiny shops. Many in this area belong to the Hazara tribe, which has traditionally faced discrimination. The Hazara are well regarded, however, for their car repairs and commerce in spare parts, trade in used clothes, and metal work, sometimes recycling containers into house gates. Women and some men are also involved in carpet weaving. But people returned from displacement with their businesses, skills, connections, and working capital eroded. This, combined with continued discrimination and an influx of new tribes, contributed to very high unemployment rates for Hazara men. Food and other basic needs, meanwhile, were reported to cost three times as much as before the war. Life in Shazimir is now very hard. In Colombia, too, the internally displaced living in urban barrios face unemployment, discrimination, and difficulties earning enough for daily survival.

### Diversification of incomes after conflict

After the horror and destruction of violent conflict, new chances sometimes emerge for poor families to come back stronger. When displacement, continuing insecurity, weak markets, or other obstacles make farming difficult or impossible, desperate rural households may be forced to take up nonfarm work. These new economic activities, which help families cope during the conflict period, sometimes also help them move ahead afterward. Households that diversify may begin to accumulate more assets than when they relied solely on farming.

As figure 5.2 illustrates, movers have indeed been able to diversify their income sources. Movers in 2005 still relied most heavily on sale of crops, as they did in 1995, but their income from regular wage jobs and from nonagricultural employment increased greatly over the period. The chronic poor have not diversified to the same extent. They have remained trapped in temporary

**FIGURE 5.2**
**Sources of income for movers in conflict and nonconflict communities, 1995 and 2005**

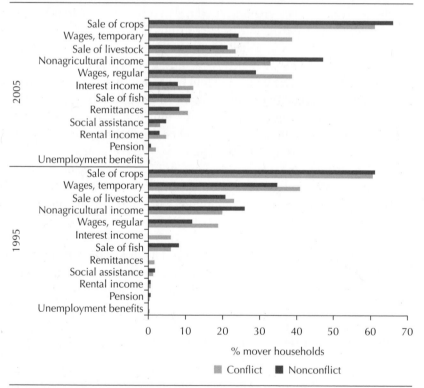

*Source:* Household questionnaire.

day jobs (61 percent, compared to 39 percent among movers). Their income from crop sales has declined and their nonagricultural income has stagnated, although their access to regular wage employment has grown (see appendix tables F.24 and F.25).

Diversification most often entailed vending, skilled trades, or migration to cities or abroad to seek work. In the conflict village of Los Rincones, Colombia, a cattle feed factory closed and farming became too dangerous because of the continuing insecurity. These changes pushed families to rely more heavily on selling in the village market, which catered to traffic from the highway. They also sent their youth to Venezuela for jobs that were reported to be well paid. In the villages of North Maluku province in Indonesia that reported high rates of poverty escapes, the end of conflict brought numerous new job opportunities for motorcycle taxi drivers, artisans, carpenters, bricklayers, and other tradesmen. These drew on skills that farmers often learned during the months of displacement from their land. In the small and poor coastal village of Kaithamavi, Sri Lanka, security restrictions on fishing and coir work forced workers to seek jobs in nearby towns and farther away. An exceptionally high 64 percent of households in this village climbed all the way out of poverty during the cease-fire years. Similarly, the relatively few households that moved out of poverty in Assam, India, most often attributed their upward climb to securing new or multiple sources of income.

Stable salaried employment, while hard to find, offered perhaps the best means of moving ahead. In communities in Afghanistan, employment by nongovernmental organizations (NGOs) was rated as highly desirable, and households with an NGO employee were rated the best off. In all countries, government workers reportedly coped better through conflict periods because their salaries were paid even if they could not work.[4]

Conversely, lack of diversification into nonfarm activities apparently played a key role in explaining low mobility rates in many peaceful communities outside the conflict zones. An unexpected finding of the study is that in Indonesia, the Philippines, and Sri Lanka, mobility rates were on average much lower in the sample villages that lay completely outside the conflict zones. For example, in Indonesia, the five peaceful East Java villages had rates of poverty escape less than half of those in the five conflict communities of North Maluku. The financial crisis of the late 1990s led to a sharp fall in the price of farm crops, especially tobacco produced in the East Java villages, while prices for farm inputs spiked. Access to nonfarm economic activities was extremely limited for these villagers, but key to mobility in the few households that found them. In Sri Lanka, the peaceful communities in the south averaged more modest levels of poverty escapes than the conflict communities in the north and east. Farmers in the south faced deteriorating market conditions for their paddy, tobacco, and cinnamon crops, and educated youth were relocating permanently to take factory jobs in Sri Lanka's towns and cities.

## Illegal economies

*Before, if I wanted to get a loan of 100,000 Afghanis [$2,000], I could get it easily from poppy dealers. They knew that I was cultivating poppy and I would give the money back. But now, since I have stopped growing poppy, even if I ask for a small loan with a very high interest rate, they don't lend me the money. They do not trust us because we are poor and we have no regular income.*

—Participant in a community timeline discussion group, Morlaw Ghano, Nangarhar province, Afghanistan

The negative side of livelihood diversification is diversification into illegal activities. Large-scale illegal activities in the study communities mainly involved poppy cultivation in Afghanistan and coca in Colombia. These countries provide cautionary tales of what can happen when illegal economies take hold.

In 2006, Afghanistan supplied 90 percent of the world's heroin, and its crop production broke all records that year (DeYoung 2006). In some of the communities visited, Afghans reported that they had climbed out of desperate wartime poverty or even became wealthy from the trade. According to Mullah Rahman from Morlaw Ghano, "From 1992 onwards, poppy prices were very high because some drug smugglers came to our community during these years. The best time of my life was from 1999 to 2004 because I earned a lot of money cultivating poppy." Similarly, some Colombians identified their time or a family member's time working on coca farms as an important, if not the most important, period of asset accumulation in their lives.

Illicit crop production in both countries is extensive, lucrative, and "pro-poor" in the sense that its production is low-skilled and labor-intensive. Afghan smallholders said that they were able to grow poppy because drug middlemen made credit readily available to them in the planting season. Moreover, the middlemen promised to return and buy the crop at a guaranteed price. Such accessible credit and reliable buyers were nowhere to be found for common crops. Moreover, poppy grows quickly and needs little water. Thus, even poor villages and poor farmers without costly irrigation systems can get in on the action. Perhaps most enticing, villagers in Nasher Khan say poppy yields five times the profits of other crops.

In the two villages visited in Nangarhar province, Afghanistan, people relied heavily on the crop to survive the wars and recover. "We had to rebuild our houses; our farms did not exist anymore. The only thing that helped our community to come out of poverty was to plant and grow poppy. It is what really led our community to prosper," explained a leader from Morlaw Ghano. Similarly, a resident of Nasher Khan reported, "People can make just 5,000 to 6,000 Afghanis [$100 to $120] per *jerib* when they cultivate wheat. Every family has an average of 4–5 jerib, but it is not enough to maintain a family with five members. When we were cultivating poppy, we could afford some luxury items like cars, or to pay for our sons' marriage." When reconstruction and development programs arrived, many Nangarhar farmers agreed to switch to wheat crops. But families across Afghanistan are struggling to earn enough growing wheat, and leaders and producers alike openly explained to our research teams that they are using poppy production as a bargaining chip to obtain desperately needed aid and attention.

In Colombia, we saw the dark side of the drug trade. Drug addicts, youth gangs, and other armed actors made daily life treacherous in the barrios of Santa María, Villa Rosa, El Gorrión, and El Mirador.

## Youth in Peril: Frustration and Optimism

*The environment for education was totally lost. People had to stay in the house in the evening. For fear of the army, the young boys had to escape because they are asked several questions [harassed] if they are found on the road.*

—Men's discussion group, Kahikuchi, Assam, India

*I want a steady job and I should have been married. I want a permanent job that is halal [legal].*

—Noviyanto, an 18-year-old youth, Patobako, East Java province, Indonesia

*We are poor. We had no food, no clothes, no bicycle, no equipment for studying, and nothing in our shelter. When we were young we had to help our parents take care of our cow and feed our livestock, so we could go to study, but then we were already tired and exhausted.*

—Male youth discussion group, Salvia Prey,
Sangkae district, Cambodia

For most of the youth and children in our study, violence, not peace, was the norm (box 5.1). War stole their sleep at night. War sent them running terrified for cover. War robbed them of their family and friends. War shut down their education and deprived them of normal childhood and teenage years. Male youth risked forced or voluntary recruitment by the different armed groups or succumbed to the lure of youth gangs, brawls, heavy drinking, and drugs. Young women and girls everywhere risked physical assault and abduction and endured prolonged seclusion.

Yet despite growing up with so much violence and insecurity, the youth in conflict countries harbored the very same ambitions for their lives as did the youth in the peaceful countries visited for the global Moving Out of Poverty study. Above all, they wanted stable jobs. In farming regions, youth said

---

**BOX 5.1**

**Militarized dreams of young children in high-conflict La Soledad, Colombia**

La Soledad, a poor village in Colombia, was occupied by FARC (Fuerzas Armadas Revolucionarias de Colombia) guerrillas for several years until the army cleared them out in 2002. Juan, a schoolteacher who stayed during the occupation, recalled the arrival of the guerrillas: "The first days were a surprise. Then we got used to it. We got used to seeing them with their big guns. They would go to the supermarket and they would not pay a thing. And nobody could say anything. We coexisted with the guerrillas, but with fear."

Despite the warnings about the armed conflict, Juan continued teaching at the school, staying on even after major attacks drove people from the village. He reflected on the changes he saw in the youth, including young children. "If you asked them before the conflict what they wanted to be when they grew up, they used to say 'driver' or 'farmer.' Nowadays they say 'policeman,' 'soldier,' 'guerrilla fighter,' and lately 'paramilitary.'" During the conflict, he noted, "the kids took any old stick and called it a machine gun, and they carried around guns, magazines, and even a grenade."

they were trapped by the lack of economic opportunities and forced to rely on backbreaking and low-paying farm work. In towns and neighborhoods, they said they simply cannot find any work that pays. Nevertheless, most of these young men and women hoped to go further in life than their parents. Most remained idealistic and want to make a difference in their communities and families.

The vast majority of youth, even in rural areas, expressed hope that they would someday work at nonfarm jobs. Youth everywhere wanted to fly planes, join the military, run for office, heal people, teach, set up trading companies, own shops, start firms, build factories, program computers, sew and weave, and enter law enforcement. They recognized clearly, however, that such occupations would remain out of reach unless they received help. In Ponky Kda, Cambodia, a group of young men and women explained that they had missed their education because of the war and could not read, but they still longed for stable, permanent jobs:

> For us it would be great if we could have someone provide us with skills training to run a business or weave. Then we could have more job opportunities. We learned that there are a few conditions in order to have a permanent job in the garment factory. If you are illiterate, then you should know how to sew. But if you cannot sew, then you can just work as a temporary worker . . . By contrast, if you can sew and you also have a good education, then you will get a high wage. On Han got only $30 per month because she is illiterate.

In the barrio of Villa Blanca in Colombia, the young women explained that they didn't have the wherewithal to find good jobs or start their own small ventures. They needed help with training and resources. Many of them had to leave school early because they became single mothers at an early age. Eighteen-year-old Onalis, from rural Los Rincones, Colombia, reported that she is managing to complete high school but will have to take a break before entering university: "The future is built in the present. I have to work first to get some money and then keep on studying."

Civil service is popular among youth because it means stable work and earnings and respect among family and friends. Some young people also saw government careers as a way to make the world better and safer. Seventeen-year-old Nicolas of El Gorrión, Colombia, said he hopes to go into public administration and direct public resources to "their proper destination."

Among civil service jobs, a government teaching position was mentioned most often, but law enforcement and army careers were also very popular among the youth in conflict areas. Badrus of Tattantok, Indonesia, declared in her discussion group, "Really, I wish to become a policewoman, but because

I have passed the age limit I just want to be a teacher. I want to become a teacher because there are none here, only students, so if you need a teacher they have to come from Pamekasan." In the village of Tucampo in the Philippines, 18-year-old Angel hoped to become a policeman because he heard that they are well paid and he would be able to support his family. Sandi, from the same village, wanted to be a soldier and help stop the war. In Dubiading, Philippines, 22-year-old Nel said he wanted to join the local militia so he could help his community and "so the number of delinquents would decrease and our youths would not be harassed by other people." Simrata, in Assam, noted that his father was a farmer and his mother a housewife, but he aspired to a different career: "I shall do any job related to the defence service. One who joins this service can fight against the enemies of his country with guns and cannons. If he can kill the enemies then he wins respect and glory. That is why I like it."

## Poor People's Priorities After Conflict

*We don't want aid. We only want support to stand on our own. If the government can build the roads and give us a factory for the young people to work, we can develop the village.*

—Men's discussion group, Pothupana,
Ampara district, Sri Lanka

We asked people for their priorities and their analysis of the most important interventions needed to assist the recovery and prosperity of communities and families. No matter how the question was asked or who answered, the pattern of responses was strikingly similar. The priorities were strong and clear: people's overriding concern was for their own economic recovery.

We asked discussion groups to draw a timeline showing the history and development of their community. They were then asked to rank the two most important events or factors that had helped or led to *community* prosperity. Over 90 percent of the responses across the communities where conflict had ended referred to economic programs and interventions. Typical responses came from three different groups in conflict-affected communities in North Maluku, Indonesia—key informants and separate discussion groups of men and women (table 5.2). They focused almost exclusively on postconflict assistance, in particular two national government-led community-based programs: the IDT (Inpres Desa Tertinggal, a program for neglected villages), and its successor, the KDP (Kecamatan Development Program). The KDP gives

**TABLE 5.2**
**Factors that led to community prosperity in conflict-affected communities in North Maluku, Indonesia**

| Community | MOP | Key informants | | Male discussion group | | Female discussion group | |
|---|---|---|---|---|---|---|---|
| | | Reason 1 | Reason 2 | Reason 1 | Reason 2 | Reason 1 | Reason 2 |
| Bodolenge | 0.68 | Building of the road | IDT, KDP programs | Building of the road | KDP program | Security | High motivation to work |
| Galalolo | 0.43 | Postconflict assistance | Monetary crisis | Help with housing | Help with rice | Clean water | Subdivision of the province |
| Barumangga | 0.42 | IDT program | KDP program | IDT program | KDP program | IDT program | KDP program |
| Lupotogo | 0.20 | Postconflict assistance | New government building | Market for agriculture | Security | Postconflict assistance | Additional business capital |
| Yasapira | 0.16 | Conflict settlement | Postconflict assistance | Determination | Education | Determination | Security |

Source: Indonesia national synthesis report (Rahayu and Febriany 2007).

block grants to community groups through procedures that require participatory planning and high levels of accountability and transparency. Communities choose the projects that they want to see implemented locally, such as the building of roads, markets, and housing; provision of business capital; basic food subsidies; and security enhancements.

In the mapping of actors and institutions involved in conflict and local democracy, we also asked community discussion groups what would help *people,* that is, individual households, recover more quickly. Once again, across communities, we found that 90–95 percent of responses had to do with interventions that would directly provide jobs, improve the business environment, and facilitate trade and employment, with improved security as a precondition.

In every one of the high-conflict sample communities in Indonesia, the first-ranked response to this question recommended improving the local economic environment and providing economic opportunities through government and reconstruction assistance, including aid to farmers, better tools, salaries for carpenters, and motorboats for fishermen. The second-ranked responses also dealt with economic assistance, such as credit, but in some cases they included building trust across rival Christian and Muslim groups; responses also emphasized the importance of people's own agency and willingness to work hard. In the Philippines, first-ranked responses in conflict-affected communities again focused primarily on economic factors; respondents called for building housing and roads, improving harbors, reestablishing palm oil plantations, extending credit and grants for businesses and cooperatives, and upgrading machinery for farmers. Many also emphasized the importance of people's own initiative and determination to recover. Second-ranked interventions were again primarily economic, focusing on recovery of livelihoods and training for improved productivity among farmers and fishermen, as well as on education (a response given by women) and better governance. In Afghanistan, in every community the primary response focused on economic recovery and livelihoods.

In Sri Lanka, the responses in many communities were dispirited. After 25 years of war and living in fear, people said that the war was blocking all opportunities and until the war ended there would be no development. Even so, they too focused on economic opportunities as the most important for recovery.

In communities in Assam, both women's and men's discussion groups also focused on livelihoods. People in the village of Morga, which was still experiencing heavy conflict involving the army, the border security force, and a variety of extremist groups, said that even though conflict continued, "people have tried to improve their life amid all of this by opening small tea gardens, fisheries, cultivating *rabi* [winter] crops, etc. This has happened mainly due to self-confidence and boldness of oneself." Their suggestions on how to improve people's well-being were both poignant and important in their implication for aid strategies. A participant in a men's discussion group said,

> If the government had discussed matters with the extremists, if it had urged them to return to the mainstream by giving them employment, and if the educated youths could have found employment, then maybe our conditions would have improved. Unemployed youths join extremist groups, and then the army, in search of them, tortures ordinary people, making life miserable for us. The government is playing with fire through the Naga Assamese border problem. Today they are neglecting the problem, but tomorrow we will lose our land to the Nagas.[5] If the central government had shown an interest in solving the problem then we would not have suffered like this. But the problem exists, as it always has, and we are never sure when we will lose our lives at the hands of the Nagas.

## Generating Household and Community Prosperity

*If we compare our livelihoods today to 1992–93, the majority of us have moved upward from the poor and destitute conditions that we faced then.*
—Discussion group, Salvia Prey, Sangkae district, Cambodia

*Even the buyers won't come to the village because of the bad road conditions. It's better if the village improves, but the ethics of traders should also improve.*
—Men's discussion group, Assam, India

We bring together two sets of data to answer the question of how to generate prosperity at the local level. First we look at data from the household dataset, and next we present data for the communities in which households are embedded. In both, the primacy of economic factors comes through clearly. At the household level, the focus is on household recovery, while at the community level, the focus is on infrastructure that enables mobility.

### Household mobility

*If, when we are sitting somewhere selling vegetables, we have to give 20–30 rupees to the police or face assault, where is the freedom?*
—Men's discussion group, Gatakpur, Assam, India

During household interviews, movers were asked to list the three most important reasons for their escape from poverty. There were no major differences between conflict and nonconflict communities (table 5.3). In conflict contexts, 60 percent of the reasons overall have to do with people's productive activities: through private sector and government jobs (21 percent combined), nonagricultural and agricultural initiatives (24 percent), and the management of multiple sources of income (15 percent). Other important factors were improvement in housing (10 percent), hard work (7 percent), and family background and assets (5 percent). Factors mentioned less often included improved economy and functioning of government, loans, women stepping out to work, migration,

TABLE 5.3

**Reasons for upward mobility of mover households in conflict and nonconflict communities**

*percentage of reasons mentioned*

| Reason | Conflict | Nonconflict | Total |
|---|---|---|---|
| Jobs | 16 | 18 | 17 |
| Nonagricultural initiative | 16 | 17 | 16 |
| New sources/multiple sources of income | 15 | 14 | 14 |
| Housing | 10 | 8 | 10 |
| Agricultural initiative | 8 | 5 | 7 |
| Hard work | 7 | 12 | 9 |
| Family factors | 5 | 6 | 5 |
| Government jobs | 5 | 4 | 5 |
| Obtained loan/credit | 3 | 3 | 3 |
| Improved economy | 3 | 2 | 2 |
| Women stepped out to work | 2 | 3 | 2 |
| Improved security (less crime) | 2 | 2 | 2 |
| Improved governance | 2 | 1 | 2 |
| Migration/remittances | 1 | 2 | 1 |
| Obtained legal title | 1 | 1 | 1 |
| Better health | 1 | 0 | 1 |
| More NGO assistance | 1 | 0 | 0 |
| Community associations/joined | 0 | 0 | 0 |
| Other | 2 | 4 | 3 |

*Source:* Household questionnaire; *N* = 663.

better health, NGO assistance, and legal titles to land (each 1–5 percent). Joining community associations was mentioned by less than 1 percent.

## Community-level prosperity

We combined information from the community questionnaire and the detailed group discussions to identify the factors that seem most closely associated with community mobility in conflict and nonconflict contexts. Although several factors emerged as important, it was rare to find all these factors present in the same communities.

The general importance of infrastructure for development and poverty reduction is well known, but the focus is usually on national infrastructure. Our results focus on the community level. Surprisingly, despite the destruction of basic infrastructure in conflict contexts, we did not find any major differences between conflict and nonconflict communities with respect to community-level infrastructure, particularly in 2005 (figure 5.3; also see appendix table F.26).

**FIGURE 5.3**
**Infrastructure and access to facilities by MOP and conflict rating, 2005**

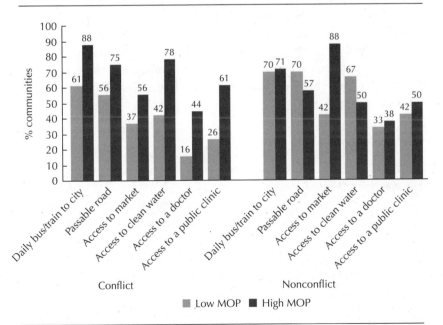

*Source:* Community questionnaire.

What is striking, however, is that among conflict communities—and *only* among conflict communities—the level of infrastructure is significantly greater in high-MOP communities than in low-MOP communities. These differences were not seen in nonconflict contexts. There was one exception, physical access to markets, where the difference associated with MOP status was even greater in nonconflict communities than in conflict communities (appendix table F.27).

What might explain this different pattern of results in conflict and non-conflict communities? We go back to the role of shock and crisis in shaking up communities and households, releasing economic dynamism as people work to recover all that they have lost. Crisis also galvanizes outside agencies to provide assistance. In this context, the presence of roads, transport, and markets all contribute directly to supporting people's economic activities. Clean water and health care are also closely associated with decreased illness and thus promote productivity. Doctors and public health clinics may be particularly important in conflict-affected communities because of the physical and emotional trauma that people have suffered.

Discussion groups held in the communities provided a deeper look at what makes a difference to community mobility. Five key factors emerged: an overall climate of fairness in markets; housing as a permanent asset; roads that connect to markets; the presence of credit facilities that enable poor people to expand their businesses; and jobs in private sector enterprises and public works projects. We found outstanding examples of one or another of these factors in different communities, as part of assistance strategies of government or NGOs, but it was rare to find all of them in any one community.

## Fair access to markets

*It is difficult for us to look for a job even as construction workers because they don't accept Muslims.*

—Usman, a 49-year-old man, Tucampo,
Parang municipality, Philippines

*Probably some of them [upper-level officials] have no knowledge of our lives . . . and are afraid to smell our cow dung.*

—Men's discussion group, Salvia Prey,
Sangkae district, Cambodia

Poor women and men are at the bottom of the heap in many ways. Economically disadvantaged, they are also distant from the decision makers whose dictates affect their ability to survive and get ahead. In discussion groups, poor people displayed a calm acceptance of some inequality as inevitable and natural. The common metaphor used was the unequal fingers of the hand, some taller than others. Yet they are tired of being trampled upon and pushed to the edges, and they feel helpless to challenge the arbitrary institutions that confront them as they try to make a living. Poor people want to participate in markets, but these markets are routinely captured by those who have more. Often the poor have to pay disproportionately high bribes and "fines" for merely trying to work their small farms, do odd jobs, or pursue tiny entrepreneurial ventures. In urban areas the lack of legal documents contributes further to their exclusion.

Discussion groups in Cambodia frequently referred to the "black is white" character of capture and corruption. The rich engage in illegal market activities and benefit with impunity; the poor are penalized when they go about their legal business and cannot get justice for offenses committed against them.

Poor people in Chakboeng, Cambodia, a fishing community, described the widespread use of illegal fishing methods by wealthy people in collusion with large traders and the fishing authorities charged with monitoring the use of illegal equipment and access to community fishing lots. While the large traders and wealthy households are allowed to get away with using prohibited equipment, bribes and "fines" are demanded from poor villagers fishing in community lots with legal equipment. Violence and intimidation against the poor were also reported in Chakboeng and other villages. A member of a community fishery group in Chakboeng narrated his experience:

> One day I put a *broul* [bamboo fishing trap] to catch fish in the river in the open fishing area. But then a number of fishery inspectors from Phnom Penh approached and forced me to take the broul out of the river unless I paid them 2.4 million riels [$600]. On behalf of the village fishery community, I spent almost a morning bargaining for a reasonable fee of 1.6 million riels [$400]. Finally, the inspectors agreed to that amount. I then had to borrow money from a Vietnamese fisherman I know and paid them. Such a case should not have happened for two reasons. My fishing equipment is allowed to be used by community fisheries, and I did this in the open area released to the community by the government in 2001. But I could not claim my rights because they had guns.

In Somrampi, Cambodia, a member of a community timeline discussion group told a similar story:

> One truck which transports our pigs or marine products is asked to pay 4,000 to 5,000 riels at each checkpoint. Small traders who transport their commodities by motorbike have to pay 500 riels each time at each checkpoint. Very often I feel that all such checkpoints are leeches that are sucking our blood from every corner of our lives. We would waste our time and spoil our goods if we tried to argue for our rights. It is really funny to us that the robbers call us troublemakers or criminals and then take money from us.

Two types of responses stand out. Despite poor people's experiences with captured markets, nobody wanted markets to shut down. Instead, they wanted assistance and guidance. Poor people everywhere spoke about how their lives had changed when local markets (and sometimes distant ones) started to function well and provided outlets for their goods. Second, even when confronted by wrongdoing on the part of the rich, poor people emphasized the importance of monitoring their own behavior, sticking together, and maintaining their self-respect, dignity, and ethical principles. Lorna, a young member of a women's discussion group in Kilaluna, Philippines, said that one should "be strong . . . stick to one's principles. The poor should also have unity." Added Linlin, "Respect oneself. No matter how rich and powerful the wealthy become, if the people in the community don't respect them, it has no use. For us poor, even if we don't have enough money, if we are respected it is still all right."

## Housing

*We have some freedom at last, because we have our house. Although we have to pay for the services, it is really good to have our space. We will take care of it because it is ours.*

—Mario, a 57-year-old man, El Gorrión,
Ibague municipality, Colombia

Although poor people need and appreciate many different types of infrastructure projects, including electricity, schools, health centers, and other basic infrastructure, housing programs seem to be the most deeply valued. The importance of housing for well-being cuts across communities of all types.[6] Having a home promotes independence, security, belonging, family harmony, credit access, space for production, and peace of mind. Being forced to abandon one's home is one of the most traumatic experiences associated with conflict. After months and sometimes years of displacement, those able to return very often face the shock of seeing their houses completely looted, damaged beyond repair, or burned to the ground. Even though housing is privately owned, when everyone in a community becomes the owner of a permanent private home, the effect goes beyond the individual. Everyone then develops a stake in community peace and prosperity.

With some notable exceptions, government, donor, and NGO programs provide only modest housing assistance in war-torn areas, so reconstruction of housing remains uncompleted for years. In addition, rather than providing better housing to *all* in need in a community, many programs use divisive strategies to figure out the most "deserving" in the community. This was most apparent in communities in Sri Lanka.

Housing is so important that upgrading temporary shelter to permanent housing is often one of the first investments that people make from years of savings. For example, in the village of Sastaing, Cambodia, people said, "Housing has improved a lot over the past 10 years. In the past, we had only small thatched houses, but now we have houses made of wood with tin roofs . . . and there are many big houses now." Recovery was harder in Ponky Kda. The village leader said, "It has taken several households almost 10 years to save enough money to build a better house. Only a few poor families whose daughters have managed to find permanent employment in garment factories in Phnom Penh or Baek Chan or Kamboul since 1999 or 2000 can afford better housing."

## Roads

*It is easier now, because there was no road before. Back then we had to take our crops on animals. We had to pay for more workers to take out five horses and hire two cowboys. You do the numbers! Now we can get a vehicle here, to our house.*

—Justo, a 38-year-old man, La Soledad,
Pasto municipality, Colombia

Roads and bridges are lifelines. But in conflict, they can become death traps. Rival factions fight to control them so that they can ferry troops, supplies, and contraband. There are also the spoils of looting and "war taxes" on civilian road traffic. When roadblocks and checkpoints by armed groups persist for months and years, people become trapped and cut off from markets, jobs, vital inputs to their livelihoods, food, medicine, clinics, schools, and places to take refuge. When the checkpoints finally come down, or at least become safer to pass through, the newly opened roads can usher in new beginnings for their villages and towns. This is especially the case when a village suddenly becomes connected by road to an active market. And when external assistance targets road construction, repairs, and transport services, this can lead to transformations in village economies.

In Sri Lanka, roads were patrolled by Tamil and army troops, and people feared road travel even during the cease-fire. Passing through security checkpoints meant, at a minimum, losing time waiting in line to hand over papers. Often vehicles were searched or completely unloaded, and goods were seized or "tolls" were charged. Not surprisingly, traders and haulers plied the roads as little as possible.

In Dubiading, Philippines, before the road was rebuilt, villagers had to transport their fish catches to markets by boat at great cost in time and money. "With the good road, they can bring their large catches to Cotabato . . . Iligan or Marawai City, where they can demand higher prices," explained men in a discussion group there. Villagers in North Maluku, Indonesia, also reported benefits from road construction following the conflict. Villagers from Riah Khillaw, Afghanistan, hoped for an improvement in transport to urban centers, so that commuters could reach jobs and small farmers could access wholesale markets. In Nasher Khan, villagers reported that road repair meant that people could now "easily move from one village to another. In the past, if someone was ill, it was very difficult to take him to the doctor because the roads were not good."

Roads are important, but unless they link to markets and unless there is demand for what people produce, economic benefits may not follow. In Ramili Qali, Afghanistan, people expressed frustration that new road construction in their area put them nowhere near any active markets that might help their livelihoods.

### Credit

*No, there was no credit system in the past and there is no credit system now. Our government has to help us by providing credit to buy things in advance, such as seeds and fertilizer.*

—Men's discussion group, Morlaw Ghano,
Nangarhar province, Afghanistan

*We want to have a little enterprise, but we cannot obtain a loan. We have
been trying to get one for seven months.*
—Estela, a 35-year-old woman, El Mirador,
Pasto municipality, Colombia

The market economy works on credit. Yet people in conflict contexts are
starved for loans. In a few places, people praised formal credit programs that
provided springboards for small livelihood activities to take off. But in the
vast majority of our sample communities, formal lending services were not
available. Where they were, the terms were widely seen to be unfavorable,
with loans too expensive, too tied up in conditions, and too loosely aligned
with the cycles of their livelihoods. Instead, people borrowed from informal
sources—from family, relatives, friends, local shopkeepers, and moneylenders. But these were small loans that could not help their livelihoods grow
quickly. The unavailability of formal credit in the aftermath of conflict hits
people especially hard when they need to rebuild houses, farms, and businesses from scratch.

Figure 5.4 compares sources of credit in conflict and nonconflict communities, showing the heavy reliance on informal sources. Just 4 percent of
communities reported the presence of commercial banks, and only 13 percent had access to government banks. As discussed in chapter 3, borrowing
from friends has a negative association with community-level movement out
of poverty. Friends are also affected by conflict and have little to give; heavy
reliance on loans from friends indicates that communities do not have access
to formal sources of credit.

In the barrios visited in Colombia, affordable loans were said to be impossible to find. People had to take debt from moneylenders to run their businesses and pay for food and other expenses. According to Josué, a 77-year-old
man in Villa Rosa, "There is a kind of loan [called] 'pay every day.' They lend
you $50, and you have to pay back $2.50 every day for 24 days. If you make
$5 in one day, you still have to pay half of that. We cannot refuse to pay two
days in a row because you will be in trouble . . . Eighty percent of the people
work with this credit."

In some conflict communities, religious organizations seem to be stepping up to fill some of the vacuum in formal credit. More than a quarter of the
conflict communities reported credit available from religious groups in 2005,
up from zero in 1995. Women in Patobako, Indonesia, for example, said
that Muslimat, an Islamic women's organization, had become an important

**FIGURE 5.4**
**Availability of credit sources in conflict and nonconflict communities, 1995 and 2005**

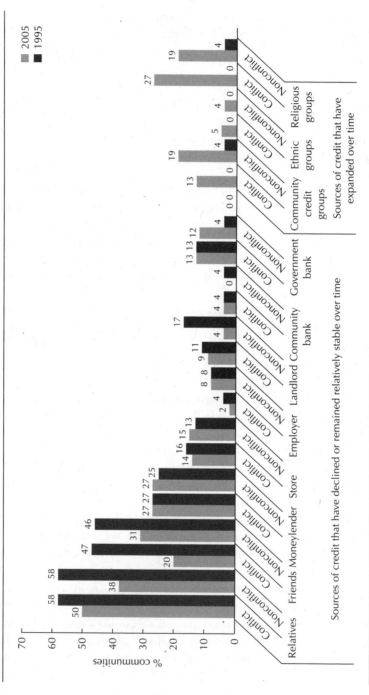

*Source:* Community questionnaire.

source of credit for them. Members could take small loans when they needed cash for household expenses or emergencies, and the terms were based on a woman's ability to repay. Reliance on ethnic associations for credit, though smaller, also increased. These developments may or may not be favorable. Religious and ethnic groups typically provide credit only to their own members, and there is some evidence that this may further the polarization of communities. In addition, like informal lenders, such groups generally give very small loans.

Reliance on community credit groups and associations also grew. Although such groups helped people cope, few of these associations, including those assisted by outsiders, were able to overcome the disadvantages of small scale. Nor did most back up their loans with business support to small enterprises, especially in the crucial area of market orientation.

Microcredit by itself can hardly be expected to help poor people overcome all barriers and move out of poverty. But when credit is combined with skills training, production of items for which there is a market, and roads that connect communities to markets, then credit becomes a springboard out of poverty. Otherwise, like revolving credit societies, microcredit keeps people revolving in poverty.

In Shazimir, Afghanistan, a microcredit program tried to start activities, but people declined to participate because they considered the loans too small and costly and feared they would be unable to repay them. In Sri Lanka, people mentioned programs run by the government, donors, and NGOs, as well as some commercial lending programs, but access to them varied widely from one community to the next. In the east, a Sinhalese community favored by the government enjoyed multiple formal sources. By contrast, Muslim and Tamil communities reported relatively few outlets, notably schemes under the NGO Sarvodaya and the government's Samurdhi welfare program, and these only provided very small loans. People said they could not get anywhere with that level of assistance, but the bigger lenders were off limits. "To get loans from the bank we need to show something as collateral, and two government servants have to recommend the loan. So poor people like us can't get loans from banks or finance companies," lamented a discussion group in Thambulla.

In Indonesia, numerous formal credit institutions were active, but their coverage was also uneven. As elsewhere, difficulties with eligibility requirements and interest rates kept poor people from being able to use them. Farmers in Yasapira explained that civil servants have the earnings and collateral to take loans, but "as for us, we do not earn much, so our income cannot support it." In Barumangga, men explained that "it's too complicated" to get credit as there are "a lot of requirements." A women's discussion group of Somrampi stressed that you had to have a lot of courage to take on debt. A bank had very recently set up an office in urban Kalisido, and many of the 700 traders in its subregency market were quickly finding its lending and savings services useful. But for Anan, a 34-year-old man from Kalisido, the new bank's credit did not seem to be available. When asked about loans, he described rates that moneylenders charge: "If we get a loan for 500,000 rupiah, we must repay 700,000 rupiah in three months." People reported that many moneylenders go around the market and housing areas offering credit for daily consumption needs. Although the interest is high, people said that they counted heavily on these loans.

The types of credit initiatives that seemed to be most appreciated were often linked to supporting livelihood activities. In Riah Khillaw, Afghanistan, a group of women said that an NGO called Handicap had come into the community and provided credit to a group of disabled people who wanted to start a business. According to Khan Bibi, a housewife, "The loans were of around 1,000 Afghanis. People bought several sheep for very cheap prices, about 200 or 300 Afghanis per sheep. Abdulfattah is a disabled man and he got 30,000 Afghanis and started a small shop in the community. Now he has improved his small shop and is saving to buy more products for his shop."

## The missing private sector

*It would be better for us as girls or women if we could have a good job in the village that could provide us with a good income, such as a teacher, village medical practitioner, or hair dresser, raising pigs and cattle, small grocery shopkeeper, dress retailer, or tailor, or improving our dry-season farming. But we don't know whether we can achieve our goals or not because we have no money, no schooling.*
—Women's discussion group, Chakboeng,
Peam Ro district, Cambodia

*Ninety percent of the people in this village are doing day labor jobs. Now some ladies from our village are going to vocational training in tailoring and handicraft production.*
—Women's discussion group, Thambulla,
Ampara district, Sri Lanka

Men and women with stable jobs in factories, businesses, hotels, and transport could be found in our study, but infrequently. In Assam, Indonesia, Sri Lanka, and Colombia, conflict-affected communities reported that factories and plantations shut down and did not reopen when security improved. As mentioned earlier, 40 percent of the study communities had no formal private employers, a rate that hardly changed over the decade. Without a private sector that generates employment, there are few stable jobs. Even in Colombia, a middle-income country, 75 percent of the income earned by the households surveyed for the study (mostly displaced) came from temporary and casual employment and only 13 percent from regular employment.

Workers across the conflict countries who wanted anything more than casual and poorly paid jobs had to go elsewhere. In the village of Sastaing, Cambodia, where landlessness is a significant problem, 70 to 80 percent of the community's workers are reported to have migrated to Thailand. In several Cambodian villages it was common for daughters to be sent to factory jobs in Phnom Penh. Young men eager to make good money in Colombia went to the countryside to work on coca fields or across the border to Venezuela. The best-off households in the north and east of Sri Lanka had family members working in Western countries, while less wealthy households could only reach the Middle East, where earnings for overseas workers were lower.

Some private firms were present as contractors in public works. These public works do provide temporary jobs in construction to poor people and hence are extremely important, particularly if they result in building needed infrastructure. In some conflict-affected communities, private medical clinics provided some employment. But in general, the formal private sector was conspicuous by its absence.

## Conclusion

The first need in poor communities recovering from conflict and violence, after a minimum level of security and safety, is economic livelihoods. Despite this basic reality, most assistance programs either do not focus on restoring incomes as a priority or give such miserly help that it does little to contribute to poverty reduction. This is misguided, as improved economic security is perhaps the most important bulwark against renewed conflict sparked by manipulative politicians and armed groups.

Poor people, particularly in conflict contexts, want to participate in markets and they want markets to function well. But they mostly find themselves pushed to the fringes. Poor people's tiny, tiny enterprises—growing a clutch of bananas or tailoring three uniforms or raising two goats—almost never provide a route out of poverty. Such microenterprises may help people cope day to day, but they rarely achieve any stability or scale. Thus, they do little to help poor people consolidate permanent assets quickly or change their bargaining power in markets.

Daring new approaches and innovations are needed at three levels. First, tiny entrepreneurs need assistance to access markets and achieve scale, particularly by aggregating goods produced for markets. Second, innovation is needed to create poor people's corporations or businesses, or what are often called social enterprises. And finally, changes are needed in the business models used by multinational corporations that own large plantations or factories, so that workers gain some limited ownership and share more fairly in profits. It is particularly important to involve young men in business. Co-owners rarely destroy factories or plantations.

Current postconflict strategies doom people to cycling in and out of poverty for the rest of their lives. Permanent housing, basic infrastructure that facilitates access to markets, markets that are fairer to poor people, access to loans of adequate size, and above all restored and stable incomes reaffirm human dignity and confidence in governments. This is the path to peace and reconciliation.

## Notes

1. Our results do not represent African communities in conflict, which are likely to be even poorer.
2. To protect the privacy of participants, this book uses pseudonyms for the study communities (villages and barrios). Cities, municipalities, districts, departments, and provinces are identified by their real names.
3. The Colombia study focused on displaced people in urban barrios. In the two rural villages in the sample, however, people described neighboring villages that had been flattened or badly damaged.
4. The exception to this seems to be in Afghanistan under the Taliban, when local teachers were fired and other government workers lost their jobs to Taliban loyalists.
5. The Nagas are another insurgent and separatist ethnic group. They have been demanding an independent state in the northeast since 1952.
6. Housing conditions were a marker of well-being on ladders of life in communities across the study. The poorest households, for example, relied heavily on shel-

ters made of temporary materials that let in rain, cold, and insects. In Indonesia, poor households made do with bamboo walls, while the rich built walls of brick. In Sri Lanka, poor dwellings were described as thatched and on tiny plots.

# References

DeYoung, K. 2006. "Afghanistan Opium Crop Sets Record." *Washington Post*, December 2, A1.

Rahayu, S. K., and V. Febriany. 2007. "Indonesia Case Study: North Maluku and East Java." Moving Out of Poverty national synthesis report. Available on the Moving Out of Poverty study Web site, http://go.worldbank.org/9ER0AOIH20.

# Aid Strategies: Can Chickens and Miserly Handouts Reduce Poverty?

*In a way, the conflict has helped us lead better lives because we became prosperous after the conflict. There has been a lot of assistance given to us by the government and by the different nongovernmental organizations.*

—APIPA, A 36-YEAR-OLD WOMAN,
Paitatu, Kauswagan municipality, Philippines

*We had nothing left. No livelihoods. No cultivated lands. Nothing. We had to start all over again.*

—DISCUSSION GROUP,
Kumputhiri, Trincomalee district, Sri Lanka

A id strategies play a critical role in the recovery of a community after the end of war. This is the paradox of conflict. All too often it takes a war or a disaster to draw attention to a community's need for assistance to help its households move out of poverty and destitution. And even with aid, mobility is not assured.

Based on the evidence in this study, it is obvious that development assistance strategies for countries recovering from conflict need to change quite dramatically. In this section we draw upon the study findings to set forth principles that are important for more effective development assistance by governments, donors, nongovernmental organizations (NGOs), and the private sector in conflict contexts. Such strategies should promote recovery from conflict and also lead to state and nation building. The section begins with a case study of a village in Afghanistan, illustrating the issues surrounding aid to war-torn communities and some approaches that can work well. We then draw upon experiences from the wider sample of 102 communities across countries to propose 10 principles for more effective aid, noting that the relevance and application of these principles will vary depending on the country and community context.

## The Case of High-Conflict and High-Mobility Ramili Qali

*When the Taliban came in 1999, they transferred about 500 people from this village by force to Kabul, then Jalalabad. About 50 families could go to Gulbahar and Panjsher and join the mujahedeen. The Taliban set fire to our houses and gardens and cut our grapevines, exploded our irrigation canals . . . Some people were killed and disabled as a result of the Taliban attack, and this fighting lasted for three years.*

—Men's discussion group, Ramili Qali,
Parwan province, Afghanistan

161

*In one year, the irrigation water, the electricity power, roads, and culverts were done by the National Solidarity Program.*
—Women's discussion group, Ramili Qali,
Parwan province, Afghanistan

The village of Ramili Qali in Afghanistan's Parwan province lies at the crossroads of geography and history.[1] Located in the agriculturally rich Shomali Plain, an hour's drive north of Kabul, it produces one of the main Afghan exports, *kishmish* or raisins. The village is on the road to Panjsher and is close to the major trade centers of Kabul, Kunduz, and Mazar-e-Sharif. Its location made Ramili Qali highly strategic during the various conflicts that roiled the area.

Community members highlighted two episodes. The first was in 1996, when the Taliban took control of the area and blew up the main upstream irrigation structures. The second was in 1999, when the frontline of the fight between the Taliban and the Northern Alliance reached the village. At that time the Taliban evacuated the whole community, and Taliban and Northern Alliance soldiers looted and laid waste to the village. The area was left as one of the most heavily landmined in the entire country, a wasteland in which nearly everything was dead or razed to the ground. These were the dire conditions facing the people of Ramili Qali when they began returning to the village in 2002 after the defeat of the Taliban.

Ramili Qali became the focus of reconstruction efforts because of its level of destruction, its proximity to the capital, and its large agricultural potential. The first step was demining, which was carried out by the nongovernmental HALO Trust in 2002. During a discussion of their community's timeline, people recalled, "Both the Taliban and Northern Alliance put a lot of landmines in the village. When we got back to the village, HALO Trust found 2,000 landmines in the village itself and 10,000 in the whole area, including the fields. The mines did not really hurt the adults, because we were trained not to go behind the red stones, but the young children did not remember." Several people were killed or maimed by the mines. Demining of the agricultural fields allowed farmers to restart their crops. The community initially chose to plant poppy as a way of getting quick cash into the hands of families who came back with "nothing but their clothes." As one farmer said, "We didn't even have one egg."

The United Nations High Commissioner for Refugees (UNHCR) quickly initiated a housing program that resulted in the restoration of 200 homes in the first year. This had a large impact, as it helped returnees settle in quickly and restart their lives. In 2003, as more people returned, free seeds and fertilizer were distributed in small quantities to farmers, enough to start planting some crops and vegetables. The discussion group said, "It was not big, but before that we did not even have enough to eat, and right after that we could sell vegetables in the bazaar." Two schools were constructed—one for girls, with funds from the coalition forces, and one for boys, with funds from the United Arab Emirates.

Discussants reported that several important events occurred in 2004, with the activities of the National Solidarity Program (NSP) judged to be the most important. As part of its participation in the NSP, the village democratically elected men's and women's councils to start a process of grassroots democracy and make decisions on grants for development. Other key events included the reestablishment of the agricultural cooperative for farmers owning vineyards, with the help of coalition forces based at the Bagram air base; distribution of wheat seeds to farmers through the alternative livelihoods program; a disarmament and demobilization program that started gathering weapons in return for funds; and paving of the main Kabul–Jabal Saraj highway. In exchange for this assistance, the community stopped poppy cultivation.

In 2005, the village received NSP grants totaling $30,000. The women's council, through a consultative process, chose to invest in two 40-kilowatt electrical generators that provided four hours of electricity at night for lighting all the houses and for television.[2] The men's council chose rehabilitation of minor irrigation canals. Both projects were implemented right away. The NSP activities seem to have contributed to the fairly rapid embracing of a culture of broad-based, participatory decision making in the village, at least for development-related matters. Discussion group members said, "This is totally normal, that people are consulted." A men's discussion group said that people returned with greater belief in themselves. "Since people went to different parts of the world, got information, and knew what their rights are, a few people alone cannot rebuild a country."

The second siphon on the major irrigation system was repaired by the Chinese government, returning irrigation to all the fields. This was a turning point in restoring livelihoods. Farmers recounted, "Of course, the grapevines did not immediately regrow and produce, but it allowed our farmers to grow other things like wheat, maize, and poppy." A village-based seed enterprise was created, and some NGOs dug wells to ease the drinking water problem.

Two factors in addition to external aid contributed to Ramili Qali's progress in the period before 2006. The first was a resourceful village chief who had a strategic vision for his community and actively sought out connections and resources outside the community. For example, during our research team's visit he appealed to them to talk to the French agricultural cooperation agency on the community's behalf. He also expressed regret that he could not get the villagers lucrative jobs at the nearby Bagram air base because he did not have a good relationship with the Afghan intermediary to the base commander, who recruited from his own people and tribe.

Second, the community was cohesive even though it included two main ethnic groups, a Tajik majority (70 percent) and a Pashtun minority (30 percent). All are Sunni Muslims, though they speak different languages. Very early in the interviews, people said that social and ethnic inequality between Tajiks, Pashtuns, and Hazara did not exist in their community as it did in other villages in Afghanistan; rather, the Pashtun minority was well integrated in the community's life. A discussion group of men said, "There is no social inequality where we live. All people live in the same condition. Since people stopped fighting, they feel unity among each other."

Potential tensions are held in check for the moment by the shared experience of devastation and by the proactive role of the village chief. The discussion was held in a part of the village that is majority Tajik. During the discussion, the *mirab,* or water supply manager, recounted an incident in which he had refused to distribute irrigation water to a Pashtun of the village, a former member of the Taliban who was hated because of the burning of the village houses. The Pashtun appealed to the chief, who forced the manager, a Tajik, to release the water to him.

The Ramili Qali example highlights the importance of quick intervention after conflict to provide security, especially through demining, followed immediately by steps to restore housing and livelihoods. Legitimacy was established at the local level through the creation of elected local councils for women and men, which in turn organized consultations with villagers on priorities for spending the funds coming in from outside. The community decided collectively to give up poppy plantation in return for substantial assistance to start other livelihoods, particularly irrigated agriculture.

However, as government and international assistance waned, farmers in Ramili Qali began thinking about returning to poppy cultivation, both as a last resort for subsistence and as a potential bargaining chip. In 2006 UNHCR continued building houses, but by then the flow of external resources was starting to dry up. As livelihoods were not yet fully reestablished, the community started debating whether it was worth risking a return to poppy cultivation. Turning back to poppy, they reasoned, might attract international and government attention and restart the flow of resources to help the community continue on the path to recovery. Moreover, poppy traders and drug lords could potentially provide large amounts of quick credit, as they were doing in other villages.

Despite the influx of assistance, Ramili Qali still had many unmet needs at the time of our team's visit. One common complaint was lack of credit to start or expand businesses. Tools, fertilizers, medicine for livestock, and other inputs were priced so high as to be unaffordable, but there was no source of credit other than the family and some shopkeepers who would sell on credit. Women said, "We cannot farm because we do not have the necessary tools. We need to borrow money to improve our lands, but we cannot get loans." The business environment remained difficult, as there were no traders in the village. Raisins were taken to Qara Bagh and Charikar to be sold there. The textile factory in Gulbar had not reopened, and there were no private sector companies in or near the village.

In light of the assistance that poured into Dash-e-Rabat, one may be tempted to assume that enough was done for recovery, and that if people did not prosper it was somehow their fault. We end this section with a reminder of the total devastation experienced by this village and other villages in conflict zones. Recovery from such devastation and the rebuilding of community, social relations, and livelihoods take more than two or three years. In 2006, after several years of aid, people in Ramili Qali estimated that they had recovered only half of their pre-Taliban production levels, and that full recovery would take another five to seven years. A women's discussion group recounted:

> All the grapevines and walnuts and apples were dried and burnt. The newly planted trees take a lot of time to grow: for example, grapes take seven years to become fruitful. All the livestock and poultry were stolen; during the Taliban, all the valuable materials of the households were stolen and others were burnt. The Taliban were cutting the trees but not eating the fruit, and this is a sin. Our youth were martyrs. My four nephews were killed on the same day.

Not every community received as much help as Ramili Qali. We found great variation across countries in the quality, levels, and types of assistance received, as well as variation within each country. Communities in Assam were the least likely to mention receiving any assistance at all. What help did arrive came through the local government in most cases and occasionally through local NGOs. Communities in Assam also had the lowest moving out of poverty rates and very high levels of overall poverty. In Cambodia, the researchers found a strong association between village recovery and the levels of development assistance. In Chakboeng, where local recovery was strong, the community reported 14 projects during the study period, while remote, conflict-ridden, and impoverished Koh Phong had just one project. Communities in Indonesia affected by the intercommunal conflict in North Maluku mentioned the largest number of government assistance programs, although indigenous NGOs also played a role. Communities in Afghanistan, Colombia, and the Philippines reported government, international, and NGO assistance, although problems emerged with respect to waning attention and inadequate levels of support.

## Implications for Aid Strategies

*When we got here the [neighborhood] committees started, and I was tell-*
*ing them to let us choose where we were going to live the rest of our lives,*
*but they would not let us do so. That was already decided. Democracy is*
*mistreated. They did not say, "How would you like your houses?" The one*
*with power is like God, doing whatever he wants with people.*
                        —Gustavo, a 46-year-old man, Villa Rosa,
                                    Cartagena municipality, Colombia

*There are conflicts between the displaced and the roofless [homeless].*
*There are always conflicts because of the aid the displaced receive. Most of*
*the institutional help is for the displaced and just a little for the roofless.*
*The leaders are in charge of dividing people.*
                        —Women's and men's discussion groups, Villa Blanca,
                                    Floridablanca municipality, Colombia

This section suggests 10 principles for aid strategies based on the study findings. The relevance and application of these principles will be unique to each context and will vary even within the same country and over time. We focus primarily on the local level. Our rationale is simple. When something happens in thousands and thousands of communities, it aggregates to the national level. At the same time, this change in thousands of communities is not possible without shifts in political leadership, policies, programs, capacity, and resources at the national and international levels. In other words, we are proposing that national reconstruction policies be informed by local realities and develop large-scale national programs to reach thousands of communities soon after conflict ceases.

### One: Establish security

Until security, law, and order are established, life after conflict cannot return to normal. People will not invest whatever limited resources they have when they are waiting to see if another conflict breaks out, threatening to destroy all their investments once again. International peacekeepers can play important roles in securing peace, but such forces need to stay for long periods to prevent a return to conflict, as in the Philippines and Afghanistan.[3]

All communities have mechanisms to resolve disputes and manage conflicts. These measures are sometimes cruel and divisive and sometimes fair and effective. Some of these mechanisms, or new ones, should be encouraged with a sharp eye to supporting a culture of fair justice across social, ethnic, religious, caste, and gender groups. In some communities new mechanisms will emerge almost spontaneously, as seen in a few communities in Indonesia and the Philippines. But in other places active intervention will be needed to make this happen. This was the case, for example, in Afghanistan, where the National Solidarity Program helped spur the formation of men's and women's councils. These weakened the power of exclusionary religious councils, composed mostly of village religious elders, that were known for harsh treatment of women's infractions.

Sometimes army and police presence provides a boost to security, but at other times it contributes to insecurity. Accountability and capacity of the army and police are important issues, and this may point to a role for third-party monitors or international peacekeepers. When the army is deployed to help rebuild destroyed community infrastructure, this can sometimes be an effective means for reestablishing discipline and credibility and reconstructing the country.

### Two: Move quickly to address a development emergency and coordinate among donors

When people have lost nearly everything, their needs are immediate and huge. In Ramili Qali, most evacuated families returned in 2004 and 2005 precisely because the international aid community mobilized quickly and effectively to first clear the fields and community of mines and then moved immediately into building houses. Villagers resorted to poppy in the first season to earn quick cash and then were able to start planting crops and vegetables with relatively meager resources. As a result, a substantial 58 percent of poor households moved out of poverty in Ramili Qali. Yet in 2006, the discussion groups estimated that it would take the village another seven years to recover fully. All told, recovery would require at least a decade of uninterrupted peace and sustained investment. Unfortunately for Afghanistan, both security and the economic situation have worsened since 2006. Peacekeeping and reconstruction assistance has flagged, and government corruption has soared.

The lesson here is that development assistance, whether from government, NGOs, or international agencies, needs to arrive quickly, adjust to evolving needs over time, and stay for as long as is needed. Yet most international assistance to postconflict communities is slow in coming and ends too soon. Recovery from the traumas of conflict is a lengthy process, and assistance programs need to continue for at least a decade. Nearly all large programs that successfully reach poor people and reduce poverty in peacetime continue for at least that long, if not longer.[4]

To be effective, donor-driven assistance programs need to be coordinated by national governments or their appointees. Transparent management, by both the government and the donors themselves, is of paramount importance. When each donor pretends that others do not exist and assumes that it alone knows best, the effect on the ground is pathetic. Such assistance rarely benefits poor people; it merely keeps donors busy in the business of aid and probably crowds out the private sector.

### Three: Give generous grants rather than miserly handouts

To rebuild their lives, people in postconflict communities need cash. Such assistance lifts poor people out of poverty firmly and quickly so that they can get started again and move toward relative prosperity, rather than cycling in and out of poverty. Poor people do not lack initiative or courage; what they lack is material resources. Development debate still carries a whiff of the attitudes associated with the false notion of a "culture of poverty": if you give poor people anything more than a pittance, they will get lazy and spoiled on the dole. Another influential concept that is often applied inappropriately is that people's need and demand for particular goods and services should be judged only by their willingness to pay.

Getting money into people's hands is the most demand-oriented tool, as they decide how to use the resources. There is now a vast literature on conditional cash transfers (see, for example, Grosh et al. 2008). For quick recovery in postconflict settings, unconditional, generous cash grants are needed to help poor people invest in permanent economic assets that allow them to generate income streams over time.

After the Helsinki peace agreement ended the fighting in Aceh, Indonesia, a variant of the Kecamatan Development Program was used to reach conflict victims and reintegrate ex-combatants. Starting in 2006, it was implemented in one-third of Aceh and reached half a million people living in ex-combatant households. Communities discussed the needs of households and decided that the priority was not rebuilding community infrastructure but providing cash to individuals and groups. People bought engines and motorcycles, a priority no outsider would have foreseen. The amount of land farmed by ex-combatants doubled in one year, and asset ownership increased significantly. A recent evaluation shows that the share classified as poor in the communities recovering from conflict in Aceh decreased by 11 percentage points (Barron et al. 2009), contrasting with a less than 1 percentage point decline (from 17.5 to 16.7 percent) in Indonesia's national poverty reduction rate in the previous decade, between 1996 and 2004 (World Bank 2008).

Development assistance in conflict contexts needs to serve as a launching pad, not a 100-step ladder.

## Four: Provide accessible credit, supported by advice

In postconflict communities, there is typically a huge unmet need for loans that are not tiny but are large enough to provide real help. Loans should be easy to access, they should not require endless paperwork, and they should come with business support to help people avoid investing in losing ventures. In the communities visited in Afghanistan, nobody had access to banks, community associations, or any organized credit programs. They borrowed small amounts when they could from friends and family or from private moneylenders and traders. When people did receive credit, it was seldom linked to helping them produce for and connect to larger markets beyond the village. Typically, women start tiny, tiny ventures raising a few chickens or goats, which quite frequently die, or they sew a few clothes or sell cooked food. They copy each other, with the result that their enterprises quickly saturate local demand for eggs, clothes, cooked food, or whatever else they are producing. These initiatives are important, but they do not add up to a leap out of poverty.

Microcredit can make a difference when it is supported with market linkages, improvements in production quality, and aggregation through marketing groups. The microcredit programs encountered in the study villages seldom met this standard. Sri Lanka is celebrated among microcredit advocates for reaching 60 percent of all households with microcredit through many different microfinance providers. This broad coverage is important, but it does not mean that microcredit helps people move out of poverty and stay out of poverty. A recent evaluation of the government-run Samurdhi program concludes that there is little evidence that the microcredit program results in poverty reduction. Only 4 percent of all Samurdhi participants receive loans from the microcredit program, with the poor having the lowest probability of doing so (Glinskaya 2003).[5] Poor people in some of the study communities appreciated the Samurdhi credit program, but it did not receive high ratings as a launching pad out of poverty.

In short, most microcredit programs in the sample communities were not transformational. There are promising innovations in financial services for poor people, and these need to be developed and adapted for people living in conflict contexts.

## Five: Use inclusive rather than narrow targeting

Providers of development assistance, whether NGOs, governments, or donors, have become obsessed with targeting and fine-grained targeting criteria. Who is the poorest, the most excluded, the most worthy of receiving aid? This determination to target only the poor does not always serve the poor, as clever individuals along the distribution channels can find a thousand different ways to capture the benefits unless there are transparency of information, independent media, and external monitors from NGOs or international agencies.[6] The Samurdhi program in Sri Lanka, for instance, has had such extensive mistargeting that an evaluation concludes that the program would have been better off with no targeting at all (Glinskaya 2003).

One way to avoid the need for targeting is to offer so little that the very poor will self-select into programs. Typically this means subsidized food programs offering coarse, low-quality grains and public works offering below-market wages, benefits of little interest to the well-off. Such an approach can help get food and cash into poor people's hands, but it is largely a coping strategy rather than a launching strategy for the poor. It helps, but it penalizes the poor to achieve efficiency gains.

Research shows that geographic targeting based on community or sub-district poverty is easier and more effective than within-community targeting. In communities where fighting has been on religious, social, or political grounds, and where ex-combatants need to be reintegrated, there are many painful fissures to be healed. The last thing such a community needs is another divisive measurement exercise to dictate who has suffered the most or who is most deserving based on external criteria. The only exception is to specify that traditionally excluded groups, based on ethnicity or gender, must be included. Beyond this, people in communities know each other's needs, and when supported by the presence of external facilitators who are accountable, communities can usually discuss their needs and make wiser choices than can outsiders.

In Aceh, Indonesia, where cash grants were given out, an evaluation notes that even though the project was meant for conflict victims, only 44 percent of conflict victims received assistance, while 40 percent of the money went to nonvictims. Those who did receive the help valued it highly, and overall villagers rated the program as highly successful. However, it is important to note that the goal of social cohesion and reintegration of ex-combatants was not met. In fact, the ex-combatants in program villages were more disliked than in control villages, probably because the empowerment approach did not include embracing previous combatants (Barron et al. 2009). Without the "leakage" to others in need, including ex-combatants, the project probably could have resulted in more conflict in these areas.

In Sri Lanka, in the villages of Kaithamavi and Manivaliin Jaffna district, people pointed out that housing was being supplied by five different agencies, each with different targeting criteria, different conditions, and different sizes and forms of grants. Even so, not everyone who needed a house obtained a house. The requirement that beneficiaries provide land records meant that the poorest people, who typically had no titles or had been pushed out by others' fraudulent claims, usually did not receive housing. Given the small grant sizes, many houses remained incomplete for years, as people put any additional cash toward food and livelihood activities. This stood in contrast to the experiences in Ramili Qali, Afghanistan, and Paitatu, Philippines, where new houses, often bigger than people's old houses, were built quickly and distributed equitably in a coordinated way. This helped overcome bitterness and energize the community.

## Six: Build unity—neutrality is not enough

Many NGOs and international development agencies pride themselves on their neutrality when they work in conflict contexts. They shouldn't. Neutrality, in the sense of not favoring one side over another, is necessary but not sufficient. What is needed is a proactive strategy to reach out to all groups in these deeply fractured communities and assist them in healing old wounds and burying sources of conflict. This happens not through pious platitudes but through actions—actions that lay the foundation for knitting a nation back together.

Going back to the Aceh example, it is unrealistic to expect deeply hurt and divided communities to come back together if aid is given in ways that further divide and if it is not supported by any efforts to change the culture of war, hurt, loss, and hatred. The Aceh evaluation notes that the level of acceptance of ex-combatants is lower among civilian victims in project areas. This is not surprising; victims need help, and other people, including ex-combatants who are not victims, may also need help. Social tensions, divisions, and conflicts in these communities did not go down over the two-year period, nor did levels of trust in government increase.

Contrast these results with those in the Philippine community of Paitatu, where the building of houses for everyone became a means of fostering unity among previously warring groups (see chapter 4). When Christian pastors and Muslim imams worked side by side to build the houses that would improve people's lives, they modeled behavior that led to reconciliation. This work was made possible in part by the active role of a committed Muslim leader, Camlon Moner. By the end of the project, community groups reported higher unity and tolerance across Muslim and Christian groups and higher levels of trust—trust not only in their community leaders, but in their local government, armed groups, and even the army, which coordinated the housing reconstruction. This community was not attacked again by the Islamic separatists, and it became a refuge for both Muslims and Christians in subsequent years. All this happened against the backdrop of broad efforts to support community-based initiatives and actively spread a culture of peace. The government, NGOs, and international aid agencies invested in the training of leaders and community facilitators, and they used radio, television, and posters to spread the message. Community success was celebrated and publicized at all levels, from local to national.[7]

In conflict-affected contexts, religious organizations, however well intentioned, may play roles that are unhelpful and even dangerous. They often reach out only to members of their own religion and employ only from this group. World Vision is one of the largest Christian relief and development organizations, working in over 90 countries with a budget of $1.6 billion. Despite the scale of its works, it did not stand out in any of the study communities as particularly beloved or trusted. Instead, discussants in both Sri Lanka and the Philippines voiced suspicion, perceiving the organization to favor Christian groups and possibly to be seeking conversions among Muslims and other non-Christians. Faith-based organizations can contribute to healing only if they openly practice fairness and actively seek to build bridges across social divides while engaged in development work in war-torn areas. It would also help if Christian organizations hired Muslims and Muslim organizations hired Christians, making a practical commitment to breaching the religious and other social fissures in the places where they work. In short, they should borrow from Camlon's approach to building intercommunal trust and solidarity.

Reconciliation across social divides often goes hand in hand with justice. Transitional justice mechanisms, truth and reconciliation panels, and various local traditions and rituals can play a role in helping people let go of the past. What is relevant will vary by context.

## Seven: Promote local ownership, local knowledge, and local ways

The development rhetoric is rife with platitudes about the importance of local ownership, putting developing countries in the "driver's seat," and supporting local initiative at the national and local levels. This approach works better in countries already strong enough to take a stand against donor whims. It works least well in the poorest countries, where international funds make up the major share of the national budget, and in countries recovering from conflict. International aid agencies are permeated by a culture of interagency competition.[8] There is a disdain for the indigenous at all levels, especially when it comes to addressing large national problems. Simultaneously, there is often an assumption that the "primitive" is good enough for poor countries when the real need may be to leapfrog to the latest technology.

We highlight two of the many painful examples recounted by Ashraf Ghani, Afghanistan's first finance minister. In 2001 Afghanistan had three different currencies in circulation, which looked identical but traded for different values. Ghani wanted to replace them with a new currency. The International Monetary Fund warned that the change would take years, and the United Nations calculated that introducing a new currency would require

8,000 bureaucrats. The Afghan finance team went ahead and replaced the currency nationwide in four months. The secret was to gain the cooperation of the *hawala* dealers, indigenous money traders who handle most of the internal and external money transfers throughout the country. When their cooperation was solicited on behalf of the nation, they rapidly collected and burned the old currency and replaced it with the new (Ghani and Lockhart 2008, 208–9).

The second example shows that sometimes local knowledge calls for adopting the most modern technology. Before the first presidential elections in Afghanistan in 2004, the Afghan government team urged UN staff to purchase the latest iris-recognition technology to identify voters at polling stations. The new technology would replace the old manual system of giving out cardboard cards and inking voters' fingers to show that they had voted. It would create a reusable biometric database for future elections and would cut down on voter fraud, theoretically allowing just one mistake in 10 million compared to the 30 percent voter fraud expected under the old system. The $140 million cost would be offset by fees generated by the issuance of identity cards and other legal documents. Nonetheless, the new technology was not adopted. The reason the UN gave was simple: a donor had provided $10 million worth of cardboard and would have been offended had it not been used. After the election, many people reported voting multiple times after washing the supposedly indelible ink off their fingers (Ghani and Lockhart 2008, 77–78). In the 2009 elections, allegations of voter fraud were even more widespread.

At the community level, the results of dysfunctional behavior among donors are even more visible. Examples in the study communities included poorly designed programs that nobody wants, different projects with different conditions in the same sector of the same community, aid so stingy that it made little difference to anyone, and training that went nowhere. Food aid shipped in from overseas sometimes depressed local rice and wheat prices so that local farmers struggling to recover from conflict gave up and grew nothing—or turned to growing poppy.

### Eight: Prioritize key sectors

Compared to the clear priority given by local people to economic recovery, the priorities of aid strategies seem muddled. Aid does not, for the most part, concentrate on reviving people's livelihoods. And when it does, the assistance is usually too meager: it helps people cope day to day but does not enable them to build permanent assets and move out of poverty permanently. In short, it is not transformational.

Figure 6.1 reports the types of development projects received in the study communities in the last 10 years. It is striking that the nonconflict communities received more development projects overall than the conflict-affected communities (probably because it is easier to work in peaceful settings). The most common types of projects were schools and roads. Education is a basic human right, and investment in schools is critical for the next generation, but schools do not directly help the short-term economic recovery of families. Roads help tremendously, but only if they connect communities to market towns. Only 16 percent of the conflict-affected communities reported receiving assistance with agriculture and only 7 percent received any finance/credit projects. Yet there is great need for grants and credit to restart economic activities in conflict-affected communities. Health is important as a basic human right as well as for economic livelihoods, and there are no differences between health projects in conflict and nonconflict communities.[9]

Conflict-affected communities need everything that poor communities need and more. Given the strong importance that people attach to stable and adequate income streams, we recommend five priority sectors for aid to thousands of communities: housing, direct and generous cash and other support

**FIGURE 6.1**
**Development projects in conflict and nonconflict communities, 1995–2005**

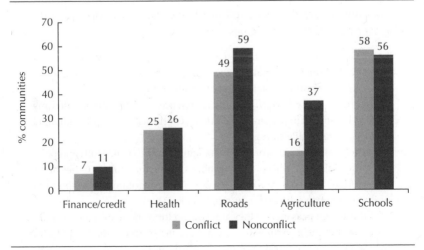

*Source:* Community questionnaire.

to individuals, rural roads that connect producers to markets, credit linked to markets, and public works that provide employment along with training in construction and related trades. With the exception of roads, these priorities are not reflected in aggregate aid flows to the conflict-affected communities in the study. Nor do aid strategies focus on attracting the private sector to invest, innovate, and create employment in war-torn countries.

### Nine: Support capacity building for income generation, especially among youth

Capacity building is needed at all levels. But it needs to be embedded in a wider culture of change, so that people will be able to use their new skills and will have incentives to do so. At the community level, two needs stand out. One is for training and capacity building that enables people to succeed in markets. The other is for vocational training and capacity building that creates economic opportunities for unemployed and underemployed youth.

Development practice is dominated by a supply-driven approach that often churns out training courses that have no practical purpose. Desperate people in needy communities may welcome these courses, but only until they realize that they do not lead to anything.

Examples from several communities in Colombia are extreme but true. In Villa Rosa, Colombia, the research teams met María, a 50-year-old woman, who cheerfully exclaimed, "I have lots of those diplomas. I have 28!" We give five examples that speak for themselves. The first demonstrates hope; the second, waiting; the third, wasted resources; and the fourth, optimism despite being overtrained. The fifth signals reality.

> I have taken a course as a community leader, another in confection, another in first aid, cooperation, bakery, soy management, industrial machines in the SENA [a government agency that offers job training] . . . All these courses helped me, because I acquired some experience. I will be able to offer my services because I am prepared to do that. (Gloria, a 40-year-old woman, El Gorrión, from her life story)
>
> There came a social worker who taught us how to make dolls and bags. She always said, "We will contact you about selling the stuff," but they never called. What we need here is credit, because we earn nothing doing this kind of thing. (Women's discussion group, Villa Rosa)
>
> If you are a peasant and they give you aid for working the land, you can move on. But the government . . . you have never been a shoemaker, and they bring you a shoemaking course. They gave us those bakery courses. We

wanted that money to use in the countryside. (Carlos, a 52-year-old man, Santa María, life story)

In 1998 I did a shoemaking course in the SENA. It was a time when I had no work. Between 1998 and 1999 I did a bakery course and then a mechanics one. With ANDAS [a solidarity group] I have been in many courses on democracy, human rights, and leadership. Being here, building houses, we did many courses on family violence, how to live in a community, and self-esteem. I did a leadership course between 2001 and 2002. After that, there was another course on cooperation with another 40 people. We were going to create a cooperative, but I already belonged to one downtown. We had courses on FTA, repair, justice and truth law, the 025 code of the Constitutional Court, between 2004 and 2005. This year I have not had that much time. (Gustavo, a 46-year-old man, Villa Rosa, life story)

The institutions, they've lost some power because evil stories are told among us. It is said that they have mismanaged the resources, that they always take their share and they only give training. Most of the communities need that money to survive, not to be trained. That's why they [institutions] have lost their image. (Ferley, a 34-year-old man, El Gorrión)

Youth are at a crossroads after conflict, yearning to start their adult lives, but with few salable skills. Public works, vocational, and on-the-job training that gives young men and women skills in construction-related trades and manufacturing will be very helpful. In addition, bridging schools that help youth complete interrupted schooling and advance to tertiary and technical education are much needed and can help the children of poor families enter the middle class.

## Ten: Create a culture of accountability

No matter how one looks at the root causes of conflict, the quality of politicians matters. We have documented a few of the thousands of examples of corruption, capture, venality, and violence experienced in communities recovering from conflict. The political culture has to change at all levels. However, for a new government whose hold is still fragile, bringing about change at the national level is the most difficult, as different groups fight for power. Hence, we recommend a focus on creating and spreading a culture of accountability and active citizenship from below, while working on changes at the top.

Our results show that dysfunctional governance is pervasive at the local level in conflict contexts. Neither local elections nor citizen representation functions the same way in conflict and nonconflict communities in the same countries. However, people in communities are hungry for responsive and accountable government.

Most governments and aid agencies still think that community-driven approaches are meant for NGOs that work in a few communities, not for large entities that have to worry about an entire country or several countries. Evidence built up over a decade of work, however, shows that it is feasible to implement nationwide community-driven programs that create a local culture of transparent and accountable governance while they deliver basic infrastructure and support to raise incomes. Over time these programs can be adapted to focus on monitoring other basic services or community needs. In fact, the evidence demonstrates that when properly designed, such programs become critical in connecting citizens to the state in ways that build nations and deepen government legitimacy.

One such program is the Kecamatan Development Program (KDP), initiated in 1998, when fiscal crisis in Indonesia was followed soon after by regime change. The KDP, a $1.6 billion program financed by the Indonesian government and several donors, including the World Bank, gives communities block grants and an open menu of projects to choose from. The process of open discussion by community groups, proposal writing, and monitoring is guided by paid facilitators, and transparency is practiced with respect to all decisions and money flows. The program is completely managed by Indonesians and is open to public audit. Journalists are encouraged to visit project sites without securing prior permission.

A second example is the National Solidarity Program (NSP) started in Afghanistan in 2003, right after the fall of the Taliban, while the government in Kabul was still creating itself. This nationwide program too helped build community-level infrastructure. Most notably, it created new elected community councils, with separate councils for women and men, to seed a new set of participatory decision-making bodies at the local level. National exchanges between regions and communities allow the program to adjust and change. The NSP is now completely managed by Afghans; community outreach is facilitated by partner organizations, mostly NGOs. Programs like KDP and NSP are generating and nurturing a new cadre of leaders for their countries.

## Conclusions

*During the mujahedeen time, before the Taliban, disputes were solved by religious scholars and elders. During the Taliban there was no one in this*

*village and this place was a battlefield. After the Taliban, a new thing happened: NSP came here and people elected a village council. Problems are now solved through this village council.*
—Discussion group, Ramili Qali,
Parwan province, Afghanistan

Aid strategies in conflict contexts need to shift to reflect the realities of local communities. Substantial aid and assistance for recovery, whether from government, NGOs, or international agencies, are critical. The assistance should begin *immediately* after conflict ceases and continue for 7 to 10 years. It must be adequate in size and scope to restore homes and incomes, and it must be implemented in a way that rebuilds social relations, trust, and people's sense of belonging as citizens. Encouragement to the private sector to invest should be a critical part of recovery strategies.

Assistance is most effective and appreciated when it focuses first on economic rehabilitation and recovery of all households in the community. Because everyone then becomes more invested in peace, such economic assistance may also help protect against future conflict. However, given that most conflicts have deep roots in social cleavages, it is important that aid be administered in ways that heal and reconnect social rifts. Most assistance programs ignore this uncomfortable social reality.

The problems that plague aid programs and strategies at the international and country levels are also evident at the local level in our sample communities: too many actors, not enough coordination, short attention span, conditionality, and different strategies for the same types of projects in the same locale. This results in resources being scattered and wasted. This will only change when agencies involved in development assistance also drop the divisiveness between them.

## Notes

1. To protect the privacy of participants, this book uses pseudonyms for the study communities (villages and barrios). Cities, municipalities, districts, departments, and provinces are identified by their real names.
2. The field researchers wrote that if you visit the village at night, you will not find anyone to talk to; everyone is watching Tulsi, an Indian television soap opera telecast in Afghanistan.
3. Paul Collier and his colleagues argue that international peacekeeping forces are among the most effective uses of development assistance (Collier 2007; Collier, Hoeffler, and Söderbom 2008).

4. See *Ending Poverty in South Asia* (Narayan and Glinskaya 2007). This message also emerged strongly from the Chinese, Indonesian, and Indian program and policy experiences discussed at the learning conference in Shanghai in 2006.
5. See also GTZ and Ministry of Finance and Planning (2008).
6. So widespread is the collusion to rip off government funds that monitors have been threatened and harmed. In India, the National Rural Employment Guarantee Scheme promises 100 days of employment in public works to every household. To its great credit, the program includes social audits and is subject to the Right to Information Act, which allows any citizen to ask for information about any government program. However, several social activists have been murdered while conducting such audits and speaking out. Nonetheless, the sheer scale of the project is having a deep impact on the flow of migrant labor from poorer states to the agricultural belt in Punjab, forcing higher wage rates for labor in Punjab.
7. Fearon, Humphreys, and Weinstein (2009) conducted a panel study of a community-driven reconstruction program supported by the International Rescue Committee in northern Liberia. Despite the program's limited resources (it provided a single "quick impact project" of $2,000 to $4,000 in each of 42 randomly selected communities), the authors found strong evidence that the program was successful in increasing social cohesion in the communities that received it. The program also enhanced democratic political attitudes and increased confidence in local decision-making procedures. However, the panel study found little evidence that enhanced material well-being resulted from this relatively limited program.
8. See Ghani and Lockhart (2008) for stunning examples.
9. Ghobarah, Huth, and Russett (2003) present evidence that wars shorten lives, both during the fighting and long after it stops. They attribute their results to populations' greater exposure to the risk of death, disease, and disability as well as to the reduced public and private resources available for health care during and after wars. Justino (2006) provides a useful review of the literature on the significant health and nutrition consequences of conflict.

# References

Barron, P., M. Humphreys, L. Paler, and J. Weinstein. 2009. "Community-Based Reintegration in Aceh: Assessing the Impacts of BRA-KDP." Conflict and Development Team, World Bank, Jakarta.

Collier, P. 2007. *The Bottom Billion: Why the Poorest Countries Are Failing and What Can Be Done about It.* New York: Oxford University Press.

Collier, P., A. Hoeffler, and M. Söderbom. 2008. "Post-Conflict Risks." *Journal of Peace Research* 45 (4): 461–78.

Fearon, J. D., M. Humphreys, and J. Weinstein. 2009. "Development Assistance, Institution Building, and Social Cohesion after Civil War: Evidence from a Field Experiment in Liberia." Paper presented at Center for Global Development seminar, Washington, DC, March 4.

Ghani, A., and C. Lockhart. 2008. *Fixing Failed States: A Framework for Rebuilding a Fractured World*. New York: Oxford University Press.

Ghobarah, H. A., P. Huth, and B. Russett. 2003. "Civil Wars Kill and Maim People—Long after the Shooting Stops." *American Political Science Review* 97 (2): 189–202.

Glinskaya, E. 2003. "An Empirical Evaluation of the Samurdhi Program in Sri Lanka." Paper presented at the Second World Bank Conference on Inequality, Washington, DC, June 9–10. Originally prepared as a background paper for the Sri Lanka Poverty Assessment.

Grosh, M., C. del Ninno, E. Tesliuc, and A. Ouerghi. 2008. *For Protection and Promotion: The Design and Implementation of Effective Safety Nets*. Washington, DC: World Bank.

GTZ and Ministry of Finance and Planning. 2008. "Outreach of Financial Services in Sri Lanka." Colombo. http://www.microfinance.lk/pdf/1227096039.pdf.

Justino, P. 2006. "On the Links Between Violent Conflict and Chronic Poverty: How Much Do We Really Know?" HiCN Working Paper 18, Households in Conflict Network, University of Sussex, Brighton, UK.

Narayan, D., and E. Glinskaya, eds. 2007. *Ending Poverty in South Asia: Ideas that Work*. Washington, DC: World Bank.

World Bank. 2008. World Development Indicators Online. Washington, DC.

# Concluding Reflections

*There is no peace with hunger.*
*Only promises and promises and no*
*fulfillment. If there is no job, there is no*
*peace. If there is nothing to cook in the*
*pot, there is no peace.*

— OSCAR, A 57-YEAR-OLD MAN,
El Gorrión, Colombia

ountries recovering from conflict present perhaps the strongest case for development assistance. When poor countries become involved in political conflict and violence, they are in danger of falling into conflict traps; conflict traps in turn are strongly associated with rising poverty. The case for focusing on the "bottom billion" has already been powerfully made. We draw upon perspectives from below, from some of the bottom billion, to summarize our findings and draw out implications for aid strategies.

Effective development assistance in conflict-torn countries is not about incremental change or incremental increases in aid. It is about transforming development assistance and the ways in which it is delivered. It is about turning aid approaches upside down.

## National-level politics is the problem, but national politics alone is not the solution

Civil conflict is a fight between competing armed groups, or between armed groups and the state, and it is a fight over resources. At the national level, issues of sovereignty are paramount. States face two primary challenges, security and legitimacy, the two preconditions for state building. Patience, consistency, and tenacity are needed to help weak but legitimate states deepen legitimacy and security while strengthening their capacity. Once basic security is established, development, inclusion, and peace do not follow automatically but must be built. This cannot be done by focusing only on a country's capital city; rather, it requires nationwide programs that reach thousands of rural communities and small towns in the far-flung periphery. Security forces are needed to maintain peace, and these forces may be local, national, or perhaps international, depending on the context. But their job can come to an end only if local people develop a stake in peace, so that they resist violence and do not surrender their young boys as recruits to armed groups of one ideology or another.

When will this happen? There are two answers. It will happen when people in thousands and thousands of communities experience economic recovery that makes life better than before. And it will happen when people in these thousands and thousands of communities have developed a taste for and demand fair and accountable leaders and governance.

## Economic recovery is critical, but it needs to go beyond macroeconomics

After security, people's first priority—as we heard over and over again—is their own economic recovery, not national economic recovery. Our data are very clear on this. When people are poor to begin with, when what little they own has been destroyed, and when they have little education, no amount of microcredit will get them out of the hole. Rather, people need direct and generous grants to rebuild their lives. Money heals. Money helps people economically, and with encouragement money helps people let go of past grudges. In this way it can start people on the path of tolerance.

Programs that provide free housing and "rich people's toilets" to replace stinking open pits can help lift people out of depression after conflict. They can start the process of allaying suspicions and building trust in supporting institutions, including the government, the army, religious groups, and other nongovernmental organizations (NGOs). Proper housing is the first sign of dignity and hope, of belonging to a community, of a return to normality. However, housing assistance is typically partial, so people go without completed houses for years; often, when materials are given, they are only enough to build houses that are *smaller* than what people had before. Governments and donors often waste much time and effort dividing up communities into those who will receive help and those who will not, increasing divisiveness further.

## Market-led recovery is central, but poor people need help to succeed in markets

Jobs and incomes for millions of people can be generated only through market-led recovery—but with a new twist. When 70 to 90 percent of people in a community are poor, recovery depends critically on markets in which poor people become producers and consumers on fairer terms. Almost no development assistance focuses on markets in any systematic way. Typically, programs select a few families and hand out a few tools and inputs such as seed and hoes, or in a few cases sewing machines. But they do not help poor producers enhance the quality of their product, connect to markets, and aggregate their goods for marketing in order to achieve scale and bargaining power. Markets can lead recovery; the paradox is that poor people need grants to prepare for and succeed in the marketplace.

Microcredit programs were numerous in the communities visited, but their results on the ground appeared thin. Some had so many conditions attached to them that people refused to engage with them. Most programs offered inadequate amounts of help. Giving a goat or three chickens to selected individuals does little to move a community out of poverty. There is also the problem of duplication. When everyone in a village produces the same thing, local markets quickly become saturated, as there is very little absorptive capacity when the majority of the people are poor. Yet external agencies are fooled because they don't stay long enough to see the long-term results, and poor people, being polite, may express appreciation for whatever they receive.

Helping poor people's economic activities in small ways, dubbed the "livelihoods approach," has been popularized by the UK Department of International Development. But tiny, tiny production efforts do poor people little good unless they can access markets and sell at a fair price There is little evidence of market orientation in the assistance that NGOs, governments, and international agencies are providing to poor people in conflict contexts. The worlds of "livelihoods" and market-led growth have yet to come together.

## Nation building requires inclusive development and a culture of reconciliation and peace

The killer in ethnic, religious, or tribal conflict is the "small identity," based on loyalty to a group that is narrower than the nation-state. Politicians regularly use narrow identities and the inequalities associated with them to stoke the fires of conflict. As young people in war-torn Sri Lanka reminded us, Sri Lankans don't think of themselves as Sri Lankan but as Tamil or Sinhala or Muslim. Assistance provided in conflict-affected environments typically fails to invest in building national identities; this is harmful and needs to change.

Clearly, when there are inequalities in markets, politics, and societies that affect the life opportunities of different groups, grievances need to be addressed. However, even in the worst-hit Sri Lankan communities, the solutions that all three groups focused on was ending war and building peace, not continuing war and continuing to kill each other. People just want to get on with their lives, take care of their families with dignity, and let others get on with their lives as well.

Two approaches are vital, though the forms and details will vary depending on the context. First is the principle of inclusion in development programs. In conflict-affected contexts, this means actively reaching across the most painful social divides and including everyone. In some contexts the key divide is between Muslims and Christians; in others it is between Muslims of different sects or clans; in still others it is between the followers of different leaders or members of different tribes.

Community-level groups and associations whose memberships cut across social divides are important in poverty reduction and economic development, and also in maintaining peace. The power of unity can even deflect war, as witnessed in several communities in the Philippines. During the devastating all-out war waged by the government in the Mindanao region in 2000, joint action by Muslims and Christians allowed communities to avoid attacks by both government soldiers and insurgents. Bullies attack the weak and divided, not the strong and united.

Second, the culture of war has to be replaced actively by a culture of reconciliation and peace. There are many ways of doing this: through truth and reconciliation commissions, through creation of peace zones, and through quick resolution of conflicts using a variety of dispute resolution mechanisms at different levels. In our sample the most vigorous large-scale effort from below was in the Philippines, where 82 peace zones were created across Mindanao, often with active citizen participation. The zones were supported by the government, donors, NGOs, Christian churches, and Muslim imams. But it was the culture of peace, spread through stakeholder meetings, community facilitators, and investments in communities, that made a difference in changing beliefs.

While top-down political leadership, policies, resources, and programs are critical, the culture of peace and the transformation of narrow identities into broad national identities will happen only when thousands of communities directly engage in this effort in ways that make sense in their particular environment. Local leaders have a huge role to play in creating this virtuous cycle.

## People are ahead of politicians

In conflict contexts, politics at the local level is dysfunctional. None of the usual measures of democracy behave normally; instead, they misbehave. In conflict communities, local elections, and even the responsiveness of local government, have perversely negative effects on poor people's mobility. Conversely, corruption and bribery, which have doubled in a decade, seem to facilitate moving out of poverty in conflict contexts. But despite everything, people still show up at meetings, they still participate, and they still form groups to help each other. This civic behavior improves local governance and helps nudge village councils that represent different ethnic and religious groups to start functioning in ways that promote cooperation and community prosperity.

The challenge, of course, is doing this on a large scale while regime changes and fiscal crises are convulsing the nation-state. Here, the experience of nationwide, bottom-up, community-driven programs is instructive.

## Large-scale, community-driven programs foster a culture of accountability

Until recently, community-driven development was thought to be the domain of utopians and labor organizers. There is now growing evidence that investing in communities works, even when countries are going through seismic political and economic crises, as in Indonesia in 1998 and Afghanistan in 2003.

Beginning with the Kecamatan Development Program (KDP) in 1998, the Indonesian government has incorporated community-driven development as a key poverty reduction strategy aligned with its decentralization program. It has invested $1.6 billion in programs covering every province and almost every village in Indonesia—experimenting, making adjustments, learning, and adjusting again. Implemented through the Indonesian government, the programs provide block grants directly to the subdistrict and village levels, and inclusive community groups decide how to spend the money. Rigorous evaluations and many independent audits conclude that less than 1 percent of program funds are misused and that construction costs for program-built infrastructure are less than half the costs for government-built infrastructure.

In Afghanistan, the $1 billion National Solidarity Program (NSP) was the brainchild of Ashraf Ghani, then the country's finance minister. It was designed by Scott Guggenheim, who also designed the community-driven program in Indonesia. The NSP was started in 2003, soon after the defeat of the Taliban. While not problem-free, it now reaches every secure province in Afghanistan. In the absence of any state presence, the NSP established elected community councils for men and women and in a few places for youth.

In addition to building local infrastructure and delivering livelihood programs, the Indonesian and Afghan programs have generated thousands of leaders, facilitators, and community organizations that can facilitate decentralized, inclusive decision making. Large transparent programs with decentralized governance make their biggest contribution by promoting culture shift, encouraging ordinary people to hold their leaders accountable for use of government finances. When thousands of citizens demand accountability, they are helping to build legitimate and sovereign states from below. The culture of accountability at the top will also need to change, with transparent national budgets subject to public scrutiny, and international scrutiny if international funds are involved. International agencies, however, cannot demand a transparent national budget while keeping their own expenditures in the same country opaque.

## International aid strategies are muddled

The problems with international aid strategies have become issues of public debate. We highlight several problematic features of current development assistance orthodoxy, adopted even by NGOs. This approach can be characterized as social welfare to help poor people cope rather than entrepreneurial and economic development to help poor people prosper. The current orthodoxy is to give loans, not grants, and in small amounts; target narrowly, deciding who deserves help and who does not; and spread resources across households and communities and then move on to other areas. These approaches keep poor people in conflict contexts in poverty or hovering near the poverty line. Our research results would reverse the current orthodoxy: give grants, not loans; give a lot, not a little; cover broad geographic areas and all social groups rather than target narrowly; concentrate, saturate, and stay in a place for a long time, until systemic change becomes deeply embedded; and finally, build on poor people's initiative and organizations creating economic opportunity and access to markets.

## Religious organizations can be dangerous

In conflict contexts, religious organizations can be dangerous and fuel divisiveness. Religious organizations will have to act in radically different ways if they want to have positive effects in conflict communities. When religious organizations become bridging organizations, reaching out and working with people of other religions without trying to change anyone's faith, they become a force for reconciliation and unity. There were striking examples of this behavior in some of the peace zones in the Philippines. When religious organizations start providing basic services and credit, particularly across religious groups, the negative side effects can disappear.

The world of development assistance and poverty reduction needs more people like Camlon Moner, the barangay captain in the Philippines who overcame many problems to bring resources to his community and unite Muslims and Christians who had been killing each other for decades. The world of development assistance needs more Scott Guggenheims, anthropologists and social scientists who can translate an understanding of local contexts into nationwide programs and policy design. The world of development assistance needs more "searchers," experts who are willing to ask questions and design solutions that fit a particular place at a particular time in history. Finally, the world of development assistance needs more people who value the indigenous without either romanticizing everything that is local or dismissing indigenous strategies as automatically inferior.

Development isn't about big things; development is about little things done on a big scale.

PART **2**

# Country Case Studies

# Violence, Forced Displacement, and Chronic Poverty in Colombia

*Patti Petesch and Vanessa Joan Gray*

*I lost part of my life with displacement, the work of more or less 10 years. I lost my animals, my economic stability. I wasn't myself anymore . . . I haven't been able to recover my land, no one knows who's the owner. Some other people got in there. Who's going to evict them?*

— ESTEBAN, A 64-YEAR-OLD MAN,
Santa María, Cartagena municipality

*Displaced people are discriminated against. Employers don't give them any jobs because they wonder if they are guerrillas.*

— CARLOS, A 21-YEAR-OLD MAN,
Villa Blanca, Floridablanca municipality

Since the late 1980s, violence by several armed organizations has claimed the lives of tens of thousands of Colombians. Armed conflict in Colombia is primarily a rural phenomenon, although there are important exceptions, and the nation's violence disproportionately affects its poorer citizens (UNDP 2003). Of the world's estimated 23.7 million internally displaced persons (IDPs), some 3 million are in Colombia; only Sudan contributes a larger share to the global total (UNHCR 2006, 5). This chapter provides a case study of eight Colombian communities that were directly affected by violent conflict, with the goal of identifying factors that contribute to their recovery. Six of the study communities are urban neighborhoods, or barrios, that have become IDP resettlement areas. The other two are rural villages that were taken over by illegal armed groups for extended periods.

By their own measures of well-being, the eight study communities saw 77 percent of their population remain in chronic poverty over the decade-long study period, from 1995 to 2005. Persistent political violence provides a key explanation for this dismaying poverty rate. Indeed, an important finding from this research is that the displaced people in this study did not always find safe refuge after fleeing their villages. The political violence, waged primarily in the countryside, followed many of them into their urban resettlement barrios. There was, nevertheless, significant variation among the eight study communities in the extent to which people were able to recover from conflict and displacement. This study uses these variations in mobility outcomes to explore the relationship between conflict and poor people's mobility. It asks why some communities provided more opportunities than others for recovery, however limited.

The exceptionally long duration of the armed conflict in Colombia has resulted in the coexistence of multiple forms of organized violence, most of which constrain or block poor people's opportunities for upward mobility.

**193**

Given this context, we found three factors to be particularly important for understanding the low levels of mobility experienced.

First, individuals who are marked by conflict and displacement encounter few livelihood options. They face severe discrimination in labor markets and exclusion from other economic opportunities. Although these disadvantages were widespread in the study communities, the communities that were close to active markets generally experienced more mobility than those that were not.

Second, confidence in local officials is very low due to problems of corruption, but communities with the highest levels of mobility reported higher levels of cooperation with their elected officials and local government. While displaced people greatly value the assistance provided to them, the help is mainly designed to meet immediate subsistence needs rather than to support recovery and escape from poverty.[1]

Third, a crucial mechanism that struggling communities can use to get ahead, collective action by poor people themselves, is under direct siege in Colombia. Community leaders in five of the communities were assassinated or fled due to threats, and often this was associated with the wider political violence. Ordinary people often perceived the loss of their leaders as an even more severe and lasting blow to their community's prospects than the harmful effects of the violence on their livelihoods.

We open the chapter with background on key economic, political, and social trends in Colombia during the study period. We then describe the study design and use of subjective poverty measures. The next section presents mobility outcomes in the study communities and explores the nature of the violence these communities experienced and its impacts on livelihoods. This is illustrated by a comparative case study of mobility in the two conflict-affected villages, Los Rincones and La Soledad.[2] Next, the chapter considers how local democratic functioning and grassroots collective action shape mobility in contexts of violence. These findings are highlighted by a comparative case study of mobility in two of the urban barrios, Santa María and El Mirador. We close with a few reflections on the policy implications of the study findings.

## The National Context

Colombia presents a study in clashing political, economic, and social trends. It has achieved macroeconomic stability and steady economic growth for most of the period since World War II, but the country also suffers from high levels of poverty and inequality. It has one of the world's oldest traditions of regular elections and civilian rule, but its history is marked by numerous civil wars, and exclusionary institutions continue to shape the society.

Unlike most of its neighbors, Colombia has had strong economic growth for decades, except for a sharp contraction in 1999. Per capita income exceeded $2,700 in 2006, giving the country middle-income status (World Bank 2007). Even so, 60 percent of the population lived in poverty in 1995, and this rate increased with the recession in the late 1990s (World Bank 2002, 12).[3] Economic recovery between 2002 and 2004 helped move 1.4 million people out of poverty, and by 2006 the national poverty rate had declined to 45 percent (World Bank 2005, 2008). Yet despite this progress, Colombia ranks third in inequality among countries in Latin America and the Caribbean, which is one of the most unequal regions of the world (World Bank 2008).

State weakness has played a significant role in these uneven development patterns and in causing and prolonging violent conflict in Colombia. In the less accessible parts of the territory, the central government has not consistently monopolized the use of force, provided infrastructure and social services, or protected property and personal security. Thus, the country is afflicted by multiple forms of organized violence even as it remains under democratic rule.

For decades, leftist guerrillas, right-wing paramilitaries, transnational drug-trafficking organizations, and U.S.-backed government forces have used violence to control resources and territory, particularly in rural areas far from the nation's population centers. In conflict zones, life and property are not protected by the rule of law, and 97 percent of violent crimes go unprosecuted. Rule by lethal force is commonplace, but even that form of "order" is unstable because of the intense competition for dominance among armed groups. Measured in the numbers of internally displaced persons, child soldiers, and active landmines, few conflicts have exacted a more staggering humanitarian toll than the war in Colombia.[4] According to the Colombian Commission of Jurists, political violence killed nearly 20 people per day on average in 2000, the midway point in this study's observation period (Tate 2007, 33). Rural civilians make up the majority of conflict victims, and forced displacement is the impact suffered most widely (UNDP 2003).

Forced displacement in Colombia is part of a pattern of migration with origins in the 1920s. Sparsely occupied lands and booming resource sectors (coffee, bananas, gold, emeralds, oil, coca) have pulled migrants toward some regions, while violence and the concentration of land ownership have expelled people from other regions. In areas lacking an effective government presence, conditions were amenable to the growth of insurgent armies and, later, drug-trafficking organizations and paramilitary groups. Today some areas are under martial law. Since 2002 the Álvaro Uribe administration has reduced the power of the nation's largest guerrilla organization, the FARC (Fuerzas Armadas Revolucionarias de Colombia). It has negotiated a mass demobilization of paramilitaries and incarcerated hundreds of illegal combatants. Security in the cities, in key production areas, and on the main highways has improved significantly. Nevertheless, the insurgency has not been vanquished. A new paramilitary group, Águilas Negras, is assassinating and intimidating civilians, even in the capital city. The illegal drug trade is thriving. And the majority of the nation's departments continue to send and/or receive significant numbers of displaced people (UNHCR 2007).

Generations of Colombians have lost family members, property, and livelihoods to violence. The effects of violence have combined with those of large-scale migration to weaken family and community bonds. One of the damaging consequences of the conflict's long duration is that the criminality and social problems associated with postconflict settings are present even though war is still being waged on several fronts.

## Research Framework and Design

The key question in the Colombia study is how and why some conflict-affected communities were more able than others to recover and provide opportunities for poor people's mobility. The research design approaches the challenge of understanding mobility with few prior assumptions.

An analytic model of empowerment was used to broadly frame the analysis. It consists of interaction between two sets of factors: (a) a change in the assets and capabilities of poor individuals or groups to take purposeful actions, or exercise *agency*; and (b) a change in the *opportunity structure*, which involves the dominant social norms and structures within which poor and disadvantaged actors must work to advance their interests.[5] This chapter focuses especially on community-level opportunity structures that affect mobility, including the strength of the local economy, the functioning of local democracy and governance, and the nature of social cohesion.

A key principle of the research design for the global Moving Out of Poverty study was to build on existing datasets and mobility analyses to the fullest extent possible. The analytic focus and sampling design for the study in Colombia were informed by a mobility study of 2,322 displaced households conducted by the Universidad de los Andes in Bogotá, the Bishop's Conference of the Catholic Church, and the World Bank.[6] The original research and sampling design for the Colombia Moving Out of Poverty study, which featured a balanced sample of barrios and villages, had to be discarded after the data collection began.[7] The problems were due to a combination of ongoing security risks and the unwillingness of some localities to participate in a study about conflict and development issues. The team also had difficulty finding barrios with large IDP populations. As there are no refugee centers in Colombia, the displaced are widely scattered across poor urban barrios and squatter communities. Many have made their way from very difficult temporary housing conditions on squatter lands to more permanent lots, as described below.[8]

## Study sample and datasets

The sample of eight communities contains two rural villages, both conflict affected, one of which experienced a brief episode of mass displacement. The remaining six communities are urban barrios. Of these six, five are relatively new IDP settlements and one, El Mirador, is an established barrio that received a significant influx of displaced people during the study period (map 8.1). Table 8.1 presents the sample communities covered by the study.

We do not claim that this small sample is necessarily representative of Colombia's 3 million IDPs. Nevertheless, the mobility trends found in the eight communities seem to be consistent with larger and more representative studies of the displaced, as discussed below.

The study sample at the household level varies with the data collection tools (see appendix C). Focus groups of residents from the eight study communities identified the mobility status of a total of 862 households. The researchers then used stratified random sampling to select a subset of 252 households that received an extensive household questionnaire. A subset of 81 individuals from these survey households also gave open-ended individual life story interviews. In addition, the dataset includes a quantitative community profile and eight qualitative community synthesis reports, which were compiled from focus group discussions and key informant interviews in each community.

Table 8.2 indicates the household sample distribution across the four mobility groups used in the Moving Out of Poverty research. *Movers* are those households that started poor but escaped poverty during the study's observation period of 1995 to 2005. *Chronic poor* started poor and remained in poverty throughout the period. *Fallers* were not poor at the start but fell into poverty, while the *never poor* households did not experience poverty at any

## MAP 8.1
## Colombia with study municipalities

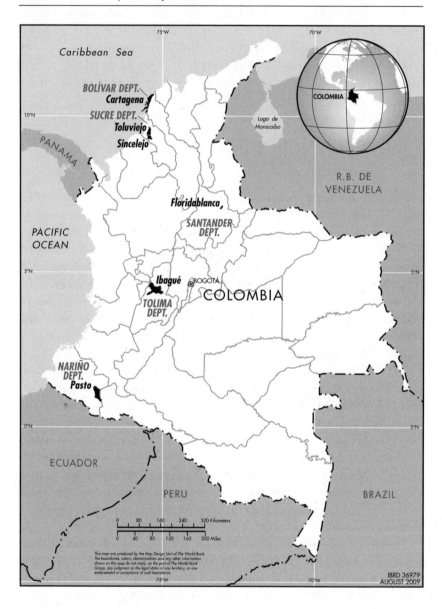

## TABLE 8.1
### Profile of Colombia study communities

| Community | Urban/ rural | Municipality | Department | Study period (years) | Displacement status |
|---|---|---|---|---|---|
| La Soledad | Rural | Pasto | Nariño | 10 | Brief period of mass displacement |
| Los Rincones | Rural | Toluviejo | Sucre | 10 | Conflict affected but little displacement |
| El Mirador | Urban | Pasto | Nariño | 10 | Established barrio with significant IDP presence |
| Villa Blanca | Urban | Floridablanca | Santander | 5 | New IDP settlement |
| El Gorrión | Urban | Ibagué | Tolima | 4 | New IDP settlement |
| Santa María | Urban | Cartagena | Bolívar | 7 | New IDP settlement |
| Villa Rosa | Urban | Cartagena | Bolívar | 6 | New IDP settlement |
| San Feliz | Urban | Sincelejo | Sucre | 6 | New IDP settlement |

*Source:* Community profiles.
*Note:* The study communities are identified by pseudonyms in this chapter.

## TABLE 8.2
### Distribution of Colombia sample households by mobility group
*number of households*

| Mobility group | Ladder of life | Household questionnaire |
|---|---|---|
| Movers | 97 | 48 |
| Chronic poor | 671 | 169 |
| Fallers | 33 | 12 |
| Never poor | 61 | 16 |
| Undetermined status | 0 | 7 |
| Total | 862 | 252 |

*Source:* Ladder of life focus group discussions and household questionnaire with individuals.

point during the study period. The measures used to classify households into the four mobility groups were determined by focus groups that participated in the "ladder of life" exercise, discussed in greater detail below.

### Design issues

For the Colombia study, an attempt was made to find communities that were at least 10 years old. The intent was to provide a longer perspective on the experience of displacement, assuming that displaced people would have moved in at the creation of the community. In practice, however, it proved to be difficult to find communities that met all the sampling criteria, including those pertaining to age.

The ladder of life activity, described below, begins its exploration of changes in well-being only at the moment when people arrived in the sample barrios—that is, *after* they had lost their houses, land, livestock, equipment, and nearly everything else. Nonetheless, many of those who narrated their lives could not help but recall their experiences prior to their displacement and arrival in their new barrios. Had the study examined mobility trajectories that were not associated with particular communities, it would have revealed an even more dramatic picture of widespread loss of assets and falls into poverty. On the other hand, the study may also overestimate the shock of conflict to the extent that it does not capture displaced households that had the means to avoid moving to the difficult resettlement barrios or that recovered enough to be able to move away from them. Nevertheless, the comparative study approach does provide insight into the factors that shaped the differences in recovery and mobility *in these study communities.*

### Locally defined poverty measure

In the Moving Out of Poverty study, definitions of who is poor and who has escaped poverty are determined by the subjective perceptions of local people. In each sample community, focus group members work together to create a figurative "ladder of life" that illustrates the different levels of well-being in their community. After extensive discussion about mobility up and down the ladder, they designate a "community poverty line" (CPL) on their ladder to indicate the step at which a household is no longer considered poor by local standards. Relative to other countries in the study, Colombia has the highest CPL—that is, the Colombian respondents' expectations were higher in terms of the physical assets, food security, occupational status, quality of family life, access to basic services, and other characteristics that a household must have to be no longer deemed poor. It seems that in Colombia local perceptions of who is poor and who is not are informed by lifestyles and norms that extend beyond the immediate surroundings of the sample communities. The widespread presence of color televisions in the households surveyed for the Colombia study, bringing continuous exposure to wealthy lifestyles, may be among the factors shaping expectations of well-being and views about poverty.

The particular descriptions of what it takes to be "not poor" were multidimensional and had many similarities from one study community to the next. A nonpoor household should have reliable income, often from both husband and wife working, along with adequate housing and diet. Additional characteristics of nonpoor households include children enrolled in higher education, access to a full range of public services, and strong family cohesion. Across different communities, the better-off households and barrios did not have to worry about flood waters seeping into their homes and washing their belongings down streets and hills.

The annex to the present chapter presents the ladder of life compiled by the women's focus group in El Gorrión, a brand-new settlement in the municipality of Ibagué. With help from the government, international donors, and national nongovernmental organizations (NGOs), the community relocated en masse to new housing, leaving behind repeated flooding and other hardships in their previous settlement. When describing the best-off households in the community, those that occupy the ladder step just above the CPL, the group said, "They have food and everything they are supposed to have." A 34-year-old woman added that physical assets are not all that distinguish the better-off: "They treat their children better, because they're relaxed. They're not so worried."

In both San Feliz and Villa Blanca, two of the newer barrios in the study still struggling to obtain services, focus groups reported that there are no nonpoor households residing in their barrio. To find households that are not poor, it was necessary to look elsewhere. In San Feliz, discussants described nonpoor households in nearby Villa Angel: these families have comfortable homes and all basic services, and the barrio is not at risk of flooding. The men's focus group in Villa Blanca described the top step of their ladder as occupied by households with multiple earners and stable income, a finished house with a "washing machine, stereo, and adequate food," and children who are studying. But households with these characteristics in Villa Blanca were still seen to be poor by people living there. The nearby barrio of La Paz, however, has households that are not poor, according to the men in Villa Blanca. These nonpoor households have even better houses and access to all services such as phone, water, electricity, gas, and cable. La Paz has good streets, transportation, a health post, sports areas, schools, and churches. There is more commerce than in Villa Blanca.

In the village of Los Rincones in the department of Sucre, the perceptions about who is poor and who is not were surprisingly similar to those in the urban barrios. To find nonpoor households, Los Rincones residents said, you need to travel 15 kilometers to Toluviejo, where people have factory and government jobs, enjoy basic public services, and have good houses with drainage. The village of La Soledad in the department of Nariño, by contrast, had better-off households: they live in brick homes, own up to 3 hectares of land and three cows, and are able to send some of their children to high school. Yet while these landowning families do not need to work as day laborers, they live in fear that armed actors will steal their potato crops or seize their land. The most affluent households in La Soledad have up to 10 acres of land, cars, and more secure second homes in the nearby city of Pasto, where they educate their children.

## Impact of Conflict-Related Difficulties on Mobility Prospects

In this section we present mobility outcomes at the household and community levels, describe the nature of the violence experienced in the study barrios and villages, and begin to examine the impacts of the violence on livelihoods and prosperity.

Of the 862 households sorted on the ladders of life, 77 percent remained trapped in poverty over the study period. Households that started poor and moved out of poverty totaled 13 percent, while households that were never poor or that fell into poverty were 7 percent and 4 percent, respectively (figure 8.1).

Statistics on poverty levels in conflict-affected areas of Colombia's countryside are not available; however, the general rural poverty rate is 68 percent (World Bank 2008). The higher poverty rates found in the eight communities sampled for this study are similar to those indicated in larger and more representative IDP studies. Based on a 2004/05 household survey of 2,322 displaced households from 48 municipalities and 21 departments, Ibáñez and Moya (2007) found that 95 percent of the households were below the poverty line and close to 75 percent experienced negative or zero asset recovery after displacement. The displaced households in their sample also faced soaring unemployment, large declines in earnings compared to their former rural incomes, and scarce access to formal credit (less than 7 percent of the sample had obtained formal credit).

**FIGURE 8.1**
**Distribution of Colombia sample households by mobility group**

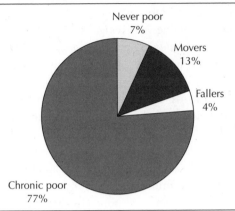

Never poor
7%

Movers
13%

Fallers
4%

Chronic poor
77%

*Source:* Ladder of life focus group discussions.
*Note:* Statistics do not total 100% due to rounding.

Problems with food security also afflicted many of those who participated in the Moving Out of Poverty study. The key informants interviewed locally reported periods of extreme food shortages in five of the six urban barrios, indicating that many households lacked the means to purchase food. People in the rural village of La Soledad also reported inadequate food supplies during some months of the year, likely due to conflict conditions that constrained villagers' freedom of movement and food production.

## Community mobility outcomes

The finding that close to 80 percent of the sample households remained in chronic poverty obscures significant variations in community-level mobility patterns. The study uses two principal indexes to measure community-level mobility. One is the moving out of poverty (MOP) index, which indicates the proportion of households in a community that were initially poor but moved up and out of poverty over 10 years, crossing the community poverty line. In three of the Colombian communities, a substantial number of households (90 in total) were reported to have escaped poverty. In three others, as described above, not a single household managed to move out of poverty over the study period. In a fourth, only one household crossed the CPL. Thus, to better capture differences in mobility rates among the study communities, we turned to a mobility measure that did not require crossing the CPL.

The alternative index, mobility of the poor (MPI), focuses on households that were poor at the outset of the study period but experienced some mobility: that is, they managed to move up one or more ladder steps, but not necessarily across the poverty line. An average of 67 percent of the initially poor households in the sample moved up at least one step. Table 8.3 provides the MPI averages for each of the study villages. By this measure, the IDP barrios can be sorted into two distinct groups of four "high-mobility" barrios and two "low-mobility" barrios. The two villages also differ from each other in terms of MPI, with their two rates falling in between the two sets of high- and low-mobility barrios.

Table 8.3 also reveals that the age of a community does not seem to affect mobility. The newer barrios registered both high and low rates of MPI, while the more established communities seemed to struggle more with recovery. However, the MPI measures do correspond closely to perceptions of the focus groups in each community about whether it is easier or harder to make a living now than at the beginning of the study period, and about the future prosperity of the community.

The exceptionally high MPI rates in the four high-mobility barrios reflect the fact that their residents very often arrived in the new settlements with only

**TABLE 8.3**
**Colombia study communities ranked by mobility index**

| Community | MPI | Study period (years) | Easier/harder to make a living than used to be | Community will be more/same/less prosperous in 10 years |
|---|---|---|---|---|
| *High-mobility barrios* | | | | |
| El Gorrión | 1.00 | 4 | Easier | More |
| Villa Rosa | 0.99 | 6 | Easier | More |
| Santa María | 0.99 | 7 | Easier | More |
| San Feliz | 0.82 | 6 | Easier | More |
| *Low-mobility barrios* | | | | |
| Villa Blanca | 0.35 | 5 | Harder | Same |
| El Mirador | 0.23 | 10 | Harder | Same |
| *Villages* | | | | |
| Los Rincones | 0.60 | 10 | Harder | Same |
| La Soledad | 0.38 | 10 | Harder | Less |

*Source:* Focus group discussions.

*Note:* MPI = initially poor who move up ÷ initially poor.

what they could carry by hand after desperately fleeing violence or threats of violence in their villages. Most of these households managed some manner of recovery from their utter destitution, but few could make the climb all the way out of poverty. The obstacles confronting the low-mobility barrios are explored more fully below.

Basic services became widely available in the barrios during the study period, so the level of services does not seem to be linked to MPI. Nearly all the study communities had access to electricity and clean water,[9] but residents frequently noted that paying for these services was very difficult for them. El Mirador is the only community with landline phone service; however, cell phones seem to be widely used across the sample.[10] In addition, the survey indicates that children everywhere are attending school. Survey responses also show that parents in all the communities hoped their children would reach university or obtain other forms of postsecondary education. Given the study participants' improved access to public services and schooling for their children, one can make sense of the perception voiced in most focus groups that their barrios and villages (if not the local economy) had become more prosperous over the study period.

## Violence and crime affecting study communities

Though tales of escape from danger in the countryside were common, so too were reports of violence in the urban areas where people had sought refuge (table 8.4). Indeed, a central finding in the Colombia study is that unlawful conduct by armed groups—predation, battery, death threats, even assassination—marked the lives of poor people both before *and after* their forced displacement.

Forms of violence related to the wider political conflict were reported in all of the communities except Villa Blanca (table 8.5). Guerrillas or paramilitaries took over the two study villages. Focus groups also reported that paramilitaries were present in two of the barrios, and there was private mention of their presence in a third. In four barrios, study participants said that violent organizations were operating in their barrios but did not specifically name them. Violent youth gangs threaten four of the six barrios. In the three newest settlements, residents also identified episodes of police brutality that were mainly associated with the frightening period when they formed the new barrio after collectively squatting on the land. This process, in which displaced or otherwise needy people enter vacant lands en masse to form squatter communities, is known in local parlance as *invasión de tierras*, or land invasion.

The collection of data on a violent conflict that is ongoing is inherently problematic (Kalyvas 2006). The process is dangerous for both the researchers and the study participants, and informants have more motives than usual for dissembling and more reasons for being inaccurate. In our study, some people were eager to show their communities in the most favorable light possible. Others declined to participate at all. People within the same locality sometimes had widely varying perceptions of the nature of current and past security problems and their effects.[11]

In presenting a picture of unremitting violent conflict, tables 8.4 and 8.5 do not detail the even more extensive reports of everyday crime and other social problems.[12] These include, for instance, widespread mentions of robbery, rape, drug selling, drug abuse, domestic violence, child exploitation,

**TABLE 8.4**

**Security conditions and trends in Colombia study communities**

| Community (ranked by MPI) | Presence of violent conflict during study period[a] | Extent of time at risk of violent conflict | Conflict intensity[b] |
|---|---|---|---|
| *High-mobility barrios* | | | |
| El Gorrión | Yes | Out of range | Low |
| Villa Rosa | Yes | < 6 months | Low |
| Santa María | Yes | > 5 years | Low |
| San Feliz | Yes | < 1 day | No conflict |
| *Low-mobility barrios* | | | |
| Villa Blanca | No | Not applicable | No conflict |
| El Mirador | No | Not applicable | Low |
| *Villages* | | | |
| Los Rincones | Yes | < 2 years | High |
| La Soledad | Yes | < 5 years | High |

*Source:* Community profiles with key informants and authors' analysis of Moving Out of Poverty study data.

a. The data in this column are from a community profile questionnaire administered to local key informants. They were asked: "During the past 10 years, were there any periods of violent conflict in the community? By conflict, we do not only mean major violent events but also conflicts that resulted in a small number of deaths or injuries or limited property damage." The key informant in El Mirador was one of the only sources in that barrio who did not report extensive violence (see table 8.5). Because of such discrepancies in the quantitative data, the authors compiled the ratings in the final column from the study's detailed qualitative accounts.

b. A high conflict intensity rating indicates reports of multiple deaths associated with organized armed actors, combined with extended periods of insecurity. A low intensity rating indicates reports of isolated incidents of insecurity and deaths associated with organized armed actors. The ratings do not reflect reports of everyday crime and violence or the activities of youth gangs, which were often present.

child neglect, and disputes over services and land. In many places police and legal services were said to be unresponsive or absent. It is clear, however, that while residents may view these forms of violence and conflict as part and parcel of their daily lives, they also associate their persistence with the wider political conflict. For instance, urban study participants sometimes linked the armed conflict and drug trafficking to the juvenile delinquency and common crime in their neighborhoods.

A crucial impact of these multiple forms of violence was to reduce people's sense of agency in their own lives. For example, La Soledad and Los Rincones villagers recounted a series of grim experiences resulting from their powerlessness in the face of armed actors. They were forced to deliver messages and observe curfews. They were prevented from using local roads, rivers, and bridges and from tending their crops and animals. They were forced into work details to build and repair infrastructure. They were sometimes ordered to cease commerce and at other times obliged to supply food and merchandise. Their livestock was stolen and consumed. Their homes and fields as well as those in neighboring villages were commandeered and converted into battlefields. Their community leaders were co-opted, bullied, and murdered. Some children were recruited into the drug economy and others were conscripted to serve as soldiers, guerrillas, and paramilitaries. For many of the parents now in barrios, it was the latter threat that ultimately drove them into the ranks of Colombia's IDPs.

Moreover, organized violence was not limited to rural areas. In all, people in five of the eight communities reported that multiple murders, sometimes referred to as "social cleansing," had occurred locally during the study period. The events were usually associated with illegal groups, but not always. Occasionally victims were said to be members of gangs, drug addicts, supporters of an armed group's rivals, or "bad folks," but more often study participants did not give clear information about the identities of either the perpetrators or the victims in these assassination waves. Nor did they ascribe motives to the killers. For example, people in San Feliz reported that in 2002, unspecified armed "outsiders" came into the neighborhood and had been present ever since. They said, "Nobody knows where they're from or what they want," but they noted that residents of the community had been forcibly carried off, never to return. San Feliz residents said they were not sure what the victims might have been doing that made them targets, whether the victims had ties with an armed group, or whether the perpetrators were members of a security force or an illegal army.

**TABLE 8.5**
**Reports of armed actors and related violence in Colombia study communities**

| Report | La Soledad | Los Rincones | El Mirador | Villa Blanca | El Gorrión | Santa María | Villa Rosa | San Feliz |
|---|---|---|---|---|---|---|---|---|
| *Illegal armed groups present in community* | | | | | | | | |
| FARC | ca. 1995 | | | | | | | |
| Unspecified guerrillas | | | | | ✔ | | | |
| Paramilitaries | | 1998, 2001–04 | | | ✔ | | ca. 2002 | |
| Youth gangs | | | ✔ | ✔ | ✔ | | ✔ | |
| Unnamed armed actors | | | ✔ | | ✔ | ✔ | | ✔ |
| *Violent incidents associated with illegal armed groups or government forces* | | | | | | | | |
| Forced displacement from present location | Massive, 2002 | Selective | | | | | Flyers on targeted groups | Death threats posted |
| Forced displacement from previous locations (most often in countryside) | | | ✔ | ✔ | ✔ | | | |
| Assassination of community activists | | JAC president killed, position left vacant | | | Leader of land invasion killed | Leader of land invasion killed; Co-Agro squatter killed, wife raped; arson | | |

| | Mid-1990s | 2003 | 2004 | | | |
|---|---|---|---|---|---|---|
| Multiple murders, some referred to as "social cleansing" | by FARC | | | | | ✓ |
| Local leaders forced to flee or cease political activity due to threats | Community groups ceased to meet 2001–03 | Series of inspectors fled, so municipality has stopped appointing | Gangs threaten JAC | Leader (successor to one killed) disappeared after threats | Community leaders forced out; some fled | JAC president and activist priest forced to flee |
| Neighbors forcibly removed and never returned | | ✓ | | Guerrilla in restaurant | | ✓ |
| Kidnapping | | ✓ | | | | |
| Murder | | | ✓ | ✓ | | |
| Extortion by armed actors | ✓ | ✓ | | | | |
| Youths recruited or conscripted by illegal armies or groups | ✓ | ✓ | | | | |
| Police brutality | By army | | During land invasion | During land invasion | | Especially during land invasion |

*Source:* Authors' analysis of Moving Out of Poverty study data.

*Note:* JAC = Junta de Acción Comunal (Community Action Board). Co-Agro (a pseudonym) is the local peasant organization.

These multiple forms of violence undermined the study participants' prospects for mobility in several ways. To examine the relationship between conflict and poor people's mobility, we move first to the countryside for a comparative exploration of the two study villages, Los Rincones and La Soledad. We then examine factors that are important for understanding displaced people's experiences with conflict and mobility in the urban barrios.

## Continuing Risks in the Countryside: Los Rincones and La Soledad

The two study villages are located in regions where illegal armies have been active for decades, and both were directly occupied by illegal armed forces during the study period. Surprisingly, the villages still experienced some mobility of their poor residents (figure 8.2). No one in Los Rincones escaped poverty, but three-fifths of Los Rincones's poor households (90 out of 149 starting poor) climbed up at least one step during the study period. La Soledad saw a few poverty escapes (12 households out of 107 starting poor), but less overall mobility of its poor than Los Rincones (29 moved up a step but stayed below the CPL).[13] What factors might have contributed to these outcomes?

**FIGURE 8.2**
**Mobility outcomes in Los Rincones and La Soledad, Colombia**

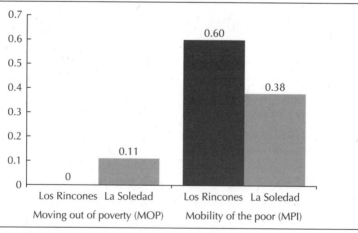

Source: Focus group discussions.

## Market access and labor migration reduce vulnerability in Los Rincones

Los Rincones sits along the main highway to Cartagena, a major city on the northern coast that bustles with foreign and domestic tourists but also endures extensive problems of poverty, crime, and corruption. Paramilitary and guerrilla forces had been waging battles in the nearby hills of Montes de María since the 1980s. Between 2001 and 2003, paramilitary groups occupied Los Rincones. While there was no mass displacement, some villagers did flee in the wake of assassinations, death threats, and other forms of intimidation. People in Los Rincones mentioned the fate of a neighboring village and former commerce partner, Chinulito, which was now under military occupation. One Los Rincones resident referred to Chinulito as having been "erased from the map."

The single biggest economic effect of the violence in Los Rincones was the 1995 closure of a cattle feed factory after death threats and extortion. The factory was by far the largest provider of jobs, with 300 workers taking turns in three shifts. The next major employer was the public works department, but perhaps only 10 villagers helped maintain area roads and these jobs also disappeared with the conflict. Local merchants also report being greatly affected. "People used to come here to buy clothes . . . beds, mattresses and so forth," explained a 38-year-old man. Local people said the paramilitaries did not force them to close their shops, as happened in some other villages, but steady bribes had to be paid to stay in business. Even street vendors selling to motorists on their way to Cartagena paid *vacunas*—protection money, literally "vaccines"—and they were told what days they were permitted to sell on the street. "As a vacuna, you could give them some meat, pork or cattle, cheese or milk," explained a 64-year-old.

More generally, the surrounding violence brought most of the agricultural activity to a standstill because it was too risky for area farmers to go out and work their lands and tend livestock. Those who attempted to maintain their farming activities had to pay bribes. Landowners, sharecroppers, and farm laborers were all affected. When asked, study participants could think of no one locally who benefited at all from the conflict. A focus group of women mentioned that some local youths gained by joining the armed groups because there were no jobs and the groups paid well, allowing youths to help their families. But they hastened to add that if the young recruits didn't do as they were told, they would simply be killed.

Since the end of the paramilitaries' occupation in 2003, villagers said, local shops were doing better, but not as well as before the conflict. The old cattle feed factory had been turned into a ranch, but it employed only 20 workers and the pay was much lower than in the factory. According to residents, a worker now barely earned enough to cover food costs.

With continuing insecurity in the surrounding area, people were relying less on farming and doing more informal trading, selling "pork meat, fruits, pies," explained a 43-year-old woman. Travelers along the highway kept the local market active. In addition, most of the village youths went off to Bogotá or Venezuela for six or seven months a year to work. According to a focus group of men, migration to Venezuela has helped many in the village accumulate some capital, which "upon their return, they can invest in housing, land or other things like machinery or consumer electronics." The community also has a new high school that is used by students from other areas. It opened after everything was destroyed in neighboring Chinulito.

Residents of Los Rincones pointed out that besides teachers, there were still no government authorities to be found in the village, not even a policeman. "Now we are too scared to have a Junta de Acción Comunal," a man explained. He was referring to the local community action board, or JAC, formed by the government to mobilize citizens for development projects. The JAC president had been killed by the paramilitaries, and no one dared take over the post. The village had obtained basic infrastructure through the JAC, but these activities ceased when the violence began, and at the time of the study, they had yet to resume.

## Remoteness stalls recovery in La Soledad

La Soledad is a highland village located in the southwestern corner of Colombia, 27 kilometers from the city of Pasto and near the border with Ecuador. Problems in La Soledad also began in 1995 with the growing presence of FARC guerrillas in the area. In 2002, pitched battles between the FARC and the Colombian army resulted in the displacement of the entire village to the city of Pasto for several months. The village was peaceful in 2005 when the study was conducted, but villagers expressed fears that armed groups and fighting could return.

As the guerrillas expanded their control in the late 1990s, the villagers' potato and dairy farms suffered enormously. Informants would let the guerrillas know when farmers had made sales, and guerrillas would then show up to take their cut. Travel and commerce were disrupted. The FARC forced some farmers to grow poppies; others had to abandon work on their farms to clear paths and do other work for the guerrillas. Public and civic programs disappeared, including government training, technical assistance, and credit to the village. During the worst periods of violence, it became too dangerous to farm, crops were lost, homes were looted, and farm animals perished or were killed.

Since the army cleared out the guerrillas in 2002, recovery has been slow and difficult. People know of few alternatives to growing potatoes. Security concerns remain high. A 42-year-old man explained that jobs have disappeared and farmers still consider it too risky to plant: "Before, it was easier to get a job. There are not any now. After the displacement, the ones who had money either left town or don't offer jobs any more. Before, people used to grow a lot of potatoes. People don't grow any now." The poorest families that had worked as farm laborers were most affected by the conflict, according to a discussion group of women. With scant livelihood options in the village, a man said, "People are migrating to dangerous places where they grow coca. A lot of people have gone away." To make matters worse, the land was no longer worth anything because the village was considered a combat zone. Fear of a resurgence of armed conflict sapped people's motivation to work. State authorities had not returned, leaving great needs unattended: "Since the conflict, nobody watches over the village. People are afraid of coming. Even the teachers won't come. Before, the mayor used to come, but not anymore," lamented a 34-year-old woman.

On the positive side, villagers reported that repairs and improvements to the school were completed in 2003 and that new water connections reached village homes in 2005. Residents had worked collectively to improve the road into the village. These additions have improved their lives, they said, compared to 10 years ago.

### Understanding differences in village mobility

In the study villages, many people risked their lives to hang on to their homes and farms despite the presence of armed actors. When asked why they did not try to leave their economic and security problems behind by migrating, a group of men in Los Rincones said the IDPs in the nearby town were even worse off. "I ran into a person who went to Sincelejo and he's eating out of garbage cans," related a villager. In remote La Soledad, people explained that they simply did not know where to go to find a better life.

Somehow many villagers not only survived but also made small movements up the ladder. Poor people in Los Rincones experienced more mobility than those in La Soledad, and this seems strongly associated with Los Rincones's active local market and location along a highway, which helped people cope with the loss of jobs and farming. In La Soledad, by contrast, no such nonfarm opportunities could be found. In both villages, residents regretted the large number of young people forced to leave the community to seek work, but opportunities for migrants in the north of the country seemed more promising.

Beyond these differences, the two villages shared much in common. People in both places expressed appreciation for some new construction in the wake of the army's victories, but they said that it remained harder to make a living than a decade ago. Few held hopes that the years ahead would bring greater prosperity. In La Soledad, a group of men explained that the future of the village depended on whether there would be peace and the government would provide more services like gas and sewerage and support for farmers. Similar perceptions were voiced in Los Rincones. And in both localities people expressed great frustration that government officials had not yet returned to their posts and that it remained too risky to revive their village councils.

## The Scramble for Urban Livelihoods

If rural villagers face limited economic opportunities because of the continuing risks of conflict, the options in the urban barrios seem scarcely better. Displaced people living in the barrios have lost loved ones, friends, and neighbors, along with most of their assets, and they typically possess few contacts or skills that would help them make new lives in the city. Their hardships are compounded as they crowd into makeshift settlements lacking basic infrastructure and struggle to obtain housing, documentation, social services, and jobs. "I was on my way up and displacement caught me without warning. Before displacement everything was normal. Now I cannot save, I have no investments, no steady job. I earn only enough to put some food on the table," related a 47-year-old man in El Gorrión.

Pushing carts and carrying crates slung over their shoulders, young and old in the study barrios spent long days seeking buyers for their wares in what they called *el rebusque* (the hustle). Some men had found temporary work in construction or hauling, and others drove motorcycle taxis (despite local ordinances against this form of transport). Many women worked as domestics or took in laundry, earned money as hairstylists or seamstresses, or peddled rice or coconut sweets. Some made handicrafts at home after participating in training workshops. For the majority of urban study participants, the constant reality was that jobs were difficult to find, poorly paid, and temporary. And the competition from all the other IDPs in similar circumstances was intense.

More than 80 percent of the households surveyed for this study indicated that over the past year a household member had been unemployed and unable to find a job. Low levels of literacy and education are no doubt one factor. Nearly 60 percent of the household sample, for example, had not completed primary school.

As shown in table 8.6, temporary and casual employment provides the most important income source in every study community. Just two communities, Santa María and Villa Rosa, report a substantial number of workers earning wages from regular employment. Both are high-mobility barrios on the outskirts of Cartagena, an important growth center in the country's economy.

As expected, crop sales provide a key income source in the two rural villages. They are also important in urban Santa María, however, and the reasons for this are discussed in the second comparative case study below. Otherwise, the urban households report dramatic reductions in earnings from crops and livestock over the study period, as one would expect among a population forced to abandon farming.

In Villa Blanca and El Gorrión, residents were forcibly relocated from their original IDP settlements to barrios farther away from the urban center. In both cases, the increased distance from city markets brought hardship. In El Gorrión, where mobility of the poor was high but almost no nonpoor households resided, people expressed appreciation for the reduced crime, improved public services, and housing assistance that followed their move away from Villa del Sol, an illegal and violence-ridden settlement near Ibagué's central markets. But for many, their new location made earning a living far more difficult, as they had to commute or rely on more costly and less active local markets. Explained Jairo, a 36-year-old resident of El Gorrión: "Yes, for me opportunities to work have declined. . . . When we lived in Villa del Sol near the plaza, we could buy fruit, find sales, buy things more cheaply, and sell prepared food. While from here, so far away, you can't do this. It's more difficult."

When asked in focus groups how violence affected local livelihoods, displaced people rarely mentioned the economic impact of specific incidents or periods of violence. They were more likely to respond with descriptions of the persistent and severe stigma they faced because they lived in places seen to be war zones.[14] Indeed, they directly linked their limited ability to recover to the often acute discrimination from employers, neighbors, and law enforcement, many of whom tended to associate the displaced, their places of origin, and

**TABLE 8.6**

**Current and initial sources of household income in Colombia study communities**

*percent*

| Community | Regular employment | | Temporary/casual employment | | Crop sales | | Livestock sales | | Nonagricultural household businesses | |
|---|---|---|---|---|---|---|---|---|---|---|
| | Current | Initial | Current | Initial | Current | Initial | Current | Initial | Current | Initial |
| El Gorrión | 13 | 30 | 77 | 43 | 13 | 36 | 3 | 27 | 33 | 23 |
| Santa María | 23 | 13 | 57 | 20 | 67 | 80 | 0 | 37 | 17 | 10 |
| Villa Rosa | 33 | 13 | 83 | 50 | 0 | 53 | 0 | 30 | 30 | 33 |
| San Feliz | 3 | 7 | 74 | 45 | 7 | 74 | 0 | 29 | 26 | 23 |
| Villa Blanca | 17 | 14 | 86 | 56 | 3 | 50 | 0 | 22 | 6 | 11 |
| El Mirador | 13 | 20 | 53 | 30 | 0 | 47 | 0 | 40 | 17 | 13 |
| Los Rincones | 3 | 0 | 89 | 77 | 31 | 37 | 0 | 9 | 3 | 3 |
| La Soledad | 0 | 0 | 57 | 50 | 50 | 47 | 33 | 33 | 7 | 3 |
| Total | 13 | 12 | 73 | 47 | 21 | 53 | 4 | 28 | 17 | 15 |

*Source:* Household questionnaire.

*Note:* Percentages refer to the proportion of households reporting each income source. Remaining income sources average less than 10% of total responses. "Current" refers to the year of the study, 2005; "initial" refers to the beginning of the study period, which varies by community.

the barrios where they resettled with Colombia's armed groups. Rightly or wrongly, the nondisplaced feared that contact with or proximity to displaced people might be dangerous and even life-threatening.

A 29-year-old displaced man in Villa Blanca explained, "As far as job opportunities, the displaced have black tape across their foreheads . . . That you're displaced is all that matters to them, not who you are as a person." Many urbanites also scorned the "backward" attitudes and practices of the mostly rural IDPs. As for poor people who were not IDPs, they felt that their circumstances had worsened because the influx of displaced people had intensified competition for work, housing, and services.

The experiences of the six study barrios suggest that relocation to urban centers is not enough to fuel mobility and recovery among the displaced. For a great many, adequate livelihood opportunities are simply not accessible because of their limited assets, skills, and connections, and because of the intense stigma of being associated with conflict. For some villagers as well as IDPs, the remoteness of their communities adds greatly to their hardships.

## Limited Government Functioning and Recovery Assistance

This section details study participants' perceptions of local governance and their experiences with local service providers. The high-mobility barrios generally displayed higher satisfaction with the performance of local governments, suggesting that democratic functioning at the local level played some role in the mobility patterns found. The data, however, present a mixed picture of the role of outside agencies and identify serious obstacles to service delivery and community initiatives that might improve the well-being of study participants. These obstacles include the absence of effective local government in some places and residents' limited influence over the agencies that shape their lives. Violence against community leaders, weak social capital, and social divisions within the communities have further constrained opportunities for mobility.

### Reforms and their limits

In the mid-1980s, the Colombian government initiated a series of reforms to foster more political inclusion and redress some of the socioeconomic disparities believed to fuel the armed conflict. Among the most important of these reforms were the new Constitution of 1991 and the introduction of direct mayoral elections in 1988 and direct gubernatorial elections in 1991. New legislative bodies were created at the municipal and departmental levels.

Mechanisms were put in place to reallocate public resources to traditionally marginalized populations.

Unfortunately, these efforts were undermined in three ways. First, the reforms encouraged political participation but did not offer protection for the physical safety of local officials, movement activists, and community leaders seeking substantive change. Members of these groups are overrepresented in statistics on victims of political violence (Gutiérrez Sanin and Ramírez Rueda 2004). In 2002 alone, for instance, 184 Colombian trade union members were murdered, and a similar number received death threats (ICG 2003, 7). Second, in some conflict regions the reforms emanating from Bogotá helped galvanize support among agribusiness elites for reactionary violence. Virulent opposition to the electoral gains of leftist political parties, and to the unprecedented resource rights granted to indigenous and Afro-Colombian communities by the new Constitution, contributed to an increase in material and political support for paramilitary violence in some localities (Oslender 2007). Finally, mechanisms designed to decentralize governance and redirect state resources to the local level also increased violence and instability as armed actors often intensified their efforts to influence municipal officials and capture public procurements to finance their activities (Siegle and O'Mahoney 2006). In some places, agents of illegal armies actually became elected officials.

The Colombian government's efforts to address the root causes of violent conflict extended beyond political reform to include investment in social programs. Legislation passed in 1993 created a nationwide health insurance program and a system (known as SISBEN) for better targeting social assistance. Meanwhile, public investments during the 1990s greatly expanded access to electricity, potable water, and sewerage. These efforts improved basic social services and reduced poverty somewhat, but in rural areas where conflict is most acute, the gains were less impressive. In 1999 nearly 80 percent of the rural population was poor compared to 55 percent in urban areas (World Bank 2002, 12). Enrollment in primary school of children ages 6 to 11 was 88 percent nationally in 2001, but only 70 percent in rural areas. Enrollment in secondary education plummets to less than 15 percent for the rural school-age population (Vélez 2003, 611–13). Ibáñez and Moya (2007, 34) found the mean years of education for IDP household heads to be less than six years, while the urban sample of household heads in this study reported four years. Among rural families facing acute danger, disrupted livelihoods, and the prospect that their offspring will be inducted into an illegal armed group, urban-rural disparities in education and basic services are an additional reason to flee to cities. It is important to stress, however, that this study suggests that most IDP migration is due to the push of violence rather than the pull of development factors (see also Engel and Ibáñez 2007).

During the study period, the government established a legal and institutional framework to provide rights and services to IDPs (Law 375, 1997). Government programs support IDP recovery through provision of housing and income-generation initiatives as well as education and health care; however, this study suggests that access to these programs is very uneven. In addition, many grassroots, national, and international organizations are engaged in the effort to respond to the humanitarian needs of Colombia's large IDP population. Local perceptions about the effectiveness and functioning of some of these programs are examined below.

## Mixed reviews for local governments

Eighty percent of the household sample for this study believed that the local elections most recently held in their locality were clean, and more than 60 percent said they had voted. Barrio focus groups praised the municipal governments of Cartagena and Ibagué, which had supplied substantial housing assistance to the displaced, and three agencies of the national government, Red de Solidaridad, Defensoría del Pueblo, and Bienestar Familiar, which provided relief, legal aid, and social services, respectively. Despite these positive comments, people generally perceived that they had little influence over local politics, and they generally rated the performance of elected officials and bureaucrats as low. Villagers in La Soledad and Los Rincones were emphatic about their neglect by the government, and barrio residents frequently lamented the government's weak presence in their communities.

Men and women throughout the study acknowledged changes in the workings of local democracy over the past decade, but they were divided over whether these changes were having a positive or negative impact on their communities. Table 8.7 reveals that in communities with higher MPI, there was a perception that cooperation between local leaders and elected representatives had improved. And in the two barrios with the highest MPI, focus groups reported that it had become easier for ordinary citizens to engage with their local government.

Of the four high-mobility barrios, three received significant assistance from their city government. El Gorrión, the barrio with the highest MPI, received the most extensive support: the city of Ibagué donated lots with deeds, provided construction supplies, and paved the streets for some 800 residents. The barrio of Villa Rosa was constructed by families chosen in a lottery administered by the municipal government of Cartagena in concert with a Swiss foundation and a local nonprofit partner, Fundación Apoyar. Located on the distant outskirts of Cartagena, Santa María was the barrio with the third-highest MPI, but it did not receive comparable outside assistance. Instead, Santa María enjoyed a significantly higher level of community organization, an asset that is discussed later in the chapter. The barrio ranking fourth in MPI, San Feliz, received support from the municipal government in the form of road construction and electricity.

Lower on the MPI scale are the two villages, which received little government aid, but the village that fared better was located near a highway that the national government had paved. El Mirador, the oldest barrio in the study, had suffered several years of neglect by the city of Pasto at the time of the study and had the lowest mobility. The barrio of Villa Blanca also had low MPI but was a new development constructed by the city of Floridablanca. It is possible that the timing of the study—immediately after residents had been relocated from another barrio into their homes—explains the divergent result. Construction had not yet been completed in 2005.

In addition to variations among the study communities in their perceptions of local government performance, there were also variations in

**TABLE 8.7**
**Perceptions on the functioning of local democracy in Colombia study communities**

| Community | Cooperation among community leaders/ council and elected leader | | Trend in access to local government |
|---|---|---|---|
| | Current | Initial | |
| *High-mobility barrios* | | | |
| El Gorrión | Yes | Yes | Increased |
| Villa Rosa | Yes | No | Increased |
| Santa María | Yes | No | Decreased |
| San Feliz | No | No | Same |
| *Low-mobility barrios* | | | |
| Villa Blanca | No | No | Decreased |
| El Mirador | No | Yes | Decreased |
| *Villages* | | | |
| Los Rincones | Yes | Yes | Decreased |
| La Soledad | No | No | Increased |

*Source:* Local key informants (cooperation among leaders) and focus groups (trend in access).

perceptions at the household level. In general, households that had never known poverty had a brighter view. From the household questionnaire, we find a significant contrast between the mobility group that we classify as never poor and the respondents in the other three categories—the movers (who were poor initially but moved out of poverty), the fallers (who fell into poverty), and the chronic poor (who had known only poverty). The median responses to the questionnaire reveal that the never poor mostly perceived government to act on behalf of *all* people, while the movers, fallers, and chronic poor responded that their government was run by a few big interests looking out for themselves. Similarly, the never poor were somewhat satisfied with the way that democracy works in their local government, while the other mobility groups reported being somewhat dissatisfied. The never poor felt that few government officials engaged in bribery and corruption in the country, while the rest felt that most government officials did.

The household survey included a question about whether public and NGO authorities generally acted in the public interest rather than in their own self-interest (figure 8.3). Local politicians and government officials at the municipal and departmental levels received the lowest ratings: only 19 percent and 22 percent, respectively, of respondents indicated that these groups acted in the interest of everyone. "They disappear," scoffed a resident of El Mirador. "You hear them promising so many things on the TV and radio, and after the election, it's goodbye. You never see them around here again." Similar views of officialdom were voiced throughout the study communities. Health care providers and teachers scored much higher, however. NGO staff ranked close to community leaders, with ratings about evenly split for both. The following sections look in more depth at people's views of some of these actors.

### Community assistance: Appreciated but inadequate and unaccountable

People in all the communities voiced great appreciation for the aid they had received, though outside support to the two rural communities lasted only a few months. In the urban barrios, many residents were beneficiaries of long-term housing assistance, food aid, vocational training, and counseling services from multiple sources. The donors that people cited included municipal governments (Cartagena and Ibagué); the Catholic Church (Pastoral Social); agencies of the national government (Red de Solidaridad, Defensoría del Pueblo, and Bienestar Familiar); the U.S. government (U.S. Agency for International Development); the United Nations; the Red Cross; and local and foreign NGOs.

**FIGURE 8.3**

**Confidence ratings in public authorities and NGOs, Colombia study communities**

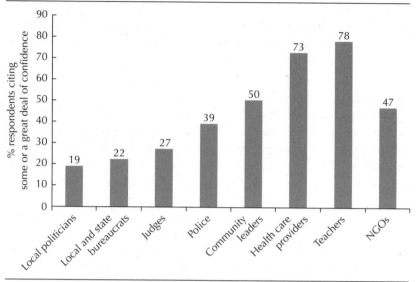

*Source:* Household questionnaire.

Three forms of aid, material and nonmaterial, mattered most to study participants. First, many were extremely thankful to have a solid roof over their heads (box 8.1). This was particularly true of those who had fled their homes in terror, perhaps on foot and carrying children, and of those who had spent months in miserable temporary housing made of materials such as plastic sheeting that failed to keep the rain out. At the time of the study, many urban participants were living in newly constructed homes on donated or invaded lots. Second, urban residents widely praised the psychological and social support services they had received, saying these had helped them cope with past traumas and had improved interpersonal relations in their families and neighborhoods. Third, they made special mention of the agencies that assisted them in filing legal and human rights claims, attributing concrete gains to such advocacy and legal services.

While expressing appreciation for the aid they received, participants also described circumstances in which they were powerless to protect or improve their well-being. By definition, most of the displaced people had lost homes and property. Many had also endured the murder or disappearance of loved ones and had personally suffered abuses such as extortion, death threats, or assault. In the face of these horrific circumstances, participants often described frustrating experiences with outside agencies that failed to provide services or provided them unfairly.

In rural La Soledad and Los Rincones, residents endured periods in which armed combat raged near their homes and fields, but no agency offered them protection or safe haven. Villagers reported that after the intense fighting subsided, the relief assistance they received was of very short duration, and their villages were subsequently abandoned by state and nongovernmental agencies alike.

In all eight locations, people cited the lack of law enforcement as a factor contributing to the violence in their community. More than 60 percent of households surveyed felt that authorities would not protect them effectively or would not protect them at all if someone tried to make them leave their land or property. In Los Rincones, people reported abusive treatment by the national army. There were also reports of street vendors suffering police harassment, of shop owners being forced to pay bribes to police to keep businesses running, and of policemen stealing from members of the community.

In El Gorrión, recipients of housing assistance felt exploited by the obligations they had incurred to a financial institution. In addition, they asserted that aid agencies had created deep divisions in their community, and they reported that a university-affiliated NGO was poorly managed and had misappropriated funds earmarked for their community. There and in other barrios, residents also expressed frustration over the emphasis on training programs when what they really needed was money and loans "to survive" or to help them find jobs or run their own businesses.

In urban areas, poor performance and lack of accountability by private contractors and firms also caused hardship and sometimes created divisions among community members. In Villa Blanca, a contractor delivered new housing units unfinished and then abandoned the project, leaving residents without recourse. In San Feliz, residents described a local electric company's unfair business practices and lack of transparency. They said the company pays a resident of the barrio to report on how many light bulbs and appliances his neighbors' households are using each month, and then the company sends a single bill to the entire community. If some households fail to pay their share, the electric company punishes the entire community by suspending service, and the company also refuses to supply records of usage or payments. The situation created great tension between the community and the contractor as well as between the paying and nonpaying community members.

**BOX 8.1**
**Partial recovery in Villa Rosa: Alicia's story**

---

Alicia is a 35-year-old married mother of three with one grandson. Her experience underscores the importance of governmental and NGO assistance to families in the wake of displacement. Yet although this support was combined with Alicia's own skills, creativity, and persistence, the family has been unable to recover the assets, earnings, and security they had before being displaced.

Alicia and her husband owned a small general store in a village in Caquetá in 1998. They had arrived there four years earlier, and prospered for a time. But insurgents stepped up their presence in the area during a campaign to take Florencia, the capital of Caquetá. They ordered local peasants out, sealed off the town, and obliged Alicia and her husband to supply them with food and clothes. Alicia recalled, "Out there the law is whatever they [the guerrillas] say. . . . Things got worse. We no longer had our little store because they took it over, but we still had all of our debts. Then the threats started. They sent us letters saying, 'Move out or we'll get you.' And that's how we came to be displaced."

The family was forced to leave behind their business, the home they owned, and all their belongings except what they could carry. They went to Cartagena. "Thank God we had relatives who would take us in. Otherwise we would have ended up like some displaced people do, living under a bridge or in the street," said Alicia. They thought that Cartagena's booming tourist sector would provide opportunities, but "it didn't turn out that way."

Alicia considers displacement to be the worst event of her life. She and her husband were affected "by the fear that we carry inside us. We thought that those people might come after us." Displacement was even more traumatic for her children, who had to begin working and street peddling in Cartagena to help the family survive. Remarkably, Alicia reports that the adversity strengthened the bonds of her close-knit family.

For the first three months in Cartagena, the family slept on the floor in the home of Alicia's cousin in Santa María. They received no formal assistance during that period because they had no information about where to go or how to sign up. Eventually they obtained some mattresses and other items from the Red Cross and food assistance from the city government and from World Food Aid. Later that year, the family invaded a nearby lot and built a flimsy structure known as a *rancho*, with plastic sheeting as a roof. Her husband sold fish for a while and then found a job in a store, but neither income lasted long.

Alicia and her family lived in the Santa María rancho for almost five years, until they were forcibly removed by police in 2003. After the eviction, however, came the best thing to happen in her life: the family was selected for resettlement in a new housing project in Villa Rosa. The city donated and deeded the lots, Fundación Apoyar supplied construction materials, and Alicia and her family built their new home.

Obtaining housing may have been the result of luck, but other gains in Alicia's life point to her resourcefulness. She taught her children how to survive hard times and proudly describes preparing fried foods for her children to sell on the street just as her own mother did. Alicia regrets having had to leave school after the sixth grade, but she has managed to get her children into private schools, with scholarships, in Cartagena. She says her self-confidence has grown in the face of adversity: "I've managed to accomplish things I never would have dreamed of doing, such as walk into an office and fight for my rights."

In addition to the housing assistance, Alicia credits vocational programs with helping her move forward. She learned how to cook professionally in a food service training program run by SENA, a national government agency, and the Fundación Apoyar, and she put her new skills to work when she was elected head of a community kitchen in the barrio. But she lost her position when funding for the program ended. Alicia also completed courses in ceramics and small business administration provided by SENA and the Red de Solidaridad Social. She yearns for the opportunity to use her skills and energy either in a small business or working in a hotel kitchen.

Life remains difficult. Alicia opened a small store and the family gets by on the meager returns from this business, as her husband is unemployed. "I rely on loans to run the store," she reports, "and when I applied for a bank loan they turned me down because we live in Villa Rosa."

Asked if she participates in local organizations, Alicia explains, "No, I don't belong to any community groups, but we have been trying to form one. We knocked on doors but didn't get any support. The agencies that brought in the vocational training told us they'd provide support for the community to get organized, but they haven't been back . . . I'd like to [join an association] as a way of helping myself and helping others, and also to make the government take our existence into account." Alicia adds that she collaborates informally with two neighborhood women who also run small street vending businesses. The local director of the Red de Solidaridad Social also helps when he can. "Right now we're applying for a jobs program with SENA. What we're fighting for is that the displaced get job opportunities without so much red tape. The government says it's helping the displaced but that is false."

Describing herself as not the kind of person to remain "stuck," Alicia says that what she needs most is gainful employment. "In Villa Rosa my life is neither so good nor so bad. I thank God that at least we have housing. Things are not so good because one needs a bit of seed capital to work with in order to be able to live with dignity, and for one's children to have dignified lives. . . . But I don't feel too bad because at least I have somewhere to live and my children are studying."

Bearing out such reports from participants, a study of resettlement programs in Colombia found that while strong municipal governments can bring important benefits, the programs are generally characterized by "insufficient and inconsistent funding (unfulfilled promises), land speculation and opportunistic behavior among bureaucrats, and limited assistance or protection throughout the reintegration period" (Muggah 2000, 145).

## Community Activism and Cohesion under Siege

A vast literature spanning more than half a century speaks to the importance of neighborhood associations in bringing concrete benefits to poor urban settlements in Latin America and other developing regions. These local networks are vital both for channeling demands to government authorities and other external partners and for catalyzing self-help efforts.[15] People repeatedly praised local leaders and groups that fought for the resettlement barrios. Nevertheless, the continued presence of political conflict had a profoundly damaging effect on the functioning of local collective action and on social cohesion—an important reason why these barrios did not provide better opportunities for mobility.

### Selective violence in the barrios

Five of the study communities experienced the removal of their local community leaders, three by assassination. In some cases the new leader who took over was described as an "outsider," and the community organization was then seen to lose its legitimacy, autonomy, and effectiveness.[16] In other instances the community organizations simply ceased to function because no one dared fill the vacuum. In either case, displaced people felt greatly deprived and perceived the loss of their leaders and independent organizations as even more damaging to their community's well-being than the effects of violence on the local economy.

The development of the Colombian IDP barrios appears to follow a life cycle that initially parallels that of other squatter settlements in Latin America—in Lima, Mexico City, Rio de Janeiro, Santiago, and elsewhere—and then departs sharply as local leadership and cohesion are shattered by the political violence. Squatter communities typically face many challenges in the initial years as they struggle to secure legal status, housing, and services, but solidarity is high. Grassroots leaders and groups often play pivotal roles in community development in this early period. As new squatter settlements become consolidated, the autonomy, solidarity, and membership of neighborhood associations are often weakened by diverse pressures, especially internal competition among rival leaders and co-optation of leaders by political parties seeking votes. Fisher (1984) argues that the ebbing of collective action may also reflect a graduation from the more confrontational tactics that were necessary during the hazardous period of land invasions. With consolidation, neighborhood associations can deploy less risky strategies to promote educational and economic activities, as did the Co-Agro Peasant Association described below. Or they may help settle local disputes, organize neighborhood crime prevention activities, or work directly with contractors to negotiate new services or improvements to existing ones.

Community organizations carried out all these local initiatives in the Colombian IDP barrios we studied. But understandably, they seemed to flounder when local leaders were assassinated or forcibly removed. It appears that even the limited power and resources available to these local leaders make them targets. Sanchez and del Mar Palau (2006) found that decentralization triggered heightened violence against local politicians in areas of Colombia where illegal armed groups were active after the mid-1990s.

In Villa Rosa, which lies 15 kilometers from the center of Cartagena, the community leadership split into two factions in 2003. Residents explained that the more powerful members of the council were associated with the paramilitaries and the others with the guerrillas. They described an ongoing campaign of intimidation; a few activists were forced from their posts, and others labeled as sympathetic to the guerrillas had to flee the barrio altogether. Former activists say they are now too fearful to get involved in community activities. People feel they have nowhere to turn if problems arise. The World Food Program and other programs ceased operating in Villa Rosa because of this split, and people express anxiety about community development programs that are passing them by.

In Santa María, the local leader of the land invasion was assassinated in 1996, and two other community leaders were killed in 2003. As described in box 8.2 on page 234, Santa María's local peasant group, which was seeking title to the plots of land its members cultivate, was the target of murder, rape, and arson orchestrated by the landowners. In both Villa Rosa and Santa María, community activists were named in death threats distributed in pamphlets or posted around the barrio. Also in 2003, the local council in El Gorrión split in two after the murder of Don Jorge, the barrio's revered community leader who had led the land invasion. Don Jorge's successor to head the council received death threats and then disappeared.

In San Feliz, located in the northern city of Sincelejo near the Atlantic coast, residents were too nervous to assemble a focus group on the topic of conflict, but a small group did agree to meet downtown, outside the neighborhood. A JAC president and a local priest actively involved in community development had both been forced to leave the barrio, but people say they do not know why. Nor do they dare inquire about the reasons, fearing retaliation. When probed on the presence of local conflict, the focus group chose to talk about less sensitive topics such as disputes with their electricity and water providers. In a private conversation, however, a woman confided that paramilitaries had been active in the area since 2002.

Local leaders in the rural study villages were also targets of violence. In La Soledad, civic associations ceased to meet for the three years that FARC guerrillas and the national army engaged in combat nearby. In Los Rincones, the president of the JAC was assassinated. Los Rincones residents said the municipality had given up appointing inspectors to their village after a series of appointees had fled their post in fear. For several years, paramilitaries obliged community leaders in Los Rincones to do their bidding. A Los Rincones councilwoman's account of being forced to hang Christmas decorations may seem innocuous, but her description of the experience conveyed her impotence and anguish.

## Low social capital

A striking finding from the Colombia data is the exceptionally low level of household membership in organizations of any kind. "No, not one, not a single group," reported a poor 52-year-old woman from Villa Blanca when asked whether she belongs to any local organizations. "You know for this you have to have a good mind, know how to talk, and have been educated." Overall, 0.69 is the average number of associations that a household in the sample belongs to (figure 8.4). This pattern, moreover, seems to extend beyond the communities of the displaced. Polanía Reyes (2005) found average memberships in voluntary organizations to be 0.64 in a representative sample of four major Colombian cities.[17]

Social capital refers to the norms and networks that enable collective action, and there is growing evidence of its importance to conflict mediation and peace (Barron, Smith, and Woolcock 2004; Varshney 2003). A hopeful sign from the study is that participation in community organizations appears to be on the rise. While at the beginning of the study period only 18 percent of the household sample belonged to at least one organization, a decade later 46 percent did. Some of this growth is due to the spread of community housing organizations for the displaced.

Civic engagement is also very weak, although there seem to be strong urban-rural differences. Participants in the six barrios widely reported that

**FIGURE 8.4**

**Average household membership in organizations, Colombia study communities**

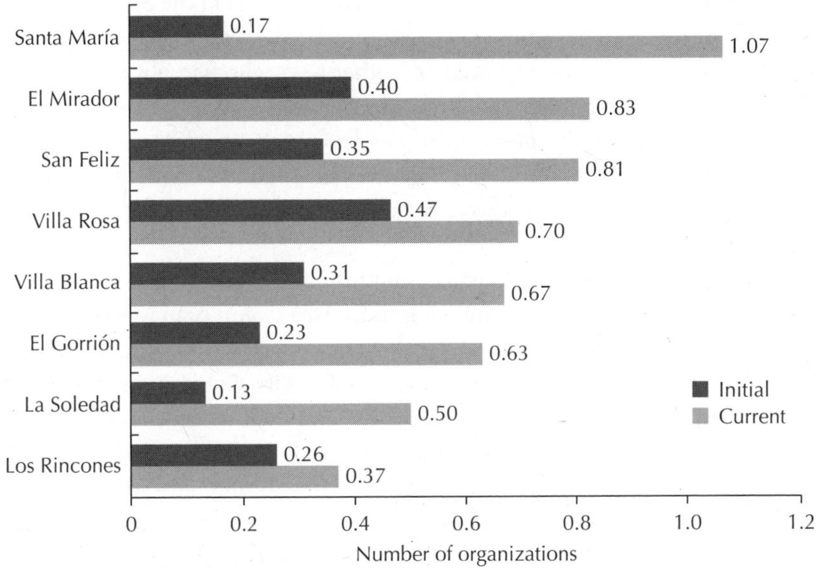

Santa María    0.17    1.07

El Mirador    0.40    0.83

San Feliz    0.35    0.81

Villa Rosa    0.47    0.70

Villa Blanca    0.31    0.67

El Gorrión    0.23    0.63

La Soledad    0.13    0.50

Los Rincones    0.26    0.37

■ Initial
■ Current

0    0.2    0.4    0.6    0.8    1.0    1.2

Number of organizations

*Source:* Household questionnaire.

they do not feel that residents participate meaningfully in decisions about important community affairs. Some in the study explained that while people may attend community activities, they do not have a voice. Villagers, by contrast, reported that they do have a say in local decisions.

## Fractured social cohesion

Diverse factors undermined social cohesion among the displaced, with pervasive organized violence being particularly important. High crime rates made it unsafe for residents to visit neighbors and attend meetings. Moreover, the fact that some barrio residents committed crimes in their own neighborhoods diminished community trust. When surveyed about trust, 83 percent of respondents said that you cannot be too careful in dealing with people; 74 percent thought levels of trust had not changed over the study period.

Divisions related to displacement status, regional origins, and ethnicity also weakened the social fabric. Barrio residents commented that because their neighbors hailed from many different regions and cultures, it was more difficult for everyone to organize and act collectively. According to Constanza of El Gorrión, for instance, "Here people are from all over Colombia—Boyacá, the coast, Putumayo . . . We try [to get along], but we don't know who is who. Where I'm from, we were very united, but here we don't know each other."

People reported divisions between IDPs who possessed a government ID card designating them as displaced and other IDPs who had not managed to acquire one. Also reported were divisions between victims of displacement and people who were homeless for other reasons. Key informants acknowledged some form of social group differences in all but one of the study communities, and such divisions were seen to contribute to violence in half of the study communities.

With respect to ethnic divisions, the number of survey households for this study that self-reported as indigenous or Afro-Colombian was very small (7 and 22 households, respectively). But 90 percent of these households were in the chronic poor mobility group. Nationally, Afro-Colombian and indigenous people represent about a fifth of all IDPs, even though they make up less than 14 percent of the country's population (World Bank, forthcoming). Ethnic discrimination and mistreatment of Afro-Colombians and members of Colombia's indigenous groups do exist, but a mestizo or light-skinned campesino just arriving from a remote conflict area is also likely to suffer marginalization or abuse. The more reliable social cleavage is that whiter, more European-looking Colombians are less likely to reside in slums of any type, even if they have been victims of violence or displacement, because they more often have the resources to go elsewhere.

Rather than ethnic divisions, the qualitative evidence emphasizes divisions between displaced and nondisplaced people, between new arrivals in the city and those with long residence, and between the displaced and homeless populations. External agencies, moreover, seem to contribute to these differences. "There are conflicts between the displaced and the homeless. There are always conflicts because of the aid they [the displaced] receive. Most of the institutional help is for the displaced and just a little for the homeless," related a 32-year-old woman.

Overall, the study found diverse economic, political, and social obstacles to recovery among both IDPs and conflict-affected villagers. Pervasive insecurity ensures weak access to markets, poor governance, and fragile social capital; at the same time, these deficiencies contribute to persistent insecurity. The result is an opportunity structure that severely constrains both individual initiatives to escape poverty and collective efforts to support more prosperous communities. A look at two urban barrios reveals these processes in greater depth.

# People Pulled Together and Apart: Santa María and El Mirador

Santa María is a large urban settlement of 40,000 located in metropolitan Cartagena, a port city that attracts tourists and businesses from around the world. On the other side of the country is El Mirador, a 33-year-old barrio of 4,000 in Pasto, a city in the Andes near the border with Ecuador. Both communities enjoyed better infrastructure and services than were present in the other study barrios.[18] Both also struggled with waves of IDP arrivals and with violence and crime over the study period. Despite these similarities, the mobility outcomes for the two barrios differed dramatically, with Santa María showing greater movement out of poverty (figure 8.5).

An important point of contrast between the two communities is that the Santa María residents who participated in the focus groups were all members of the Co-Agro Peasant Association.[19] The study period in Santa María dated from 1998, the year when many people had arrived impoverished in the barrio and begun their active engagement with this dynamic community organization. In contrast, El Mirador, founded in 1971, was the only study barrio not overwhelmingly populated by newly arriving and struggling IDPs, and the socioeconomic status of its households was more heterogeneous.[20] Why didn't these advantages help El Mirador be more resilient?

### Santa María: A tale of collective mobility

Santa María received thousands of IDPs in 1997 when paramilitary groups gained ascendancy over the two leftist guerrilla groups, the ELN and FARC, which had been active in the department of Bolívar and in neighboring departments. Another massive round of displacements occurred in 2002, when government forces tried to gain control of strategic and economic zones in the department. The second wave of violence coincided with a period of "social cleansing" murders by armed actors within Santa María itself. In the words of 56-year-old Nelly, "countless bodies appeared in the streets." A few people provided a more abstract view of the period as one in which different armed groups eliminated adversaries and vied for control. Death notices were hung on lampposts and several community leaders were assassinated. Among the victims were leaders of the 1996 land invasion of Santa María. People said that conditions had improved since 2004, but criminal homicide and political assassinations still occurred.

**FIGURE 8.5**
**Mobility outcomes in Santa María and El Mirador, Colombia**

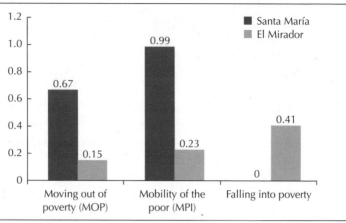

*Source:* Focus group discussions.

In the Santa María focus groups, perceptions about the effects of violence and crime on local livelihoods split along gender lines. The men's focus group portrayed the violence as largely in the past, and men felt the neighborhood did not deserve its bad reputation. As for hurting local livelihoods, a 56-year-old man argued, "Nah, the local economy stays the same, because if I sell avocados [and a violent incident occurs], I'm still going to keep selling avocados." In the women's focus group, however, participants expressed more fear. "You're always very nervous. Somebody gets killed, or two or three people." The women pointed out that just days earlier a young motorcycle taxi driver had been seized on the highway and was not seen again. Other women reported waves of "social cleansing" killings, murders of community leaders, muggings, theft, family violence, and attacks on women.

The women's focus group also contradicted the men's view that violence did not affect local commerce, arguing that people were reluctant to shop where murders had occurred. One woman described the influence of superstition and another told of shopkeepers receiving 24 hours' notice to leave the barrio. Overall, though, it was reported that the local economy rebounded quickly because another shop would open soon after one closed. Despite the crime, most stores stayed open late.

Nor did the violence seem to interfere with a steady pace of community improvements. "Every day we're more prosperous," said a 62-year-old male resident of Santa María. "Now they're going to pave the streets. Before, we didn't have buses. There's water, electricity, better housing, and new projects are coming." Residents credited the local government and the arrival of basic services, including schools and a health clinic, with greatly improving their lives.

In addition, people believed that joining the Co-Agro Peasant Association had made a real difference to their well-being. The group grew from 30 members in 1995 to 200 a decade later. Members enjoyed access to farm plots of up to 2 hectares in a nearby farming area of 89 hectares, and 50 members had parcels elsewhere. They grew corn, cassava, rice, and ñame (a tuber), and some had erected ranchos, small shacks, on their parcels for cooking meals and storing tools. A road was built to the farming area in 1999, but there were no buses from the barrio or downtown Cartagena. Nor did the farming area have irrigation, farm machinery, or basic services.

The association held periodic meetings and an annual assembly. Members managed their individual parcels autonomously, but they collaborated by sharing labor, exchanging produce, helping each other during times of illness, and petitioning together for legal title to their parcels. Co-Agro was also a major conduit for aid from the Colombian government, which had supported a food pantry and community kitchen, health brigades, family planning and prenatal nutrition services, and agricultural extension programs.

While most of Co-Agro's members were men, its president was a woman and very highly regarded. She reported that about half of Co-Agro's members relied on sales of their crops as their principal source of income. She noted that members were better off than many other Santa María residents: they earned income from their harvests, and their households benefited from access to fresh food. One man, comparing Co-Agro members to his neighbors who are not members, said, "We are super well off compared to them."

Many Co-Agro farmers supplemented their farming with informal trading or sporadic work in construction or hauling. A few ran small shops or businesses. Many wives also contributed income, typically by peddling baked sweets or doing domestic work for hire. Men in focus groups expressed great frustration at the low earnings from the work available locally and the willingness of others to work for miserable wages.

A key goal for Co-Agro was to increase crop output, but problems of drought, pests, and lack of irrigation made it difficult to scale up. The most severe constraint was the lack of land titles (box 8.2).[21] Uncertain tenure status impeded members' access to credit and programs, which in turn prevented them from implementing projects such as aquaculture. Members nonetheless said that Co-Agro was succeeding thanks to the unity and perseverance of its members. As one put it, "Even though we only have machetes—we have no tractors or machinery—oh, well, at least we have aspirations."

**BOX 8.2**
**Violence against Co-Agro**

---

"There are problems with some people who want to get us out of here," acknowledges a 66-year-old member of the Co-Agro Peasant Association. "Now some alleged owners have appeared and they won't let us work in peace," reports another member. "They haven't stopped us from farming, but they tell us 'we'll get you out tomorrow' and 'we're going to burn your houses to the ground.'"

Co-Agro has been the target of repeated violence. In 2001 a young Co-Agro member was murdered on his plot of land, his wife was raped, and their dwelling was burned to the ground. According to Co-Agro's president, the perpetrator was a resident of Santa María hired to carry out the crime. When she confronted him he confessed, but he was not brought to justice. In 2006 there were two more arson attacks on Co-Agro ranchos.

Co-Agro's leaders said neither the attacks nor the threats had deterred them, but they felt the impact nonetheless. All but four families did not live on their parcels, partly because they could not afford to build a rancho and partly out of fear of being killed. According to one of the association's founding members, "Some folks have stopped coming to meetings . . . They are afraid, they think that there could be a massacre here, and since they are coming from areas with terrible violence they don't want to go through anything like that again."

---

## El Mirador: Heightened competition on many fronts

The displaced population surged in El Mirador in 2000 when combat between guerrilla and government forces intensified in the surrounding countryside. As in Santa María, there was a period of "social cleansing" in El Mirador, and some residents credited the killings with bringing a temporary reduction in gang violence, armed robbery, and other crime. Unlike in Santa María, however, focus groups cited steadily worsening trends in crime and violence after the assassination wave, with rival youth gangs perceived as the most acute problem.

People described roving gangs with a dozen or more members, some as young as 11 and many addicted to drugs. "One can't go out because they'll rob you." Taxi drivers were said to refuse to enter the barrio at night. Mothers said they did not let their children go anywhere unaccompanied for fear that they would be robbed or beaten. A man reported that children leaving school were routinely threatened and extorted. A woman described a brutal incident in which "they tied up an old man like a cow and stripped him of everything, including his shoes."

As a result, local shop owners in El Mirador installed security gates and closed earlier. But focus group participants generally perceived the rise in criminality as a consequence rather than a cause of economic decline. A 68-year-old woman named Gabriela said, "The violence is partly due to the unemployment situation. It's that people have no money and there are no jobs. . . . Many of them [the gang members] have a wife and children. They are suffering and that's why they make others suffer." Rosario, 36, expressed a similar opinion: "There are lots of young people that would like to work, but they don't have jobs, so they rob."

Residents also linked local gang activity to external drug trafficking organizations, citing drug pushing by gang members and crimes committed by addicts to feed their habits. It was often noted that youths in El Mirador were recruited to work in regions where drug crops were cultivated, and the life stories recorded in this barrio revealed that many displaced people had spent part of their lives in areas where coca leaves or opium poppies were grown.

According to a 56-year-old male resident of El Mirador, "Things used to be better in this neighborhood. People had gardens where they grew corn, they kept hens. There were brick factories . . . People lived better when there were fewer people here. It started getting crowded and then came the crime." Another older man also associated his increased hardships with the arrival of IDPs: "Outsiders have come in, the displaced. Those of us who more or less got by as street peddlers used to make 8,000 or 10,000 pesos a day. Now we're lucky to make 2,000 pesos."

Economic changes were also identified as causes of the barrio's rising hardships. Focus groups cited the opening of a large department store and a supermarket. According to one man, "It's unfair competition. . . . They put in a supermarket and offer consumers lower prices . . . The small retailer cannot offer prices like that." Study participants also lamented the disappearance of jobs due to factory closings. "Before, there was a lot of industry. Ten years ago we had Coca-Cola, Bavaria, Postobón [beverage manufacturers], and they generated plenty of jobs. Not anymore," observed a 59-year-old man. Others mentioned additional factory closings, while a 40-year-old woman perceived a more generalized decline: "I believe things have changed a lot as far as jobs, and also in the way workers are treated."

It was mentioned that women had more livelihood options, often because they were more willing to engage in lower-status and lower-paying jobs such as domestic work, taking in washing, and vending foods on the street. "Here the only jobs to be found are for women," commented a man. People also observed the high proportion of female-headed households among El Mirador's IDPs. Focus groups and life stories from the barrio described wives who migrated to El Mirador after losing their spouses to the conflict, mothers whose sons had gone to work in coca fields or other parts unknown, marriages that had collapsed under the strain of long-term separations, and wives who worried constantly about the safety of husbands who had remained behind to tend farms in violent areas. Among the El Mirador women who recounted their life stories, those who had lived in coca-growing areas recalled those periods as ones of asset acquisition and prosperity.

With few options locally for earning income, both newly arrived and longtime residents spoke of financial hardships in El Mirador. A displaced woman explained, "Nowadays I get by doing laundry and selling any little thing. I buy and resell toothpaste, soap, corn. Washing clothes I get paid between 1,500 and 2,000 pesos, depending on how dirty they are. With that I earn enough for no more than a little soup. Right now I'm doing well if I earn 5,000 or 6,000 pesos a day." A 76-year-old woman described grim circumstances in her household. "They pay my daughter 5,000 pesos per day for cooking. My son finds what he can out on the streets . . . Paying 50,000 pesos a month for rent, sometimes we eat and sometimes we don't."

IDPs across the study barrios reported difficulty paying for food and utilities, but in El Mirador these hardships were compounded dramatically by a lack of affordable housing. In the other barrios, which were some distance from an urban center, many families had managed to obtain housing lots through programs, or they could occupy lots illegally or rent them for nominal fees. In contrast, poor IDPs who sought refuge in El Mirador had few options but to pay costly rent. Purchasing lots was not possible because of their high costs.

Another factor that disadvantaged residents of this barrio was the demise of older organizations and the low level of organization among IDPs. In the mid-1990s, community activists led by the local JAC got the streets paved and a school built. But in recent years the JAC has not been very active. Many in the barrio had no knowledge of any community organizations at all, though there were several for the displaced that operated locally and dispensed aid. There were also indications that the beneficiaries of the aid were perhaps not the neediest among El Mirador's displaced residents.

## Understanding differences in barrio mobility

In the case of high-mobility Santa María, it is reasonable to expect that its relative proximity to Cartagena's diverse and active economy afforded opportunities not found in Pasto. Regular wage employment was much more prevalent in Santa María than in El Mirador (table 8.6). Moreover, crop sales by members of Co-Agro provided crucial income in Santa María that was entirely absent in El Mirador, and thus better mobility in the former barrio can be at least partly attributed to the presence of a strong community organization. This organization also served as a valuable conduit for government and NGO assistance. When asked about future trends in prosperity, a Co-Agro member replied, "It has to be three times better, because more and more aid programs are arriving."

In low-mobility El Mirador, residents blamed a decade of deterioration on intense competition for jobs and on violent crime by local youth gangs. Compared to Santa María, El Mirador suffered more harmful effects related to Colombia's illegal drug economy. People also frequently stated that life was difficult because they needed cash for purchasing food and basic services *and* paying high rents—but they could earn almost no cash income. Moreover, El Mirador's long-standing community associations experienced decline, and organization among IDPs was weak. Residents held out few hopes that their community would improve in the future unless the government got involved.

## What Makes for Community Resilience and Recovery?

In the two case studies and other findings presented above, three factors seem to play important roles in mobility processes, but their contributions to wider poverty escapes are heavily constrained by the broader conflict context.

First, a community's proximity to active markets can support mobility, but even in the communities near markets, adequate livelihood opportunities were still not accessible to a large share of men and women in this study. Root causes included severe problems of violence, the stigma of displacement and conflict, and the scarce financial, physical, human, and social assets in the communities.

Second, people associate the prosperity of their communities with the presence of public services and programs, including humanitarian relief and social assistance, but these currently seem insufficient for helping poor people escape poverty. It is encouraging that the government's recently launched Juntos program, which seeks to move 1.5 million poor and 350,000 displaced families out of poverty, is designed to address problems of access to and effectiveness of assistance programs.[22]

Three, violence directly undermines local collective action and social cohesion, but when community organizations can retain their leaders and their autonomy, they can serve as important agents of self-help efforts. They may also provide delivery of services and access to economic opportunities.

These findings point to four areas for policy attention. First and fore-most, law and order for *all* Colombians must be paramount. An important finding from this study is that there was no clear dividing line in most of the barrios between political violence and other types of local mayhem. Police stations were widely seen as unhelpful, while community efforts to resist vio-lence appear largely ineffective. Much higher priority needs to be placed on strengthening local institutional capacities for the prevention of crime and violence. As long as citizens and community leaders are in physical jeopardy, there will be less progress in the areas of economic opportunities, effective local governance and services, and collective action.

Second, the concentration of humanitarian and development resources on urban sectors needs to be reconsidered. The study villages received a few recov-ery schemes in the immediate aftermath of violence and were then promptly forgotten. A more active government presence is necessary to consolidate peace and to rebuild infrastructure, services, and economies in the rural areas.

The conventional rural-urban economic divide seems to be blurred for many people affected by conflict. When they can or must, villagers engage in petty trades, and urban barrio residents farm. A farm plot is an especially valuable asset that many villagers and IDPs alike long to own and work. Land reform, titling programs, and extension services can help poor groups in both urban and rural areas access new land or recover lost property and boost their farming productivity. These are promising approaches that would build on the agricultural skills and interest among this population. But unless and until the rule of law and well-functioning markets are present, these assets will simply be "transferred again to the ones who have the power of guns."[23]

For households that need to supplement farming or that cannot farm, the qualitative data suggest that informal businesses are more remunerative than activities involving street vending, temporary jobs, or domestic work. While training programs to help individuals pursue small business ventures were often available, few people could access loans for start-up capital. Most relied on friends, moneylenders, and sometimes local credit associations for loans. In addition, more than 70 percent of surveyed households reported that government rules and regulations make it somewhat or very difficult to set up a business. Small changes in rules accompanied by wider access to sav-ings and credit services could support more inclusive market opportunities.

Third, home ownership seems to be an especially critical asset for groups affected by conflict. Owning a home brings material security, and the house is a key productive asset for those who run home businesses or are engaged in rental markets. Having a home also helps restore peace of mind and a sense of belonging. The numerous housing organizations among the displaced are serving a pressing need and aspiration where they function effectively.

Finally, new initiatives are needed to buttress the security and autonomy of grassroots leaders and institutions of the displaced. More people escaped poverty in Santa María than in any other community, and the effectiveness of the Co-Agro Peasant Association was crucial to this outcome. The gains nevertheless appear fragile. What happens if the urban farmers lose their land, to which they do not hold title? What happens if the same horrific fate befalls their gifted leader as has happened to countless other organizers?

In addition to addressing the threats to physical safety and the security of assets, policy makers and external agencies seeking to assist victims of conflict need to pay much greater attention to how their actions affect local capacity to exercise agency. Public policies and programs shape the incentives facing community organizations and profoundly influence their membership, priorities, and capacities for decision making and action. These groups have struggled to find creative and effective ways to close infrastructure gaps, reduce crime and violence where they live, and address pressing economic and social problems. They are on the front lines where the battles against violence, exclusion, and stigma are fought.

In some cases, the effects of well-intentioned community programs for the displaced have run counter to the goals of building local organizational capacity, trust, and social cohesion. There is now a large literature on community development models that help reduce these hazards. The approaches work in part by equipping local groups to avoid harmful partnerships through mechanisms that support information access, inclusive and participatory processes, accountability, and organizational strengthening (Ackerman 2003; Narayan 2002; Narayan and Ebbe 1997). Such empowerment practices have been in use for years, but the lessons about their importance for successful community development do not seem to be spreading. The slow uptake in part reflects the limited understanding of local-level institutions among international agencies and those in the development economics field more generally.

Participants in the Moving Out of Poverty study attached high importance to community unity and activism, and they appeared conscious of the potential benefits of collective action. Most had voted in recent elections held in their communities and were attentive to the results. Whether they were pleased with a new mayor or not, their interest in who held a local office suggests a measure of vibrancy in Colombian democracy. Moreover, barrio residents attributed the presence and quality of the services they received to their community leaders and organizations, indicating an awareness of the value of social capital. In a violence-scarred society, this resilience and willingness to work together may offer a promising start for future recovery.

# Annex: Ladder of Life for El Gorrión

**FIGURE 8A.1**
**Ladder of life for El Gorrión, prepared by a women's focus group**

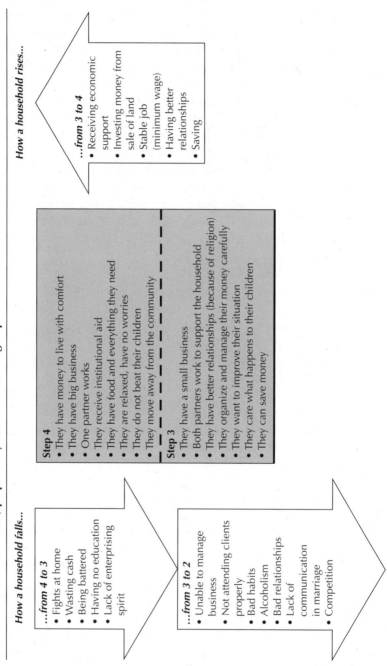

*How a household rises...*

**...from 3 to 4**
- Receiving economic support
- Investing money from sale of land
- Stable job (minimum wage)
- Having better relationships
- Saving

**Step 4**
- They have money to live with comfort
- They have big business
- One partner works
- They receive institutional aid
- They have food and everything they need
- They are relaxed, have no worries
- They do not beat their children
- They move away from the community

**Step 3**
- They have a small business
- Both partners work to support the household
- They have better relationships (because of religion)
- They organize and manage their money carefully
- They want to improve their situation
- They care what happens to their children
- They can save money

*How a household falls...*

**...from 4 to 3**
- Fights at home
- Wasting cash
- Being battered
- Having no education
- Lack of enterprising spirit

**...from 3 to 2**
- Unable to manage business
- Not attending clients properly
- Bad habits
- Alcoholism
- Bad relationships
- Lack of communication in marriage
- Competition

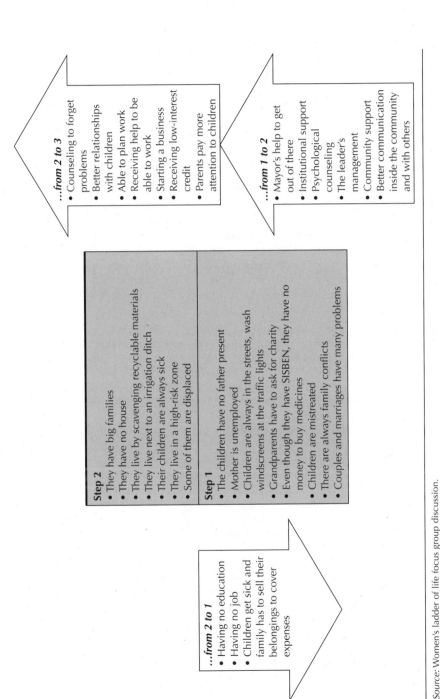

**...from 2 to 3**
- Counseling to forget problems
- Better relationships with children
- Able to plan work
- Receiving help to be able to work
- Starting a business
- Receiving low-interest credit
- Parents pay more attention to children

**...from 1 to 2**
- Mayor's help to get out of there
- Institutional support
- Psychological counseling
- The leader's management
- Community support
- Better communication inside the community and with others

**Step 2**
- They have big families
- They have no house
- They live by scavenging recyclable materials
- They live next to an irrigation ditch
- Their children are always sick
- They live in a high-risk zone
- Some of them are displaced

**Step 1**
- The children have no father present
- Mother is unemployed
- Children are always in the streets, wash windscreens at the traffic lights
- Grandparents have to ask for charity
- Even though they have SISBEN, they have no money to buy medicines
- Children are mistreated
- There are always family conflicts
- Couples and marriages have many problems

**...from 2 to 1**
- Having no education
- Having no job
- Children get sick and family has to sell their belongings to cover expenses

*Source:* Women's ladder of life focus group discussion.
*Note:* Bold solid line between steps 2 and 3 indicates the community poverty line. Bold dashed line between steps 3 and 4 indicates the official poverty line.

# Notes

The Colombia study is part of the global Moving Out of Poverty study led by Deepa Narayan in the Poverty Reduction and Economic Management (PREM) Network of the World Bank. For a discussion of key study concepts and data collection methods, see chapter 1 and the appendixes to this volume. Also see volume 2 of the Moving Out of Poverty series (Narayan, Pritchett, and Kapoor 2009) and the study methodology guide (Narayan and Petesch 2005).

The Colombia country study was directed by Sergio Prada at Centro de Estudios Regionales, Cafeteros y Empresariales (CRECE) in Manizales, Colombia. The "Colombia National Synthesis Report" was written by María Teresa Matijasevic, Liliana Velázquez, Carolina Villada, and Mónica Ramírez and is available on the Moving Out of Poverty study Web site (http://go.worldbank.org/9ER0AOIH20). Portions of the analysis and findings presented in this chapter, such as the three-tiered community typology, draw directly from the synthesis report, but we also returned to the original study data to conduct additional analysis.

We wish to thank Mohini Datt, Soumya Kapoor, Kalpana Mehra, Niti Saxena, and Emcet Tas for their excellent research support. Jairo Arboleda, Ana María Ibáñez, María Teresa Matijasevic, Deepa Narayan, Sergio Prada, Ashutosh Varshney, and Liliana Velázquez provided detailed and helpful feedback on earlier versions of the chapter.

1.  Ana María Ibáñez, economics professor at Universidad de los Andes, personal communication, June 25, 2008.
2.  To protect the privacy of participants, this chapter uses pseudonyms for the eight study communities (villages and barrios). Cities, municipalities, and departments are identified by their real names.
3.  The contraction in 1999 was followed by a period of low growth, but real economic growth rebounded from 1.9 percent in 2002 to 6.8 percent in 2006 (World Bank 2007).
4.  For background on the armed conflict and its humanitarian impacts, see policy briefing notes by the International Crisis Group (ICG 2003, 2006).
5.  For elaboration of the empowerment framework, see Petesch, Smulovitz, and Walton (2005). For refinements to the framework and discussion on applying it to examinations of mobility, see Narayan and Petesch (2007).
6.  The sampling framework for this IDP survey builds on the Survey of the Internally Displaced People and the RUT system, an initiative to collect data on households displaced by conflict. The survey has been administered by the Bishop's Conference of the Catholic Church since 1987, and it contains information for more than 32,000 households.
7.  The original research design emerged after extensive consultations with the Universidad de los Andes researchers involved in the larger IDP study, as well as with experts in the World Bank, national government, other universities, civil society, and Catholic Church. The study was conceived to yield information on how the recovery experiences of displaced populations who remained in urban settlements compare with those of displaced populations who returned to their villages. The 10 sample communities were divided evenly between urban and

rural, and they also varied in their growth contexts and in the intensity of conflict or displacement. After repeated efforts in the field, however, the research team discarded three of the five original rural sites and ran into problems working in many of the original urban IDP settlements sampled as well. Due to budget and schedule constraints, and after considerable consultations and investments in identifying suitable substitutes for the study communities, the research design was reframed to focus on urban IDP barrios and the sample was reduced from 10 to 8 communities.

8. Ana María Ibáñez points out that this disbursed settlement pattern among IDPs no doubt complicates the delivery of displacement assistance but may in the long run ease resettlement into the city (personal communication, June 25, 2008).

9. The exceptions are lack of access to clean water in the two younger barrios of Villa Blanca and San Feliz.

10. In Los Rincones, for instance, one study participant commented that there are some 60 cell phones in the village.

11. The urban data are often unclear about exactly who is perpetrating the violence. In some cases local conflicts (involving individual crimes, youth gangs, family feuds, personal animosities, local political rivalries, or disputes between neighborhoods) may be linked to the wider conflict or to the predation activities and strategic goals of armed factions at the national level. High-profile kidnappings have received more attention than everyday crime and other social problems in the media and literature on the type of urban crime and violence that is associated with the armed groups. Other studies on Colombia have found that violence is most likely to be reported accurately where it is infrequent; in places where violence levels are higher, there is a scarcity of accurate data (Rubio 1999). These caveats notwithstanding, certain patterns did emerge from the study, but more detailed ethnographic work with longer periods of fieldwork would be needed to understand how local mobility processes are influenced by battles for political control that extend beyond the study communities. While the rapid data collection methods used in the study made it difficult to surmount these hurdles, the field researchers nevertheless did a remarkable job of uncovering information about these sensitive issues.

12. See Moser (2004) for a more complete classification of categories of urban violence.

13. The statistics on falling into poverty are not presented here because there was only one faller between the two villages, a household residing in La Soledad. In Los Rincones, there were no nonpoor households to fall into poverty, but a total of nine poor households did become more impoverished.

14. See Arboleda, Petesch, and Blackburn (2004, chap. 3) for similar accounts of illegal armed groups controlling poor urban barrios, the problems of intense stigma faced by these residents, and the harmful impacts of crime and violence on family life.

15. For two thoughtful discussions on grassroots activism in urban squatter communities, see Fisher (1984) and Moser (1989).

16. Perlman (2007) observed rising violent crime and declining social capital in the favelas of Rio de Janeiro during nearly the same time period as this study covers. In her study favelas, residents' associations lost independence as competing drug factions, some with ties to Colombia's drug economy, steadily gained control of

community organizations. After decades of diverse and successful community activism, the only active local groups left at the time of her study seemed to be those sponsored by churches.

17. The average for this sample drops to 0.64 as well if Santa María is excluded. The Santa María sample specifically consisted of members of the Co-Agro Peasant Association, while organizational membership was not a sampling criterion in the other study sites. Sudarsky (1999) also found low levels of social capital in Colombia.

18. At the time of the study, in 2005, Santa María had five community centers, three schools, and a newly opened health clinic. Residents also described an array of outside agencies that delivered training programs, workshops, and counseling services. El Mirador's physical infrastructure was also quite good, but study participants identified a pattern of deterioration in recent years. El Mirador was the only study community with extensive telephone service, a post office, a plaza for daily commerce, and access to the Internet. The barrio also had electricity, water, and sanitation, but the sewerage system was taxed beyond capacity and causing public health problems. There was an elementary and a secondary school, a Catholic church, and a doctor's office, but the neighborhood health clinic closed in 2003 after having served the community since 1972.

19. The peasant association is identified here by a pseudonym to protect its members.

20. Focus groups in El Mirador identified 61 nonpoor households (among 118 households sorted) at the beginning of the study period, but this number fell to 47 over the decade as the barrio struggled with changes in the wider economy, the influx of IDPs, and rising gang violence and crime. In contrast, Santa María had just six never poor households (out of 89 sorted). It should be noted that areas of Santa María also date back decades and contain many non-IDPs, although the sample for this study mainly consists of newly arrived IDPs.

21. The farmland was cleared in 1990 by eight families that had the authorization of the caretaker and the absent landowner. A few years ago, a woman—believed to be the second wife of the man who owned the land at the time it was cleared—filed a legal claim to evict the tillers and won. Co-Agro, with the assistance of a private attorney and a public defender appointed by the Defensoría del Pueblo, responded by filing an appeal, which was still undecided at the time of the study.

22. The Juntos program helps families understand their rights and entitlements so they can access the range of programs that they need to move themselves out of poverty. See www.accionsocial.gov.co.

23. Sergio Prada, personal communication, May 11, 2008.

# References

Ackerman, J. 2003. "State-Society Synergy for Accountability: Lessons for the World Bank." Civil Society Team, Latin America and the Caribbean Region, World Bank, Washington, DC.

Arboleda, J., P. Petesch, and J. Blackburn. 2004. *Voices of the Poor in Colombia: Strengthening Livelihoods, Families and Communities*. Washington, DC: World Bank.

Barron, P., C. Smith, and M. Woolcock. 2004. "Understanding Local Level Conflict in Developing Countries: Theory, Evidence and Implications from Indonesia." Social Development Papers, Conflict Prevention and Reconstruction Paper 19, World Bank, Washington, DC.

Engel, S., and A. M. Ibáñez. 2007. "Displacement Due to Violence in Colombia: Determinants and Effects at the Household Level." *Economic Development and Cultural Change* 55 (2): 335–65.

Fisher, J. 1984. "Development from Below: Neighborhood Improvement Associations in the Latin American Squatter Settlements." *Studies in Comparative International Development* 19 (1): 61–85.

Gutiérrez Sanin, F., and L. Ramírez Rueda. 2004. "The Tense Relationship between Violence and Democracy in Colombia, 1974–2001." In *Politics in the Andes: Identity, Conflict, Reform,* ed. J. Burt and P. Mauceri, 228–46. Pittsburgh: University of Pittsburgh Press.

Ibáñez, A. M., and A. Moya. 2007. "Do Conflicts Create Poverty Traps? Asset Losses and Recovery for Displaced Households in Colombia." Background paper for Moving Out of Poverty Study, Poverty Reduction and Economic Management Network, World Bank, Washington, DC.

ICG (International Crisis Group). 2003. "Colombia's Humanitarian Crisis." Latin America Report 4, International Crisis Group, Bogotá and Brussels.

———. 2006. "Tougher Challenges Ahead for Colombia's Uribe." Latin America Briefing 11, International Crisis Group, Bogotá and Brussels.

Kalyvas, S. 2006. *The Logic of Violence in Civil War.* New York: Cambridge University Press.

Moser, Caroline O. 1989. "Community Participation in Urban Projects in the Third World." *Progress in Planning* 32: 71–133.

———. 2004. "Urban Violence and Insecurity: An Introductory Roadmap." *Environment and Urbanization* 16 (2): 3–16.

Muggah, R. 2000. "Through the Developmentalist's Looking Glass: Conflict-Induced Displacement and Involuntary Resettlement in Colombia." *Journal of Refugee Studies* 13 (2): 133–64.

Narayan, D., ed. 2002. *Empowerment and Poverty Reduction: A Sourcebook.* Washington, DC: World Bank.

Narayan, D., and K. Ebbe. 1997. *Design of Social Funds: Participation, Demand Orientation and Local Organizational Capacity.* World Bank Discussion Paper 375. Washington, DC: World Bank.

Narayan, D., and P. Petesch. 2005. "Moving Out of Poverty Methodology Guide." Poverty Reduction Group, Poverty Reduction and Economic Management Network, World Bank, Washington, DC.

———. 2007. "Agency, Opportunity Structure, and Poverty Escapes." In *Moving Out of Poverty: Cross-Disciplinary Perspectives on Mobility,* ed. D. Narayan and P. Petesch, 1–44. Washington, DC: World Bank; New York: Palgrave Macmillan.

Narayan, D., L. Pritchett, and S. Kapoor. 2009. *Moving Out of Poverty: Success from the Bottom Up.* New York: Palgrave Macmillan; Washington, DC: World Bank.

Oslender, U. 2007. "Violence in Development: The Logic of Forced Displacement on Colombia's Pacific Coast." *Development in Practice* 17 (6): 752–64.

Perlman, J. 2007. "Elusive Pathways Out of Poverty: Intra- and Intergenerational Mobility in the Favelas of Rio de Janeiro." In *Moving Out of Poverty: Cross-Disciplinary Perspectives on Mobility*, ed. D. Narayan and P. Petesch, 227–71. Washington, DC: World Bank; New York: Palgrave Macmillan.

Petesch, P., C. Smulovitz, and M. Walton. 2005. "Evaluating Empowerment: A Framework with Cases from Latin America." In *Measuring Empowerment: Cross-Disciplinary Perspectives*, ed. D. Narayan, 39–67. Washington, DC: World Bank.

Polanía Reyes, S. V. May 2005. "Capital Social e Ingreso de los Hogares del Sector Urbano en Colombia." PhD diss., Department of Economics, Universidad de los Andes, Bogotá.

Rubio, M. 1999. *Crimen e impunidad: Precisiones sobre la violencia.* Bogotá: Tercer Mundo.

Sanchez, F., and M. del Mar Palau. 2006. "Conflict, Decentralization, and Local Governance in Colombia, 1974–2004." Documento CEDE 2006–20, Centro de Estudios sobre Desarrollo Económico, Universidad de los Andes, Bogotá.

Siegle, J., and P. O'Mahoney. 2006. "Assessing the Merits of Decentralization as a Conflict Mitigation Strategy." Paper prepared for USAID's Office of Democracy and Governance as a supporting study for the revision of the *Decentralization and Democratic Local Governance Programming Handbook*. Development Alternatives, Inc., Washington, DC.

Sudarsky, J. 1999. "Colombia's Social Capital: The National Measurement with the BARCAS." World Bank, Washington, DC. http://poverty2.forumone.com/library/view/4627/.

Tate, W. 2007. *Counting the Dead: The Culture and Politics of Human Rights Activism in Colombia.* Berkeley: University of California Press.

UNDP (United Nations Development Programme). 2003. *El conflicto, callejón con salida.* National Human Development Report 2003 for Colombia. Bogotá: UNDP.

UNHCR (United Nations High Commissioner for Refugees). 2006. *Measuring Protection by Numbers.* Geneva: UNHCR.

———. 2007. *Supplementary Appeal for IDPs in Colombia: Protection and Durable Solutions for IDPs in Colombia.* Geneva: UNHCR.

Varshney, A. 2003. *Ethnic Conflict and Civic Life: Hindus and Muslims in India.* New Haven, CT: Yale University Press.

Vélez, E. 2003. "Education." In *Colombia: The Economic Foundation of Peace*, ed. M. Giugale, O. Lafourcade, and C. Luff, 611–52. Washington, DC: World Bank.

World Bank. 2002. "Colombia Poverty Report." Colombia Country Management Unit, PREM Sector Management Unit, Latin America and the Caribbean Region, Washington, DC.

———. 2005. "Country Assistance Strategy Progress Report for Colombia for 2003–07." World Bank, Washington, DC.

———. 2007. *World Development Indicators.* Washington, DC: World Bank.

————. 2008. "Country Partnership Strategy for the Republic of Colombia for the Period FY 2008–2011." Colombia and Mexico Country Management Unit, Latin America and the Caribbean Region, World Bank, Washington, DC.

————. Forthcoming. "Peace Programmatic II: Reparation for Especially Vulnerable Victims of the Armed Conflict in Colombia." Colombia and Mexico Country Management Unit and Sustainable Development Sector Management Unit 3, Latin America and the Caribbean Region, World Bank, Washington, DC.

# From Milkless Cows to Coconut Trees: Recovery from All-Out War in Mindanao, Philippines

*Katy Hull and Chona Echavez*

> *People cannot work on their farms when there is conflict. All are afraid and suspicious of each other. This causes poverty, more than that brought about by natural calamities.*
>
> — RENATO, A 50-YEAR-OLD MAN,
> Newsib, Tulunan municipality

> *Before the road rehabilitation, we could hardly bring our products to the center. Transporting patients for medical assistance and evacuation during conflict was a big problem. Now the road is passable and a lot better than before.*
>
> — DOLORES, A 49-YEAR-OLD WOMAN,
> Newsib, Tulunan municipality

U sman lives in the barangay of Abanang in Mindanao, the easternmost island in the Philippines.[1] All of Usman's assets, including his plow, were destroyed in the war in 2000. "I lost all my household utensils and few clothes that were left. Bullets also destroyed the roof of the shanty." In spite of his hardships, Usman rates his levels of social well-being at the time as moderately high because of his good relationships with his family and his community.

In the barangay of Lomamoli, Akmed has found his livelihood impeded by interclan rivalries. "There were times when warring factions had an encounter near my farm. I could not harvest at that time . . . But we could still support ourselves because my wife is a teacher."

Manuel claims that his life has improved since "our community has been governed by a good leader who is supportive of our needs." He notes that a new road to his barangay, Bakimati, has allowed for more economic opportunities.

Tina, in Dubiading, works two jobs to ensure her family's survival. In 2003 she found employment as a cook for a construction company, but she considered her wage to be inadequate for the family's needs. "So I found an additional livelihood—I accepted cake orders. This is better than my work for the construction company because nobody tells me what to do and I can charge 120 pesos for one layer of cake."

Usman, Akmed, Manuel, and Tina have each had a different experience of conflict and of recovery from conflict. But they have one thing in common: between 1996 and 2006 their households moved out of poverty. The stories of these four individuals are at once idiosyncratic and emblematic of the experiences of others who have crossed the poverty line in Mindanao. This chapter explores factors that have enabled some households to move out of poverty on the island while others remain trapped in poverty. It pays

**249**

particular attention to community, as opposed to household, factors, since community-wide mobility ratings and qualitative analysis indicate that Usman's, Akmed's, Manuel's, and Tina's chances of moving out of poverty were highly dependent on the villages in which they lived.

The chapter begins by describing the nature and origins of conflict in Mindanao. The second section traces the impact of conflict on communities in the sample, comparing the experiences of communities where many people moved out of poverty during the study period with those where only a few did. It demonstrates that the high-mobility communities have been shielded from the worst ravages of internal and external conflict, while those with low mobility have been afflicted by continuous violence.

The intermediary mechanisms that enable communities to move out of poverty are discussed in the third and fourth sections, which address the roles of external assistance and local leadership in boosting economic opportunities and strengthening community cohesion. We uncover significant differences in the kinds of external assistance that high- and low-mobility communities have received, with the former benefiting from deeper investments in infrastructure and basic services. Leaders, whether formal or informal, have helped attract and channel this assistance in high-mobility villages, while in low-mobility villages elected officials continue to struggle to turn the fortunes of their communities around.

The fifth section investigates women's changing social and economic opportunities during and after conflict. It demonstrates that a permanent change in the status of women depends in large part on economic opportunities and sociopolitical structures in the postconflict environment. The chapter concludes with some policy recommendations.

## Separatism, Land Disputes, and *Ridos*: Faces of Conflict in Mindanao

The Mindanao conflict is rooted in a long history of interference in local traditions and neglect of socioeconomic needs. It remains unresolved to this day. The 10 communities that are the focus of this chapter report three major triggers for conflict between 1996 and 2006: war between rebel forces and government troops, land disputes between Muslim and Christian communities, and family feuds, known as *ridos*, mainly between Muslim clans. A number of authors have conducted exhaustive research on the causes and nature of conflict in Mindanao (for example, Buendia 2005; Gutierrez and Borras

2004). The more modest goal here is to provide insight into the impact of conflict on economic mobility in the communities sampled for the Moving Out of Poverty study.

## A 500-year struggle between center and periphery

The "all-out war" that the Joseph Estrada administration declared against Muslim separatists in 2000 has its roots in long-running tension between the center and periphery. Originally inhabited by indigenous groups, Mindanao was exposed to Islam through trade in the fourteenth century. By the time Spain colonized the Philippines in 1565, the island was predominantly Muslim. Spanish and subsequently American colonizers attempted to integrate the Muslim people of Mindanao, known as the Moro or Bangsamoro, into mainstream Christian society, albeit by different means. While Spain pursued a policy of forced conversion to Christianity, the United States adopted an official stance of noninterference with local traditions. However, the imposition of Western legal norms, such as a ban on slavery, and the promulgation of public education were perceived as part of a concerted effort by American occupiers to inculcate Christian values (Gowing and McAmis 1974).

When the Philippines became independent in 1946, Mindanao was yet to be peaceably integrated into the nation. A separatist movement gathered strength under various guises: the Muslim Independence Movement of the 1960s; the Moro National Liberation Front (MNLF), organized in the 1970s; and the Moro Islamic Liberation Front (MILF), which broke away from the MNLF in the late 1970s. Negotiations between the MNLF and the government led to the creation of the Autonomous Region in Muslim Mindanao (ARMM) in 1990, comprising the three regions on mainland Mindanao and the Sulu archipelago. The MILF rejected the compromise inherent in regional autonomy and continued to pursue its stated objective of secession and creation of an Islamic state of Bangsamoro, by force if necessary.

In February 2000, a series of bombs attributed to the MILF left 45 dead and dozens injured. President Estrada declared "all-out war" against the MILF. True to its name, the war had a devastating impact. In villages suspected of being rebel outposts, residents were evacuated, homes and other buildings were razed, crops were lost, and animals were stolen or killed. Seven of the 10 communities in this study—Abanang, Glikati, Tucampo, Bakimati, Kilaluna, Paitatu, and Bulipobla—were directly affected by the all-out war.[2] The impact of the conflict on communities in this study is described in greater detail below.

Coming to power in 2001, President Gloria Macapagal-Arroyo declared a policy of "all-out peace." But a final agreement between the government and the MILF remains elusive, and the fragile peace continues to be punctuated by sporadic skirmishes.

## Fighting for land and power

The land conflict between Christians and Muslims in Mindanao, like the separatist struggle, has its roots in historical insensitivity to the cultural traditions of Muslim communities and neglect of their economic needs. In the 1950s and 1960s, the Philippine government encouraged landless Christian farmers from Luzon to settle first in Cotabato and then in Lanao del Norte, provinces of Mindanao populated mainly by Maguindanao and Maranao Muslims, respectively. The government operated under *jura regalia*, a Spanish colonial doctrine holding that communal lands remain under government control. This ran in direct contravention of Moro customs of land ownership.

Waves of state-sponsored settlement were accompanied by even larger influxes of voluntary immigrants from the Visayas, the island group north of Mindanao (Wernstedt and Simkins 1965). Even in cases where Christian settlers bought land from their Muslim neighbors, the sale could be contested, since land, in Moro tradition, belongs to the clan rather than to the individual. In some cases Christian settlers, believing they had purchased land fairly, found themselves approached by clan members who demanded additional payments. In other cases, Muslims attempted to retake by force land that they believed to be rightfully theirs. Christians organized units to protect themselves against Muslim attack; Muslims dubbed these forces the ILAGA, or Ilonggo Land Grabbers Association (the Ilonggo are people from Iloilo province in the Visayas). Confusion and anger prevailed.

Three communities in the sample—Bakimati, Paitatu, and Newsib—have been particularly exposed to land conflict over the 1996–2006 period. In each case, the conflict has decades-old antecedents. The case of Newsib is typical. Christian migrants from central Visayas settled there in the 1960s, believing that they had legitimately bought lands from the chief of Tulunan municipality. Their Muslim neighbors accused them of illegally occupying the land, the Christians formed self-protection units, and the conflict quickly escalated. "Every three or four years, conflict between Muslims and Christians would erupt, causing a massive evacuation and claiming lives on both disputing sides," recalled Julio, a 63-year-old resident of the barangay. The area became a virtual no-man's-land until a peace accord was brokered in 1986. The peace was shattered in 1999 when an elderly Christian settler was murdered while working on his farm.

Over the course of four decades, Christian migrants have been more successful economically than Muslims, and they have also become more powerful, socially and politically. This has fueled Muslim resentment of their Christian neighbors and their anger at perceived favoritism toward Christians on the part of the central government. Land conflicts tend to be an expression of these tensions. In the words of Camlon, the village leader of Paitatu, "The land dispute is not really the root of the problem. It has become an instrument that feeds the ongoing conflict between Muslims and Christians at the expense of many lives."

## Taking the law into their own hands

Ridos, or blood feuds, are linked to the Maranao notion of *maratabat* (honor). When a family believes that its honor has been compromised, a rido enables family members to exact revenge, thereby reclaiming lost prestige. Since Moro families are large (as many as six nuclear families may live together under the same roof), ridos have the potential to involve entire communities in reprisals and counterreprisals between clans.

Ridos have affected half the communities in the sample over the 1996–2006 period. They are often linked to a struggle for political power. Mayoral elections sparked a rido in Lomamoli in 1988, when the elected incumbent was murdered by supporters of his defeated opponent. Elections for barangay chairman caused a rido in Tucampo in 2003, when a candidate shot his political rival. And although they are most common within the Maranao community, ridos are by no means exclusive to them. Dubiading, which is arguably the most peaceful community in the sample, was once blighted by a corrosive feud between the barangay's most powerful Christian and Muslim families.

Although ridos are a highly localized form of conflict, their persistence is tied to the broader political and socioeconomic context in Mindanao. In areas distant from the organs of the state and normative values of legality and justice, traditional notions of honor and vengeance persist. And the absence of significant economic opportunities provides poor incentives for peace. Indeed, as will be demonstrated further on, in communities where economic opportunities have increased, ridos have tended to abate, since fighting parties have greater incentives to resolve their feuds.

## Conflict and basic needs

Cavanaugh (2000) posits that conflict is rooted in the denial of three basic human needs: recognition of ethnic identities and cultures; participation in society and access to services; and security, including access to adequate housing and food and physical safety. On these counts one can discern a potent combination of historical sources of conflict in Mindanao. Past governments have denied the religious and cultural traditions of Muslim people. Christians have been perceived as gaining privileged access to economic opportunities and political power. Regional infrastructure, education, health, and housing needs have been neglected, and communities are exposed to constant insecurity due to the ravages of conflict.

Since democracy was restored in the Philippines in 1986, successive national governments have implicitly acknowledged that the sources of conflict in Mindanao lie in the historic neglect of the region and its people. The administration of President Corazon Aquino established the Mindanao Economic Development Council in 1992 to promote socioeconomic development in the region. Just prior to the outbreak of all-out war in 2000, President Estrada toured Mindanao to promote a large investment program to develop agriculture and infrastructure in the region. The administration of President Arroyo is pursuing a two-pronged approach to peace that consists of both high-level negotiations with the MILF and a program of rehabilitation and development of conflict-affected areas.

Assistance from external donors has also expanded since the all-out war. Supported by a $33.6 million World Bank loan, the Philippine government created a social fund in late 2002 that devolves decision making to local communities to foster sustainable development in the ARMM. The social fund program aims to support social and economic infrastructure and services, food security, employment opportunities, and better local governance. Participating communities have chosen from various projects derived from a local needs assessment, ranging from water and sanitation systems to health services to capacity building for women's groups. To encourage ownership, local and municipal governments are required to contribute 5 percent and 10 percent, respectively, of project costs (ARMM Social Fund Project 2006). In addition, the Japan Bank for International Cooperation has provided a $19.8 million loan to finance small infrastructure projects in the ARMM conflict-affected areas. This chapter will consider the extent to which this assistance has helped meet the basic needs of the poor and heal the wounds of conflict in our small sample of communities.

## The Impact of Conflict: Lives and Livelihoods Forestalled

The correlation between poverty and conflict in Mindanao has been well documented. The second-largest island in the Philippines, Mindanao is rich in agricultural resources and accounts for more than half of the country's foreign exchange reserves.[3] Yet it is beset by poverty: in terms of real per capita income, the five poorest provinces in the Philippines are in Mindanao, with the bottom four in the ARMM (map 9.1). Human development indicators tell a similar story.[4]

The precise economic impact of conflict on Mindanao cannot be quantified. Schiavo-Campo and Judd (2005) note that when the direct costs of the conflict are measured in terms of damage to productive assets, they appear relatively low on account of a low initial stock of capital and infrastructure. But the indirect costs—including the inhibition of investment, which has hampered agricultural productivity—are bound to be much higher, although they are difficult to measure. It is also impossible to assess the extent to which conflict has forestalled household prosperity, particularly among poorer households at risk of becoming locked in permanent poverty. In the sample of communities in our study, focus group discussants almost unanimously described a growth in inequality over the decade studied. Reflecting on the impact of the conflict, Jamilah, a 38-year-old woman in Abanang, commented, "Wealthy people are like coconut trees because they never lose their fruit. As time passes by, they will continue to bear fruit, or income in this sense. On the other hand, the poor are like milking cows that no longer have any milk to spare."

Aiming to step beyond broad studies on the relationship between conflict and poverty in the Philippines, this chapter draws on the voices of numerous participants who testify to the ravaging effects of conflict on their livelihoods and social fabric. It pays particular attention to the experiences of the three communities with the lowest and highest levels of movement out of poverty in order to detect key differences in the factors that mediate the impact of conflict on community prosperity.

The study uses two basic indexes to derive community-wide mobility ratings. Both are based on the initial poor set, those households that were poor at the beginning of the study period. The moving out of poverty index (MOP) measures extent of upward mobility by the initially poor *across the poverty line* in a community during the study decade. The mobility of the poor index (MPI) measures overall upward mobility by the initially poor, *irrespective of whether or not they crossed the poverty line*. In both cases, the "poverty line" is

## MAP 9.1
## The Philippines with study municipalities

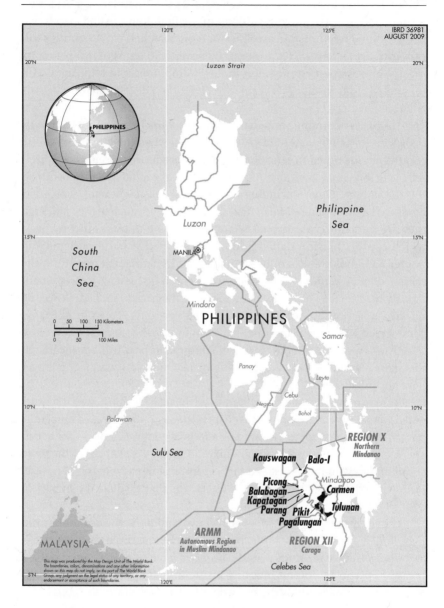

determined by focus groups in the community based on local conceptions of what it means to be poor.

In spite of the conflict, people have been able to move out of poverty in Mindanao (table 9.1). Of the three communities with the highest levels of MOP, one has been subject to a destructive external conflict and two have experienced significant internal discord. Bakimati, a community that has experienced MPI, albeit with lower-than-average MOP, has been subject to both external and internal conflict.

Table 9.1 does not reveal immediately noticeable differences in the conflict experiences of the communities with the highest and lowest mobility levels. In the high- and low-MOP categories alike, two of the three communities have experienced significant internal conflicts and two of the three are so-called peace zones. Abanang, the barangay with the highest MOP level, has

**TABLE 9.1**
**Economic mobility and conflict ratings in Mindanao study communities**

| Level of MOP/ community | Municipality | Economic mobility rating | | Conflict rating | | |
|---|---|---|---|---|---|---|
| | | MOP | MPI | External | Internal | Peace zone |
| High | | | | | | |
| Abanang | Baloi | 0.38 | 0.41 | High | | |
| Lomamoli | Balabagan | 0.35 | 0.48 | Low | ✔ | ✔ |
| Dubiading | Picong | 0.29 | 0.49 | Low | ✔ | ✔ |
| Moderate | | | | | | |
| Glikati | Pikit | 0.25 | 0.27 | High | | |
| Tucampo | Parang | 0.23 | 0.34 | High | ✔ | |
| Bakimati | Kapatagan | 0.20 | 0.47 | High | ✔ | ✔ |
| Kilaluna | Carmen | 0.20 | 0.23 | Low | | ✔ |
| Low | | | | | | |
| Paitatu | Kauswagan | 0.19 | 0.37 | High | ✔ | ✔ |
| Newsib | Tulunan | 0.17 | 0.19 | High | ✔ | |
| Bulipobla | Pagalungan | 0.00 | 0.04 | Low | | ✔ |
| Average | | 0.23 | 0.33 | | | |

Source: Authors' analysis from ladder of life focus group discussions and other Moving Out of Poverty study data.

Note: MOP = initially poor who move out of poverty ÷ initially poor. MPI = initially poor who move up ÷ initially poor. External conflict: high = more than 10 deaths; low = less than 10 deaths. Internal conflict: ✔ = presence of major rido(s) or land conflict(s). Peace zone: ✔ = presence of a peace zone. The study villages are identified by pseudonyms in this chapter.

faced a high level of external conflict, as have Paitatu and Newsib, barangays
with some of the lowest levels of MOP in the sample. Closer investigation of
the impact of conflict on these six communities does, however, reveal important differences in the intensity of external conflict, the depth of internal
strife, and the effectiveness of peace zones in containing violence.

### The bottom three

Bulipobla, Newsib, and Paitatu, the three communities with the lowest levels
of MOP, have all experienced the direct effects of the conflict between the
government and the MILF. The all-out war was just the most dramatic expression of an ongoing struggle between the center and periphery that played out
in these communities over the course of a decade. In addition to the 2000
battle, Bulipobla experienced other conflicts in 1997 and 2002, and Newsib
was the site of a clash between the Armed Forces of the Philippines (AFP)
and the MILF in 2003. In Newsib and Paitatu, the separatist conflict also
overlapped with a long-standing conflict over land between Christian and
Muslim communities.

Suspected by the government of being a MILF hiding post, Paitatu was
hard hit by the all-out war. One hundred people were injured and 13 died in
the violence.[5] Houses and farmland were damaged by fire and bombs, and
animals and vehicles were stolen or destroyed. To survive, many people sold
the remainder of their assets at low prices. Two Paitatu villagers spoke for
countless others when they recalled the ordeal. Abram said, "We were so weak
because we did not have food to eat, but the worst was we just watched our
children starve, for we could not do anything but run." And Badriah recalled,
"Not a single house was left, all were burned, everything, including the mosque
and the madrassa. They took all things that were still useful. They also burned
the vehicles that were left here . . . Most people were forced to sell their draft
animals at a very low price, sometimes less than half of their real cost."

Although few people in Bulipobla lost their lives to conflict over the
course of the decade (hence the community's classification as low-conflict),
the evacuation from the village was deeply damaging to community prosperity. Whereas most villages in the sample were evacuated for between three
months and a year as a result of the all-out war, the residents of Bulipobla
spent a total of three years outside their community between 1997 and 2003.
Evacuation prevented residents from engaging in farming, the only occupation they knew, and "people just depended on the rations that were given by
different organizations," according to Tata, a 43-year-old woman. It is hardly

surprising that Bulipobla, the only community in the sample in which no one moved out of poverty, was also subject to the longest evacuation. "The evacuation is one of the main reasons why we are still trapped in poverty. We have not been able to regain the livelihoods we lost during the conflict," said Risa, age 31.

The residents of Newsib and Paitatu also experienced regular evacuations due to internal conflicts over land as well as clashes between the AFP and the MILF. "Any conflicts that cause evacuation are the main reason for our poverty, because after each evacuation farmers go back to square one," said Jennifer, a resident of Newsib.

Given the intensity of the conflict in these communities, outsiders and residents alike have exhibited a rational reluctance to invest. Business in Newsib has "no strong foundation," said Romulo, because potential investors are inhibited by "the many conflicts and evacuations." Investment has dropped "because of fear of possible eruption of the conflict," and even casual commerce has been affected since "people are afraid to pass through the village road," according to Camlon, the village leader in Paitatu. For most, agriculture represents too great a risk, given that it entails significant upfront investment with medium-term returns. Those who have witnessed the destruction of their crops on more than one occasion no longer respond to an end to fighting as a signal to return to their fields. Following their evacuation in 2000, farmers in Paitatu did not go back to work for fear they would be attacked by the military or caught in the crossfire.

Education is another form of investment that is affected by conflict, since many families cannot afford to support their children's schooling. "Our parents cannot work so they do not have anything to give us to support our studies," noted Jesse, a villager in Newsib. Young people are forced to abandon their studies early and turn their attention to day-to-day survival. Camlon, in Paitatu, noted that "school activities stopped on the onset of war and took time to return to normal. All the more, it is hard to interest a child in returning to the same grade level where he was enrolled the previous year."

Ethnic, religious, social, and economic differences seem to be more sharply drawn, on average, in the low-MOP communities. In Bulipobla and Paitatu, discussants accept that these divisions have sometimes led to violence (table 9.2).

The qualitative data confirm that land conflict between Christian and Muslim households has been at once an expression of deep internal divisions and the cause of further deterioration of communal bonds. In Newsib, residents' evacuation experiences in 1999 were unequal: Christians were given

TABLE 9.2
**Ethnoreligious divisions in Mindanao study communities**

| Level of MOP/ community | Ethnoreligious mix | Extent to which social differences divide community (1=no division, 5=very great division) | | Do social differences lead to violence? |
|---|---|---|---|---|
| | | 2006 | 1996 | |
| *High* | | | | |
| Abanang | 99% Muslim (Maranao); 1% Christian | 1 | 1 | No |
| Lomamoli | 100% Muslim (predominantly Maranao) | 1 | 1 | No |
| Dubiading | 95% Muslim (Maranao); 5% non-Muslim (predominantly Catholic) | 1 | 1 | No |
| *Moderate* | | | | |
| Glikati | 100% Muslim (Maguindanaon) | 1 | 2 | Rarely |
| Tucampo | 90% Muslim (80% Iranon, 10% Maguindanaon and Maranao); 10% Christian | 2 | 2 | No |
| Bakimati | 100% Muslim (90% Maranao, 5% Iranon, 5% Maguindanaon) | 1 | 1 | No |
| Kilaluna | 60% Christian; 30% indigenous; 10% Muslim | 1 | 1 | No |
| *Low* | | | | |
| Paitatu | 99% Muslim (Maranao); 1% Christian[a] | 2 | 3 | Sometimes |
| Newsib | 60% Muslim (Maguindanaoan); 40% Christian | 1 | 1 | Rarely |
| Bulipobla | 99% Muslim (Maguindanaoan); 1% Christian | 2 | 2 | Sometimes |

*Source:* Community profiles.

a. Although Paitatu itself is predominantly Muslim Maranao, the surrounding areas are populated by Christian settlers.

a military escort to an evacuation center, where they received relief goods, while Muslims stayed with their families in a nearby municipality. Christians themselves recognize that they suffered less during the evacuation. "We could return [to our farms] during the daytime and go back to the evacuation center in the evening," noted Maria. Perceived favoritism of the government toward

Christians has fueled the flames of Muslim resentment. Amara, a 45-year-old woman in Newsib, commented, "The Christians benefited most from the services of the military because they escorted them whenever they went to their farms."

Focus group discussions indicate that land conflict in Newsib has frayed the social fabric of the community. Discussants note that organizations and cooperatives are inactive, their members scattered, and they identify lack of cooperation as a factor affecting community prosperity. For one discussant, at least, the weakness of communal ties is unsurprising: "Lack of cooperation," Lando observed, "is expected between conflicting residents within one community."

But recent events in Paitatu and in Bakimati, another community beset by land conflict, indicate that deep divides between Christians and Muslims are by no means irreparable. External support and strong local leadership have helped build bridges between residents in these communities, as we discuss further on. Residents of Paitatu report that divisions based on religion and ethnicity are lower in 2006 than they were in 1996 (table 9.2). And there are signs that the newfound spirit of cooperation is beginning to yield economic benefits: while levels of MOP in Paitatu and Bakimati are relatively low, at 0.19 and 0.20, respectively, their mobility of the poor indexes (MPI) are higher than the 0.33 average across the sample (table 9.1).

## The top three

Like all communities in the sample, the three with the highest levels of MOP—Abanang, Lomamoli, and Dubiading—have experienced violence between the government and separatist forces, along with internal strife. But for these communities, unlike those in the bottom mobility bracket, external conflict has been a horrendous anomaly rather than a constant reality. And they have managed to strengthen internal cohesion, despite family feuds.

Of these top three, Abanang was the only community to be directly targeted by the government in the all-out war. The impact of the conflict must not be understated: almost 100 houses were destroyed and residents were evacuated. Farmers, in particular, suffered. Arvin, age 20, remembered, "We experienced the repercussions of that armed struggle for about a year. During that year, it was difficult to recover because a number of residents had lost their means of livelihood. The farmers could not start planting. They lost the income that they were supposed to obtain from the crops that they left because of the armed conflict and they incurred some debts. They were unable to pay for the fertilizers they had borrowed and used in the previous planting cycle. That delayed their recovery."

But in contrast to the long evacuations experienced by residents of the bottom three communities, the residents of Abanang began to return in June 2000—just three months after the war began—and were not forced to leave their community again. The conflict has not seemed to foster a fear of returning to productive economic activities, since the threat of recurrence has been relatively low. After one year "we no longer feared that another conflict incident might occur in our community," added Arvin.

Lomamoli was not directly affected by the all-out war, and the impact in Dubiading was low because of community unity among Christian and Muslim groups. Discussants acknowledged that travel, trade, and the prices of commodities were temporarily affected. But relative to other communities in the sample, they experienced minimal negative effects of the war. Instead of evacuating, Lomamoli and Dubiading hosted evacuees from neighboring villages, many of whom chose to remain even after the immediate threat of violence subsided. While the all-out war brought death and destruction for most communities, in Dubiading it prompted life-affirming preparations. "When Erap [Estrada] declared all-out war, the first thing we did was assemble, both Muslims and Christians, and we planted food for life," said Bob, a 67-year-old community leader in Dubiading. "We planted bananas and cassava because we anticipated that if we were not directly affected, we would become the receivers of evacuees."

Dubiading's only direct experience with the separatist struggle over the course of the decade was itself a testimony to the depth of community cohesion. In 2002 the MILF prepared to attack a military camp stationed nearby. Muslims living in the upland were the first to spot the approaching MILF forces and rushed down to warn the CAFGU—the local militia, manned almost exclusively by Christians—of a pending attack. The warning gave the CAFGU time to prepare, and together with the AFP they repelled the MILF over the course of a single day. For one CAFGU member, the experience was a powerful indicator that community affiliations can trump religious ones. To his surprise, said Jimmy, his Muslim neighbors "thought of us like brothers."

None of the three communities in the top MOP bracket has been exposed to the kind of land conflicts that have divided Christians and Muslims in Newsib and Paitatu for decades. Abanang, where the population is almost entirely Muslim Maranao (table 9.2), has not experienced any significant internal conflict. Lomamoli and Dubiading, on the other hand, have continued to experience interclan rivalries, with violence erupting in 1988, 1996, and 2003 (Lomamoli) and 1996 and 2003 (Dubiading). Like any other form of conflict, ridos hamper economic activity. Nimfa, in Lomamoli, noted that due to a conflict in 1996, "our men could not work in the upland farms; they just stayed in the house because they were afraid to be seen by the enemy." Bob, age 67, a community leader who has firsthand experience of the effects of ridos in Dubiading, reflected, "When a family dispute arises, its negative effects range from insecurity to loss of freedom and loss of opportunity. What I mean by loss of opportunity is, even if they are on the verge of improving, once a family feud arises, their resources are automatically diverted to safety measures. They sell their cattle because they cannot work. They sell their land to buy guns and ammunitions . . . they cannot engage in business or move freely."

While the economic effects of ridos must not be minimized, the extent of the damage has been contained in Lomamoli and Dubiading. Unlike land conflict, with its debilitating effects, ridos have not eroded community cohesion entirely. Table 9.2 indicates that perceived divides along ethnoreligious lines are low in the high-MOP communities, and residents do not consider violence to have been based on religious, ethnic, or social divisions. Indeed, Dubiading has experienced a high level of community cooperation in spite of a religious divide between its Muslim majority (95 percent) and Christian minority (5 percent), with residents coming together to construct a day care center in 1995 and convert a police headquarters in 1998. Moreover, peace zones have played a vital role in limiting the impact of internal conflict in these two communities.

## The potential role of peace zones

The community profiles captured in table 9.1 suggest that peace zones are not automatic harbingers of prosperity. Although the presence of a peace zone is associated with movement out of poverty in Lomamoli and Dubiading, in Paitatu and Bulipobla it does not appear to have yielded significant economic dividends. Investigation of the role of peace zones in these four communities suggests that while they are by no means a panacea for the devastating effects of conflict, they can be instrumental in building a firm foundation for community cohesion and economic prosperity. Much, however, depends on the extent to which the initiative is a product of genuine grassroots demands for peace.

Peace zones sprang up in Mindanao in the late 1980s and became increasingly popular in the second half of the 1990s as a way of fortifying the tentative cease-fire between the government and the MNLF. Usually, local people made a public declaration of peace and sought compliance from warring factions. The concept has since been co-opted by nongovernmental organizations (NGOs), donors, and even the national government in an attempt to implant a culture of peace in war-torn communities in Mindanao (Rood

2005). The peace zones have been described as "one of the most significant signs of hope in the midst of what oftentimes appears as a bleak situation" (Gaspar, Lapad, and Maravillas 2002).

Dubiading's peace zone, which predates the trend toward community-driven peace building in the late 1980s and 1990s, provides insights into the origins and possible benefits of local peace initiatives. Following the suspected murder of a wealthy landowner by local rivals in 1952, two families, one Christian, one Muslim, became locked in a violent conflict. Through the efforts of Bob, the son of the murdered landowner, the dispute was finally put to rest some two decades later. Bob's experience in settling the rivalry between sworn enemies convinced him of the potential for a wider peace. His idea first met with resistance. "When we created the zone of peace it was not immediately accepted," he recalled. "It was not only the people in the barangay who did not believe in it, but also the public officials, my brothers, and other members of my family. They were all saying, 'That will not push through. That will not succeed' . . . However, I did not stop there because I believe in positive thinking. One step forward is better than nothing at all."

In 1976 Bob finally convinced local leaders, including separatist commanders, to sign on to the notion of a 1 square kilometer zone of peace in which all violence would be banned. The concept was disseminated on local radio, creating a "chain reaction" as it gained credibility and a grassroots following. Astutely, Bob observes that the peace zone has not prevented conflict but rather has "sanitized" or "modified" it. Sanitizing conflict, he explained, means "putting things in the proper perspective. Even if the problem cannot be prevented, we can ensure that it happens in a more humane way. For instance, we have to identify a place where we will not quarrel. Even if we meet our enemies, we will not scold them, we will not hurt them, we will not kill them. It started that way . . . if we meet our enemy in that particular area, the zone of peace, we will not quarrel there. We will wait for the enemy to go out of the boundaries of the zone and then we will have all the firecrackers that we need. That is it."

The peace zone concept rests on the creation of a credible division between areas of conflict and nonconflict, thereby enabling pockets of normalcy even during periods of heightened tension. Bob responded to the 2003 feud in Dubiading by delineating an area in which fighting was permitted. This precluded the rido from drawing in nonclan members or affecting trade. Jimmy, age 38, said, "He [Bob] divided the marketplace and placed a flag to signify the demarcation of where they could fight. He told conflicting parties that they could have their war as long as they did not cross the boundary.

While they were having a war on one side, trade continued on the other side of the boundary."

Dubiading's peace zone is certainly the most established and arguably the most successful in the sample. By contrast, Lomamoli's peace zone is a relatively recent creation. Local and international civil society organizations worked with local leaders to create a zone of peace in the municipality of Balabagan and the surrounding barangays in the early 2000s (Bush 2004). The ex-mayor invited community organizers from Lomamoli to a six-month training and leadership program in 2004, in which they were taught leadership skills and the "culture of peace." The peace zone concept took root in Lomamoli as local organizers immediately applied their training to a consultative process for the installation of a community water system.

Peace zones have played an important role in minimizing the effects of conflict in Dubiading and Lomamoli, but they do not seem to have had a significant impact in two low-MOP barangays, Paitatu and Bulipobla. What explains these differing experiences? Certainly, all peace zones are not created equal. Bulipobla's peace zone was not a locally driven initiative, deriving instead from President Arroyo's designation of the community as a "sanctuary of peace" in 2004. Although discussants note that the change in status gave some evacuees confidence to return to the village, it occurred too late to protect Bulipobla from the worst ravages of war, and its robustness is yet to be tested. That Paitatu's status as a peace zone does not figure in focus group discussions is itself a testimony to an absence, as yet, of a genuine grassroots connection with the initiative, which has been driven by NGOs and the United Nations (Confesor 2005).

## The Paradox of Conflict: Bringing Assistance to Neglected Communities

Violent conflict has had a negative impact on economic outcomes in Mindanao. But discussants recognize a paradox: the conflict has also drawn the attention of the government and NGOs to economic deprivation in the region, ushering in unprecedented levels of assistance. The observation of one participant, Omar in Glikati, is echoed throughout the community reports: "Ironically, the changes [infrastructure improvements] in the community right now are because of the conflict episode that we experienced."

All communities in the sample have benefited in some way from external support following violent conflict. Especially in the aftermath of the all-out war, they have received new infrastructure and health care facilities, renovated

housing, and livelihood assistance. But community questionnaires point to
a disparity in access to infrastructure and services between villages with high
and low levels of MOP (tables 9.3 and 9.4). According to survey results, the
three high-MOP communities had marginally better access to water in 1996
and electricity in 2006; they also had greater availability of health and educational facilities, particularly secondary schools. When we dig deeper into
the experiences of these communities, the differences in the kinds of assistance received, and the resulting impact on residents' economic opportunities, become clear.

## High-MOP communities: Promoting economic activity and community cohesion

External assistance has led to significant infrastructure improvements in the
three communities with the highest MOP. By 2006 all three had a central
supply of water and electricity and good road access to neighboring villages
and urban centers. This was not always the case. In 1996 the bridge that

**TABLE 9.3**
**Access to infrastructure in Mindanao study communities**

| Level of MOP/ community | Most households have access to clean water | | Community has access to electricity | | Road between village and nearest city is passable all year |
|---|---|---|---|---|---|
| | 2006 | 1996 | 2006 | 1996 | 2006 |
| *High* | | | | | |
| Abanang | ✔ | | ✔ | ✔ | ✔ |
| Lomamoli | ✔ | ✔ | ✔ | | ✔ |
| Dubiading | ✔ | ✔ | ✔ | | ✔ |
| *Moderate* | | | | | |
| Glikati | ✔ | | | | ✔ |
| Tucampo | ✔ | ✔ | ✔ | | ✔ |
| Bakimati | | | ✔ | | ✔ |
| Kilaluna | ✔ | | ✔ | ✔ | ✔ |
| *Low* | | | | | |
| Paitatu | ✔ | | ✔ | | ✔ |
| Newsib | ✔ | ✔ | ✔ | | ✔ |
| Bulipobla | ✔ | | ✔ | ✔ | ✔ |

*Source:* Community profiles.

**TABLE 9.4**
**Access to services in Mindanao study communities**

| Level of MOP/ community | Primary school | | Lower secondary school | | Upper secondary school | | Health clinic | |
|---|---|---|---|---|---|---|---|---|
| | 2006 | 1996 | 2006 | 1996 | 2006 | 1996 | 2006 | 1996 |
| *High* | | | | | | | | |
| Abanang | ✔ | ✔ | ✔ | ✔ | | | | |
| Lomamoli | ✔ | ✔ | ✔ | | ✔ | | ✔ | |
| Dubiading | ✔ | ✔ | ✔ | | ✔ | | ✔ | |
| *Moderate* | | | | | | | | |
| Glikati | ✔ | ✔ | ✔ | | ✔ | | ✔ | ✔ |
| Tucampo | ✔ | | | | | | ✔ | |
| Bakimati | ✔ | ✔ | ✔ | | ✔ | | ✔ | |
| Kilaluna | ✔ | ✔ | ✔ | | | | | ✔ |
| *Low* | | | | | | | | |
| Paitatu | ✔ | ✔ | ✔ | ✔ | | | ✔ | |
| Newsib | ✔ | ✔ | | | | | ✔ | ✔ |
| Bulipobla | ✔ | | | | | | ✔ | |

*Source:* Community profiles.

connected Abanang to its principal marketplace collapsed, and in 1997 residents lived without power or a proper water supply for a year. Lomamoli was without electricity until 1999, and although it is classified as having access to water in 1996 (table 9.3), the source was a spring located some distance from the village center. Dubiading's residents depended on private power generators until 2003, and the main road was in bad condition until it was paved in 2004.

Lomamoli and Abanang have both benefited from initiatives to install clean water supplies since the end of the all-out war. In 2005 a government agency sponsored the installation of five public wells in different areas of Abanang. The entire community has benefited from the project, especially those households living close to one of the wells.

In Lomamoli, the impact of a program to increase access to water has been even greater. Prior to 2005, residents were forced to fetch water from a spring located a kilometer from the village center. Those who could, transported the water by car, motorcycle, bicycle, or animal cart; others made the journey on foot, pulling carts or simply lugging the heavy containers home by hand. "We used a cart to transport containers to the source and back to our homes," recalled Hannah. "We would wait a long time at the spring because there were many people who needed water." Two NGOs, the Peace and Equity Foundation and Community Organizers Multiversity, helped bring running water to Lomamoli. The NGOs also encouraged the formation of a "people's organization" that was partially responsible for installation of the water system. The initiative, which eventually consisted of more than 50 faucets, has been a resounding success, and focus groups describe it as the most important factor affecting community prosperity. The combined improvements in water and electricity have eased the burden of domestic work and enhanced productivity in Lomamoli. Hannah said, "Before, there were no [electric] rice cookers, unlike now. Now, people have washing machines, we no longer go to the spring to wash our clothes . . . and refrigerators so we can sell ice or ice candy." Jimmy concurred: "It minimizes the burden on people, especially farmers, because before, after they worked in their farms, they still had to fetch water."

Thanks to the attention it has received from the national government, Dubiading has benefited both from systematic electrification and from major improvements in its roads. In 2003 Gloria Arroyo visited the village as part of a tour of Mindanao. Witnessing conditions in the barangay, she ordered its immediate electrification and construction of a road connecting it to the neighboring municipality. Discussants recognize the positive impact of basic infrastructure development on their economic opportunities. A regular electricity supply means that fishermen can now keep their catch fresh for up to three days. Hamid reflected that before the road was paved, Dubiading was "like an island." Farmers now have easy access to markets that they could previously reach only by boat, and fishermen can engage in commercial activities. "Before, it was so difficult to sell all their catch that sometimes they would opt to throw it away or give it to their neighbors rather than see it spoil," said Hadji Assad. "With the good road, they can bring their large catches to Cotabato . . . Iligan or Marawai City, where they can demand higher prices."

Abanang has likewise benefited from a systematic upgrading of its road systems over the course of the decade. Following a visit by then vice president Arroyo in 1996, the bridge connecting the village to the closest market was repaired. Traders, government employees, and students who had been cut off from their places of business, work, and study were able to resume their activities. In the wake of the all-out war, a more comprehensive program of road repair got underway, this time under the auspices of the local government unit and provincial government. Discussants noted that economic opportunities improved following the rehabilitation of the roads: private vehicles could pass through the village and farmers could transport their goods.

In addition to infrastructure improvements, the communities with the highest mobility have enjoyed a better level of social services, in particular secondary education (table 9.4). The establishment of a public secondary school has brought meaningful changes to the community of Lomamoli, saving time and money previously used for travel to schools outside the village and encouraging attendance. The school building also serves as a community center.

The relationship between improvements in social services and economic mobility is also evident in Glikati, a community with an MOP level just below that of Dubiading's (table 9.1). In 2004 an NGO, Balay Inc., built a high school. Previously, the cost of travel and risk of conflict had prohibited children from attending school; since the school's construction, the majority of children continue their studies through the upper secondary level. The high school has also brought positive economic externalities for the adult residents of Glikati: women have set up convenience stores and stalls around the school and more men provide motorcycle transport as a form of secondary income.

External interventions have had discernible economic and social effects in these communities. First, infrastructure assistance and the growth of public services have helped boost economic opportunities, whether in traditional agricultural or fisheries sectors or alternative livelihoods. In Dubiading, access to private employment is deemed to have improved from "somewhat difficult" to "not so hard if help is available from relatives or friends."[6] Residents testify to a strong relationship between infrastructure development and private sector activity. Tina, a 49-year-old woman, emphasized the importance of the new road to the village. "The Christian businessmen here in Dubiading, such as those who buy steel and plastics, can now easily deliver their products to other communities because their vehicles can now enter the barangay. The road is good, unlike before, when the tires of the trucks got stuck in the mud. . . . Now, it is easier to go back and forth from Dubiading to Kapatagan and vice versa." A men's focus group concurred: "People used to have difficulty going to other barangays. They had to walk for miles, bringing torches to light their way. The picture is different at present. Presently, there are tricycles, jeepneys, and other private vehicles of high class. As for fishing, other fishermen from Lanao del Norte enter the barangay to fish and they hire local residents to guide them. The guides then get paid and [are] given a share of their catch."

Second, external assistance has helped reinforce a positive cycle of peace and prosperity in these communities. To return to the paradoxical relationship between conflict and external assistance, it could be argued that Abanang, Lomamoli, and Dubiading have suffered from "just enough" conflict to benefit from external assistance: Abanang was a direct target in the all-out war, while Lomamoli and Dubiading were located in close proximity to separatist hot spots and were well known for ridos. But, as will be discussed below, each of these communities has demonstrated a capacity for internal cohesion. In other words, the containment of conflict appears to have encouraged external agencies to make significant investments in infrastructure and social services.

External investments have in turn increased stability in these communities. In some cases, infrastructure improvements have had a direct impact on security. Discussants in Lomamoli noted, for instance, that since the barangay was electrified their enemies cannot "just enter at will" once the sun goes down; residents now feel able to leave their homes without fear of violent reprisals. In other cases, the impact of external assistance on internal stability has been more subtle, gradually shifting incentives for reconciliation between opposing groups. Electrification of Dubiading "reduced the number of family feuds, especially between those who live in the mountains and coastal areas," reported Hadji Assad, since families living in the upper barangay must now approach those living near the power supply to have their electricity connected. Similarly, paving of the road means that "families in conflict would prefer negotiating their disputes so they could travel without any hassle." Bob, also in Dubiading, reflected, "Ridos have reduced tremendously because the people would like to take advantage of the road. They want to construct their houses near the road and they cannot do that if they do not have peace with their enemies. So peace and the road have developed a symbiotic relation. One cannot live without the other . . . and they corresponded to each other's need."

## Low-MOP communities: Plastering over the cracks

The three communities with the lowest levels of MOP have also benefited from external assistance. Echoing discussants elsewhere, Sarah, a resident of Paitatu, noted, "In a way the conflict has helped us to lead better lives" because of the "assistance given to us by the government and NGOs." But in contrast to the high-MOP communities, those with low MOP remain hampered by poor basic infrastructure and social services.

Saying nothing about the *quality* of infrastructure and services, the quantitative data only hint at the extent of deprivation in low-MOP communities (tables 9.3 and 9.4). Focus group discussions reveal that in 2006, Bulipobla, the only community that experienced no MOP over the decade, had only sporadic supplies of electricity and water and no farm-to-market road. Roads in Paitatu remained in poor condition, and the community did not receive full electricity until 2005. Discussants recognized that the continued short-comings in their infrastructure have limited their economic opportunities. "If we are able to resolve the problems in infrastructure like having a farm-to-market road, it would then be easier for the farmers and fishermen to trans-port their products, reducing operating costs," said Mahmud, a 37-year-old man in Bulipobla.

Only Newsib has experienced significant improvements in its road sys-tem. But new roads have not led to more remunerative opportunities. While the barangay road was constructed by the government, its upkeep and exten-sion have become the responsibility of a palm oil plantation, which has expanded its presence in the community over the course of the decade. The plantation has created jobs in the community, but the quality of these jobs is poor. Many farmers sold their land to the corporation and now work as day laborers—an occupation that all discussants associate with the poorest of the poor in their communities. Fabian noted that in spite of the new roads, "the standard of living of individual households is still not improving: in fact, most households have a harder time now than before."

In contrast to the high-MOP communities, none of the low-MOP com-munities had a high school in 2006, and only one, Paitatu, had a lower sec-ondary school during the study period (table 9.4). Bulipobla lacked even a primary school until an international organization, Community and Family Services International, provided one in the wake of the all-out war. But the school was destroyed in renewed fighting in 2003. "The NGO was disappointed with what happened because they were expecting that they could help the children in our area," Mahmud noted. After the school was destroyed, "the NGO was at a crossroads, considering whether or not they would continue their funding." The residents of Bulipobla contributed to rebuilding the elementary school and the NGO remained tentatively engaged in community affairs.

External assistance in low-MOP communities is best characterized as piecemeal. Income-generating projects such as business and credit support programs have often failed to take root because of the absence of a basic infrastructure comprising roads, water, and electricity. As a result, access to private sector activities remains severely curtailed in all three communities; discussants describe finding private sector employment as "very difficult" in both 1996 and 2006.[7] Residents of Bulipobla named a livelihood assistance program provided by the ARMM Social Fund as the second most important factor affecting community prosperity (the elementary school being the most important factor). But they noted that despite ample assistance, people remain trapped in poverty. A credit program failed because, in the absence of linkages to external markets, the women were unable to generate follow-up income. Likewise, in Paitatu, income diversification opportunities remain limited by poor roads and restricted access to neighboring markets. "Compared to 10 years ago," Amil reflected, "we still have the same source of living, which is farming and no others. There is no improvement."

In contrast to the experiences of communities with high MOP, external assistance in low-MOP communities has tended not to reinforce a positive cycle of peace and prosperity. Perhaps high levels of violence in Bulipobla and Newsib have dissuaded organizations from initiating significant infrastructure improvements. Certainly, the destruction of Bulipobla's elementary school in 2003, less than three years after it was built, must have been a chastening experience for external organizations hoping to facilitate lasting improvements in the barangay.

Paitatu is, however, a partial exception to this pattern. Although it has not received the same level of infrastructure assistance as the high-MOP communities, relief efforts, including the rebuilding of a mosque and houses and the installation of a water system, have helped repair the rift between Christian and Muslim groups. The barangay captain, a Muslim named Camlon, reflected on the transition from deep distrust to mutual understanding as the community received assistance from Christian relief agencies:

> Before, whenever we heard a Christian name, we would immediately feel angry because of the long experience of conflict we have had with the Christians. Imagine three decades of life lived in violence . . . In May of 2000, Christians came here with government agencies to provide help, yet people were still suspicious. It took some time before we trusted their intentions . . . It is hard to imagine that a group of Christian pastors would help build a mosque, houses, and a water system for a Muslim community. I never heard of any religious group doing so much to break down barriers and bridge the gap between two historically opposed groups for the sake of peace.

In addition to material support, external relief brought a fresh perspective to residents who suffered from an ingrained mistrust of their neighbors. Ties between Christians and Muslims strengthened when Paitatu residents worked together in a United Nations initiative to construct a reservoir. In

2003, as surrounding villages erupted in violence, Paitatu remained peaceful. "This was unusual," reflected the barangay captain, Camlon, "because in the past whenever there were problems close to our barangay, we were the first to evacuate." A perceptible shift in attitudes took root, even though the land conflict had not been resolved. "This is the only time that Paitatu has experienced a sense of community, with people living close to each other, cooperating and helping one another."

Paitatu has begun to experience the mutually reinforcing relationship between external assistance and community cohesion documented in the high-MOP communities. It has already achieved significant mobility of the poor (MPI), albeit without much MOP (table 9.1). Its barangay chairman reflected, "We cannot deny that there are still a lot of people here who experience poverty. In fact you can see that for yourself. And it is a lie to say that we no longer need assistance, but life today is better than before. People are now secure and can concentrate on their livelihoods without fear of war and evacuation. That, with the [provision of] basic services, could result in economic stability."

## Democracy and Economic Mobility

As we have seen, the impact of conflict, the extent of postconflict assistance, and the level of social cohesion can hinder or help economic mobility. But to what degree have local democratic institutions and local leaders been instrumental in facilitating these outcomes?

### Perceptions of governance and democracy

Across communities, our study found vast disparities in perceptions of government at its most local and more distant levels, with the former viewed much more favorably than the latter. Youth participants in Glikati, for example, view corruption as a minor problem within the barangay, but they consider it to be ubiquitous at the municipal level. In Abanang, participants are satisfied with the performance of their barangay leaders, but some believe that the municipal mayor "deprived the community of all assistance because we opposed him in the last election." The contrasting perceptions of local and national government are reflected in table 9.5: throughout the sample, while villagers perceive corruption to be limited among local officials, they view it as pervasive at the national level.

**TABLE 9.5**
**Perceptions of the quality of governance and democracy in Mindanao study communities**

| Level of MOP/ community | Corruption: national[a] | | Corruption: local[b] | | Participation[c] | Responsiveness[d] | Influence[e] |
|---|---|---|---|---|---|---|---|
| | 2006 | 1996 | 2006 | 1996 | | | |
| *High* | | | | | | | |
| Abanang | Most | A few | Almost none | Almost none | ✓ | | ✓ |
| Lomamoli | Most | Most | A few | A few | | ✓ | ✓ |
| Dubiading | Almost all | Almost all | A few | A few | ✓ | ✓ | ✓ |
| *Moderate* | | | | | | | |
| Glikati | Most | Most | A few | A few | ✓ | ✓ | ✓ |
| Tucampo | Most | Most | A few | A few | ✓ | | ✓ |
| Bakimati | Most | Most | Almost none | Almost none | ✓ | ✓ | ✓ |
| Kilaluna | Most | Almost none | Almost none | Almost none | ✓ | ✓ | ✓ |
| *Low* | | | | | | | |
| Paitatu | Almost all | Most | Almost none | A few | ✓ | ✓ | ✓ |
| Newsib | Almost none | Almost none | Almost none | Almost none | ✓ | ✓ | ✓ |
| Bulipobla | A few | Most | Almost none | Almost none | ✓ | ✓ | ✓ |

*Source:* Male focus group discussions.

a. Responses to questions: What proportion of government official/civil servants in this country are corrupt? And 10 years ago?

b. Responses to questions: What proportion of government official/civil servants in this village take or demand bribes? And 10 years ago?

c. The majority of discussants agree that more people now participate in important community decisions than 10 years ago.

d. The majority of discussants agree that the local government now pays more attention to what "people like you" think when important decisions are made.

e. The majority of discussants agree that over the past 10 years the ability of the people in the community to contact the local government and influence its actions has increased.

These findings are consistent with the historical tensions between center and periphery in Mindanao. Indeed, in villages that have been directly
targeted in the all-out war, a distrust of national government is palpable. In
Glikati, residents find the continuous presence of the military unnerving,
while there is at least tacit support for the MILF. In Abanang, one discussant, Vicente, was more explicit: "If we follow MILF governance, this will
bring forth progress in the community." Yashir noted that the all-out war
was "declared by a democratic government . . . How can you say, then, that
democracy could help to promote prosperity of the community?"

Overall in Mindanao, discussants in both the low-MOP and the high-
MOP communities tend to have positive perceptions of the quality of local
democracy. In Bulipobla, Noli, a 42-year-old man, said, "The barangay officials
today are good. The barangay chairman knows how to handle the community
and works in a consultative aspect, unlike those past politicians who decide
on matters without consulting the people." Wadud, a 43-year-old man from
Paitatu, was similarly complimentary: "Our voices are given more attention
compared to 10 years ago. Our barangay chairman immediately responds to
problems raised by us the best way he can."

There were exceptions. Not all communities are pleased with their local
governments. In Lomamoli, a 29-year-old female discussant commented that
community leaders do not consult residents about community affairs: "they
only decide among themselves." A majority of male discussants believe that
neither their level of participation nor their influence has increased over the
past decade. In Dubiading, when asked whether people in the community
influence decisions of local government, a 30-year-old man observed, "If the
people would think that the decision made by the barangay chairman is not
good, it would still be the one followed."

In Dubiading, perceptions of the effectiveness of the barangay leadership (which is dominated by Muslims) split cleanly along religious lines.
For instance, of the 12 focus group discussants, the five Muslim men believe
that many people participate in community decision making, while the one
Christian man and six Christian women perceive decision making to be dominated by a few. The women said that Christians are not informed when community meetings take place, and the Christian man, Minggoy, observed, "The
ones who make decisions are those who are powerful, such as the barangay
chairman [a Muslim]."

Our results indicate that there is no simple relationship between democracy
and economic mobility in communities with social cleavages. In these environments the role of informal leaders may become particularly important.

## Informal leadership

Community survey questions on the quality of governance and democracy pertain to formal leaders and institutions only. But, as demonstrated by the experience of two of the high-MOP communities, Lomamoli and Dubiading, in some communities informal leaders and institutions may be perceived as more effective than their formal counterparts.

In Lomamoli, there is strong evidence to suggest that the sultan, a traditional leader, remains influential because formal leaders and representative institutions have failed to deliver peace and prosperity effectively. Asked how changes in democracy have affected the community, focus group discussants report a negative impact. It is easy to see why: elections are dreaded as a time of heightened tension and violence. Following mayoral elections in 1988, an elected incumbent was murdered by political rivals, and subsequent elections have been neither free nor fair. And for the residents of Lomamoli, formal political processes represent pain without gain since, once elected, barangay officials are largely ineffectual and corrupt. "They do not listen to us . . . they keep the money for themselves," observed Aliyah.[8] Under these conditions, the sultan retains a vital role: he is considered a provider of "moral and financial support," more powerful than the current barangay chairman.

While Bob, the founder of the zone of peace in Dubiading, is an important figurehead for that entire community, the small Christian minority in particular clings to him as their chosen representative. Since Christians represent only 5 percent of the population of this barangay (table 9.2), they have little hope of gaining a foothold in representative politics and perceive exclusion from community affairs. "There is no other person that we could easily approach except for Bob," said Tina, a participant in a women's focus group. But Bob's significance for Christians is due to his ability to overcome rather than reinforce sectarian politics. Although he considers himself a Christian, Bob's mother was Muslim, and this mixed background provides him an unparalleled degree of moral authority in the community. A women's focus group explained, "The high respect that is bestowed on Bob and his family has been theirs ever since [the declaration of the peace zone] . . . People have gotten used to approaching him every time they have concerns. Even Muslims look up at him because his mother was a Muslim."

As part of the zone of peace initiative, Bob runs a peace committee to mediate internal conflicts. In contrast to barangay meetings, gatherings of the peace committee are regarded as open to all: indeed, the committee derives its legitimacy from its inclusiveness. As will be explored in more detail below, the committee is an important outlet for those normally excluded from formal politics. Bob explained, "Everyone—men, women, children, the elderly, and married people—is free to throw in his or her opinion or question the validity of the litigants."

In sum, the experiences of these two communities suggest that where formal political processes are viewed as corrosive and corrupt, or elected officials as nonrepresentative, informal leaders may retain a high degree of influence. The snapshot of the relationship between local democracy and economic mobility presented by table 9.5 remains incomplete unless we consider the combined role of formal *and* informal leaders and institutions in advancing peace and community prosperity.

## Leaders as peacemakers

The experiences of the communities in the sample confirm the assertion by Barron, Diprose, and Woolcock (2006) that "local leaders play a large role in helping shape the specific 'cultural realm' which regulates conflictual action." As respected and well-off members of the communities, leaders prove indispensable in resolving ridos. In Lomamoli, the former mayor of the municipality, a local congressman, and the sultan each helped resolve family feuds. To end the rido in 1996, the ex-mayor appealed to the congressman, who agreed to pay 150,000 pesos to assuage each of the warring parties. By virtue of the respect he commanded in the community, the sultan both led his clan in conflict and harried them to peace: "family feuds have started to subside through the efforts of the sultan," remarked Hannah. In Dubiading, Bob is the arbitrator of disputes and the guarantor of peace. Warring factions tend to approach him for advice. "Uncle Bob then works on it," explained Hamid, a participant in a men's focus group. "He tells the conflicting parties, 'This person does not want to join your dispute. You will answer to me if you inflict harm on him.' That is the reason why those who are experiencing family feuds return. Almost all of us here have family grudges but we remain here because Uncle Bob is our warranty."

In highly fractionalized communities, leaders face a particularly sensitive task in bridging the divide between ethnic and religious groups. Postconflict assistance threatened to exacerbate tensions between Christians and Muslims in Newsib and Paitatu, localities in which Christian minorities have wielded disproportionate influence in local economic and political institutions. As discussed above, Muslims were antagonized by unequal access to emergency relief in Newsib. Barangay officials attempted to redress the imbalance; they "saw that Christians benefited the most from the assistance" and "tried to conduct a survey to locate the Muslims and convince them to return" so they could receive a share of the relief goods, according to Teodula. Their efforts have started to yield dividends: the majority of discussants perceive improvements in the levels of popular participation (table 9.5) as Muslims have begun to participate in traditionally Christian-dominated community affairs. Romulo reflected that "10 years ago the Muslims did not join meetings, they did not even stay in the center of the barangay for very long." This pattern has begun to change as Muslims gain faith that their local representatives are acting in their best interests.

In Paitatu, Camlon, the barangay captain, ensured the equitable distribution of external assistance, thereby diffusing a potential source of conflict between Christians and Muslims and between rich and poor. In 2000, in the wake of the all-out war, an NGO donated 12 houses; one year later a government agency provided a further 94 to replace all those damaged in the fighting. Camlon was in charge of allotting the homes. "We trusted him at first because we did not have any other choice," noted Abram, a Muslim discussant, but "he proved to be good and showed that he is helping the community, not for his own benefit but for the benefit of the residents of Paitatu." Badriah added, "We trusted him to choose the first beneficiaries of the initial 12 houses. He picked one family from each of the 12 big clans in the barangay. Later the rest of the residents were each given their own house. In fact, his house was one of the last to be built."

## Representation and external assistance

In a number of communities in the sample, leaders, whether formal or informal, can be credited with a vital role in attracting external assistance. In some cases this is closely linked to their role as peacemakers. Through his efforts to forge a permanent zone of peace, Bob has contributed to Dubiading's renown, making the village an obvious stop-off in President Arroyo's 2003 Mindanao tour even though it was not directly affected by the all-out war. By raising the profile of the village, Bob has helped ensure that it benefits from the attention of the national government. Similarly, Camlon, the barangay captain of Paitatu, has helped forge his village's reputation among relief organizations as a "model of transformed community," leading to an influx of assistance and accelerated economic mobility of the poor.[9]

In Bakimati, another community with high MPI levels, focus group discussants link the entry of NGOs, and their provision of infrastructure and livelihood programs, to the presence of Mayor Martha, elected in 2001. One of the mayor's first acts was to forge a peace covenant between warring factions. "Ever since the peace covenant was signed there have been a lot of people coming into our community," noted Rose, age 25. "These NGOS were not present before Mayor Martha took over as our municipal mayor." The community has since witnessed a large influx of external assistance, resulting in rehabilitated housing, electricity supplies, and a health center. According to Temil, "The best thing that has happened to our community is when we had our electric connection; this was due to the efforts of our municipal mayor." Rose added, "Since having our own health center, the children's mortality rate has dropped because we have been able to avail ourselves of free medical services."

The link between political representation and external assistance is not limited to the presence of effective leaders, however. Dubiading's change of administrative status in 2003 demonstrates that institutional mechanisms may also be essential for ensuring that external assistance is channeled toward communities in need. Between 1995 and 2003, Dubiading was in effect a "ghost barangay," deprived of political recognition by a corrupt mayor who knew that a majority of the residents opposed him. As a result, "we were never considered for any project from either the local or the national government," observed Hadji Assad. With the election of a new mayor in 2003, Dubiading's status as a barangay was restored. Assistance that had previously gone to a neighboring community began to flow in, leading to improvements in law and order, access to clean water, and a larger volume of trade.

## Women during and after Conflict: From Victims to Decision Makers?

Research on the impact of conflict in diverse settings indicates that despite its many harmful effects, it can present a window of opportunity for social and economic change. "Long years of separation and exposure to new social environments and attitudes, new perceptions of the role of the family and its members, and forced migration in search of employment, all contribute to continued dismantling of existing social institutions and the establishment of new ones" (Sørensen 1998, ix). Women can be direct beneficiaries of these changes. Indeed, one researcher claims that conflict in Mindanao has transformed "subservient and economically dependent Moro women into independent and assertive decision makers in their homes and in the community" (Margallo 2005). But the experiences of women in the sample communities indicate that this transformation is by no means automatic and will largely depend on the economic and institutional opportunities available to them in postconflict society.

## Opening the window of economic opportunity

Researchers observe that conflict can force women to take on roles in traditionally male domains because of the scarcity of male labor and the higher risk of violence against men (Bouta and Frerks 2002). The impact of conflict on women in Mindanao bears out these observations. Bob, the peace activist in Dubiading, noted that conflict affects men and women differently. Men are the direct targets in ridos, land conflicts, and separatist battles; as a result, they "do not go out, to avoid getting shot," and women "are the ones working in the mountains." Participants in other barangays told similar stories. Hannah, in Lomamoli: "[During the conflict] the men could not go to the mountains, to their farms. When their enemies knew that they were going to the mountains, they would block them . . . The women were the ones who visited the farms. We went there to check whether or not somebody harvested the crops." Gina, also in Lomamoli: "We [women] took care of the farms . . . We cooked [and sold] fried cassava for us to get by." Romulo, in Newsib: "During conflict, only the women are allowed to go out and coordinate with their neighbors about the evacuation . . . Women at this time are freer than men."

But conflict can of course impede the socioeconomic opportunities of women as well as advance them. "If war had not happened, I would have finished my education. I would not have resorted to marrying at an early age," reflected Ambao from Tucampo. Armed conflict between the AFP and MILF in Glikati in 1997 broke up a women's organization that had provided start-up capital for small businesses. When its members were evacuated, the organization collapsed. Returning to the village after a year, the women were too busy rebuilding their individual lives to revive the group. And while conflict forced growing numbers of women into the labor force in Lomamoli, they did not automatically experience their altered status as a form of liberation. Indeed, all female participants say that they were greatly burdened by their new responsibilities during the conflict.

Whether upheaval due to conflict translates into lasting, positive economic changes for women depends to a large extent on the level of economic opportunities in their community. In the high-MOP communities, where postconflict assistance has ushered in improved infrastructure and social services, women have tended to benefit. In Dubiading, Tina is just one of a number of women who have profited from infrastructure improvements since 2003. The road has brought in new private sector employers, such as the construction company where Tina works as a cook, and the increased traffic has meant a viable consumer market for her cake business. Her economic opportunities have multiplied. "I saw a great change in my life starting in 2004," said Tina. "That was the time that I had work that I could depend on. My husband's income has helped us too but in our household we are really depending on my income."

As those primarily responsible for the household chores, including fetching water and washing clothes at the spring, women have been the greatest beneficiaries of the new water and electricity systems in Lomamoli. Their household burdens are lighter, and with refrigeration they can generate additional income selling ice candy. In Bakimati, a community with below-average MOP but the third-highest level of MPI, the construction of a farm-to-market road means that women "can now sell along the road because there are now more vehicles passing by the area," according to Rose. "Before, it was only men who were able to find a means of livelihood and women would just have to stay at home." Most women are involved in "buy and sell businesses now and are given more opportunities to sell in our local market," added Mariam.

The building of new facilities such as schools and clinics also brings new opportunities for women. In Glikati, the community with the fourth-highest level of MOP, Tina reported, "Since the high school was built people find other means to earn by selling cooked food and snacks near the school. It is a good opportunity for the people, especially the women." Tuks, a 40-year-old woman in Glikati, agreed: "Before, it was just my husband who worked for the family. He was a fisherman and a farmer . . . Now, my husband still farms but I have a small convenience store that I manage. The store helped us so much, especially since we are located at the back of the high school where many students come and buy candies and other goods."

But in communities where postconflict assistance has not resulted in significant improvements in basic infrastructure and services, women's economic opportunities are even more limited than those of their husbands, brothers, and sons. In spite of well-intentioned efforts to boost the economic independence of women through credit and livelihood assistance schemes, women have found it difficult to generate additional sources of income in the low-MOP communities. According to Khalid, a male discussant, the credit scheme for women in Bulipobla failed in part because they had no prior business experience. The providers "should have conducted livelihood seminars before giving the funding," he observed. Even more important, poor access to markets meant that women starting up businesses were almost bound to fail. Infrastructure improvements, including better transport and road connections to neighboring towns and villages, are essential if women's economic ventures are to succeed.

## Airing their thoughts

In addition to broadening the scope for women's economic participation, postconflict societies can provide women with new roles in informal peace processes, civil society, and community-driven development, which may eventually lead to a greater role in formal politics (Bouta and Frerks 2002; Sørensen 1998). Research on Mindanao indicates that with the support of government agencies and NGOs, women have gained confidence in advocating for peace, although their role in formal politics remains limited (Margallo 2005).

The experiences of several communities in the sample provide some, albeit scant, evidence of a growing role for women in formal politics in recent years. In both Dubiading and Bakimati, women have reached unprecedented levels of political power. "Women are beginning to get involved in leadership," observed Bob. "One example is . . . the vice mayor, the second in command. When the barangay chairman is not there, she is the one who decides things." In Bakimati, Mayor Martha is particularly popular among female focus group discussants. Mariam reflected, "Finding a means of livelihood is easier since she became our mayor. If there are ever conflicts, they are now easily pacified, and there are more NGOs that have extended some assistance to our barangay."

But it is in the realm of informal politics and community associations that women have tended to achieve prominence. As discussed above, Dubiading's peace committee offers an inclusive organization for those, such as Christians, women, and youth, who tend to be excluded from formal community-level politics. Bob observes gradual changes among Maranao women, whose freedom to participate in public gatherings has been heavily circumscribed until recently: "Little by little, Maranao women were influenced by our liberated ways to the point that they can now participate in the conflict resolution litigation . . . Slowly, they are liberated. Slowly, they are able to speak out, ask questions, and observe the procedures in a conflict resolution exercise."

In Bakimati, women have benefited from a spike in associations, networks, and organizations since the end of the all-out war. Two organizations in particular have helped promote women socially and economically. One, which provides dressmaking training and start-up capital to women, has 300 members in the barangay. The other is an association of health workers. In Glikati, where associational life remained dormant in the wake of conflict in 1997, a new women's association was organized in 2006.

Women's growing role in community and associational structures has contributed to perceptible shifts in attitudes in traditionally patriarchal societies. Bob claims that women's increased voice has empowered them to reject arranged marriages: "In fact, many of them are already liberated to say, 'No, I will not be married to that man.'" Slowly but surely, attitudes regarding polygamy are changing. "Old folks who have been practicing polygamy are starting to campaign against it . . . The campaign came from them and not from us," Bob noted. In Glikati, women testify to their own empowerment. "The NGO helped me so much in knowing what I want. I can openly say what is on my mind," declared Shainah, age 52. Twenty-six-year-old Mirah said, "I open my thoughts. I can say what I want to say. Right after the conflict, I learned that if I do not air my thoughts I will continue to struggle." She concluded, with a laugh, "Nobody can say what I can or cannot do."

But evidence from Lomamoli suggests that even if women benefit from greater economic opportunities in the postconflict period, this will not automatically translate into higher social or political status in traditionally patriarchal societies. Institutional shifts are required to facilitate an increase in women's public profiles. Female focus group discussants testify that their role in community decision making remains heavily circumscribed. "Women are not good in discussions like that . . . we would answer incorrectly if we were to join such a meeting," said two participants, Hannah and Gina. According to Hannah, women in the community respond to the orders of the sultan: if he were to tell them to participate in community meetings, they would do so. The implication is that until he gives such an order, these women will stand on the sidelines.

## Conclusion: Movers' Stories in Perspective

Usman, Akmed, Manuel, and Tina, the four movers whose stories started this chapter, are individuals, and their life stories are theirs alone. But Usman, Akmed, Manuel, and Tina are also products of their environments, and their stories would certainly be different if they were living somewhere else. If Usman lived in Kilaluna instead of Abanang, he would have been deprived of the united community that was a crucial source of support during the all-out war. If Akmed were from Bulipobla rather than Lomamoli, his household would have less chance of generating the dual income that proved vital for economic mobility. If Manuel lived in Newsib instead of Bakimati, he would have benefited less from strong leadership and good governance. And had Tina lived anywhere other than Dubiading, she might have experienced less confidence in her own abilities to turn her household's fortunes around.

This chapter has attempted to identify factors that have enabled communities to move out of poverty in Mindanao. Toward this end, it has focused on key differences in the conflict and postconflict experiences of communities with high and low levels of poverty mobility. These differences are summarized in table 9.6.

The impact of conflict on each of the communities in the sample should not be underestimated. But a comparative study of the experiences of high- and low-MOP villages reveals significant differences. In the bottom three communities, external conflicts were characterized by an almost unremitting struggle between center and periphery, resulting in long periods of evacuation, while drawn-out land conflicts placed Christians and Muslims at loggerheads. In the top three communities, external conflict was an irregular occurrence, and internal conflicts, where they occurred, did not fractionalize entire communities. Whereas the peace zone concept has been largely foisted on the low-MOP communities by external organizations, in high-MOP Dubiading and Lomamoli it has been driven by a grassroots demand for stability. This in turn has helped institutionalize a culture of coexistence, and even cooperation, among neighbors.

While all the communities have benefited from external assistance in the wake of the all-out war, in high-mobility communities external assistance has brought a comprehensive overhaul of basic infrastructure—roads, water, and electricity—as well as significant improvements in health and education services. In low-mobility communities access to consumer markets is constrained by inadequate roads, and basic infrastructures and services remain poor. In these cases, external support has often only plastered over the cracks, providing economic assistance programs with little long-term sustainability.

Local leaders and representative institutions have played a vital role in forging peaceful conditions and attracting external assistance. Informal leaders have compensated for ineffective or unrepresentative institutions in two of the high-MOP communities, Lomamoli and Dubiading. In low-MOP communities local leaders have faced an unfortunate combination of deep conflict scars and inadequate support from external organizations. It should be no surprise that in these cases, good leadership has yet to translate into economic mobility.

**TABLE 9.6**
**Key characteristics of Mindanao study communities with high and low MOP**

| Community mobility level | External conflict | Internal conflict | Peace zones | External assistance | Local leadership | Women's position |
|---|---|---|---|---|---|---|
| High MOP | Episodes can be severe but are isolated | Nonexistent or contained; religious divides do not spark violence | Well-established, internally driven, effective | Key infrastructure and basic services | Positive impact on community prosperity has translated into MOP; informal leaders mediate religious divisions and compensate for ineffective governance | Increased economic and in some cases political roles in postconflict society |
| Low MOP | Multiple severe episodes | Long-standing and ongoing land conflicts, associated with religious divides | Recent, externally imposed, untested | Small-scale livelihood assistance; key infrastructure still lacking | Positive impact on community prosperity has yet to translate into MOP | Return to traditional roles after conflict |

*Source:* Authors' analysis of Moving Out of Poverty study data.

In communities affected by conflict, women's transition from "subservient and economically dependent" actors to "independent and assertive decision makers" (Margallo 2005) is far from automatic. Only high-mobility communities provide the economic opportunities conducive to a long-term reconfiguration of gender roles. But even in these cases, a shift in local institutions is required to ensure the incorporation of women in community decision making.

## Policy implications

On the basis of the experiences of the 10 communities in the sample, and in particular those with the highest and lowest levels of MOP, it is possible to suggest five broad policy recommendations.

*A lasting peace must be generated from the bottom up*
The experiences of the three highest-mobility villages point to a potentially virtuous cycle between internal cohesion, external assistance, and economic incentives for peace. But this mutually reinforcing relationship depends in part on genuine grassroots demands for peace. This does not imply that the government, NGOs, or donors should wait passively for autonomous local peace movements to spring up. Rather, it suggests that external parties must identify budding movements and potential leaders and pay adequate attention to local capacity building and leadership training programs to help reinforce an indigenous culture of peace.

*External assistance should provide sustainable opportunities for income generation and economic diversification*
In stark contrast to the communities with the lowest levels of MOP, each of the high-mobility communities has experienced major improvements in its basic infrastructure, boosting the commercial viability of agriculture and expanding off-farm opportunities. Although outside agencies will be reluctant to make significant infrastructure investments in communities that are still highly vulnerable to destructive conflict, small leaps of faith may be required, since the economic opportunities ushered in by external assistance can themselves boost incentives for peace. External agencies must step beyond emergency relief and stand-alone livelihood assistance projects and search for opportunities to contribute to the lasting expansion of economic possibilities.

*The national government must accelerate its efforts to support development in Mindanao*
While the testimonies of some discussants point to deep-seated disaffection with the central government, the experience of high-MOP communities indicates the benefits that can accrue to those that have received Manila's attention.

The notion that the future of peace rests on efforts to boost development in Mindanao has not been lost on the national government: service delivery, infrastructure development, livelihood support, land tenure reform, affirmative action for Muslims, and community-based reconciliation programs have been on the agenda since 2003. A radical rethinking is not required. Rather, with the help of its development partners, the government must step up its current program to reverse a history of insensitivity to Moro traditions and neglect of socioeconomic needs.

*Local representative institutions should strive to incorporate minorities*
While both high- and low-mobility villages testify to the vital role played by local leaders in promoting peace and prosperity, a significant divide emerges in some communities where particular groups have rallied behind informal, rather than formal, leaders. To resolve a long-term legitimacy gap that could prove particularly damaging when individual informal leaders disappear from public life, local democratic structures should encourage the participation of potentially marginalized groups. Depending on communities' circumstances, one approach may be to incorporate informal leaders themselves into representative institutions. Programs to enhance the voice of ethnic and religious minorities and to ensure their representation on local decision-making bodies could also prove vital.

*Women's leadership and economic potential must be realized*
In communities with low MOP, women have tended to return to their traditional private sphere after war winds down, despite short-term shifts in gender roles during the conflict. The experience of some of the high-MOP communities, on the other hand, indicates the importance of women's ongoing contribution to household income and community cohesion. The postconflict period presents a window of opportunity for women. While this transition may be in part automatic (for instance, infrastructure assistance can make new economic opportunities available to women), community-based organizations and NGOs can play a crucial role in strengthening women's leadership capacity through appropriate assistance and training.

An integrated strategy that combines local-level institution building with high-level support for economic development would help make stories like Usman's, Akmed's, Manuel's, and Tina's a reality for many more people in Mindanao. Such a strategy could help poor people move themselves out of poverty. Or, to borrow the analogy provided by Jamilah from Abanang, it could turn milking cows that no longer have any milk into coconut trees that never lose their fruit.

# Notes

The Mindanao study is part of the global Moving Out of Poverty study led by Deepa Narayan in the Poverty Reduction and Economic Management (PREM) Network of the World Bank. For a discussion of key study concepts and data collection methods, see chapter 1 and the appendixes to this volume. Also see volume 2 of the Moving Out of Poverty series (Narayan, Pritchett, and Kapoor 2009) and the study methodology guide (Narayan and Petesch 2005).

Lead researchers for the Mindanao study were Erlinda Montillo-Burton, Chona R. Echavez, and Imelda G. Pagtulon-an. Mary Judd and Ashutosh Varshney provided useful comments on earlier versions of the chapter.

1. To protect the privacy of participants, this chapter uses pseudonyms for the 10 study villages (barangays). Cities, municipalities, provinces, and islands are identified by their real names.
2. There was no fighting between government troops and the MILF in Lomamoli, Dubiading, and Newsib in 2000. However, Dubiading and Newsib were the sites of skirmishes in 2002 and 2003, respectively.
3. Bananas, coconut oil, iron ore, and pineapple are the principal export products.
4. According to the United Nations, real per capita income was lowest in Sulu, followed by Tawi-Tawi, Basilan, Maguindanao, and Zamboanga del Norte. Human development rankings were lowest in Sulu, followed by Maguindanao, Tawi-Tawi, and Basilan (UNDP 2005).
5. Five people were killed in gunfire, six died due to sickness during evacuation, and two women died while giving birth in the forest during evacuation.
6. Discussants were asked to rate the ease of finding private employment in both 1996 and 2006, with 1 representing "very easy" and 6 representing "very difficult." In Dubiading they rated access at 5 in 1996 and 3 in 2006.
7. Discussants in Paitatu, Newsib, and Bulipobla rated the ease of finding private employment at 6 ("very difficult") in both 1996 and 2006.
8. Similarly, in Tucampo, where barangay elections caused a rido in 2003, there is broad dissatisfaction with the quality of local democracy (table 9.5).
9. See "Inudaran Projects" on the Web site of Pakigdait Inc., http://pakigdaitinc1.tripod.com/hedlyn002.htm.

# References

ARMM Social Fund Project. 2006. *Community Development Assistance (CDA) Component Operations Manual*. Manila: World Bank.

Barron, P., R. Diprose, and M. Woolcock. 2006. "Local Conflict and Community Development in Indonesia: Assessing the Impact of the Kecamatan Development Program." Indonesian Social Development Paper 10, World Bank, Jakarta.

Bouta, T., and G. Frerks. 2002. *Women's Roles in Conflict Prevention, Conflict Resolution, and Post-Conflict Reconstruction: Literature Review and Institutional Analysis*. The Hague: Netherlands Institute of International Relations Clingendael.

Buendia, R. 2005. "The State-Moro Armed Conflict in the Philippines: Unresolved National Question or Question of Governance." *Asian Journal of Political Science* 13 (1): 109–38.

Bush, K. 2004. *Building Capacity for Peace and Unity: The Role of Local Government in Peacebuilding.* Ottawa: Federation of Canadian Municipalities. http://www.inter national.canurb.com/pdf/Peace_ENG.pdf.

Cavanaugh, K. A. 2000. "Understanding Protracted Social Conflict: A Basic Needs Approach." In *Reconcilable Differences: Turning Points in Ethnopolitical Conflict,* ed. C. Irvin and S. Byrne, 65–78. West Hartford, CT: Kumarian Press.

Confesor, N. 2005. "The Philippines: In Search of a 'Transformed' Society—Building Peaceful Social Relations—By, for, and with the People." Paper prepared for "Dialogue in the Social Integration Process," expert group meeting at the United Nations, New York, November 21–23.

Gaspar, K. M., E. A. Lapad, and A. J. Maravillas. 2002. *Mapagpakamalinawon: A Reader for the Mindanawan Peace Advocate.* Davao City, Philippines: Alternative Forum for Research in Mindanao and Catholic Relief Services/Philippines.

Gowing, P., and R. McAmis. 1974. *The Muslim Filipinos.* Manila: Solidaridad Publishing House.

Gutierrez, E., and S. Borras Jr. 2004. *The Moro Conflict: Landlessness and Misdirected State Policies.* Policy Studies, no. 8. Washington, DC: East-West Center.

Margallo, S. 2005. "Addressing Gender in Conflict and Post-Conflict Situations in the Philippines." Social Development Papers, Conflict Prevention and Reconstruction Paper 20, World Bank, Washington, DC.

Narayan, D., and P. Petesch. 2005. "Moving Out of Poverty Methodology Guide." Poverty Reduction Group, Poverty Reduction and Economic Management Network, World Bank, Washington, DC.

Narayan, D., L. Pritchett, and S. Kapoor. 2009. *Moving Out of Poverty: Success from the Bottom Up.* New York: Palgrave Macmillan; Washington, DC: World Bank.

Rood, S. 2005. *Forging Sustainable Peace in Mindanao: The Role of Civil Society.* Washington, DC: East-West Center.

Schiavo-Campo, S., and M. Judd. 2005. "Mindanao Conflict in the Philippines: Roots, Costs, and Potential Peace Dividend." Social Development Papers, Conflict Prevention and Reconstruction Paper 24, World Bank, Washington, DC.

Sørensen, B. 1998. *Women and Post-Conflict Reconstruction: Issues and Sources.* WSP Occasional Paper 3. Geneva: United Nations Research Institute for Social Development.

UNDP (United Nations Development Programme). 2005. *Peace and Conflict Prevention: Human Security.* Philippine Human Development Report 2005. New York: UNDP.

Wernstedt, F., and P. Simkins. 1965. "Migrations and the Settlement of Mindanao." *Journal of Asian Studies* 25 (1): 83–103.

# Disturbing the Equilibrium: Movements Out of Poverty in Conflict-Affected Areas of Indonesia

*Patrick Barron, Sri Kusumastuti Rahayu, Sunita Varada, and Vita Febriany*

> *In 1995 we were free to enter the two communities, Christian and Muslim. But in 1999, the conflict occurred. In 2002 when we returned from evacuation, the intimate harmony between the two religions began to loosen up.*
>
> —A 68-YEAR-OLD MAN,
> Galalolo, North Maluku province

> *Assistance from the government has helped recovery. People became more confident to return. There is now trust and good relations. The assistance to farmers in 2004 and 2005 from North Halmahera district included tractors and vegetable and peanut seeds.*
>
> —MEN'S DISCUSSION GROUP,
> Yasapira, North Maluku province

I ndonesia's postcolonial history can be read as an ambitious attempt to pursue the dual objectives of reducing poverty and building national cohesion. When Sukarno declared the country's independence in 1945, he inherited a nation that ranked among the world's poorest, despite its massive natural resource wealth. It was also one of the most religiously, ethnically, and culturally diverse. A lack of progress on poverty reduction helped bring about his fall in 1967; by then, per capita annual income was around $50 (Suryahadi, Sumarto, and Pritchett 2003).

The incoming New Order government under General Suharto premised its legitimacy on an aggressive strategy of national development. In Suharto's eyes, this required improving macroeconomic management, attracting foreign investment, and building physical, health, and education infrastructure across the country. But it also involved a concerted effort to maintain strong, centralized control by the state. Village governance structures were homogenized under a 1979 law to ensure that officials governed in the remotest corner of Papua as they did in urban areas of Java. A military command system saw army personnel stationed in every village. Any source of conflict that could undermine Indonesia's ethnic and religious harmony, and hence jeopardize the economic "miracle," had to be contained. Despite egregious human rights abuses and a lack of basic political freedoms, for many years the development strategy seemed to be working. By 1991 real per capita gross domestic product (GDP) had reached $610, a result of annual growth of 4.6 percent that peaked at over 9 percent in 1995. Poverty fell from 54.2 million people in 1976 to 22.5 million in 1996—from 40 percent to just over 11 percent (Suryahadi, Sumarto, and Pritchett 2003).

The house of cards collapsed with astonishing speed. The Asian financial crisis revealed just how rotten Indonesia's financial and economic institutions really were. As the extent of bad debt, much of it involving Suharto's cronies, was exposed, money fled the country and the banking system all but failed. In July 1997, $1 bought around 2,400 rupiah. By January 1998, the currency had devalued to Rp 18,000 per $1, a 750 percent depreciation (World Bank 2006). Poverty more than doubled in 1998, barely falling in 1999. The basic bargain of the Suharto years, in which Indonesians traded their freedoms in return for economic growth and stability, no longer held.

A wave of violence swept the country, challenging the basis of the Indonesian nation. Communal conflicts broke out in the Maluku islands, Sulawesi, and Indonesian Borneo. Old separatist conflicts in Papua and Aceh, at either end of Indonesia's archipelago, reignited. More localized forms of violence, including land conflicts, vigilante lynchings, and local political unrest, also erupted. One account, based on incidents reported in provincial newspapers in 14 provinces (excluding Papua and Aceh), estimated 10,247 deaths from communal violence in 1997–2001 (Varshney, Panggabean, and Tadjoeddin 2008). But the real impacts of the violence were undoubtedly underreported (Barron and Sharpe 2008). The failure of institutional legitimacy was compounded by increasing poverty levels and, in particular, limited opportunities for young men to obtain salaried employment. Indonesia has immense ethnic and religious diversity—almost 300 ethnic groups speaking 250 languages are spread across 17,000 islands. Imagining a coherent national community (Anderson 1991) has always been a difficult and delicate task. As a vicious cycle of violence, increased poverty, and eroded institutions led to social fragmentation, some observers began to speculate whether Indonesia could hold together.

The postcrisis period saw an uneven recovery from the paroxysms of poverty and conflict. Indonesia's economic woes proved more enduring than those in most other Southeast Asian countries. Economic growth inched up slowly, reaching 4.5 percent by 2003. Nevertheless, 2005 growth rates were still below the precrisis figures and far from the peak achieved in 1995. The improvement in economic performance was insufficient to absorb the increase in the labor force; as of 2009, unemployment remains widespread and continues to rise. Nor has growth been enough to seriously address the problem of poverty (Suryahadi, Sumarto, and Pritchett 2003). In 2006 poverty stood at nearly 18 percent, using the Indonesian statistics bureau's measure of about $1.50 expenditure per day (BPS 2008).[1] According to the World Bank (2006), 42 percent of Indonesians were living on less than $2 per day.

The incidence of poverty and the extent of poverty reduction are uneven across the national territory. Wide differences in per capita GDP persist between western and eastern Indonesia. In Java and Bali, poverty rates in 2006 were 15.7 percent, and in remote Papua, 38.7 percent. There are also great differences within regions and provinces. Some regions that produced agricultural and fishery commodities for export (like pepper, palm oil, rubber, nutmeg, cloves, copra, and shrimp) were hit less hard by the financial crisis. They experienced an initial rise in prosperity after the crisis because of the huge decrease in the value of the rupiah and increase in export earnings.[2]

Similarly, while the level and impacts of violent conflict have fallen since the 1998–2001 period, they are still severe. A nationwide survey in 2003 found almost 5,000 deaths from conflict in the preceding year (Barron, Kaiser, and Pradhan 2009). The two separatist conflicts and the intercommunal violence have eased, but more localized forms of conflict have taken their place, collectively accounting for significant impacts (Barron and Sharpe 2008; Welsh 2008).

Levels and impacts of violent conflict, and trends over time, also vary extensively between and within regions. The 2003 survey found high or medium levels of conflict in 109 rural districts (*kabupaten*) and towns (*kota*), around one-quarter of the Indonesian total (NPRC 2005). Further evidence on large-scale and local conflicts points to significant regional and local variation, with violence concentrated in a number of "hot spots" (Varshney, Panggabean, and Tadjoeddin 2008).

Unexpectedly, the Moving Out of Poverty study of 10 Indonesian communities revealed higher rates of poverty reduction in the villages that experienced large-scale conflict than in areas without large-scale intercommunal conflict. After describing the study's approach and sample, we explore the factors that may account for the relatively rapid and inclusive recovery in the high-conflict area, and we compare these findings with conditions and trends in the more peaceful region. The analysis highlights the importance of several factors that influence poor people's mobility: postconflict aid, the decentralization of the public sector, income diversification, and community-level collective action. We then discuss how the nature of conflict itself can shape mobility prospects, and conclude with a synthesis of the main findings.

## The Study in Indonesia

The Moving Out of Poverty study seeks to understand variations in the extent to which people can move out of poverty and stay out of it, and how experiences of conflict affect such moves. Previous analyses of poverty in Indonesia, such as the World Bank's comprehensive poverty assessment (2006), have focused on macro factors that drive poverty. The present study aims to complement this in several ways.

First, it focuses on variations and changes in poverty levels and patterns at the community level. This allows for an exploration of the *local factors* that help account for variance in poverty across communities. Second, it tracks the movements of households and individuals in and out of poverty. This helps us understand how the *characteristics of households* partially determine their poverty situation.[3] A third purpose of the study, and the primary focus of this chapter, is to look at how *conflict* affects people's movements out of, or into, poverty.

Violent conflict has often been identified as a driver of poverty. Lost productivity from violent conflict and crime outside of war zones is estimated to amount to $95 billion per year (Geneva Declaration Secretariat 2008, 100). Countries experiencing civil wars suffer an annual reduction in GDP of 2.0–2.2 percent (Collier 1999; Hoeffler and Reynal-Querol 2003; Restrepo et al. 2008). Civil wars tend to cost between $60 billion and $250 billion (Collier, Chauvet, and Hegre 2008). Incomes are reduced by around 15 percent and the portion of people living in absolute poverty increases by about 30 percent (Moser 2006).

Yet while the macro impacts of violence on poverty may be almost universally negative, the poverty-conflict nexus at the micro level is more complicated. Conflicts create winners and losers, and some people may be enriched by violence.[4] Different forms of conflict may have different poverty impacts. Conflicts can also lead to postconflict responses that change poverty dynamics. Aid, or efforts to strengthen local institutions, may help some move out of poverty. In contrast, if aid is captured by (former) elites, it can consolidate poverty among the marginalized.

## Constructing the sample

The study compared movements out of poverty in areas that experienced high levels of conflict with mobility in peaceful areas in another part of the country. Intra-area analysis is used to examine in more depth the reasons for variations in poverty movements between communities and, below that, between households. The methodological principles used for the various Moving Out of Poverty studies are outlined in chapter 1 and the technical appendixes; only a brief note on how these principles were applied to the Indonesian case is necessary here.

The sampling strategy tried to maximize variation in factors that might be associated with levels and changes of poverty. We chose to study the provinces of North Maluku and East Java (map 10.1) because of differences in their histories of conflict, detailed in the next section. But they also differ in almost every other respect (table 10.1).

**MAP 10.1**
**Indonesia with study provinces**

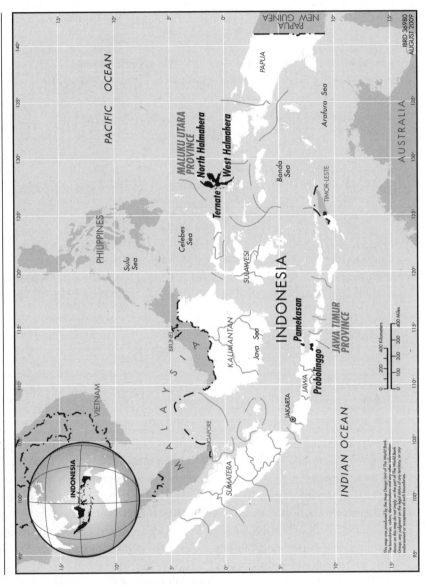

**TABLE 10.1**
**Profile of the Indonesia study provinces**

| Characteristic | North Maluku | East Java |
|---|---|---|
| Conflict (1995–2005) | High-intensity intercommunal violence | No intercommunal conflict |
| Remoteness (distance from Jakarta) | Remote | Not remote (same island as Jakarta) |
| Province size | 140,256 square km[a] | 47,158 square km |
| Population size (2005) | 884,000 | 36,535,527 |
| Regional GDP per capita (2004) | Not available because of the conflict | Rp 1,782,391 |
| Poverty rate (2004) | 12.4% | 20.1% |
| Inequality (2004) | Lower | Higher |
| Sources of income and commodities | Farming annual crops (cloves, coconut, nutmeg, lemon), fishing, carpentry, transport, civil service | Farming seasonal crops (tobacco, rice), fishing, trading |
| Religious diversity in the study communities | Diverse (split between Christians and Muslims) | Not diverse (almost all Muslims) |
| Ethnic diversity | Diverse (mixed local ethnic groups) | Not diverse (across province mainly Javanese; within sampled communities, mainly Madurese) |

*Sources:* Conflict: Community synthesis reports on the 10 Moving Out of Poverty sample communities. Province size: BPS 2005b, except as noted. GDP and poverty rate: BPS 2005a. Income sources and religious/ethnic diversity: community profiles (see table 10.3 for details).

a. This figure includes the water in the territory of North Maluku. If only land is included, the size is 33,278 square kilometers (Yanuarti et al. 2004).

Within provinces, districts were selected to maximize variation in growth over the 1995–2005 period. In North Maluku, North Halmahera district and Ternate municipality/city have relatively high growth, and West Halmahera has lower growth; in East Java, Probolinggo was the high-growth district and Pamekasan the lower-growth district.[5] Ten communities were then selected to maximize variation in conflict levels using the government's 2003 Village Potential Statistics (PODES) survey, other conflict reports, and information from local key informants. Table 10.2 shows the communities chosen for the study by growth and conflict levels.[6]

The sample communities also varied in terms of their religious and ethnic diversity, with those in North Maluku being more diverse (table 10.3).

**TABLE 10.2**
**Distribution of the Indonesia study communities by growth and conflict levels**

|  | Growth (district level) | |
| --- | --- | --- |
| Intercommunal conflict | Low | High |
| None (East Java) | Kacokerre, Pamekasan district Tattantok, Pamekasan district Kramrrak, Pamekasan district | Patobako, Probolinggo district Kalisido, Probolinggo district |
| High (North Maluku) | Galalolo, West Halmahera district; Bodolenge, West Halmahera district | Yasapira, North Halmahera district; Lupotogo, North Halmahera district Barumangga, Ternate district |

*Source:* Community profiles.
*Note:* The study communities are identified by pseudonyms in this chapter.

**TABLE 10.3**
**Major ethnic and religious groups in the Indonesia study communities, 2005**

| Province/ community | Rural/urban | Ethnicity | Religion |
| --- | --- | --- | --- |
| *East Java* | | | |
| Kacokerre | Rural | Madurese (99%), Javanese | Muslim (100%) |
| Kalisido | Semi-urban | Madurese (70%), Javanese, Batak, Chinese | Muslim (97%), Christian, Buddist |
| Patobako | Rural | Madurese (60%), Javanese, Batak, Chinese | Muslim (97%), Christian, Buddist |
| Tattantok | Rural | Madurese (100%) | Muslim (100%) |
| Kramrrak | Semi-urban | Madurese (100%) | Muslim (100%) |
| *North Maluku* | | | |
| Galalolo | Rural | Sanger (45%), other smaller groups | Christian (60%), Muslim (40%) |
| Bodolenge | Rural | Sahu (54%), other smaller groups | Christian (100%) |
| Yasapira | Rural | Tobelo (60%), other smaller groups | Muslim (87%), Christian (13%) |
| Barumangga | Urban | Tidore (60%), other smaller groups | Muslim (90%), Christian (10%) |
| Lupotogo | Semi-urban | Tobelo (90%), other smaller groups | Muslim (75%), Christian (25%) |

*Source:* Community profiles.

## Methodology

Twenty-six researchers conducted fieldwork in Indonesia between July and September 2005. Within each community, an integrated package of quantitative and qualitative instruments was used (see appendix C for a list of data collection methods). The qualitative work included 81 focus group discussions and 156 individual life story interviews conducted across the Indonesian study locations. "Ladder of life" focus groups in each village placed households in their community on different steps of a figurative ladder to document their poverty experiences over 10 years. These groups also set the community poverty line (CPL) in their village. The rankings of individual households in relation to the poverty line were then used to generate a number of indexes tracking local poverty dynamics over the 1995–2005 period; these in turn provided the basis for comparative analysis of poverty mobility patterns across communities. The qualitative fieldwork also probed the processes by which individuals and communities became richer (or poorer) and the factors favoring or constraining such movements. Quantitative work included a survey of 372 households that could be used for statistical analysis of these patterns and to shed further light on factors that significantly helped individuals move out of poverty.

## Experiences of Conflict in the Study Communities

North Maluku and East Java had very different experiences of violent conflict over the study period, 1995–2005. Communities in North Maluku endured widespread, deadly intercommunal violence between 1999 and 2000, which caused almost all the people in the sample villages (at least on Halmahera) to evacuate for three years. In contrast, East Java was chosen to represent areas with no intercommunal conflict. The area experienced low levels of violent conflict, with most incidents localized. These had smaller, but nonetheless important, impacts on the social and economic life of those communities.

### Widespread violence in North Maluku

The previously peaceful region of North Maluku experienced a series of ethnic, political, and religious riots from 1999 to 2000. Ethnic conflict over the proposed establishment of a new subdistrict (*kecamatan*) in an area with significant natural resources escalated into a province-wide religious war.[7]

The violence began in the Kao gulf in Malifut, a rural subdistrict in northern Halmahera. It involved indigenous ethnic Kao and a community of migrants, the Makians, who had been relocated to the area by the government in 1975. While the Kao accepted the presence of migrants on their customary land, Makians in the political and social elite lobbied to form a separate subdistrict in the area. In May 1999 the government issued a regulation mandating the split. The Kao opposed the new subdistrict, claiming that the area was their traditional land and that the new boundaries cut through their community. The recent discovery of gold in the area made the issue more contentious.

Tensions peaked on August 18, 1999, when a Makian attack destroyed two Kao villages. Had the district government acted impartially, the violence might have halted at this point. But the government ignored Kao demands for compensation for the villages. Two months later several thousand Kao attacked Malifut, driving the entire community from Halmahera and destroying the new subdistrict (Wilson 2005). While religion was peripheral to the initial outbreak, the fact that the Makians were Muslim and the Kao largely Christian set the scene for the religious carnage that followed.

Makians displaced by the attack fled to the provincial capital of Ternate. On the evening of November 3 an anti-Christian riot erupted in Tidore, destroying all the Christians' houses and churches and killing several dozen people.

Three days later, rioting started in southern Ternate. The security forces did little to prevent the attacks: 31 people were killed and a large number injured. Six churches and 353 houses were destroyed. The almost 13,000 Christians living in the city fled to police and military bases and to the sultan's palace and were soon evacuated to North Sulawesi province. Violence then broke out across the province. Fighting in Tobelo city led to the deaths of over a thousand people in the surrounding subdistrict in just a few days. Hundreds of Muslims died in attacks on villages by a Christian militia, the Pasukan Merah (Red Force). Similarly, battles between villages devastated the subdistrict of Galela, and most Christians fled to Tobelo (Wilson 2008, 96–129).

While Christians and Muslims were fighting across the province, political conflict came to the fore in Ternate, the administrative heart of North Maluku. The violence here was between two Muslim factions divided by ethnicity and politics. The clashes became known as the *putih-kuning* (White-Yellow) conflict, after the colors worn by the opposing groups. Throughout 1999 the North Maluku political and bureaucratic elite had divided into two ethnopolitical factions, one surrounding the sultan of Ternate and the other the Central Halmahera district head. Tensions grew over several issues, notably the governorship and the location of the provincial capital, issues that held enormous implications for the ethnic and patronage networks of each leader.[8]

On December 27, 1999, a fight broke out between members of the Pasu-kan Kuning (Yellow Force, representing the sultan of Ternate) and a group of youths. The following morning, clashes between the Yellow and White forces swept through the city. When the Yellow Force set fire to dozens of houses owned by Tidore migrants, thousands came on boats from Tidore and fought the sultan's forces, who were defeated.

These events were quickly forgotten as thousands of displaced Muslims began arriving from Tobelo. Muslims set aside their political rivalries and sought to retaliate against Christians in the Kao region and Tobelo/Galela on Halmahera, forming the Jihad Force. The attempted attacks against Kao were halted by military and police. The militia that traveled to Galela faced much less resistance from the security forces (Wilson 2008, 147–76). The first target of the Jihad Force was the main Christian stronghold of Duma village in Galela. Approximately 250 Christians died. Unable to attack Tobelo city, the Jihad Force disbanded, and most members returned to their homes or to refugee camps in Ternate.

After 10 months of terrible carnage, the region was free of major violence. But around 4,000 people had lost their lives in North Maluku, making it perhaps the worst communal violence in Indonesia's transition to democracy. Approximately 300,000 people were displaced from their homes, and much of the province's infrastructure was destroyed, particularly on Halmahera island.

The conflict between Christians and Muslims in 1999–2000 devastated all five of our sample villages in North Maluku. In Barumangga village, the earlier White-Yellow conflict also led to deaths. Specific examples illustrate these consequences.

In Galalolo, West Halmahera, around 600–700 houses were destroyed and three people died. One informant described his experience: "My parents' house was burned to the ground, their goats were lost, and everything else was damaged or lost." In Bodolenge, in the same district, around 100 Mus-lims left to live in another village located 13 kilometers away. Relationships between Christians and Muslims quickly deteriorated, even though some of them were related to one another. The Muslims never returned. Two Muslims and three Christians were killed.

In Yasapira, North Halmahera, about 200 people died and another 20 were injured; 168 families were evacuated and did not return until 2003. All property was destroyed, including 764 houses. All the school buildings were burnt down and hundreds of cattle were lost. A male villager in Yasapira recalled, "Children saw what happened and were traumatized. Children who could talk told their mothers, 'Mum, don't carry us on your back, because later they will kill us.'" The psychological scars remain. Women said they still felt tense and men reported that they rarely slept well; when they did it was only "the light sleep of chickens," as one man put it.

In Lupotogo, North Halmahera, the conflict destroyed 175 houses as well as hundreds of cattle and goats. Mosques and shops were also destroyed. Here, however, relationships have returned to their preconflict standing, and at the present time the Christian and Muslim communities are close.

Other forms of conflict were also present in North Maluku but had smaller impacts. These included water and land border disputes (Bodolenge); demonstrations over civil servant exam results and over land compensation, the latter of which led to loss of life (Galalolo); conflicts between the army and community (Barumangga); and the killing of a Javanese motorcycle taxi driver (Yasapira).

## Localized conflicts in East Java

East Java was chosen as an area with no intercommunal conflict. However, fieldwork quickly revealed that everyday forms of conflict exist in this area, including occasional political violence. The scope of violence is limited, and the fighting attracts little attention outside of the communities concerned. East Java as a whole experienced at least 254 deaths from collective violence between 1990 and 2003 (Varshney, Panggabean, and Tadjoeddin 2008), but most of these resulted from strictly local clashes. A survey of conflicts reported in local newspapers for seven East Javanese districts in 2001–03 found 158 deaths (Barron and Sharpe 2008).[9]

Conflicts in East Java tend to involve vigilante actions in response to issues such as theft, accusations of witchcraft, and sexual indiscretion, as well as battles between youth groups, in particular different martial arts (*silat*) groups. Within the sample for the local newspaper survey, there was variation in dominant forms of conflict (and types of impact) depending on whether districts were located on the Java mainland or on Madura, an island off the east coast of Java. Of the Moving Out of Poverty districts, Pamekasan is on Madura and Probolinggo is on Java; however, most people in Probolinggo are ethnic Madurese, and patterns of conflict there tend to fit with those prevalent on Madura. Vigilante responses to theft and perceived witchcraft were frequent in the Madura districts studied; on the Javanese mainland, fights between youth gangs were more common. One consequence was that conflicts on Madura were more likely to lead to deaths, while on Java they more frequently resulted in property damage or injuries (Barron and Sharpe 2008).

Some examples from the Moving Out of Poverty fieldwork illustrate. In Patobako, a conflict over the election of the head of an Islamic women's group split the community and tensions nearly spiraled into violence several times. In Kacokerre in 1999, a mob killed two *dukun santet*, reputed practitioners of witchcraft who were alleged to be responsible for a strange illness that was afflicting some community members. Such localized conflicts had relatively limited impacts, but they did affect communities. As we will discuss further on, the fact that conflicts tended to pit people from the same village against each other led to a weakening of trust and damage to relationships in some villages.

### Population changes as a result of conflict

In addition to its impact on lives, property, and social relations, large-scale conflict can lead to population shifts (figure 10.1). In all five sample communities in East Java, the population increased at least slightly during the study decade. In high-conflict North Maluku, the number of people declined in three communities and increased in two. In Galalolo, one of the communities that experienced a decline, the population has fallen to one-third of what it was. This situation was a result of the conflict of 1999 and 2000. In the case of villages whose population decreased, some of the people who evacuated did not return because of the trauma that they had experienced. In the case of the villages whose population increased, many victims of the conflict moved to these communities for reasons of safety.[10]

## The Growth-Poverty-Conflict Nexus

The study generated a number of indexes aimed at measuring household and community mobility during the study period. The net prosperity index (NPI) measures net upward mobility (upward minus downward) in a village, indicating whether the share of upward movement was greater than the share of downward movement. The mobility of the poor index (MPI) shows the extent of upward mobility by those who were poor 10 years ago, irrespective of whether they crossed the community poverty line or not.[11] The moving out of poverty index (MOP) captures the extent of upward mobility by the poor across the community poverty line. For all three indexes, the numbers refer to percentages of the population in the community; for example, MOP of 0.47 means that 47 percent of those beneath the community poverty line in 1995 moved above it and were still above it in 2005.

**FIGURE 10.1**
**Population changes in the Indonesia study communities, 1995–2005**

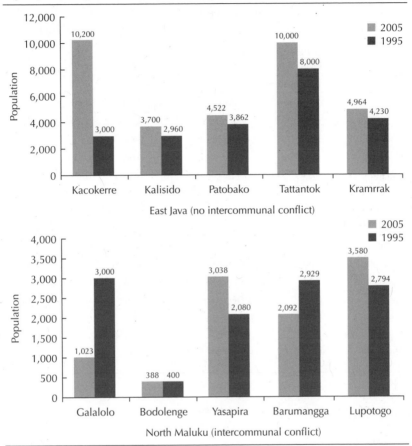

*Source:* Community profiles.

Table 10.4 shows the scores on the three indexes, along with district growth rates and the perceived change in inequality for each village studied. For the latter measure, women's and men's focus groups were asked to define inequality and then say whether inequality in their community had increased, decreased, or remained the same over the 10-year study period.

The study found that high levels of conflict were not associated with smaller movements out of poverty. Furthermore, preexisting poverty levels and growth rates were not strongly correlated with the ability of community members to move out of poverty.

**TABLE 10.4**
**Growth, inequality, and mobility in the Indonesia study communities**

| Province/ community | Growth (district level) | Increase/decrease in community inequality over 10 years (according to female/ male focus groups)[a] | NPI | MPI | MOP |
|---|---|---|---|---|---|
| *East Java (no intercommunal conflict)* | | | | | |
| Mean | | Mixed | 0.50 | 0.60 | 0.17 |
| Kacokerre | Low | Increased | 0.82 | 0.89 | 0.00 |
| Kalisido | High | Decreased | 0.66 | 0.79 | 0.42 |
| Patobako | High | Decreased | 0.50 | 0.64 | 0.17 |
| Tattantok | Low | Decreased (F), increased (M) | 0.48 | 0.50 | 0.05 |
| Kramrrak | Low | Increased | 0.04 | 0.19 | 0.19 |
| *North Maluku (intercommunal conflict)* | | | | | |
| Mean | | Decreased | 0.29 | 0.47 | 0.38 |
| Galalolo | Low | Decreased | 0.40 | 0.43 | 0.43 |
| Bodolenge | Low | Not available | 0.38 | 0.88 | 0.68 |
| Yasapira | High | Decreased | 0.33 | 0.40 | 0.16 |
| Barumangga | High | Decreased (F), increased (M) | 0.29 | 0.46 | 0.42 |
| Lupotogo | High | Decreased (F), same (M) | 0.06 | 0.20 | 0.20 |
| Mean of high-growth communities | High | Decreased | 0.37 | 0.50 | 0.27 |
| Mean of low-growth communities | Low | Increased | 0.42 | 0.58 | 0.27 |

*Sources:* Ladder of life and other focus group discussions.
a. Where no distinction is made between female (F) and male (M) focus groups, there was no significant difference in their responses regarding community inequality.

Several patterns stand out. First, as a group, communities in high-growth districts did not see greater improvements in welfare or upward mobility than those in lower-growth areas. Indeed, while the mean rate of movement out of poverty (MOP) was the same across high- and low-growth areas, overall mobility (MPI) and net prosperity (NPI) were both higher in the low-growth districts. This was particularly true in North Maluku, where overall upward mobility was stronger in villages in the low-growth district. Bodolenge, a village in a low-growth district of North Maluku, had the highest MPI and MOP scores. This suggests that district-level growth does not necessarily result in greater poverty reduction or upward mobility for the poorest in communities. Levels of growth vary even within districts. And variation in how households can access the benefits of growth is key in determining mobility, and the extent to which they can do so is not correlated with the level of growth (figure 10.2).

Second, movements out of poverty were greater in areas that were highly affected by conflict than in those that were less affected (figure 10.3). Net increases in prosperity (NPI) and upward mobility (MPI) are higher in low-conflict East Java than in North Maluku. However, such increases do not equate to movement across the poverty line. Indeed, three of the four villages that saw the greatest movement out of poverty are in high-conflict North Maluku. Given that the baseline year (1995) was four years before the conflict began in North Maluku and also before the Asian financial crisis, it is surprising to find that many people there are doing better now than they were then.

**FIGURE 10.2**
Changes in poverty rates in Indonesia study communities in high- and low-growth districts, 1995–2005

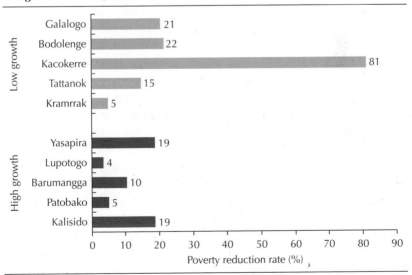

*Sources:* Ladder of life focus group discussions.

FIGURE 10.3

**Net prosperity index (NPI), moving out of poverty index (MOP), and mobility of the poor index (MPI) in the Indonesia study communities**

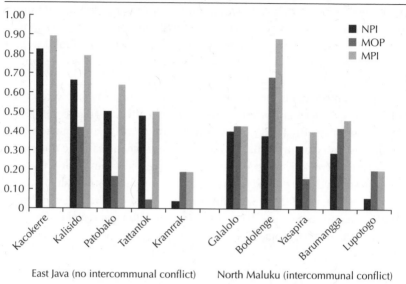

East Java (no intercommunal conflict)          North Maluku (intercommunal conflict)

*Source:* Community mobility matrixes derived from ladder of life focus group discussions.

Third, there is a large degree of variation within districts. In Probolinggo district in East Java, one village, Kalisido, did better than the others in the district on all three measures. In Kramrrak in Pamekasan district, scores are lower than in the other villages in that district, although a small number of households did move above the poverty line. In North Maluku, Bodolenge saw increases in net prosperity and large increases in upward mobility of the poor, and this was enough to push a large number of people over the poverty line. The other village studied in the same district, Galalolo, fared worse.

Experts have recognized growth as an important driver of poverty reduction (e.g., Dollar and Kraay 2002; Ravallion and Chen 1996; Sachs 2008). However, higher growth at the district level in North Maluku and East Java was not associated with movement out of poverty at the village level. Similarly, the conflict literature has emphasized the negative impacts of violence on poverty levels (e.g., Collier 2007). Yet higher-conflict villages saw greater movement out of poverty than did others.

These counterintuitive findings suggest a need to look more closely at what might be called the micro dimensions—the relationships between growth, poverty reduction, and conflict at the local level. The rest of this chapter seeks to explain why villages (and poor villagers) have largely been able to recover in violence-stricken North Maluku while movements out of poverty in East Java, which has not experienced widespread violence, have been smaller. We do so by looking at the experience of communities and households, examining variation at the provincial, village, and household levels.

## The Role of Aid

Postconflict aid and investment to rebuild North Maluku helped speed recovery from the conflict in the province. A large part of this was aimed at rebuilding houses and public infrastructure such as roads and providing clean water. Special government postconflict assistance for Maluku and North Maluku provinces totaled around $106 million over the 2001–04 period.[12] External donors, including the U.S. Agency for International Development, AusAID, the Asia Foundation, the government of the Netherlands, the European Union, the United Nations Development Programme, and the World Bank, among others, provided assistance in 2001–02 totaling an estimated $50 million (ELSAM 2002). While not all of this aid was used effectively, and some was captured by elites (Smith 2008), cumulatively it did help many villagers recover their assets, and it provided opportunities for upward mobility. Infrastructure development and targeted support, in particular for farmers, were far greater after the conflict than in the preconflict period.

In the villages in East Java, government assistance continued at similar levels over the course of the research period, with no spike in assistance. Aid in this province also tended to focus on public goods, with little assistance to individuals that could have expanded income-generating opportunities for poor people.

### Postconflict assistance in North Maluku

The most significant assistance mentioned by the villagers in postconflict areas was the BBR program (Bantuan Bangunan Rumah, or Assistance with Housing Materials). This program helped community members after they returned home. It provided assistance for rebuilding houses and funds to rebuild community buildings, accompanied by cash grants to finance consumption and investment (table 10.5). Men and women in the North Maluku villages stated that the program was very helpful for those who lost their homes and land during the conflict. Some of the rebuilt homes were of better quality than those that existed before the conflict.

In addition to housing assistance, a number of public infrastructure programs also helped develop the conflict-affected areas. Compared to the preconflict situation, when it received only a little infrastructure assistance, North Maluku received significant infrastructure aid after the conflict ended (table 10.5). The two villages with the highest rates of movement out of poverty, Bodolenge and Galalolo, both had new roads built after the conflict.

Many of these forms of postconflict development assistance were new to North Maluku. The province's remoteness, and perhaps its earlier status as a district within a province, had led to underinvestment in key infrastructure and other forms of assistance such as the provision of credit. The immense need after the conflict, and the province's new visibility, changed this.

In North Maluku, also, much of the assistance was in the form of private goods. Initial postconflict aid included provision of food and temporary shelter in the camps to which displaced villagers fled. During and immediately after the conflict, when few had the means to buy or grow food, villagers also received subsidized rice through the Raskin program.

Importantly, the aid helped improve money-making opportunities for many poor villagers. It included provision of training in agricultural skills as well as in other industries that helped some diversify their income-generating activities away from sole reliance on farming. Also provided were basic productive assets (farming equipment, seeds, fertilizer, etc.) and technical assistance (in areas such as fertilizing techniques and pest elimination) to boost productivity.

Grants also came through revolving funds programs, notably IDT (Inpres Desa Tertinggal, or Presidential Instruction for Neglected Villages) and KDP (Kecamatan Development Program). Communities and village leaders in Barumangga and Bodolenge asserted that these two programs were the most important factors in raising community prosperity. IDT provided grants of Rp 20 million in cash to villages regarded as having been left behind in development. Decisions on use of the funds were left to groups in the communities, and funds could be used for development of productive infrastructure or for group economic activities. Like IDT, KDP targets the poorest communities. In particular, women's productive groups supported through the program were reported to have made a difference, using the credit as capital for cake making and other business ventures. The role of KDP is discussed further below.

Despite concerns from some villagers and observers about unequal aid distribution, and some skimming of funds by government officials and contractors, people in all five villages largely agreed that postconflict aid had significantly boosted community prosperity and helped the poor. In Lupotogo, a woman reported that after the conflict "there was government aid in the

**TABLE 10.5**
**Infrastructure assistance and key factors that helped prosperity in North Maluku, Indonesia**

| Community | Assistance received 1995–2000 | Assistance received 2001–05 | Factors that helped community prosperity |
|---|---|---|---|
| Galalolo (MOP = 0.43) | | Postconflict housing construction (2002) | Assistance (restoration) after the disturbances |
| | | Construction of new district offices (2003) Road project (2005) | Clean water Help with housing, postconflict assistance Help with rice |
| Bodolenge (MOP = 0.68) | Drinking water project (1997) | Postconflict housing construction (2002) | Construction of a road to the village (1984) |
| | | Building of a tourist site along the beach and a road into the tourist site (2004) | Government programs in the form of a revolving fund (IDT, KDP) and clean water. |
| | | Building of two public sanitary facilities and a resting place in the tourist site (2004) | Surfacing of the road with asphalt (1990) |
| | | Change of water pumps for water supply (2004) | |
| Yasapira (MOP = 0.16) | | Postconflict housing construction (2002) | Help through revolving funds Postconflict assistance Mutual assistance Education assistance |
| Barumangga (MOP = 0.42) | | Road project (2003) | IDT program KDP program |
| Lupotogo (MOP = 0.20) | | Road project (2002) Postconflict housing construction (2002) | Postconflict assistance Additional business capital Markets for agricultural products |

*Sources:* Key informant interviews and focus group discussions.
*Note:* KDP = Kecamatan Development Program; IDT = Presidential Instruction for Neglected Villages.

form of fishing boats, carpenters' tools, cooking tools, etc. Without that aid, what could we do for life, as everything was destroyed at that time?" A man in Bodolenge noted, "We now earn more than before because of aid from the government and NGOs. We now have more modern agricultural equipment and tools for carpentry."

## Regular development assistance in East Java

Compared to North Maluku, East Java received more "regular" aid and development assistance. It did not receive postconflict assistance, however, and levels of aid varied little over the 1995–2005 period (table 10.6).

**TABLE 10.6**
**Infrastructure assistance and key factors that helped prosperity in East Java, Indonesia**

| | Assistance received | | Factors that helped |
|---|---|---|---|
| Community | 1995–2000 | 2001–05 | community prosperity |
| Kacokerre (MOP = 0) | | Road project (2001) | Paving of the road with asphalt |
| | | | Health cards, social safety net, green card/health insurance (2005) |
| | | | Raskin rice subsidies |
| | | | Aid program providing seed/fertilizer |
| Kalisido (MOP = 0.42) | Sinking of artesian wells (1995) | Road sealing (2003, 2004) | |
| | Road project (1995) | | |
| | Market access | | |
| | Construction of artesian well | | |
| | Other government assistance | | |
| Patobako (MOP = 0.17) | Installation of electricity (1995) | | Paving of the road with asphalt |
| | Asphalting of road (1995, 1997) | | Installation of electricity |
| | Sinking of artesian well (1999/2000) | | Clean water |
| Tattantok (MOP = 0.05) | | Road project (2005) | |
| Kramrrak (MOP = 0.19) | Road project (1997) Development of wharf (2000) | Inauguration of special clean water channel to Branta (2003) | Construction of a dock |
| | | | Construction of clean water channels |
| | | | Increases in education |
| | | | Financial aid program for small traders |

*Sources:* Key informant interviews and focus group discussions.

In East Java, aid tended to take the form of infrastructure development. Other targeted programs did exist (Raskin rice subsidies, financial aid, and seed/fertilizer assistance), and communities reported some of these as having beneficial effects. However, by and large development assistance tended to follow patterns from before 1995. This may have increased overall community wealth—indeed, East Java saw greater increases in net prosperity than North Maluku—but it had less impact in empowering the poorest.

Little of the aid in East Java related to the agricultural sector, the main source of livelihoods in that province. There was little agricultural extension work, and neither government nor nongovernmental organizations (NGOs) made efforts to help people move into nonagricultural jobs. This meant that when market prices for crops went down, community members had few means to protect themselves. In East Java, as we will note later, changes in crop prices, particularly related to the financial crisis, had major negative impacts, more so than in North Maluku. But the assistance given to villagers after the crisis was minimal, certainly less than that which supported villagers' recovery from the shock of conflict.

### Varying impacts of aid: Mechanisms for assistance

Aid had different impacts in different villages. This resulted in part from differences in the levels and forms of assistance. However, the *mechanisms* through which aid was given were an even greater determinant of varying impacts.

Compare the experiences of Bodolenge, Yasapira, and Lupotogo villages in North Maluku. Sixty-eight percent of those in Bodolenge who were poor in 1995 managed to move out of poverty; in contrast, only 16 percent of the poor in Yasapira and 20 percent in Lupotogo were able to move above the poverty line. Different experiences with aid were not the only reason for this variation, but aid was important.

Informants in Bodolenge cited the Kecamatan Development Program, a World Bank–supported national government program, as being particularly important in helping villagers move out of poverty. In 2004 the village received a grant of Rp 37.5 million to fund saving and credit groups and groups concerned with income-generating activities. The groups used the money to purchase agricultural inputs, including seeds, and finance small start-up businesses. Other funding from the program was used to develop a nearby tourist spot, improving the road and facilities there, and to change the generator for the water pump to ensure a supply of drinking water. A female villager in Bodolenge noted, "The impact was that the community could enjoy the recreation place and generate income by selling things there.

This creates job opportunities and also generates village income because each tourist must pay Rp 1,000 to enter, plus a parking fee of Rp 3,000 for motorbikes and Rp 5,000 for cars."

There were a number of reasons why the KDP community-based mechanisms had big impacts in Bodolenge. First, communities were involved in selecting projects for funding, and they chose those they knew would have the greatest impact. Second, the inclusion of the poorest villagers in decision making and implementation helped ensure that the projects benefited those most in need of assistance. Sixty percent of those who moved out of poverty in Bodolenge cited KDP as a key driver of their increased prosperity.[13]

To summarize, the makeup and extent of aid and the ways in which it was delivered all affected poverty trajectories. Aid levels stayed stagnant in East Java over the research period but grew greatly in North Maluku. While there was certainly elite capture of some resources there (Smith 2008), aid did flow to those who most needed it. Aid in North Maluku was also of a type that helped the most impoverished, especially through the housing program, and helped boost productivity and skills. Infrastructure development also had a larger impact in North Maluku because of the low starting point (by comparison, many of the villages studied in East Java already had basic transportation infrastructure before 1995).

## Decentralization and District Splitting

The research period corresponded with the implementation of thoroughgoing decentralization across Indonesia (Usman 2001). Before the introduction of regional autonomy, Indonesia's governmental system was centralized, with the majority of decisions made at the national level. After the change, most decisions (with the exception of those related to defense and security, foreign policy, monetary matters, religion, and justice) became the responsibility of the regional governments, in particular those at the district/town level.[14] Local governments now spend 37 percent of the country's budget, up from 20 percent in 1999, making Indonesia one of the world's most decentralized states (Murshed and Tadjoeddin 2008).

At the same time, a process of *pemekaran* ("flowering") has led to the establishment of many new provinces, districts, and subdistricts.[15] The first new province was North Maluku, which was formed from several districts of Maluku in October 1999. By 2005, 7 new provinces had been formed from 26 former provinces, while 161 new districts/towns were established from 279 old districts and towns (NPRC 2005).

These dual processes of decentralization and division have restructured center-periphery relations and changed the way power is accessed and exercised at the local level. There is much debate in Indonesia, as in the broader literature, on the success of decentralization. Hypothetically, the devolution of power and division of areas can bring services closer to the people and increase the accountability of policy makers and service providers (Tabellini 2000; Tendler 2000; Wade 1997). There may be a better match between the supply of and demand for public goods in more decentralized countries (Crook and Manor 1998; Faguet 2004).

On the other hand, increased corruption may be associated with fiscal decentralization (Treisman 2000). In the case of Indonesia, some have argued that decentralization has led to increased capture of resources by elites, at times resulting in violent conflict between elites and the different ethnoreligious groups they represent (see Nordholt and Van Klinken 2007).

As noted above, the process of decentralization and division (actual and anticipated) helped drive the conflict in North Maluku. However, the field research also provided evidence of how this process has led to some improvements in service delivery and local democracy. In North Maluku, the creation of the new province and new districts required an expansion of the public sector, which in turn created new opportunities for secure employment. This helped some communities prosper and allowed some households to move out of poverty. In contrast, in East Java, where such administrative subdivisions did not occur, there was less impact.

### Economic impacts

Villagers reported that the establishment of new districts in North Maluku had a positive impact on their welfare. The establishment of new district offices in Tobelo (which became the capital of the new district, North Halmahera) and Jailolo (which became the capital of West Halmahera) helped create new centers of growth. This led to a rise in the demand for the construction of office buildings, an influx of people to the area, and more economic and employment opportunities, including an increase in the number of civil service positions.

Tobelo and Lupotogo, a study village adjacent to Tobelo, became centers of economic activity in the northern part of the island of Halmahera (North Maluku), with many new opportunities and jobs created. Many people moved to villages surrounding the new district capitals, including Lupotogo and Yasapira. With the population growth came a rise in demand for various products, including foodstuffs produced by local people.

Certain sectors grew rapidly. In particular, the formation of new districts required new office buildings for government agencies and houses for civil servants. This created opportunities in the construction industry and work for carpenters, bricklayers, and other tradespersons. Such changes are discussed further below.

There were also some negative impacts. The population influx increased competition between locals and newcomers for other work opportunities. In such situations, the winners will be those who have skills and expertise, and the newcomers tended to be more highly skilled than the local population. At the same time, the number of jobs in supporting industries has increased in the new districts. While the best jobs may not go to the poorest people, or even to the local population, locals can take advantage of the positive impacts of increased growth.

Improvements in infrastructure also followed decentralization. In North Maluku villages near the new district capitals, the majority of roads have been improved, and only a few of the district roads are still unsealed. The transport situation has improved, with public transport easily available and many new job opportunities for drivers.

These effects were not present to the same extent in the districts studied in East Java. No new districts or provinces were created in this province. The only change was the move of Probolinggo district's capital to Kraksaan subdistrict, where Kalisido (one of the study villages) is located. This had positive impacts, including the building of a new housing complex, provision of cellular telephone signal, electrification, and the arrival of private banks. But the effects were not as great as in North Maluku because this was not the establishment of a new district capital but merely a move of the capital from one area to another.

## Expansion of the public sector

The creation of the new district capitals led to more positions for civil servants. Some were transferred from other regions, but many new civil servants were appointed from local communities. The results of the household survey show that the main factors that raise household prosperity are associated with employment, livelihoods, and income. Civil servants have stable, fixed salaries and also receive pensions. In North Maluku, people frequently said that becoming a civil servant was an important way to ensure that one would not fall into poverty. A woman in Galalolo commented, "Regional subdivision has created work opportunities. There are now public service admission tests in Jailolo. In the past people had to go to Ternate or Ambon for the test."

While becoming a civil servant could help prevent falls into poverty, it was not strongly associated with movements out of poverty. Those who obtained work in the government typically were already graduates and had connections; those with little education and no connections had difficulty in becoming civil servants. Moreover, it is normally necessary to pay a bribe in order to become a civil servant, and it was mainly middle-class individuals who could afford such payments. As a result, the impacts of civil service expansion were unlikely to directly move people out of poverty.

Nonetheless, when a person becomes a civil servant this creates a safety net for family members and sometimes others in the village and can lead to trickle-down effects. North Maluku now has a greater number of civil servants per capita than East Java. In the absence of thriving large industries, these positions create important sources of wealth for communities.

## Local governance and democracy

Local governance is another key factor in creating prosperity and allowing movements out of poverty. The devolution of power to the local level appears to have positive impacts in lifting people out of poverty. This was more true in North Maluku than in East Java. North Malukan villagers reported greater confidence in local government than did those in East Java. North Malukans also displayed greater satisfaction with their local democracy in 2005 (figure 10.4). Perceived levels of official corruption were lower in North Maluku (37 percent of respondents reported bribery or corruption) than in East Java (51 percent).

Within districts, there is marked variation in perceptions of local governance and democracy. This highlights the importance of village-level governance in translating the (potential) gains from devolution into benefits for the poor. There was no clear correlation between households' impressions of democracy and the percentage of people in a community who moved out of poverty. However, in certain communities key elements associated with local democracy have played important roles in their development.

In East Java, increased ability to contact and influence the local government is partly due to the presence of village representative councils (Badan Perwakilan Desa, or BPDs), which began to be directly elected during the course of the research.[16] The BPD transmits community demands to local government. It is expected to assist in resolving conflicts, particularly if the village government is not functioning adequately (Bebbington et al. 2006). At the time of the study, BPDs were not present in all communities. In two East Javanese communities where BPDs were functioning, community members cited them as an important reason why democracy was enhancing community prosperity.

**FIGURE 10.4**
Satisfaction with local governance and democracy in the Indonesia study provinces, 2005

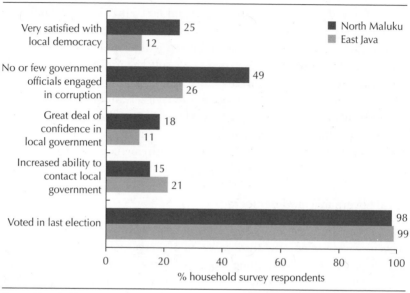

*Source:* Household questionnaire.

In North Maluku, BPDs were not yet present in many villages, but other local institutions helped create prosperity. Bodolenge, which has experienced the greatest movement out of poverty among the sample communities, benefited from decentralization. Informants noted that almost no local officials were involved in bribe taking or other forms of corruption. Good local leadership also spurred local collective action, with residents coming together to build a road to the subdistrict capital. In this community, 70 percent of residents also felt that the local government listened to community aspirations before making decisions.

In contrast, in Lupotogo the aid and infrastructure development projects that did arrive were implemented through mechanisms that did not involve the community, and villagers were not involved in selecting, designing, or implementing projects. The gap between the government and the governed was one reason for this. Around two-thirds of households surveyed in Lupotogo said that local government was paying less attention to community aspirations than in the past. The programs that Lupotogo received thus had slight impact on poor people, in part because of lack of community involvement, in part because of the apathy of the local government.

The men's focus group in Lupotogo reported that local government attention to the community's interests had increased over the 10-year period. However, they believed that this stemmed largely from the local government's fears of demonstrations against it rather than from any real desire to improve the prosperity of the poor. In contrast, the women's group said that local government attention to the community had declined. In the past the government built and widened the roads, provided lighting and telecommunications, and cleaned the market. Yet the road was now damaged, and although it was a priority for the community, no steps were taken to fix it.

## Diversification of Livelihoods

A key reason why more people were able to move out of poverty in North Maluku was the greater diversification of livelihoods there compared to in East Java. This was in part the result of the types of crops grown. However, the conflict, and more important, the response to the conflict, also led to a diversification of livelihoods away from sole reliance on farming in North Maluku. This movement increased prosperity and helped some people move out of poverty.

In East Java rice is the primary crop, with other seasonal crops such as tobacco and pulses also grown. There was little change in the crops grown over the 10-year period. In most of the East Javanese communities, prosperity is linked closely to market prices in a given year and to the quality of crops. The latter in turn depends on the way crops are cultivated and on seasonal climatic conditions. While rice requires ample rainfall or an abundant water supply, tobacco prefers dry conditions. One villager in Kacokerre noted wryly, "There is no rain in the rice-growing season, yet rain falls when tobacco is planted." People in other villages echoed this observation.

In contrast, farmers in North Maluku traditionally have grown crops that are harvested once a year (such as cloves) and those that can be harvested year-round (coconuts and nutmeg). These require little care and are less vulnerable to seasonal climate changes.

Because crops are harvested once a year rather than seasonally, many people in North Maluku have other occupations they pursue while waiting for the harvest. These include trade, carpentry, laying bricks, driving, and doing day labor. As a result, there is less overall reliance on agriculture in North Maluku than in East Java, and more diversity in income sources.

This became important when the conflict hit. With their established occupational sidelines, villagers in North Maluku, including poor people, developed a wide array of skills. This made it easier for them to take advantage of the economic boom associated with postconflict aid and the new district capitals. After being displaced by the conflict, many farmers returned to find their fields destroyed. However, they had other skills that they could put to use as opportunities arose. Displaced people also acquired new skills out of necessity.

The experience of Pak Solomon, a 36-year-old man from Yasapira who moved out of poverty, illustrates this process. He dropped out of school in his second year of junior high and became a farmer, helping his father-in-law for two years. Solomon learned how to drive from his brother and sometimes filled in for him in his driving job. With this experience, he was able to get a full-time job driving a public bus. With savings from the work, he bought 3 hectares of land, which he planted in nutmeg. From his earnings as a driver and farmer he built a house and bought a motorcycle. Both were burned during the conflict.

During his time as a refugee with a family in Ternate, Solomon was able to find a job as a driver. With this income he bought a machine to grate coconut that he planned to use when he returned home. With the arrival of postconflict aid, many new houses and offices were being built, and a friend helped him find work in construction. The BBR assistance also allowed him to build a new house for himself. In 2005 another friend helped him find work as a logging laborer in a distant location called Wasileo, far from his family. Solomon finally returned to Yasapira to become a farmer again after buying 8 hectares of land in Wasileo and another 3 hectares in Yasapira. On this he plants nutmeg, coconut, and chocolate.

Pak Solomon is typical of many upwardly mobile villagers in North Maluku, who move in and out of farming and other occupations depending on opportunities and needs. The skills used for these jobs are often gained through nonformal education, as many of those who moved out of poverty in North Maluku did not complete secondary school. Informal typing and sewing courses, learning how to make cakes and *jamu* (traditional herbal medicines), learning fishing and trading skills from family or friends: all are important in providing poor villagers with practical skills they can use.[17]

In East Java, where farmers have depended on certain crops for years and aid has been limited, few opportunities exist in sectors beyond agriculture. As a result, East Javanese households have not had many opportunities to diversify their income sources.[18] More respondents to the household survey in North Maluku (26 percent) than in East Java (16 percent) mentioned that now it is easier to obtain work with private employers. Sixty-six percent of respondents in East Java said it had become more difficult to obtain work with private employers, while 48 percent of respondents in North Maluku said the same.

Those who did move out of poverty in East Java tended to do so through hard work, but often this was not enough. The example of a chronically poor man from Tattantok illustrates. Pak Udin had been working since the age of 10 in a series of odd jobs. By age 15 he was breaking rocks, earning Rp 10,000 for a full truckload. During the tobacco harvest he would work as a day laborer, cutting the crop. For a while he taught at an Islamic prayer house, but he returned to harvesting tobacco when he married. Overall, his income has risen slightly, but he has not yet crossed the community-defined poverty line. Udin's dependence on the weather to ensure a quality tobacco crop makes him vulnerable. He laments, "This year, 2005, my tobacco has not sold; much of it is ruined from the rain. Now I still work as a tobacco laborer for someone, but because the tobacco doesn't sell, I haven't been paid yet. If it continues like this, how can there be any prosperity?"

The postconflict rebuilding and creation of new districts in North Maluku also directly supported the diversification of livelihoods. Some of the aid programs taught new skills and gave housing, mentoring, and financial support, while public works projects created opportunities for construction. In the private sector, opportunities also arose for *ojek* (motorcycle taxi) drivers, artisans, and other tradesmen. In Yasapira, porters carry luggage at the ferry terminal, and in Galalolo, people sell petrol (gasoline) in plastic bottles from stalls set up in front of homes.

Farmers in North Maluku also began experimenting with new crops, particularly vegetables such as beans, tomatoes, and chilies, which yield monthly or seasonally instead of annually. Reasons for this included technical assistance provided by government and NGOs on the use of fertilizers and pesticides. New equipment for soil preparation was also provided; in the past farmers used a hoe but now they plough with hand tractors, and there is a wider availability of seeds.

## Trust, Social Cohesion, and Collective Action

The conflict in North Maluku resulted in total devastation and disturbed social, economic, and political relations and roles. Tremendous need and the desire for rapid recovery motivated the community to work together closely to rebuild infrastructure and the local economy, in the process enhancing community-level collective action. A desire to ensure that such violence did not occur again strengthened relations between groups. In contrast, in East Java, where conflict was more limited, no such shock occurred. Levels of collective action and trust remained the same, limiting opportunities for those previously marginalized to move ahead.

## Conflict experience, diversity, and collective action

Communities in North Maluku are more ethnically and religiously diverse than those in East Java,[19] and they also experienced far more destructive conflict. We might hypothesize that this would lead to lower levels of intra-community trust and collective action in North Maluku than in East Java.[20] However, the study found that many dimensions of collective action were higher in North Maluku, and that the conflict was one cause of this.

Overall, in both provinces, trust has grown within villages. While the general level of trust in other people is still relatively low, with less than half of household survey respondents saying they could trust others, it has increased. Such increases are larger in North Maluku than in East Java, with 46 percent noting improvements in the former compared to 36 percent in the latter. In North Maluku, trust often crosses religious divides. As one man in Lupotogo noted, "There is trust and good relations here. For example, when something bad happens to Muslims, for example when someone dies, we Christians visit them, and vice versa."

Collective action, by a number of measures, is also higher in North Maluku. Around 96 percent of households surveyed in the North Maluku villages said they had participated in communal activities in the past year, compared to 81 percent in East Java. Seventy-six percent of households in North Maluku said they would be very likely to help if a neighbor's house burned down, compared to 58 percent in East Java. This question likely held particular salience for many of the respondents in North Maluku since many did lose their homes during the conflicts and received assistance from neighbors in the rebuilding process. Village leaders in North Maluku concurred, saying that the villagers, now and 10 years ago, were likely or very likely to work together to solve water problems and very likely to help others in difficulty.

Group membership is both a key determinant and a consequence of high capacity for collective action. As figure 10.5 shows, membership in community groups is high in both provinces and has risen since 1995. While there are more groups in East Java, the increase in group membership between 1995 and 2005 is greater in North Maluku.

Differences in the characteristics of group membership between the two provinces may have an effect on mobility. North Malukan households are more actively involved in income-generating and savings/credit groups than are East Java households. In North Maluku, participation in savings/credit groups more than doubled in the research period. Such groups are of particular importance for movements out of poverty. In contrast, informants in East Java were far

**FIGURE 10.5**
**Group membership in the Indonesia study communities, by province**

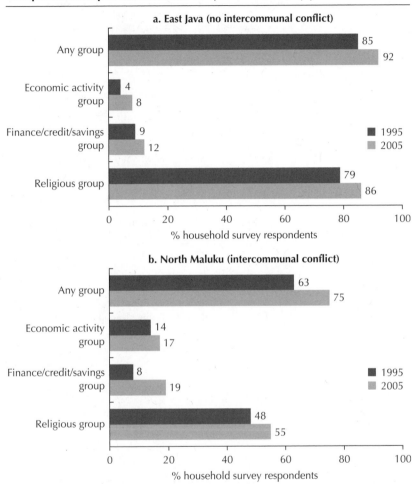

a. East Java (no intercommunal conflict)

b. North Maluku (intercommunal conflict)

*Source:* Household questionnaire.

more likely than those in North Maluku to cite religious groups as most important to them. Four of the five East Java villages said that membership in religious bodies was more important than membership in other kinds of groups
(table 10.7). In North Maluku only two study villages, Lupotogo and Yasapira,
which had the lowest MOP ratings in the province, deemed religious groups to
be most important. Membership in religious groups does not appear to play
an important role in moving people out of poverty.

**TABLE 10.7**
**Most important groups and organizations in the Indonesia study communities**

| Province/community | Number of organizations | | Most important groups in the community |
|---|---|---|---|
| | 2005 | 1995 | 1995 and 2005 |
| East Java (no intercommunal conflict) | 129 | 98 | |
| Kacokerre (NPI = 0.82, MOP = 0.00) | 6 | 5 | Nahdatul Ulama (religious group) |
| Kalisido (NPI = 0.66, MOP = 0.42) | 62 | 42 | Cooperative (financial group) |
| Patobako (NPI = 0.50, MOP= 0.17) | 43 | 36 | Sholawat (religious group) |
| Tattantok (NPI = 0.48, MOP = 0.05) | 4 | 3 | Jana'atus AS (religious group) |
| Kramrrak (NPI = 0.04, MOP = 0.19) | 14 | 12 | Nahdatul Ulama (religious group) |
| North Maluku (intercommunal conflict) | 103 | 71 | |
| Galalolo (NPI = 0.40, MOP = 0.43) | 22 | 20 | Karang Taruna (youth group) |
| Bodolenge (NPI = 0.38, MOPI = 0.68) | 14 | 14 | Farmers' group (production/trade) |
| Yasapira (NPI = 0.33, MOP = 0.16) | 33 | 13 | Religious group |
| Barumangga (NPI = 0.29, MOP = 0.42) | 17 | 12 | Posyandu (health group) |
| Lupotogo (NPI = 0.06, MOP = 0.20) | 17 | 12 | Church group (religious group) |

*Source:* Community profiles.

The four communities with the greatest movements out of poverty all cited nonreligious groups as being the most important now and 10 years ago. Of these, only one, Kalisido, is located in East Java, and it is the village with the highest MOP in that region. In Bodolenge in North Maluku, which saw the greatest proportion of people move above the poverty line, the number of people participating in savings/credit groups increased from 8 percent in 1995 to 30 percent in 2005. A male focus group in Bodolenge highlighted the benefits of a mutual savings group that formed after the conflict: "With this organization, the life of the community has become better. By our mutual savings, our houses that were destroyed during the conflict can be constructed through the *gotong royong* [communal group] way. The goal of this organization is community well-being. Everyone in our community is a member."

In most communities, savings/credit groups are known as *arisan*. These rotating savings clubs are built upon mutual trust, since members will not invite anyone to join who they think might not continue to contribute to the savings pool after receiving their pay-out. Coleman (1990), Geertz (1962), and Putnam (1993) have all cited these groups as one of the most important outgrowths of the gotong royong ideology, the Indonesian tradition of villagers coming together to work for the betterment of the community. High levels of involvement in such groups reflect high levels of trust between community members and their ability to work together in times of need.

### Reasons for greater collective action in North Maluku

There are several possible reasons that participation in collective action increased more in North Maluku than in East Java. First, the tremendous needs in the postconflict period meant that people had to work together to pool resources and labor to get their lives started again. The conflict in North Maluku caused most members of the community, from all strata, to lose their material assets. A feeling that everyone had suffered and was starting from scratch helped community members move beyond tensions from the past to work together for mutual benefit. Residents tried to make the most of their situation, even if they could not return to farming because their lands were destroyed. They had to, in the words of one person, "start together from zero." Even elites had to participate in and encourage collective action to help rebuild their personal economic lives, and this spilled over into broader opportunities. The conflict thus had a leveling effect that helped reduce preconflict inequalities (see table 10.4). In East Java, which did not suffer a massive external shock, social, political, and economic structures remained more rigid.

In four of the five North Malukan villages (Bodolenge, Galalolo, Yasapira, and Lupotogo), residents cited the importance of social networks in helping them obtain work after the conflict. In Yasapira and Lupotogo, these networks were particularly important for gaining employment in coveted fields such as construction and public transportation. Residents shared skills and knowledge about employment opportunities and openings for new businesses. Social capital thus substituted for other forms of capital, such as financial assets, which were depleted during the conflict. Having the trust of fellow residents and working through informal networks could make a significant difference in the likelihood of upward mobility. In East Java, where conflict did not greatly affect the local economy, there were fewer opportunities for poor villagers to use their social networks to get ahead.

The second reason for greater collective action in North Maluku is that after the conflict in that area, communities made conscious efforts to try to improve relations between groups in order to ensure that conflict would not erupt again. In Yasapira village in North Maluku, which is 87 percent Muslim, a focus group discussion member noted that attempts were made to be inclusive in decision making to avoid any recurrence of tensions: "More people are involved in important affairs to avoid suspicions and bad feelings . . . to consider the feelings of Muslims and Christians." In the *pela gadong* system, which was used frequently before the conflict, Christians and Muslims worked together to resolve conflicts and gain mutual benefit. Informants stated that this system was resurrected after the conflict to support recovery. One Christian informant noted that as a result "there is [now] trust and good relations . . . when something bad happens to the Muslims, the Christians visit them, and vice versa, for example when someone dies."

As a result, religious divisions have decreased in importance. Figure 10.6 shows whether respondents perceived large or small distinctions in their communities based on religion, social status, or wealth. Even though Muslims and Christians were involved in a devastating conflict, the majority of North Maluku households reported that such distinctions were not large, either before or after the conflict. But not surprisingly, when people were asked whether distinctions had led to conflict since 1995, three times as many respondents in North Maluku (30 percent) as in East Java (10 percent) said that they had. This understanding that religious or social differences could lead to major problems if not managed well has helped ensure proactive attempts to limit such tensions.

This perhaps accounts for the high level of involvement by villagers in community meetings in North Maluku. In the East Java villages, 24 percent of respondents to the household survey reported having attended a community meeting in the past year. In North Maluku, this figure was 50 percent. In the two communities with the greatest movement out of poverty, attendance was 62 percent (Bodolenge) and 67 percent (Galalolo).

Finally, there was a strong traditional basis for collective action in North Maluku that could be reenergized after the conflict. Prior to the conflict,

**FIGURE 10.6**
**Perceived distinctions due to religion, social status, or wealth in the Indonesia study communities, by province**

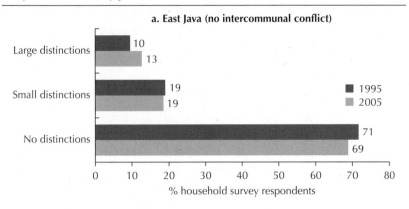

a. East Java (no intercommunal conflict)

Large distinctions: 10 (1995), 13 (2005)
Small distinctions: 19 (1995), 19 (2005)
No distinctions: 71 (1995), 69 (2005)

■ 1995
■ 2005

% household survey respondents

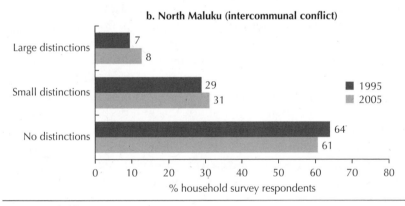

b. North Maluku (intercommunal conflict)

Large distinctions: 7 (1995), 8 (2005)
Small distinctions: 29 (1995), 31 (2005)
No distinctions: 64 (1995), 61 (2005)

■ 1995
■ 2005

% household survey respondents

*Source:* Household questionnaire.

the Christian and Muslim populations of North Halmahera had a largely peaceful coexistence, primarily due to the traditional *hibua lamo* system. A form of gotong royong mutual assistance, this system called upon Christians and Muslims to work together to resolve conflicts, and religious heads were expected to lead these efforts. Residents focused more on ethnic commonalities than on religious differences (Kooistra 2001). Key informants in the study indicated that this system also mandates mutual help between Muslims and

Christians. Although some of the literature argues that the influx of migrants from other areas of North Maluku and elsewhere weakened this system (Kooistra 2001), members of the study communities stated that this system was as strong as before the conflict. The system was upset by the violence, but community members reported that it never lost its legitimacy, and it thus could be reactivated once tensions subsided.

## The Nature of Conflict and Postconflict Recovery

As we have seen, the influx of postconflict aid, decentralization, opportunities for income diversification, and enhanced social capital all provided superior opportunities for wealth generation in North Maluku, and the leveling effect of the conflict meant that the poor also managed to benefit. A final, and important, factor is the nature of the conflict itself—the form it takes, the actors involved, and the duration of its impact. Compared to the communal violence that convulsed North Maluku, violence in East Java was sporadic, often stemming from disputes between individuals or from common crime. These localized incidents had less overall impact on the province. Yet in East Java, movement out of poverty was more limited than in North Maluku. Our analysis suggests that the difference in the nature of the conflict as much as in the scale of violence helps determine whether and how communities, leaders, and outside agencies respond to conflict. This in turn shapes opportunities for mobility among the poor.

Several examples from East Java provide illustration. In Kacokerre in 1999, a man and his wife were accused of being *dukun santet* (practitioners of black magic) and were killed. Before the killings the local people had been restless because of the appearance of a strange sickness that had caused several deaths. Victims' stomachs would become swollen, they would lose their eyesight, and within one or two months death would follow. The dukun santet had often asked villagers for assistance in the form of labor or goods. If the requests were not met, it was said, the person concerned soon found his stomach bloated. The murders of the dukun santet 10 years ago have been a continuing source of stress for the community. A man was arrested in connection with the murders and sentenced to eight years in prison, but most people in the community do not believe he was the murderer. Suspicions and tensions persist.

In Patobako, a conflict over the election of the head of an Islamic women's group split the community, and tensions nearly erupted into violence several times. The incumbent head, who had served for 20 years, lost to a new candidate in an election. But she refused to concede defeat, claiming correct electoral procedures were not followed. The dispute threatened to escalate into a *carok*, a traditional duel to defend honor that frequently ends in the death of one of the contenders. The village head stopped the conflict from escalating, but this led to an uneasy peace. Supporters of both sides would swear at each other over the village mosque's loudspeaker. Two months after the election, seating at a wedding service was still segregated to separate supporters of the two candidates.

A third case in Kramrrak involved a series of hijackings of local fishing boats over the 2001–04 period. Pirates would attack the boats late at night and steal fishing nets. It was an open secret that the marauders came from Gili Raja, a nearby island. Villagers from Kramrrak could get their nets back the next day by going to Gili Raja and paying a fee for their return. Resentment between the two villages has festered.

In their impact on lives and property, these isolated conflicts in East Java are clearly much less serious than the wave of violence that swept North Maluku. Though such incidents occasionally resulted in deaths—as of the dukun santet—the toll is nowhere near the thousands of deaths and massive destruction caused by the religious war. However, such localized incidents in East Java apparently had a more negative effect on poverty mobility than did the widespread violence in North Maluku. A closer look at the distinct characteristics of the violence in the two areas can help explain why.

A first and important difference is the proximity of the actors involved in conflict. In North Maluku, villagers typically said the people who started the violence lived outside the community where the violence took place. They usually did not know the exact causes of the conflict, but they almost uniformly blamed "outsiders." As one Muslim man in Yasapira explained, the perpetrators of the conflict were "strangers who wanted to destroy everything."

In none of the five research communities in North Maluku did villagers blame those of other religions who lived in the same village for the outbreak of conflict. This was true even in Bodolenge, the one village where the minority religious group had left and not returned. A man in Bodolenge recounted, "Before the riot we always lived in peace and all were relatives, the Muslims as well as the Christians. My younger sibling who took refuge in Manado is Muslim; in the riot we took refuge together." As result, it was not too difficult to rebuild social ties, and villagers made conscious efforts to do so. This, as discussed earlier, apparently helped some of the poorest improve their situation.

In the East Java communities, participants in conflict almost always came from the same village. In both the Kacokerre and Patobako incidents, villages were split by the disputes. This eroded trust and social cohesion and discouraged the development of the types of collective action that occurred in North Maluku. These two conflicts are indeed fairly representative of those occurring in the Madura area. One study of violent vigilante conflicts in Madura (where three of the communities were located) found that 50 percent of them involved actors who lived in the same village, and the majority of fatalities occurred in intravillage conflicts (Barron and Sharpe 2008). In Kramrrak, the conflict was between people from different villages, but these villages were close by each other.

A second important difference has to do with the length of the conflicts in the two provinces. In North Maluku, the fighting in each village lasted only three days or so, even though the province-wide conflict lasted much longer. While the impacts of such conflicts were long-lasting—it took villagers years to rebuild infrastructure and to get over their losses—tensions subsided rather quickly. The conflicts were never fully "solved"; people still do not know who instigated the clashes and perpetrators have not been brought to justice. Yet conflict issues were addressed relatively quickly through peace restoration activities, such as the joint symbolic replanting of trees by 15 Christians and 15 Muslims in Jailolo subdistrict. The government and subdistrict-level police facilitated the ceremony; a ceremonial agreement, known as the Hibualamo Declaration, demonstrated commitment from both sides to move forward with joint and peaceful reconstruction. Restorative justice in the form of post-conflict aid also helped communities move on. Security conditions are now conducive to progress.

In East Java, by contrast, many tensions were not dealt with effectively, and resentment and mistrust persist. Village institutions also played a larger role in dealing with conflict in North Maluku than in East Java. In North Maluku, village leaders saved some people by evacuating them; in East Java, village leaders were more likely to be seen as involved in the conflict.

Third, the different types of conflict—ethnic battles provoked by outsiders in North Maluku, recurrent criminal violence in East Java—also led to different community-level responses. High levels of crime in East Java have prompted the establishment of *poskambling* (community security posts) in which young men "guard" the villages overnight. The negative economic impacts of such systems have been demonstrated elsewhere. In Lampung province, for example, weariness from having to stand guard overnight has affected men's productivity, and the presence of guard posts sends a signal that the villages are not safe, scaring away outside investment (Barron and Madden 2004). Clearly, this has an impact on the ability of poor people to prosper; the fact that impoverished men have to spend time on guard duty further limits their ability to get ahead. In Kramrrak, too, local conflicts forced some villagers to change the areas they fished in, and the "fees" for reclaiming stolen nets may also have affected the local price of fish. Notably, Bodolenge in North Maluku, which had the highest proportion of people move out of poverty, was the only village reporting almost no theft.

To summarize, comparative analysis of East Java and North Maluku shows that the nature of conflict can play as great a role as its scale in determining how communities and individuals get by and get ahead. In East Java, levels of conflict were low. (Again, this study focuses on intercommunal conflict, and the conflict intensity ratings in table 10.2 refer to the presence of inter-communal conflict and not to everyday crime and violence.) However, the conflict that did take place, primarily criminal violence, had a large impact on social cohesion because the protagonists lived in close proximity. It produced tensions that were longer lasting and resulted in the need for nonproductive activities to ensure security, with negative economic repercussions. In North Maluku, by contrast, three years of sorrow experienced by most villagers led to investments in activities to build social capital, prevent conflict from reemerging, and create new opportunities for victims. This provided a basis for many poor people to improve their livelihoods. The analysis also shows that over the long run, persistent underlying social tensions and latent conflict can have serious negative impacts. Suspicions undercut trust and social capital, a requisite for widespread economic development.

## Conclusions and Implications

All the Indonesian communities studied experienced enhanced prosperity over the study period. There was, however, greater movement out of poverty in four of the five villages of North Maluku, which experienced massive communal conflict, than in the villages of East Java, which were not affected by widespread violence. In North Maluku, villagers largely managed to recover and indeed improve on their preconflict economic situation, despite the devastation of the area. In lower-conflict areas of East Java there was upward mobility, but this did not successfully push the poor above the poverty line. These findings run contrary to what we might expect. The international literature has overwhelmingly focused on the deleterious impacts of conflict on poverty. Our research suggests that, in contrast, violence can at times result in downstream positive impacts for the poorest.

This finding is not as surprising as we might think. Historians have long noted that progress in the West has been contested at every point, with violence a major force for change (see, for example, Bayly 2004). Cramer has noted that "many changes that come to be seen as progressive have their origins in social conflicts that have taken a violent turn. This is the paradox of violence and war: violence destroys but is often associated with social creativity" (2006, 279). Thus, conflict (often violent) and prosperity essentially go hand in hand (Bates 2000).

Our sample communities presented two very different sets of opportunities for the poor to advance. In East Java, villagers who improved their situation over the 10 years tended to work hard in the same occupation they had before, normally farming, or else they migrated temporarily to other areas before returning. Given that opportunities for migration were limited, often hard work was the only option. But this was rarely enough to lift people above the poverty line and keep them there.

While opportunities for the poor remain much as they have always been in East Java, new options have arisen from the dust of conflict in North Maluku. The conflict, and the response to it, disturbed the equilibrium that kept many villagers trapped in poverty. Political, social, and economic structures all changed, creating new opportunities.

First, the analysis highlights the importance of *postconflict aid*. North Maluku saw an influx of aid and investment to try to rebuild the province. While the effects of this were by no means universally positive, in general it gave communities a boost that helped move some people out of poverty. Where aid was delivered in ways that substantively involved communities, it was more likely to lead to empowerment and greater mobility.

Second, North Maluku after the conflict saw an *expansion of the public sector*, which created secure employment opportunities. The splitting of Maluku province to create the new province of North Maluku increased the number of civil servant positions and created new centers of growth. Competition over access to the resources of new districts and subdistricts played a role in driving the conflict (Wilson 2008), and it could well be a basis of future violence.[21] But public sector expansion nonetheless provided secure sources of income that were not there before.

Third, North Maluku saw a greater *diversification of livelihoods* than did East Java. This was partly a function of the types of crops grown in North Maluku. With only one harvest a year, villagers tended to develop other occupational skills that they could draw on after the conflict. Aid programs, and the expansion of the public sector, also led to new opportunities for income diversification.

Fourth, the conflict in North Maluku strengthened *community-level collective action*. A traditional system for organizing activities required members of communities to work together. The shock of the conflict affected this system. However, once the conflict subsided, the system was reconstituted and was strengthened by the need to work together to address staggering postconflict problems. Local elites had to participate in and encourage collective action to help rebuild their personal economic lives. Increases in group participation were greater than in East Java, which suffered no massive external shock and where rigid social, political, and economic structures remained in place.

Finally, a comparative analysis of East Java and North Maluku shows that conflict and violence are present even in so-called no-conflict areas. Hence, the *nature of conflict* can play a greater role than the scale of conflict in determining impacts on societies. In East Java, levels of violent conflict were low. But the conflict that did occur, primarily criminal violence, damaged social cohesion because the protagonists usually lived in the same village. In contrast, villagers in North Maluku did not in general blame their neighbors for the violence, perceiving it to be the work of external provocateurs.[22] As a result, it was not too difficult to rebuild social ties and, indeed, villagers made conscious efforts to do so. Investments in social capital–building activities were made to prevent the reemergence of conflict, and this also provided opportunities for many poor people to improve their economic welfare.

This is not to say that provoking conflict would be an effective, let alone acceptable, poverty reduction strategy. In the communities visited in North Maluku, households suffered immensely during the conflict and its aftermath, losing lives, livelihoods, and property. The scars of war will take generations to heal. As Collier (2007) has argued, areas with a history of conflict are more prone to new outbreaks, thus creating future risk of economic retraction.

Yet the study does show that where conflict is occurring, or has occurred, well-designed responses after conflict ends can in some cases lead to improvements in the lives of the poorest. The provision of postconflict aid and development projects can boost local economic opportunities. Particular forms of aid such as rebuilding public and private infrastructure, providing training in new skills, and providing access to credit are especially helpful. The use of participatory development approaches can strengthen social cohesion and also help ensure that the poorest people benefit.

Indeed, the community in our sample where poor people did best was one of the worst hit by conflict. In Bodolenge, 68 percent of the poor managed to move out of poverty between 1995 and 2005. The village also sits in a district,

West Halmahera, where growth has been low. Yet here, good local leadership, development assistance, and strong collective action helped drive mobility.

The research also showed that more limited types of conflicts, those that do not rise to the level of widespread communal violence, have impacts on poverty that need to be considered. The communities in East Java were not devastated in the same way as were those in North Maluku. Yet the conflicts that did occur, and the tensions that remain, have had an impact on the ability of villagers to support each other in improving their economic situation. Using a "conflict lens" to understand poverty can be useful, even in areas where conflict is less acute or invisible to outsiders.

## Notes

The Indonesia study is part of the global Moving Out of Poverty study led by Deepa Narayan in the Poverty Reduction and Economic Management (PREM) Network of the World Bank. For a discussion of key study concepts and data collection methods, see chapter 1 and the appendixes to this volume. Also see volume 2 of the Moving Out of Poverty series (Narayan, Pritchett, and Kapoor 2009) and the study methodology guide (Narayan and Petesch 2005).

We are grateful to the team from the SMERU Research Institute in Jakarta who conducted the study in Indonesia. Lead researchers Sri Kusumastuti Rahayu and Vita Febriany wrote the national synthesis report, "Indonesia Case Study: North Maluku and East Java," which is available on the Moving Out of Poverty study Web site (http://go.worldbank.org/9ER0AOIH20). We also thank Chris Wilson for contributing in-depth analysis of the conflict in North Maluku and providing insightful comments. Comments from our two peer reviewers, Scott Guggenheim and Ashutosh Varshney, and from Dave McRae helped strengthen this chapter. Deepa Narayan, Patti Petesch, Soumya Kapoor, and all the members of the global Moving Out of Poverty team in New Delhi and Washington initiated and facilitated the Indonesia work. We appreciate their encouragement, support, guidance, and valuable suggestions during the process of writing this chapter.

1. Rp 151,997 per month per capita, using an exchange rate of US$1 = Rp 9,141.
2. According to Suryahadi, Sumarto, and Pritchett (2003), agriculture was the only sector that still recorded positive growth during the crisis.
3. The longer Indonesia paper, which this chapter draws on, examines these issues in depth (Rahayu and Febriany, forthcoming).
4. Indeed, it has been argued that the decision to take up arms, or to mobilize people to do so, is often a "rational choice" based on perceived economic gains from participating in violence (Collier and Hoeffler 2004).
5. Local GDP data from the Indonesian statistics bureau for 1996–2002 were used to determine high- and low-growth areas. Two high-growth districts in North Maluku were selected to ensure there was an urban village (in Ternate) in the provincial sample.

6. To protect the privacy of participants, this chapter uses pseudonyms for the 10 study villages. Cities, districts, subdistricts, and provinces are identified by their real names.

7. The reasons for this war, the events leading up to it, and the impacts are complex. This section provides a brief overview; for an in-depth discussion, see Wilson (2008).

8. Through most of 1999, the sultan was the leading contender to become the province's first governor. This threatened the political ambitions of his rivals and also the dominance in the local government and bureaucracy of the Makian and Tidore migrants. Many believed the sultan would give bureaucratic positions to his supporters—Ternatans and Halmaherans, including Christians. In addition, many Muslims were angry that he had protected Christians in the November riots and had apparently supported the Kao in the dispute over Malifut. In mid-December, several of the sultan's political opponents began mobilizing their followers to counter this dominance. These militias were known as the Pasukan Putih (White Force).

9. Of the Moving Out of Poverty locations, Pamekasan district was included in the newspaper survey, while Probolinggo was not. Seventeen deaths were reported in Pamekasan between 2001 and 2003.

10. In most areas population data were not disaggregated by gender. The exceptions were Barumangga (1,031 men and 1,061 women in 2005) and Bodolenge (205 men and 183 women).

11. Because official government poverty lines are generated only down to the district level, the study generated village-specific community poverty lines. This was done in focus group discussions. In all but one of the villages, communities assessed the poverty line to be roughly the same as the official district-level poverty line. In Kacokerre, the community put the poverty line lower than the official line. We use the CPL in each community as the basis for determining whether its residents have "moved out of poverty" or not.

12. Estimate from correspondence with Claire Q. Smith of the London School of Economics, who draws on data from Bappenas, the national planning agency. No disaggregation between the two provinces is available.

13. The experience of Bodolenge with KDP fits well with evidence from other parts of Indonesia. An evaluation of the program's second phase (KDP2) found consumption gains for poor households that were 11 percentage points greater in areas that had the program than in matched control locations (Voss 2008). The proportion of households in the same study that moved out of poverty (at the $2 a day poverty line) was 9.2 percent higher in KDP2 locations than in control areas. Vulnerable households near the poverty line were also less at risk of falling into poverty in KDP2 locations.

14. Key decentralization laws are Statute No. 22/1999 (concerning regional government) and Statute No. 25/1999 (concerning financial balance between the central and regional governments). Both were fully implemented in 2001. After three years of implementation, the laws were amended through Statute No. 32/2004 and Statute No. 33/2004.

15. The government administration of Indonesia is divided at several levels down to village administration. Provinces (*propinsi*) are divided into districts (*kabupaten*) in rural areas and municipalities (*kota*) in urban areas, with kabupaten and kota essentially performing the same functions. Within these are subdistricts (*kecamatan*), which are further divided into rural (*desa*) and urban (*kelurahan*).

16. Since then, an amendment to the village governance laws has meant that BPDs are once again appointed from above.

17. Of course, formal education is also important. Higher levels of education were correlated with movements out of poverty, although this was not significant at the 5 percent level (see Rahayu and Febriany, forthcoming).

18. Quotes from various informants in the East Java villages illustrate: "There are no teenagers with the creativity to identify business opportunities; there are only those who are looking for work" (Kalisido). "It is increasingly difficult to obtain work overseas. In Malaysia people are arrested by the police and sent home to the village to become farmers again" (Kacokerre). "It is hard to find work, and a job overseas requires capital" (Tattantok). "It is difficult to find work, especially as public servants; even though many people have educational certificates or tertiary degrees, it is necessary to have money" (Kramrrak). "I am a graduate of a tertiary school but I can't find work anywhere, so in the end I became a seller of spiced fruit" (Kramrrak).

19. As discussed earlier, the conflict in North Maluku led to segregation of ethnic and religious groups, sometimes temporary and sometimes prolonged. However, in all but one village studied (Bodolenge), people from different religious groups have returned to their village.

20. Miguel and Gugerty (2005), for example, have argued that social sanctions against shirking from collective action may be more difficult to enforce across ethnic groups, weakening cooperative outcomes.

21. As of 2009, tensions persist in North Maluku over who won the 2007 gubernatorial election. These have already erupted into violence (a gubernatorial candidate's house was burned down in 2008). However, to date there has been no escalation into widespread violence of the type that hit the province in 2000.

22. Sometimes those within the village were involved. However, for a number of reasons, including a desire to move on after the conflict, most villagers interviewed chose to ignore this.

## References

Anderson, B. 1991. *Imagined Communities: Reflections on the Origins and Spread of Nationalism*. London: Verso.

Barron, P., K. Kaiser, and M. Pradhan. 2009. "Understanding Variations in Local Conflict: Evidence and Implications from Indonesia." *World Development* 37 (3): 698–713.

Barron, P., and D. Madden. 2004. "Violent Conflict in 'Non-Conflict' Regions: The Case of Lampung, Indonesia." Indonesian Social Development Paper 2, World Bank, Jakarta.

Barron, P., and J. Sharpe. 2008. "Local Conflict in Post-Suharto Indonesia: Understanding Variations in Violence Levels and Forms through Local Newspapers." *Journal of East Asian Studies* 8 (3): 395–423.

Bates, R. H. 2000. *Prosperity and Violence: The Political Economy of Development.* New York: W. W. Norton.

Bayly, C. 2004. *The Birth of the Modern World, 1780–1914: Global Connections and Comparisons.* Malden, MA: Blackwell.

Bebbington, A., L. Dharmawan, E. Fahmi, and S. E. Guggenheim. 2006. "Local Capacity, Village Governance, and the Political Economy of Rural Development in Indonesia." *World Development* 34 (11): 1958–76.

BPS (Badan Pusat Statistik). 2005a. "Gross Domestic Regional Product (GDRP) Per Capita by Province and District, 2005." Table 10.1.1 (in Indonesian) on the Statistics Indonesia Web site at http://www.datastatistik-indonesia.com/ component/option,com_tabel/kat,10/.

———. 2005b. "Number of Population by Province." Table 1.1.1 on the Statistics Indonesia Web site at http://www.datastatistik-indonesia.com/component/ option,com_tabel/kat,1/.

———. 2008. "Data dan Informasi Kemiskinan Tahun 2007. Jakarta.

Coleman, J. S. 1990. *Foundations of Social Theory.* Cambridge, MA: Harvard University Press.

Collier, P. 1999. "On the Economic Consequences of Civil War." *Oxford Economic Papers* 51 (1): 168–83.

———. 2007. *The Bottom Billion: Why the Poorest Countries Are Failing and What Can Be Done about It.* New York: Oxford University Press.

Collier, P., L. Chauvet, and H. Hegre. 2008. "Conflicts: The Security Challenge in Conflict-Prone Countries." Copenhagen Consensus 2008 Challenge Paper, Copenhagen Consensus Center.

Collier, P., and A. Hoeffler. 2004. "Greed and Grievance in Civil War." *Oxford Economic Papers* 56 (4): 563–95.

Cramer, C. 2006. *Civil War Is Not a Stupid Thing: Accounting for Violence in Developing Countries.* London: Hurst.

Crook, R. C., and J. Manor. 1998. *Democracy and Decentralization in South Asia and West Africa: Participation, Accountability and Performance.* New York: Cambridge University Press.

Dollar, D., and A. Kraay. 2002. "Growth Is Good for the Poor." *Journal of Economic Growth* 7 (3): 195–225.

ELSAM (Institute for Policy Research and Advocacy). 2002. "Nasib Masyarakat Korban Konflik Ambon" (in Indonesian). *Asasi Newsletter* (Jakarta), July–August. http:// elsam.minihub.org/txt/asasi/2002_0708/04.html.

Faguet, J. 2004. "Does Decentralization Increase Responsiveness to Local Needs? Evidence from Bolivia." *Journal of Public Economics* 88 (3/4): 867–94.

Geertz, C. 1962. "The Rotating Credit Association: A 'Middle Rung' in Development." *Economic Development and Cultural Change* 10 (3): 241–63.

Geneva Declaration Secretariat. 2008. *The Global Burden of Armed Violence.* Geneva: Geneva Declaration Secretariat.

Hoeffler, A., and M. Reynal-Querol. 2003. *Measuring the Costs of Conflict*. Washington, DC: World Bank.

Kooistra, M. 2001. *Indonesia: Regional Conflicts and State Terror*. London: Minority Rights Group International.

Miguel, E. A., and M. K. Gugerty. 2005. "Ethnic Diversity, Social Sanctions, and Public Goods in Kenya." *Journal of Public Economics* 89 (11/12): 2325–68.

Moser, C. 2006. "Reducing Urban Violence in Developing Countries." Policy Brief 2006–01, Brookings Institution, Washington, DC.

Murshed, S. M., and M. Z. Tadjoeddin. 2008. "Is Fiscal Decentralization Conflict Abating? Routine Violence and District Level Government in Java, Indonesia." MICROCON Research Working Paper 7, University of Sussex, Brighton, UK.

Narayan, D., and P. Petesch. 2005. "Moving Out of Poverty Methodology Guide." Poverty Reduction Group, Poverty Reduction and Economic Management Network, World Bank, Washington, DC.

Narayan, D., L. Pritchett, and S. Kapoor. 2009. *Moving Out of Poverty: Success from the Bottom Up*. New York: Palgrave Macmillan; Washington, DC: World Bank.

Nordholt, H. S., and G. van Klinken. 2007. *Renegotiating Boundaries: Local Politics in Post-Soeharto Indonesia*. Leiden, Netherlands: KITLV Press.

NPRC (National Poverty Reduction Committee). 2005. "Strategi Nasional Penanggulangan Kemiskinan" (National Poverty Reduction Strategy). Komite Penanggulangan Kemiskinan (National Poverty Reduction Committee), Jakarta.

Putnam, R. D. 1993. *Making Democracy Work: Civil Traditions in Modern Italy*. Princeton, NJ: Princeton University Press.

Rahayu, S. K., and V. Fabriany. Forthcoming. "Moving Out of Poverty: Understanding Freedom, Democracy, Governance, and Growth from the Bottom-Up. Indonesia Case Study: North Maluku and East Java." SMERU Research Report, SMERU Research Institute, Jakarta, Indonesia.

Ravallion, M., and S. Chen. 1996. "What Can New Survey Data Tell Us about Recent Changes in Distribution and Poverty?" Policy Research Working Paper 1694, World Bank, Washington, DC.

Restrepo, J., B. Ferguson, J. M. Zuniga, and A. Villamarin. 2008. "Estimating Lost Product Due to Violent Deaths in 2004." Background paper for the Small Arms Survey, Conflict Analysis Resource Center (CERAC), Geneva and Bogota.

Sachs, J. D. 2008. *Common Wealth: Economics for a Crowded Planet*. New York: Penguin.

Smith, C. Q. 2008. "The Impact of State Capture on Emergency Aid: UNDP's 'Post-conflict' Recovery Programme in Indonesia." Development Studies Institute, London School of Economics and Political Science.

Suryahadi, A., S. Sumarto, and L. Pritchett. 2003. "The Evolution of Poverty during the Crisis in Indonesia." Working paper, SMERU Research Institute, Jakarta.

Tabellini, G. 2000. "Constitutional Determinants of Government Spending." IGIER Working Paper 162, Innocenzo Gasparini Institute for Economic Research, Bocconi University, Milan.

Tendler, J. 2000. "Why Are Social Funds So Popular?" In *Local Dynamics in an Era of Globalization*, ed. S. Yusuf, W. Wu, and S. Evenett, 114–29. New York: Oxford University Press.

Treisman, D. 2000. "The Causes of Corruption: A Cross-national Study." *Journal of Public Economics* 76 (3): 399–457.

Usman, S. 2001. "Indonesia's Decentralization Policy: Initial Experiences and Emerging Problems." Working paper, SMERU Research Institute, Jakarta.

Varshney, A. R. Panggabean, and M. Z. Tadjoeddin. 2008. "Creating Datasets in Information-Poor Environments: Patterns of Collective Violence in Indonesia (1990–2003)." *Journal of East Asian Studies* 8 (3): 361–94.

Voss, J. 2008. "Impact Evaluation of the Second Phase of the Kecamatan Development Program in Indonesia." World Bank, Jakarta.

Wade, R. 1997. "How Infrastructure Agencies Motivate Staff: Canal Irrigation in India and the Republic of Korea." In *Infrastructure Strategies in East Asia*, ed. A. Mody, 109–30. Washington, DC: World Bank.

Welsh, B. 2008. "Local and National: 'Keroyakan' Mobbing in Indonesia." *Journal of East Asian Studies* 8 (3): 473–504.

Wilson, C. 2005. "The Ethnic Origins of Religious Conflict in North Maluku Province, Indonesia, 1999–2000." *Indonesia* (Southeast Asia Program, Cornell University) 79 (April): 69–91.

———. 2008. *Ethno-Religious Violence in Indonesia: From Soil to God.* New York: Routledge.

World Bank. 2006. *Making the New Indonesia Work for the Poor.* Jakarta: World Bank.

Yanuarti, S., Yusuf, J. R. Marieta, and M. W. Tryatmoko. 2004. *Konflik Maluku Utara: Penyebab, Karakteristik, dan Penyelesaian Jangka Panjang.* Jakarta: Lembaga Ilmu Pengetahuan Indonesia.

# Community Well-Being and Household Mobility in Postconflict Cambodia

*Cambodia Development Resource Institute*

> *Poverty is caused by lacking income or by not being able to earn a living. For example, if we want to go fishing, all the fishing areas are owned. If we go to those areas—especially with fishing nets borrowed from the creditor—we are arrested and the authorities take our borrowed fishing nets. How can we survive?*
>
> —CHRONICALLY POOR MAN,
> Preysath, Kampong Svay district

> *We now have full rights to speak, and no one warns us not to voice our concerns or ask for help. But the authorities also have the right to ignore our concerns. They have the power to force us to follow the law, but we have no way to force them to cease their misbehavior.*
>
> —A YOUTH,
> Chakboeng, Peam Ro district

# 11

Political stability and good governance are widely assumed to be prerequisites for social and economic development. Countries that experience political upheaval and violent conflict tend to perform less well than countries that enjoy peace and stability. At the local level, however, the linkages between conflict, well-being, and governance are not yet adequately understood. This chapter aims to deepen understanding of these relationships by analyzing how conflict and the onset of peace have affected well-being and local governance in nine villages in Cambodia, a country that was synonymous with genocide and violent conflict during the last decades of the twentieth century.

The nine villages vary according to their location and geophysical endowments, such as proximity to markets and natural resource assets. These factors have shaped the livelihood strategies of households and their capacities to diversify income sources and access services, markets, and employment. The nine villages also experienced various levels of armed conflict and realized peace at different times. At first glance it appears that the villages where fighting ended prior to or early in the study period of 1993–2003/04 performed better than villages where fighting was more intense and lasted longer. One possible explanation for this relationship is that households in villages that experienced the so-called peace dividend earlier were able to concentrate their efforts on income generation for a longer period of time than villages where armed conflict was more protracted.

Upon closer scrutiny, however, it appears that the timing of the end of armed conflict is not always a reliable predictor of a community's overall well-being and its performance in terms of household mobility. For example, one village with heavy and protracted fighting was among the strongly performing villages, while several other villages where fighting stopped relatively early performed poorly or moderately. A focus on when the conflict ended can obscure other important factors, notably the scope and scale of conflict and its effect on economic activity, which were not consistent across all villages. Also important are the ways in which armed conflict may have interacted with or affected other key factors that influence well-being and mobility.

The relationship between armed conflict on the one hand and community well-being and household mobility on the other, therefore, is puzzling. Our research suggests that peace and stability enable certain villages to perform well over time *when favorable circumstances are in place*, including good soils and water resources, accessible location, and well-targeted development assistance. Peace and stability are not sufficient for promoting strong performance in the absence of these key advantages. And villages that are well-endowed with such resources may still perform well despite the presence of armed conflict.

The community findings also reveal that local governance in the post-conflict period is a key factor affecting community well-being and household mobility. All nine study villages experienced problems with law and order, such as theft and youth gang violence, during the transition to peace. The communities that were heavily dependent on forestry and fishing resources, however, faced more severe governance challenges due to conflicts over access to and control of these resources. Attitudes toward and expectations of officials are changing in light of widespread corruption and perceived failures on the part of officials to resolve resource conflicts fairly and enforce laws effectively. Although some better-off households can benefit from weak governance because they are able to form relationships with officials, the costs associated with corruption act as a shock to poor households. The governance challenges associated with the postconflict period have been exacerbated by the rapid and uneven transition to an open market economy without the supporting legal and institutional frameworks in place to regulate property, manage natural resources, and address crime and violence.[1]

The next section provides a brief overview of the impacts of Khmer Rouge rule and armed conflict on Cambodia and reviews trends in economic growth, poverty reduction, and inequality during the 1993–2003/04 study period. Next, the chapter highlights the main characteristics of community well-being and household mobility in the study villages. Brief case studies of four villages illustrate the leading factors that shaped recovery from conflict at the community level. The penultimate section discusses governance issues in the postconflict period, and the chapter concludes with a summary of key observations and a few reflections on policy implications.

## Civil War and Its Aftermath

Cambodia was torn by civil war for nearly a decade prior to the victory of the Khmer Rouge in April 1975. During the period from 1975 through early 1979, the Khmer Rouge became synonymous with genocide as urban elites and figures associated with the former regime were killed and a broad swath of the population died from hunger and ill health. Estimates of the number of deaths range from 1 million to 2 million. In 1979, Vietnamese forces invaded Cambodia and established the People's Republic of Kampuchea (PRK).[2] Fighting between the PRK and the Khmer Rouge and other resistance forces continued in many parts of the country throughout the 1980s.

The Paris Peace Agreements were signed in 1991, leading to the repatriation of 360,000 refugees in 1992, national elections in 1993, and a massive infusion of reconstruction and development assistance under the auspices of the United Nations Transitional Authority in Cambodia (UNTAC). Khmer Rouge factions, however, continued armed resistance in many parts of the country until 1998, when the last combatants laid down arms.

The civil war and the Khmer Rouge period left the country's economy in shambles. During the 1980s the PRK government tried to manage a planned economy with support from Vietnam, the Soviet Union, and east bloc communist countries.[3] It was not until the UNTAC period of the 1990s that major donors such as the United Nations, the World Bank, the Asian Development Bank, and Western bilateral aid agencies established operations in Cambodia, along with many international nongovernmental organizations (NGOs). This period also coincided with the emergence of a more vibrant free market economy that gradually reached rural areas as infrastructure and security permitted. The single most important aspect of the economic recovery after 1979 was the challenge of restoring agricultural production to address food security issues. The new government instituted a policy known as *krom samaki* (solidarity groups), in which agricultural production was organized collectively.[4] In many areas the krom samaki failed, and local officials organized land distributions to households as early as 1979 and the early 1980s (Gottesman 2004). Given the fragile state of agriculture during these years, access to common property resources became important in enabling people to sustain their livelihoods. People's access to these resources, however, was constrained by fighting and by the presence of landmines and unexploded ordnance in the areas surrounding villages.

Education and health systems were also in disarray. Educated elites such as doctors, nurses, and teachers had been targets of the Khmer Rouge, and many who survived eventually fled to refugee camps along the Thailand-Cambodia border. The fighting during the 1980s and 1990s took a tremendous human toll, visible in the large numbers of disabled people (wounded soldiers, civilian landmine victims) and widowed heads of households. Years of war and Khmer Rouge rule eroded social capital in the form of trust and capacity for cooperative action. The large-scale movements of people in the aftermath of the Vietnamese invasion and the subsequent repatriation of refugees dealt a further blow to community cohesion.

After the invasion, a governing apparatus had to be rebuilt at all levels of the political administration. The few surviving intellectuals, meaning anyone with a high school education or above, were generally placed in senior positions at the national level. Given the nature of the political and armed conflict, loyalty was stressed over competency, and many subnational positions were filled along patronage lines favoring family, friends, and acquaintances (Gottesman 2004). During the 1980s the local administration focused on security, limiting local travel by citizens and enforcing conscription practices in support of the government's defense efforts against the Khmer Rouge and other resistance groups. In areas where fighting was particularly intense, military units played a significant role in local governance. In other areas where security permitted, some local officials tried their hand at development, but such efforts were largely dependent on outside assistance. With the emergence of peace, the role of local governance has shifted more toward administration and development.

Postconflict recovery has been markedly uneven across the national territory and across economic sectors. Economic growth in Cambodia was quite rapid during the study period, averaging 7.1 percent per year between 1994 and 2004. This growth has been largely driven by export-oriented garment manufacturing and tourism. Growth in the agriculture sector, however, has been slow and erratic, averaging 3.3 percent per year. This is the sector where about 70 percent of Cambodians continue to work. Agricultural production actually fell over the three years from 1999 to 2002 because of widespread droughts and floods. Productivity remains low, at 2 tons per hectare. Only 7 percent of arable land is irrigated, and fewer than 10 percent of households benefit from extension services. Land tenure is generally insecure and the number of landless households is increasing.

Poverty fell by about 1 percentage point per year during the study period, from 47 percent in 1993/94 to 35 percent in 2004. Rural poverty, however, has remained high, falling from 43 percent to 34 percent, while in Phnom Penh poverty fell from 11 percent to 5 percent. Although poverty rates have fallen, inequality increased over the decade. The Gini coefficient for national consumption increased from 0.34 to 0.40 between 1993/94 and 2004. Inequality rose sharply in rural areas, from 0.26 to 0.36; it remained constant albeit higher at 0.43 in urban areas. The high poverty rates and rising inequality in rural areas, along with high inequality in urban areas, may be the result of an unequal distribution of benefits from growth that is narrowly based in urban areas, while the majority of the population (85 percent) and the poor (91 percent) live in the rural areas (World Bank 2006, 2007).

## Performance of the Study Households and Villages

The nine study villages were originally selected to represent agro-ecological zones for a study on rural livelihoods in 2001 (Acharya and Chan 2002).[5] These nine villages were visited again in 2003/04 to conduct the Moving Out of Poverty study, and once more in 2004/05 to conduct the second wave of the rural livelihoods study (map 11.1). In 2004/05, 890 of the original 1,010 households were surveyed again, thus creating a panel dataset that enabled researchers to measure changes in community and household well-being over the three-year interval.

Villages were grouped into three well-being performance clusters according to their consumption, income, and poverty rates (table 11.1). Strongly performing villages experienced rising consumption and incomes as well as

**TABLE 11.1**
**Profile of Cambodia study communities**

| Village | District | Performance on consumption, income, and poverty measures |
| --- | --- | --- |
| Sastaing | Thma Koul | Strong |
| Chakboeng | Peam Ro | Strong |
| Salvia Prey | Sangkae | Strong |
| Koh Phong | Chhloung | Moderate |
| Troula Trav | Lvea Aem | Moderate |
| Ponky Kda | Odongk | Moderate |
| Somrampi | Kampot | Poor |
| Kdadaum | Santuk | Poor |
| Preysath | Kampong Svay | Poor |

*Source:* FitzGerald et al. 2007, based on Moving Out of Poverty study data.
*Note:* The study villages are identified by pseudonyms in this chapter.

**MAP 11.1**
**Cambodia with study communities**

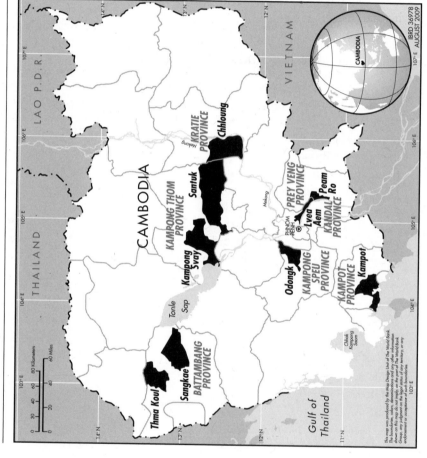

falling poverty rates. Moderately performing villages achieved income and/or consumption growth, or poverty reduction, but not both. Poorly performing villages were unable to achieve substantial gains on any of these measures.

Table 11.2 presents mobility outcomes for the 890 households in the panel according to annual per capita consumption. The three basic categories of well-being include the poor, moderately poor, and well-off.[6] Just over half of the households did not change their well-being status over the study period, 2001 to 2004/05. These "nonmoving" households consisted of the comfortably rich (24 percent of the total), the static middle (14 percent), and the chronic poor (14 percent). Just under half of the households changed status, with 26 percent moving up and 22 percent moving down, for a net gain of 4 percent. Ten percent of the households moved from very poor to moderately poor status, and another 4 percent became well off. Among the moderately poor, some climbed into wealth (12 percent) but others fell into deepening poverty (7 percent). Even higher rates of falling (15 percent) were experienced by the comfortably rich group.

The distribution of these mobility groups across the nine study villages gives us a picture of how each community fared in terms of its well-being and mobility performance (figure 11.1). The strongly performing villages of Sastaing, Chakboeng, and Salvia Prey have more upwardly mobile and better-off households, while the poorly performing villages of Somrampi, Kdadaum, and Preysath have more downwardly mobile and chronic poor households. In the three moderately performing villages of Koh Phong, Troula Trav, and Ponky Kda, households appear to be moving in opposite directions as the number of better-off and upwardly mobile households is more or less offset by a similar number of downwardly mobile and chronic poor households.

**TABLE 11.2**
**Distribution of mobility groups in the Cambodia household sample**

| | | 2004/05 | | |
|---|---|---|---|---|
| | *Status* | *Very poor* | *Moderately poor* | *Well off* |
| | *Very poor* | Chronic poor (14%) | Moving out of poverty (10%) | Rags to riches (4%) |
| *2001* | *Moderately poor* | Deepening poverty (7%) | Static middle (14%) | Climbed into wealth (12%) |
| | *Well off* | Riches to rags (3%) | Falling into poverty (12%) | Comfortably rich (24%) |

*Source:* FitzGerald et al. 2007, based on 890 panel households in the nine study communities.

**FIGURE 11.1**

**Distribution of mobility groups in the Cambodia study communities**

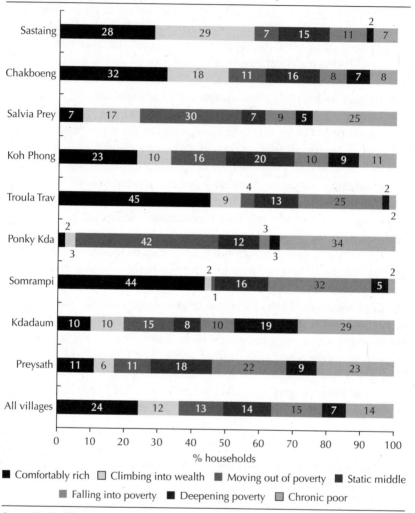

Comfortably rich ☐ Climbing into wealth ■ Moving out of poverty ■ Static middle
■ Falling into poverty ■ Deepening poverty ☐ Chronic poor

*Source:* FitzGerald et al. 2007, based on 890 panel households in the nine study communities.

According to the survey responses for the rural livelihoods study, comfortably rich households have the most assets, earn the most from each source of income, have the largest landholdings, and are the most productive. They are able to accumulate assets and diversify income sources, and they are therefore better positioned to withstand shocks associated with illness or severe weather. These households rely primarily on agriculture and self-employment and are less reliant on wage labor than other households. They use credit, including from private providers and moneylenders, largely for productive purposes such as agricultural or business inputs.

Upwardly mobile households have the second-largest landholdings after the comfortably rich. They have benefited from improved dry-season rice productivity, but they are less reliant on agriculture than in the past and more reliant on self-employment and wage labor. Some members of these households migrate for work within Cambodia or in Thailand. In poorer natural resource–dependent communities, where economic opportunities are more limited, households may earn income from illegal fishing and forest activities.

Households in the static middle are fairly evenly distributed across the strongly, moderately, and poorly performing villages, but their characteristics may vary from one village to the next. In some villages they have more in common with upwardly mobile households, while in others they are closer to the poor. These households spend more on health and education than do poor and downwardly mobile households, but they are earning more from selling labor than in the past.

Downwardly mobile households tend to be concentrated in poorly performing communities. They have smaller landholdings or no agricultural land and are less productive than other households. They are more likely to engage in wage labor or run small businesses than to rely on agriculture. They tend to use credit to cope with food shortages or shocks. They have fewer earners and more dependents. They spend more on crises and less on education. Shocks such as a natural disaster or an episode of ill health have a "cascading effect" leading to lower productivity, distressed land sales, and debt.

The chronic poor households also tend to be concentrated in the poorly performing villages. They have a higher dependency ratio and often have sick, old, disabled, or female household heads. These households have no or very few assets, rely on one or two income sources, and are landless or have very little land. As a result, they continue to rely on common property resources and/ or sell their own and their children's labor in order to survive. They use loans to eat and repay other loans and are unable to spend enough on health and education. Serious illness often incapacitates or kills (FitzGerald et al. 2007).

## Postconflict mobility factors and processes

As described above, the scope, scale, and duration of armed conflict varied significantly across the country. Although they were not selected for this purpose, the nine villages visited for the study encompass a great deal of this variation. A conflict typology is presented to help frame the analysis about the effects of conflict on local mobility processes between 1993 and 2003/04. Areas that experienced the most conflict, in terms of its duration and intensity, are designated "red," those that experienced the least conflict are "green," and those falling in between are "yellow."

Table 11.3 shows the distribution of study villages according to this conflict typology, along with the mobility typology of strong, moderate, and poor community performance. The years in the table indicate when conflict ended in each community. Of the four green-area villages, two were free of violent conflicts by 1984 and the other two were secure by the time of the 1993 national elections. The single yellow-area village was generally secure by day but was subject to occasional raids at night, as it was situated near transit points for Khmer Rouge troops. The four red-area villages experienced intense and protracted armed conflict until the mid- to late 1990s.

There seems to be little systematic relationship between the mobility performance of the study communities and the date when conflict ended. There were strongly performing communities in areas of peace (e.g., Chakboeng) and of protracted conflict (Sastaing). And there were poorly performing communities in both contexts as well. While it was expected that Kdadaum, a red-area village where fighting only ended in 1998, would perform poorly, poverty has also remained extensive in Somrampi, which achieved peace in 1993. To better understand the range of factors apart from conflict that may shape mobility in the study villages, we first compare the conflict and recovery experiences of two green-area villages with very different mobility outcomes. We then compare two red-area villages with contrasting performances.

Before moving into the village-level case studies, it is important to note that the significance of prolonged conflict cannot be discounted. Two of the three

**TABLE 11.3**
**Distribution of Cambodia study communities by conflict area and mobility performance**

| Mobility performance | Conflict area | | |
| --- | --- | --- | --- |
| | Green | Yellow | Red |
| Strong | Chakboeng (1984) | Salvia Prey (1994) | Sastaing (1998) |
| Moderate | Troula Trav (1984) | | Koh Phong (1998) |
| | Ponky Kda (1993) | | |
| Poor | Somrampi (1993) | | Preysath (1997) |
| | | | Kdadaum (1998) |

*Source:* FitzGerald et al. 2007, based on Moving Out of Poverty study data.
*Note:* Dates indicate the year conflict ended.

poorly performing villages, Preysath and Kdadaum, are in red areas, where fighting was intense and protracted, not ending until 1997/98. Meanwhile, two of the three strong performers, Chakboeng and Salvia Prey, were in green or yellow areas where fighting ended well before or very early in the study period. Hence, after the case studies we spend some time focusing on how conflict can impede poor people's access to opportunities in order to shed light on how conflict interacts with other factors to affect community performance.

## Exploring Strong and Weak Performance in Two Peaceful Villages

Let us first compare the green-area villages of Chakboeng and Somrampi. Over half (50 percent) of Chakboeng's surveyed households are comfortably well off (32 percent) or upwardly mobile (18 percent); additionally 11 percent escaped poverty. In Somrampi 44 percent were comfortably rich, but only 2 percent were upwardly mobile and only 1 percent escaped poverty. Large differences can also be seen in the rates at which households fell into poverty or experienced deepening poverty: in Chakboeng the downward movers composed 23 percent, and in Somrampi, 36 percent. What explains Chakboeng's much stronger mobility outcomes?

Chakboeng has enjoyed peace and stability since 1984, the longest period of the nine villages visited. Peace arrived in Somrampi in 1993, after years of sporadic conflict involving the Khmer Rouge. While this is nearly a decade later than in Chakboeng, Somrampi experienced peace several years before the red-area study villages (table 11.3). As explored below, however, the early onset of peace can certainly contribute to a village's recovery and rising prosperity, but it does not guarantee it; villages that face numerous other disadvantages may remain poor even after they are peaceful.

Chakboeng benefits greatly from its location near the trading center of Neak Leoung. It has very fertile soils, and agriculture is the main economic activity in the village. The new PRK government devoted agricultural development resources to this area, and farmers gradually adopted modern farming techniques. These include the use of tractors or hand tractors for land preparation and pumps for irrigation, as well as high-yielding seed varieties and chemical fertilizers and pesticides. A focus group of female youth explained the profound changes that these advances brought to the village:

> Farm machinery has been widely used since 2000 because it is easier than using draft animals . . . The area of a morning plowing with a hand tractor is equal to 10 mornings using draft animals . . . and there is no need to spend time grazing cattle and buffaloes. It provides more time for doing other things.

In the late 1980s three irrigation wells were dug in the village. Access to pumped water enabled farmers to cultivate about 610 hectares of high-yielding dry-season rice varieties. The village was eventually designated as a model development area by the Ministry of Agriculture and received support from UNICEF (United Nations Children's Fund) in the late 1980s and early 1990s. Other organizations helped extend irrigation coverage in 2002 by an additional 50 hectares.

Chakboeng also enjoys access to good fishing areas, and fishing is the second most important livelihood. The activity was restricted to a few hundred meters around the village from the mid-1980s to the year 2000, and there were frequent conflicts between fishing lot owners and local fishermen. Several fishing lots were then released back to Chakboeng commune. Although this has contributed to the marked increase in community well-being, there has been a sharp decline in fish stocks due to a lack of effective measures against fishing with illegal equipment.

The village of Somrampi, which displays much weaker performance on mobility outcomes, lacks the agricultural infrastructure needed to translate peace into prosperity. About 70–80 percent of the village households grow rice, but the soil is not fertile, little chemical fertilizer is used, and production depends on rain. Yields in the village are low, about 0.9 ton per hectare. Twenty households with land near the sea have been heavily affected by a rise in tidal levels, which has damaged rice fields.

Somrampi also struggles with rising environmental pressures on fishing livelihoods. Marine fishing involves about 85 percent of households in the village, most of whom have fishing tools and boats. This livelihood is especially important for the nearly one-third of village households that are landless and rely on access to marine resources, fishing, and collecting crabs along the shore. But the stocks have been dwindling because of overfishing. As with inland fishing, marine fishing varies in scale according to the size and type of boat as well as the fishing gear used. The demand for small marine fish increased during the last years of the study period, encouraging the use of illegal fishing nets with a very fine mesh. Although the use of illegal nets carries strong punishments, bigger fishermen can still use them because of their cozy relationships with key authorities. Members of a focus group from Somrampi explained:

> Everybody knows that this fishing activity is illegal and should be controlled by the fishing authorities, who may come once or twice per month. However, those who practice it have good connections with the fishing authorities . . . and colluders may inform the owners when the authorities come.

Somrampi has received only modest development assistance. Compared to Chakboeng, there has been little support for agricultural production.

Access to good roads has been in place only since 2003, after the renovation of the national road connecting Kampot provincial town to Kep resort. This improvement has promoted better communication and the marketing of local marine products, and several organizations have helped build a primary school as well as facilities for literacy training.

## Contrasting Performance in Two Villages with Protracted Conflict

Let us now turn to two red-area villages where fighting persisted into the late 1990s. The mobility performance of Preysath is considerably lower than that of Sastaing. Just 11 percent of Preysath's households are comfortably well off, and another 17 percent are upwardly mobile. In Sastaing, these rates jump to 28 percent and 36 percent, respectively. Moreover, Preysath's group of chronic poor households (23 percent) is more than three times as large as Sastaing's, and its group of downwardly mobile households (31 percent) is twice as large. Do similar or different factors shape mobility processes in communities with protracted conflict?

Preysath achieved full peace only in 1997, which may have contributed to its weak performance. The intense fighting included frequent gun battles with occasional bomb explosions. Many landmines were laid in the area during the conflict; while most have since been cleared, some remain. The poor security in the area constrained people's freedom of movement, limiting their ability to fish and farm rice, as well as their access to common property for land clearance and harvesting of forest products. Most households had little or no land and were unable to clear any new forest land because of the fighting and the danger of landmines. According to a focus group from the village:

> Prior to the defection of Pol Pot troops to the government [in 1996 and 1997], most villagers were scared to sleep in the house, and most of the time slept on the ground close to security trenches. Every time Khmer Rouge or government troops came to the village, they took our chickens and ducks, or burned our houses if we were not willing to give our belongings to them. It was bad luck for those who went fishing and met them. They would ask us to get out of our boat and then take everything we had.

During this period, many people eventually fled to other villages.

In addition to enduring severe and protracted conflict, Preysath is also disadvantaged by its heavy reliance on fishing, the main occupation for most residents, and on rainfed rice farms. It is very remote, and boats are the primary means of reaching urban markets and the provincial center. When peace finally arrived, people were able to fish freely and clear forest land for agriculture, although problems with theft persisted. Road conditions remained poor, but market access nevertheless improved for local products, including fish, paddy, and livestock. And about half of those who fled the village during the years of conflict returned to the village.

As in the other fishing villages in the study, local incomes suffered greatly as fish stocks declined in the postconflict period. With improved market access and security, people started to use more sophisticated fishing gear. The decline in fishing income then prompted more people to shift to rice farming. In some cases, households have been clearing inundated forest land, which in turn has affected fish breeding and led to a further decline in fish stocks. Beginning in 2000, the village also experienced problems with drought that contributed to its poor recovery.

Preysath has received little development assistance. Caritas, an international NGO, and UNICEF provided two credit schemes to the village in the late 1990s and early 2000s, but both failed after a few years. These organizations also helped promote dry-season rice production that requires pumping water from the river. There has not been any other agricultural assistance or effort to improve the road.

In the strongly performing village of Sastaing, peace arrived in 1998, a year later than in Preysath. But the two villages' experiences with conflict and recovery present a stark contrast.

Sastaing enjoys good soils and irrigation infrastructure, as well as easy access to nearby markets. With irrigation, Sastaing's farmers produce both wet-season and higher-yielding dry-season rice. The village also benefits greatly from its location near National Route 5, which provides good access to nearby markets. Ironically, the war contributed to improved agricultural productivity in Sastaing. The poor security conditions during the conflict prompted farmers to mechanize agricultural production, and this in turn raised productivity. The rising incidence of cattle and buffalo theft in the area beginning in 1993 led villagers to start selling off their livestock in order to acquire hand tractors. As a result, the village was able to increase rice yields, at least up until 2000, when the area began to experience prolonged floods followed by drought.

Migration and remittances from family members play a significant role in Sastaing's economy, as 60 percent of households are landless. Since 2000, migration to the nearby Thai border or into Thailand has increased dramatically. About 70–80 percent of the community's economically active persons between the ages of 15 and 40 are working in Thailand. Many young women also migrate to Phnom Penh to work in the garment sector.

Fishing in open-access ponds and streams and in inundated forests is also common in Sastaing. In discussions for the study, villagers repeatedly mentioned the widespread use of illegal fishing tools, such as electric shocks, chemical substances, and finely meshed nets. This resulted in a sharp decline in fish stocks and fishing income between 1999 and 2003. Since 2004, however, there have been several notices of serious actions against illegal fishing activities from the national government, and local authorities have had success in combating these activities as well.

Sastaing has received considerably more development assistance since the mid-1990s than has Preysath. Roads around Sastaing have been upgraded, partly as a result of assistance provided to a nearby village where approximately 80 returnee households resettled. A gravel path was constructed in 1997 and other improvements have taken place since then as a result of the government's local development program, SEILA. Social services, including education and health, have improved. NGOs have helped support a village rice bank project as well as a self-help group credit scheme. A villager who participated in a focus group observed, "Ten years ago, we did not have medical practitioners or a hospital. At that time we had to spend our rice or gold in exchange for treatment or medicines . . . Now we have medical practitioners providing services in the village."

It is important to note that the differences in the performance of the two red-area villages were already emerging before the end of the conflict. For example, the intense and protracted fighting in remote Preysath limited the amount of land people could farm. The little land that was farmed had poor-quality soils, so production was limited. This retarded overall community performance and slowed household mobility. In Sastaing, armed conflict also affected people's efforts to farm, but it was not as disruptive as in Preysath. Fertile soils and irrigation enabled people to obtain higher yields on what land they were able to cultivate. This offset to a certain extent the impact of conflict by enabling more households to accumulate capital assets (such as hand tractors) with which to intensify farming practices and increase overall productivity. With the onset of peace, the strong differences in farm productivity, local endowments, access to markets, and development assistance accentuated the divergence in prosperity experienced by these two villages.

## Conflict and Access to Opportunities

The four village case summaries identify several factors that interact to promote (or hinder) community well-being and household mobility. These include geophysical endowments, access to natural resource assets, community location and accessibility, development assistance, and timing of the end of conflict. This section draws from across the study villages to examine these factors more fully. First, however, it is useful to look at the role of the land reform that was implemented during the conflict in these primarily agricultural villages. Land acquisition established the foundation upon which households could eventually accumulate assets and diversify income sources, the keys to upward mobility.

## Land acquisition

In all nine study villages, formation of the krom samaki (solidarity groups) was followed by a distribution of agricultural land. In two of the nine sites, people were allowed to reacquire the land they held prior to the Khmer Rouge regime. In other villages, lots of land were distributed to households but the formula used for parceling out the lots varied somewhat. In some villages households with more members received more land than smaller households, while in other villages land was divided equally among households regardless of their size. Efforts were usually made to provide households with lots of similar quality in terms of their elevation, location, and so forth.

In well-performing Chakboeng, the krom samaki functioned until 1987, the longest of any of the study villages. In 1988 and 1989, land was distributed to former krom samaki members, about 0.16 hectare per adult. Households were also able to clear forested land for agricultural purposes. About 12 percent of the households do not have farmland and rely instead on wage labor and access to common property resources. In most other villages the rates of landlessness are much higher.

A krom samaki functioned in poorly performing Preysath from 1979 to 1983, and it was seen to be effective in helping poor farmers earn a living. In 1983 land was distributed to households according to the number of members. As a result, larger households received more land than smaller households. It also appears that some people, including local government officials, received a disproportionate share of land. According to a focus group of male youths, government authorities benefited excessively during the land distribution by giving plots to their relatives and "others who are rich." The youths commented that "some households in this community hold two to four plots of arable lands while the poor without connections hold only one plot."

During the early 1980s, poorly performing Somrampi was the site of a state-owned salt mining operation whose workers did not belong to the village krom samaki. When the krom samaki disbanded, agricultural land was divided only among its members. About half of the adults in the village each received 0.13 hectare, but the salt mine workers did not receive any land, leaving many landless.

In many villages households were able to acquire additional land by clearing forest areas, but this also depended on the amount of available labor and on security and governance conditions. Larger households, which tended to acquire more land through distribution, also had more hands available to clear land for farming when security conditions permitted. Villagers in strongly performing Chakboeng in the green area have been able to clear additional land since the early 1980s. In the poorly performing red-area village of Preysath, on the other hand, people were officially allowed to clear additional land, but they were generally unable to do so because of heavy fighting and the presence of landmines. In other red-area villages such as Sastaing, moreover, local leaders and the military restricted mobility into areas where people could be harassed by or consort with Khmer Rouge soldiers. This too prevented people from clearing and farming the land.

Certain provisions of the peace agreement played an important role in land acquisitions. In Salvia Prey, a strongly performing village, 100 refugee households were resettled in 1992. Nearly all of them were considered poor upon their arrival, as they had no land and very few financial resources. In 1994, inundated forest land that had once been inaccessible to villagers because of the presence of Khmer Rouge forces was distributed to the returnee households, with each household receiving about 1 hectare. Many of them, however, did not have the financial or human resources required to clear the land and eventually left the village. A focus group from Salvia Prey explained:

> The returnees have nothing. Many of them have sold out their land received when they were resettled in this village. This is because they lacked money to clear their lands and start growing rice. Therefore they had to rely entirely on wage labor in the village or along and/or across the Cambodia-Thai border, and collecting morning glory and edible insects to survive.

## Natural resource assets

In addition to access to farmland, access to fisheries and nontimber forest products during and after the conflict shaped the recovery of communities from conflict. The case of poorly performing Preysath can illustrate. Intense and protracted fighting there acted as a brake on natural resource exploitation by area farmers by restricting their access to both fisheries and forests.

But once the fighting ended, these areas reverted to open-access common property. In the case of fisheries, therefore, the conflict helped maintain fish stocks at a sustainable level, but when the fighting ended the stocks were quickly depleted by excessive harvesting. In the case of forests, the continued presence of landmines and ongoing banditry may have acted to forestall rapid exploitation, even after the conflict ended.

The two red-area villages of poorly performing Kdadaum and moderately performing Koh Phong show similar patterns of natural resource degradation, with the important exception that the intense exploitation coincided with rather than followed the conflict. During the armed conflict, the government granted forest concessions near the two villages to large companies, and governance of the forest areas passed from the state sector to private commercial interests. These companies had the necessary resources with which to reach accommodations with armed groups, and they colluded with both government and Khmer Rouge forces to preserve their own access to timber for harvesting. Ordinary villagers, meanwhile, had little or no access to the forest because of both the corporate concessions and the continued fighting. When the conflict ended, people found that the forests had been severely degraded. This had a significant negative effect on community well-being and on mobility among households that had depended on these resources.

Although armed conflict restricted access to natural resource assets in resource-dependent villages, thus undermining community well-being and retarding mobility, it does not follow that the absence of armed conflict resulted in well-regulated access. For example, the green-area villages of Chakboeng and Somrampi have both experienced conflict over access to fishery resources. In the well-performing village of Chakboeng, the impact of dwindling fish stocks has been largely offset by the intensification of rice production and diversification of income sources, including expanded trade with nearby markets. In more remote and poorly performing Somrampi, however, the problems of dwindling marine resources are exacerbated by the fact that poor soils and low productivity limit the scope for intensification and diversification of agriculture. The effect is to push people toward low-paid wage labor.

## Location and access

A community's location and infrastructure affect its market access and trade, the availability of social services, and the amount and type of development assistance it receives. The most direct links between location, access, and armed conflict can be observed in the two poorly performing red-area villages of

Preysath and Kdadaum and in the moderately performing red-area village of Koh Phong. All three villages are in remote locations, and Khmer Rouge forces were stationed in surrounding forest areas that were difficult for government forces to penetrate. In the remote village of Preysath, market access was severely impeded by armed conflict and banditry and by the lack of roads.

The armed conflict also affected circulation to and from red-area villages by delaying the construction of roads and other infrastructure, which in turn affected the level and type of other assistance. For example, in Kdadaum and Koh Phong, roads that connected the villages to commercial and administrative centers were not built until 2002. Although assistance remained meager even after that, the roads have connected the village to local markets and have opened up areas for other types of economic activities.

Armed conflict did not severely disrupt trade and market access in the strongly performing red-area village of Sastaing, which is located near a national highway and local markets. In this case, a favorable location helped the village overcome the negative effects of fighting. In the strongly performing green-area village of Chakboeng, road conditions were not ideal during the 1990s, but security-related problems did not impede access. As a result, area producers were able to get their products to market and traders regularly came to the village. An accessible location and favorable agricultural conditions in addition to peace and stability, therefore, made this an attractive area for development investments. In several other green-area villages, on the other hand, poor access and remote location made it difficult for people to take advantage of peace and stability. The poorly performing village of Somrampi was hampered by poor road conditions, while the moderately performing village of Troula Trav is virtually inaccessible during some seasons of the year.

## Development assistance

There appears to be a strong relationship between village performance and levels of development assistance and a somewhat less strong relationship between conflict intensity and levels of development assistance. Table 11.4 shows that the three strongly performing villages all benefited from substantially more assistance than did moderately and poorly performing villages. It also reveals that three of the four red-area villages had a low number of development interventions during the study period, while villages in the green and yellow areas show a mixed picture in levels of assistance. But the presence of conflict in a particular area does not reliably predict development assistance trends. For example, the red-area village of Sastaing had one of the highest numbers of development interventions among all villages, while Troula Trav, a green-area village, had among the lowest.

The strongly performing villages of Chakboeng, Salvia Prey, and Sastaing all report extensive development assistance. Green-area Chakboeng received a number of government and NGO development interventions to support agricultural production and promote public health. It also appears that some households in red-area Sastaing indirectly benefited from similar types of assistance provided to 80 returnee households who were resettled near the village. The government assistance was provided in the late 1980s, and there was some NGO activity as well. This was certainly the case in yellow-area Salvia Prey, where significant levels of reconstruction and development assistance were provided in support of about 100 returnee households from the refugee camps along the Thailand-Cambodia border. According to local leaders in Salvia Prey:

> We were lucky to receive an influx of rural development programs from NGOs in the early 1990s. It is impossible to recall all the development activities we have received . . . Development aid flowed into the village immediately after the resettlement of returnees in our village.

The absence of conflict in Chakboeng enabled the government to focus early development interventions in that area. In Salvia Prey and perhaps to a lesser extent in Sastaing, development interventions were provided to support returnees who were coming back from refugee camps after the peace agreement was signed. In each of these three cases, development assistance also appears to be somewhat integrated with complementary services that support agricultural production, and with social services. These include road construction, irrigation (except in the case of Salvia Prey), and credit services, as well as clean drinking water, health care, and schools.

Prolonged armed conflict, poor location, and inaccessibility help explain the much lower levels of development interventions in the three other red-area villages. Poorly performing Preysath and Kdadaum received little or no support for agricultural production and virtually no support for infrastructure and public health. The same is true for moderately performing Koh Phong, another red-area village where practically no development interventions were provided because of its remote location and heavy fighting.

Three green-area villages also have not received many development interventions. These include the poorly performing village of Somrampi as well as the moderately performing villages of Troula Trav and Ponky Kda. In these three villages, location has probably played a significant role in limiting the

**TABLE 11.4**
**Number of development interventions in Cambodia study communities, by conflict area, 1992–2004/05**

| | Conflict area | | | | | | | | |
| | Green/yellow | | | | | Red | | | |
| Sector | **Chakboeng** | Troula Trav | **Salvia Prey** | Ponky Kda | Somrampi | **Sastaing** | Koh Phong | Kdadaum | Preysath |
|---|---|---|---|---|---|---|---|---|---|
| Agriculture | **6** | 0 | **5** | 0 | 0 | **3** | 0 | 0 | 2 |
| Credit | **4** | 0 | **3** | 2 | 4 | **4** | 0 | 0 | 1 |
| Health care | **1** | 1 | **1** | 1 | 1 | **3** | 1 | 1 | 0 |
| Water | **3** | 1 | **3** | 0 | 0 | **1** | 0 | 0 | 0 |
| Roads | **0** | 0 | **2** | 1 | 1 | **3** | 0 | 1 | 0 |
| Education | **0** | 1 | **2** | 1 | 1 | **0** | 0 | 1 | 1 |
| Total | **14** | 3 | **16** | 5 | 7 | **14** | 1 | 3 | 4 |

*Source:* FitzGerald et al. 2007, based on Moving Out of Poverty study data.
*Note:* Strongly performing villages are shown in bold.

amount of assistance. It may be that these villages were not located in areas specifically targeted by the development community or that they somehow did not meet the criteria for assistance. In the case of Troula Trav, development assistance arrived almost by accident when the Cambodia Development Resource Institute provided support for drinking water wells after conducting research for this study in the village.

## Timing

When the fighting actually ended also had important implications for community well-being and household mobility. One way that conflict affects village life is through its impact on public security. Nearly all of the villages reported problems with theft and robbery, particularly during the period of transition from conflict to peace. Several green-area villages reported that theft and robbery seemed to increase in the early to mid-1990s, coinciding with the UNTAC period. In the red-area villages, it appears that theft and robbery were widespread during the fighting and then in some cases intensified once the armed conflict was over.

For example, Khmer Rouge units established themselves in the forest areas near Preysath and conducted military operations from this base. As various units began to defect to the government, other units remained in the forests and essentially became bandits. Another example concerns Koh Phong village, where armed conflict had been particularly intense during the early to mid-1990s. Around the middle of the decade units negotiated to defect to the government, but other units continued fighting while at the same time taking up banditry. Thus, the red-area villages did not always see a sudden end to fighting and the immediate resumption of peace. Rather, armed political conflict transformed into security issues associated with banditry, which in turn affected people's capacity to clear new land and conduct trade. According to a focus group in Preysath:

> The village security was really terrible . . . in 1993 and 1998. There were a lot of thieves and robbery. We were restless every night . . . Prior to 1998, the thieves lived in the inundated forests. They came to the village and shot at us very often. They took all our valuable belongings and sometimes raped women. We rarely dared to go fishing far from the village.

The timing of the end of conflict also affected the capacity of villages to cope with other shocks and disadvantages. As noted above, all nine study villages experienced severe flood and drought during the second half of the study period. Households in the green-area villages of Chakboeng and Salvia

Prey had sufficient time after the end of conflict in their areas to accumulate productive assets and diversify income sources before the floods and drought hit, and they were thus better able to withstand the negative effects of these disasters. In the red-area villages of Preysath and Kdadaum, however, the period between the end of the fighting and the onset of drought was by comparison quite brief. Households in these two villages did not have sufficient time to accumulate productive assets, expand land, and develop infrastructure before the drought hit. As a result, overall village well-being either stagnated or declined, even though some households were able to benefit from peace. In red-area Sastaing and Koh Phong, the advantages conferred by more productive soils to some extent offset the disadvantage of protracted fighting, possibly helping to account for their better performance outcomes.

For several villages the end of conflict also brought improved access to natural resource assets. This enabled people to expand farmland, collect wood and nontimber forest products, and fish more openly. In poorly performing Kdadaum, however, forest concessionaires had already established control over nearby forestland by the time peace arrived. Consequently, as noted above, constraints on local people's access to the forested areas were already well in place, limiting their ability to clear new land and harvest forest products. In essence, one set of constraints imposed by the fighting was replaced by another set of constraints imposed by the concessionaires.

## Summary

Peace and stability enable certain villages to perform well over time under favorable circumstances, but peace alone is not enough to promote strong performance in the absence of development assistance and other advantages. At the same time, armed conflict in itself does not necessarily override favorable circumstances such as productive soils and easy market access. It seems, however, that when armed conflict is combined with unfavorable circumstances, including poor-quality soils, remote locations, and poor market access, as well as a lack of development assistance, community well-being and household mobility will almost invariably be affected adversely.

The mode of land acquisition after the krom samaki disbanded established the foundation upon which households could eventually accumulate assets and diversify income sources. Households with more adult members were able to acquire larger landholdings through state land distribution and by clearing forest land where security permitted. Location and transport infrastructure have also played important roles with respect to market access and natural resources as well as development assistance. Strongly performing, green-area Chakboeng, with fertile soils and good market access, enjoyed peace and stability for a relatively long period and received substantial support for agricultural development. Households were able to concentrate on asset accumulation, which enabled many of them to better cope with flood and drought in the second half of the study period. In the strongly performing red-area village of Sastaing, good soils, favorable location, and substantial development assistance offset the effects of protracted conflict. Although ongoing fighting constrained the ability of most households to farm and clear additional land, good-quality soils enabled them to produce more than most other villages during the fighting and eventually enabled them to withstand weather shocks.

In poorly performing green-area Somrampi, poor soils, declining natural resources, and bad roads offset the potential benefit of a longer period of peace. In the poorly performing red-area village of Preysath, remoteness, protracted conflict, and banditry exacerbated problems of poor soils and a lack of access to markets, natural resources, and development assistance. Poorly performing red-area Kdadaum also has poor soils, and households were not able to expand their areas of cultivation due to the fighting. This constrained agricultural production and households' ability to accumulate assets and diversify income sources, which in turn weakened the ability of many of them to withstand the flood and drought shocks that occurred shortly after the fighting ended. Because of their remote locations and poor access, these villages have also lagged behind in terms of development assistance.

## Governance and Mobility in the Postconflict Era

As armed conflict subsided, governance emerged as a key factor affecting community well-being and household mobility. In particular, the weak governance of natural resources and a lack of law and order imposed formidable constraints on the recovery and prosperity of the study villages. All the villages experienced problems with human security, such as theft and youth gang violence. Communities heavily dependent on fisheries and forest products also frequently experienced conflicts over access to and control of those resources.

### Natural resource plunder

The process that links the wider Khmer Rouge armed conflict with local conflicts in resource-dependent areas involved the formation, expansion, and consolidation of patronage networks involving the Cambodian military, other government officials, and private sector actors. Cambodians refer to these relationships using the term *khnang*, which we will loosely translate as "strongback." The fighting in red areas in the 1980s and 1990s provided the context in which patronage ties were nurtured at the local level. In some areas, the military acquired control over large areas of land and sometimes played a key role in local governance.[7] These relationships eventually evolved into powerful governance forces located outside the official state structure and established a precedent for managing forests once the political conflict ended. Although forest concessions were terminated in 1997, powerful traders and other outside investors were able to continue logging operations in collusion with various military authorities and high-level forestry officials.

Strongback relationships are also an important factor in the enforcement of fishing regulations. Individuals with strong patronage support are routinely perceived to be able to benefit from illegal fishing techniques because they can escape punishment from local authorities. In the fishing villages visited for this study, the strongback networks did not appear to involve the military as they did in the forest villages, but they did involve high-ranking officials at the provincial level, as well as others responsible for enforcing fishing regulations at the local level. Villagers in Salvia Prey provide this account:

> People undertaking large-scale illegal activities are untouchable because they have strong backing from high officials . . . and most of them are impossible to approach . . . too powerful . . . and it is impossible to break this relation under the current system . . . Many illegal fishing tools have recently been destroyed by the provincial Department of Forests and Fisheries in collaboration with commune authorities, but the owners were not arrested because they are untouchable.

The weak governance of natural resource assets in the postconflict period has had a profound impact on community well-being and household mobility in the resource-dependent villages. Forestry and fisheries are both extractive industries that feature similar governance problems with arbitrary enforcement of rights and regulations. A focus group of young men from Kdadaum explained:

> Sometimes we [are arrested by] the forest authorities while we are being hired to carry wood . . . We have to spend 200,000 riels to be free from arrest. If not, our cart will be kept at their provincial office and we will be put into custody if we are not able to escape quickly . . . There are so many kinds of authorities who claim to be competent to arrest us, and we do not know which one is which. We are afraid of all kinds of people carrying weapons and wearing black or green clothes.

In the red-area forest villages of Kdadaum and Koh Phong, logging activities are very lucrative and have attracted powerful and wealthy outside investors. These concessionaires have the means to provide equipment and transport and to make the necessary political and social connections (through strongbacking) that enable their operations to skirt the laws on logging. Local communities have little recourse against such forces. The manner in which these outside investors engage local workers in the industry and restrict access to the forests has a powerful effect on community well-being and household mobility. A field report noted:

> Although the community has been adversely affected by forest access restrictions and its controversial implementation, people still depend on the forest. Corruption tends to generate unequal access to the forest. The rich households continue to have access to large-scale logging, while about 50 percent of households, especially middle-level households that have the means for transportation business, transport wood for the big traders. The medium households also access forest byproducts and sometimes engage in small-scale logging. The poor collect edible insects and forest byproducts and work as wage laborers for large-scale loggers.

Fishing is similar in many ways to forestry as an extractive mode of production. The competition for access to and control over fisheries pits local villagers against outside traders and investors and also against other households within the village. As in timber extraction in Kdadaum and Koh Phong, a household's chances in the competition for fishing access depend in large part on the mode of transport and equipment at its disposal. For example, better-off households in the green-area villages of Somrampi and Troula Trav usually have larger boats with bigger engines and are therefore more mobile in terms of where they are able to fish. Poorer households have smaller boats and engines that limit the fishing areas they can reach. The poor also use simple fishing gear that limits the size of their catch.

The use of illegal fishing techniques and equipment is an important factor that helps determine the extent to which people are able to benefit from fishing. Those who use the illegal means are perceived to be better off than those who do not. The well-off fishers are also understood to have strongback support among local officials and others mandated to enforce fishing regulations. Villagers from the moderately performing red-area village of Koh Phong report that people who have connections and can afford bribes can "freely go fishing and use illegal fishing tools without any worry of being arrested." They also say, "Corruption is getting worse. Good governance is something good only on paper. In reality it's totally different."

In the case of villages where fishing represents an important source of income and food, people reported that access to fisheries was restricted either by poor security (e.g., Koh Phong, Sastaing) and/or by the private management of fishing lots that denied open access (e.g., Chakboeng, Troula Trav). In the green-area village of Troula Trav and the red-area villages of Chakboeng, Koh Phong, and Sastaing, the fishing lot reforms of 2000 and the introduction of community fisheries since 2002 were followed by a rapid decline in fish stocks due to overfishing with illegal equipment. In this sense, the overriding problem is one of enforcement of the rules and regulations. According to villagers in Troula Trav,

> Not all fishing lots were given back to the community, as announced. Those who infringe the law normally are those top government officials. They become richer and richer with just a piece of paper which they show us, a sub-decree. People in this commune are mostly illiterate and of course are tired of the routine and unchanged corrupt practices of the higher authorities, especially fishery inspectors.

## Human security

Many of the study villages reported that theft and robbery were widespread during the fighting. In some cases this intensified in the early to mid-1990s as Khmer Rouge units defected to the government side. Sometimes the rise in thefts during the transition to peace could be attributed to a breakdown in authority as the old regime was perceived to have lost its mandate to govern, especially after the election in which the ruling party lost.

In the red-area village of Preysath, theft and robbery became deeply engrained in the daily lives of people and had a profound effect on their ability to trade and earn livelihoods during the conflict period. Villagers there reported:

> We had to transport our fish to sell in Kompong Thom. Most of the time, our fish were spoiled and could not be sold by the time we reached the market. Many people were arrested or required to pay money whenever we traveled out of the village. We live with serious fear of war, theft, and robbery. Whoever had good buffaloes or cattle saw them subjected to robbery or stolen by the gun-holders. We have no time to worry about better earnings while keeping our lives from all types of threats . . . We had to ask permission to buy milled rice for our consumption from the standing police. Otherwise we would be accused of being a food supplier to Pol Pot.

Similarly, villagers in red-area Sastaing said that theft had increased. "We dared not leave our house because we worried about security . . . During the second national election, there were many cases of cattle and buffalo theft."

**BOX 11.1**
**Somrampi: The trap of poor governance and continued insecurity**

Somrampi is the one green-area village where few poor villagers were able to escape poverty and many people fell into deeper poverty over the study period. According to local villagers, the lack of security and the difficult governance environment have impeded their efforts to recover since conflict ended there in 1993.

Somrampi's residents say that better-off fishermen who have good connections with the fishing authorities use illegal nets with impunity. As a result, fish stock are dying off as small marine life gets swept away in the nets. In addition, authorities at checkpoints disrupt travel and commerce in the village and along nearby roads, harassing poor fishermen and small traders on motorcycles and demanding payments in the name of security. Explained one villager, "Very often I feel that all of these checkpoints are leeches that are sucking our blood from every corner of our lives. We would waste our time and spoil our goods if we tried to argue for our rights."

The village has also suffered from a surge in local crime and violence that accompanied the end of the war. But the police response has been both inadequate and corrupt. In the initial years after the conflict, the community continued to be plagued by robberies and kidnappings. While these problems are now under control, competing groups of violent gangs endanger local people. The gangs are sometimes described as tied to gambling networks or comprising different groups of Muslim and Khmer youth or youth of rich and poor families who come together to fight. Villagers expressed

But toward the end of the study period, villagers in this well-performing village noted important improvements in security and attributed some of this to effective efforts to confiscate guns, as well as overall improvements in well-being with the arrival of peace.

Although the incidents of theft and robbery in green-area villages as well as banditry in red-area villages were reported to have abated after the UNTAC period and the defection of Khmer Rouge forces to the government, such crimes spiked again in many villages during the latter part of the study period. In the poorly performing red-area villages, people felt that such crimes were largely the result of poverty exacerbated by the effects of flood and drought on the poor and the very poor since 2000. In the green-area village of Somrampi, people also attributed the increase in crime to gambling as well as to poor governance and policing (box 11.1).

**BOX 11.1  continued**

concern that only "two out of 10" criminals are caught by the police, and many of these are released when they are found to be the children of high-ranking officials and police. But when poor youths are caught, the "parents lose fame and reputation and also have to pay some amount to free their children from jail . . . some families sell out their land or cattle for such payment." Indeed, villagers repeatedly expressed frustration over problems of "irresponsible authorities" and rising corruption, and they feel powerless to seek recourse:

> We do appreciate the recent developments in the village, which we have never had before. But talking about corruption, it is really worse here. Who should we complain to about such social illnesses? All are the same. They are good at being leeches, but have no responsibility. For instance, they said they are police and/or fishing authorities, but when there are marine robberies happening to our villagers, and then we report to them for intervention, they say it is beyond their responsibility and try not to listen to us. We don't know what their roles really are, probably just coming to collect money from us.

When asked about their members of Parliament, one villager responded, "The MPs have never shown up after elections. And to become an MP they should be a member of a particular political party first. And if the party is corrupt, they become more concerned with their party interests rather than respond to our needs. Who then will help us to clear up our thorny paths of life?"

Around 2000, all of the study villages also began experiencing problems with youth gangs that engaged in fighting and in some cases drug use. Villagers attributed the gangs' emergence to various factors, including the arrival of outside laborers and increased competition for work (as in Kdadaum), pornography (Sastaing), migrants returning to villages, and alcohol. A villager from Koh Phong reported, "For the past two years we have been having the so-called 'big brothers' who are frequently fighting one another after being drunk . . . Both boys and girls do not usually go out at night . . . because of the frequent fighting among the gangsters." Villagers in Kdadaum spoke of a general decline in morality and lack of respect for village elders and traditional values:

> From 1993 to 1998, we thought that security and human safety in our village were good because the young people paid respect to the older people and the livelihoods were not as difficult as now. Since it was not

hard for people to earn a living, there was no theft or robbery. . . . It is different now . . . the morality of people has declined. For example, many people now like drinking wine and easily go with many partners . . . There are many cases of corruption and the police can no longer provide justice to innocent people. To earn one's livelihood is more difficult and as a result there are more thieves and robbery.

In many of the villages, local authorities and the police seem unable or unwilling to intervene in problems with youth. In some situations, they are reluctant to act in cases that may involve the children of higher officials or other powerful people. In other cases, they refuse to act unless they are paid to do so. Another reason for such inaction is that officials may be unsure of their mandate and authority. As with theft and robbery, however, the situation regarding youth gangs seems to be improving in at least some of the green-area villages, including Chakboeng and Troula Trav, as a result of interventions by government authorities.

Another important area pertaining to human security that appears to be improving in nearly all the study villages is domestic violence. The improvement is attributed to several factors, including greater public awareness about the issue due to media campaigns, education provided by NGOs, and more active intervention by local authorities. People generally considered poverty to be the cause of domestic violence and largely associated it with drinking by men. And to the extent that people viewed domestic violence as contributing to a household's downward mobility or stagnation in poverty, the decrease in abuse can be expected to contribute to improved household mobility in the years ahead.

## Attitudes and perceptions of local governance

Strong, moderate, and poorly performing villages reported similar concerns and observations about poorly functioning institutions and corrupt government officials. There is more variation across the different mobility groups, as better-off households are able to benefit from weak governance and corruption while poor and destitute households, unable to pay corruption costs and without powerful connections, generally suffer.

The experiences of the nine study villages suggest there is an uneasy fit between modern notions of democracy and human rights and Cambodia's deeply rooted traditional norms and values such as respect for authority and elders. Hierarchical power relations are a pervasive feature of Cambodian society, and relations between persons of lower and higher status are often personalized and cast in terms of family and kinship networks. Those with lower status must show respect for those with higher status, and they are not expected to question or challenge those in positions of authority. At the same time, those with higher status and greater power are expected to show respect for and provide protection to those with lower status (Pak et al. 2007).

Recent studies (e.g., Ballard 2007) suggest, however, that Cambodians hold increasingly mixed views of their leaders because of the latter's failure to meet traditional expectations. Results from the Moving Out of Poverty focus groups bear this out. High officials, law enforcers (police, military), and people with powerful commercial interests were characterized as abusive, corrupt, self-interested, and greedy. They were frequently described as using their wealth and power to buy rights and authority and to oppress others. This was especially so in the natural resource–dependent villages of Chakboeng, Somrampi, and Troula Trav, as well as in the red-area villages of Preysath, Koh Phong, and Kdadaum. As one focus group in Kdadaum reported:

> It is easy to buy power here since the pockets of all officials are open . . . Those with power just make a few trips to the forest and cut trees; then they can earn enough money to cover their expenses for a position . . . It would be fortunate for us if they did not use their power to reap profits from us, but that is not the case. Normally they threaten other villagers for money . . . How can the poor survive? . . . The poor are normally the victims, and the powerful people are those who benefit . . . Unlike before, the powerful should not be respected. But what can we do? They have guns and always make money from our back.

Governance failures concerning natural resources and human security are widely perceived to have affected community well-being and household mobility. The relationship between governance, corruption, and power pervades the daily experiences of many villagers, and their perceptions are changing about the local leaders and higher officials who have responsibility for regulation of natural resources. Male youths from the village of Kdadaum said,

> People who have power are those who have money, so [they also] have rights to forest logging . . . The poor who work for the rich do not have power because they dare not argue against or bargain for good remuneration . . . The rich know many key concerned authorities not only in this commune but in other places and levels and so can smoothly operate their wood-cutting business.

Although many people do not have a clear sense of the concept of good governance, they readily equate power with corruption and recognize that this relationship is essentially antithetical to good governance. They also equate power with social and economic status: those who were rich have power and authority while those who were poor have no power. Power is also closely associated with the distribution of well-being. Those with power are able to use it to accrue more assets. In short, those with power can act as they desire without fear of punishment. In this sense, power is closely tied to corruption.

The introduction of democratic processes such as local and national elections and participatory development planning has combined with media and NGO education campaigns to raise awareness and expectations about ordinary people's rights. This process has also provided new standards against which leaders and their performance are being judged—and often found wanting. One reason for this is that beneath the veneer of liberal institutions and values, neo-patrimonialism continues to flourish, and very real tensions were evident in the study villages. When measured against liberal democratic norms and values, leaders are failing to deliver, while at the same time the patronage system is serving clients less well than in the past as greed outweighs benevolence among the wealthy and powerful. As a result, trust in and satisfaction with authorities are generally low, especially in relation to higher officials and forestry and fishing authorities. A focus group in Chakboeng captured these tensions:

> We now have full rights to speak, and no one warns us not to voice our concerns or ask for help . . . but the authorities also have the right to ignore our concerns . . . The difference is that they have the power to force us to follow the law, but we have no way to force them to cease their misbehavior.

People's concerns about the relationship between power and corruption were most evident in the natural resource–dependent villages, where access to and control over resources were seen to be highly biased in favor of the well off and powerful. In these and other villages, the unequal distribution of corruption benefits and impacts appears to be an important factor in determining household mobility. Those with power and wealth are able to use their assets to accrue even more power and wealth, while poor and very poor households are prevented from improving their situation. "Between 1993 and 2004," explained a villager from the moderately performing green-area village of Troula Trav, "the well-being of some people improved because some people respect law whereas some do not. The people who respect the law have lower living conditions than the people who do not respect the law."

Although high-level authorities are perceived to be corrupt and abusive, villagers tend to be more satisfied with local authorities. Most villagers believe that local authorities are at least somewhat concerned with the welfare and interests of their constituents. For example, a villager from Somrampi observed, "Fortunately, our commune leaders are more responsive to us, actively encouraging village development planning. We don't know how much money they have for our development plan. But at least they are close to us and have shared concerns." In villages where armed conflict ended only recently, the opening up to markets and development assistance has given villagers a more positive view of their local leaders than in villages that have been open and peaceful for a longer period of time.

In sum, the findings from these nine villages support other studies (e.g., Pak et al. 2007) suggesting that neo-patrimonialism still dominates Cambodian political culture, and that so-called liberal democratic institutions, processes, and values have been unevenly and uneasily grafted onto this base. Patronage networks exist alongside formal roles and responsibilities, with real power and decision making located within the patronage network rather than in formal institutions. Patronage networks provide clients with political and economic protection and chances for advancement. Such networks exist throughout the society and enable those with power and influence (or powerful connections) to extract wealth and resources, including from the natural resources. Corruption is a feature of patronage relationships and is endemic at all levels of society and decision making.

As discussed above with respect to natural resource exploitation, during the armed conflict patronage relationships began to take on an increasingly commercial orientation. Actors with ties to strongback networks could collude with authorities at different levels of government to obtain access to and control over resources and trade. These commercial alignments eventually limited local people's traditional access to resources and hence their access to livelihoods. The result has been to inflame resentments about the privileges of power and wealth enjoyed by elites and high government officials.

People believe that the diminished capacity of local officials to resolve problems such as theft and youth gang violence is also linked to the armed conflict, albeit indirectly. The rampant banditry and lawlessness that emerged in many areas during and immediately after armed conflict demonstrated that local officials had little power to maintain social order, just as they had little authority or capacity to resolve conflicts over natural resources. Strongback relationships formed during the conflict have flourished during peacetime to the extent that people of influence and their offspring are often able to act with impunity and disregard for the law.

## Conclusion

This study suggests that there is no direct relationship between conflict and mobility. We find high-performing communities in areas that experienced many years of peace as well as in an area that saw few years of peace. But, obviously, the consequences of conflict do weigh on the economic, social, and political life of the Cambodian villages visited. The negative impacts of armed conflict, particularly in communities where it ended later in the study period, were magnified in less-accessible areas with poor soils and other disadvantages, resulting in overall poor community performance and low levels of household mobility. In these villages, households did not have sufficient time to accumulate assets with which to withstand the impacts of the flood and droughts that struck many parts of Cambodia during the latter part of the study period. In more accessible villages or ones where fighting was less severe and the conflict ended earlier, more households, especially those with ample available labor, were able to acquire land, accumulate other productive assets, and diversify income sources. This positioned them to better manage adverse weather and other shocks.

This study also reveals that higher levels of development assistance were repeatedly associated with improved community performance, and that the accessibility of villages in addition to their conflict-affectedness may affect overall assistance levels. Roads seem to be particularly important because they enable trade and also allow diverse forms of assistance to flow into a community. Coordinated interventions focusing on integrated support for transport infrastructure, clean drinking water, agricultural production, and social services seemed important in the villages with the highest levels of prosperity. The exact balance between these priority areas would need to be determined through a collaborative planning process involving all principal actors.

The scope and scale of the conflict and the timing of peace also had a significant impact on the governance of natural resource assets. Generally speaking, the armed conflict and political struggle that took place during the 1980s and 1990s created conditions in which powerful state and commercial actors could gain access to and control over natural resource assets and other commercial opportunities at the expense of local communities. The process also had an impact on the environment and on the sustainability of the resource base. Steps need to be taken to prevent or reduce such opportunities.

Once security is obtained, armed forces should be withdrawn from resource-sensitive areas and the management of resources handed over to the appropriate civilian authorities who are mandated, trained, and equipped to regulate access to and control over valuable natural assets. Local institutions such as community fishery and forestry oversight bodies need to be established as soon as possible in postconflict areas. Where possible, development interventions in natural resource–dependent areas should support enforcement and the mediation of conflicts over resources, along with the diversification of income sources in order to reduce pressures on local resources.

The postconflict transition from national security to national development is vitally important. Although the Cambodian state ultimately prevailed in the armed conflict, the many governance failures identified in the nine villages suggest that the state has not yet successfully managed the transition from an authoritarian regime focused on security and political control to a democratic state that emphasizes an equitable and transparent allocation of productive resources for local and national development. The governance challenges associated with the political transition underway during the study period have been exacerbated by the rapid and uneven transition from a closed to an open market economy without supporting legal and institutional frameworks in place to regulate property rights, manage natural resource assets, and address local crime and conflict. The policy lesson is that institutions of peacetime governance need to be established and strengthened as a matter of priority from the outset. The experience of Cambodia shows that while this is necessary, it is also a long and difficult process.[8]

## Notes

The Cambodia study is part of the global Moving Out of Poverty study led by Deepa Narayan in the Poverty Reduction and Economic Management (PREM) Network of the World Bank. For a discussion of key study concepts and data collection methods, see chapter 1 and the appendixes to this volume. Also see volume 2 of the Moving Out of Poverty series (Narayan, Pritchett, and Kapoor 2009) and the study methodology guide (Narayan and Petesch 2005).

The Cambodia study was led and financed by the Cambodian Development Research Institute (CDRI) in Phnom Penh and builds on their earlier village panel dataset. Lead researchers were So Sovannarith and Ingrid FitzGerald. This chapter was written by Dr. Brett Ballard, formerly senior research adviser at CDRI and currently agriculture and rural development adviser for AusAID. It presents a synthesis of "Trends in Community Well-being and Household Mobility in Nine Cambodian Villages," a report prepared by CDRI and available on the Moving Out of Poverty study Web site (http://go.worldbank.org/9ER0AOIH20). The chapter also introduces additional material and analysis concerning the role of conflict in shaping community well-being and household mobility in the nine study villages. The penultimate section on governance issues in the postconflict era draws directly from the original CDRI report. Mia Hyun and Tim Conway from the World Bank were helpful in setting up the study, and Verena Fritz, Mia Hyun, Deepa Narayan, Patti Petesch, Sophorl Pete Pin, and Ashutosh Varshney provided valuable comments on the chapter.

1. This observation of the postconflict transition is based on correspondence with Mia Hyun, World Bank poverty specialist in Cambodia, May 9, 2008.
2. See Chanda (1986) for an account of the events and political circumstances leading up to the Vietnamese invasion.
3. See Mysliwiec (1988) for a discussion of international aid to the PRK from 1979 through 1987.
4. See Boua (1983) for a first-hand account of the krom samaki system in the early 1980s. This account suggests that the groups also played an important security role during this time.
5. To protect the privacy of participants, this chapter uses pseudonyms for the nine study villages. Districts and cities are identified by their real names.
6. The moderately poor group includes households that fell within a band of 20 percent on either side of the poverty line.
7. Boua (2003) and Gottesman (2004) observed this phenomenon throughout the country. Gottesman observed that during the 1980s Cambodian military units evolved into "a lucrative patronage system that supported itself and propped up local civilian authorities" and that with increasing autonomy came "the pursuit of revenues, specifically the exploitation of natural resources." Around the Tonle Sap lake, "local military units engaged in extensive fishing activities . . . sometimes using explosive devices." Military authorities also controlled the timber business, and "since 1983, the Ministry of Agriculture had been complaining of unauthorized timber commerce by a wide range of military organizations" (2004, 229–30).
8. Mia Hyun, World Bank poverty specialist in Cambodia, correspondence, May 9, 2008.

# References

Acharya, S., and S. Chan. 2002. "Facing the Challenges of Rural Livelihoods: A Perspective from Nine Villages in Cambodia." Working Paper 25, Cambodia Development Resource Institute, Phnom Penh.

Ballard, B. 2007. "Local Governance and Poverty Reduction." In *We Are Living with Worry All The Time": A Participatory Poverty Assessment of the Tonle Sap*, ed. B. Ballard, 245–73. Phnom Penh: Cambodia Development Resource Institute.

Boua, C. 1983. "Observation of the Heng Samrin Government 1908–1982." In *Revolution and Its Aftermath in Kampuchea: Eight Essays*, ed. D. P. Chandler and B. Kiernan. New Haven, CT: Yale University Southeast Asia Studies.

———. 2003. "Cambodia, Ten Years after UNTAC." In *Post-Conflict Reconstruction in Japan, Republic of Korea, Vietnam, Cambodia, East Timor and Afghanistan*, ed. N. Azimi, M. Fuller, and H. Nakayama, 121–26. Proceedings of an international conference held in Hiroshima, November 2002. New York: United Nations Institute for Training and Research.

Chanda, N. 1986. *Brother Enemy: The War After the War*. New York: Collier Books.

FitzGerald, I., and S. So, with S. Chan, K. Sithen, and T. Sokphally. 2007. "Moving Out of Poverty? Trends in Community Well-being and Household Mobility in Nine Cambodian Villages." Cambodia Development Resource Institute, Phnom Penh. http://go.worldbank.org/9ER0AOIH20.

Gottesman, E. 2004. *Cambodia after the Khmer Rouge: Inside the Politics of Nation Building*. Chiang Mai, Thailand: Silkworm Books.

Mysliwiec, E. 1988. *Punishing the Poor: The International Isolation of Kampuchea*. Oxford: Oxfam UK.

Narayan, D., and P. Petesch. 2005. "Moving Out of Poverty Methodology Guide." Poverty Reduction Group, Poverty Reduction and Economic Management Network, World Bank, Washington, DC.

Narayan, D., L. Pritchett, and S. Kapoor. 2009. *Moving Out of Poverty: Success from the Bottom Up*. New York: Palgrave Macmillan; Washington, DC: World Bank.

Pak, K., H. Vuthy, E. Netra, A. Sovatha, K. Sedara, J. Knowles, and D. Craig. 2007. "Accountability and Neo-Patrimonialism in Cambodia: A Critical Literature Review." Working Paper 34, Cambodia Development Resource Institute, Phnom Penh.

World Bank. 2006. *Halving Poverty by 2015? Poverty Assessment 2006*. Phnom Penh: World Bank.

———. 2007. *Sharing Growth: Equity and Development in Cambodia*. Equity and Development Report 2007. Phnom Penh: World Bank.

# Sri Lanka: Unequal Mobility in an Ethnic Civil War

*Patti Petesch and Prashan Thalayasingam*

*If there is a program in a village where there is a majority of Muslims, they benefit more than other ethnic groups. In a village where there is a majority of Tamil families, the Tamils get more benefit than other groups. There is no equal distribution.*

— FEMALE YOUTH,
Thambulla, Ampara district

*Democracy is only something that is at the beginning of our country's name and nothing more. The country's official name is the Democratic Socialist Republic of Sri Lanka. This is the only place that there is democracy. It is just a word added to the name. It doesn't mean anything else.*

— MALE AND FEMALE YOUTH,
Nelutanga, Hambantota district

CHAPTER 12

Mrs. Pushpamalar lost her house in 1985, in 1987, and again in 1990. Each time it was burned to the ground by the Sri Lankan army. "To save our lives," she recalled, "we escaped into the forest and stayed there for some time. In 1990, 110 sacks of rice were also burnt." During one army raid, she and other fleeing villagers became cornered on a beach, where she witnessed the army kill her sister's sons and other children. While these memories continue to haunt her, by the time study teams visited her village in 2006, Mrs. Pushpamalar and her family had managed to pull themselves up and out of poverty. They did so despite the armed conflict that continued to rage around them.

After the traumatic events of 1990, the family struggled for years to secure shelter and work. Mrs. Pushpamalar's life took a turn for the better when she relocated in 1997 to Nilakulam, a mostly Tamil village in the Eastern province of Sri Lanka that has received numerous families displaced by conflict.[1] Her cousin, a member of Parliament who represents a Tamil political party, helped them secure land in the village. Mrs. Pushpamalar first took a job breaking stones in the area quarries; her husband did wage labor and eventually learned masonry skills. Slowly they accumulated enough savings from their wages, supplemented by a loan from her sister, to build a home and complete their children's education. In 2003 they opened a small shop which Mrs. Pushpamalar now runs with her son while her husband continues with his masonry.

Mrs. Pushpamalar credits her family's recovery to her close relationship with her husband and to advice that she received from a previous landlord, who talked about the importance of saving and a housewife's role in this. "After coming here, I started to apply those [lessons] in my life. We saved together, so we were able to run our life without expecting from others." When asked whether they now have enough saved to cope with an emergency,

Mrs. Pushpamalar responded that their savings will be enough "if anything happens naturally, but if there is any problem due to the conflicts, I am not sure." Now age 53, Mrs. Pushpamalar says she and her husband plan to work five more years. "We believe in ourselves a lot."

Between 1983 and 2009, the Liberation Tigers of Tamil Eelam (LTTE) waged an armed struggle to carve out a separate Tamil state from the Northern and Eastern provinces of Sri Lanka. This chapter presents firsthand accounts of people living through the civil war there and explores their perceptions of the factors affecting recovery and poverty reduction in their communities from 1990 to late 2005. This period includes several years of fragile peace after a cease-fire was declared in 2002, and it predates a new spiral of violence that began in 2006 when a government offensive reasserted authority over Tamil-controlled areas of the country. In January 2008 the government formally withdrew from the 2002 cease-fire agreement. After intense combat, they declared the LTTE defeated in May 2009.

Mrs. Pushpamalar's account of being propelled by conflict into deeper poverty, followed by difficult but successful years of recovery, resonates with many other life stories shared for this study. In her village of Nilakulam, in fact, 44 percent of the households that were considered poor in 1990 had escaped poverty by 2005, according to local standards. An important factor underpinning this mobility was the 2002 cease-fire agreement between the government and the LTTE. But another study village located in the very same district saw just 17 percent of its poor households climb out of poverty over the same period. In two other conflict-affected districts visited for the study, a similar pattern emerges, with one village having much more poverty reduction than the other. This chapter explores each of these three districts in turn, seeking to understand the reasons for such striking differences in the recovery and mobility of the paired communities.

Our analysis finds that factors that are often thought to be important for mobility may not be so crucial in conflict contexts. A town in Jaffna district with the largest market and most diverse economy in the sample did not provide high mobility for its poor households over the 15-year study period. But a Jaffna village with far fewer local economic opportunities saw many of its poor residents escape poverty. Its inclusive recovery is all the more surprising because it experienced far more intense conflict than the town. Rather than more favorable economic or conflict conditions, what distinguished this high-mobility village was the presence of strong collective action and social cohesion. These factors also emerge as important to mobility differences in another community pair. In addition, our findings reveal that the ethnic composition of a community makes a difference, creating either advantage or disadvantage in access to government, civic and donor resources, and opportunities for economic diversification, including remittances.

We begin our examination with a brief introduction to development trends in Sri Lanka and the forces leading up to the civil war. This is followed by an overview of the study design and sample and of the community-level mobility outcomes that frame the study's comparative analysis. The next two sections examine the three pairs of study villages in the North and East, exploring the principal economic, political, and social factors that may have contributed to the large mobility differences between the paired communities in each district. A fifth section synthesizes findings from focus groups conducted with youth on their aspirations for themselves and their communities. We close with brief policy reflections.

## The Tinder Box: Rising Expectations, Slow Growth, and Ethnic Exclusion

Sri Lanka is a multiethnic country. About three-quarters of its 21 million people are Sinhalese, and a large share of Sinhalese are Buddhists. Another 18 percent are Tamils, who are primarily Hindu or Christian. The Tamils are heavily concentrated in the Northern, Eastern, Western, and Central provinces.[2] Muslims account for 7 percent, with the largest concentrations living in the cities and in the Central, Southern, and Eastern provinces.

For decades, Sri Lanka has given priority to human development investments, and these have had important payoffs. The country now enjoys rates of life expectancy, child mortality, and gender parity in literacy that are comparable with those of developed countries (Glinskaya 2000). These advances have been combined with relatively strong macroeconomic growth in recent years. But all this has been insufficient to reduce the large income and regional inequalities that divide the country and fuel its conflicts.

The World Bank's 2007 poverty assessment for Sri Lanka portrays striking disparities in growth and poverty reduction between the capital of Colombo and the rest of the country. In the Western province where Colombo is located, gross domestic product grew on average 6.2 percent annually between 1997 and 2003, compared to 2.3 percent in the other provinces. These statistics, however, exclude the Northern and Eastern provinces, where data collection has not been possible for years due to the conflict; the income and regional disparities would likely grow even wider if data for those areas were available. Inequality in Sri Lanka increased rapidly over the 1990s and into the present century, mirroring the trends in Bangladesh, India, and Pakistan over the same period (Sengupta 2006).

In 2002 the poverty headcount for the Colombo district was just 6 percent. But poverty rises to a high of between 32 and 37 percent in four districts toward the south of the country that are reported to have per capita incomes similar to those in the east (World Bank 2007, x). The World Bank concludes that if the inequalities between Colombo and the rest of the country had been smaller, "30 percent growth in average consumption by 2002 would have reduced poverty by more than 15 percentage points nationally instead of the observed 3 percentage points" (2007, xi).

Two major conflicts have roiled Sri Lanka in recent decades. A Sinhalese insurgent group called Janatha Vimukthi Peramuna (JVP, or People's Liberation Front) tried to violently overthrow the government first in 1971, and when their grievances were not addressed, again in 1989. The government violently suppressed the 1989–91 insurrection, leading to almost 60,000 deaths.[3]

The second conflict, led by the LTTE, began in 1983 and evolved into a civil war over the issue of a separate homeland for ethnic Tamils. Over the next two decades, roughly 70,000 people were killed, 750,000 were displaced internally, and another 700,000 fled overseas (Ariyaratne 2003, 33). Norway helped mediate a successful cease-fire that took effect in February 2002. But the peace talks broke down in 2003, and support for a political solution declined. The 2004 election brought to power a coalition that viewed the government's policy as too conciliatory toward the LTTE, and violence escalated after the 2005 election of a strongly nationalist (that is, pro-Sinhalese) president. After intensive combat, extensive civilian casualties, and a humanitarian crisis due to mass displacement and the internment of tens of thousands of civilians in camps, the army regained full control over the Jaffna peninsula in the far north and declared victory in May 2009.

There is a diverse literature on the sources of Sri Lanka's civil war. Sirimal Abeyratne (2004) argues that both the JVP and LTTE insurrections are rooted in the same social and economic forces. The country's investments in human development, especially education, raised capabilities and expectations among youth for good jobs. But economic policies that favored import substitution industrialization, and the continued support provided to rural agriculture through subsidies and irrigation-based development schemes, produced low economic growth for much of the 1960s and 1970s. The economy could not keep pace with the changing labor force, and unemployment soared. This encouraged Sri Lanka's youth to mobilize against the state around ethnic grievances and perceptions of economic discrimination. By the time the economic crisis of the mid-1970s pushed the government to undertake policy reforms—which did yield stronger growth in the following decades—the first JVP uprising had already broken out, and rebellion among Tamils was gathering momentum.

Donald Horowitz's account (2000) of the seeds of conflict focuses on constraints derived from the country's ethnically based political parties and other weaknesses of the electoral system. These made it impossible for the government to mediate the ethnic tensions gripping the society, and indeed served to exacerbate them. Most notably, intense electoral competition between the two leading postindependence political parties gave rise to increased ethnic posturing and pandering to the Sinhalese majority among the electorate. This led in turn to increasing pro-Sinhalese nationalism: the Parliament in 1956 passed the Sinhala Only Act, imposing Sinhala as the official language, and in 1972 Parliament enacted legislation that was widely perceived to discriminate against Tamil university applicants. In this environment, steps toward political accommodations to ease ethnic tensions, such as proposals for modest decentralization reforms in the 1950s and 1960s, proved impossible to move forward. Opposition parties seeking to enlarge their base of support seized on the decentralization issue and tapped into popular opposition to compromising with the Tamils (Horowitz 2000, 132–33). This sentiment only intensified with the economic hardships of the 1970s, and violent anti-Tamil riots spilled into the streets of Colombo in that period.

The political process then prolonged the civil war once it broke out. Jayadeva Uyangoda (2007) draws attention to the continuing inability of the government to produce a credible program of decentralization, which in turn undermined peace talks and led to persistent political stalemate between the government and the LTTE. He also attributes the duration of the conflict to the stubborn determination of both sides to seek a military solution.

Successive attempts at peace negotiations revealed the extent of this intractability. Both parties lacked the will to make difficult compromises that could jeopardize their power base. Each successive attempt at peace gave way to greater belligerence and political posturing. The fieldwork for the study concluded just as the government was launching a major offensive that took over territory held by the LTTE.

## Research Design

The study found that some poor households are more resilient than others and are even able to escape poverty despite experiences of intense violence,

recurring displacement, and protracted insecurity. This chapter focuses particularly on community-level factors and processes that affect mobility in conflict contexts. The analysis is informed by concepts of agency and opportunity
structure elaborated by Narayan and Petesch (2007). This theory holds that
poor people's choices and the actions they take to advance their well-being
are heavily shaped by the public, market, and civic institutions of their communities and by the prevailing values and norms that influence what people
perceive they can and cannot do.

The fieldwork began in a period of relative peace in September 2005.[4]
Two months later, however, the election of a strongly nationalist president was
followed by renewed clashes between the army and the LTTE. These changing security circumstances meant that the sample had to be modified, and
the quantitative data collection that was to follow the qualitative fieldwork
unfortunately could not be completed. Except for a small set of closed-ended
questions that were posed to key informants and focus groups in the study
communities, the dataset for this examination was compiled exclusively
from qualitative tools involving open-ended key informant interviews, focus
groups, and individual life stories such as the one that opened the chapter.

The 2004 tsunami struck the north, east, and south coasts, killing more
than 30,000 people and leaving tens of thousands displaced or missing. Of
the districts visited for this study, Ampara in the East was particularly affected.
The impacts of the massive disaster there and elsewhere in the study regions
were woven into discussions about the conflict and trends affecting the recovery and prosperity of communities.

## Community sample

The sample covers nine villages selected from six districts in the Northern, Eastern, and Southern provinces of the country (table 12.1 and map 12.1). These
three regions were chosen because the LTTE conflict has been confined largely
to the North and East since 1983, while the South and East were important
arenas for the JVP conflict of 1989 to 1991. This chapter focuses on mobility
processes in the seven villages visited in the North and East. The two villages
in the South serve mainly as a control and are not examined fully here. The
JVP conflict that occurred there largely predates the observation period of the
study, and the area is now relatively peaceful.

Within each region, the villages were selected to provide variation in growth
and conflict intensity during the study period.[5] In the East, ethnic variation was
also introduced to capture this important characteristic of the region. The study
sample is much too small to be considered representative of welfare, conflict,

**TABLE 12.1**
Conflict intensity and ethnic composition of Sri Lanka study communities

| Province/district | Village | Conflict intensity | Ethnicity |
|---|---|---|---|
| *North* | | | |
| Jaffna (high growth) | Kaithamavi | High | Tamil |
| | Manivali | High | Tamil |
| Mannar (low growth) | Pesavankalai | High | Tamil |
| *East* | | | |
| Trincomalee (low growth) | Nilakulam | None | Tamil |
| | Kumputhiri | Low | Muslim |
| Ampara (high growth) | Pothupana | High | Sinhalese |
| | Thambulla | None | Muslim |
| *South* | | | |
| Matara (high growth) | Welumbe | None | Sinhalese |
| Hambantota (low growth) | Nelutanga | None | Sinhalese |

Source: Moving Out of Poverty study data.
Note: For an explanation of growth and conflict intensity ratings, see note 5. The study communities are identified by pseudonyms in this chapter.

or ethnic conditions in Sri Lanka as a whole, but it does provide a framework for a comparative analysis of mobility factors and processes and of how these are affected by the conflict environment at the community level.

## Mobility measure

In each village, separate focus groups of men and women held detailed discussions about what helps and hinders the prosperity of households in their community. The groups created a "ladder of life" on which they ranked households in the village according to their level of well-being, from the poorest and worst off to the richest and best off. They then considered how and why households at the different steps might move up the ladder to a higher level of well-being, become stuck at the same level, or fall down to a lower level. Finally, they designated a "community poverty line," the level above which households are no longer considered poor by local standards.

Table 12.2 presents a sample ladder of life from a men's focus group in the village of Kaithamavi in the heavily conflict-affected Jaffna district in the North. The bold line between steps 2 and 3 of the ladder shows where the focus group placed the community poverty line. It is noteworthy that housing conditions are a central marker of well-being status at all steps of the ladder;

**MAP 12.1**
Sri Lanka with study provinces and districts

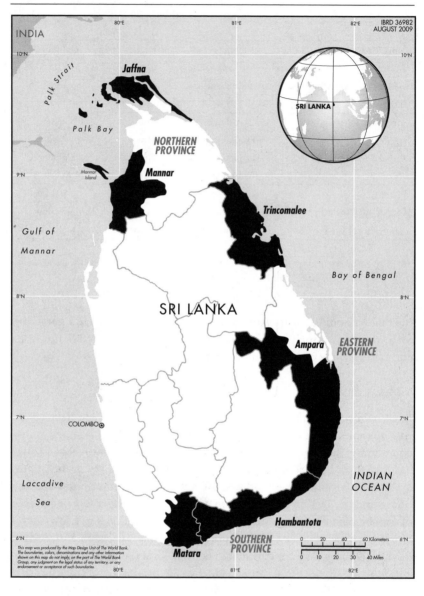

**TABLE 12.2**
**Sample ladder of life in Kaithamavi, Sri Lanka**

| | |
|---|---|
| Step 4 (richest) | Their main income source is remittances from abroad. |
| | They have houses with modern facilities. |
| | Education level is better than others. |
| | They can invest in business. |
| Step 3 | They are educated up to a certain level. |
| | They have better housing conditions than those lower down. |
| | They are government employees, shop owners, and foreign migrants. |
| Step 2 | They do daily wage labor. |
| | They did not receive assistance from the government. |
| | Some are resettled civil servants. |
| | They don't have permanent houses. |
| Step 1 (poorest) | Most of them have thatched houses, not proper houses. |
| | Houses are badly damaged by the war. |
| | They have large families. |

*Source:* Male ladder of life focus group discussion.
*Note:* Bold line indicates the community poverty line.

indeed, owning a home in good condition is often a characteristic of non-poor families across the communities in this study. Typically this means that the house is constructed of permanent materials such as brick or cement and sand. The step just above the poverty line also frequently features permanent jobs, such as in the civil service, better-educated children, some remittances, and land for agriculture and livestock. In the more developed Sinhalese communities of Welumbe in the South and Pothupana in the East, the poverty line was placed a bit higher than elsewhere. In Welumbe, civil servants and those owning 2 acres of land were still seen to be poor; in Pothupana, the step just below the community poverty line had homes made of brick and farms of 4 acres.

Households at the bottom step are often seen to be disadvantaged in terms of their family composition: they may be large families with many dependents, female-headed families, or households with more female, elderly, disabled, or ill members, sometimes all surviving on a single income. Youths in the poorest families often have to perform daily wage labor to help make ends meet. At the top step, by contrast, it is common for households to run businesses or have large landholdings and to receive remittances from family members working abroad (though remittances are not always the main income source as they are in this sample ladder). The importance of remittances revealed by the focus groups is consistent with findings of other studies.[6]

During the focus group discussions that generated the ladder in table 12.2, the men explained that step 2 comprises about 60 percent of the village and that most of these households used to be better off before the conflict. But their homes were completely destroyed, so they now live in rented homes and temporary shelters and do not run any businesses. The men reported that it is very hard to cross the community poverty line to reach step 3: "We can't do our work freely because of the situation in the country. We are even afraid of building new houses and starting a new business because of this situation." Despite these difficult circumstances, as we shall explore below, many of Kaithamavi's poor were able to pull themselves up to steps 3 and 4 during the study's recall period of 15 years.

It is important to note that only those households that had returned to and were residing in the village in 2005 were included in the ladder exercise. There were not sufficient resources to track down the displaced households that had resided in the study villages in 1990 but had relocated elsewhere permanently since then. The qualitative evidence suggests that the statistics may understate the extent of resilience and mobility among better-off groups because the households and household members with more resources and better connections in 1990 were also more likely to have migrated to peaceful areas of the country or abroad when the war set in.[7]

## Mobility outcomes

The ladder of life created by focus groups was used to calculate each community's performance on poor people's mobility. Households that started below the community poverty line in 1990 but rose above it during the 15-year study period were said to have moved out of poverty. We generated a moving out of poverty (MOP) index for each village by dividing the number of households that moved out of poverty by the number of households identified as poor in 1990.

This study found very large differences from one community to the next in their poverty reduction performance over the 15 years (table 12.3, column 3). To frame the analysis, we use the striking differences in MOP ratings between matched pairs of villages visited in three districts: Kaithamavi and Manivali in Jaffna district, Nilakulam and Kumputhiri in Trincomalee district, and Pothupana and Thambulla in Ampara district. In each pair, one village is identified as high-mobility (shown in bold in table 12.3) and the other as low-mobility, based on their relative MOP ratings. This creates a simple two-part typology for the comparative analysis.

When the peaceful South is included, three of the four villages in the sample with high MOP are located in high-growth districts. The other high-MOP village, Nilakulam, is a relatively new community of displaced households and its sampling profile is low growth. Taken together, these outcomes suggest that a community's poverty reduction performance is associated with the strength of the district economy.

The MOP outcomes, however, do not suggest any association between mobility and conflict. Experiences of intense conflict do not necessarily impede very high rates of mobility, as Kaithamavi and Pothupana demonstrate. Conversely, some of the low-mobility communities experienced less intense conflict or none at all during the study period.[8]

The only ethnic pattern that emerges is that in the East, the two Muslim communities did not perform as well as the comparison villages that are Tamil and Sinhalese. The sample is certainly too small to draw policy conclusions, and people from every village described disadvantages due to their ethnicity, but for the Muslim villages the data strongly suggest that the disadvantages of their minority ethnicity are more severe than for the two other groups. Concerns related to caste differences surfaced rarely in the discussions, except when focus groups were probed specifically about issues of

**TABLE 12.3**
**Mobility outcomes of Sri Lanka study communities**

| Province/district | Village | MOP | Conflict intensity | Ethnicity |
|---|---|---|---|---|
| North (average MOP 0.25) | | | | |
| Jaffna (high growth) | **Kaithamavi** | **0.44** | High | Tamil |
| | Manivali | 0.18 | High | Tamil |
| Mannar (low growth) | Pesavankalai | 0.14 | High | Tamil |
| East (average MOP 0.30) | | | | |
| Trincomalee (low growth) | **Nilakulam** | **0.44** | None | Tamil |
| | Kumputhiri | 0.17 | Low | Muslim |
| Ampara (high growth) | **Pothupana** | **0.39** | High | Sinhalese |
| | Thambulla | 0.20 | None | Muslim |
| South (average MOP 0.19) | | | | |
| Matara (high growth) | Welumbe | 0.24 | None | Sinhalese |
| Hambantota (low growth) | Nelutanga | 0.13 | None | Sinhalese |

Sources: Ladder of life focus group discussions, conflict timeline discussions, and key informant interviews.
Note: MOP = no. of households that cross community poverty line ÷ no. of households initially poor.
High-MOP villages are shown in bold. For an explanation of conflict intensity ratings, see note 5.

social inequality (or in the case of Welumbe in the South, in reference to political allegiances during the JVP uprising). When caste was mentioned, almost everyone reported that these differences had become relatively unimportant or were disappearing altogether, especially among youth.

By comparison with villages in the North and East, the two villages from the peaceful southern region averaged lower rates of MOP. Again, this area of the sample, where conflict occurred between 1989 and 1991, is used mainly as a control and is not explored in depth in this chapter. These communities do, nonetheless, face problems, including agricultural stagnation, scarce non-farm income opportunities, youth moving in large numbers to the country's urban areas to seek work, and weak local democracy and governance.

## Mobility and Conflict in the North

Conflict on the Jaffna peninsula has taken many twists and turns, and the three communities visited in the Northern province experienced the most severe and protracted conflict in the sample.

The LTTE controlled the North throughout the mid-1980s, but the Indian Peace Keeping Force (IPKF) captured Jaffna city in 1988 after extensive combat.[9] The Indian troops withdrew amid controversy in 1990, and the LTTE regained control of Jaffna and held it until an army offensive known as Operation Jayasikkuru (Victory Is Assured) drove the Tigers out in 1995. The LTTE recaptured Jaffna once again in 1998. Active fighting finally ended when the cease-fire agreement was signed in 2002, but fear and insecurity continued to surround the three study communities in the North throughout the study period.

In the LTTE-controlled areas, the armed group operates as a de facto government, administering justice and collecting taxes. However, the government continues to provide and finance most public services in these areas. As Uyangoda explains, "The LTTE's role is to administer the public services, in a tacit understanding with the state that the public servants also obey the LTTE's orders and instructions" (2007, 41).

The intensity and duration of active combat vary significantly across the conflict area, and this affected the conflict experiences of the study communities. But whether there was armed combat raging in close proximity or not, civilians throughout the Northern and Eastern provinces were drawn into the conflict and deeply affected by the deaths and injuries of loved ones, repeated episodes of displacement and property loss, and forced recruitment of male youth into armed groups. They also suffered forced taxation and their physical mobility was restricted by road blocks, searches, requirements for passes, and the threat of landmines. Fear and anxiety were pervasive. Moreover, the wider insecurity often made it too risky for villagers to farm or work in coastal areas and forests, thus depriving them of their livelihoods. Nonetheless, out of necessity people found ways to carry on with their lives.

Throughout this period, the different armed forces repeatedly evacuated tens of thousands of civilians across Jaffna, which is largely populated by ethnic Tamils. In 1990 the Tigers ordered a mass evacuation of Muslims from Jaffna district (this period also coincides with Tamil-Muslim riots and Muslim displacement in a study village in the East). When describing their displacement experiences, study respondents spoke of relatives and neighbors who were killed, injured, or lost while seeking refuge. They also reported people of all ages pouring onto the main highway on foot, especially in 1995; often their savings were stolen by different armed groups as they fled for their lives. Many evacuated to crowded makeshift centers set up in temples, schools, and camps, where they survived on government relief and humanitarian aid from nongovernmental organizations (NGOs). A few risked their lives taking boats to India or to other parts of Sri Lanka, including Mannar and Puttalam, but refugee conditions were reported to be equally difficult there and many soon returned.

While waves of displacement affected all three of the study communities in the North, residents of Manivali, a low-MOP village, faced the shortest periods away from their homes. They experienced a month-long evacuation in 1987, with the arrival of the IPKF in Jaffna, and another displacement in 1995 for six months during the army offensive. Kaithamavi's first evacuation was not until 1990, but it was followed by others in 1995, 1996, and 2000, with many households only coming back to the village after the 2002 ceasefire. Like the Manivali villagers, residents of Pesavankalai were evacuated in 1987, but then people were forced to flee again in 1990, 1994, and 1997, with most residents only returning in 2002.

Along with its briefer periods of evacuation, Manivali had other advantages that would seem to promise an easier recovery from episodes of violence and displacement. A semi-urban community, it hosted Jaffna's largest market and a diverse local economy. But in fact, this community registered a much lower level of poverty escapes (18 percent) than did Kaithamavi (44 percent), a village that was far more affected by the conflict and had less favorable market and infrastructure conditions (table 12.4).

The next two sections look more carefully at the impacts of conflict on Manivali and Kaithamavi and at the economic, political, and social factors that shaped their recovery after 2002. Why were more households in Kaithamavi able to escape poverty than in Manivali?

**TABLE 12.4**
**Profile of study communities, Jaffna district, Sri Lanka**

| Village | MOP | Conflict intensity | Ethnicity |
|---------|-----|--------------------|-----------|
| Kaithamavi | 0.44 | High | Tamil |
| Manivali | 0.18 | High | Tamil |

*Sources:* Ladder of life focus group discussions, conflict timeline discussions, and key informant interviews.

## Manivali: Grappling with inequality and continued strife

Before the civil war, local people recounted, low-mobility Manivali was a peaceful and thriving community with a large market and many opportunities. Fishing, agriculture, tobacco cultivation, and cigar making, among many other livelihoods, provided good incomes for the town's 950 families. There were also two medium-size factories where local youth found jobs manufacturing iron nails and aluminum products.

But the war took a heavy toll on the town. Many better-off families shut down their factories, farms, and businesses and fled permanently from the region. And when Manivali's residents returned in 1996 after being displaced for half a year, they encountered extensive property damage and loss: 280 houses had been completely destroyed and another 150 partially damaged, much of the livestock had been killed, and farming and fishing equipment had disappeared. Traditional livelihoods became difficult or impossible to continue. For example, coastal activities involving fishing, coir work,[10] or harvesting Palmyra palm faced security restrictions, and it became too risky to transport goods by canoe. Farming also suffered, with most people ceasing their paddy and tobacco cultivation. Renewed investment in livestock was deemed too risky. And with the reduction and disappearance of so many economic activities, so too went many wage work opportunities for Manivali's poor—shedding light on the comparatively low rate of MOP found there. Focus groups reported widening inequality.

Some of the town's remaining nonpoor families coped by switching to vegetable crops, running grocery shops and other small businesses, and receiving remittances from family members working abroad. Overseas migration was relatively rare among the town's families but increased with the war, and many people cited remittances as a key reason that some households had been able to prosper during the conflict. The source of the remittances also made a difference. In Manivali's ladder of life discussion group, the men carefully distinguished the families receiving assistance from kin working in the Middle East—which placed them just above or below the community poverty line—from the better-off families whose relatives were working in countries such as the United Kingdom and Canada. One woman said her household had escaped poverty because her husband went to work overseas: "After my husband went to France, my confidence increased."

In addition to remittances, Manivali's better-off found other opportunities. During the several years before 2002 when travel restrictions were in place, local farmers and businesses were able to make large profits because there was no competition from outside the area. Once the roads opened, however, profits declined as traders from Colombo reached the local market with lower-cost goods, including cheaper vegetables.

Irregularities with land ownership in the wake of displacement also seem to have brought benefits to the town's wealthier groups. Some displaced families returned in 1996 to find fraudulent claims on their property, but they lacked the necessary titling documentation to prove ownership.[11] When asked directly about how the local land disputes were being handled, focus groups did not identify any leader or institution helping people resolve them. A World Bank–financed housing assistance program and other government schemes helped only about 50 households that could provide property titles and demonstrate a low income. At the time of the visit, some of the town's landless were living on temple lands in makeshift housing. The situation has been further complicated by a sharp increase in land prices due to a rise in purchases by better-off families with remittances.

Along with land disputes, people returned from displacement to face dangers of shootings and landmines as well as roundups, arrests, and prolonged detentions by the Sri Lankan army, which was suspicious of the town's connections to the LTTE. Trust was shattered as neighbors betrayed neighbors to the army and people began disappearing. According to one resident:

> Some people have gained by betrayals to the army. Some of these
> [betrayed] people have been shot. Mainly the LTTE members' families,
> heroes' families, and the people involved in pasting notices have been
> treated badly by the army. Some government officers escaped by showing
> their [government] identity cards. EPDP [a Tamil political party] members
> also got some favoritism.

People also reported growing problems of theft, alcoholism, and violence among groups of youth. "Nowadays youths are not obeying the elders. Elders are scared to talk to youth about their habits, because they fear they might be attacked. Teenagers at the age of 15 are also drinking alcohol, smoking cigarettes . . . There are five bars in this area," explained a local man. Manivali used to have a group of youth who collaborated to protect the community from theft, but this ceased functioning with the conflict. Community meetings are said to be poorly attended, and if a community project is undertaken, such as a cleaning campaign, only the committee members participate. "No one is interested in doing this work anymore," said an informant. When asked about the functioning of local democracy, focus groups had little to say on the topic. "No, we don't have democracy because of the war," explained a discussion group of young women and men. Another discussion group of men said corruption is very high. "Political parties sometimes come here and campaign, but nothing is done."

Following the cease-fire, in 2003 and 2004, the town did receive two microcredit schemes. In 2005 the local Women's Rural Development Society began another loan program for women, financed by the United Nations Development Programme. But the women's focus group indicated that while these initiatives have helped some people launch small ventures such as home-based sewing and craft businesses, the lending opportunities "were not uniformly shared within the community." Despite the cease-fire and new credit opportunities, people reported that it is now much harder than in the past to find work or make a profit in the local market. There is a growing presence of motorbikes, cell phones, and other symbols of affluence in the village, but these mask growing inequality. Overall, focus group members in Manivali described a widening gap between the best off and worst off. In high-MOP Kaithamavi, they described the opposite: there, inequality was seen to be shrinking.

### Kaithamavi: Forging paths to recovery and peace

By comparison with Manivali, the village of Kaithamavi, where many people moved out of poverty, has seen more widespread recovery. But local people in this community of 684 households generally do not attribute their improved conditions to economic factors. Before the conflict, Kaithamavi's workers mainly engaged in fishing, coir work, and some farming. After 1990, however, all of these activities became difficult to carry out, no matter whether the area was under LTTE or army occupation at a given moment. Coastal livelihoods remained subject to crippling restrictions, even with the cease-fire:

> When we go to sea, we have to produce a national identity card and get a pass and when we come back we can get the identity card by giving the pass. Fishing is allowed from 6 a.m. to 1 p.m. But within this time duration it's difficult to go to sea and come. Women are allowed to do coir work during 7 a.m. to 12 noon. But coir work cannot be done always. They can go to the sea only when water level is low, which may be in the

morning or the evening depending on the tides and seasons. If the high-security zone is removed, we can do our work freely. If we could not finish our work and come out [by the curfew], the army punishes us. Sometimes they hit us. Also we have to stay in queue carrying the coir bags for a long time to get a pass.

In the face of repeated displacements and continuing insecurity and travel restrictions, many households have been forced to look beyond the village to bring in income and rebuild their lives. Some have found work in other villages in masonry and carpentry, skills often learned during displacement. As in Manivali, women are doing sewing in their homes. Some people somehow found a way to accumulate savings during displacement and then launched new businesses such as bakeries, grinding mills, and grocery shops when the cease-fire took effect. Some households have sent family members overseas.

When questioned about local democracy, both the men's and women's focus groups echoed the group in Manivali that said there was little to talk about. One man from Kaithamavi declared, "We have to stop the war first to talk about democracy," and a woman stated, "We don't know where [democracy] is. It is just a concept. It is not there in this country." Another man reported that he had been turned away from voting in two elections because someone had already voted in his name before he arrived: "This is the democracy we have in this society. We don't want to talk about those groups." Another man added that it's senseless to talk about the local government because its powers are severely limited by the war: "We want peace first. After that the local government can function."

While formal political processes are seen to hold little relevance, villagers report that local groups and collective action play valued roles in the life of the community. To resolve disputes within the community, for example, people can use the Social Service Centre, the Maha Sangam (a community group), or the Fisheries Society. But people say their internal problems are minor, and their main concern is trying to get the army to lift the high-security zone and move out of the area. Villagers organized a petition, engaged in picketing, and wrote letters to the government, the president, and the army commander protesting the presence of the army camp and the denial of access to large areas of land adjacent to their village. Fifty families with houses in the security zone remain homeless. People also fear the army presence because of the danger of retribution from the army as well as from the Tigers if either side perceives that villagers are cooperating with the other. The villagers have yet to get any response to their petitions, but their efforts demonstrate the social cohesion and capacity for collective action that has been the hallmark of this village.

Kaithamavi attracted more extensive reconstruction and development assistance after the cease-fire than did Manivali. The municipal council built a water system in 2002 when people began returning and then new roads in 2004 and 2005. GTZ, the German development agency, provided financing and material to rebuild 19 houses. In 2004 the Women's Rural Development Society in the village became the liaison for a World Bank–financed housing project that benefited an unspecified number of families in the first phase and 71 families in the second phase; it was widely considered the most important support yet received.[12] There are also various private and governmental loan funds that people said they can access, although there is reluctance to borrow large amounts for fear of a renewed outbreak of war.

Nearly all of Kaithamavi's families are participating in some way in Samurdhi, the country's largest antipoverty program, which began in 1995 and became fully operational in the North and East after the cease-fire. The program provides small financial grants. The maximum grant is 1,000 rupees (approximately $10), which is given to a family of more than five members whose total monthly income is less than 500 rupees. Samurdhi also extends microloans on a rotating basis to groups of five, and additional benefits are available to help families with births and funerals. The program requires beneficiaries to provide voluntary labor in local public works, such as a 2004 latrine reconstruction project in the village.

### Key factors: Internal cohesion and external assistance

Both of the Jaffna communities endured displacement and destruction during the study, but Kaithamavi's conflict experiences were far more severe. Nevertheless, Kaithamavi went on to experience much more inclusive recovery, even though Manivali had a large market and a more diverse economy.

In both communities local livelihoods were greatly damaged by the civil war. People who had enough means coped by sending family members abroad to work and by investing in small businesses. Poorer people survived by engaging in traditional fishing and handicraft work when conditions allowed and by seeking wage labor wherever they could find it. Rather than economic advantages, what distinguishes high-mobility Kaithamavi from lower-mobility Manivali is that the former received more external assistance and displayed stronger social cohesion and institutional capacities for collective action. While insecurity due to the war is pervasive in both localities, villagers in Kaithamavi do not report the problems of alcoholism, criminality, and youth violence that are present in Manivali.

These findings suggest that in risky cease-fire environments, a community's capacity to come together and tackle problems collectively takes on great importance for preventing criminality and ensuring that any opportunities available are widely shared by community members. It may be that Kaithamavi's more intense experiences with conflict helped bring the community together and foster more cohesion and mutual dependence.[13] The villagers came together to protest the high-security zones, and although these efforts were unsuccessful, they reflected local institutional capabilities that were no doubt important for obtaining and administering the reconstruction and social assistance received. In Manivali, by contrast, it seems that better-off groups were able to take advantage of the disarray in land titling. The World Bank–financed housing reconstruction program, which required property titles, is likely to have exacerbated the difficulties for homeless people in a community where there was no local recourse for land disputes or provision to recover legal documents lost during conflict and displacement.

Manivali also received less public and NGO support. Samurdhi, the government's signature antipoverty program, only arrived there in 2004, a decade after it was instituted in Kaithamavi. It is not clear whether this was because Manivali was seen to be less needy, or whether the town's leaders and networks were perhaps less proactive in seeking the program. The official reason given for the lack of coverage of Samurdhi in the North and East is the conflict, but this does not explain why some areas received help and others, affected similarly by conflict, did not. Whatever the case, the contrasting levels of community cohesion, grassroots activism, and external assistance seem to be the most important factors explaining the sharp differences in poverty reduction seen in these two Tamil communities in the North.

## Mobility and Conflict in the East

The obstacles facing the two pairs of communities visited in the Eastern province are similar to those encountered in the North. Villagers here also struggled with persistent insecurity, displacement, restrictions on mobility, difficulties in carrying out their traditional farming and fishing livelihoods, and weak local government. However, there were important aspects of their experiences with conflict and recovery that differed from those in the North. With one notable exception, much of the conflict in the sample villages had passed by the early 1990s. Also important, the population in the East is divided among three ethnic groups, with Tamils and Muslims each composing roughly 40 percent and Sinhalese the remaining 20 percent.[14] Discrimination, fear, and even violence between Tamils and Sinhalese and between Tamils and Muslims affected the villages visited. Much of this strife was not seen to be related directly to the civil war, although the conflict environment no doubt exacerbated ethnic tensions.

The village with the highest mobility among the four in the East is Nilakulam, and it is also the only Tamil community in the sample from this province. The village is young and small, and like Kaithamavi it displays very strong collective action and high levels of external assistance. The other high-mobility village is Pothupana, a Sinhalese village that is decidedly less cohesive. But Pothupana has nevertheless prospered from years of special assistance under a governmental resettlement and irrigation program. By comparison, the two low-mobility Muslim communities faced more difficulties in accessing economic opportunities and public resources over the study period. Their minority ethnic status within the district seemed to play an important role; nonetheless, residents of the newer of the two Muslim villages expressed only limited concern about ethnic disadvantages relative to the many other hurdles they faced.

All these factors come into play in a comparison of the high- and low-mobility study villages in each of the two districts visited in the East, Trincomalee and Ampara.

## Trincomalee district: Risks and opportunities shaped by ethnicity

The two villages in the Trincomalee district are low-mobility Kumputhiri, which is home to 660 Muslim households, and high-mobility Nilakulam, a small and new village of 104 Tamil households (table 12.5). Villagers from both endured mass displacement due to the conflict, but the more established community of Muslims experienced greater hardships in its recovery.

Kumputhiri was evacuated by the army in 1990 in response to an LTTE attack that killed 30 villagers. After resettlement in 1991, villagers were again attacked by the LTTE. The Muslim village then experienced a long period of relative peace until three farmers who were guarding their lands were killed

**TABLE 12.5**
**Profile of study communities, Trincomalee district, Sri Lanka**

| Village | MOP | Conflict intensity | Ethnicity |
|---------|-----|--------------------|-----------|
| Nilakulam | 0.44 | None | Tamil |
| Kumputhiri | 0.17 | Low | Muslim |

Sources: Ladder of life focus group discussions, conflict timeline discussions, and key informant interviews.

in 2003 by the Tigers. The army stationed a security post in the village, but people remained very fearful.

Nilakulam experienced a prolonged evacuation from 1983 to 1990, and most of its original families never returned. Over time, as conflict ebbed in the East, the village was resettled by Tamil families who had been displaced across the conflict region, with the majority arriving in the village for the first time after 1998.

### Kumputhiri: Limited economic opportunities and partnerships

The 2002 cease-fire did not much improve economic opportunities for the Muslim community of Kumputhiri. Villagers no longer needed to hand over bags of rice and other goods as tribute to the LTTE, but it remained too risky for them to work in nearby coastal and forest areas. The area was nominally under army control, but villagers still had to pay fees to the LTTE for passes to enter those areas, and even then they faced danger in doing so. People used to gather wood and engage in shifting cultivation in forest areas, but in 2005 they reported:

> We have to pay 50 rupees to go to the woods to bring a cartload of fire-wood. But even though we pay 50 rupees sometimes they catch us and ask us to pay 15,000, 20,000, or even 25,000 rupees to release the cart. If we go to argue with them they will kill us. In 2003 the LTTE killed three people who were safeguarding their cultivation lands.

Security restrictions such as those described in the Jaffna area also deterred people from fishing and harvesting coastal resources such as shrimp and using the sea for coir production. A garment factory in the village used to provide some jobs, but it never reopened after the evacuation in 1990.

As a result, since the cease-fire most of Kumputhiri's workers have relied mainly on wage labor in nearby paddy fields and quarries. Others engage in brick making, masonry, and carpentry. The few better-off households in the village run small shops, lease farmland, and receive remittances from family members working abroad. Emigration can bring new hardships: young women, in particular, take low-paying, high-risk jobs overseas as domestic workers. Some poorer households seek work in the Middle East, where the pay is reported to be very low. Still, emigration and remittances have allowed some to improve their well-being. When recounting her life story, a woman who moved out of poverty in Kumputhiri said, "First high point is 2003, when I went abroad. The second high point is when my husband went abroad."

Both of the Trincomalee villages have strong community leadership. Yet, although it is larger and more established, Kumputhiri has been unable to form as many productive links with external partners as has the younger

Tamil village. Kumputhiri's Mosque Committee plays many roles—mediating local disputes, providing information on job opportunities, convening meetings, coordinating with external actors, and organizing community activities. A leading concern has been to gain access to the same services and entitlements enjoyed by the non-Muslim communities that surround the village. In particular, the community has been fighting to gain access to water for household consumption as well as for irrigation, but without much success. "The government should build wells for us and we should be treated equally. We can't accept this discrimination. The government has to give us what they give to other villages," said the focus group of women. The Mosque Committee has occasionally turned to the police, members of Parliament, and even government ministers for help. "But they don't support us," complained the men's discussion group. "The media also do not report on our problems. We are rejected by all."

Kumputhiri's member of Parliament helped the village gain housing in the 1980s and electricity in 1993 (for the 40 percent of the village that could afford the initial connection fees). The MP was with the ruling United National Party. Since the victory of the more nationalistic Sri Lanka Freedom Party in 2004, the women's group explained, the village no longer receives attention from the government.[15]

The Samurdhi welfare program provides modest benefits to 60 percent of Kumputhiri's residents. However, local people asserted that all but perhaps 5 percent of the village should be eligible. There have been troublesome delays and irregularities in payments, and villagers reported at the time of the visit that no payments had been made for the last three months. People also resented the fact that they did not get any additional assistance after the tsunami, although other villages in their area did.

### Nilakulam: More options and success with mobilizing

By comparison with Kumputhiri, Nilakulam, which experienced higher mobility, offered more local opportunities for earning a living and greater access to external resources.[16] With the cease-fire, travel resumed to the popular Nilaweli beach, and Nilakulam was well positioned near the main road to the beach, allowing vendors to hawk handicrafts and other items. Other local livelihoods that villagers say became easier after the cease-fire include farming on leased land, raising cattle, making cement blocks, running small businesses, weaving Palmyra products, doing masonry and carpentry work, and securing government and NGO jobs. Continuing security problems after the cease-fire, however, prevented villagers from venturing long distances for work.

In Nilakulam, 50 percent of households receive Samurdhi, compared to 60 percent in Kumputhiri. But the program seems to be more active and appreciated in Nilakulam because its loans, though modest, are accessible, and it also provides funeral and wedding benefits. While a greater proportion of the population of Kumputhiri was identified as poor according to the Samurdhi criteria, the Nilakulam beneficiaries were clearly more active, accessing the other components of the program. Problems of poor coverage and payment delays are not reported in Nilakulam as they are in Kumputhiri.

Perhaps more important, NGO-supported projects and loan schemes are mentioned with much greater frequency in Nilakulam. The many partnerships are a reflection of the village's active Rural Development Society (RDS), which was formed in 1998 to bring services into the new community. Among other things, the RDS helped secure a well, a community center, a school, and a daycare facility, and it organized annual sports events. Its president is held in high esteem. But Nilakulam still lacks electricity, transport facilities, and health care, which makes people's lives more difficult. In addition, as in the villages of the North, land issues persist. The community is sited on temple lands, and households are paying taxes with the expectation of one day receiving deeds.

People say that the local government has generally not been helpful in addressing community needs, and the village instead has had to mobilize on its own behalf. In 2003, for instance, the RDS organized a large strike along the main road to protest the community's omission from the official map. The strike attracted the attention of the police and government officials, and Nilakulam was included on the map thereafter. Community members see this victory as the most important factor contributing to Nilakulam's prosperity because they are convinced that the recognition helped them secure resources from NGOs that work in the area.

People in Nilakulam hope that if there can be peace in the region, the community will continue to prosper. A male youth said that the village helped elect a doctor from a nearby village to the council, and "we believe that he can work for the community." By contrast, a female youth from Kumputhiri was considerably less sanguine about the prospects for democracy and its contribution to the welfare of her community, saying, "We do not think anything will change in the future."

### Ampara district: Different starting points and mostly different hurdles

The Ampara villages in the study number nearly 300 households each, and both depend heavily on paddy rice farming. And as in Trincomalee, it is the Muslim village that experienced lower mobility and fewer opportunities among the two visited (table 12.6). But the disadvantages of ethnicity play

**TABLE 12.6**
**Profile of study communities, Ampara district, Sri Lanka**

| Village | MOP | Conflict intensity | Ethnicity |
|---------|-----|--------------------|-----------|
| Pothupana | 0.39 | High | Sinhalese |
| Thambulla | 0.20 | None | Muslim |

*Sources:* Ladder of life focus group discussions, conflict timeline discussions, and key informant interviews.

out somewhat differently in Ampara. In this case the high-MOP village is populated by Sinhalese, a minority group in local (but not national) politics and, like the Muslims, threatened by the LTTE. In fact, Pothupana experienced a major LTTE attack and was also plagued by strong internal divisions. Yet many people found ways to escape poverty there.

In 1990 the villagers of Muslim Thambulla endured intense violence between Tamils, Muslims, and a small group of Burghers (Eurasian descendents of colonial settlers). Prior to this time, the three ethnic groups reportedly lived together without any problems in a single village, and some Muslims were even members of the LTTE. But when the LTTE murdered two Muslim civilians from the village in 1990 as part of a larger Tamil campaign against Muslims, the Muslim LTTE combatants left the armed group to help their fellow Muslims prepare to retaliate. Muslim politicians within the government helped arm the Muslim group. But after waves of retaliation and a major attack that resulted in several deaths on both sides, the Muslims collectively abandoned their lands and resettled permanently in a separate community. Villagers reported that 15 years later they were still fearful of venturing into Tamil areas.

Sinhalese Pothupana was attacked by armed groups during the JVP uprising in 1989. A more severe attack came in 1999, when a small armed group of LTTE combatants descended at night on a hamlet adjoining Pothupana and killed 44 men, women, and children. But it is important to note that reports of the attack mixed together anguished accounts of LTTE brutality against unarmed civilians with references to local rivalries that seemed to have little to do with the civil war. The massacre, as local people call it, came on the heels of a wave of retaliatory violence that began with an unspecified incident involving Sinhalese traders and a Tamil owner's cow. The dispute resulted in the murder of a Sinhalese, and when police became involved, one or two Tamils were shot as well. Other accounts of violent incidents in the East during the study period also mention the presence of private disputes and suggest that the war was being used as cover.[17]

*Thambulla: Unequal options and returns*

Over the course of the 1990s, the new village of Thambulla obtained permanent housing, a school and technical college, electricity, roads, and drainage. All these amenities, participants said, helped the village's very large poor population improve their well-being, if not necessarily escape poverty. The atmosphere of lawlessness that prevailed after the 1990 spate of violence subsided. Sometimes local people sounded false alarms of Tamil invasions and then looted households and farms as people fled. But some of the villagers spreading these rumors were caught and brought to the police.

Most of Thambulla's workers do daily wage labor or lease land from owners of area paddy fields. But unlike farmers in the other study communities, the farmers who lease land here say they are paid in kind with bags of rice equivalent to just an eighth of their paddy's total yield.[18] The village competes with others for irrigation water and is at a disadvantage because it is farther downstream. As a result, farm jobs are scarce and returns from leasing land very low. As elsewhere in the region, some people make bricks and others work in local quarries, particularly between the paddy harvesting seasons. A few of the best-off people in the village run shops, have family members working overseas, or have found jobs with the government or NGOs. A women's group explained that overseas migration is a particularly important strategy used by large families to avoid impoverishment. It also helps get young people out of the country so they cannot be forcibly recruited by the LTTE. There is some mention of female youth trying to take up work in garment factories, but without access to transport this is very difficult.

Islamic banks provide some credit in the community, but a focus group of women explained that to get bank loans people must "show something as collateral, and two government civil servants have to recommend the loan. So poor people like us can't get loans from banks or finance companies." They reported that Samurdhi loans are available, but that the amounts loaned are too small to finance anything beyond small-scale, low-return activities.

Nonetheless, Thambulla's key informant and both the men's and women's focus groups named the antipoverty program as one of the two most important factors contributing to prosperity in the village. There are 180 families participating in Samurdhi, while another 98 families have been identified as eligible but have yet to receive benefits. In addition to the revolving credit program, Samurdhi has also provided food stamps and assistance with construction of a water tank for irrigation.

The people of Thambulla also spoke highly of their *grama sevaka* (local government officer). He has effectively resolved local land disputes and was appealing a regulation with the government that requires every family to have a minimum of 10 perches (1 perch = 25 square meters of land). If the requirement were reduced to five perches, this would ease dowry pressures on poor families with many daughters, because land is frequently included in the dowry. In fact, the dowry is perceived as "the biggest crisis of this village," creating special hardship for parents with several daughters because of the high costs of giving them away in marriage. The cost is particularly high for this community because it is relatively remote. Parents pay heavily, including by providing land, in order to entice prospective sons-in-law to look beyond the disadvantages of the community and its location.

In other respects, Thambulla's villagers expressed disappointment with the local government, even though the village has received several projects.[19] The men's group reported a decline in participation in community decision making and activities since the onset of the conflict. They explained that local people are never consulted when government opportunities become available or when the Samurdhi officer is deciding on who should be eligible for benefits. They also estimated that perhaps 90 percent of government officials are corrupt and take bribes. And they held out little hope that local democracy might improve in the years ahead.

### Pothupana: The favored village

Pothupana's economy provides a stark contrast to Thambulla's. The area in which the community is situated was developed as one of Sri Lanka's first large-scale irrigation and resettlement schemes in the 1950s, and in 1990 the government named Pothupana one of Ampara's two "Productivity Villages." Members of Parliament from different areas of the East visited the village after it received this distinction. Ampara's representative provided electricity and a turmeric drier. Villagers say the arrival of electricity along with the agricultural extension services provided in the 1990s greatly advanced the community.

After the LTTE killings of 1999, however, paddy fields sat abandoned, cattle were sold off, and trade with neighboring Tamil communities became greatly strained. A climate of fear prevailed, even though the army placed two additional camps in the area and some villagers were trained and stationed as home guards. Some families left the community altogether. Others with exposed houses near the edge of the village slept with friends who had safer homes in the center or moved their households there. But fears of LTTE attacks continued. When sharing her life story, a poor woman reported that her husband had been killed by the LTTE in 2004 while he was working on a tractor in a field that they leased. "We didn't know until he was shot that they [the LTTE] were there."

Farming resumed after the 2002 cease-fire, but local people report the village to be less prosperous than in the early 1990s, mainly due to shrinking profit margins for rice. Villagers also grow turmeric, coconut, ginger, vegetables, maize, cowpea, cashew, and areca nut. Turmeric was profitable in the late 1980s and much of the 1990s, but increased competition and a fungus in the late 1990s pushed farmers to try other crops. The village economy also struggled after the tsunami because extensive rice donations drove down the market price. Some households, however, began producing and selling bricks to meet the demand created by post-tsunami housing reconstruction. In addition, several people are working in government jobs, including with the armed forces and police. An elderly woman who has moved out of poverty in Pothupana, for instance, explained that she was able to do this because her two sons secured jobs with the police and the navy, and together they are saving and also cultivating crops "so we can be well prepared for the future." In addition, the village employs 30 home guards. About 25 young women commute daily to garment factories, and other women are receiving training in sewing and handicrafts.

A focus group of women from Pothupana identified no fewer than six available credit sources: Sarvodaya (an NGO), the Samurdhi program, the local funeral group, a local group of paddy cultivators, private lenders, and agricultural unions. The men's and women's focus groups identified fertilizer subsidies and credit from Sarvodaya and from Ceylinco, a private firm, as the top factors helping Pothupana prosper. Nevertheless, the women said that default rates are high because there is so much credit available: "What happens is that people take loans from each and every place and they won't bother to pay the money back and they cheat the company. Even the groups who provide the loans try to pull down the other group." Villagers also said that credit for fertilizer and pesticides is usually not available from these programs, so farmers instead rely on costly loan sharks, causing them to fall into debt "one harvesting season after another."

When discussing the quality of local democracy and governance, villagers acknowledged that the government had improved the education of youth in the village and had provided opportunities based on merit, such as scholarships. But beyond this they had little favorable to report about government functioning. When asked about democracy and its future in the country, the women's focus group in Pothupana replied that Sri Lanka is not a democratic country, and "if we bribe 50 rupees now, in 10 years we will have to bribe 100 rupees." The women also reported that with the exception of Samurdhi, government schemes often had limited effectiveness and were tainted by their association with partisan politics: "When the parties change in the local government, then the policies and the people who are benefited change. So we don't think that they contribute anything to economic opportunities. Last time they built a well near the house of a party supporter." While elected officials may be more accessible than earlier, the women said this has little effect: "They are all just sitting there. They don't pay attention to the development of the village." The male youths from the village were also discouraged about the possibilities for local democracy to help the village prosper, saying, "We have only one Sinhala member of Parliament for the whole of Ampara district. The politicians are not worried about the real issues. They just work for the votes during election time."

Another hurdle facing the villagers of Pothupana is the presence of strong social divisions that impede collective action. The divisiveness dates back to 1956, when the area was settled by people brought in from three different districts who then organized themselves into three separate groups according to their areas of origin. A focus group of female youth describes some of the tension that followed:

> There is no equality at all. There are people from three districts in this village. Their customs, traditions, and the ways they behave in society, even their attitudes, are very different from one area of the same village to the other. If there is some common thing to be done, people get divided in these groups. These things have been happening for many years now. No matter what we initiate in the village, it falls apart because of this.

The young women went on to explain that both the local temple committee and the association of turmeric producers became inactive in large part because of the lack of transparency, mismanagement, and breakdown in trust between people from different areas living in the community. But the youths also said that these divisions are declining among the younger generations.

### Ethnicity and the mechanisms of inequality traps

The term "inequality trap" refers to pervasive inequalities in economic, political, and social opportunities that combine and persist over time to keep people poor (Bebbington et al. 2008; Rao and Walton 2004; World Bank 2005). In the East, ethnicity clearly emerges as critical to understanding the processes generating the much lower mobility in the two Muslim communities visited. Again and again, the cases reveal how ethnicity colors local politics and government functioning, access to economic opportunities, and the capacities of civic leaders and networks to advance community interests. In the context of public and market institutions weakened by conflict, the Tamil community that could marshal strong unity and collective action, Nilakulam, experienced the highest mobility in that province. In the other village with high mobility, Pothupana, there is little unity, but it does not seem to be necessary in a locality heavily advantaged by a majority ethnic composition and extensive public and private partnerships.

It is noteworthy that Sinhalese Pothupana benefited from years of government support for its farming. It is the only community visited in the North and East that does not feature numerous reports of family members going abroad for work. This is a testament to the benefits of public investment and also to the presence of more extensive private and NGO resources than were found in the other communities visited. If Pothupana villagers do not perceive the Samurdhi program to be very important, this makes sense in a community that has many other promising opportunities. And if people in the village don't particularly get along, this also seems less important in a community where basic services are already available and the economy is more diversified.

The large differences in initial conditions notwithstanding, public resources seem to reinforce rather than ease inequalities among the study villages. In her evaluation of Samurdhi, for instance, Glinskaya (2000, 19) finds that relative to Sinhalese households, Sri Lankan Tamils, Indian Tamils, and Muslims are less likely to receive Samurdhi (due in part to the limited coverage of Samurdhi in the North and East). Compounding these difficulties in targeting the poor, the private sector and NGOs seem to follow rather than substitute for the services, infrastructure, and capacity building provided by government. Villagers in Pothupana enjoy more diverse credit sources than the others in the sample from the North and East.

A study of the effects of conflict on social capital was conducted in 1998–99 in seven communities in the North and East. The authors found that "bridging" social capital—connections between groups of different ethnicities or between actors inside and outside a given village—had been actively undermined by both the government and the LTTE in order to ensure a loyal base of support (Goodhand, Hulme, and Lewer 2000). In the more stable areas under either LTTE or army control, "bonding" groups (connecting people of similar religion or ethnicity) expanded in importance, with temples and mosques in particular taking on higher profiles. The Moving Out of Poverty study confirmed these divisive processes.

The study found that bridging ties did quickly reemerge with the cease-fire in 2002. But the ethnic composition of the villagers clearly shaped the extent of these partnerships and the advantages derived from them. Nilakulam and Thambulla, for instance, are the two new communities rising out of conflict and displacement, but they have markedly different mobility trajectories. In Tamil Nilakulam, lack of access to electricity, land, and water remain urgent problems, but people have come together to agitate successfully for access to development opportunities available in the area and to create new ones. Mobility out of poverty in Nilakulam is the highest among the sample villages in the East. Muslim Thambulla presents a contrasting picture. The relatively weak political power of Muslims in the country combined with inattention and corruption in the local government mean that Muslim villagers have few reasons to expect many dividends from political connections or collective action. But in 2004, due to the efforts of a Muslim member of Parliament, 10 households in Thambulla managed to access water service and 20 others tapped in illegally. This was highly appreciated.

## Youth in Conflict: Looking beyond Uncertainty and Unfairness

*We don't know what will happen in the future given the context of the war. If this war ends, then that is all we need.*
  —Focus group of female youth, Pothupana, Ampara district

*Actually there isn't anything that can't be done by the youth, because they are powerful. If one is courageous and helps others she can be powerful.*
  —Female youth, Nilakulam, Trincomalee district

In each of the study villages, separate focus groups of female and male youths discussed their aspirations for themselves and their communities. Their discussions make clear that conflict interacts with inequalities in education, ethnicity, gender, and other hardships to affect youths' aspirations and their access to opportunities. The youth hold high hopes for their future, but they are realistic in judging that they will not be able to achieve these aspirations without peace. On the one hand, they express deep anxiety and a feeling of lack of control due to the disadvantages that surround them. On the other hand, they voice optimism and confidence that they, as young people, hold great power to get ahead and make their communities better—if only there can be peace. Several of the youth focus groups identified specific activities that their local youth organizations had accomplished for their communities.

Speaking for many in the study, a young man from Kaithamavi described a fundamental challenge for youth: "We need to get better jobs than the jobs our parents do." A good education is understood to be at the heart of this. But youths from poorer families and poorer communities widely reported strong inequalities in access to quality education and thus in the kinds of jobs available to them after they complete their education. When asked about wider problems of inequality, another young man of Kaithamavi specifically focused his response on problems with education:

> There is no equality at all. It is only a concept and not a practical one. The rich people here get a better education and the poor people can't have access to better education because they can't pay fees to these schools . . . We have to go to the small schools and there are no facilities for these students. Education is not equal to all. Job access is not equal to all.

Ethnic inequalities also feature prominently in the youths' discussions of the obstacles they face, including in the Tamil villages. In Tamil Nilakulam, youths said that when local villagers are caught illegally tapping into the power lines, they are fined and arrested, while those from the nearby Sinhalese village can tap power lines with impunity. And in Tamil Kaithamavi, young people resent having to speak Sinhala in Jaffna: "Army soldiers arrest us if we don't speak it sometimes. We have no freedom to speak our own language." Youths from the non-Tamil villages, meanwhile, reported that despite the cease-fire they are fearful of traveling to Tamil areas. In Pothupana, as indicated above, youths feel disenfranchised with just a single Sinhalese member of Parliament from the district.

Female youth confront gender inequalities. Everywhere, women are identified and identify themselves primarily as housewives, despite the important economic contributions that most bring to their households. "My mother is a housewife and she is working at a small shop near our home, where she gets a small income," reported a youth from Kumputhiri. In Manivali women tend cows and sell milk, and they also do handicrafts and garment work in their homes. In Kaithamavi women do these kinds of jobs as well as coir work along the coast when the army permits. In Thambulla, women weed the paddy fields, and in Pothupana the female youths reported that women do most of the paddy cultivation. In Welumbe in the South, the female youths said, "Women have less freedom, because when they are done with cinnamon peeling they have housework to attend to, and then if they are making cigars they do that late into the night." The young women of Muslim Kumputhiri face restrictions on their physical mobility, both by custom and because of the war. There are no job opportunities available to women, they said, so women often do home-based activities such as sewing and vegetable gardening. Their aspirations center mainly on getting married.

Male and female youth alike expressed frustration over their lack of freedom to travel within and beyond their own villages because of the insecurity of the civil war. Young men are targets of harassment and forced recruitment by the different armed groups; male youths of Manivali defined freedom as the ability to "go anywhere at any time." But women have the least freedom of all, as females traveling alone face threats of violence even during peacetime. "We do not let women move around on the roads after 8 p.m. to avoid incidents," reported youths in Nilakulam. The young women in that village reported that they had to stop their education because the school is too far away, saying, "Women cannot go wherever they want because they will be abused." In Muslim Thambulla, "Females have to ask permission [to leave their homes] and males always accompany us."

In most communities, youths say that multiple disadvantages interact to keep them from realizing their personal aspirations. In Kaithamavi, for instance, young women said they face a lack of facilities in the village, transport problems, social norms that prevent women from coming home late ("society will gossip and say bad things about us"), language problems ("we have to do everything in Sinhalese"), and the closure of the nearby factory. In Pothupana, young men spoke of living in fear because of the civil war. They lamented their inability to get a good education, both because of the war and because of the poor schooling opportunities available locally.

But it is equally evident from the discussions that these young people have not resigned themselves to a future that is permanently constrained by conflict and by the many other obstacles they face. They see themselves as more educated and aware than their parents, and several youths in the study openly said that their expectations for their own well-being and that of their community exceed those of older generations. A young man named Anton from Kaithamavi explained that while his father is a mason and his mother a housewife, he runs a shop and is saving to expand it because he sees a demand. Another youth from Kaithamavi reported that his father is a fisherman and his mother makes ropes, but he is employed as a tradesman by a local business. He learned his skills on his own and on the job, but again, like many youths across the study, he would like to see improved educational and work opportunities so that young people could get better jobs in the future. In Pothupana, male youths said they need better roads, a rice mill, and computer facilities: "If we get good infrastructure, especially roads, we can develop the village ourselves."

The youths appeared well informed about and actively engaged in the political and civic life of their communities. Young people in most communities hang posters, organize and attend rallies, and do other work for political parties during the campaign seasons, many with the hope of snagging jobs in the public sector through their political patrons. In Manivali the female youths said that "young people's ideas are keenly considered" when decisions are made on community affairs. And they said their divisional secretary secured resources to construct a training center after local youth requested one. Likewise, in Kumputhiri, the male youths reported that more people are participating now in community affairs, and they argued that "young people are the source of power in our village, so they are encouraged." In Nilakulam, young men reported that they work together to guard the community at night, and they recently organized a large protest over water problems in the village. Pothupana youths said that their Buddhist youth association has helped give youth a stronger collective voice in the village. The young people there worked together to evict squatters who had taken over an important gathering place for youth and others near the temple. The young men also reported that youth did not previously participate in decision making in the village, but with more education they have been getting involved in helping to combat local corruption and foster more open decision making. In Thambulla, youths said they participate in all important local affairs, including Samurdhi meetings, the Shramadana programs of the NGO Sarvodaya, and community meetings with local government officials. They also described the work of a youth club called Unity that offers classes in computer use, Sinhala language, and sewing.

Comments by male youths in Nilakulam reflect the complex internal and external struggles facing young people across the villages visited. Because the civil war makes their future so uncertain, they said, they "cannot plan anything in this condition." But still, the young men from this village of displaced families have fought back against adversity and fully expect that their lives in Nilakulam can be better still:

> We have a dream about our village in our mind. We see our village with roads in good condition, no temporary housing, a good playground, school-going teenagers, no army camp, a good water supply, and people with good, consistent jobs. We hope this dream of prosperity will come true in 10 years.

## What Matters for Poverty Reduction in Fragile Contexts?

> *We cannot predict it [future prosperity of the village]. It depends on either peace or war. If we get peace in the country, the village will be prosperous after 10 years by hard work of each and every one in the village. We have resources of Palmyra palm, sea, and land.*
>
> —Men's discussion group, Kaithamavi, Jaffna district

*We have facilities to do jobs such as in the forest, the paddy fields, and the sea, but people do not like to do much because they have fear of the war so they think it is enough to get food and basic things. We wish to move from here because our children also will have to face the same problem in future.*
—A man who has moved out of poverty,
Kumputhiri, Trincomalee district

*Peace, politics, and freedom. Those should be there to have democracy.*
—A discussion group of male youth, Thambulla, Ampara district

The 2002 cease-fire made a large difference in the lives of the communities visited in the North and East of Sri Lanka. In a relatively short period, markets were resurrected, farmers returned to their lands, houses and other infrastructure were rebuilt, community activism resurfaced, and families recovered some semblance of their earlier peaceful lives. But it is clear from this study that communities varied widely in the extent to which they were able to recover in this period and reduce poverty.

Intense periods of combat between the armed groups resumed shortly before the data collection ended in late 2005. Hence, in reflecting on the messages emerging from this inquiry, it must be stressed that they stem from circumstances made possible by three to four years of fragile security.

Neither a community's initial economic and infrastructure conditions nor the intensity and duration of the conflict it experienced turned out to accurately predict success in reducing poverty during the cease-fire period. Instead, the comparative case studies show that social cohesion and collective action, ethnicity, external development resources, economic diversification, and remittances from abroad played strong roles in shaping poor people's mobility processes. These factors often intertwined: for instance, strong cohesion and collective action sometimes enhanced poor people's access to external resources. Most significantly, ethnic and religious divides exercised a pervasive influence over the other factors, profoundly shaping access to livelihoods and external resources as well as incentives for collective action. With these linkages in mind, the study offers three general messages for policy makers and for researchers pursuing further investigation.[20]

1. *The quality of local democracy and governance can do much to support (or thwart) the opportunities that underpin recovery on the ground.* The nation's extensive poverty beyond the Western province reflects fundamental weaknesses of the Sri Lankan state and its failure to serve all citizens equitably. Politics is widely perceived to be rife with corruption. Whatever public investment a village did manage to snare was often associated

with a particular member of Parliament—partisan spoils rather than the work of a professional and responsive bureaucracy. Issues of ethnicity have affected Sri Lanka's political and policy environment since independence. Successive parties have achieved electoral success by portraying themselves as champions of specific ethnic groups, and political parties continue to play the ethnicity card to garner support. As a result, there is a general belief that narrowly defined ethnic agendas drive much of the political and governmental process in Sri Lanka. This may help explain why in those communities that seem to be doing well since the cease-fire— where substantial public assistance has flowed in for reconstruction and where people perceive more access to their elected officials—study respondents still strongly insist that there is no real democracy. Even in Nelutanga, a remote Sinhalese village of the South that is completely outside of the conflict zone at present, a villager described democracy as "an empty word now, without any meaning." Along with the more standard problems of government effectiveness, people everywhere raised basic questions about legitimacy, fairness, and representation.

A notable exception to people's sharply negative perceptions of their government is the Samurdhi antipoverty program. It was present in every community, although its workings varied widely from one village to the next in ways that did not seem to have much to do with need. For some people, its presence may represent a stamp of citizenship, government recognition, and belonging that is more significant than its modest grants, loans, and other projects (CEPA 2006). The existence of the Samurdhi program in a community conveys official recognition of the deprivation and poverty that exist there, and often this triggers other types of assistance to Samurdhi recipients from NGOs and private organizations. Still, evaluations of the Samurdhi program corroborate reports in several study villages of poor targeting, meager assistance levels, and unreliable disbursements. Glinskaya (2000) finds that Samurdhi missed 36 percent of the households in the lowest expenditure quintile while around 40 percent of its budget went to relatively well-off households. She also reports that the benefits are well targeted to the country's poorest regions and that the poor outcomes mostly reflect difficulties with targeting on the ground within communities. Again, in Jaffna and Trincomalee districts, Samurdhi was more appreciated and active in the study communities that showed more cohesion and social capital. Mobilization of villagers for the shared labor and savings components of the program requires a degree of community organization and a sense of collectivity. The study shows that communities with these characteristics are better able to utilize the full range of services provided by the Samurdhi program.

2. *Policies need to be sensitive to the ethnic composition of communities and should strive to reduce the formidable barriers that disadvantaged groups encounter in accessing opportunities.* The study reveals that in the conflict zones of the East, where settlement patterns have become largely segregated by ethnicity, trust between groups was shattered by the war and remained strained during the cease-fire years. Young and old everywhere voiced fears of traveling to, trading with, working in, and seeking public services in communities of different ethnicity from their own. Tamils, Sinhalese, and Muslims still moved about, got on with their livelihoods, and received services, but with far more difficulty in such a divisive environment.

   The poverty reduction performance of the two Muslim villages was substantially lower than that of the Tamil and Sinhalese villages visited in the East, with the latter two reporting many more opportunities for accessing markets, wage work, credit, and external partnerships. In the district of Ampara, to cite one example, numerous young women in the Sinhalese village found factory work, but young women in the Muslim village did not, although they expressed an interest in it. Of all the groups that contributed to the study, Muslim women seemed most affected by barriers to their mobility. Poor security, discrimination outside the community, and cultural norms all combine to restrict Muslim women's ability to travel and work beyond their communities.[21] Few loan programs were reported in the Muslim villages, while the Sinhalese village of Pothupana has so many credit schemes that people play them off one another. Initiatives are needed to help to rebuild relationships and organizations that cut across ethnic and religious lines, so that disadvantaged communities and individuals can participate more fully in market and civic opportunities and access public services.

3. *Policies should recognize the importance of social cohesion and collective action for inclusive recovery processes. However, conflict can profoundly alter the functioning of these bonds, which can hinder as well as help movements out of poverty, depending on the local context.* Kaithamavi in Jaffna suffered greatly during the conflict, and its local economy was largely crippled. But widespread poverty reduction still followed the cease-fire. With strong cohesion, community organization, and diverse grassroots groups, people mobilized to address the challenges facing them, and the community kept at bay the crime, youth violence, and alcoholism that plagued the other Jaffna community, Manivali. Kaithamavi also attracted more support for its recovery. From the comparative case study in the district of Trincomalee, collective

action again emerges as an important dimension that distinguishes the village with the highest mobility, Nilakulam. There people took to the streets to get their squatter community of displaced families literally placed on the map, which in turn put the village on the radar of NGOs.

By contrast, conflict ushered in increased inequality and exclusion for Manivali. Its better-off households found ways to adapt to and even benefit from the situation by sending family members overseas and by taking advantage of local opportunities wherever they might be found—including land ownership irregularities or monopoly practices made possible by security restrictions that kept out market competition. Meanwhile, poor people who depended on farming and coastal resources struggled to cope by working at poorly paying and unreliable petty trades, wage labor, and construction. They had few leaders or organizations to which they could turn to ease their difficult recovery.

The influence of local cohesion and collective action, in and of themselves, on movement out of poverty should not be overstated. High-mobility Pothupana displayed little unity but found other paths to inclusive growth due to varied central government investments. Meanwhile, Muslim communities are well known for being close-knit, but their disadvantaged ethnic status combined with the harsh external environment constrained the ability of these villages to forge external partnerships and attract resources.

Recovery assistance should be responsive to these variations in local cohesion and organizational capacities. In less promising environments, such as Manivali's, external resources will be unlikely to contribute to poverty reduction unless complementary investments are made to address local problems of exclusionary and weak institutions and violent crime.

Perhaps the most hopeful news from the study is that young men and women across Sri Lanka express aspirations for peace in their communities. Now that the war has ended, governments, donors, and NGOs should work with Sri Lankans, young and old, to restore cohesion and trust across social groups and build a future of peace, prosperity, reconciliation, and fairness.

## Notes

The Sri Lanka conflict study is part of the global Moving Out of Poverty study led by Deepa Narayan in the Poverty Reduction and Economic Management (PREM) Network of the World Bank. For a discussion of key study concepts and data collection methods, see chapter 1 and the appendixes to this volume. Also see volume 2 of the Moving Out of Poverty series (Narayan, Pritchett, and Kapoor 2009) and the study methodology guide (Narayan and Petesch 2005).

Lead researcher for the Sri Lanka conflict study was Prashan Thalayasingam at the Center for Poverty Analysis (CEPA) in Colombo. This chapter draws on "Moving Out of Poverty in Conflict-Affected Areas of Sri Lanka," a paper prepared by CEPA and available on the Moving Out of Poverty study Web site (http://go.worldbank .org/9ER0AOIH20). In addition, new analysis was conducted for this chapter from the very rich qualitative field reports prepared by CEPA. Shonali Sardesai, Per Wam, and Ashutosh Varshney provided helpful comments on the chapter.

1. To protect the privacy of participants, this chapter uses pseudonyms for the nine study villages. Cities, districts, and provinces are identified by their real names.

2. The "Indian Tamils" are concentrated mainly in the central highlands, where they first came to work on colonial tea estates in the 1800s. The "Sri Lankan Tamils" are considered to be native to the island, having arrived in ancient times.

3. The JVP was initially Marxist and multiethnic, but its platform evolved into one stressing Sinhalese nationalist causes. Its members campaign against political compromises with Tamils.

4. For more detail, see the synthesis report on the Sri Lanka research (CEPA 2006).

5. Because of the absence of district-level growth data, unemployment data where available were used as a proxy indicator for growth. Sample selection based on conflict intensity was determined by available data at the district level on the number of internally displaced people in the North and East and on the number of reported killings in the South. However, the final intensity ratings provided in table 12.3 are derived from a systematic review of the qualitative data on conflict, with the high-conflict communities reporting at least five combatant or noncombatant deaths along with extensive injuries, displacements, or property destruction in the village. It is important to note that the four "no-conflict" villages all experienced episodes of conflict in the late 1980s or early 1990s—but this is prior to the 1995 initial study year for the global comparative analysis.

6. The World Bank's Sri Lanka poverty assessment (2007, xv), examining 2003/04 survey data from the country's Central Bank, found that transfers represented 37 percent and 24 percent, respectively, of household incomes in the Northern and Eastern provinces (although data for some of the poorest areas in these provinces were not available). This compares to 16 percent of incomes in the Western province. Consistent with reports on the importance of transfers at higher steps of the ladder, Glinskaya (2000) finds that 7.5 percent of households in the top quintile receive private transfers compared to 2 percent of households in the lowest quintile.

7. A quote from a male discussion group in Kaithamavi is illustrative of many other responses to study questions about migration trends in the village: "The people who left permanently had wealth and relatives in other areas of the country. After getting enough foreign earning, people move to developed areas or to foreign countries where they can live peacefully."

8. It is important to note that the four "no-conflict" villages all experienced episodes of conflict in the late 1980s or early 1990s, associated with either the JVP or the Tamil insurgency. But because 1995 marks the initial study year for the cross-country comparative analysis in this volume, these communities are classified as no-conflict here.

9. The government of Sri Lanka invited the IPKF to prepare the North and East for fulfillment of new peace terms at a time when the Sri Lankan military was needed elsewhere to quell JVP unrest.

10. Women in the coastal villages visited for the study frequently engaged in making ropes, mats, and other handicrafts that they refer to as coir work. The fiber for these very durable goods is made by harvesting coconut husks and soaking them in sea water. But the imposition of high-security zones along the coasts made it difficult for many women to continue this work, and the market has also been affected by competition from synthetic products.

11. In Pesavankalai, most people also lacked their deeds when they returned in 2002 to find their village completely leveled. In this case, however, the government intervened and provided lots along with deeds, and NGOs followed quickly with housing assistance.

12. However, villagers also reported that the housing materials and finance provided were insufficient to allow people to rebuild their homes completely. And many other families did not make it into the scheme and still need help with rebuilding their houses.

13. Shonali Sardesai (World Bank), personal communication, September 16, 2008.

14. In Trincomalee and Ampara districts where the study took place, Muslims outnumber Tamils. In the third district of the East, Batticaloa, Tamils make up three-quarters of the population and Muslims the remainder (International Crisis Group 2008).

15. In this election the Sri Lanka Freedom Party campaigned as the United Peoples Freedom Alliance in coalition with a number of other leftist and nationalist parties.

16. Because of its status as a receiving area for the displaced, Nilakulam is not typical of other villages in this area. According to Per Wam of the World Bank, the majority of villagers in Trincomalee depend on agriculture and own 1–2 hectares of paddy land. During much of the study period, the LTTE controlled some 70 percent of the land area in Batticaloa, including all the best agricultural land. The biggest obstacles facing small farmers were difficulties obtaining fertilizer and other inputs and getting their produce to market. They also faced problems moving around because of army checkpoints in government-controlled zones, but the government did run services in health and education, as did the LTTE (personal communication, October 6, 2008).

17. See Kalyvas (2006) for important conceptual and empirical work on the frequent presence of malicious opportunism in the context of civil wars.

18. In Kumputhiri, for instance, there are reports of daily wages of 350 rupees on area paddy fields, but there is work for only 20 days a month—or none at all if there is no rain.

19. Relative to those in Trincomalee, the Muslim politicians of Ampara are better connected politically, with ambitious leaders in Parliament and elsewhere. Thus, they are able to deliver quite extensive "pork" to their constituents (Per Wam, personal communication, October 6, 2008).

20. We recognize that the sample is too small to draw definitive policy conclusions about the importance of factors such as ethnicity or social capital for poor people's

mobility. Significantly, the Sri Lanka poverty assessment finds *no* correlation between a household head's religion or ethnicity and the incidence of poverty (World Bank 2007, 28). It may be that the importance of ethnicity emerges more strongly from community-level than from household-level analysis. However, the World Bank's data, as indicated earlier, exclude the Northern and Eastern provinces, which have the greatest presence of minority ethnic groups.

21. It is important to note that some young Muslim women are being sent overseas for jobs, cultural strictures notwithstanding. They are sent mainly as domestic workers to the Middle East. Families apparently believe that if dire economic circumstances compel their young women to work outside the country, they will be better off working in Muslim countries, within a familiar religious and social setting.

# References

Abeyratne, S. 2004. "Economic Roots of Political Conflict: The Case of Sri Lanka." *World Economy* 27 (8): 1295–1314.

Ariyaratne, R. A. 2003. "Sri Lanka: On the Edge of Internal Displacement." *Forced Migration Review* 17: 33–34.

Bebbington, A., A. Dani, A. de Haan, and M. Walton. 2008. "Equity, Inequality Traps and Institutions: Cross-Disciplinary Views." In *Institutional Pathways to Equity: Addressing Inequality Traps*, ed. A. Bebbington, A. Dani, A. de Haan, and M. Walton. Washington, DC: World Bank.

CEPA (Centre for Poverty Analysis). 2006. "Moving Out of Poverty in Conflict-Affected Areas of Sri Lanka." Produced by CEPA for the World Bank. Available on the Moving Out of Poverty Web site, http://go.worldbank.org/W5GYDQE5N0.

Glinskaya, E. 2000. "An Empirical Evaluation of Samurdhi Program." Background paper for Sri Lanka Poverty Assessment, Report 22-535-CE. World Bank, Washington, DC.

Goodhand, J., D. Hulme, and N. Lewer. 2000. "Social Capital and the Political Economy of Violence: A Case Study of Sri Lanka. *Disasters* 24 (4): 390–406.

Horowitz, D. L. 2000. *Ethnic Groups in Conflict*, 2nd ed. Berkeley: University of California Press.

International Crisis Group. 2008. "Sri Lanka's Eastern Province: Land, Development and Conflict." Asia Report 159, International Crisis Group, Colombo and Brussels.

Kalyvas, S. N. 2006. *The Logic of Violence in Civil War*. New York: Cambridge University Press.

Narayan, D., and P. Petesch. 2005. "Moving Out of Poverty Methodology Guide." Poverty Reduction Group, Poverty Reduction and Economic Management Network, World Bank, Washington, DC.

———. 2007. "Agency, Opportunity Structure, and Poverty Escapes." In *Moving Out of Poverty: Cross-Disciplinary Perspectives on Mobility*, ed. D. Narayan and P. Petesch, 1–44. New York: Palgrave Macmillan; Washington, DC: World Bank.

Narayan, D., L. Pritchett, and S. Kapoor. 2009. *Moving Out of Poverty: Success from the Bottom Up*. New York: Palgrave Macmillan; Washington, DC: World Bank.

Rao, V., and M. Walton. 2004. "Culture and Public Action: Relationality, Equality of Agency, and Development." In *Culture and Public Action*, ed. V. Rao and M. Walton, 3–36. Stanford, CA: Stanford University Press.

Sengupta, R. 2006. "Globalisation and Inequality: The Global Scenario and South Asia." In *Does Inequality Matter? Exploring the Links between Poverty and Inequality*, ed. P. Thalayasingam and K. Arunasalam, 193–233. Colombo: Centre for Poverty Analysis.

Uyangoda, J. 2007. *Ethnic Conflict in Sri Lanka: Changing Dynamics*. Washington, DC: East-West Center.

World Bank. 2005. *World Development Report 2006: Equity and Development*. New York: Oxford University Press.

———. 2007. *Sri Lanka Poverty Assessment: Engendering Growth with Equity: Opportunities and Challenges*. Report 36568-LK. Washington, DC: World Bank.

# Post-Taliban Recovery and the Promise of Community-Driven Development in Afghanistan

*Deepa Narayan, Emcet Tas, and Philibert de Mercey*

*People were happy when the Taliban went away and the elections took place. But we were disappointed when previous commanders were appointed to the official posts. The drought and the lack of confidence in our government reduced the level of life in this country.*

—MALE FOCUS GROUP,
Shazimir, Kabul province

*Because of the conflict and also migration, the local economy was very poor and people endured many problems. The only thing that helped this community come out of poverty was to plant and grow poppy. Poppy is really what led this community to prosper.*

—QAYOUM, A MALE SHOPKEEPER,
Nasher Khan, Nangarhar province

**CHAPTER 13**

The windy Shomali Plain to the north of Kabul city is home to a rural community, Ramili Qali, located on the road leading to the rich Turkestan plains.[1] Once a peaceful agricultural community, Ramili Qali found itself in the midst of war in the mid-1990s. The conflict shattered the community beyond recognition, transforming its fertile expanses into battlefields and its rich soils and vineyards into a landmined wasteland. Villagers' properties were looted and destroyed. Facing imprisonment, destitution, and death, a majority of the community's inhabitants fled, leaving behind the ruined shell of a village.

## The Story of Ramili Qali

This experience of war and destruction was new for Ramili Qali. Before the Taliban era, the Shomali Plain was one of the most peaceful and economically vibrant regions of the country. Primarily a desert until the late 1970s, the region was settled after the Karmal government built an irrigation system on the Panjsher River in 1978. Thanks to its favorable location at the crossroads of main trade routes, the area prospered and became a commercial center in the following decades. Local farms produced a variety of agricultural goods, including one of the country's main exports, *kishmish* (raisins), which were sold in central Afghanistan and in neighboring Iran and Pakistan.

Before the Taliban takeover, Afghanistan's war-torn history included 13 years of *mujahedeen* resistance to the Soviet incursion, followed by a decade of civil war among armed political parties (or mujahedeen factions) called *tanzims*. These earlier conflicts did not devastate Ramili Qali. In fact, some villagers even earned extra income by smuggling weapons. But the rise of the Taliban to power in 1996 brought a major downturn. "When the Taliban first came to this area, they set our houses and our gardens on fire, cut down our

**419**

grapevines, and exploded the two siphons of the main water intake on the Panjsher River," recalled Abdul Qaher, a 43-year-old vine grower.

The destruction of the water system made it almost impossible for the villagers to survive, let alone farm. Looking for a more peaceful environment with new livelihoods, they pooled their resources to migrate and resettle in other communities. Pir Mohammed, a 60-year-old farmer, testified, "We left all of our properties and went to other places. About 450 families went to the Kashmir region of Pakistan, 50 families went to Panjsher, and another 50 were in Iran."

For the small group of households that stayed in Ramili Qali, the situation became steadily worse, with no proper irrigation and frequent harassment by the Taliban. In 1999 intense fighting around Kabul resulted in the establishment of a militia frontline in the village and evacuation of the remaining villagers. Abdul Qaher testified, "The Taliban put some of our men in jail and the weakest ones died there. They deported everybody else—women, children and men—to camps in Kabul and Jalalabad. Many of these refugees escaped and settled in Kashmir, where most of our villagers had moved three years ago." The conflict eventually turned Ramili Qali into an abandoned village, a battlefield for the Taliban and the Northern Alliance, while most of its inhabitants subsisted under harsh conditions in Kashmir. The women of the village said, "We were in a very bad condition in Kashmir. A lot of people were jobless and unhappy away from home . . . The children got used to stealing from people."

Nevertheless, the capacity of the refugees to stay together during these difficult times strengthened social bonds, kept good memories alive, and fostered a common desire to return and rebuild the community from scratch. After the fall of the Taliban regime in 2001, the Ramili Qali refugees returned in groups, only to find their community in ruins. "When we got back to the village, there were 2,000 landmines in the village itself, and 10,000 in the whole area including the fields," said Abdul Qaher. The region's economic resources, including its grapevines and water systems, had been destroyed.

In such a desolate environment, the returnees needed to push hard to reinitiate income flow. Thanks to its proximity to the capital city and its well-known economic potential, the Shomali Plain attracted numerous assistance programs after the Taliban ouster, which provided the momentum that Ramili Qali needed. These programs first addressed the emergency situation by establishing security, demining the fields, reconstructing shelters, rebuilding schools, and distributing seeds and fertilizers to farmers. As one villager pointed out, "Of course, our grapevines did not regrow immediately, but [external aid and infrastructure building] allowed our farmers to grow other things like wheat, maize, and poppy." Such short-term coping mechanisms—particularly poppy cultivation—played a significant role in the initial recovery of the community. They prevented many villagers from sliding into deeper poverty and allowed them to earn the income or credit necessary to establish more diverse livelihoods in construction, shopkeeping, and trade.

Over the long run, the interaction between foreign assistance and the villagers' capacity to unite for the collective good led to even more successful recovery paths. Putting the long-term development of their community before their individual interests, the villagers adhered to the government-imposed ban on poppy cultivation in 2004, securing in return several additional development projects. Similarly, villagers showed their preference for reconstruction over war by participating in the Disarmament, Demobilization, and Reintegration program and turning in old militia weapons in exchange for cash and jobs. They also proactively approached nongovernmental organizations (NGOs) and donors through their village leaders in order to maintain the influx of long-term community development programs, which they succeeded in attracting even years after the war ended.

The arrival of the National Solidarity Program (NSP) in 2003 reinforced these recovery efforts. The program helped establish inclusive institutions at the village level, and it worked with a partner NGO to deliver key development projects.[2] For example, the NSP strengthened the local agricultural cooperative, which supported agricultural production and other services related to transportation and exportation of products. It also facilitated capacity building at the community level by replacing the armed local leaders—previously appointed by commanders—with two democratically elected community development councils (CDCs), one each for men and women.[3] These councils became directly involved in the reconstruction process by inspecting and supervising NGO activities and development projects. They also solved local disputes, coordinated the distribution of limited water supplies, and organized an autonomous program to prevent the spread of drug use among youth.

These inclusive community institutions also encouraged participation among women and youth in Ramili Qali. The women's CDC made the decision to use part of an NSP grant to install electricity in the village, and young women started to leave their homes during the day to attend school or work at local NGOs—two remarkable developments in a country with a long history of strict gender norms that largely proscribe a role for women outside the domestic sphere. "I want to become a doctor, as there is no clinic in our area, and I would like to establish a clinic and hospital in this village," said Sogufa, an 18-year-old female student, showing her desire to contribute to community development. For both women and men, the rise of self-confidence and hope has been an important complement of the inclusive post-Taliban environment in Ramili Qali. Male youth stated their belief in change, even in commonly rigged areas like politics: "Before, we had no contact with the district government, but now we can easily go to the district and meet the *uluswal* [district manager] when we face any problem . . . There will be more positive changes 10 years from now, especially with respect to bribes, corruption, and administrative reforms. We are optimistic about our future."

In 2006, a decade after the horrific events that destroyed Ramili Qali, the villagers were confident that their community had a brighter future ahead. Pir Mohammed said, "There is security where we live. Many improvements like electricity, water, schools, and roads have already been prepared for us, and we can expect these things to get better in the future." Abdul Qaher's testimony was a tribute to the social aspects of participatory development: "We can now get informed about events through television and radio. People can voice their problems through the council." All the villagers agreed that "everybody benefits from these changes because [they] are all in the same boat."

Events since 2006, however, have cast doubt upon the villagers' hopes for security and prosperity. Security has degraded considerably since 2006 due to an increase in the activities of both opposition factions and criminal groups. The United Nations now considers most of the southern half of the country to be at high or extreme risk. In addition, most provinces and districts surrounding Kabul are deemed unsafe. Attacks on foreign or governmental forces and on civilians have increased steadily, with peaks every summer. The security situation impedes both rule of law and economic development processes in areas already deprived of government and aid presence, thus generating discontent and encouraging collaboration with opposition groups. A renewed effort to break this vicious circle is underway, with a large set of military operations to be followed immediately by a massive injection of aid money in the most problematic areas.

## An Inclusive Approach to Reconstruction

*A proverb says: When a brick is dislodged from its place, it is very difficult to place it correctly again.*
—Sultan Ahmad, a 45-year-old man, Zakwak Ulya, Herat province

Ramili Qali went through near-complete destruction after the mid-1990s and then recovered rapidly in the post-Taliban era (figure 13.1). Many rural

**FIGURE 13.1**
**Collapse and recovery of community well-being in Ramili Qali, Afghanistan**

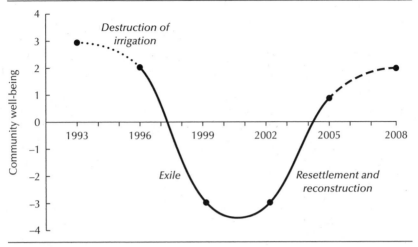

Source: Household questionnaire.
Note: Community well-being is consolidated from ratings of individual well-being on a ladder of life.
The solid line represents the study period.

communities in postconflict Afghanistan shared similar experiences of war and destruction.[4] Nationwide, more than two decades of war left behind a devastated infrastructure, weak institutions, and crushed livelihoods. The conflict displaced over 6 million people, many of whom lived or continue to live in exile. It shredded the social and institutional fabric of a peaceful nation, eventually turning it into a safe haven for extremist movements and illegal groups at the turn of the twenty-first century. While many communities, especially in the eastern and southern parts of the country, were struggling, others like Ramili Qali recovered with the help of a combination of factors, including external assistance and community-driven reconstruction.

This chapter examines six communities, five rural and one urban, to highlight the conditions that seem to have influenced postconflict transition paths in the relatively secure northern half of Afghanistan (map 13.1). By examining communities that experienced different trajectories of war and different postconflict environments, we try to learn about the factors that affect people's quest for recovery. We explore the interactions between individual and collective mobility efforts on the one hand and postconflict livelihood opportunities, external assistance, local democracy, and social links on the other hand. As we try to capture the underlying sources and sequencings that

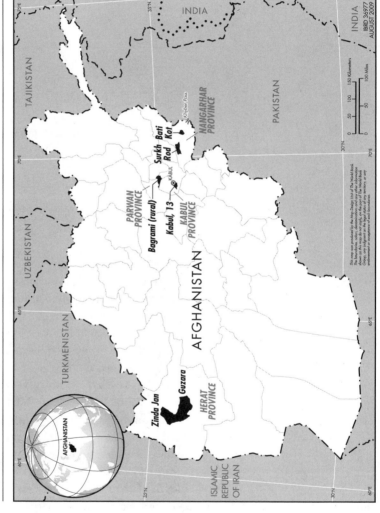

**MAP 13.1**
**Afghanistan with study districts**

yielded successful transitions, we encounter both disappointment and hope in local people's testimonies.

The people of Afghanistan began a new quest for postconflict normalization and development after the removal of the Taliban regime and the installation of an interim government in 2001. Thanks in part to growing international attention and aid, the new government implemented a wide range of national reconstruction and development programs. In the years following the removal of the Taliban, foreign aid made up as much as 40 percent of the national income and nearly 90 percent of government expenditures, contributing to an astonishing growth rate of 29 percent in 2002 and 13 percent (on average) between 2003 and 2006.[5] Despite this impressive performance, aid-driven aggregate growth did not always translate into successful local recovery, mainly because of four problems.

First, a significant portion of the foreign aid was used in 2001–02 to finance short-term humanitarian needs, while long-term reconstruction projects remained underfunded. In 2004 Afghanistan had the lowest aid per capita figure among all postconflict reconstruction cases (Rubin et al. 2004), and the country has received only 60 percent of $25 billion that was pledged by the international community in 2001.[6] Second, the persistent threats by Taliban commanders and the frequent Taliban attacks on aid workers continue to limit the outreach of development programs, especially outside the periphery of secure city centers like Kabul and Jalalabad. Third, there are growing concerns that the limited government funds have not always been used in the best possible way. Due in part to limited human capital in Afghanistan, aid absorption by the local population was constrained, and hence the funds were often spent on national projects run by foreign contractors rather than delivered directly through participatory community programs (Ghani and Lockhart 2008). Finally, drought gripped the heavily agricultural economy, becoming more intense toward the end of the 1990s and stretching into the early years of the next decade.

These problems contributed to two discouraging trends.[7] One was a surge of illegal activities centered around poppy farming and the narcotics trade, both of which have thrived since 2001, even in communities that had no previous history of poppy cultivation.[8] Illegal opium revenues were estimated to reach nearly $3 billion in 2005, an amount equivalent to half of the legal economy of Afghanistan (UNODC 2005). The other trend was a new wave of internal migration, a rural exodus that has altered the social texture and economic geography of the country. The control of remote regions by armed groups and illegitimate rulers, usually aided by the drug economy, continues to deepen rural poverty traps.

Despite persistent constraints and unmet expectations, the end of the war also brought security, legitimacy, freedom, and new opportunities to many. In this study, we found that even in the most difficult circumstances, small amounts of external assistance can make a difference when its goals are in harmony with local priorities and its delivery is supervised by community-driven development programs. This may be seen as an alternative path to postconflict reconstruction, one that builds on the hard work of millions of rural Afghans and combines state-building efforts from above with inclusive practices on the ground.

In the rest of this chapter, we give primacy to these local perspectives. We begin by introducing the Moving Out of Poverty study in Afghanistan and discuss the study's sampling framework, methodology, and data. We then turn to local people's explanations of individual and collective mobility factors and sequencings in the post-Taliban period. Next comes a detailed analysis of the three opium-producing communities in our sample, focusing on the motivation for and impacts of poppy cultivation. In the following section, the promising role of participatory local institutions, particularly the community-led NSP program, is explored in the context of evolving social norms and youth aspirations. We conclude with a few policy insights and recommendations to promote state-building efforts at the local level.

## The Moving Out of Poverty Study in Afghanistan

### Methodology

The Moving Out of Poverty study aims to explain why and how people move out of poverty over extended periods of time. It underscores the importance of context specificity and poor people's own perspectives about the factors that help or hinder economic mobility. Throughout, the focus is on long-term poverty dynamics and collective or individual pathways out of (and sometimes into) poverty. The quantitative and qualitative data are triangulated through pluralist research methods that gather detailed accounts of contextual realities. In the case of conflict-affected countries, these accounts help give a more complete picture of the drastic social, economic, and political changes induced by wars and the impact of these factors on mobility.[9]

One of the distinctive aspects of the study is that it lets local people define and explain, in their own terms, the transition paths that they and other members of their communities have followed. In other words, the study uses subjective measures of well-being developed in each community instead of applying universal definitions in different contexts. Community focus groups rank local households according to their perceived levels of well-being over the last 10 years, placing them on different steps of a figurative ladder called the ladder of life (table 13.1). The focus groups then collectively decide on a poverty threshold for their community, called the community poverty line (CPL). In order to avoid—or at least minimize—the bias of self-assessment in household responses, the community ladder of life exercise is taken as the basis of community well-being and mobility measures.

Every household is placed on a step of the ladder in 2006 and in 1995. The results are used to create a community mobility matrix that shows upward and downward movements of each household over the study period, both in absolute terms and relative to the CPL. Aggregate measures of mobility at the community level, or mobility indexes, take into account the movements of *all* households in a given community, as identified by community focus groups. For example, the ratio of the number of poor households who crossed the

**TABLE 13.1**
**Ladder of life in Riah Khillaw, Herat province, Afghanistan**

| | |
|---|---|
| Step 8 | Families that receive remittances from abroad |
| Step 7 | Government officials |
| Step 6 | Landowners |
| Step 5 | Skilled workers |
| Step 4 | People with a few *jerib* (up to 1 hectare) of land |

CPL —

| | |
|---|---|
| Step 3 | Disabled people |
| Step 2 | Families with no agricultural land |
| Step 1 | People with no land and no private house |

**Ladder of life in Ramili Qali, Parwan province, Afghanistan**

| | |
|---|---|
| Step 7 | Ministers and drug lords with power |
| Step 6 | Those who hold key positions in the government |
| Step 5 | People who can afford luxuries like a car |
| Step 4 | Tailors, shopkeepers, NGO employees |

CPL —

| | |
|---|---|
| Step 3 | Teachers and government employees |
| Step 2 | Low-skilled employees (waiters, guards, cart vendors) |
| Step 1 | The poorest, with no land |

*Source:* Ladder of life focus group discussions.
*Note:* The Riah Khillaw focus group created a ladder with eight steps and the Ramili Qali group created one with seven. Step 1 is the poorest step in each case. Bold lines indicate the community poverty line.

CPL over the study period to the number of initially poor households determines the "moving out of poverty" rate (MOP). Similarly, the ratio of the number of all households that moved up on the ladder of life over the study period to the total number of households in the community determines the "prosperity" (recovery) rate, or PI (see chapter 1 and appendix B for details).

Along with the objective measures of economic well-being that are collected through household surveys (for example, on initial assets, income, and credit sources) and key informant interviews (for example, on the presence of markets or infrastructure in the community), the subjective poverty measures constructed through community focus group discussions constitute the quantitative basis of the study. They are complemented by qualitative research methods that gather rich open-ended testimonies by women, men, and youth, both individually (through life story interviews) and in groups (through focus group discussions). These testimonies highlight the underlying factors that have influenced economic mobility as well as the social and institutional characteristics of the study communities.

## Sampling

In Afghanistan, the research methods explained above were applied in six relatively secure communities in four provinces—Kabul, Nangarhar, Herat, and Parwan. Given the interest in long-term mobility dynamics, the study period covered the 10-year period that began with the Taliban takeover of the government in 1996. It therefore covers approximately equal periods under the Taliban regime (1996–2001) and the post-Taliban government (2001–06).

The focus was on collecting rich and detailed accounts of collective and individual experiences *within* the relatively secure communities that were visited, rather than on maximizing the number of selected communities or the national representativeness of our sample. In particular, although sample selection tried to maximize the diversity of community conflict trajectories in the last two decades, even the communities that were severely affected by the most recent Taliban conflict were stable and at the reconstruction phase by the study's end in 2006.[10]

Nevertheless, a number of additional, observable community characteristics were also considered in the selection of provinces and communities so as to enhance diversity and sample variation. These included the degree of conflict-affectedness, proximity to a large city or a neighboring country, presence of poppy-related activities, degree of drought-affectedness, exposure to international aid, representation of the three main ethnicities in the country (Pashtun, Tajik, and Hazara), and an ad hoc vulnerability rating recently developed by the Afghan Ministry of Rural Rehabilitation and Development (MRRD 2005).[11] The resulting sample, summarized in table 13.2, entails a mixture of these characteristics.

Five of the selected communities were rural villages located within a two-hour drive of the capitals of their respective provinces, while one village near Kabul city, Shazimir, had the characteristics of an urban community. By design, the focus was on small villages of only a few hundred households, as the primary purpose of the study is to provide a detailed analysis of collective and individual pathways out of poverty within the socioeconomic realities of the selected communities. Although chosen with care, the sample represents a minute fraction of the country's estimated 38,000 communities (CSO 2005), and our conclusions do not necessarily carry over to other communities across Afghanistan. In particular, one must be cautious about the applicability of our conclusions to the parts of the country that were still conflict-affected and had not yet progressed to the reconstruction phase.

## Nuances in mobility outcomes across communities

A unique feature of the Afghan study is the presence of the governmental transition as an objective, nationwide "landmark" in the middle of the study period. This allowed the respondents to compare two drastically distinct periods, the first characterized by massive destruction and the second by postconflict recovery and reconstruction. It also implied similar covariant movements in mobility outcomes across communities (table 13.3).

An examination of the mobility indexes reveals some of these co-movements and other interesting patterns present in the sample. First, since the researchers imposed no limit on ladder of life rankings, each community's ladder of well-being differed in terms of its poverty thresholds and its number of steps. In addition, 84 percent and 68 percent of female and male focus group participants, respectively, placed the (subjective) community poverty line above the (objective) official poverty line (figure 13.2). Second, there have been similar and moderately large recovery trends over 10 years in *all* the study communities. On average, over 40 percent of all households in the sample experienced some degree of upward movement, reflected in the prosperity index (PI). Among the households that were initially poor, an average of 47 percent moved out of poverty (MOP). Third, the differences between the prosperity index and the *net* prosperity index (NPI) indicate that downward movements were also significant, especially in low-MOP communities.

Finally, there were moderately large differences in the moving out of poverty rates both within and across provinces. On average, 35 percent of

**TABLE 13.2**
**Profile of Afghanistan study communities**

| Community | Province | District | Main ethnicity | No. of households | Impact of conflicts | | | |
|---|---|---|---|---|---|---|---|---|
| | | | | | Soviet | Tanzims | Taliban | |
| Shazimir | Kabul (urban) | Kabul, 13 | Hazara | 400 | low | high | high | |
| Ramili Qali | Parwan | Bagram | Tajik | 550 | high | moderate | high | |
| Morlaw Ghano | Nangarhar | Bati Kot | Pashtun | 150 | high | moderate | moderate | |
| Nasher Khan | Nangarhar | Surkh Rod | Pashtun | 200 | high | high | moderate | |
| Zakwak Ulya | Herat | Guzara | mixed | 490 | high | moderate | moderate | |
| Riah Khillaw | Herat | Zinda Jan | Pashtun | 300 | high | low | moderate | |

Source: Community profiles.
Note: The number of households was estimated by a group of elders in each community, since official statistics for villages are not available. The study communities are identified by pseudonyms in this chapter.

**TABLE 13.3**
**Mobility outcomes in Afghanistan study communities**

| Province | Community | No. of steps on ladder of life | CPL | PI | NPI | MOP | FRIP | FRI | MRI | PSP |
|---|---|---|---|---|---|---|---|---|---|---|
| Kabul | Shazimir | 5 | 3 | 0.34 | 0.30 | 0.29 | 0.10 | 0.10 | 0.41 | 0.61 |
| Parwan | Ramili Qali | 7 | 5 | 0.41 | 0.27 | 0.58 | 0.22 | 0.24 | 0.22 | 0.52 |
| Nangarhar | Morlaw Ghano | 6 | 4 | 0.36 | 0.24 | 0.34 | 0.54 | 0.66 | 0.14 | 0.65 |
| Nangarhar | Nasher Khan | 7 | 4 | 0.53 | 0.43 | 0.61 | 0.50 | 0.50 | 0.11 | 0.82 |
| Herat | Zakwak Ulya | 7 | 4 | 0.37 | 0.12 | 0.40 | 0.09 | 0.19 | 0.36 | 0.34 |
| Herat | Riah Khillaw | 8 | 4 | 0.46 | 0.33 | 0.61 | 0.25 | 0.25 | 0.25 | 0.65 |
| Mean | | | | 0.41 | 0.28 | 0.47 | 0.28 | 0.32 | 0.25 | 0.60 |
| Standard deviation | | | | 0.07 | 0.09 | 0.13 | 0.18 | 0.19 | 0.11 | 0.15 |

*Source:* Figures are derived from ladder of life focus group discussions among men.
*Note:* CPL figures indicate the first step at which households are no longer considered poor. PI = prosperity index (all households that move up ÷ total number of households). NPI = net prosperity index (all households that move up less all households that move down ÷ total number of households). MOP = moving out of poverty index (initially poor who move above CPL ÷ initially poor). FRIP = falling of the rich into poverty index (initially rich who move below CPL ÷ initially rich). FRI = falling of the rich index (initially rich who move down ÷ initially rich). MRI = mobility of the rich index (initially rich who move up ÷ initially rich). PSP = percentage of households in community starting poor. Standard deviations measure the variance across communities. The high-MOP communities are shaded.

**FIGURE 13.2**

**Relationship of the community poverty line to the official poverty line according to focus groups of men and women, Afghanistan study communities**

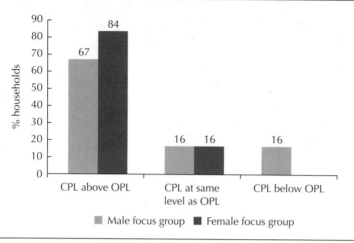

Source: Community focus group discussions with men and women.
Note: N = 91; OPL = official poverty line.

households in the low-MOP communities of Shazimir, Morlaw Ghano, and Zakwak Ulya moved out of poverty between 1996 and 2006. The corresponding average was 60 percent in the high-MOP communities of Ramili Qali, Nasher Khan, and Riah Khillaw.

On the one hand, the presence of moderately large and similar recovery rates across provinces suggests that nationwide recovery developments influenced postconflict mobility trends. This is also implied by the fact that the households immediately below or above the CPL had similar characteristics across the sample. Households at these steps often consisted of farmers, daily laborers, shopkeepers, and government employees. On the other hand, diverse poverty reduction rates across communities suggest that community-specific trends were not negligible. For example, the communities of Nasher Khan and Morlaw Ghano are both in Nangarhar province, but the poverty reduction rate in the former was almost twice as large as in the latter. While the CPL (according to the male focus group) was placed between steps 2 and 3 in Shazimir, it was placed between steps 4 and 5 in Ramili Qali.

These nuanced mobility patterns necessitate a closer look at the underlying local conditions. This is not possible in our household survey, since there are large covariate movements across communities and a small number of observations per community. However, the rich qualitative accounts gathered through key informant interviews, open-ended life stories, and focus group discussions among men, women, and youth provide lively illustrations of the factors and interactions that influenced socioeconomic movements in each community. The rest of the chapter centers on these local testimonies, which may help reshape future reconstruction efforts by bringing local people's concerns to the fore.

## Mobility in a Context of Endless War

*The government has collected the illegal armed groups' weapons and there are numerous security checkpoints in the city. There are also reconstruction projects and economic opportunities. People want to work, not fight.*

—Nadir Ali, a male shopkeeper, Shazimir, Kabul province

*If poor people work hard and they have courage, they can attain economic power.*

—Shirin Gul, a female laborer, age 47,
Zakwak Ulya, Herat province

Armed conflicts come in many forms. Sometimes they emerge at the national or international level and filter down to involve local actors. Sometimes they start in particular neighborhoods or villages and expand to become national in scope. Some conflicts arise from internal disputes and serve to divide societies; others are externally imposed and reinforce social unity by creating a common enemy. In Afghanistan all these forms of conflict have come together in a span of only two decades.

The Soviet invasion in 1979 triggered a nationwide resistance movement that went on for 13 years, reaching its peak after the mujahedeen factions unified in 1985 against the "common threat." The victory of the jihadists against the Soviets was followed by a deadly power struggle among the tanzims. This lasted from 1992 until 1996, when the Taliban seized control of the government.

International forces removed the Taliban regime in 2001 and helped broker an agreement for an interim authority headed by Hamid Karzai, who subsequently won the presidential election in 2004. The restoration of legitimate government appeared to mark the beginning of a more stable era in Afghanistan. This cautiously optimistic perception prevailed throughout the second half of our study period, despite a rising Taliban insurgency. The situation worsened significantly in 2006 as Taliban threats and attacks, initially confined to the southern and eastern provinces, started spreading to provinces that had been historically safer. As a result, insecurity is rising again, reducing foreign investment and leading the Afghanistan government to make security the first pillar of its National Development Strategy (Government of Afghanistan 2008).

Afghan participants in the Moving Out of Poverty study generally viewed the different conflicts in their country's recent history as one big war, rather than as multiple episodes with varying intensities and independent consequences. They perceived this war to have had long-lasting effects that are still felt even in communities that were not directly involved in the fighting. Local testimonies from four rural communities in our sample indicated that they were either severely or moderately affected by the earlier Soviet and tanzim wars, even though most villagers did not participate as combatants (table 13.2). Similarly, the four communities from Nangarhar and Herat provinces were not directly affected by the Taliban aggression in the mid-1990s, yet local testimonies revealed that these villages still felt the consequences of war through insecurity, limited economic opportunities, corruption, forcible recruitment, and illegitimate actions by commanders. Besmillah Khan, a farmer from Nasher Khan in Nangarhar, recounted, "During the six years of the Taliban regime, [Nangarhar] suffered from violence and corruption. [The Taliban] killed our villagers and burned our houses. They collected unfair taxes, controlled all of our actions, and sent our young people to fight." Similar stories were heard across other sample communities. Fazel Haq, from Riah Khillaw in Herat, recalled, "During the Taliban regime, no entrepreneur wanted to invest in Afghanistan, no construction took place, and poverty was at its peak. We were an unrecognized, illegitimate state, so we did not have any economic relationship with the rest of the world."

In addition to the instability and lack of economic opportunities, a drought in 1999–2004 severely affected agricultural livelihoods in four of the five rural communities in our sample.[12] According to government estimates, 60 percent of Afghanistan's 2.3 million hectares of irrigated land have been ruined since the first signs of drought in 1997 (Government of Afghanistan 2006).[13] The adverse effects of the drought were still visible in Nangarhar and Herat during our fieldwork in 2006. Akhtar Gul, a drought-affected farmer from Nasher Khan, said, "We had more water in the past, but since the drought is still a problem and the government is not paying attention to our situation, our condition is worsening year by year." Other farmers added,

"We will be better in the next 10 years only if the government takes immediate action and builds a new irrigation system."

In this context of massive destruction and natural disaster, it is hardly surprising that three-fourths of the most commonly mentioned reasons for downward shifts in community well-being were related to conflict or drought and their consequences, most importantly unemployment and lack of economic opportunities (table 13.4). At the household level, the three most important causes of downward mobility were also related to these community-level factors: lack of stable employment, job loss, and shocks to agricultural production such as high input prices and bad harvest due to drought (figure 13.3).

What were the factors that helped households and communities recover, move out of poverty, and take part in the postconflict reconstruction process? In the remainder of this section we discuss the sources and sequencings that influenced upward mobility and successful transition paths at both the community and household levels.

**TABLE 13.4**
**Reasons for community downward mobility, Afghanistan study communities**

| | Reasons for downward mobility | |
|---|---|---|
| Community | Cited by key informants | Cited by male (M) and female (F) focus groups |
| Shazimir | 1. Conflicts (Taliban regime) | M: Civil war, corruption |
| | 2. Conflicts (tanzim wars) | F: Unemployment, land conflicts |
| Ramili Qali | 1. Destruction (irrigation structure) | M: Taliban conflict |
| | | F: Forced migration, destructions |
| | 2. Conflict (Taliban regime) | |
| Morlaw Ghano | 1. Conflict (Soviet invasion) | M: War and corruption |
| | 2. National policies (ban on poppy) | F: Ban on poppy |
| Nasher Khan | 1. Drought (lack of irrigation) | M: Drought, war, and corruption |
| | 2. National policies (ban on poppy) | F: Civil war, kidnapping |
| Zakwak Ulya | 1. Conflict (communist regime) | M: Drought, migration |
| | 2. Drought (lack of irrigation) | F: Poverty, unemployment |
| Riah Khillaw | 1. Conflict (Taliban regime) | M: Poverty, unemployment |
| | 2. Drought (lack of irrigation) | F: Low prices, lack of irrigation |

*Source:* Community focus group discussions with men and women.
*Note:* The high-MOP communities are shaded.

**FIGURE 13.3**
**Most important reasons for household downward mobility, Afghanistan study communities**

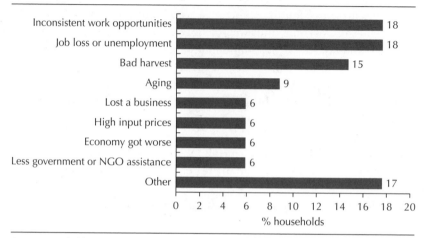

*Source:* Household questionnaire with households that fell into poverty over the study period. *N* = 34 responses. The category listed as "other" includes family size, rise in housing cost, decline in remittances, too much debt, and more corruption.

## Community-level effects of security and reconstruction

*Now that we have an elected national government, people are free of the previous regimes and their oppressions and destruction. We have security. People can do what they want. Now, there are economic and social activities. War is over.*

—Haji Kazam Ali, a 70-year-old man, Shazimir, Kabul province

Despite the looming insurgency in the second half of the study period, study participants perceived a real change in the security environment. About 70 percent of the households in our sample indicated that their community went from being "generally violent" to "generally peaceful" between 1996 and 2006. Accordingly, the most important community mobility factors in the post-Taliban era were related to improvements in national security and to building of basic infrastructure (table 13.5). These seem to have laid the groundwork for diversification of livelihoods and other paths to recovery.

After relative security was established, the communities in our sample started to erase some of the marks of war. Demolished water structures, roads, schools, and clinics were targeted for rebuilding with the help of infrastructural development programs (table 13.6). Demining of agricultural fields and

**TABLE 13.5**
**Reasons for community upward mobility in Afghanistan study communities**

| | Reasons for upward mobility | |
|---|---|---|
| Community | Cited by key informants | Cited by male (M) and female (F) focus groups |
| Shazimir | 1. Security (end of Taliban) <br> 2. Infrastructure (road construction) | M: New government, access to water <br> F: Return from exile, education |
| Ramili Qali | 1. Infrastructure (irrigation structure) <br> 2. Other reconstruction projects (schools, shelters, demining) | M: Agricultural inputs, NSP <br> F: Other reconstruction projects |
| Morlaw Ghano | 1. Infrastructure (canal building) <br> 2. Alternative livelihoods (surge in poppy prices) | M: Infrastructure <br> F: Skill accumulation in exile, security |
| Nasher Khan | 1. Security (end of Soviet regime) <br> 2. Alternative livelihoods (poppy cultivation) | M: Reconstruction projects, schools <br> F: Security, infrastructure |
| Zakwak Ulya | 1. Reconstruction projects (road construction) <br> 2. Security (victory of mujahedeen) | M: New government, security <br> F: NSP, reconstructions |
| Riah Khillaw | 1. Security (Daud regime) <br> 2. Infrastructure (electricity project) | M: Schools, infrastructure <br> F: Education, literacy and skills training |

*Source:* Community focus group discussions with men and women.
*Note:* The high-MOP communities are shaded.

**TABLE 13.6**
**Infrastructure improvements in Afghanistan study communities during the study period**

| Community | Electricity | Roads | Irrigation, pumps, or canals | Schools or clinics | Clean water |
|---|---|---|---|---|---|
| Shazimir | | ✔ | | | |
| Ramili Qali | ✔ | | ✔ | ✔ | ✔ |
| Morlaw Ghano | | | ✔[b] | | ✔ |
| Nasher Khan | | ✔[a] | ✔ | | ✔ |
| Zakwak Ulya | ✔ | | | ✔ | ✔ |
| Riah Khillaw | ✔ | ✔ | ✔ | | ✔ |

*Source:* Community profiles.
*Note:* The high-MOP communities are shaded.
a. Nasher Khan benefited from road construction around the city of Jalalabad.
b. Morlaw Ghano is located in a well-irrigated, government-owned farming area, and its irrigation structure was unharmed during the wars.

installation of proper water channels in Ramili Qali played a crucial role in reducing short-term vulnerabilities and allowing the community's traditional livelihoods to recover. Communities close to major cities particularly benefited from the reconstruction of roads, which restored villagers' access to markets and nonfarm employment opportunities. "The construction of our road has been very helpful for us. In the past people could not bring their goods to the market. Now it is easier to bring goods to the city on time and sell them," commented a respondent in Riah Khillaw, Herat. Another interviewee from the community of Shazimir near Kabul added, "There is a saying: time is gold. Thanks to this road, shopkeepers save at least half an hour going to the bazaar every day. People also save some money on taxi fares since the distance is now shorter."

Infrastructural developments and better security appear to have promoted the trend toward commercialization of agriculture in rural settings. In particular, given the proximity of the communities in our sample to large cities, the newly rehabilitated water structures and more secure transportation facilities enabled farmers to grow a greater variety of crops and sell them in the nearby markets at higher prices. In Ramili Qali, the testimony of Reza Gul on the favorable effects of security and market access is representative of other rural communities in our sample: "During the time of the Taliban, there weren't any buyers for our products. Raisins were cheap, because the Taliban blocked the roads and people could not export to foreign countries . . . Now, our men can go to Charikar and Qara Bagh [nearby markets] and they know about the prices. Our products generate a good income these days." New infrastructure also contributed to the emergence of new livelihood opportunities. For example, in Riah Khillaw, the new electricity structure enabled women to work as tailors and embroiderers at night, a development that villagers welcomed: "The fact that both women and men can work together and generate income for the family is an improvement for the community."

In addition, newly built schools, clinics, and water wells improved community well-being. In Zakwak Ulya, Herat, the villagers said that "after the NSP came to our village, we could manage to rehabilitate our school, to construct a clinic, to dig wells for drinking water, to build *hamam* [public baths]. Now we are going to start constructing a water supply system to each house." Female respondents in Nasher Khan, Nangarhar, mentioned that "in the past, there were a lot of diseases in the community, but now they have decreased because we have clean water, thanks to the help of international organizations." In Shazimir, Fatima, a 35-year-old tailor, said,

"Schools for the children are opened and there are teachers. Now, we can send our children to the school, which can help them to get better jobs and move up in the future."

While basic infrastructure was a prerequisite for future community development, infrastructure projects by themselves were not sufficient for recovery; complementary developments had to take place simultaneously. In remote regions that lacked access to urban markets or electricity, for example, the benefits from roads or irrigation projects were limited. Villagers in Zakwak Ulya, Herat, said, "During the season we sell our fruits at a very cheap price and in a very short time because we don't have cold storage to keep them and we can't reach different cities. Exporting to Iran is an issue; it is more expensive and difficult to penetrate the border these days. The lack of access to markets will cause farmers to fail." Others stressed that infrastructural developments must be synchronized with the government's import and agricultural policies so as to allow local producers to compete with cheap products coming from abroad. Sher Ahmad, a 60-year-old farmer, advised that "the government should impose import restrictions, buy our products in large quantities at a fair price, or distribute seeds and fertilizers to reduce our costs. Right now, all kinds of fruits come from Iran and we cannot compete with them."

Although NGOs did not have a large presence in rural Afghanistan before 2001, they have played a significant role in facilitating complementary developments in some communities. In Riah Khillaw, Herat, a newly installed electricity structure, connected from a nearby village in Iran, allowed an NGO to launch a computer training program that helped youth gain skills for nonfarm occupations. Similarly, construction of a new school by an NGO in Nasher Khan and the start of several vocational training programs helped villagers move into higher-paying jobs such as teaching, engineering, and government work. In Ramili Qali, villagers mentioned their gratitude for the seeds and fertilizers that had been distributed by NGOs. In five of the six communities visited for the study, employment with NGOs was seen as the most important change in livelihood opportunities.

The relatively secure environment and postconflict reconstruction efforts generally had a positive impact on community recovery paths, although some variance in the amount and type of assistance was observed within and across provinces (see box 13.1 for the case of urban Shazimir). To further explore the sources of poverty mobility and recovery in postconflict contexts, we turn next to individual and collective experiences and local people's mobility efforts.

**BOX 13.1**
**Lack of economic catalysts and postwar collapse in urban Shazimir**

---

Shazimir is a dense, urban residential community near Kabul.[a] A small rural village until the latter part of the twentieth century, the community expanded during the communist regime and became a cosmopolitan conglomerate that hosts three ethnicities (Hazara, Tajiks, and Pashtuns), two religious sects (Sunni and Shi'a Muslims), and two spoken languages (Dari and Pashto). For years, people from different backgrounds, primarily unskilled workers from neighboring provinces, came to this area to find cheap shelter and job opportunities in the city, and they established new livelihoods such as metal recycling, carpet weaving, and sale of spare parts. The community was doing quite well before the fall of the communist regime.

The spread of the tanzim wars to the area in 1992 divided the community along ethnic lines, leading many people to take up arms. As everywhere, conflict brought destruction and mass migration: "When the tanzim came, people were killed or injured during the fights; nearly every family had at least one *shaheed* [martyr]. A lot of people fled the community to take refuge in Pakistan and Iran." In 1996 the community was captured by the Taliban, which made the situation worse. "There was a psychological opposition between the armed commanders and the people . . . People were threatened, robbed and killed. Many people fled the community."

The remaining inhabitants of Shazimir and a small number who returned after the Taliban ouster received some external assistance, since aid programs were concentrated around Kabul, but this assistance usually focused on emergency problems rather than on long-term development. In rural settings, infrastructure and agricultural reconstruction projects could sometimes lift entire communities out of poverty, at least in the short run (as in the case of Ramili Qali). By contrast, the external assistance schemes in urban Shazimir were not very helpful in terms of facilitating community-wide economic recovery, as community cohesion was low, everyone had different livelihoods, and assistance did not focus sufficiently on improving economic opportunities and helping small businesses. Some new livelihoods were established through new technologies, computers, telecom companies, and jobs in NGOs, but they were insufficient to rebuild the community economically.

The community's proximity to Kabul—although it first seemed like a virtue—eventually encouraged many more people to leave Shazimir. As Rustam, a 30-year-old laborer, testified, "After the fall of Taliban, everyone was happy and returned to the country after losing everything during the war.

*continued*

But they could never get back to their businesses or normal life. Three-fourths of the people in this community are jobless." According to Mir Afghan, a 55-year-old shopkeeper, "Now, most people are jobless and they can be driven to commit crimes . . . If credits were provided with low or no interest, or if the government provided some work opportunities in this community, people would be able to recover. People in this community are very hard working. They could totally change the shape of their lives, if they had financial opportunities."

Lacking economic catalysts that could have promoted recovery paths, Shazimir had the second-lowest MOP rate in our sample. The postconflict developments were not favorable enough to keep this urban community, once a mosaic of different ethnicities and social groups, united in the post-Taliban era. Ghulam Jan, a 35-year-old electrician, said, "Many returnees left the community again to go to Iran and Pakistan, because there were no opportunities for them [here]." Although concerned that their village could soon become deserted, other villagers confessed that they too were considering migration.

a. For a review of the latest trends in urban poverty in Afghanistan, see Schütte (2005).

---

## Mass migration, rise of economic opportunities, and individual mobility paths after resettlement

*If the government and NGOs create work like road construction, then everyone will get opportunities to work as a laborer. It will be good if people can get work here instead of going for work somewhere outside the community.*
—Mina Abdullah, a female tailor, Riah Khillaw, Herat province

More than two decades of insecurity and economic paralysis in rural Afghanistan have left many people with but one option: to leave. The migration story of Belqis, a middle-aged woman, illustrates the repeated displacements that families all over the country have endured during the different episodes of war.

> As security and the economy were getting worse day by day, we had no choice but to migrate to Pakistan in 1987. We moved to Peshawar and started a new life. In 1995, we returned to our homeland and stayed in my father-in-law's house in Kabul. As the security situation was worsening there, we moved back to our former place in Ghorband [Parwan province] in 1999. After the wars ended in 2001, we used our savings to open up a dry-cleaning shop in [Shazimir]. We started a new life and we are doing better so far.

In a nation with millions of displaced people and refugees, our field teams encountered similar stories in all the communities visited for this study. Generally, migration was not a voluntary decision but an urgent necessity, forced by security threats or a stagnant economy in people's home villages. "During the war, many people left for Iran and Pakistan and stayed there, because they are better off now in those countries. But we haven't seen anyone who was not affected by the wars, became better off here, and then left," said Ehsan from Shazimir. In addition, migration was often undertaken collectively, by entire communities, rather than individually. In all the villages in our sample, people chose their migration destination according to the presence of friends and relatives, who helped them in their new surroundings by providing shelter, jobs, and moral support.

As in the case of Ramili Qali in Parwan, described at the beginning of the chapter, these mass migration experiences strengthened social links among villagers and fueled their collective desire to return. Yasin, a 38-year-old farmer from Nasher Khan in Nangarhar, recalled, "There was no hope for us in Pakistan and we were only waiting to see our country achieve independence [so we could] return. We felt very happy when we were able to come back, but at the same time we were afraid to see what had become of our village." Even though they knew their houses and properties had been looted or destroyed, many villagers still returned to their home communities as soon as the wars ended. This was the experience of Karim, a 55-year-old man from Riah Khillaw in Herat:

> When we went to Iran, in 1984, I had a lot of difficulties because it was not like our country. The first two years were difficult because I was not able to find a job; I was indigent. Then my brothers found me a job, I worked hard and learned new skills in masonry . . . I returned to Afghanistan after our community became safe and progressed faster in my own village by cultivating my own land. Now, I am an official employee and I also work on my lands. The level of my life is good.

Migration entailed many social and economic risks, even if it was undertaken collectively, and it was a traumatic experience for many. Nevertheless, it brought some social and economic benefits at both the community and household levels. On the one hand, villagers in urban Shazimir testified that "many people left and many people returned. People are more helpful and cooperative with each other now, because they all suffered together." Migrants' friends and relatives who remained at home also benefited from migration, although to a smaller extent. Households that received remittances from abroad were usually placed on the highest step of the community ladder of well-being (see table 13.1). However, regular remittances and other types of family donations were rare—on average, less than 10 percent of the households indicated that they received gifts from family and friends between 1996 and 2006. The most important benefits of migration came through exercise of individual agency, both during exile and after resettlement in postconflict communities.[14] Collectively, a majority of household responses in our sample indicated that the three most important sources of upward mobility were availability of more economic opportunities, better security, and steady employment in the postwar period (figure 13.4). Local testimonies reveal that individuals and households who learned new skills abroad ended up benefiting most from the new occupations and livelihoods that became available after the wars. Masood, an elderly male farmer from Zakwak Ulya in Herat, described the advantages of those who had migrated and returned: "During migration, many became literate in Iran. They can now work in the government and foreign organizations. They have a good income compared to everybody else." Similarly, women in Herat utilized the tailoring and embroidery skills they acquired in Iran, while lower-skilled male returnees found employment in construction projects as daily wage laborers, carpenters, or

**FIGURE 13.4**
**Most important reasons for household upward mobility, Afghanistan study communities**

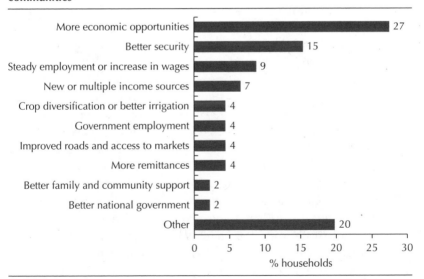

*Source:* Household questionnaire with households that moved out of poverty over the study period. N = 91 responses. The category listed as "other" includes improvements in national economy, health, education, and access to government services; migration; less corruption; and more responsive local government.

mechanics. Naim, a middle-aged farmer from Ramili Qali, proudly said, "I benefited from the masonry skills I learned in Pakistan. I am also familiar with agricultural work. This helps me earn some extra income next to farming. My economy is very good compared to 10 years ago."

Mismatches between the skills learned abroad and the opportunities available in the villages after return were, of course, possible. "Some people learned an occupation that was not applicable in the community, such as welding, tailoring, or carpentry. These people left the community once again and went to the city," said Niaz Gul, a young farmer in Nasher Khan, Nangarhar. In some cases the returnees found better-paying jobs in cities, which helped their households recover through remittances.

Even those who never migrated or learned new skills, however, could also exercise individual agency in the postconflict environment. Often they had to do so to keep their households from slipping downward. Drought-affected farmers and civil servants in Herat and Nangarhar—two groups below the community poverty line—worked in others' fields and commuted to other agricultural areas or to cities in order to acquire additional wage employment and supplement their regular income. Need drew some women, traditionally confined to the home, into the paid workplace as well. While 40 percent of the surveyed households had more than a single source of income, 15 percent indicated that both men and women in their households were active income earners.[15] In Riah Khillaw, Herat, villagers testified that "a female training and education center was opened last year and all the females of the community participate in this course. Women do tailoring in their houses, so both women and men work together."

Examples of hard work and successful transitions were encountered again and again in all the study communities. Najiya, an elderly female farmer from Riah Khillaw, stated, "My husband and I worked the land and also cared for livestock in the past. I used to have 10 sheep [10 years ago]; now I have 15. Because we have worked very hard on our land to cultivate vegetables, wheat, and other crops, we have been able to get enough food from our land." Many people emphasized that only through hard work could they accumulate enough earnings to invest in the future of their children. Shrifa, a young tailor in Nasher Khan, Nangarhar, said, "There is a person in our community who really worked very hard as a watchman to provide education for his sons. Now one of his sons is a doctor, one is an engineer, and one is a teacher. They live in the city and have a very good income." In urban Shazimir, where unemployment was high and mobility low, villagers claimed that "only if people are not interested in working hard is it difficult to move from one step to the next. If they work hard, moving up is not difficult."

To sum up, security and reconstruction efforts at the community level, combined with skill accumulation, hard work, and livelihood diversification at the household level, constituted the most important mobility factors in postconflict environments. However, in communities heavily affected by wars, these combined efforts often fell short. It is not surprising, therefore, that opium production has emerged as a lifeline for millions of households in postconflict Afghanistan. Focusing on the three communities in our sample where poppy was grown on a large scale, we next examine the sources of the opium economy and its effects on mobility outcomes in different contexts.

## Unfulfilled Promises and the Surge of the Opium Economy

*Karzai's government banned poppy cultivation, which was a big blow to our economy as people lost their main economic resource. Now a lot of people are jobless, and the income they get from wheat or other crops is not enough for their families. Our government did not provide us with an alternative livelihood, so if the situation continues like this, we are determined to cultivate poppy again.*

—Haji Mohammad, an elderly man,
Morlaw Ghano, Nangarhar province

Over two decades of war, individuals and armed groups coped with scarce economic opportunity by devising a wide range of livelihood activities—including some that were illegal. For example, the militias employed men as local commanders and recruited youth as combatants. It was common for men who had connections in armed groups to engage in smuggling goods. Such war activities were also observed in our sample. In Kabul, people reported that weapons smuggling was a good source of extra income during the tanzim and Taliban wars, while in Herat and Nangarhar, farmers said that the Taliban and the commanders pushed them to cultivate poppy in order to raise funds for the militias.

After the wars ended, the regions that did not immediately benefit from external reconstruction assistance, or that were exogenously constrained in their ability to diversify livelihoods, turned to illegal activities once again. Opium production was by far the most important of these; it kept expanding during and even after our study period.

By 2006, the opium sector exceeded half the size of the entire legal economy of Afghanistan, and it grew further after the study to account for 90 percent of the world's opium production in 2008 (Government of Afghanistan

2008). It was the opium processors and traders who profited most; small-scale poppy farmers in rural areas received a minor share of total revenues from the narcotics trade. Even so, the average annual income of poppy growers was roughly equal to the per capita income in the country in 2006. Farmers regarded poppy as an important source of income in the absence of alternative livelihoods, as no other crop could command such a high sale price. Research by the United Nations Office on Drugs and Crime (UNODC 2006) indicates that poppy cultivation reemerged in the post-Taliban era mainly as a coping strategy to address vulnerabilities rather than to enhance luxury consumption. Nearly 58 percent of the interviewed poppy farmers from poppy-growing regions of Afghanistan indicated that they grew poppy either to cope with poverty or because of the absence of livelihood alternatives and foreign aid. On the other hand, about 30 percent said that they were drawn to poppy by its high sale price compared to other crops (figure 13.5).

The two main poppy-dependent communities in our sample are Nasher Khan and Morlaw Ghano in Nangarhar province, one of the main poppy-growing provinces in Afghanistan. They illustrate interesting differences in the motivations of poppy growers and the ultimate impact of poppy cultivation on postconflict recovery paths. We now examine the postconflict mobility characteristics of these two communities in a comparative framework in

**FIGURE 13.5**
**Motivations for poppy cultivation in Afghanistan**

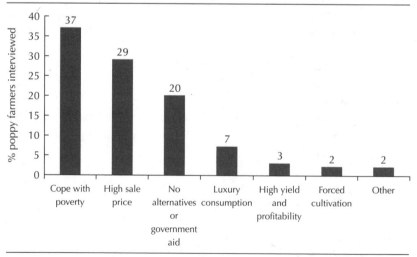

*Source:* UNODC 2006.
*Note:* The category listed as "other" includes lack of water during summers, high food prices, low sale prices for wheat and cotton, demand from addicts, and lack of enough land for other forms of farming.

order to understand the links between individual and collective mobility efforts, on the one hand, and the interactions between the government ban, external assistance, and livelihood diversification opportunities, on the other hand. For the sake of further comparison, box 13.2 presents the experience of Ramili Qali, a community that had no history of poppy cultivation before 2001 but turned to poppy briefly between 2002 and 2004.

**BOX 13.2**
**Ramili Qali: Giving up poppy in exchange for aid**

Poppy cultivation in Ramili Qali has a short history. Farmers resorted to the crop briefly in the immediate aftermath of the Taliban ouster, while they were waiting for their fields to be demined and their grapevines to regrow. After the government prohibited poppy cultivation in 2004, making the delivery of future aid contingent on compliance, the villagers in Ramili Qali voluntarily abandoned poppy cultivation. They did so in part to receive the highly beneficial development projects that were delivered to the area, but also because the main sources of well-being in this rich agricultural region had traditionally been grapevines and raisins. The decision to abandon poppy cleared the path for more aid-led development in the post-Taliban period. Since 2004, Ramili Qali has remained "clean," and the large sums of foreign aid it has received in return have enabled the community to restart traditional livelihoods and recover a measure of its erstwhile prosperity.

The villagers unanimously cited external assistance and reconstruction projects as the most important positive mobility factors in their village. However, the ex-poppy growers also voiced concern that the government's attention to their situation has diminished in recent years, especially in regard to the delivery of alternative livelihood programs.[a] They debated whether poppy cultivation might be used as a weapon to attract the government's attention and induce officials to keep their promises, leading to a second wave of aid-driven mobility. "We got some help, but not as much as Helmand or Kandahar provinces received through the alternative livelihoods projects. If we restart poppy cultivation now, maybe we can get more assistance and prosper more rapidly," said Abdul Qayum, a poor man. Although the issue was still debated in the village council in 2006, it seemed unlikely that Ramili Qali would risk the ongoing reconstruction programs for limited gains from poppy cultivation.

a. Projects that promote the replacement of opium-related activities with legal income sources, called alternative livelihoods projects, delivered large funds to poppy-dependent provinces. In 2006, $490 million was committed for this nationwide program. Nangarhar, as one of the main poppy-producing provinces, received around $70 million in the same year (Altai Consulting 2005).

### Poppy-dependent livelihoods in Nangarhar

*The government is not helping us at all. It does not allow us to cultivate
poppy. We don't know how we are going to survive.*
—Khudai Noor, a 25-year-old farmer,
Nasher Khan, Nangarhar province

Nasher Khan and Morlaw Ghano are located near the city of Jalalabad, the
provincial capital of Nangarhar and the largest city in the eastern region. Both
villages went through similar war trajectories during the communist regime,
and they received little external aid or development assistance in the post-
Taliban period. Like many other communities in Nangarhar, they also have a
long history of poppy cultivation. While Nasher Khan was heavily affected by
the drought during our study period, Morlaw Ghano, located in a green area
near the Sharq Canal, has always been well irrigated. Despite this apparent
advantage, however, Morlaw Ghano had the *lowest* recovery rate among the
five rural communities in our sample, while Nasher Khan had the *highest*. In
this section we explore the sources of these dramatic differences with a particular focus on poppy-related recovery dynamics.

Nasher Khan was subject to violent conflict and forced displacement
during the Soviet aggression in the late 1970s. This led to the familiar series
of events that we observed all over the country, starting with war and destruction, continuing with mass migration and accumulation of off-farm skills,
and ending with postconflict resettlement and reconstruction. "We were
eagerly waiting for our village to be evacuated so we could return. The Rus-
sians left our village in 1992 and people started coming back. Only then did
life return to normal," recalled Mohammad, a 38-year-old farmer. By "normal," Mohammad actually referred to an unusual situation characterized by
dependency on a single source of income. To reinitiate local livelihoods in a
dry and desolate region after many years spent in exile, villagers turned to a
familiar crop that did not require much water or effort to grow: poppy. "Due
to the conflict and also to migration, the local economy was very poor and
people endured many problems. We had to rebuild houses; farms did not
exist anymore . . . The only thing that helped this community to come out
of poverty was to plant and grow poppy. Poppy is really what led this community to prosper."

With the arrival of poppy dealers, who provided credit, seeds, and fertilizers to subsidize poppy cultivation, Nasher Khan rapidly became a well-
functioning poppy economy. Ahmad, an experienced poppy grower,

explained that most villagers earned six times what they could have earned by cultivating wheat or barley. He added, "We used to have two [poppy] harvests in this area, one at the beginning of spring and other at the end of summer. Sometimes we even had three harvests, when it was a good year with enough water." These earnings helped households move up and out of poverty, even allowing them to "afford some luxuries like cars and marry [their] sons."

After four years of increasing prosperity, Nasher Khan fell into the hands of the Taliban in 1996. Soon after, the drought took hold, reducing harvests and eroding the community's well-being. "When the Taliban came, drought also came into our district. Crops were reduced by 80 percent, which was a heavy economic blow to the whole region," said Ali, a middle-aged poppy grower. In addition, the Taliban started to collect *ushur*, a tax under Islamic law, which cut further into the earnings from poppy growing. Even so, the villagers said, "Given the difficult circumstances, at least the people were able to survive, thanks to poppy."

After the fall of the Taliban, Nasher Khan received very little external aid. Most of what did arrive was in the form of humanitarian assistance rather than alternative livelihood programs. Meanwhile, the drought, and the village's lack of adequate irrigation, continued to constrain cultivation. The villagers' savings from the glory days of poppy dwindled rapidly, and they desperately needed additional income sources. Fortunately, rehabilitation of the roads around Jalalabad in the post-Taliban period and the reopening of the brick factories near the village provided some nonfarm employment that helped prevent falls into poverty.

Just as the drought was easing and farmers were making plans to resume poppy production, the government passed a law that prohibited opium cultivation in Afghanistan. The villagers in Nasher Khan referred to this as "the most important disruption to economic mobility," since it rendered their major source of income illegal *without* delivering any alternative livelihoods or installing an improved irrigation system to support cultivation of other crops. It was up to the villagers to finance the transition to alternative crops or off-farm activities, but they had few ways to obtain funds to do so. Ali added, "Before, if I wanted to get a big loan, I could get it easily from poppy dealers. They knew that I was cultivating poppy and I will give the money loan back. But now, even if I ask for a small loan with a very high interest rate, nobody lends me the money." Other villagers confirmed Ali's testimony, saying, "They do not trust us because we are poor with no regular income."

The villagers in Nasher Khan were thus left to their own devices in their quest for postconflict recovery. Ironically, it was their pre-Taliban displacement experiences that came to their rescue. Since they had accumulated nonfarm skills in construction and other low-skilled professions during the forced migration, they were somewhat prepared for livelihood diversification. The village's proximity to Jalalabad, which prevented its farmers from secretly growing poppy, also helped them obtain off-farm employment. So did the reopening of the brick factories outside the village. Consequently, in the post-Taliban era, Nasher Khan saw growing income diversification that facilitated recovery and prosperity at the community and household levels.

In Morlaw Ghano, a different set of dynamics were in place, even though the two communities had had similar conflict experiences in the pre-Taliban period. Once a prosperous community whose farms had thrived since construction of the Sharq Canal in 1965, Morlaw Ghano was laid waste by the Soviet invasion and the subsequent communist regime, which bombed the area and burned forests around the village. There was an increase in crime and insecurity, as hundreds of thousands of refugees passed by the village on their way to Pakistan. As the security situation became unbearable, a majority of the community's inhabitants left their fields and properties and fled the village. "Many people in the community got physical and mental problems during the war against the Russian troops, and they migrated to other countries like Pakistan," remembered Nasir, an elderly man who stayed in the village. He added, "After the fall of communist regime, some of the refugees returned, but after a short time they fled again due to the fighting between the mujahedeen, never to return."

By the early 1990s, Morlaw Ghano was partly deserted. At the same time, the growing presence of drug dealers and mujahedeen commanders in Morlaw Ghano encouraged those villagers who could not leave the community to start growing poppy for a quick recovery. One villager commented, "Poppy is a very ancient crop here. It has been growing for centuries and centuries. During the mujahedeen wars, poppy cultivation was very common, even though the prices were not very high."

Morlaw Ghano was one of the rare communities in Nangarhar that was not affected by the drought. As a result, villagers in Morlaw Ghano continued to benefit from poppy cultivation throughout the Taliban period, unlike the people of Nasher Khan, who were forced by drought to seek nonfarm livelihoods. The poppy potential of Morlaw Ghano's well-irrigated fields turned the village into a magnet for drug dealers, who mainstreamed poppy cultivation with the help of the Taliban. Anwar, a 40-year-old farmer, said, "Our economy, mostly agricultural, was very good during the Taliban, because we had water, good poppy harvest, and a seller to buy our crops." This was true even though the Taliban charged rent for government-owned agricultural farms or redistributed land titles unfairly to its supporters. Rahman, a middle-aged poppy grower, emphasized that the community still managed to prosper: "People started to come to our village from abroad to buy poppy, so prices became higher and higher [increased by tenfold] during the Taliban. This was a boom to our economy and wealth. The best time of my life was from 1996 to 2004, as I earned a lot of money cultivating poppy."

Not surprisingly, during the Taliban regime the community became increasingly dependent on poppy as its inhabitants continued to pursue opium-led pathways out of poverty. The life story of Alhaj Saifor, an elderly driver, illustrates:

> In 1984, I went to live and work as a driver in Pakistan, because our life here was very sad. The Russian soldiers had taken the village from the mujahedeen and my 14-year-old was killed during the fights . . . At the end of 1992, I returned to [Morlaw Ghano] but my house was destroyed and my land was ruined. My sons started cultivating poppy and we got a good income. That year, I stopped working as a driver because we were getting a lot of money from poppy . . . I was very happy that I could buy three cows for my family with my savings. I reconstructed my house, in which we are living now, little by little with my savings. I want to stay in my community for the rest of my life.

The fall of the Taliban in 2001 did not lead to major changes in Morlaw Ghano. The community did not receive external assistance or development programs. Unlike the returned migrants of Nasher Khan, who brought diverse skills back with them, many refugees from Morlaw Ghano never returned to the village. Moreover, the village was located relatively far from Jalalabad, with no direct transportation link to facilitate daily commuting. Morlaw Ghano, therefore, had little way to diversify its livelihood sources away from poppy—and also no real reason to do so. The villagers were able to maintain the well-functioning drug economy in a drought-free and now also more secure environment.

A decade of poppy-led growth in Morlaw Ghano eventually came to an end with the government ban in 2004. When it happened, the villagers had very few alternatives other than shifting to other crops and growing vegetables like potatoes and watermelons, which brought in a fraction of what they used to earn from poppy. Only the households that had accumulated enough savings could afford trucks to bring goods and vegetables to markets in neighboring villages. Not everyone in the village had such savings, since farmers cultivated poppy on small plots of land and whatever they had accumulated over the years had been reinvested in poppy seeds or spent on household necessities. "Our economy is dependent on agricultural land. If we are not allowed to plant poppy, we need another crop that would let us survive," said Walid, one of many villagers who moved out of poverty during the poppy boom under the Taliban. He added, "Now, instead of poppy, wheat is being planted and people do not receive much compensation for it. In the past, people were able to buy cars, jewels, and gold. To make a good life is more difficult now." Omra, a 50-year-old female farmer, stated, "We used to be able to buy things and save money. Now, we only have money to have three meals a day and it is impossible to save. Sometimes we are sick but we cannot afford to pay for our treatment."

Given the years of dependence on poppy, the government ban naturally contributed to the reversal of mobility trends in Morlaw Ghano. "Everyone was wealthy in the past, but now there are more and more poor people in the community. Poverty is growing," said Malali, a young female farmer. Shimal, a 45-year-old male employee, complained that the lack of alternative livelihoods contributed to the community's desolation since the poppy ban: "There are no new working opportunities here. Life is getting more and more difficult. In Pakistan, there are jobs for everyone, so people go there with their families and together they earn enough to survive." Many villagers asserted that people were moving out of Morlaw Ghano because of poverty, and they feared that their community might end up deserted in the near future if alternative livelihoods could not be found.

### Learning from the two poppy stories: Self-induced transition paths in Nasher Khan

*This area has been badly affected by wars and then by drought. We are still suffering the consequences. But at least people can now go to Jalalabad, to Kabul, to Khugyani, and to other places to find a job if they cannot find one here.*

—Adeib Satar, a former commander and poppy grower,
Nasher Khan, Nangarhar province

The recovery and poverty reduction rates of Nasher Khan and Morlaw Ghano in the post-Taliban era were clearly influenced by their relative dependence on poppy and their vulnerability to changes in the drug economy. Both villages grew rapidly in the early years of the post-Soviet era, thanks to high demand for poppy and the availability of credit sources, and this favored poverty reduction. In the Taliban era, their paths diverged. While the drought encouraged Nasher Khan to diversify its income sources as early as the mid-1990s, Morlaw Ghano remained solely dependent on poppy until the crop was banned in 2004. Since then, Nasher Khan has prospered, while Morlaw Ghano has fallen on hard times.

An examination of the community-level dynamics reflects these distinct recovery paths in the two communities. First, it is apparent that there has been some poverty reduction in the last 10 years even in Morlaw Ghano, thanks to years of poppy cultivation. Thus, there is a modest increase in the number of households on the middle steps just above the CPL, and a downward shift in the number of households on the lowest steps (figure 13.6, lower panel). Although very few transitions appear to have taken place in the upper well-being categories, primarily due to the fact that poppy cultivation was small-scale, the postconflict recovery experience of Morlaw Ghano has nevertheless been more or less linear, with households at each step on the ladder progressing one or two steps upward relative to their initial position. In contrast to this, the upward movements in Nasher Khan have been dramatic, with households initially on the lower steps transcending the middle categories and reaching prosperity over the course of 10 years (figure 13.6, top panel).

These differences seemed to have been influenced by the latest migration experiences and by alternative income activities that the villagers were able to adopt in the absence of poppy income and external aid. In Morlaw Ghano, a majority of the prosperous households left the community permanently after the poppy ban in 2004 in order to look for better alternatives elsewhere. Those who stayed in the village were the poorer households that could not afford to migrate. In Nasher Khan, by contrast, the most successful households stayed in the community despite the drought and the Taliban regime, and they started exploring alternative livelihood sources as early as 1996. These households commuted to nonfarm jobs in the nearby city and brought their incomes back to the village, contributing to community prosperity as well as their own.

What were first thought to be unfortunate events in Nasher Khan—the drought and the Taliban regime—helped the community cope better in the long run by initiating an income diversification movement. Morlaw Ghano, on the other hand, remained heavily dependent on poppy throughout the 1990s and took a severe hit once its only source of recovery was banned.

**FIGURE 13.6**
**Shifts over 10 years in distribution of households on the community ladder of well-being, Nasher Khan and Morlaw Ghano, Afghanistan**

*Nasher Khan*

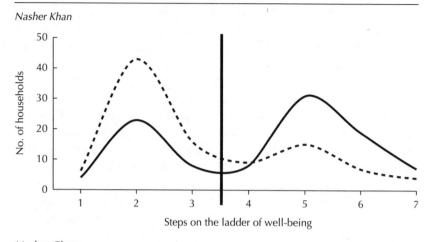

Steps on the ladder of well-being

*Morlaw Ghano*

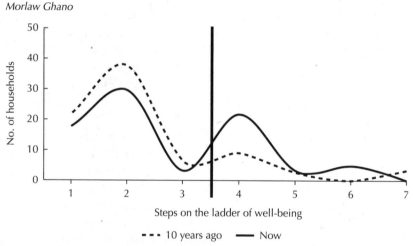

Steps on the ladder of well-being

- - - 10 years ago    —— Now

*Source:* Household questionnaire.
*Note:* Step 1 on the ladder is the lowest, or poorest; step 7 is the highest, or richest. The bold vertical line indicates the community poverty line. The dashed and the solid lines indicate the number of households on each step on the ladder in 1996 and 2006, respectively. Comparison of the two curves reveals the community mobility trends over the study period.

In addition to varying patterns of poppy dependence, the extraordinary mobility dynamics over 10 years and the uneven distributions of households on the ladder steps suggest that the two communities also faced additional postconflict constraints. On the one hand, Nasher Khan seems to have experienced a nonlinear mobility trend, in which households either stayed stuck on the lower steps or else jumped over the middle steps just above and below the CPL to reach the higher ones. This suggests the presence of poverty traps in the community.[16] On the other hand, a great majority of the households in Morlaw Ghano were either on the lowest steps of well-being or just above the community poverty line even 10 years ago, which suggests that the community was highly vulnerable even before the ban on poppy was imposed.

Villagers' testimonies confirmed that there were indeed additional constraints besides the prohibition of poppy. In Morlaw Ghano, they mentioned that "the prices of goods and food have increased. Most of our lands belong to the government and we take little profit . . . Most people below [the CPL] have very little land and will stay at the same level if the government does not build factories or give away free land." In Nasher Khan, villagers stressed the need for external assistance to promote diversified, nonfarm livelihoods: "The government should provide more loans and credit. It must build industries and create jobs for people. It also needs to support the farmers and improve our irrigation system for future droughts." The poor households in both villages added that one can move upward on the ladder of well-being if there are credit sources and more agricultural and nonfarm opportunities. They agreed that "if you do not get help, it is impossible to move."

In the absence of alternative diversification strategies or any kind of reward for adhering to the poppy ban, people in the two communities— particularly Morlaw Ghano—decided in 2006 that they had no choice but to restart poppy cultivation.[17] "The *uluswal* [chief of the district] told us that if people in other districts cultivated poppy, then we could also do so," said the villagers in Morlaw Ghano. Similarly in Nangarhar, the villagers said, "The people in Shinwar and Khogyani districts restarted, but we couldn't [because it was already too late in the season]. Next year we will also start cultivating poppy again." After all, since the government did not deliver alternative livelihoods or aid, it did not have much to take away as a punishment for growing poppy illegally. Unlike Ramili Qali in the Shomali Plain, which received numerous development projects in return for abandoning poppy (box 13.2), Nasher Khan and Morlaw Ghano had nothing to lose and everything to gain from giving opium poppy another chance.[18]

## The Promise of Local Democracy and Community-Led Development

*Local democracy is better now than 10 years ago, and it will be better in the next 10 years. Our people can go to school and university, girls can go out of the country to get education, and women can work. We wish that in the future everyone will have a job according to their merit and talent.*
—Abdul, a male youth, Riah Khillaw, Herat province

*Freedom is to take part in all the problems in the community, to get information, and to try to solve them.*
—Khan Bibi, a 60-year-old housewife, Riah Khillaw, Herat province

*One finger can do nothing alone; five fingers can do more things if they are together.*
—A male youth, Morlaw Ghano, Nangarhar province

In postconflict Afghanistan, as we have seen, reconstruction programs and people's own efforts have been *partially* successful in creating opportunities for economic recovery and poverty reduction. These efforts have been constrained by insufficient resources, unfulfilled promises, and lack of livelihood alternatives in rural contexts. In addition to economic factors, however, social and political factors play an important role in shaping prospects for mobility in the postconflict period. Local democratic institutions, social capital, and new social norms have influenced individual and collective mobility efforts and have also had an impact on the future of grassroots state-building efforts.

Traditionally, rural communities in Afghanistan are ruled by a group of unelected leaders and nonparticipatory institutions: the *malek* (village chief), the *shura* (village council of elders), and the *mullah* (religious leader). These local institutions are socially exclusive, for the maleks typically inherit their status from the family, the new shura members are appointed by the other members of the council, and the retiring mullahs choose their own successors. Not surprisingly, in the communities visited for our study, these exclusive institutions were perceived to be very powerful. "The chief of the village has political power. He is also the richest. The malek can put someone in prison and he can release him from the prison," said the villagers in Riah Khillaw. In Nasher Khan, Sangar, a young day laborer, said, "The chief of the village, the elders of the village, and the mullah have more power because people obey what they say. The workers have less power because people do not even listen to their opinions."

Alongside these nonparticipatory local institutions, people in rural Afghan communities also have customary social networks and other informal support mechanisms. These have thrived in spite of—or perhaps because of—the divisions and displacements induced by the wars. A fundamental social unit in rural Afghanistan is the *qawm*, a solidarity group based on kinship, residence, or occupation that can cut across ethnic or tribal lines. These informal mechanisms often provide a safety net at the local level, as indicated by illustrations of cohesion, cooperation, and trust from our sample. A typical household had participated in an average of 3.5 community activities in the previous year: the average number of activities ranged from 1.5 (in Ramili Qali) to 7.9 (in Riah Khillaw). Over 90 percent of households in the sample trusted that their neighbors would help them during crises. Similarly, 82 percent of households believed that people in their community would come together and pool their efforts to solve a community problem.

After the fall of the Taliban, the national and local governance institutions in Afghanistan underwent significant changes in connection with post-conflict state-building efforts. At the national level, the Bonn Conference of 2001 instituted a transitional authority, which set a timeline for the adoption of a new, democratic constitution and the creation of state institutions. The first elections in three decades were successfully held to elect the executive and the legislative branches of government in 2004 and 2005, with voter turnout of 80 percent and 50 percent, respectively.

A parallel democratization process has taken place at the community level as well. Participatory development programs, notably the National Solidarity Program, aim to strengthen democratic governance at the local level and build mutual trust between the national government and its citizens. These political reforms have challenged the nonparticipatory nature of traditional village institutions. In addition, they are trying to integrate people's own support mechanisms with formal local institutions and with the development efforts of the national government.

### The National Solidarity Program and community-led development

*Before the Taliban, disputes were resolved by religious scholars and elders. After the Taliban, a new thing happened: NSP came here and people elected a village council. Problems are now solved through this village council. Now there is an elected local government that represents people and that people can contact easily.*

—Abdul Qaher, a 43-year-old vine grower,
Ramili Qali, Parwan province

One of the boldest development programs implemented by the Afghan government after the Taliban ouster was the National Solidarity Program.[19] The program was launched in 2003 by the Afghan Ministry of Rural Rehabilitation and Development in order to support rural reconstruction and development efforts in needy communities through small- to medium-size grants and community-driven projects. It is based on the concept of participatory assistance, previously unknown in Afghanistan, which aims to empower local actors by letting them decide on and manage reconstruction projects. As of its sixth year, the NSP has reached over 22,000 communities and 359 districts in all 34 provinces of Afghanistan. It has financed over 46,000 community projects, 25,000 of which have been completed.

The program allocates $200 per household, for an average of $33,000 and a maximum of $60,000 per community. In order to be eligible for development programs through the NSP, communities are required to have a democratically elected community development council (CDC). In other words, the purpose is to enhance local democracy, capacity building, transparency, and accountability at the village level while supporting local development projects. The first step in the NSP-funded development process, therefore, is to help communities conduct a secret ballot election in which each neighborhood elects one or more representatives to the CDC. Communities can choose to have separate CDCs for men and women or opt to have both groups sit on the same council. Each elected CDC works with an NGO partner assigned by the ministry to identify community priorities and oversee the preparation of a community development program.

The CDC then chooses one of the proposed projects for implementation and sets the rules for project management, such as when to release the funds and how to supervise the work. By allowing democratically elected councils to control the implementation of projects, including the associated resources, the NSP aims to develop local skills in participation, consensus building, accounting, monitoring, operations, and maintenance. The program also seeks to link the CDCs to other government agencies, NGOs, and donors to improve future access to services and resources. As of 2009, there are nearly 22,000 elected CDCs in all 34 provinces of Afghanistan.

In our sample, some of these benefits were observed in the communities with the second-, third-, and fourth-highest levels of MOP, namely, Ramili Qali, Riah Khillaw, and Zakwak Ulya. All three participated in NSP-sponsored programs in the post-Taliban era. In particular, these three communities benefited from the social effects of the participatory processes initiated by CDC elections, including improvements in empowerment, gender norms, and youth aspirations. In addition, they appeared more likely than lower-MOP communities to have responsive local leaders and strong relations with the government (table 13.7). Since we have already discussed the workings of NSP-related mechanisms in Ramili Qali, we now turn to the comparative cases of Riah Khillaw and Zakwak Ulya, both located in Herat province.

Riah Khillaw and Zakwak Ulya are located in the fertile western part of Afghanistan, near the Iranian border in the west and the Turkmenistan border in the north. As in the Nangarhar study villages, many people in these two communities were forcibly displaced by the Soviet war and the communist regime during the 1980s. This was followed by collective resettlement after the fall of the Soviets. Thanks to the availability of irrigation and water intakes in the two communities, the resettled villagers were able to resume rich agricultural livelihoods, allowing the two communities to recover promptly. Although the arrival of the Taliban was associated with destruction of some infrastructure, neither of the villages was seriously affected by the Taliban regime.

Zakwak Ulya and Riah Khillaw were hit by drought in 1996 and 2001, respectively. This initiated a transition to off-farm employment through migration, skill accumulation, and diversification of income sources, much as was observed in several other study communities. In Zakwak Ulya and Riah Khillaw, the shift toward alternative livelihoods was aided by the proximity of these communities to Herat city and an industrial park near the Herat airport. Proximity to the Iranian border was also an advantage; many households were familiar with the culture and language of Iran, facilitating cross-border trade and migration.

In the post-Taliban era, both Riah Khillaw and Zakwak Ulya received significant external assistance programs through NGOs, international organizations, and the Afghan government. The most important, according to the villagers, was the NSP. Mawlawi, an elderly farmer from Riah Khillaw, said,

> After the formation of the interim administration and a transitional government, the reconstruction process started all over Afghanistan and also in our area. These projects helped the community to prosper. First, foreign forces based in Herat airport distributed food and medicines to villagers. Most importantly, the NSP program came to our area and we created a community development council, separately for men and women. We managed to rehabilitate our school, construct a clinic, and dig wells for drinking water.

The projects implemented through the NSP addressed a wide range of issues, including infrastructural developments, income generation projects, and acquisition of off-farm skills. In Riah Khillaw, Abdul Aziz testified that

**TABLE 13.7**
**Presence of local institutions and participatory development programs in the Afghanistan study communities**

| | Shazimir | Ramili Qali | Morlaw Ghano | Nasher Khan | Zakwak Ulya | Riah Khillaw |
|---|---|---|---|---|---|---|
| *Reconstruction* | | | | | | |
| Presence of reconstruction projects | Limited | Extensive | Limited | Limited | Extensive | Extensive |
| *Community institutions* | | | | | | |
| Form of community governance | Malek | CDC | Malek | Malek | Malek | CDC |
| Elected community council | No | Yes | No | No | Yes | Yes |
| Presence of NSP | No | Yes | New[a] | New[a] | Yes | Yes |
| Leader perceived to play a positive role in community development | | Yes | Yes | | Yes | Yes |
| Strong local governance | No | Yes | No | Yes | Yes | Yes |
| Strong relationship with national government | No | Yes | No | Yes | Yes | Yes |
| Impact on livelihoods | Weak | Strong, positive | Weak | Strong, negative | Strong, positive | Strong, positive |
| Other local institutions | Elders | Elders, agricultural cooperative | Elders | Elders | Elders, agricultural cooperative | Elders, agricultural cooperative |
| *Community participation* | | | | | | |
| Voice and participation | Weak | Strong | Moderate | Strong | Strong | Strong |
| Change in voice and participation over study period | Positive | Positive | Positive | Positive | Positive | Positive |
| Women's participation in community affairs | No | Yes | No | No | Yes | Yes |

*Source:* Community profiles.
*Note:* The high-MOP communities are shaded.
a. The National Solidarity Program had just arrived in Nangarhar province at the time of this research.

"the target of the NSP programs is to help the community and to improve livelihoods. Now we have a CDC that we did not have 10 years ago, and through this CDC we were able to construct a clinic and public baths for our village." Respondents from Zakwak Ulya added that "schools have been reconstructed and the entire community is sending their children to the schools, both boys and girls. Improvement in education is good for our community."

What made the NSP different from other assistance programs, besides its broad coverage and implementation at the national level, was the inclusion of local people's opinions, priorities, and other input in the local reconstruction process. Instead of delivering assistance based on fixed blueprints, the program allowed the elected community representatives to identify and address the community's most urgent problems. The democratically elected CDCs for women and men contributed to the development of community participation and collective action. In Riah Khillaw, the villagers said, "Before, the local government communicated with the elders, who acted according to their own opinion . . . Now the CDCs cooperate with the government and NGOs to implement NSP projects. The people in the community are involved in all the activities." In Zakwak Ulya, the villagers also testified that "there were no councils or consultation groups 10 years ago. Now there is an NSP council in the village and people can solve problems more easily."

The diffusion of participatory practices at the community level seems to have also led to greater social cohesion and unity. "In our community, almost everyone takes part in every decision; people are united," said Mriam, a middle-aged woman from Zakwak Ulya. This unity allowed the villagers to voice their concerns collectively and induced the local government to become more responsive to community concerns. "Before, only commanders could talk to the governors . . . Now, people have more voice. Even if we want to meet the governor, we can. Our government pays more attention to community problems than before." Khan Bibi, a housewife from Riah Khillaw, also explained that the community started lobbying representatives and powerful individuals in the government to ensure future service delivery: "Mohammed Nasir, a member of *welayati shura* [the elected provincial council], is from our community. We get together to approach him and he helps the community get electricity and water."

The villagers' emphasis on their *own* actions and improvements attained through the social institutions created by the NSP suggests that these participatory mechanisms meant as much to them as the actual reconstruction works. This appeared to be especially true for women (box 13.3). "Now, the people in the community are aware of how to get information about the development of the community," said female focus group discussants in Zakwak Ulya. "The

## BOX 13.3
## A gender revolution, yet to come

---

*Men are free outside the home and women are free inside the house. According to the Islamic rules of our society, men are freer. It is our tradition and our culture.*

—A man, Morlaw Ghano, Nangarhar province

*Our people are always talking about Islam, but they don't know anything about what real Islam says about education and women. They do not know that Islam said education is necessary and important for both men and women. Women should take part in business, jobs, and politics. Islam gives us these rights but our people and parents take them away.*

—A female youth, Riah Khillaw, Herat province

The traditional position of women in the Afghan society is clearly defined: they are considered to represent the honor of the family, so they are confined to their homes and the private sphere, where their behavior is closely observed. National projects aimed at gender reform date back at least to King Amanullah Khan's initiative in 1921 to open the first primary school for girls and raise the legal marriage age. But repressive regimes kept strict gender laws in place decade after decade. After the restoration of democracy in 2001, the new 2003 constitution gives women rights equal to those of men for the first time in the history of modern Afghanistan: "Any kind of discrimination and privilege among the citizens of Afghanistan is prohibited" (art. 22); "all the citizens of Afghanistan have equal rights and duties before the law" (art. 23).

Despite the constitutional reform, the strict norms segregating women continue to be widely observed all over the country. In all the surveyed communities, women were subject to traditional confinement and to male control over their lives. Ezmaray, an 18-year-old woman in Riah Khillaw, testified that "in our society, girls have the least freedom because we cannot go to school or take decisions about our lives and future. We cannot even go anywhere without a *mahram* [a male family member as chaperone]." In Nangarhar, one woman said, "For two years I could not visit the neighbors next door, because my husband forbade me to set foot out of the house." In Shazimir, the Hazara women could not complete our ladder of life sorting exercise because they knew only a few of the 95 households living in a small neighborhood of 10 short streets. In Morlaw Ghano, the young girls protested that "men are privileged because they can marry whenever they want, whomever they want, and they can study more than girls." Although women were sometimes involved in economic life, especially on family farms, having women at work was usually

*continued*

considered to reflect a household's poverty. Women's incomes were viewed as "extra" earnings rather than regular contributions to household income.

Women's status in Afghanistan is among the worst in the world and is reflected in dismal well-being indicators. Female life expectancy does not exceed 45 years, and the maternal mortality ratio ranges between 1,600 and 1,800 deaths per 100,000 live births. Only 40 percent and 10 percent of girls enroll in primary and secondary school, respectively (United Nations 2006).

Yet changes in the role of women are slight but perceptible, the result of an egalitarian constitution, increased access to schools and health facilities, and newly formed participatory institutions at the local level. In three of our six sample communities, the implementation of the National Solidarity Program, with its rules for grassroots participation, allowed women to gain a measure of freedom and social inclusion. Women were given their own CDCs, which allowed them to debate community issues and make independent decisions free of the dominating influence of men. Delivery of the NSP projects was contingent on women's participation in community elections and in the selection of reconstruction projects. While women in Ramili Qali chose to implement a community-wide project, namely, electricity supply, the women's CDC in Riah Khillaw chose to implement a literacy course for the illiterate women in the village. Through the NSP, therefore, women have gained access to capacity-building programs, learned to make community decisions, and gained influence and self-confidence in the public sphere.

Future generations of Afghan women are likely to be more aware of their rights and their social and economic potential than the current one. As Sheharaz, a young student from Riah Khillaw, said, "Having knowledge and education can increase freedom. If you are educated and you know about the rights of men and women, you can request your rights and ask to work outside the house or even outside the community." There is no gender revolution yet in Afghanistan, but programs like the NSP are helping to enhance women's status in local communities and in this way to gradually institute a new set of gender values in Afghan society.

---

NSP is helping the community a lot with their projects. Women have freedom to work and to get education, and we also have a female CDC and a training center in the community. We can all participate in the community development activities and problems." In Riah Khillaw, women emphasized the economic inclusion of females as a result of the NSP: "A female training and education center was opened last year and all the women of the community participate in this course. Women do tailoring in their houses. That the women can work and get an income for the family is an important change in our village."

## Dominance of downward mobility factors in Zakwak Ulya

The social developments facilitated by the NSP were similar in Zakwak Ulya and Riah Khillaw, and appear to have been equally beneficial in both villages. So what explains the different mobility paths of these communities? The comparative mobility statistics indicate that while the prosperity (recovery) rates measured by the PI in the two villages were similarly high (around 40 percent), the net upward movements measured by the NPI differed considerably: in Zakwak Ulya, only 12 percent of the households experienced upward mobility, whereas in Riah Khillaw 33 percent did.

Local testimonies from the two communities reveal that the mobility differences between Riah Khillaw and Zakwak Ulya can be largely explained by economic factors that led to falling mobility in Zakwak Ulya. In particular, the drought, lack of infrastructure, and absence of binding restrictions on agricultural imports contributed to downward mobility among the primarily farmer population of Zakwak Ulya. Ehsanullah, a young farmer, asserted, "More attention has to be paid to the agricultural sector. The fruits of this area do not grow in any other part of Afghanistan, but we still sell them at a very low price. We do not have cold storage to keep the fruits fresh, so we cannot take them to different cities or foreign countries." Deena, also a farmer, added, "The drought and lack of markets for agricultural products are the factors that make it harder for people in this community to move up. If there were more and better markets to sell agricultural products, we could move up more easily." Nezammuddin, a middle-aged farmer who fell into poverty over the study period, emphasized competition from imports: "Most of the people in our community are farmers who work in the fields. We do not earn enough profits because most of the agricultural products are imported from Iran." Another villager added, "If the government controls the import of fruit and cereals from Iran, Pakistan, and China, we can move up. Otherwise, we cannot compete with them."

In contrast to the situation in Zakwak Ulya, in Riah Khillaw the impact of drought and other constraints did not pose major obstacles to recovery. "There were lots of problems with water distribution in the past. Sometimes people were fighting for water," explained a male discussion group. "One year ago, a development program started in the community [to fix the water shortages] and we do not have these problems anymore." The community also has access to electricity, which helps ensure proper agricultural storage conditions. A newly reconstructed road has eased the access to the city markets. "Construction of this road has been very helpful for us. In the past people could not bring their goods to the cities. Now it is easier to take goods to the market on time." Zohra, a recently trained tailor, added that diversification opportunities helped Riah Khillaw to recover: "In the last 10 years, concrete masonry, ceramic, and metal works have started in the village, occupations that people learned in Iran. Thanks to electricity, women started to do tailoring and embroidery work. We now depend less on farms."

Overall, the social and political changes brought by the NSP seem to have facilitated community well-being and transitions out of poverty, but they did not directly address economic vulnerabilities and downward mobility factors at the household or community level. This was particularly true in Zakwak Ulya, where downward movements were driven by exogenous factors like the community's location and the impact of drought. In short, inclusive and participatory elements embedded in projects sponsored by the NSP worked better and promoted upward mobility in Riah Khillaw, where more favorable initial conditions and alternative vulnerability-reducing mechanisms were already present. This in turn may point to certain complementarities between sociopolitical factors that promote upward movement and postconflict economic alternatives that prevent falling.

## Youth participation and future aspirations

*Young people should participate in community affairs. They have the energy and the knowledge to do something for the future and improvement of the community.*
—Tahira, a 20-year-old woman, Nasher Khan, Nangarhar province

*We have a shura [village council] for adults and another shura for young people. We meet together twice a month. The chief of the shura collects a monthly fee from each member and when someone has a problem we give this money to him or her.*
—Parisa, an 18-year-old woman, Riah Khillaw, Herat province

Many societies struggle with containing the energy, emotions, and aspirations of their youth. During wars or in postconflict environments, youth suffer disrupted schooling, a paucity of legal economic opportunities, and in some cases forcible conscription by insurgents. The result, especially for young men, is often despair. Yet we encountered a cautious optimism among the youth in our study communities. Their perspectives on the links between mobility, power, democracy, and social relations provide a glimpse of what the future may hold for the communities in our sample.

The youth in the visited communities expressed their belief that economic mobility is closely tied with different forms of power. "Power means to have good health, to be physically strong, to have authority in the community and to have higher education," said the male youth group in Nasher Khan, Nangarhar. "It means to have money, to have land, or to have a high post in the government, so you can move out of poverty." Young female discussants in Shazimir thought that "power helps people to get education, to earn a good income, and to get a better life. If someone is powerful, he or she earns the respect of the family and the society." Nabila, a 22-year-old woman from Riah Khillaw, Herat, summarized by saying, "There is a strong relationship between being free, being powerful, and moving out of poverty. You cannot be rich and not powerful, or be poor and powerful."

Young people said that power can be obtained in several ways. In Ramili Qali, the female youth said that "some obtain power via hard work, knowledge, and education; some obtain power from the barrel of a gun; others obtain it by trafficking narcotics." In Morlaw Ghano, Nangarhar, young people believed that they themselves could also acquire power through hard work and education: "The youth can become powerful if they work hard and gain physical power. If they have a high education, they can easily find jobs and move up."

Although they came from rural communities where agricultural livelihoods were common, the youth in our sample did not feel trapped in their parents' occupations; they aspired to rise to better-paying professions. "My father is an elder and my mother is a housewife. I am a farmer now but I want to be the owner of a factory," said Sharifullah from Morlaw Ghano. Another young man added, "My father is a farmer, currently unemployed, and my mother is a housewife. I work in a printing house and in the future I want to have my own tailor shop." Especially in the high-mobility communities in our sample, with greater social cohesion, some young girls felt that their future aspirations were no longer constrained by strict gender norms. For example, in Nasher Khan, Nadia said, "My father cannot work, as he is old and weak. I am not educated but I want to learn tailoring to help my family." Similarly, 18-year-old Atifa from Riah Khillaw said, "My father is a mullah and my mother is a housewife. I would like to continue my education and become a good journalist in the future."

While the participation of youth in community institutions was limited in Kabul and Nangarhar, we encountered youth inclusion at least in one of the villages in our sample, Riah Khillaw in Herat. "Youth have an important role in the district council. Our elders know that in the future this society will be governed by the youth, so they invited us to join them," said Mostafa, a young male student. In addition to participating in the elders' shura, the youth also formed a youth council that facilitated solidarity, cooperation, and trust among young men and women in the village. Parisa, an 18-year-old woman, said, "We have a separate shura for young people, which meets twice a month. The chief of the council collects a monthly fee from each member and we use this money [to provide assistance] when someone has a problem."

These local organizations played an important part in channeling the energy of youth toward community issues and local capacity building in Riah Khillaw. In the communities where such participatory mechanisms were lacking, young people were still aware of the importance of social inclusion and yearned to participate in community decisions. In Nasher Khan, for example, young discussants testified that "the elderly do not invite the youth to community meetings, because they think that they do not need the youth's advice to make good decisions. But the youth should be active and free to participate in decision making, because they will be the wealth of our country in the future."

The youth expressed confidence that these constraints will be overcome in the future as local democracies improve and mature. "People believe in democracy, we have the possibility to raise our voices and ask for our rights," said young people in Morlaw Ghano. Those in Ramili Qali added, "If the number of educated people increases in our society, and if security, gender equality, and the human rights continue to be maintained, the local government will become [more inclusive] in the future."

## Conclusion and Policy Implications: Continuing Threats and New Opportunities

Despite early efforts at state building, Afghanistan has continued to struggle with the growing insurgency, insecurity, fragile institutions, and widespread corruption since the conclusion of our study in 2006. While opium cultivation decreased by 19 percent in 2008 (UNODC 2008a), narcotic exports still contribute one-third of the gross domestic product. Rural incomes would need to rise by at least 300 percent—from $1 to $4 a day—for opium production to become a less attractive economic activity (Ghani 2009). Because of the ongoing drought, more than 5 million people were in need of immediate food assistance in 2009; 2 million of them were mothers and children under age five. In 2008, an average household spent up to 77 percent of its income on food, compared with 56 percent in 2005 (UNFAO 2009).

As a result, Afghanistan remains highly susceptible to humanitarian crises. In this context of deteriorating national well-being, our findings on the conditions and sequencings that seem to have influenced local recovery paths can play a role in shaping future reconstruction efforts. Two key points stand out.

First, the testimonies in our sample revealed that policies must be crafted to support local people's desire to make a new beginning and get on with their lives after many years of destruction, drought, and forced displacement. Although individuals and communities took initiatives to cope and diversify their livelihoods, we found that these efforts were usually insufficient to yield successful transition paths in devastated rural and urban settings. In particular, our findings indicated that successful transitions were conditioned on the delivery of external assistance. Reconstruction of broken infrastructure, facilitation of access to markets, and provision of income diversification mechanisms to reduce dependence on agriculture seem to have been the fundamental prerequisites for postconflict mobility.

Second, our findings indicate that the community-led development efforts pioneered by the National Solidarity Program, which bundled aid with participatory institutions and implemented this package in thousands of communities across the country, need to be supported further, as the program seems to have delivered additional benefits beyond the development projects themselves. The NSP initiated the formation of the first democratic local institutions at the community level, thereby encouraging capacity building, collective discourse, and inclusive decision making. In particular, the inclusion of rural villagers, women, and in some instances youth in the NSP process appears to have promoted new understandings of democratic functioning and social cohesion, critical to keeping ethnic tensions at bay.

One of the NSP's objectives was to create inclusive and locally accountable community development councils at the local level and then to link these councils with other government agencies, NGOs, and donors to improve future access to resources. The creation of the CDCs has set the foundation for bottom-up reconstruction and state-building efforts in the future.

Furthermore, by combining the development efforts of the national government with an on-site NGO presence and the local expertise of villagers, these programs are likely to impose less administrative and financial burden on the government. Finally, higher participation and inclusive practices at the local level can help advance social change in other areas, notably the area of gender norms. The postconflict reconstruction environment presents an opportunity to overcome social obstacles in Afghan society and enable *all* Afghans to rebuild their war-torn country from the bottom up, one community at a time.

# Notes

The Afghanistan study is part of the global Moving Out of Poverty study led by Deepa Narayan in the Poverty Reduction and Economic Management (PREM) Network of the World Bank. For a discussion of key study concepts and data collection methods, see chapter 1 and the appendixes to this volume. Also see volume 2 of the Moving Out of Poverty series (Narayan, Pritchett, and Kapoor 2009) and the study methodology guide (Narayan and Petesch 2005).

The Afghanistan country study was directed by Philibert de Mercey, Alejandra Val Cubero, and Najibullah Ziar. They also wrote the "Afghanistan National Synthesis Report," available on the Moving Out of Poverty study Web site (http://go.worldbank.org/9ER0AOIH20). We would like to thank Susanne Holste, Alexandre Marc, Ambar Narayan, Patti Petesch, Meena Rafie, Ayse Sengueler, Shonali Serdasai, and Ashutosh Varshney for their valuable feedback on an earlier draft of this paper.

1. To protect the privacy of participants, this chapter uses pseudonyms for the six study villages. Provinces, districts, and cities are identified by their real names.

2. The National Solidarity Program is a government-led rural development program, supported by the World Bank along with several other donors and organizations. The program seeks to lay the foundation for a sustainable form of inclusive local governance, rural reconstruction, and poverty alleviation in the country. It builds capacity at the local level by establishing and delivering development projects through democratically elected community development councils. The councils represent the first formal representative institution at the community level in Afghanistan.

3. Both mixed and gender-specific CDCs were created. In some communities, villagers asked for separate councils for men and women, mainly because of religious reasons.

4. In this chapter, the term "postconflict" refers to the relatively stable post-Taliban conditions in the visited communities.

5. Growth figures are based on estimations of the International Monetary Fund, since official statistics do not exist for this period.

6. The partnership between the Afghan government and international donors was revised during the Paris Conference of June 2008. The new agreement includes the funding of longer-term development objectives, as outlined in the Afghanistan National Development Strategy (ANDS), and nation-building efforts. It is too early to evaluate the success of, or the donors' actual commitment to, this revised partnership. The declaration of the Paris Conference is available on the Web site of the British Foreign and Commonwealth Office (http://www.fco.gov.uk/en/).

7. For an early assessment of the links between poverty, risk, and vulnerability in post-Taliban Afghanistan, see World Bank (2005).

8. Although the poppy-cultivating communities analyzed in this chapter are not directly linked to the post-Taliban insurgency movement in Afghanistan, a recent report by UNODC (2008b) concluded that local corruption and the insurgency movement are tightly linked with the opium boom. In southern provinces where the insurgency is strong, poppy-related activities are concentrated in the hands of

a small number of drug lords, and the scale of production is large. In contrast, in the northeast and northwest provinces studied in this chapter, poppy cultivation is primarily a coping strategy for small farmers in the absence of alternative livelihoods. See the third section of this chapter for a detailed analysis of the latter.

9. See appendixes B and C of this volume for a detailed discussion of data collection tools and other methodological details of the study.

10. Although the focus on relatively stable communities reduces diversity and increases the risk of bias, the security of the research team necessitated a geographic restriction in community selection.

11. The National Risk and Vulnerability Assessment (NRVA), started in 2003, gathers information on rural livelihoods in Afghanistan and supports use of this information in programs and policies aimed at reducing poverty and vulnerability in the country. For details, see the NRVA Web site at http://www.mrrd.gov.af/ nss-vau/.

12. The four communities heavily affected by drought were all in the Nangarhar and Herat regions. The fifth rural community, Ramili Qali in Parwan, had lacked a working irrigation system since the early years of the Taliban regime. The drought was not a crucial issue in the urban community in our sample, Shazimir.

13. According to the Afghanistan Statistical Yearbook, 2.3 million hectares of arable land were estimated to exist in Afghanistan in 1980. These statistics were not updated for years because of the conflict.

14. For a detailed discussion of migration and repatriation issues in Afghanistan, see Altai Consulting (2006), Turton and Marsden (2002), and UNHCR (2004). For an overview of the link between poverty reduction and rural poverty in Afghanistan, see Ghobadi, Koettl, and Vakis (2005).

15. The researchers' observations suggest that the latter figure may be understated. On account of the prevalent gender norms, many household heads did not count home production, farming, or other cash income earned by women as part of household income.

16. As noted by Barrett and Swallow (2005), the small number of households in the transitory categories just above and below the poverty line suggest that there are two equilibria at the two extreme ends of the ladder of well-being. The lack of connections between the two equilibria suggests that there might be poverty traps that prevent the initial poor from moving up in small increments.

17. At the time of our research, in 2006, Nangarhar was among the priority provinces for the government's alternative livelihoods programs and a large USAID-sponsored program aimed at rebuilding the agriculture sector. However, the villagers in Morlaw Ghano and Nasher Khan were unaware of these developments and did not mention them in their testimonies.

18. Poppy production resumed in Nangarhar in 2006. It grew exponentially and within a year had increased by 286 percent (UNODC 2007).

19. More details about the National Solidarity Program can be found at http://www. nspafghanistan.org/about_nsp.shtm.

# References

Altai Consulting. 2005. "Mapping of Alternative Livelihoods Projects 2005." United Nations High Commissioner for Refugees, Kabul.

———. 2006. "Integration of Returnees in the Afghan Labor Market." United Nations High Commissioner for Refugees and International Labour Organization, Kabul.

Barrett, C. B., and B. M. Swallow. 2005. "Fractal Poverty Traps." Applied Economics and Management Working Paper, Cornell University, Ithaca, NY.

CSO (Central Statistics Office). 2005. "Pre-Census Household Count." Kabul.

Ghani, A. 2009. *A Ten-Year Framework for Afghanistan: Executing the Obama Plan and Beyond*. Washington, DC: Atlantic Council.

Ghani, A., and C. Lockhart. 2008. *Fixing Failed States: A Framework for Rebuilding a Fractured World*. New York: Oxford University Press.

Ghobadi, N., J. Koettl, and R. Vakis. 2005. "Moving Out of Poverty: Migration Insights from Rural Afghanistan." Afghanistan Research and Evaluation Unit, Kabul.

Government of Afghanistan. 2006. "Afghanistan National Development Strategy: A Strategy for Security, Governance, Economic Growth and Poverty Reduction." Kabul.

———. 2008. "Afghanistan National Development Strategy: A Strategy for Security, Governance, Economic Growth and Poverty Reduction." Kabul.

MRRD (Ministry of Rural Rehabilitation and Development). 2005. "National Risk and Vulnerability Assessment 2005 Database." Kabul.

Narayan, D., and P. Petesch. 2005. "Moving Out of Poverty Methodology Guide." Poverty Reduction Group, Poverty Reduction and Economic Management Network, World Bank, Washington, DC.

Narayan, D., L. Pritchett, and S. Kapoor. 2009. *Moving Out of Poverty: Success from the Bottom Up*. New York: Palgrave Macmillan; Washington, DC: World Bank.

Rubin, B., A. Stoddard, H. Hamidzada, and A. Farhadi. 2004. *Building a New Afghanistan: The Value of Success, the Cost of Failure*. Paying for Essentials Policy Paper Series. New York: Center on International Cooperation, New York University.

Schütte, S. 2005. "Livelihoods of the Urban Poor in Afghanistan—Conceptual Issues and Review of Literature." Afghanistan Research and Evaluation Unit, Kabul.

Turton, D., and P. Marsden. 2002. "Taking Refugees for a Ride? The Politics of Refugee Return to Afghanistan." Afghanistan Research and Evaluation Unit, Kabul.

United Nations. 2006. *Report to the Economic and Social Council on the Situation of Women and Girls in Afghanistan*. New York.

UNFAO (United Nations Food and Agriculture Organization). 2009. *Afghanistan: Humanitarian Action Plan 2009*. Rome: UNFAO Emergency Operations and Rehabilitation Division.

UNHCR (United Nations High Commissioner for Refugees). 2004. *Afghanistan: Challenges to Return*. Geneva: UNHCR.

UNODC (United Nations Office on Drugs and Crime). 2005. *Afghanistan Opium Survey*. Kabul: UNODC.

———. 2006. *Afghanistan Opium Survey.* Kabul: UNODC.

———. 2007. *Afghanistan Opium Survey.* Kabul: UNODC.

———. 2008a. *Afghanistan Opium Survey.* Kabul: UNODC.

———. 2008b. "Is Poverty Driving the Afghan Opium Boom?" Discussion Paper. Kabul.

World Bank. 2005. *Afghanistan—Poverty, Vulnerability and Social Protection: An Initial Assessment.* Washington, DC: World Bank.

PART 3

Technical Appendixes

# Appendix A: Researchers and Institutions Involved in Conflict Country Studies

**TABLE A.1**
**Researchers and institutions involved in conflict country studies**

| Country | Lead researchers | Other researchers | Institution | Country report | Country report authors |
|---|---|---|---|---|---|
| Afghanistan | Philibert de Mercey, Alejandra Val Cubero, and Najibullah Ziar | ACNielsen India, Masooma Essa, Aliya Wahdat, Mohammad Zarif Sediqqi, Shingul Kaliwal, Abdul Wahdood, Besmellah Alokozay, Sayed Awlia | Altai Consulting | "Moving Out of Poverty: Understanding Freedom, Democracy and Growth from the Bottom Up: National Synthesis Report for Afghanistan" | Philibert de Mercey, Alejandra Val Cubero, and Najibullah Ziar |
| Cambodia | Ingrid FitzGerald and So Sovannarith | Chan Sophal, Kem Sithen, Tuot Sokphally, Pon Dorina, Kem Sithen, Ann Sophapim, Chea Sovann, Chen Soportea, Chey Nath, Chheang Vuntha, Choun Chanthoura, Chim Charya, Hang Vannara, Heng Daravuthy, Hov Idh, Keo Ouly, Kim Sithy, Khun Chandavy, Long Kolab, Men Sam On, Ouk Leakhana, Pean Pancy, Ros Channak, Sek Vuthy, Sok Saroeun, Tang Kruy, Thun Sean Heng, Yous Samrith, K. A. S. Murshid, Pon Dorina, Chhay Pidor, Brett Ballard, Neak Samsen | Cambodia Development Resource Institute (CDRI), Phnom Penh | "Moving Out of Poverty? Trends in Community Well-being and Household Mobility in Nine Cambodian Villages" | Ingrid FitzGerald and So Sovannarith with Chan Sophal, Kem Sithen, and Tout Sokphally |

| Colombia | Ana María Ibáñez, María Teresa Matijasevic, Sergio Iván Prada, and Carlos Ariel García | Liliana Velásquez, Mónica Ramírez, Carolina Villada, Miguel Ángel Rivera, Adriana Quiceno, Lina Isabel Trujillo, Alejandra Velásquez | Centro de Estudios Regionales, Cafeteros y Empresariales (CRECE), Manizales, Colombia | "Moving Out of Poverty: Understanding Freedom, Democracy and Growth from the Bottom Up: National Synthesis Report for Colombia" | María Teresa Matijasevic, Liliana Velásquez, Carolina Villada, and Mónica Ramírez |
|---|---|---|---|---|---|
| India (Assam) | Deepa Narayan and Binayak Sen | Arijit Mukhopadhyay, Debnath Bhadra, Arijit Mukherjee, Pankaj Deka, Tilak Kalita, Chandan Das, Rupjyoti Borah, Prasanna Hazarika, Rahul Barman, Shankar Thakuria, Deuti Hazarika, Hiren Bhattacharjee, Chandan Sarma, Kamal Lodh, Bidya Sinha, Sanjay Das, Utpal Saibia, Rama Kanta Barman, Rapjuyoti Ratna, Maqbul Ali | World Bank | "Who Benefits from Conflict? Some Evidence from Assam" (in *Moving Out of Poverty*, vol. 3, *The Promise of Democracy and Empowerment in India*, ed. Deepa Narayan) | Deepa Narayan, Binayak Sen, and Ashutosh Varshney |
| Indonesia | Sri Kusumastuti Rahayu and Vita Febriany | Ruly Marianti, Wawan Munawar, Didit Wicaksana, Mutmainah, Khoirul Rosyadi, Suroso, Akhmadi, Mutmainah, Ari Ratna, Ivanovich Agusta, Heri Rubianto, Widy Taurus Sandi, Erfan Agus Munif, Sulton Mawardi, Syahidussyahar, Ervan Abdul Kadir, Nurdewa Safar, Muhlis A. Adam, Musriyadi Nabiu, Salha Marasaly, Abdulgani Fabanjo, Edy Nasriyanto Hatari, Muhammad Noor, Nurdewa Safar, Abdul Kadir Kamaluddin | SMERU Research Institute, Jakarta | "Moving Out of Poverty: Understanding Freedom, Democracy, Governance, and Growth from the Bottom Up: Indonesia Case Study: North Maluku and East Java" | Sri Kusumastuti Rahayu and Vita Febriany |

(continued)

**TABLE A.1**
*continued*

| Country | Lead researchers | Other researchers | Institution | Country report | Country report authors |
|---|---|---|---|---|---|
| Philippines | Erlinda Montillo-Burton, Chona R. Echavez, and Imelda G. Pagtulon-an | Jennefer Lyn Bagaporo, Vergil Boac, Donna Sanchez, Conralin Yap, Adonis Gonazales, Carla Vergara, Marie Clarisse Gomos, Michael Lou Montejo, Lourdes Wong, Prospercora Vega, Vicky Regidor, Betty Aposakas, Lucia Sabanal, Carol Pagtulon-an, Roxendo Ucat, Marlo Reyes, Esther Briones, Rowena Abilja | Research Institute for Mindanao Culture, Xavier University, Cagayan de Oro City, Philippines | "Moving Out of Poverty in Conflict-Affected Areas in Mindanao, Philippines" | Erlinda Montillo-Burton, Chona R. Echavez, and Imelda G. Pagtulon-an |
| Sri Lanka | Prashan Thalayasingam | Gayathri, Sujatha, Gayan, Chathura, Siriwardane, Dayal, Indira, Munas, Vigitha, Sivadeepan, Sivaharan, Rathan, Leo, Azam, Shehan, Suchith, Baanu, Shahim, Rahuman, Kosalai, Sudarshan, Braveena, Niroshan, Kannan | Centre for Poverty Analysis (CEPA), Colombo | "Moving Out of Poverty in Conflict-Affected Areas in Sri Lanka" | Prashan Thalayasingam |

*Note:* All country reports are available online at http://go.worldbank.org/9ER0AOIH20.

# Appendix B: Overview of Study Methodology

The Moving Out of Poverty study is a large, complex research program carried out in 21 diverse study regions in 15 countries around the world. The study combines both qualitative and quantitative work to explore from below the processes, interactions, and sequencings associated with household transitions out of poverty. The focus is on learning from men and women who have managed to move out of poverty in the long run, roughly over the period from 1995 to 2005. The study examines factors and processes that enable individuals to accumulate assets and explores the role of community institutions in supporting or obstructing their mobility.

This volume is the product of a special comparative research program that was embedded within the global Moving Out of Poverty study to examine the links between conflict and mobility from a micro perspective. It focuses primarily on the effects of conflict on communities and on poor people.[1]

## Description of the Conflict Study

While the development literature is replete with studies of the impact of conflict on countries' growth rates, institutions, and overall development, there have been relatively few studies that focus on the consequences of conflict for communities and for poor people's attempts to move out of poverty. The conflict study presents the voices of men and women who have lived through these experiences in a diverse set of communities. It includes case studies of seven countries: Afghanistan, Cambodia, Colombia, India (Assam), Indonesia, the Philippines, and Sri Lanka.[2] In addition, the cross-country analysis in chapter 1 provides new qualitative and quantitative evidence on the social, political, and economic factors that affect community and household mobility in conflict or postconflict contexts.

This note provides an overview of the study's technical design. It discusses the conceptual framework, the sampling strategy, two data collection instruments of particular relevance to this volume, the construction of the dependent and independent variables for the quantitative analysis, and the multivariate regression functional form.

### The conceptual framework

We started our research with broad questions.[3] What are the processes that allow some poor people to move out of poverty while others in the same community remain stuck in poverty? What is the role of social relations in moving out of poverty? How important are psychological factors and personal agency? Does local democracy make a difference?

We deliberately did not adopt any particular conceptual framework, because we knew that early marriage to concepts and measuring tools limits what you see. We wanted to explore before we started limiting. We deliberately collected too much data, using 10 different measuring tools to probe the whys and hows of poverty escapes and stagnation. We expected that this would create an enormous challenge in data analysis, and it did. We are not recommending this as a research strategy to everyone, but we think it is important in poverty studies to cast a wide net and to look beyond what one might first assume to be the correct explanation.

Our data analyses proceeded in three stages. In the first phase, which took six months, we used an inductive approach to develop a coding system for the analysis of life stories. We let the data speak to us. After reading 200 life stories, we developed categories that would "catch" most of the information emerging from people's descriptions of the key events in their lives and the processes that facilitated or hindered their accumulation of assets.

In the second phase, we analyzed 60 community pairs. The communities in each pair were selected to differ in terms of one particular variable: social stratification or democracy, collective action, and economic opportunity. In one pair, for instance, community A might differ from community B only in levels of social stratification, holding other variables constant. We analyzed these communities using a variant of the SOSOTEC technique that we learned from Robert Chambers during the earlier, Voices of the Poor study.[4] We read reports, interviews, and descriptions; cut them into strips; and sorted the ideas, gradually compiling them into subsets and larger sets and diagramming the relationships between them. Given our huge dataset, this process also took several months. The diagrams became very elaborate as our teams mapped relationships across communities and country contexts. This technique appears disorganized and time-consuming, but it surpasses all others in "letting voices emerge" during the analysis phase. In particular, it delays the imposition of expert concepts until much later.

Figure B.1 shows one such diagram created by our team for the village of Galalolo on Halmahera island in Indonesia.[5] A large proportion of the villagers in this community are farmers, mostly landless, while the rest are government civil servants working in the nearby city of Ternate. Ten years ago the community used to have more economic livelihoods, but these vanished after the monetary crisis and the resulting inflation of the late 1990s. The crisis had a positive influence on individual agency by forcing people to take initiative and search for new livelihoods in taxi driving or other small businesses. But the religious conflict between Muslims and Christians in 2000

**FIGURE B.1**

**Factors influencing movement out of poverty in Galalolo, Indonesia**

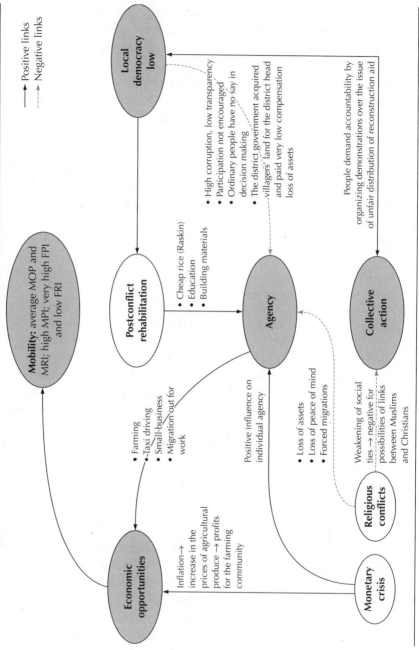

Positive links
Negative links

Local democracy low

Mobility: average MOP and MRI; high MPI; very high FPI and low FRI

• High corruption, low transparency
• Participation not encouraged
• Ordinary people have no say in decision making
• The district government acquired villagers' land for the district head and paid very low compensation loss of assets

People demand accountability by organizing demonstrations over the issue of unfair distribution of reconstruction aid

Postconflict rehabilitation

• Cheap rice (Raskin)
• Education
• Building materials

Agency

Collective action

• Farming
• Taxi driving
• Small business
• Migration out for work

Positive influence on individual agency

• Loss of assets
• Loss of peace of mind
• Forced migrations

Weakening of social ties → negative for possibilities of links between Muslims and Christians

Religious conflicts

Inflation → increase in the prices of agricultural produce → profits for the farming community

Economic opportunities

Monetary crisis

*Source:* Global research team analysis of MOP data.

led to forced displacement on a large scale and destruction of all productive assets left behind by the refugees. The conflict also hindered the scope for collective action by weakening social ties after resettlement took place in 2002. This in turn interacted with low local democracy, high corruption, unfair political practices, and nonparticipatory institutions to block poor people's efforts to move out of poverty in the postconflict context. The villagers did come together to demonstrate against corruption and unfair distribution of aid resources, and as a result, some rehabilitation programs provided economic assistance and reconstruction projects that had a positive influence on individual agency. Yet the overall movement out of poverty in this village remained only average, not high.

Is movement out of poverty in Galalolo average because poor people, for whatever reason, do not possess enough initiative? Or do poor people fail to escape poverty because their initiatives meet resistance and are blocked? Or are poor people simply excluded from the economic, social, and political opportunities that the well-off enjoy? How does collective action by the rich and poor block or facilitate economic and political opportunities?

*Key concepts: Initiative and opportunity*
The interplay of factors revealed in the community diagrams eventually led to the conceptual framework adopted for the quantitative analyses carried out in the third year. This conceptual framework, described below, guided the third and final phase of our data analysis, which was quantitative. This included multivariate regression analyses to test the role of local-level institutions in the movement out of poverty while taking into account other community and household features.

As we studied hundreds of diagrams from individual communities, two overarching concepts emerged: *initiative* and *opportunity*. The interaction between these two concepts largely structures the movement out of poverty (figure B.2).

In studying these movements, we can make an analogy with flows from physical systems. If we see that a weak flow of electric current is causing a bulb to glow faintly, it could be either because the power source is weak or because resistance to the flow of power is high, so the power is dissipated in heat. Or if we see a trickle of water flowing past us, it could be because there was little water at the source or because obstacles are blocking the flow.

We start with poor people. At the source of poverty reduction are the initiatives that millions and millions of individuals and households take to better their lives.[6] Such initiatives may involve growing new crops, using new agricultural techniques or equipment, accessing new markets, starting a

**FIGURE B.2**
**Conceptual framework of the Moving Out of Poverty study**

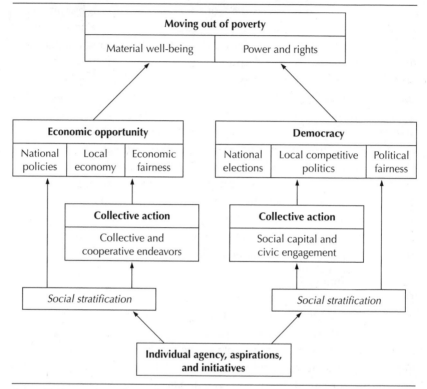

Source: D. Narayan, L. Pritchett, and S. Kapoor, *Moving Out of Poverty: Success from the Bottom Up* (New York: Palgrave Macmillan; Washington, DC: World Bank, 2009), 46.

business, getting a job, or migrating for employment. People take initiatives based on their self-confidence, agency, aspirations, and empowerment—their sense that what they do matters and has the potential to succeed.

Initiative can also be embedded in collective action, from pooled labor or savings groups to marketing cooperatives to fully cooperative firms. Both poor and rich people can act collectively, either through formal organizations or through informal groups and networks. Both usually associate with their own kind—the rich with the rich and the poor with the poor. At times the interests of the rich and poor may converge, as when everyone wants to solve a community-wide problem. At other times the rich and poor compete for influence and access to limited resources. Collective action by the poor will then meet with resistance from the rich.

It is a reality that most societies are divided, most often along lines of caste, ethnicity, gender, religion, or wealth. Economic, social, and political organizations and networks fissure along the same social divides, leading to what Tilly calls "durable inequality" between social groups.[7] Across all study regions and all topics, we find social stratification to be a conditioning factor that affects both initiative and opportunity. In conflict contexts, ethnic and religious divides sometimes polarize societies and lead to clashes.

Whether economic initiative, either individual or collective, leads to upward movement depends on the opportunities available and on access to them. We consider three aspects: national policies, local economies, and economic fairness. There is no question that progress in overall national prosperity has an enormous influence on the pace of poverty reduction. But our study is not primarily about the link between national policies and poverty, a field of inquiry for which our techniques are not well suited. Instead, we focus on the local level. How do opportunities at the very local level (as small as the village) structure the movement out of poverty? How does the fairness of economic opportunity—whether individuals from all walks of life are able to participate effectively in the economy—influence poverty reduction, at the local level and hence also at the national level?

In the political sphere, too, people participate both individually and collectively. We acknowledge the importance of electoral democracy at the national level in framing political freedom. But our focus is again at the local level. It is participation in open, competitive, *local* political processes that determines access to and influence over local governments and government-financed programs. Poor people can participate individually through elections. But organized collective action is just as important, as the ability to express common interests is key to successful participation and representation, especially among marginalized groups. Moreover, the structures of political opportunity strongly influence whether local politics helps or harms poor people in their efforts to improve their well-being. We are concerned with the efficacy of electoral accountability, the presence of political clientelism, and the extent of fairness in opportunities to participate in public decision making.

In reality, of course, boundaries between the political and the economic are always blurred and contested, and this is even more the case when political conflicts are raging. Political power can thwart or create economic opportunity, and economic success can increase power and influence in the political sphere. We stress these interconnections throughout the book because this is the reality that people most often described on the ground.

## TABLE B.1
## Countries in the conflict study stratified by income, growth, and governance

| Economy | High governance | Low governance | Very low governance |
|---|---|---|---|
| Low income (US$825 or less) | | | |
| High growth | | India (Assam) | Cambodia |
| Low growth | | | Afghanistan |
| Lower middle income (US$826–US$3,255) | | | |
| High growth | Philippines | Indonesia, Sri Lanka | |
| Low growth | | Colombia | |
| Upper middle income (US$3,256–US$10,065) | | | |
| High growth | | | |
| Low growth | | | |

Note: Income figures are per capita gross national income. Growth and governance classifications reflect the growth rate in 2004 and the average governance rating for 1996–2004. A growth rate < = 3 indicates a low-growth country. High governance rating refers to a governance average > 0 and < 2.5; low governance rating, a governance average < 0 and > –0.5; very low governance rating, a governance average < –0.5 and > –2.5. Governance average is the simple average of six components (voice and accountability, political stability, rule of law, government effectiveness, regulatory quality, and control of corruption) of the governance dataset in D. Kaufmann, A. Kraay, and M. Mastruzzi, "Governance Matters IV: Governance Indicators for 1996–2004" (Policy Research Working Paper 3630, World Bank, Washington, DC, 2005).

## Choosing the study regions

In selecting countries and regions within countries to participate in the conflict study, an effort was made to cover a variety of contexts. As shown in table B.1, the seven countries included in the conflict study differ in terms of their income levels, national growth rates, and governance environments.[8] Not surprisingly, while there is considerable variation along the dimensions, some cells of the table are empty: for example, there are no low-income/high-governance countries in the study. The conflict sample consisted of low-income and lower-middle-income countries with diverse growth performances.

Selection of regions also took into account the availability of local research institutes with the interest and capacity to carry out the multidisciplinary study in the context of violent conflicts, as well as interest on the part of national governments and World Bank country teams.

## Sampling for communities (villages, neighborhoods)

The sampling design for the individual studies ensured variation across two variables. The first variable was rate of economic growth: to select communities with different growth rates, the research teams used regional, provincial, or district-level data, depending on the lowest level available. The second variable was the intensity of the major political conflict.

Thus, the spatial sampling was devoted to finding communities within the broader region with higher and lower levels of growth and conflict. A high conflict intensity rating means multiple deaths (at least five) that were directly associated with major political violence, combined with either extensive property destruction or mass displacement. Communities with a low conflict intensity rating reported isolated incidents of deaths due to political violence and either some property destruction or some displacement. Communities were rated as "no conflict" if no deaths were reported. The ratings do not reflect incidents of everyday crime and violence or the activities of youth gangs, which were often present in the study regions. This sampling strategy was employed for districts/blocks/villages to identify study sites in the seven conflict-affected countries (table B.2). The resulting conflict sample consisted of 102 communities: half were from India (Assam), and the rest were from the six countries profiled in part 2 of the current volume.

## Sampling for households

The selection of households was based on a household sorting exercise undertaken during a focus group discussion called the "ladder of life," described more fully below.[9] The focus group tool was used to gather community perceptions of household well-being, both in the initial study period (1995) and in the current period (2005).[10] Based on the focus group rankings of households on the steps of the ladder of life, a community mobility matrix was constructed for each village. This revealed the mobility of each household over the study period. These ratings provided a useful source for selecting respondents for the household survey. Four mobility groups were considered:

- *Movers:* households that were poor in 1995 but had moved out of poverty by 2005
- *Chronic poor:* households that were poor in 1995 and remained poor in 2005
- *Fallers:* households that were not poor in 1995 but fell into poverty by 2005
- *Never poor:* households that were not poor in 1995 and remained not poor in 2005.

A classification of "poor" means households below the locally defined community poverty line, and "not poor" refers to households above it.

Once households in the community mobility matrix were stratified into these four mobility groups, a minimum of 15 households in each community

**TABLE B.2**
**Choosing locations within conflict study regions**

| Study region | Provinces/ districts | Blocks | Communities | No. of communities | No. of household surveys |
|---|---|---|---|---|---|
| | Selection criteria | | | | |
| Afghanistan | Conflict, proximity to city or borders, cultivation and trade of poppy, degree of exposure to international aid | | | 6 | 91 |
| Cambodia | Agro-ecological features, market access, and local governance conditions (panel study) | | | 9 | — |
| Colombia | Growth, conflict, and whether communities were receiving displaced populations or were themselves displaced | | | 8 | 252 |
| India: Assam | Growth and conflict | Conflict | | 50 | 746 |
| Indonesia | Type of conflict (ethnic, religious, local) | Growth | Conflict and ethnic/religious composition | 10 | 372 |
| Philippines | Study conducted only in the Mindanao region | Growth | Conflict | 10 | 300 |
| Sri Lanka | Growth and conflict | Growth | Conflict | 9 | — |
| Total | | | | 102 | 1,761 |

*Source:* MOP country synthesis reports (see appendix A).
*Note:* In all conflict regions, districts with a very high level of active conflict at the time of the survey were not chosen for reasons of safety of the field team. The Moving Out of Poverty household questionnaire was not used in Cambodia because the research was embedded in an ongoing panel study on rural livelihoods that covered 890 households. In Sri Lanka the household questionnaire could not be fielded because of renewed violence. — Not available.

were selected for the survey. We deliberately oversampled movers and the never poor because of the study's interest in learning from those who had moved out of poverty and those who had been able to maintain their wealth. Table B.3 shows the approximate desired distribution for sampling the household questionnaires in each community.

Adherence to this distribution depended on the availability of sufficient numbers of households in each of the four mobility groups. Sometimes it

**TABLE B.3**
**Desired distribution of households across mobility groups in all study regions**

|  | Now | |
|---|---|---|
| *10 years ago* | Poor or worse off | Nonpoor or better off |
| Poor or worse off | Chronic poor: 20% | Movers: 40% |
| Nonpoor or better off | Fallers: 10% | Never poor: 30% |

*Source:* D. Narayan and P. Petesch, "Moving Out of Poverty Methodology Guide" (Poverty Reduction Group, Poverty Reduction and Economic Management Network, World Bank, Washington, DC, 2005).

was not possible to match the target percentages: in very poor communities, for instance, the number of movers was limited, and therefore fewer movers were interviewed.

The household questionnaires were conducted mainly with adults between 30 and 60 years of age. The aim was to identify and understand the range of factors that helped or hindered the mobility of individuals within the larger context of their households and communities. The two multimodule questionnaires were innovative in that they collected information on social capital, personal aspirations, and perceptions of local governance, freedom, crime, insecurity, and violence, in addition to the usual demographic and economic information on assets, expenditure, health, and education. While many of the questions on expenditure and assets related to the household, the subjective questions were about the individual. The final column of table B.2 summarizes the number of household surveys collected in the conflict study regions. These varied from only 91 in Afghanistan to over 700 in Assam, for a total of 1,761 households in the study.

Two points are worth noting. First, the unit of analysis is the study region, not the country. The study made no attempt to create a nationally representative sample. In the discussion, country names are used merely as a shorthand way of identifying data from the study regions within those countries. Thus, by "Indonesia" it should be clear that we mean "the communities/households sampled for our study within the two selected regions of Indonesia" (North Maluku and East Java).

Second, the household surveys were not used to estimate numbers of poor or nonpoor or movers. Those are estimated in the community mobility matrix. The household surveys had two main uses. One was to reveal differences in reported characteristics, attitudes, behaviors, and outcomes of the movers out of poverty compared to the three other mobility groups. The second was to run multivariate regressions using the household's mobility status, as ascribed by the focus group, to establish associations between household mobility and characteristics of the household and locality. We made no attempt to establish causality or make causal claims based on these regressions, though that is one possible way to interpret the associations.

## Key Data Collection Instruments

The Moving Out of Poverty study utilizes several different instruments for data collection. This section describes the use of two key qualitative instruments: focus group discussions on "ladder of life" and on "conflict timeline and institutional mapping." These two instruments provide the basis for the community mobility and conflict intensity ratings, respectively, which serve as the foundation of the conflict study (see appendix C for a list and brief description of all data collection methods).

### Ladder of life and community mobility matrix

The community mobility ratings used in the study and regressions were based on the ladder of life household sorting exercise undertaken during community focus group discussions. This exercise, conducted in each study community, proceeded in four steps:

1. The focus group first discusses events and factors that have affected their community's prosperity over the past 10 years.
2. The group then constructs a figurative ladder of life for their community. Each step of the ladder corresponds to a category of household well-being that the group defines in terms of specific household characteristics (land ownership, assets, occupation, living conditions, social prestige, and psychological factors, among others). The process does not prescribe a set number of ladder steps, and the focus groups varied in the number of steps they used to characterize the different well-being groups in their communities.
3. As part of this discussion, each group develops its own definition of a poverty line, called the community poverty line (CPL). The ladder step just above the CPL is the step at which people are considered no longer poor in their community.
4. Once the focus group has created a detailed ladder and discussed why households in the community might move up and down the ladder, the focus group conducts a household sorting activity. Every household on a list of up to 150 households residing in the community (developed prior to the discussion) is mapped onto the ladder to denote the household's

well-being status both 10 years ago (usually 1995) and currently (at the time of the survey, usually 2005).

Table B.4 shows the ladder developed by a male focus group in the village of Bodolenge in North Maluku province, Indonesia. The group described households at the bottom step, for example, as those who can change their clothes only every three days and who rely on a public toilet to wash; while they may own a plot of land, their production is extremely low. By step 3, however, households can change their clothes twice a day, have their own rudimentary toilet, and have the means for more productive farming.

The discussion group of men in Bodolenge clustered the seven steps into three broad categories of poor (steps 1–2), prosperous (steps 3–5), and rich (steps 6–7). They reported that it was easy for households to move up or down within these three categories, but more difficult to jump across category lines. For instance, while they said it would be possible to manage one's farm plot with a little bit more effort and thus move from step 1 to step 2, they considered it more difficult to accumulate enough assets to acquire more land and move to step 3. Similarly, moving up from the middle categories to steps 6 and 7 required access to business capital, education, and large savings, which many households at the "prosperous" steps lacked. When the men were asked late in their discussions at which step a household was no longer deemed poor by the community, they indicated step 3. These discussions, then, serve to capture a complex set of multidimensional factors and processes surrounding household well-being and mobility.[11]

The final activity in the ladder focus groups is a household sorting exercise that is used to determine household mobility. The facilitator calls out the names of households in that community one by one, reading from a list of up to 150 households residing in the community that has been prepared in advance. The focus group members then identify the ladder step that each household should be placed on to denote its well-being status both 10 years ago (1995) and currently (2005).

After the focus group has completed its work, the research team constructs a community mobility matrix based on the group's household rankings. The community poverty line divides the mobility matrix into four quadrants showing which households, over the 10-year study period, have remained poor (upper left quadrant), moved out of poverty (upper right quadrant), fallen into poverty (lower left quadrant), or remained nonpoor (lower right quadrant). This study's community mobility matrixes are similar in many ways to standard transition matrixes based on measured income or consumption,

**TABLE B.4**
**Ladder of life from male focus group discussions in Bodolenge, Indonesia**

| Key reasons for downward movement | Characteristics of ladder steps | Key reasons for upward movement |
|---|---|---|
| *Conflict:*<br><br>"Before the conflict, our life was peaceful and harmonious. In the conflict, people were separated: many people took refuge in Manado, Java, and other places. The Muslims still do not want to return."<br><br>"The yield in the plantation could not be fully harvested for years, because people were still afraid. Children were not allowed to go to the plantation unless guarded by a soldier."<br><br>"All the houses were destroyed and we spent all of our savings for reconstruction."<br><br>*Unstable prices:*<br><br>"Farmers are dependent on the price of the harvest crop. If prices fall, the income of the farmers decreases and they are likely to fail." | **Step 7: RICHEST**<br>Own a beautiful house with tile floor, a ceiling, and plastered walls; have a sofa set; have sanitary facilities inside the house with ceramic floor; able to send children to school up to university; when sick, get medical treatment in Manado; use electric stove for cooking; own a TV set (21 inches), a disc antenna, and a VCD player; have a cellular phone; own farmland; have substantial savings; are able to buy many cows, looked after by other people with shared yield system; own two cars for business; work as entrepreneurs<br><br>**Step 6: RICH**<br>Have more than enough food, eat properly with chicken twice a month; drink instant coffee; own a plastered house; own a TV set (21 inches), disc antenna, video and CD player; own a fridge; have good sanitary facilities; are able to send children to college in Ternate; when sick, get medical treatment in Ternate; have more savings than those at step 5; own two motorcycles; own kerosene stove with 24 wicks; work as teachers or school principals<br><br>**Step 5: MORE PROSPEROUS**<br>Own a house painted and finely plastered; own two sets of plastic chairs; own a TV set (20 inches), disc antenna, radio, VCD player, and tape recorder; have own sanitary facility finely plastered; are able to send children up to senior high; when sick, get medical treatment in Jailolo; own a bicycle and a cart to carry goods; own a kerosene stove with 24 wicks; have more savings than those at step 4; own a motorcycle; own two cows<br><br>**Step 4: PROSPEROUS**<br>Have enough food and eat chicken once a month; change clothes three times a day; own a plastered and painted house, with floor roughly plastered; own one set of plastic chairs; when sick, get medical treatment at a public health center in Jailolo; have own sanitary facility but not plastered; own a TV set (18 inches), a radio, and a video and CD player; own a bicycle; have savings, but only a little; own a cow | *Social support mechanisms:*<br><br>"Having successful friends who give advice and encouragement about moving up is important."<br><br>*Networks:*<br><br>"Participation in groups that support business activities, such as the farmer or savings group, helps one to move out of poverty."<br><br>*Access to loans and credit:*<br><br>"With business credit and loans delivered through government programs, one can move up to the next step."<br><br>*Transportation:*<br><br>"In the past, farmers could not sell the harvest yield to Ternate, because there was no transportation overland. Now, the roads are fixed and one can take a car. The transportation is good." |

| | | |
|---|---|---|
| *Lack of education:*<br><br>"There is no human capital. Many villagers lack the knowledge necessary to expand their business."<br><br>"Children cannot go to junior high school because the roads are in bad condition." | **Step 3: LESS PROSPEROUS**<br>Have a good diet, eat rice every day; eat chicken on Christmas days; change clothes twice a day; own a semi-permanent house; own chairs made of bamboo; own a TV set (14 inches) used only to watch movies on CDs, a radio, and a tape recorder; have own sanitary facility but not permanent (walls made of jute/cement sacks and woven bamboo); able to send children up to senior high; when sick, go to the village clinic at own expense, not using health card; own a farm land with 60–70 clove trees; no savings | *Crop diversification:*<br><br>"To move up, farmers can plant monthly crops like corn and groundnut that become ready for harvesting in a short time. They should not depend on yearly plants like clove, nutmeg, and coconut." |
| *Health shocks and lack of health care:*<br><br>"Death of a family member, especially parents, is devastating. The children are not capable of managing the business left by the parents." | **Step 2: POOR**<br>Have enough food to eat, with rice twice a day, otherwise banana and kasbi (edible tuber); eat chicken on Christmas day; change clothes once a day; own a semi-permanent house (75% finished), not yet plastered, not painted; have chairs made of bamboo; have no sanitary facility, use public one; able to send children up to junior high; able to afford bicycle for children; own a tape recorder; only work as much as needed | *Hard work and family:*<br><br>"The key is to work hard, to have the will to move up, and to have an encouraging family, a supportive wife." |
| "Doctors never come to this area. There is only one nurse in this community." | **Step 1: POOREST**<br>Eat rice once a day, otherwise banana and kasbi; not thrifty, the day's earning is spent all at once, have to earn for the following day; change clothes once every three days; able to send children only up to primary school; use health card to get health treatment from a paramedic; own a semi-permanent house; have no electricity; own furniture consisting of benches; bathe at a public sanitary; own a small piece of farmland; own clove and nutmeg plantations but do not know how to take care of them, so the yield is poor; no hard work; no savings | |

*Source:* Male ladder of life discussion group in Bodolenge, Indonesia.
*Note:* Bold line indicates the community poverty line. Focus group discussants in this community placed the community poverty line at the same level as the official poverty line.

except that they are based on community-defined categories (not constructed categories like quintiles of income) and on community recall.

Figure B.3 presents the mobility matrix for 78 households in Bodolenge. The steps of the ladder in this village go from step 1, the poorest, to step 7, the richest. Each of the numbers in the cells represents a particular household (the household numbers are arbitrary labels). A household's placement in the matrix is determined by its position on steps of the ladder today, as perceived by the focus group, and 10 years ago, as recalled by the group. Household 14, for example, moved up from step 1 in 1995 to step 3 in 2005 and would be labeled a "mover." Household 10 remained at the poorest step in both periods ("chronic poor"), while household 21 remained at the richest step ("chronic rich"). Both household 36 and household 94 fell into poverty ("fallers") over the study period. In comparing mobility patterns for the whole set of households, the share of poor (on steps 1 and 2) in Bodolenge fell from 43 to 16 percent over the study period. Therefore, according to the key summary statistic for our study, 68 percent moved out of poverty (MOP = initial poor who cross the community poverty line/initial poor), so the MOP index for Bodolenge is 0.68. A greater proportion of the initially poor households, 88 percent, experienced upward mobility in general (MPI = initially poor who move up irrespective of whether they crossed the CPL). Therefore, the MPI index for Bodolenge is 0.88.

The Bodolenge focus group participants testified that the most important factor that helped them prosper was their collective spirit to rebuild the community. This was evident in the reconstruction of houses and other shelters through voluntary work and the formation of mutual groups to encourage savings among farmers. At the household or individual level, hard work and support from family or social networks were considered to be important determinants of upward mobility. In addition, better security, roads, and transportation improved access to buyers of agricultural products. This especially helped farmers in the bottom and middle categories sell their harvest and move up or accumulate greater savings. Delivery of government programs (such as the Kecamatan Development Program) and informal saving mechanisms among farmers are also mentioned as important determinants of mobility out of poverty.

In discussing reasons why households might fall down the ladder, the men's focus group in Bodolenge pointed to the shock of violent conflict combined with hardships created by a poor harvest, limited access to farmland, emigration and damage to support networks, and depletion of savings for reconstruction. At the household level, failure to diversify income sources left

## FIGURE B.3
## Community mobility matrix from Bodolenge, Indonesia, based on male focus group discussion

| Steps | | Now 1 | Now 2 | Now 3 | Now 4 | Now 5 | Now 6 | Now 7 | Total |
|---|---|---|---|---|---|---|---|---|---|
| | 1 | 10 | 11, 15, 29, 40, 73, 85, 91 **MPI** | *14* | | | | | 9 (12%) |
| | 2 | 39 | 12, 75, | 5, 18, 22, 50, 65, 67, 72, 84, 88, 90, 92 | 6, 13, 23, 26, 33, 41, 42, 43, 46, 69, 70 **MOP** | | | | 25 (31%) |
| *10 years ago* | 3 | | 99 | 8, 16, 38, 63, 68, 71, 74, 80, 83, 93 | 7, 31, 64, 66, 82 | 4, 34 | 3 | | 19 (24%) |
| | 4 | | *36, 94* | 54, 59 | 36, 56, 57, 58, 76, 77, 78, 81, 86, 89, 97 | | 30 | | 16 (21%) |
| | 5 | | | | | | | | 0 (0%) |
| | 6 | | 1, 19 | | | | 2, 47, 53, 79, 87 | | 7 (9%) |
| | 7 | | | | | | 20 | *21* | 2 (3%) |
| | Total | 2 (3%) | 14 (18%) | 24 (31%) | 27 (34%) | 2 (3%) | 8 (10%) | 1 (1%) | 78 (100%) |

Source: Male ladder of life discussion group in Bodolenge, Indonesia.
Note: The bold lines indicate the community poverty line, set between steps 2 and 3 in this community. Households whose numbers are shown in bold italic are discussed in the text. MOP refers to the proportion of the initially poor households that moved out of poverty, while MPI refers to the initially poor households that moved up (irrespective of whether they crossed the CPL) over the study period.

farmers vulnerable to unstable prices for their harvest. Lack of education and health shocks were also important reasons for falling into poverty.

## Conflict timeline and institutional mapping

A key data collection method specific to the conflict study was to collect rich contextual descriptions of the violent conflicts that took place in the community and analyze their consequences. In this activity, small discussion groups of local residents probe the forms and nature of local conflicts and their effects over time on local economic opportunities, power structures, and key institutions. These institutions often included those related to local governance, conflict mediation, and/or public safety.

The same data were collected in the sample of communities from the conflict countries where there was little or no political violence, and the study questions were framed broadly enough to be relevant to these contexts as well. The activity consists of four steps:

1. *Public safety and dispute resolution:* The focus group members discuss public safety conditions and trends, as well as mechanisms used in the community to resolve disputes. Other topics are explored, as necessary, to open the discussion in a way that builds on the strengths of each community.

2. *Trajectory of major conflicts:* The focus group members are asked to recall the most important conflicts that have affected the community in the past 10 years. Although the focus is on this period of recall, the participants can indicate other significant conflicts that have occurred earlier. Our definition of "major conflict" includes violent events that resulted in a large or small number of deaths or injuries, and extensive or limited property damage, but it excludes everyday petty theft and crime. Once the respondents have listed all of the major conflicts that they can recall, they are asked to identify the most important conflicts and explain the nature, duration, and impact of each of them in greater detail.

3. *Impact on key livelihoods:* The focus group members are asked questions about how conflict has affected key livelihoods in the community. If there have been multiple conflicts in the village, then the focus is on the most important conflict that occurred in the past 10 years.

4. *Impact on institutions:* The focus group members are asked to examine the functioning of and changes in community institutions in areas affected by conflict. These institutional dynamics are explored within the context of an important conflict or dispute that occurred in the community within the past 10 years. The purpose is to obtain a clear understanding of

the leading local institutions and of how a context of conflict has affected these local institutions, local governance, and local economic opportunities and livelihoods over time. The different actors and impacts are often identified on an institutional map.

Fieldwork in a conflict context requires extensive preparation in order to create an environment of trust and openness for data collection and ensure the safety of the field team and the study participants. In this conflict study, government authorities at all levels and representatives from opposition groups, where relevant, were familiarized with the purpose of the research and consulted on the timing of fieldwork and on measures that could be taken to ensure the safety of all involved. In addition, the research teams conducted the conflict timeline focus group activity in a private area at the end of the fieldwork, after they had gained some understanding of the conflict through a key informant interview. This helped reduce suspicions that might arise from asking the group detailed questions about the conflict and provided more time for the field team to establish trust with local people and better understand key concerns facing the community.

## Background to the Community Regressions

To construct the community regressions, we first specify (a) a measure for the dependent variable, that is, "movement out of poverty" (MOP); (b) measures for each of the conceptual variables; (c) the way we propose to distinguish between private and community impacts of some of the conceptual variables (particularly the local democracy and agency measures); and (d) the control variables included in the regressions.

### Measure for mobility: The dependent variable

Since the study is about the mobility of poor people, only those households that were poor 10 years ago, at the beginning of the study period, were included for purposes of regression analysis. Within this "initial poor set," the objective was to differentiate between those who moved out of poverty over the 10 years and those who did not. The dependent variable used in community and household regressions in the study was called "moving out of poverty" (MOP), which was based on the group of households that were initially poor and moved up and out of poverty over 10 years, crossing the community poverty line. Although we limit our regression analysis in this volume to only one dependent variable, an additional dependent variable measuring "mobility of the poor" (MPI) was also used for the regression analysis in the global study. In sum, the two indexes were as follows:

- MOP: households that were initially poor and moved up and out of poverty over 10 years, crossing the community poverty line
- MPI: households that were initially poor and moved up any distance over 10 years, irrespective of whether or not they crossed the community poverty line.

The data offered two measures that could be used to calculate the dependent variables. The first was status of and change in the household's rank on the ladder of life, now compared to 10 years ago, as identified by the ladder of life focus group discussion. The second was status of and change in the household's self-assessed rank on the ladder of life, now compared to 10 years ago, as identified by the respondent in the household questionnaire.

The dependent variable used in the study was constructed using the first measure: community perceptions of the household's mobility on the ladder of life. It is important that the mobility ratings were *not self-assessed*. This was to avoid endogeneity biases or "halo effects" that might arise in regressing a household's own perception of movement against its perception of variables measuring the conceptual categories. For instance, it may well be that people who subjectively *feel* they have more control of decision making also subjectively *feel* they are moving up—even if others perceive them as economically stagnant. By using the community's perception of mobility as the dependent variable and the individual's responses about the household as measures of the right-hand-side variables, this particular problem is attenuated, if not eliminated.

*Construction of MOP score*
The ladder of life discussion group developed mobility rankings of each household that received the survey. Focus group members recalled the household's placement on the well-being ladder 10 years ago and then determined its current step on the ladder. Based on these mobility ranks and the community poverty line, the MOP score was constructed as a binary variable (yes/no) using the following formula:

$$MOP^{h,j} = \begin{cases} 1 & if \ step^{h,j}_{t-n} < CPL^j, \ step^{h,j}_t \geq CPL^j \\ 0 & otherwise \end{cases}$$

where step is the step on the ladder of life constructed by the focus group and CPL is the community poverty line set by the group and n is the (roughly 10-year) recall period.

## Measures for conceptual categories of independent variables

The MOP dependent variables were regressed against various independent variables to produce the partial associations (no attribution of causality is expressed or implied). These included both community variables and household variables. The community-level variables were of two types: one set comes from the community instruments, such as the focus group, and the other comes from using the household responses and computing leave-out means. A list of all of the variables used in the regressions reported in this volume with their sources and coding is presented in appendix D.

*Community variables from community instruments*
There were eight community-level variables used in the regressions that were drawn either from the community-level information provided by key informants or from the focus group discussions.

- *Initial strength of the economy.* Key informants were asked about the strength of the local economy, the presence of private employers, and the difficulty of finding a job 10 years ago.
- *Access to education.* Key informants were asked to identify the presence of main educational institutions in their village (in both 1995 and 2005) including primary, lower secondary, upper secondary, technical or vocational, college or university, and other schools.
- *Social exclusion.* Two questions were combined into an index using principal components analysis (PCA). Focus group participants were asked to estimate changes in decision making on important community affairs over 10 years. The index also included a question on whether access to networks and associations within the village had increased or decreased (or had remained the same) over 10 years.
- *Access to information.* Key informants were asked to identify the presence of information sources in their village (in both 1995 and 2005) including local newspaper, national newspaper, national television station, national radio station, a community bulletin board, and public telephones.
- *Presence of and membership in local groups.* Key informants were asked to identify the presence of economic and social groups in their village 10 years ago, including financial/credit groups, religious groups, political groups, and ethnic groups.
- *Local democracy.* Key informants were asked two questions about the presence and representativeness of a village council. They were also asked whether the village held community meetings to discuss community issues.

- *Religious polarization.* This was based on demographic criteria, on the relative sizes of the two largest religious groups.
- *Corruption.* Three questions were combined into an index using PCA. The key informant questionnaire included two questions about corruption, one about officials at the national level and one about officials at the local/community level. In addition, the focus group discussion produced an estimate of corruption among government officials in the community.

## Using principal components to combine conceptually related variables

For many of the phenomena that the analyst might wish to elicit and examine, it is impossible to know with any precision which question will produce the most reliable responses. Hence, questionnaires often include questions on closely related concepts. When data are to be used in multivariate regressions, this leaves the analyst with four options. We chose to combine conceptually similar questions into a single index using principal components.

A word about the three options rejected. One is "profligacy," simply including in the regressions all of the possible variables. This has the advantage of "letting the data decide," but it has the disadvantages of creating regressions with 50 or more individual variables and of producing massive multicollinearity if the variables are in fact closely related conceptually. A second option is to choose the "best" indicator for each conceptual category. This can be done a priori, which runs the risk of choosing the empirically least successful (e.g., most subject to measurement error), or it can be done based on "horse races" of available candidates, which is the very definition of data mining. The third option is to use some index based on a weighted average of the questions. This has the advantage of reducing the numbers of variables and avoids data mining, but the weights are arbitrary. A common practice of using "equal" weights has nothing in particular to recommend it.

Principal components analysis is a commonly used data reduction technique that reduces a set of variables to a single variable. It analyzes the correlations between a set of variables and produces a set of weighted averages of the underlying variables such that (a) each captures the maximum common variation among the set of variables, and (b) each additional factor after the first is orthogonal to the previous factor. So the first factor is a linear weighted average of the set of $N$ variables with weights chosen so as to maximize the overall common variance of all the variables.

While in many ways the index produced is arbitrary, this does have three advantages. First, it is not data mining, as it does not use any information about the dependent variable in choosing the specification. Second, it chooses weights that, if the $N$ variables in the set are truly conceptually related, statistically best capture the common variation. Third, since it is a linear index, it is relatively easy to map back from the underlying variable through the regression coefficient to the association with the dependent variable.

We did the principal components analysis study region by study region, rather than imposing common weights across all study regions. The results for each study region for each PCA-constructed variable are presented in appendix E. First, whenever there are only two variables, PCA just produced equal weights. Second, the results are mostly in accord with expectations. All variables are recoded so that movements in the same direction numerically represent movement in the same conceptual direction (this is not necessarily true in the raw questions). We see that most of the PCA, therefore, produces, as expected, indexes with all positive weights, often nearly equal. But third, there is considerable variation across countries in the weights. Rather than attempt to choose the "best" fit for each study region, we just implemented the data reduction technique and used the weights produced.

The only way in which this process differed from the perfectly garden-variety PCA was that we wanted an index of conditions 10 years ago. But rather than using the PCA weights from 10 years ago, we did PCA on the current variables and then used those weights to construct an index for 10 years ago, based on the values of the underlying variables from that time.

Once we had the PCA scores, we could infer the estimate associated with each individual component variable in that index with the dependent variable (MOP or MPI). To do so, we proceeded in two steps. First, we used the PCA weights to calculate how much a change in an individual component of the index would change the index (which involved the variance of the component because PCA norms the raw variables). Next, we multiplied this value with the ordinary least squares regression coefficient for the PCA score to estimate the concomitant associated change in MOP/MPI.

## Functional Form

An ordinary least squares (OLS) model was used for running regressions. Since the dependent variable is a binary outcome (0/1), this is sometimes referred to as the linear probability model. It is well known that with a limited dependent variable, there are estimation techniques (such as probit and logit) that are statistically more efficient. This is because by imposing in estimation the constraint (which must be true) that the predictions of outcomes by the regression techniques have to be strictly between zero and one, these techniques produce lower standard errors than OLS.

We did not do this, however, for three reasons. First, the loss from not using a logit or probit estimator is only efficiency (a second-order property of estimators), not consistency, and we suspect that in this case the gains to precision are not particularly meaningful. Second, the linear probability model has ease of interpretation, particularly when moving from the underlying PCA-constructed indexes to the reporting of outcome associations. Third, with nonlinear functional forms like logit and probit, the use of the leave-out means is much more complicated.

All of the standard errors used the standard adjustment to be consistent with cluster-based sampling using the cluster techniques available in Stata data analysis software.

While a complete specification was run for the study regions in India, a relatively parsimonious model was used for the non-India study regions, where sample sizes were much smaller. The sparse specification excluded the PCA index on fairness, the PCA index for social inequality in schools, and ownership of land. Leave-out means were included only for the responsiveness of local democracy and personal agency PCAs. For the conflict sample regressions presented in this volume, a slightly different specification (with fewer explanatory variables) was used because of the smaller sample size and policy focus on conflict. These regression results are presented in appendix F.

## Notes

1. This technical note draws from appendix 2 of the second volume in the Moving Out of Poverty series, which presents a detailed discussion of the global study's methodology and sampling. See D. Narayan, L. Pritchett, and S. Kapoor, *Moving Out of Poverty: Success from the Bottom Up* (New York: Palgrave Macmillan; Washington, DC: World Bank, 2009). A technical note by the same authors that describes the sampling and methodology, entitled "Moving Up and Out of Poverty: Countries, Communities and Individuals," is available on the Moving Out of Poverty Web site (http://go.worldbank.org/5RHUMMKC70).

2. The case study of Assam was published in the third volume in the Moving Out of Poverty series and is not included in the present volume. See D. Narayan, ed., *Moving Out of Poverty: The Promise of Empowerment and Democracy in India* (New York: Palgrave Macmillan; Washington, DC: World Bank, 2009).

3. The discussion in this section replicates the conceptual framework discussion in chapter 1 of volume 2 of the Moving Out of Poverty series, with minor modifications specific to the conflict study. See D. Narayan, L. Pritchett, and S. Kapoor, 2009, *Moving Out of Poverty: Success from the Bottom Up* (New York: Palgrave Macmillan; Washington, DC: World Bank).

4. SOSOTEC stands for Self-Organizing System on the Edge of Chaos. The exercise is done in groups.

5. All local-level communities in the study (villages, barrios, etc.) are identified by pseudonyms in this book. Higher-level entities (blocks, provinces, districts, regions, states, and countries) are identified by their real names.

6. We often use the terms "individual" and "household" interchangeably, although we recognize that complicated gender and other dynamics inside the household will often keep the household from acting as a single unit.

7. Charles Tilly, *Durable Inequality* (Berkeley: University of California Press, 1999).

8. The other countries included in the global study are Bangladesh, India (Andhra Pradesh, Uttar Pradesh, and West Bengal), Malawi, Mexico, Morocco, Senegal, Tanzania, Thailand, and Uganda.

9. For the studies that used panel data, such as Cambodia in the present volume, the household samples were conducted by revisiting panel households and interviewing the same person who was interviewed for the panel before.

10. The observation periods for the country studies vary somewhat and are specified in each of the country chapters. To help people with recall, teams were instructed to select an initial study year that coincided with a major event in the country, such as the transition to a new president. In Cambodia, however, the study built on an existing panel; a baseline year of 2001 was used for sorting households, and 1993 was used as the baseline for focus group discussions of trends. The Colombia study examined mobility processes in six mostly new neighborhoods settled by large displaced populations, as well as in two conflict-affected villages. The baseline years for the new barrios vary from 4 to 10 years ago, depending on the age of the settlements.

11. These descriptions were enriched with additional qualitative data collection methods such as open-ended life story interviews with male and female participants. See appendix C for a full list of the data collection methods.

# Appendix C: Data Collection Methods

**TABLE C.1**
**Data collection methods**

| Activity | Data collection method | Purpose | Sources of information |
|---|---|---|---|
| 1 | Selective literature review | • Provide background to the key growth and poverty puzzles in the country.<br>• Help design the study. | Secondary sources |
| 2 | Key informant interview or workshop: national timeline | • Identify policy questions to be addressed by the study.<br>• Develop a national timeline of key events and policies that have helped or hindered people's movements out of poverty. | Policy experts from government, civil society, and private sector |
| 3 | Community profile | • Identify community-level factors that have helped or hindered movement out of poverty and the overall prosperity of the community over the past 10 years.<br>• Quantify and code data emerging from focus discussions based on their ratings of issues ranging from community prosperity to freedom and inequality. | Key informants<br>Focus group discussions |
| 4 | Key informant interview: community timeline | • Understand community-level events or factors that have helped or hindered movement out of poverty and the overall prosperity of the community.<br>• Gain an understanding of the local context. | Two to four key informants in a group or individually |
| 5 | Focus group discussion: ladder of life | • Identify the range of factors that help or hinder movement out of poverty or prosperity over time at the community level.<br>• Identify the range of factors that help or hinder movement out of poverty or prosperity over time at the household level, and the reasons for movement at the different levels.<br>• Identify the sequencing and interaction among factors at the household level that enable movement between different steps of the ladder of life.<br>• Identify the mobility status of specific households in the community. | One focus group of adult men<br>One focus group of adult women |

| | | | |
|---|---|---|---|
| 6 | Focus group discussion: livelihoods, freedom, power, democracy, and local governance | • Understand trends in economic opportunities for the community.<br>• Understand the impact of government rules and regulations and other factors on access to economic opportunities.<br>• Explore people's understanding of the concepts of freedom, power, and inequality, and how these concepts relate to economic mobility and well-being.<br>• Explore people's understanding of democracy and how democracy is working at the local level. | One focus group of adult men<br>One focus group of adult women<br>Depending on the local context, this activity can be conducted as one discussion, or there can be two sections discussing (a) sources of economic opportunities and the role of governance, and (b) freedom, power, inequality, and democracy. |
| 7 | Focus group discussion: aspirations of youth | • Explore youths' aspirations for earning a living and steps they are taking to prepare for their future.<br>• Explore youths' understandings of the concepts of freedom, power, inequality, and democracy, and how these concepts relate to economic mobility and well-being. | One focus group of male youths<br>One focus group of female youths |
| 8 | Two mini–case studies: community-wide events and factors affecting mobility;<br>or<br>Focus group discussion: conflict timeline and institutional mapping (for study countries affected by conflict) | • Provide in-depth analysis from a range of perspectives on two important events or factors affecting the overall economic prosperity of the community over the past 10 years.<br>• Understand public safety conditions and trends over the last 10 years and local mechanisms for ensuring safety and resolving disputes in the community.<br>• Understand the major conflicts or disputes in the community over the last 10 years.<br>• Assess how conflict affects livelihoods in the community.<br>• Examine the functioning of and changes in community institutions in areas affected by conflict. | Key informants and focus group discussions |

*(continued)*

**TABLE C.1**
*continued*

| Activity | Data collection method | Purpose | Sources of information |
|---|---|---|---|
| 9 | Household questionnaire | • Identify the range of factors that help or hinder mobility of individuals within the context of their households. | Select informants randomly within each mobility category based on the household sorting exercise undertaken during the ladder of life focus group discussion. |
| 10 | Open-ended interviews: individual life stories | • Understand how and why some individuals escaped poverty, and the factors and processes that led to their escape.<br><br>• Understand how and why some individuals managed to stay out of poverty, and the factors and processes that helped them maintain their wealth.<br><br>• Understand how and why some individuals remained trapped in chronic poverty, and the factors and processes that kept them in poverty.<br><br>• Understand how and why some individuals fell into poverty, and the factors and processes that led to their decline.<br><br>• Understand the factors and processes that come together for accumulation or depletion of assets and savings. | Adults (men or women) 30–60 years of age. A household questionnaire is completed with each informant who provides an individual life story. Identification of informants follows a process similar to selection of informants for the questionnaire. |

# Appendix D: List of Variables for Community Regressions

**TABLE D.1**
**List of variables for community regressions**

| Explanatory variable | Source | Coding/ directionality |
|---|---|---|
| *Economic opportunity* | | |
| Strength of local economy 10 years ago (rc205b) | KI | very weak=1, very strong=5 |
| Access to education (PCA index, rc301) | KI | yes=1, no=0 |
| Primary school present in village/neighborhood (rc301i) | KI | yes=1, no=0 |
| Lower secondary school present in village/neighborhood (rc301ii) | KI | yes=1, no=0 |
| Upper secondary school present in village/neighborhood (rc301iii) | KI | yes=1, no=0 |
| Technical/vocational school present in village/ neighborhood (rc301iv) | KI | yes=1, no=0 |
| College/university present in village/neighborhood (rc301v) | KI | yes=1, no=0 |
| Access to credit from friends (c223b_friend) | KI | yes=1, no=0 |
| *Local democracy (PCA index)* | | |
| Presence of village council 10 years ago (rc502b) | KI | yes=1, no=0 |
| Village council was representative 10 years ago (r2c502b2) | KI | yes=1, no=0 |
| Village had organized community meetings 10 years ago (rc410b) | KI | yes=1, no=0 |
| *Corruption (PCA index)* | | |
| Corruption in government officials at the country level (c505b) | KI | almost none=1, almost all=4 |
| Corruption in government officials in village (c506b) | KI | almost none=1, almost all=4 |
| *Social stratification* | | |
| Religious polarization[a] (polarrel_ed3) | KI | polarization=1, no polarization=0 |
| *Exclusion from social institutions and political processes* | | |
| Index of social exclusion (PCA index) | | |
| Change in access to networks and associations within the community (c919) | FGD | less access=3, more access=1 |
| Change in participation in decision making (c916) | FGD | less access=3, more access=1 |

## TABLE D.1
*continued*

| Explanatory variable | Source | Coding/ directionality |
|---|---|---|
| *Access to information* | | |
| Access to information 10 years ago (PCA index) | | |
| Local newspaper (IMrc5071b) | KI | yes=1, no=0 |
| National newspaper (IMrc5072b) | KI | yes=1, no=0 |
| National television (IMrc5073b) | KI | yes=1, no=0 |
| National radio (IMrc5074b) | KI | yes=1, no=0 |
| Community bulletin board (IMrc5075b) | KI | yes=1, no=0 |
| Public telephones (IMrc5076b) | KI | yes=1, no=0 |
| *Presence of and membership in local social groups (PCA index)* | | |
| Number of financial/credit groups 10 years ago (c402b) | KI | |
| Number of political groups 10 years ago (c404b) | KI | |
| Number of religious groups 10 years ago (c405b) | KI | |
| Number of ethnic groups 10 years ago (c405ib) | KI | |
| *Control variables* | | |
| Regional controls[b] | | |
| Afghanistan dummy | | yes=1, no=0 |
| Indonesia dummy | | yes=1, no=0 |
| Philippines dummy | | yes=1, no=0 |
| Colombia dummy | | yes=1, no=0 |
| Region East Asia | | yes=1, no=0 |
| Region Africa | | yes=1, no=0 |
| Region Latin America | | yes=1, no=0 |
| Conflict country dummy | | yes=1, no=0 |
| Conflict community dummy | | yes=1, no=0 |
| Percent of village population starting poor (com_psped) | | 0 to 100 |

*Note:* Reference questions in the community questionnaire are indicated by *c* and in the household questionnaire by *h*. Prefix *r* means variable was recoded. Suffix *a* means current (at time of the study); *b* means initial (approximately 10 years ago). KI = key informant; FGD = focus group discussion.
a. Polarization is highest where the largest and the second-largest groups are equal in size.
b. When used in regressions for the sample of conflict countries, regional dummies include only Colombia in Latin America and only the Philippines and Indonesia in East Asia. Because Afghanistan, which is in South Asia, is always included separately, the reference country is India in the overall and peaceful countries samples, and Assam in the conflict countries sample.

# Appendix E: Weights for the PCA-Constructed Indexes

## TABLE E.1
## Weights for the PCA-constructed indexes

| *Economic opportunity* | |
|---|---|
| Access to education index (rc301) | |
| Primary school present in village/neighborhood (rc301i) | 0.1900 |
| Lower secondary school present in village/neighborhood (rc301ii) | 0.4811 |
| Upper secondary school present in village/neighborhood (rc301iii) | 0.5506 |
| Technical/vocational school present in village/neighborhood (rc301iv) | 0.4151 |
| College/university present in village/neighborhood (rc301v) | 0.5069 |
| *Index of social exclusion* | |
| Change in access to networks and associations within the community (c919) | 0.7071 |
| Change in participation in decision making, 1=more, 3=less (c916) | 0.7071 |
| *Access to information index, 10 years ago* | |
| Local newspaper (IMrc5071b) | 0.4473 |
| National newspaper (IMrc5072b) | 0.4733 |
| National television (IMrc5073b) | 0.5204 |
| National radio (IMrc5074b) | 0.3485 |
| Community bulletin board (IMrc5075b) | 0.3393 |
| Public telephones (IMrc5076b) | 0.2618 |

# Appendix F:
# Additional Tables for Part 1

**TABLE F.1**

**Mean MOP of communities by conflict rating and migration trend, 1995–2005**

| Predominant migration trend | Conflict | Nonconflict | Total |
|---|---|---|---|
| Inward or no migration | 0.18 | 0.16 | 0.17 |
| Outward migration | 0.21 | 0.10 | 0.17 |
| Total | 0.18 | 0.14 | 0.17 |

Source: Ladder of life group discussions and authors' analysis.

**TABLE F.2**

**Distribution of communities by conflict and MOP rating in Assam and non-Assam portions of sample**

percentage of communities

| | Total sample without Assam | | Assam only | |
|---|---|---|---|---|
| MOP rating | Conflict | Nonconflict | Conflict | Nonconflict |
| Low MOP | 35 | 50 | 34 | 33 |
| Middle MOP | 35 | 21 | 34 | 33 |
| High MOP | 31 | 29 | 31 | 33 |
| Total | 100 | 100 | 100 | 100 |

Source: Ladder of life group discussions and authors' analysis.
Note: Total sample includes Sri Lanka.

**TABLE F.3**

**Democratic structures in conflict and nonconflict communities, 1995 and 2005**

percentage of communities

| Democratic structure | Year | Conflict | Nonconflict |
|---|---|---|---|
| Presence of village council | 2005 | 39 | 44 |
| | 1995 | 32 | 30 |
| Elected village leader | 2005 | 77 | 70 |
| | 1995 | 70 | 63 |
| Fairly elected village leader | 2005 | 73 | 65 |
| | 1995 | 61 | 44 |

Source: Community questionnaire.

**TABLE F.4**
**Democratic structures by MOP rating in conflict and nonconflict communities, 1995 and 2005**

*percentage of communities*

| | | Low MOP | | High MOP | |
|---|---|---|---|---|---|
| Democratic structure | Year | Conflict | Nonconflict | Conflict | Nonconflict |
| Presence of village council | 2005 | 37 | 58 | 39 | 38 |
| | 1995 | 32 | 33 | 28 | 38 |
| Elected village leader | 2005 | 89 | 83 | 56 | 50 |
| | 1995 | 89 | 75 | 50 | 38 |
| Fairly elected village leader | 2005 | 89 | 82 | 47 | 50 |
| | 1995 | 84 | 50 | 35 | 38 |

*Source:* Community questionnaire.
*Note:* The middle MOP tercile of communities is not presented.


**TABLE F.5**
**Representation on local councils in conflict and nonconflict communities, 1995 and 2005**

| Indicator | Year | Conflict | Nonconflict |
|---|---|---|---|
| % of councils where all social groups are represented | 2005 | 81 | 83 |
| | 1995 | 83 | 75 |
| % of council members who are women | 2005 | 25 | 18 |
| | 1995 | 8 | 11 |
| % of council members who are poor | 2005 | 50 | 60 |
| | 1995 | 40 | 38 |

*Source:* Community questionnaire.
*Note:* "All social groups" refers to ethnic, religious, tribal, caste, racial, and language groups.


**TABLE F.6**
**Representation of all social groups on local councils, by country, 1995 and 2005**

*percentage of councils*

| Year | Afghanistan | Assam[a] | Colombia | Indonesia | Philippines | Total |
|---|---|---|---|---|---|---|
| 2005 | | | | | | |
| Conflict | 100 | 67 | 50 | 100 | 86 | 81 |
| Nonconflict | 100 | n.a. | 100 | 60 | 100 | 83 |
| Total | 100 | 67 | 71 | 78 | 89 | 82 |
| 1995 | | | | | | |
| Conflict | 100 | 100 | 33 | 100 | 83 | 83 |
| Nonconflict | 100 | n.a. | 100 | 33 | 100 | 75 |
| Total | 100 | 100 | 50 | 71 | 88 | 81 |

*Source:* Community questionnaire.
*Note:* "All social groups" refers to ethnic, religious, tribal, caste, racial, and language groups; n.a. = not applicable.
a. In Assam the numbers represent only three communities.

**TABLE F.7**
**Representation on local councils and responsiveness of local government, by country, 1995 and 2005**
*percentage of communities*

| Indicator | Afghanistan | Assam | Colombia | Indonesia | Philippines | Total |
|---|---|---|---|---|---|---|
| *Representativeness of village council, 2005* | | | | | | |
| Not representative or no council | 17 | 96 | 38 | 30 | 20 | 68 |
| Representative | 83 | 4 | 63 | 70 | 80 | 32 |
| *Representativeness of village council, 1995* | | | | | | |
| Not representative or no council | 0 | 98 | 75 | 50 | 30 | 75 |
| Representative | 100 | 2 | 25 | 50 | 70 | 25 |
| *Change in representativeness of village council, trend over 10 years*[a] | | | | | | |
| Never representative or no council | n.a. | 96 | 50 | 60 | 67 | 87 |
| Representative in 2005, but not in 1995 | n.a. | 4 | 50 | 40 | 33 | 13 |
| *Responsiveness of local government, 2005* | | | | | | |
| A lot | 33 | 6 | 25 | 50 | 40 | 19 |
| A little | 33 | 66 | 25 | 40 | 50 | 55 |
| Not at all | 33 | 28 | 50 | 10 | 10 | 26 |
| *Change in responsiveness of local government, 2005* | | | | | | |
| More responsive | 67 | 8 | 38 | 80 | 60 | 30 |
| Same | 33 | 66 | 25 | 0 | 30 | 48 |
| Less responsive | 0 | 26 | 38 | 20 | 10 | 23 |

*Source:* Community questionnaire.
a. In communities without a village council or where the council was nonrepresentative in 1995. Communities that were representative in 1995 remained representative with two exceptions: one community in Afghanistan and one in Assam did not have representative councils in 2005.

## TABLE F.8
Representation on local councils by MOP rating in conflict and nonconflict communities, 1995 and 2005

| Indicator | Year | Low MOP Conflict | Low MOP Nonconflict | High MOP Conflict | High MOP Nonconflict |
|---|---|---|---|---|---|
| % of councils where all social groups are represented | 2005 | 86 | 71 | 83 | 100 |
| | 1995 | 83 | 50 | 100 | 100 |
| % of council members who are women | 2005 | 28 | 10 | 21 | 34 |
| | 1995 | 12 | 0 | 3 | 14 |
| % of council members who are poor | 2005 | 50 | 46 | 58 | 70 |
| | 1995 | 48 | 14 | 26 | 48 |

Source: Community questionnaire.
Note: "All social groups" refers to ethnic, religious, tribal, caste, racial, and language groups. The middle MOP tercile of communities is not presented.

## TABLE F.9
Trends in religious and ethnic polarization in conflict and nonconflict communities, by country, 2005
average polarization score

| Country | Religious polarization | Ethnic polarization | Country | Religious polarization | Ethnic polarization |
|---|---|---|---|---|---|
| **All countries** | | | **Colombia** | | |
| Nonconflict | 11 | 20 | Nonconflict | 35 | 4 |
| Conflict | 14 | 26 | Conflict | 25 | 11 |
| Total | 13 | 24 | Total | 29 | 8 |
| **Afghanistan** | | | **Indonesia** | | |
| Nonconflict | 0 | 5 | Nonconflict | 1 | 14 |
| Conflict | 6 | 34 | Conflict | 25 | 43 |
| Total | 4 | 25 | Total | 13 | 27 |
| **Assam** | | | **Philippines** | | |
| Nonconflict | 12 | 33 | Nonconflict | 5 | 10 |
| Conflict | 13 | 30 | Conflict | 20 | 28 |
| Total | 13 | 31 | Total | 17 | 24 |

Source: Community questionnaire.
Note: Polarization measures the size of the second-largest group (the minority) relative to the largest group (the majority) in a community; the higher the percentage, the higher the polarization. Where there is more than one minority group or the size of the minority group is not reported, polarization is computed as one-half of the total minority share in the community population. In Indonesia, the second-largest group was not recorded in the community dataset, so ethnic and religious information from the community synthesis reports was used to compute polarization.

**TABLE F.10**
**Religious and ethnic polarization by MOP rating, in conflict and nonconflict communities, 2005**

| Indicator | Low MOP | High MOP | Total |
|---|---|---|---|
| Religious polarization | | | |
| Conflict | 0.23 | 0.14 | 0.16 |
| Nonconflict | 0.09 | 0.02 | 0.11 |
| Total | 0.18 | 0.10 | 0.14 |
| Ethnic polarization | | | |
| Conflict | 0.29 | 0.34 | 0.29 |
| Nonconflict | 0.14 | 0.10 | 0.23 |
| Total | 0.23 | 0.26 | 0.27 |

Source: Community questionnaire.

**TABLE F.11**
**Government responsiveness and community safety in conflict and nonconflict communities, 1995 and 2005**

| Community safety on a 1–4 scale | Year | Conflict | | Nonconflict | | Total | |
|---|---|---|---|---|---|---|---|
| | | More responsive | Less responsive | More responsive | Less responsive | More responsive | Less responsive |
| General safety (very peaceful=1, very violent=4) | 2005 | 1.4 | 1.9 | 1.7 | 1.7 | 1.5 | 1.8 |
| | 1995 | 2.2 | 2.9 | 2.0 | 2.3 | 2.1 | 2.7 |
| Safety at home (very safe=1, very unsafe=4) | 2005 | 1.8 | 1.9 | 1.7 | 2.1 | 1.8 | 2.0 |
| | 1995 | 2.2 | 2.8 | 1.8 | 2.3 | 2.1 | 2.6 |
| Safety walking alone (very safe=1, very unsafe=4) | 2005 | 1.6 | 2.3 | 1.5 | 1.9 | 1.6 | 2.2 |
| | 1995 | 2.0 | 3.2 | 1.7 | 2.3 | 1.9 | 2.8 |

Source: Community questionnaire.

**TABLE F.12**
**Government responsiveness and trends in service provision, 1995–2005, in conflict and nonconflict communities**

*percentage change 1995–2005*

| | Conflict | | Nonconflict | | Total | |
|---|---|---|---|---|---|---|
| Service | *More responsive* | *Less responsive* | *More responsive* | *Less responsive* | *More responsive* | *Less responsive* |
| Access to clean water | 40 | 50 | 50 | −25 | 43 | 13 |
| Access to doctors | 33 | 100 | 100 | 0 | 50 | 50 |
| Access to public health clinics | −11 | 50 | 50 | 50 | 0 | 50 |
| Private health clinic | Increased | 0 | 100 | 50 | 500 | 25 |
| Quality of health care | 5 | 12 | 20 | 43 | 9 | 21 |
| Public works projects | 500 | 150 | 100 | 150 | 300 | 150 |

*Source:* Community questionnaire.

## TABLE F.13
## Democratic governance by conflict rating and country income level, 1995 and 2005

| Indicator | Year | Conflict rating | Country income | |
|---|---|---|---|---|
| | | | Low | Middle |
| Presence of village council (% of communities) | 2005 | Conflict | 15 | 89 |
| | | Nonconflict | 12 | 100 |
| | | Total | 14 | 93 |
| | 1995 | Conflict | 13 | 72 |
| | | Nonconflict | 12 | 60 |
| | | Total | 13 | 68 |
| Elected village leader (% of communities) | 2005 | Conflict | 72 | 89 |
| | | Nonconflict | 59 | 90 |
| | | Total | 68 | 89 |
| | 1995 | Conflict | 69 | 89 |
| | | Nonconflict | 53 | 90 |
| | | Total | 64 | 89 |
| Fairly elected village leader (% of communities) | 2005 | Conflict | 100 | 88 |
| | | Nonconflict | 100 | 89 |
| | | Total | 100 | 89 |
| | 1995 | Conflict | — | 13 |
| | | Nonconflict | — | 50 |
| | | Total | — | 20 |
| All social groups are represented on council (% of councils) | 2005 | Conflict | 83 | 75 |
| | | Nonconflict | 100 | 80 |
| | | Total | 88 | 77 |
| | 1995 | Conflict | 100 | 77 |
| | | Nonconflict | 100 | 67 |
| | | Total | 100 | 74 |
| % of council members who are women | 2005 | Conflict | 19 | 27 |
| | | Nonconflict | 25 | 17 |
| | | Total | 21 | 23 |
| | 1995 | Conflict | 1 | 11 |
| | | Nonconflict | 0 | 15 |
| | | Total | 1 | 12 |

— Not available.

**TABLE F.13**
*continued*

| Indicator | Year | Conflict rating | Country income Low | Middle |
|---|---|---|---|---|
| % of council members who are poor | 2005 | Conflict | 34 | 56 |
| | | Nonconflict | 70 | 58 |
| | | Total | 43 | 57 |
| | 1995 | Conflict | 10 | 51 |
| | | Nonconflict | 8 | 48 |
| | | Total | 9 | 50 |
| Local leaders respond to local concerns (% of communities) | 2005 | Conflict | 8 | 39 |
| | | Nonconflict | 12 | 40 |
| | | Total | 9 | 39 |
| | 1995 | Conflict | 21 | 61 |
| | | Nonconflict | 0 | 60 |
| | | Total | 14 | 61 |
| Most or all government officials are corrupt (% of communities) | 2005 | Conflict | 97 | 76 |
| | | Nonconflict | 82 | 60 |
| | | Total | 93 | 70 |
| | 1995 | Conflict | 50 | 53 |
| | | Nonconflict | 29 | 70 |
| | | Total | 44 | 59 |
| Most or all government officials take bribes (% of communities) | 2005 | Conflict | 59 | 24 |
| | | Nonconflict | 88 | 0 |
| | | Total | 68 | 15 |
| | 1995 | Conflict | 29 | 18 |
| | | Nonconflict | 24 | 13 |
| | | Total | 27 | 16 |
| Positive changes in democracy, past 10 years (% of communities) | | Conflict | 47 | 65 |
| | | Nonconflict | 50 | 90 |
| | | Total | 48 | 74 |
| Participation in decision making increased, past 10 years (% of communities) | | Conflict | 46 | 47 |
| | | Nonconflict | 65 | 70 |
| | | Total | 52 | 56 |
| Gap between richest and poorest increased, past 10 years (% of communities) | | Conflict | 8 | 50 |
| | | Nonconflict | 24 | 70 |
| | | Total | 13 | 57 |

*Source:* Community questionnaire.
*Note:* "All social groups" refers to ethnic, religious, tribal, caste, racial, and language groups.

**TABLE F.14**

**Mean community MOP by presence and representativeness of village council 10 years ago, all Moving Out of Poverty study countries**

| Presence of village council 10 years ago | Representativeness of village council 10 years ago | | |
|---|---|---|---|
| | Not representative or no council | Representative | Total |
| No | 0.26 | n.a. | 0.26 |
| Yes | 0.21 | 0.25 | 0.24 |
| Total | 0.25 | 0.25 | 0.25 |

*Source:* Community questionnaire.
*Note:* n.a. = not applicable.

**TABLE F.15**

**Mean community MOP by presence and representativeness of village council 10 years ago, conflict countries only**

| Presence of village council 10 years ago | Representativeness of village council 10 years ago | | |
|---|---|---|---|
| | Not representative or no council | Representative | Total |
| No | 0.12 | n.a. | 0.12 |
| Yes | 0.13 | 0.32 | 0.28 |
| Total | 0.12 | 0.32 | 0.17 |

*Source:* Community questionnaire.
*Note:* n.a. = not applicable.

## TABLE F.16
**Representativeness of village council, social divisiveness, and number of local groups/associations in conflict and nonconflict communities**

| Indicator | Conflict | | | Nonconflict | | |
|---|---|---|---|---|---|---|
| | No council | Not representative council | Representative council | No council | Not representative council | Representative council |
| Divisiveness of social differences, 1995 (no division=1, divisive to a very great extent=5) | 1.67 | 2.33 | 2.00 | 1.93 | 2.45 | 1.93 |
| Number of local groups/associations, 1995 | | | | | | |
| Main economic activity | 0.08 | 0 | 0.80 | 0.37 | 0.32 | 0.69 |
| Finance/credit | 0.13 | 0 | 0.53 | 0.61 | 1.45 | 0.76 |
| Education/health | 0.10 | 0.33 | 1.27 | 0.27 | 0.71 | 0.58 |
| Political | 1.51 | 0.67 | 1.33 | 0.67 | 1.35 | 1.15 |
| Religious | 0.97 | 1.33 | 1.80 | 0.19 | 1.18 | 0.70 |
| Ethnic | 0.15 | 0.33 | 0.60 | 0.01 | 0.04 | 0.03 |
| Total | 2.95 | 2.67 | 6.33 | 2.13 | 5.05 | 3.90 |

*Source:* Community questionnaire.

**TABLE F.17**
**Correlations between community MOP and religious polarization and number of religious groups/associations in different settings**

| | Conflict countries | | Peaceful countries (n=366 communities) |
|---|---|---|---|
| Indicator | Conflict communities (n=57) | Nonconflict communities (n=27) | |
| Religious polarization | –0.19 | –0.35 | –0.04 |
| Number of religious groups/associations | 0.02 | 0.25 | –0.16 |

Source: Community questionnaire.

**TABLE F.18**
**Trends in participation and access to associations and networks in conflict and nonconflict communities**

| Indicator | Conflict | Nonconflict |
|---|---|---|
| Average number of community activities and meetings in 2005 | 4.6 | 6.4 |
| Participation in community meetings in 2005 (% of communities) | 73 | 74 |
| Participation in community meetings in 1995 (% of communities) | 60 | 41 |
| Networks and associations are open to many in 2005 (% of communities) | 81 | 92 |

Source: Community questionnaire.
Note: Three outlier communities that had over 50 community meetings each are excluded.

**TABLE F.19**
**Actors involved in mediating disputes as reported by movers and chronic poor, in conflict and nonconflict communities**
*percentage of households reporting mediation*

| Type of actor involved in mediation | Conflict | Nonconflict | Total |
|---|---|---|---|
| *Reported by movers* | | | |
| Community leader | 70 | 71 | 71 |
| Respected leader | 46 | 54 | 49 |
| Religious leader | 39 | 49 | 42 |
| Ethnic leader | 20 | 21 | 20 |
| Police | 59 | 41 | 53 |
| Courts | 19 | 17 | 18 |
| Other government official | 40 | 48 | 42 |
| Head of associational group (e.g., microfinance or burial group) | 14 | 16 | 15 |
| Teacher | 17 | 19 | 18 |
| Armed opposition | 8 | 10 | 9 |
| Self-defense group | 12 | 10 | 11 |
| Other | 4 | 6 | 5 |
| *Reported by chronic poor* | | | |
| Community leader | 73 | 46 | 64 |
| Respected leader | 42 | 28 | 37 |
| Religious leader | 29 | 33 | 30 |
| Ethnic leader | 19 | 14 | 17 |
| Police | 48 | 69 | 55 |
| Courts | 14 | 18 | 16 |
| Other government official | 39 | 31 | 36 |
| Head of associational group (e.g., microfinance or burial group) | 11 | 20 | 14 |
| Teacher | 17 | 16 | 17 |
| Armed opposition | 11 | 8 | 10 |
| Self-defense group | 12 | 14 | 12 |
| Other | 5 | 2 | 4 |

*Source:* Household questionnaire.

**TABLE F.20**
**Actors involved in mediating disputes as reported by movers and chronic poor, by country**
*percentage of households reporting mediation*

| Type of actor involved in mediation | Afghanistan | Assam | Colombia | Indonesia | Philippines- conflict | Total |
|---|---|---|---|---|---|---|
| *Reported by movers* | | | | | | |
| Community leader | 53 | 89 | 30 | 88 | 67 | 71 |
| Respected leader | 93 | 78 | 0 | 45 | 47 | 49 |
| Religious leader | 67 | 52 | 4 | 66 | 28 | 42 |
| Ethnic leader | 36 | 48 | 0 | 13 | 20 | 20 |
| Police | 73 | 93 | 91 | 66 | 14 | 53 |
| Courts | 40 | 56 | 0 | 21 | 4 | 18 |
| Other government official | 40 | 48 | 4 | 34 | 58 | 42 |
| Head of associational group (e.g., microfinance or burial group) | 33 | 48 | 0 | 5 | 11 | 15 |
| Teacher | 33 | 67 | 0 | 16 | 4 | 18 |
| Armed opposition | 20 | 41 | 0 | 0 | 4 | 9 |
| Self-defense group | 7 | 59 | 4 | 2 | 4 | 11 |
| Other | 0 | 0 | 0 | 16 | 1 | 5 |
| *Reported by chronic poor* | | | | | | |
| Community leader | 42 | 70 | 35 | 85 | 79 | 64 |
| Respected leader | 95 | 70 | 4 | 39 | 28 | 37 |
| Religious leader | 67 | 51 | 1 | 73 | 16 | 30 |
| Ethnic leader | 37 | 32 | 3 | 18 | 14 | 17 |
| Police | 53 | 85 | 79 | 64 | 14 | 55 |
| Courts | 26 | 43 | 4 | 18 | 4 | 16 |
| Other government official | 21 | 38 | 15 | 42 | 54 | 36 |
| Head of associational group (e.g., microfinance or burial group) | 32 | 36 | 10 | 3 | 2 | 14 |
| Teacher | 32 | 57 | 4 | 9 | 1 | 17 |
| Armed opposition | 11 | 30 | 3 | 0 | 6 | 10 |
| Self-defense group | 11 | 38 | 10 | 6 | 1 | 12 |
| Other | 0 | 4 | 1 | 18 | 2 | 4 |

*Source:* Household questionnaire.

## TABLE F.21
**Percentage of movers and chronic poor who have little or no confidence in officials, in conflict and nonconflict communities**

*percentage of households reporting little or no confidence*

| | Movers | | | Chronic poor | | |
|---|---|---|---|---|---|---|
| Type of officials | Nonconflict | Conflict | Total | Nonconflict | Conflict | Total |
| Local government officials | 21 | 40 | 33 | 52 | 40 | 45 |
| State/national government officials | 28 | 45 | 39 | 58 | 44 | 50 |
| Local politicians | 38 | 52 | 47 | 66 | 49 | 56 |
| Traditional village leaders | 10 | 30 | 22 | 30 | 22 | 25 |
| Doctors and nurses in the health clinic | 12 | 8 | 10 | 22 | 12 | 16 |
| Teachers and school officials | 4 | 8 | 6 | 13 | 8 | 10 |
| Police | 41 | 27 | 33 | 49 | 32 | 39 |
| Judges and staff of courts | 40 | 43 | 42 | 56 | 41 | 47 |
| NGO staff | 27 | 18 | 21 | 40 | 27 | 32 |

*Source:* Household questionnaire.


## TABLE F.22
**MOP and number of local groups/associations by type, in conflict and nonconflict communities, 1995 and 2005**

*mean number of local associations*

| | | Conflict | | Nonconflict | | Total | |
|---|---|---|---|---|---|---|---|
| Type of association | Year | Low MOP | High MOP | Low MOP | High MOP | Low MOP | High MOP |
| Main economic activity | 1995 | 0.16 | 0.39 | 0.50 | 0.75 | 0.52 | 0.38 |
| | 2005 | 3.37 | 1.50 | 0.75 | 2.25 | 1.76 | 1.78 |
| Financial | 1995 | 0.26 | 0.28 | 0.08 | 2.00 | 0.72 | 0.47 |
| | 2005 | 2.05 | 1.83 | 1.50 | 3.38 | 3.13 | 4.20 |
| Education and health | 1995 | 0.58 | 0.28 | 0.50 | 1.00 | 0.50 | 0.41 |
| | 2005 | 0.84 | 0.50 | 1.00 | 1.38 | 0.94 | 0.74 |
| Political | 1995 | 1.00 | 1.39 | 1.00 | 1.63 | 1.10 | 0.80 |
| | 2005 | 1.47 | 1.67 | 1.92 | 2.25 | 1.30 | 1.03 |
| Religious | 1995 | 1.32 | 1.06 | 2.33 | 3.00 | 0.71 | 0.35 |
| | 2005 | 1.79 | 1.33 | 2.33 | 3.38 | 0.98 | 0.49 |
| Ethnic | 1995 | 0.16 | 0.11 | 0.17 | 0.00 | 0.03 | 0.00 |
| | 2005 | 0.26 | 0.00 | 0.17 | 0.00 | 0.03 | 0.00 |

*Source:* Community questionnaire.
*Note:* The middle MOP tercile of communities is not presented.

## TABLE F.23

**Mean strength of local economy and change in strength of local economy by MOP rating in conflict and nonconflict communities, 1995–2005**

| Level (very weak=1, very strong=5) | Year | Low MOP | High MOP |
|---|---|---|---|
| Conflict | 2005 | 2.58 | 2.72 |
|  | 1995 | 2.37 | 2.56 |
| Nonconflict | 2005 | 2.25 | 2.75 |
|  | 1995 | 2.17 | 2.25 |
| Total | 2005 | 2.45 | 2.73 |
|  | 1995 | 2.29 | 2.46 |
| *Change, 1995–2005 (%)* |  |  |  |
| Conflict |  | 9 | 7 |
| Nonconflict |  | 4 | 22 |
| Total |  | 7 | 11 |

*Source:* Community questionnaire.
*Note:* The middle MOP tercile of communities is not presented.

## TABLE F.24

**Sources of income for movers in conflict and nonconflict communities, 1995 and 2005**

*percentage of households*

| Income source | 2005 | | 1995 | |
|---|---|---|---|---|
|  | Conflict | Nonconflict | Conflict | Nonconflict |
| Sale of crops | 61 | 66 | 61 | 61 |
| Wages—regular | 39 | 29 | 19 | 12 |
| Wages—temporary | 39 | 24 | 41 | 35 |
| Nonagricultural income | 33 | 47 | 20 | 26 |
| Sale of livestock | 23 | 21 | 23 | 21 |
| Interest income | 12 | 8 | 6 | 0 |
| Sale of fish | 11 | 11 | 6 | 8 |
| Remittances | 10 | 8 | 2 | 0 |
| Rental income | 5 | 3 | 1 | 1 |
| Social assistance | 3 | 5 | 1 | 2 |
| Pension | 2 | 1 | 0 | 1 |
| Unemployment benefits | 0 | 0 | 0 | 0 |

*Source:* Household questionnaire.

**TABLE F.25**
**Sources of income for chronic poor in conflict and nonconflict communities, 1995 and 2005**
*percentage of households*

| Income source | 2005 Conflict | 2005 Nonconflict | 1995 Conflict | 1995 Nonconflict |
|---|---|---|---|---|
| Wages—regular | 20 | 15 | 13 | 14 |
| Wages—temporary | 61 | 63 | 55 | 52 |
| Sale of crops | 48 | 32 | 53 | 50 |
| Sale of livestock | 21 | 14 | 22 | 20 |
| Sale of fish | 8 | 10 | 6 | 9 |
| Nonagricultural income | 21 | 20 | 13 | 15 |
| Rental income | 1 | 1 | 0 | 2 |
| Interest income | 2 | 1 | 2 | 2 |
| Remittances | 6 | 7 | 2 | 2 |
| Pension | 3 | 2 | 0 | 1 |
| Unemployment benefits | 0 | 1 | 0 | 0 |
| Social assistance | 5 | 7 | 3 | 3 |

*Source:* Household questionnaire.

**TABLE F.26**
**Infrastructure in conflict and nonconflict communities, 1995 and 2005**
*percentage of communities*

| Infrastructure | Year | Conflict | Nonconflict | Total |
|---|---|---|---|---|
| Access to: | | | | |
| Bus | 2005 | 35 | 37 | 36 |
| | 1995 | 32 | 30 | 31 |
| Market | 2005 | 53 | 59 | 55 |
| | 1995 | 49 | 63 | 54 |
| Clean water | 2005 | 60 | 59 | 60 |
| | 1995 | 40 | 41 | 40 |
| Doctor | 2005 | 33 | 30 | 31 |
| | 1995 | 22 | 26 | 25 |
| Public clinic | 2005 | 41 | 40 | 40 |
| | 1995 | 33 | 44 | 40 |
| Private clinic | 2005 | 30 | 26 | 27 |
| | 1995 | 19 | 9 | 12 |
| Daily bus/train to city | 2005 | 75 | 74 | 74 |
| Passable road | 2005 | 67 | 61 | 65 |
| Distance to city (km) | | 22 | 24 | 23 |

*Source:* Community questionnaire.

**TABLE F.27**
**Infrastructure by MOP rating in conflict and nonconflict communities, 1995 and 2005**
*percentage of communities*

| Infrastructure | Year | Low MOP Conflict | Low MOP Nonconflict | High MOP Conflict | High MOP Nonconflict |
|---|---|---|---|---|---|
| Access to: | | | | | |
| Bus | 2005 | 37 | 25 | 39 | 50 |
| | 1995 | 26 | 17 | 44 | 50 |
| Market | 2005 | 37 | 42 | 56 | 88 |
| | 1995 | 42 | 42 | 50 | 88 |
| Clean water | 2005 | 42 | 67 | 78 | 50 |
| | 1995 | 32 | 33 | 61 | 50 |
| Doctor | 2005 | 16 | 33 | 44 | 38 |
| | 1995 | 21 | 8 | 28 | 38 |
| Public clinic | 2005 | 26 | 42 | 61 | 50 |
| | 1995 | 47 | 17 | 56 | 63 |
| Private clinic | 2005 | 32 | 17 | 22 | 50 |
| | 1995 | 16 | 8 | 0 | 25 |
| Daily bus/train to city | 2005 | 61 | 70 | 88 | 71 |
| Passable road | 2005 | 56 | 70 | 75 | 57 |
| Distance to city (km) | | 22 | 27 | 12 | 25 |

*Source:* Community questionnaire.
*Note:* The middle MOP tercile of communities is not presented.

# Index

Boxes, figures, maps, notes, and tables are indicated by *b*, *f*, *m*, *n*, and *t*, respectively.

**533**